Paris Metro

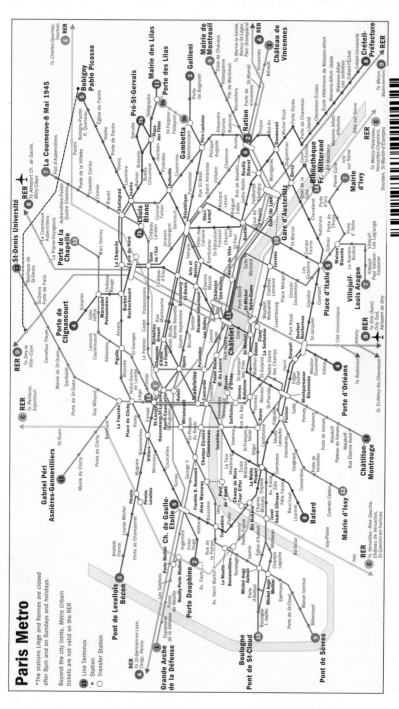

*The stations Liège and Rennes are closed after 8pm and on Sundays and holidays.

Beyond the city limits, *Métro Urbain* tickets are not valid on the RER

13 Line Terminus
○ Station
○ Transfer Station

W9-CEI-963

Paris: Overview and Arrondissements

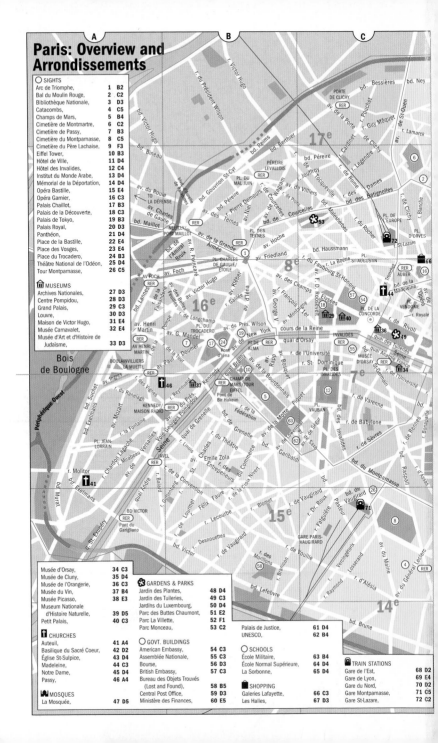

SIGHTS

Arc de Triomphe,	1	B2
Bal du Moulin Rouge,	2	C2
Bibliothèque Nationale,	3	D3
Catacombs,	4	C5
Champs de Mars,	5	B4
Cimetière de Montmartre,	6	C2
Cimetière de Passy,	7	B3
Cimetière du Montparnasse,	8	C5
Cimetière du Père Lachaise,	9	F3
Eiffel Tower,	10	B3
Hôtel de Ville,	11	D4
Hôtel des Invalides,	12	C4
Institut du Monde Arabe,	14	D4
Mémorial de la Déportation,	13	D4
Opéra Bastille,	15	E4
Opéra Garnier,	16	C3
Palais Chaillot,	17	B3
Palais de la Découverte,	18	C3
Palais de Tokyo,	19	B3
Palais Royal,	20	D3
Panthéon,	21	D4
Place de la Bastille,	22	E4
Place des Vosges,	23	E4
Place du Trocadéro,	24	B3
Théâtre National de l'Odéon,	25	D4
Tour Montparnasse,	26	C5

MUSEUMS

Archives Nationales,	27	D3
Centre Pompidou,	28	D3
Grand Palais,	29	C3
Louvre,	30	D3
Maison de Victor Hugo,	31	E4
Musée Carnavalet,	32	E4
Musée d'Art et d'Histoire de Judaïsme,	33	D3
Musée d'Orsay,	34	C3
Musée de Cluny,	35	D4
Musée de l'Orangerie,	36	C3
Musée du Vin,	37	B4
Musée Picasso,	38	E3
Museum Nationale d'Histoire Naturelle,	39	D5
Petit Palais,	40	C3

CHURCHES

Auteuil,	41	A4
Basilique du Sacré Coeur,	42	D2
Église St-Sulpice,	43	D4
Madeleine,	44	C3
Notre Dame,	45	D4
Passy,	46	A4

MOSQUES

La Mosquée,	47	D5

GARDENS & PARKS

Jardin des Plantes,	48	D4
Jardin des Tuileries,	49	C3
Jardins du Luxembourg,	50	D4
Parc des Buttes Chaumont,	51	E2
Parc La Villette,	52	F1
Parc Monceau,	53	C2

GOVT. BUILDINGS

American Embassy,	54	C3
Assemblée Nationale,	55	C3
Bourse,	56	D3
British Embassy,	57	C3
Bureau des Objets Trouvés (Lost and Found),	58	B5
Central Post Office,	59	D3
Ministère des Finances,	60	E5
Palais de Justice,	61	D4
UNESCO,	62	B4

SCHOOLS

École Militaire,	63	B4
École Normal Supérieure,	64	D4
La Sorbonne,	65	D4

SHOPPING

Galeries Lafayette,	66	C3
Les Halles,	67	D3

TRAIN STATIONS

Gare de l'Est,	68	D2
Gare de Lyon,	69	E4
Gare du Nord,	70	D2
Gare Montparnasse,	71	C5
Gare St-Lazare,	72	C2

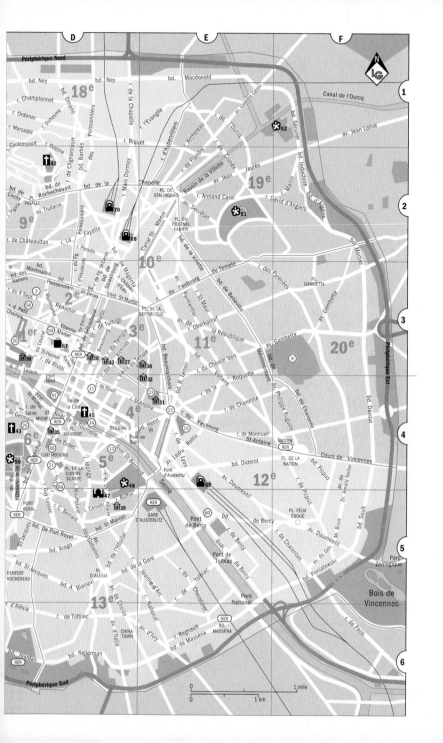

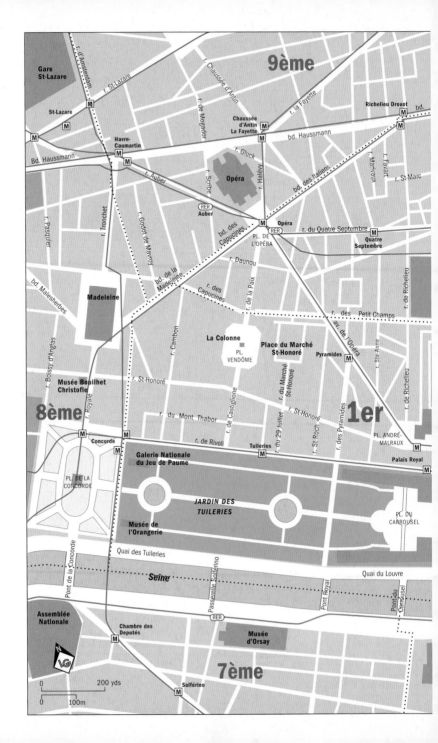

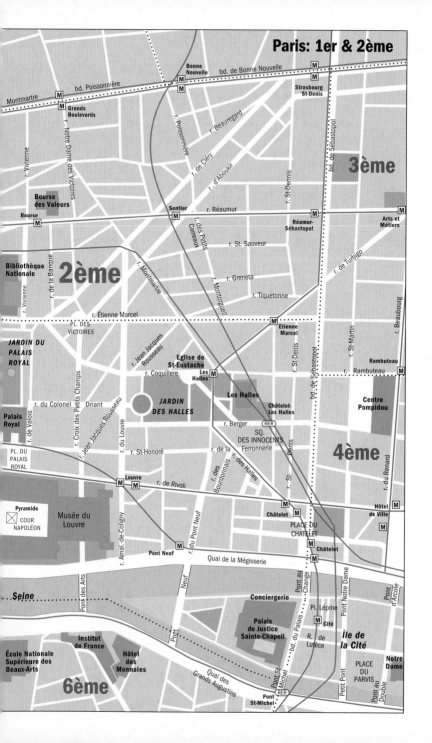

Paris: 1er & 2ème

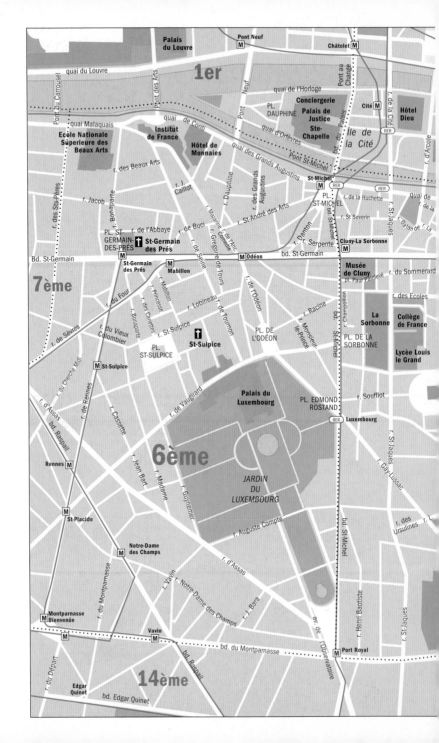

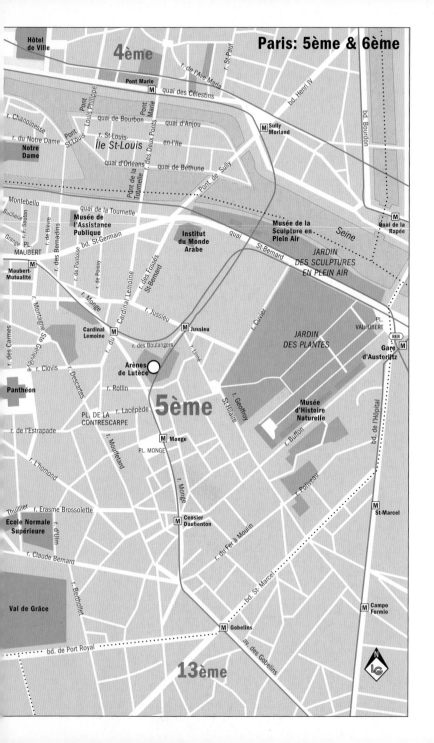

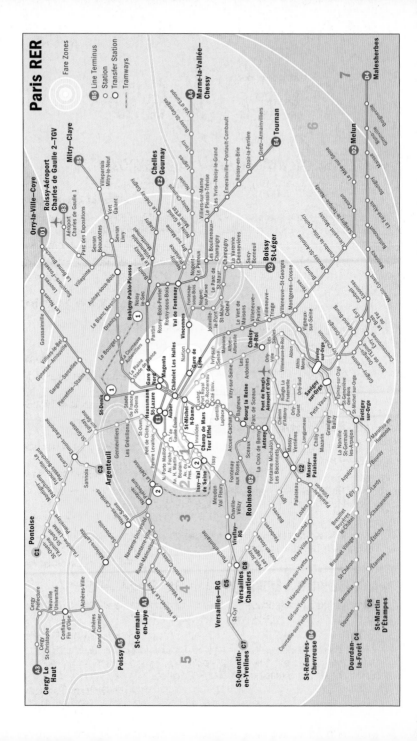

Paris RER

LET'S GO PUBLICATIONS

TRAVEL GUIDES

Australia 9th edition
Austria & Switzerland 12th edition
Brazil 1st edition
Britain 2007
California 10th edition
Central America 9th edition
Chile 2nd edition
China 5th edition
Costa Rica 3rd edition
Eastern Europe 12th edition
Ecuador 1st edition
Egypt 2nd edition
Europe 2007
France 2007
Germany 13th edition
Greece 8th edition
Hawaii 4th edition
India & Nepal 8th edition
Ireland 12th edition
Israel 4th edition
Italy 2007
Japan 1st edition
Mexico 21st edition
Middle East 4th edition
New Zealand 7th edition
Peru 1st edition
Puerto Rico 2nd edition
South Africa 5th edition
Southeast Asia 9th edition
Spain & Portugal 2007
Thailand 3rd edition
Turkey 5th edition
USA 23rd edition
Vietnam 2nd edition
Western Europe 2007

ROADTRIP GUIDE

Roadtripping USA 2nd edition

ADVENTURE GUIDES

Alaska 1st edition
Pacific Northwest 1st edition
Southwest USA 3rd edition

CITY GUIDES

Amsterdam 4th edition
Barcelona 3rd edition
Boston 4th edition
London 15th edition
New York City 16th edition
Paris 14th edition
Rome 12th edition
San Francisco 4th edition
Washington, D.C. 13th edition

POCKET CITY GUIDES

Amsterdam
Berlin
Boston
Chicago
London
New York City
Paris
San Francisco
Venice
Washington, D.C.

LET'S GO

■ PAGES PACKED WITH ESSENTIAL INFORMATION

"Value-packed, unbeatable, accurate, and comprehensive."

—*The Los Angeles Tim*

"The guides are aimed not only at young budget travelers but at the indep
dent traveler; a sort of streetwise cookbook for traveling alone."

—*The New York Tim*

"Unbeatable; good sight-seeing advice; up-to-date info on restaurants, hotel
and inns; a commitment to money-saving travel; and a wry style that brighten
nearly every page."

—*The Washington Pos*

■ THE BEST TRAVEL BARGAINS IN YOUR BUDGET

"All the dirt, dirt cheap."

—*People*

"Let's Go follows the creed that you don't have to toss your life's savings to
the wind to travel—unless you want to."

—*The Salt Lake Tribune*

■ REAL ADVICE FOR REAL EXPERIENCES

"The writers seem to have experienced every rooster-packed bus and lunar-
surfaced mattress about which they write."

—*The New York Times*

"[Let's Go's] devoted updaters really walk the walk (and thumb the ride, and
trek the trail). Learn how to fish, haggle, find work—anywhere."

—*Food & Wine*

"A world-wise traveling companion—always ready with friendly advice and
helpful hints, all sprinkled with a bit of wit."

—*The Philadelphia Inquirer*

■ A GUIDE WITH A SPIRIT AND A SOCIAL CONSCIENCE

"Lighthearted and sophisticated, informative and fun to read. [Let's Go] helps
the novice traveler navigate like a knowledgeable old hand."

—*Atlanta Journal-Constitution*

"The serious mission at the book's core reveals itself in exhortations to
respect the culture and the environment—and, if possible, to visit as a volunteer, a student, or a teacher rather than a tourist."

—*San Francisco Chronicle*

LET'S GO

PARIS

MALLORY HELLMAN EDITOR

RESEARCHER-WRITERS
OLIVIA BROWN
KATE WANG

KEVIN PAIK MAP EDITOR
LAURA E. MARTIN MANAGING EDITOR

ST. MARTIN'S PRESS ❧ NEW YORK

HELPING LET'S GO. If you want to share your discoveries, suggestions, or corrections, please drop us a line. We read every piece of correspondence, whether a postcard, a 10-page email, or a coconut. **Address mail to:**

Let's Go: Paris
67 Mount Auburn St.
Cambridge, MA 02138
USA

Visit Let's Go at **http://www.letsgo.com,** or send email to:

feedback@letsgo.com
Subject: "Let's Go: Paris"

In addition to the invaluable travel advice our readers share with us, many are kind enough to offer their services as researchers or editors. Unfortunately, our charter enables us to employ only currently enrolled Harvard students.

CONTENTS

HOW TO USE THIS BOOK

ORGANIZATION. *Let's Go: Paris* covers the city *arrondissement* by *arrondissement*, step by step; we explore every nook, taste every crêpe, and leave no rock unturned. Coverage is divided by *arrondissement*. Look at thumbnail maps throughout the book for location reminders. Chapters are organized by activity or necessity: Accommodations, Food, Sights, Museums, Entertainment, Shopping, Nightlife, and Daytrips. The chapters cover *arrondissements* in ascending numerical order, with the exception of the Entertainment chapter, which is divided by types of entertainment. Within each *arrondissement*, sights are listed geographically and food and accommodations are listed by value.

PRICE DIVERSITY AND RANKINGS. Within each *arrondissement*, we rank food and accommodation establishments by value (from best to worst). Each listing is followed by a price icon (❶-❺); see p. xi for a price range breakdown. Our favorite establishments are marked with the *Let's Go* thumbs-up (🖫).

TRANSPORTATION INFO. *Let's Go* mentions the nearest **Metro** station to most establishments. When there is no Metro icon (Ⓜ) it means that no Metro station is close to the listing. Check the **Essentials** chapter for more information on transportation and the **Map Appendix** for maps.

FEATURES AND SCHOLARLY ARTICLES. Throughout this book, you'll find sidebars and longer articles—built-in reading material for waiting in line or hanging out in a cafe. You can read researchers' tales **From the Road,** learn what's been going on **In Recent News,** dive into the **Insider's City** with mini-walking tours, find explanations of items you'll see **On the Menu,** discover **Hidden Deals** and the best **Big Splurges,** and much more. Don't miss the book's **Scholarly Articles:** a history of postwar Parisian intellectuals from a leading scholar (p. 78), and discussions of 18th-century garden design (p. 326) and 19th-century urban planning (p. 273).

COVERING THE BASICS. The first chapter, **Discover Paris,** contains highlights of the City of Lights, complete with new **Suggested Itinerary** maps. The chapter is organized around the Right and Left Banks of the Seine River. **Essentials** has all the info you'll need to navigate Paris's airports, train stations, and Metro system. Take some time to peruse the **Life and Times** chapter, which sums up the history, culture, and customs of Parisians. For study abroad, volunteer, and work options in Paris, the **Beyond Tourism** chapter is all you need. The **Practical Information** chapter contains a list of local services, from dry cleaning to fitness clubs, while the **Appendix** has a phrasebook with a list of useful French phrases to help you navigate common situations in French.

FINALLY. Remember to put down this guide once in a while and strike out on your own—Paris is full of more sights and suprises than any book can cover.

A NOTE TO OUR READERS. The information for this book was gathered by *Let's Go* researchers from May through August of 2006. Each listing is based on one researcher's opinion, formed during his or her visit at a particular time. Those traveling at other times may have different experiences since prices, dates, hours, and conditions are always subject to change. You are urged to check the facts presented in this book beforehand to avoid inconvenience and surprises.

RESEARCHER-WRITERS

Olivia Brown   *1er, 2ème, 5ème, 6ème, 9ème, 10ème, 14ème, 15ème, 18ème, 19ème, 20ème*

A British expat researching the streets of Paris in style, Olivia managed to prove her legitimacy in both the grittiest Anglophone pubs and the trendiest French clubs. From exploring the seedy environs of the Place Pigalle to investigating some of the ritziest establishments in the city, Olivia tore up a tremendously diverse route. This adventurous History concentrator was able to fact-check her museums and monuments with unparalleled finesse. From finagling her way into an exclusive Louis Vuitton party to fending off countless frisky waiters, Olivia proved a gorgeous match for the City of Love.

Kate Wang   *île de la Cité, île St-Louis, 3ème, 4ème, 7ème, 8ème, 11ème, 12ème, 13ème, 16ème, 17ème*

"Are you Chinese? I love Chinese women," was probably the most frequent (and disturbing) comment Kate received on the road. But whether she soundly knocked the politically incorrect away with her perfect accent or simply blew them away with her personal style, Kate Wang took Paris by storm. Stylish, linguistically proficient, and budget-savvy, Kate was *Let's Go*'s dream researcher as she paraded through the city that had already been her home for a semester of study at the Sorbonne. Her spot-on writing takes *Let's Go*'s "witty and irreverent" style to a whole new plane.

CONTRIBUTING WRITERS

Verena Andermatt Conley teaches Romance Languages and Literatures at Harvard University. She has published extensively; her most recent work deals with post-war Parisian intellectuals.

Charlotte Houghteling has worked on Let's Go's *Middle East*, *Egypt*, and *Israel* titles. She wrote her senior thesis on the development of department stores during the Second Empire and recently completed her M.Phil at Cambridge on the consumer society of Revolutionary Paris.

Sara Houghteling was a Researcher-Writer for *Let's Go: France 1999* and has taught at the American School in Paris. She recently earned her MFA in creative writing from the University of Michigan.

Meredith Martin is a Ph.D. candidate in the Department of the History of Art and Architecture at Harvard University.

ACKNOWLEDGMENTS

LET'S GO

MAL THANKS: Her tireless, devoted, and obscenely hardcore ☒RW's, who made her remember on a day-to-day basis exactly why she loves this job. Laura Martin, a goddess in human form, who made this book (and series) possible in every respect. Kevin, for acknowledging that I don't understand maps and behaving accordingly. The plaid-and-paisley chair for not even smelling bad. Jenny and Carl for keeping the Citypod love alive. Proofers, Prod, Dunkin' Donuts hazelnut-iced-coffee-black, HBO's *Big Love* (sans Bill Paxton's ass), The Neighborhood, and BABIES.

Not done. Mal also thanks the Genzyme Corporation for its persistent motivation and strength. Trader Joe's, if only for the cheese. My wonderful roommates for understanding why I'm never actually home. My parents, for giving me my endearingly tiny stature and the encouragement that never ceased, even in this book's final hours of production. Fleurette Hackshaw and Tara Ellsley for teaching me French. God, as a rhetorical device. Helen, as a rhetorical device. The city of Cambridge for never ceasing to let me fall in love. Everyone who hired me, even when they knew better.

Everyone who reads this book, because when it comes down to brass tacks, it's all about you. Enjoy.

KEVIN THANKS: Mal, Kate, and Olivia for all their hard work and that je-ne-sais-quoi. Paris Pratique Par Arrondissement, Tanjore, and talking cats. Cliff, Mariah, Shiyang, Tom, and the rest of the office for a great summer. Mom, Dad, Karen, and Christopher for just about everything else.

Publishing Director
Alexandra C. Stanek
Editor-in-Chief
Laura E. Martin
Production Manager
Richard Chohaney Lonsdorf
Cartography Manager
Clifford S. Emmanuel
Editorial Managers
August Dietrich, Samantha Gelfand,
Silvia Gonzalez Killingsworth
Financial Manager
Jenny Qiu Wong
Publicity Manager
Anna A. Mattson-DiCecca
Personnel Manager
Sergio Ibarra
Production Associate
Chase Mohney
IT Director
Patrick Carroll
Director of E-Commerce
Jana Lepon
Office Coordinators
Adrienne Taylor Gerken, Sarah Goodin

Director of Advertising Sales
Mohammed J. Herzallah
Senior Advertising Associates
Kedamai Fisseha, Roumiana Ivanova

Editor
Mallory Hellman
Managing Editor
Laura E. Martin
Map Editor
Kevin Paik
Typesetter
Teresa Elsey

President
Brian Feinstein
General Manager
Robert B. Rombauer

ABOUT LET'S GO

NOT YOUR PARENTS' TRAVEL GUIDE

At Let's Go, we see every trip as the chance of a lifetime. If your dream is to grab a machete and forge through the jungles of Brazil, we can take you there. If you'd rather bask in the Riviera sun at a beachside cafe, we'll set you a table. We write for readers who know that there's more to travel than sharing double deckers with tourists and who believe that travel can change both themselves and the world— whether they plan to spend six days in London or six months in Latin America. We'll show you just how far your money can go, and prove that the greatest limitation on your adventures is not your wallet, but your imagination.

BEYOND THE TOURIST EXPERIENCE

To help you gain a deeper connection with the places you travel, our fearless researchers scour the globe to give you the heads-up on both world-renowned and off-the-beaten-track attractions, sights, and destinations. They engage with the local culture, only to emerge with the freshest insights on everything from local festivals to regional cuisine. We've also opened our pages to respected writers and scholars to hear their takes on the countries and regions we cover, and asked travelers who have worked, studied, or volunteered abroad to contribute first-person accounts of their experiences. In addition, we've increased our coverage of responsible travel and expanded each guide's Beyond Tourism chapter to share more ideas about how to give back while on the road.

FORTY-SEVEN YEARS OF WISDOM

Let's Go got its start in 1960, when a group of creative and well-traveled students compiled their experience and advice into a 20-page mimeographed pamphlet, which they gave to travelers on charter flights to Europe. Four and a half decades later, we've expanded to cover six continents and all kinds of travel—while retaining our founders' adventurous attitude toward the world. Laced with witty prose and total candor, our guides are still researched and written entirely by students on shoestring budgets, experienced travelers who know that train strikes, stolen luggage, food poisoning, and marriage proposals are all part of a day's work.

THE LET'S GO COMMUNITY

More than just a travel guide company, Let's Go is a community. Our small staff comes together because of our shared passion for travel and our desire to help other travelers see the world the way it was meant to be seen. We love it when our readers become part of the Let's Go community as well—when you travel, drop us a postcard (67 Mt. Auburn St., Cambridge, MA 02138, USA), send us an e-mail (feedback@letsgo.com), or post on our forum (http://www.letsgo.com/connect/forum) to tell us about your adventures and discoveries.

For more information, visit us online: www.letsgo.com.

1 2 3 4 5

PRICE RANGES>>PARIS

Our researchers list establishments in order of value from best to worst; our favorites are denoted by the Let's Go thumbs-up (👍). Since the best value is not always the cheapest price, we have incorporated a system of price ranges for quick reference. Our price ranges are based on a rough expectation of what you will spend. For **accommodations,** we base our price range off the cheapest price for which a single traveler can stay for one night. For **restaurants** and other dining establishments, we estimate the average amount that you will spend in that restaurant. The table below tells you what you will *typically* find in Paris at the corresponding price range.

ACCOMMODATIONS	RANGE	WHAT YOU'RE LIKELY TO FIND
1	under €31	Mostly hostels; expect a basic dorm-style room and hall bathrooms. There may be lockout and/or curfew.
2	€31-50	Small hotels, usually farther from major tourist attractions. Expect basic, comfortable rooms and hall bathrooms.
3	€51-75	Small hotels in more central areas, and with more amenities or better decor than those in lower ranges. Most rooms have shower and/or toilets, TV, and phone.
4	€76-95	Nicer hotels in convenient areas, with attention to decor and atmosphere. Rooms should have shower and toilet, as well as TV and phone.
5	above €95	Upscale hotels. If you're paying this much, your room should have all the amenities you want, and it should be exceptionally charming and comfortable.

FOOD	RANGE	WHAT YOU'RE LIKELY TO FIND
1	under €11	Mostly take-out food, like sandwiches or falafel. Also some cafes and crêperies.
2	€11-15	Small restaurants, cafes, and brasseries; you'll usually get a basic 1 or 2 course sit-down meal.
3	€16-25	Nicer restaurants or specialty cafes (often themed or fusion cuisine), usually featuring lunch or dinner *menus*; expect at least 2 courses (*plat* and *entrée* or dessert) and good service.
4	€26-35	Restaurants with great atmosphere, great service, and great food. You'll usually get a *menu* with 2 or 3 courses, wine, and coffee.
5	above €35	Classy, dressy restaurants with amazing food and flawless service: a memorable dining experience.

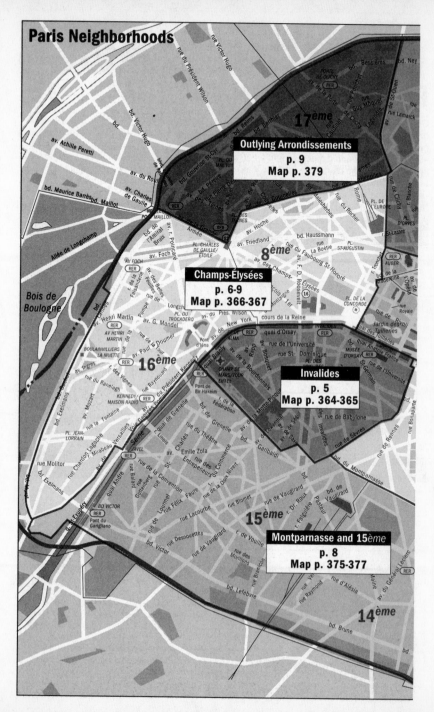

Paris Neighborhoods

17ème

Outlying Arrondissements
p. 9
Map p. 379

8ème

Champs-Élysées
p. 6-9
Map p. 366-367

Invalides
p. 5
Map p. 364-365

16ème

Montparnasse and 15ème
p. 8
Map p. 375-377

15ème

14ème

Bois de
Boulogne

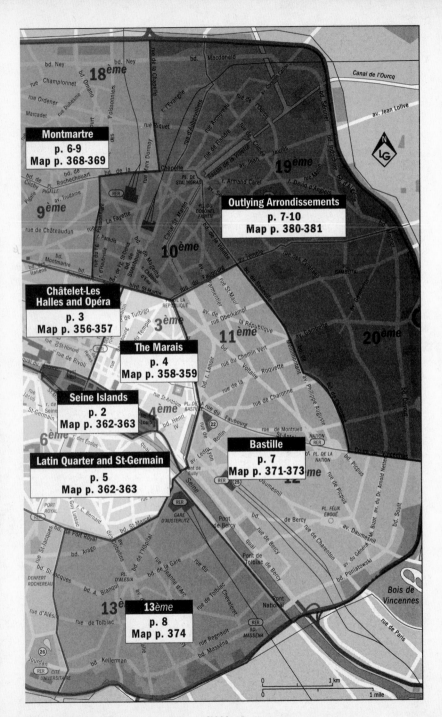

Montmartre
p. 6-9
Map p. 368-369

Outlying Arrondissements
p. 7-10
Map p. 380-381

Châtelet-Les Halles and Opéra
p. 3
Map p. 356-357

The Marais
p. 4
Map p. 358-359

Seine Islands
p. 2
Map p. 362-363

Latin Quarter and St-Germain
p. 5
Map p. 362-363

Bastille
p. 7
Map p. 371-373

13ème
p. 8
Map p. 374

0   1 km
0   1 mile

DISCOVER PARIS

When Abbot Suger commissioned the Basilique de St-Denis in the 12th century, his vision shattered the architectural conventions of the day. No one had ever seen a church so luminous or a construction so seemingly weightless. The completed cathedral was met with awe, applause, and, in some cases, derision. The unconventional "Gothic" style conceived in the outskirts of Paris soon became the international standard of cathedral design. Many of Paris's iconic monuments were first received with controversy—the Eiffel Tower, the Louvre Pyramid, and the Centre Pompidou have all been denounced as insults to the "traditional" architecture of the Parisian landscape. Such cycles of revolution and assimilation are an essential characteristic of Paris's identity. *Liberté*, *Egalité*, and *Fraternité* have been transformed from incendiary tenets of the Revolution into the bedrock of the French nation. Jean-Paul Sartre, a radical activist in the 1968 student uprisings, is now a bastion of Parisian intellectualism.

The growth and adaptation characteristic of cities and civilizations are certainly not unique to Paris. What Paris does with singular beauty, however, is integrate the new into the fabric of the old, devoting equal reverence and energy to the two. From tortuous medieval alleyways to broad 19th-century boulevards, from Notre Dame's gargoyles to the futuristic structures of the Parc de la Villette, from the exquisite masterpieces of the Louvre to the establishment of avant-garde galleries in the Marais, from the relics of the first millennium to the celebrations of the third, Paris presents itself as both a harbor of tradition and a hotbed of innovation. Paris is everything that one expects and at the same time a constant surprise; a living monument to the past and a city full of the life of the present.

FACTS AND FIGURES

AGE: 2257 years old in 2007

POPULATION (METRO AREA): 11,174,743

(CITY PROPER): 2,144,700

URBAN AREA: 2723 sq. km.

LAND AREA: 86.928 sq. km.

YEARLY VISITORS TO THE EIFFEL TOWER: 6,230,050

REVOLUTIONS: 4, to date

PERCENTAGE OF ANNUAL INCOME SPENT ON WINE: 15

KINGS NAMED LOUIS: 15

LENGTH OF THE SEINE WITHIN PARIS: 13 km.

VARIETIES OF CHEESE: 80

ESTIMATED "ROMANTIC ENCOUNTERS" PER DAY: 4,959,476

FILMS FEATURING GERARD DEPARDIEU: 157

WHEN TO GO

Spring weather in Paris is fickle, with rainy and sunny days in about equal numbers. Of the summer months, June is notoriously rainy, while high temperatures tend to hit in July. Occasional heat waves can be uncomfortable (and in extreme cases, devastating—a 2003 hot spell killed hundreds), and muggy weather aggravates Paris's pollution problem. In August, tourists move in and Parisians move out for vacation. Smaller hotels, shops, and services close for the month. While the Champs-Elysées and the Eiffel Tower are mobbed with sightseers, many of Paris's best festivals are held during the summer (see p. 95) and parts of the city can be quite peaceful. In the fall, the tourist madness begins to calm down. Despite winter cold and rain, there isn't much snow. In the off season, airfares and hotel rates drop, travel is less congested, and the museum lines are shorter.

Avg Temp (lo/hi), Precipitation	January			April			July			October		
	°C	°F	mm	°C	°F	mm	°C	°F	mm	°C	°F	mm
Paris	1/6	34/43	56	6/16	43/61	42	15/25	59/77	59	8/16	46/61	50
Versailles	1/6	34/43	56	6/14	43/57	42	14/24	58/75	59	8/15	46/59	50
Reims	-1/4	30/40	46	4/16	40/60	48	13/24	56/76	66	6/14	43/58	66

NEIGHBORHOODS

The **Seine River** flows from east to west through the heart of Paris. Two islands in the Seine, **Île de la Cité** and neighboring **Île St-Louis,** are situated in the geographical center of the city. The Seine splits Paris into two sections: the **Rive Gauche** (Left Bank) to the south of the river and the **Rive Droite** (Right Bank) to the north. Modern Paris is divided into **20 arrondissements** (districts) that spiral clockwise outward from the center of the city. Each *arrondissement* is referred to by its number (e.g. the Third, the Sixteenth). In French, "Third" is said *troisième* (TRWAZ-yem) and abbreviated "3*ème*"; "Sixteenth" is said *seizième* (SEZ-yem) and abbreviated "16*ème.*" The same goes for every *arrondissement* except the First, which is said *premier* (PREM-yay) and abbreviated 1*er.*

The neighborhoods below are listed in chronological order, starting with the Seine Islands. This is the structure that we will employ throughout the book.

ÎLE DE LA CITÉ AND ÎLE ST-LOUIS

see map p. 362-363

It's appropriate that all distance points in France are measured from *kilomètre zéro,* a circular sundial in front of Notre Dame on Île de la Cité. After all, if any place can be called the heart of Paris, it is this slip in the Seine. Île de la Cité is situated in the very center of the city and at the center of the Île de France, the geographical region surrounding Paris. It was the first part of the city to be settled (by the Gauls; see **Life and Times,** p. 59) and the first spot to be named "Paris." From the 6th century, when Clovis crowned himself king of the Franks, until Charles V abandoned it in favor of the Louvre in the 14th century, the island was the seat of the monarchy. Construction of the **Notre Dame** cathedral began here in 1163, and the presence of the cathedral along with other historically significant buildings (including **Ste-Chapelle** and **La Conciergerie**) ensured that the island would remain a center of Parisian religious, political, and cultural life—and, now, a major center of interest to tourists.

Île St-Louis had less illustrious beginnings. Originally two small islands—the Île aux Vâches (Cow Island) and the Île de Notre Dame—the Île St-Louis was considered suitable for duels, cows, and little else throughout the Middle Ages. In 1267, the area was renamed for Louis IX after he departed for the Crusades. The two islands merged in the 17th century under the direction of architect Louis Le Vau, and Île St-Louis became a residential district as a result of a contractual arrangement between Henri IV and the bridge entrepreneur Christophe Marie, after whom the **Pont Marie** is named. The island's *hôtels particuliers* (mansions) attracted an elite citizenry including Voltaire, Mme. de Châtelet, Daumier, Ingres, Baudelaire,

Balzac, Courbet, George Sand, Delacroix, and Cézanne. In the 1930s, the idiosyncratic inhabitants declared the island an independent republic.

Île St-Louis still retains a certain remoteness from the rest of Paris. Older residents say *"Je vais à Paris"* (I'm going to Paris) when leaving by one of the four bridges linking Île St-Louis and the mainland. All in all, the island looks remarkably similar to its 17th-century self, retaining a rich depth of history as well as a genteel tranquility. While tourists might clog the streets on weekends, the island is nonetheless a haven of boutiques, specialty food shops, and art galleries that can provide for a pleasant wander.

RIVE DROITE (RIGHT BANK)

The *Rive Droite* has long been considered the more fashionable side of the Seine. The first four *arrondissements* comprise what has historically been central Paris and contain the oldest streets in the city, along with many of its most famous sights and best (if not cheapest) restaurants, nightlife, and shopping.

FIRST ARRONDISSEMENT

see map p. 356-357

The 1*er* is the *arrondissement* where visitors are most reminded of Paris's royal history. Its most famous sight, the **Louvre,** was home to French kings for four centuries, and the surrounding **Jardin des Tuileries** was redesigned in 1660 by Louis XIV's favored architect, André Le Nôtre. Today, the bedchambers and dining rooms of the *ancien régime* house the world's finest art, and the Sun King's prized gardens are a playground for sunbathers, children, and tourists alike. Royalty still dominates the 1*er*, though: Chanel, Cartier, and the Ritz Hotel hold court in the imposing **place Vendôme.** Less ritzy souvenir shops crowd **rue du Rivoli** and **Les Halles,** while elegant boutiques line **rue St-Honoré,** also home to the Comédie Française, where actors still preserve the tradition of Molière. Farther west, smoky jazz clubs rule the night on **rue des Lombards.**

 LET'S NOT GO. Although above ground the 1*er* is one of the safest regions of Paris, the area's metro stops (Châtelet and Les Halles) are best avoided at night.

SECOND ARRONDISSEMENT

see map p. 356-357

The 2*ème* has a long history of trade and commerce, from the lovely 19th-century **passageways** (prototype shopping malls) to the **Bourse,** where stocks and bonds have been traded for hundreds of years. The oldest and most enduring trade of all, prostitution, has thrived on **rue St-Denis** since the Middle Ages. East of r. St-Denis, many small, inexpensive restaurants and hotels make the 2*ème* an excellent place to stay. **Rue Montorgueil** is lined with old-fashioned *boulangeries* and other food shops and cafes. The area known as **Etienne-Marcel** bursts with fabulously cheap clothing and great sales in more expensive stores—come here to get outfitted for wild nights of clubbing. For those tired of searching for the perfect top (or out of money from buying several perfect tops) and up for a laugh, the Opéra Comique, now the **Théâtre Musicale,** can be found between bd. des Italiens and r. de Richelieu.

'OP TEN PLACES TO GET AN EYEFUL

1. Père Lachaise Cemetery.
Practically a city in its own right, immense Père Lachaise is riddled with famous dead folk, including Jim Morrison, Oscar Wilde, and Edith Piaf. Your mausoleum should look so good (p. 232).

2. Parc André Citroën. Probably the most unconventional "park" you'll ever witness. Avant-garde heaps of metal and other pieces of "art" dot the landscape in a surprisingly pleasant arrangement. For the best view of the whole affair, try a hot-air balloon ride (p. 223).

3. Ste-Chapelle. Go on a sunny day, and the light streaming through the stained glass windows will literally leave you breathless (p. 185).

4. Cité des Sciences et de l'Industrie. A perfect stop after the Parc de la Villette. Don't miss the Explora Science Museum, a haven for the playful and young at heart, complete with an IMAX-esque cinema to take in the sights on an enormous screen.

5. Parc de la Villette. Mellow out and then take a stroll through the trippily unconventional Promenade des Jardins, which features the colorful Garden of Dunes and Wind. You might want to ride out your relaxation here before moving on to the terrifying Garden of Childhood Fears (p. 231).

THIRD AND FOURTH ARRONDISSEMENTS: THE MARAIS

see map p. 358-359

see map p. 358-359

The Marais ("swamp") was drained by monks in the 13th century and land-filled to provide building space for the Right Bank. With Henri IV's construction of the glorious **Place des Vosges** at the beginning of the 17th century, the area became the city's center of fashionable living. Leading architects and sculptors of the period designed elegant **hôtels particuliers** with large courtyards. Under Louis XV, the center of Parisian life moved to the *faubourgs* (then considered suburbs) St-Honoré and St-Germain, and construction in the Marais ceased. During the Revolution, former royal haunts gave way to slums and tenements, while the majority of the *hôtels* fell into ruin or disrepair. The Jewish population, a presence in the Marais since the 12th century, grew with influxes of immigrants from Russia and North Africa—and was tragically depleted during the Holocaust. In the 1960s the Marais was declared a historic neighborhood. A 30-year period of gentrification and renovation has restored the Marais to its pre-Revolutionary glory.

Once-palatial mansions have become exquisite museums, and the tiny twisting streets have been adopted by hip bars, avant-garde galleries, and some of the city's most unique boutiques. **Rue des Rosiers**, in the heart of the 4*ème*, is still the center of the city's Jewish population. Superb kosher delicatessens neighbor Middle Eastern and Eastern European restaurants, and on Sundays, when much of the city is closed, the Marais remains lively. The Marais is also unquestionably the center of gay Paris, with its hub around the intersection of **rue Ste-Croix de la Brettonerie** and **rue Vieille-du-Temple.** Recent heavy tourism has encroached upon the Marais's eclectic personality, threatening to reduce it to commercial blandness. However, the district still retains its signature charm: an accessible, fun, and friendly mix of old and new, queer and straight, cheap and chic, classic and cruisy, hip and historic. No pilgrim to Paris should miss it.

RIVE GAUCHE (LEFT BANK)

The *"gauche"* in Rive Gauche once signified a secondary, lower-class lifestyle, the kind flaunted by the perennially impoverished students who stayed there.

Today, the Left Bank's timeless appeal is ensured by its inexpensive cafes and bars, great shopping and sightseeing, and timeless literary caché.

FIFTH AND SIXTH ARRONDISSEMENTS: LATIN QUARTER

see map p. 362-363

The *6ème* and the western half of the *5ème* make up the *Quartier Latin*, named for the language used in the *5ème*'s prestigious *lycées* and universities prior to 1798. The *5ème* has been right in the intellectual thick of things since the founding of the **Sorbonne** in 1263, and its hot-blooded student population has played a major role in uprisings from the French Revolution to the insurrection of May 1968 (**Life and Times,** p. 62). The cafes of the legendary **boulevard St-Germain** in the *6ème* were the stomping grounds of Hemingway, Sartre, Picasso, Camus, and just about everyone else who was in Paris during the first half of the 20th century.

Many feel that the Latin Quarter has lost its rebellious vigor since 1968, citing the replacement of the old cobblestones (used by students as projectiles) with paving as proof. Yet while areas like **boulevard St-Michel** (the boundary between the *5ème* and *6ème*), with their chain stores and hordes of camera-toting tourists, are notable victims of commodification, the smaller byways of the student quarter hold fast to their progressive, edgy, and multiethnic tone. Dusty bookstores, art-house cinemas, smoky jazz clubs, and international eateries abound. **Place de la Contrescarpe** and **rue Mouffetard,** both in the *5ème*, are quintessential Latin Quarter; the Mouff' has one of the liveliest street markets in Paris. Despite its high-class fashion and ostentatious wealth, the *6ème* is home to two of Paris's most vibrant cultural staples: literary cafes and art galleries. In addition to the classic intellectual haunts of St-Germain-des-Prés, there is a thriving literary life around **Carrefour de l'Odéon.**

SEVENTH ARRONDISSEMENT

The *7ème* became Paris's most elegant residential district in the 18th century. The 1889 completion of the **Eiffel Tower** at the river's edge, though met with mixed feelings at the time, ensured a continued spotlight on

6. Parc de Belleville. A great place for the entire family to take in the sights and sounds of the suburban Parisian landscape. Complete with a playground at the entrance, numerous scening footbridges, and some amazing fountains (p. 234).

7. Parc Monceau. A wonderful place to take that special someone, weather permitting. Lounge in the shade and people-watch in the company of such wonders as an Asian pagoda and Romanesque ruins (p. 214).

8. Parc des Buttes-Chaumont. Enjoy the gorgeous modern incarnation of what once was a dumping ground for criminal corpses and a repository for horse carcasses. Not convinced? Check out some on the winding paths or the Roman temple atop a cliff (p. 232).

9. Tennisium. The tennis fans at this internationally acclaimed museum are as entertaining to observe as the sport-related artifacts themselves. Catch some of the best tennis games in history in the Tennisium's archives.

10. Passages and Galeries. The literal underground hangout of the poshest French bourgeoisie. Come here to see, be seen, or even pretend to shop among Paris's most frivolously decadent (p. 192).

DISCOVER

see map p. 364-365

the area. The World's Fairs that followed helped to cement the landmark in Parisian history. Many of the neighborhood's stunning residences have been maintained as foreign embassies, while the **National Assembly** and the **Invalides** add historical merit and traditional French character to this section of the Left Bank. Between the grass of the **Champ de Mars** and the fashionable side streets surrounding **rue de Sèvres,** the 7*ème* offers both the most touristy and the most intimate sights in Paris. Predictably, the area is expensive when it comes to food and accommodations.

EIGHTH ARRONDISSEMENT

see map pp. 366-367

For all its legendary wealth and glamor, the 8*ème* actually began life as a gloomy mire. The military set up camp in the swamp after the 1789 Revolution, but it wasn't until the mid-19th century that the area really took off. During the Second Empire, when Haussmann engineered the *grands boulevards* and finished construction of the **place de l'Etoile,** the 8*ème* came alive with social and commercial activity.

The 8*ème* today is past its prime. Its broad boulevards are still lined with vast mansions, expensive shops, and grandiose monuments, but there's little sense of movement or style. The **Champs-Elysées,** once synonymous with fashion, now rents to charmless establishments ranging from cheap to exorbitant. Much of the *arrondissement* is occupied by office buildings and car dealerships, making most of the 8*ème* comatose after dark. Only the Champs throbs late into the night, thanks to flashy nightclubs and cinemas and droves of tourists spilling over onto its sidewalks. A stroll along **avenue Montaigne, rue du Faubourg St-Honoré,** or around the **Madeleine** will give a taste of what life in Paris is like for those with money to burn. Don't expect hidden deals in this neighborhood—low prices here generally mean low quality. From a big-picture perspective, however, the 8*ème*'s *grands boulevards* are still magnificent, and the area has a small selection of excellent museums.

NINTH ARRONDISSEMENT

see map p. 368-369

The 9*ème* is a diagram of Paris's cultural extremes. The lower 9*ème* boasts the high art of the magnificent **Opéra Garnier** and the high-class *couture* of swanky department stores **Galeries Lafayette** and **Au Printemps.** The upper 9*ème*, near the northern border with the 18*ème*, offers a striking contrast: low-brow porn shops, X-rated cinemas, and prostitution characterize the neon-lighted area known as **Pigalle.** Separating these two sectors is a sleepy, residential neighborhood—the 9*ème*'s geographical center. There are plenty of hotels, but many to the north are used for the local flesh trade. Nicer but not-so-cheap hotels are available near the respectable and central bd. des Italiens and bd. Montmartre.

LET'S NOT GO. Place Pigalle and Ⓜ Barbès-Rochechoart are notorious for prostitution and drugs, both of which become apparent at an early hour. The area is heavily policed, but travelers (particularly young women and those traveling alone) should still exercise caution.

TENTH ARRONDISSEMENT

The **place de la République** was once a hotbed of Revolutionary fervor, but Haussmann put an end to that with some clever urban planning (see **Haussman-**

nia, p. 273). Since then, the 10ème has quieted down. In general, the area is one of striking juxtapositions—regal statues scrawled with graffiti and peaceful, sunny squares next to boulevards packed with seedy wares. Most travelers only visit the 10ème to use one of the *arrondissement's* two train stations, but even though the 10ème doesn't draw tourists, parts of it are well worth exploring. Good, cheap restaurants abound, and the blossoming area near **Canal St-Martin** makes for pleasant wandering.

see map p. 370

> **LET'S NOT GO.** The 10ème is far from most tourist sights, and certain areas may be unsafe at night; take care around the bd. St-Martin and parts of r. du Faubourg St-Denis at any time of day. Use caution west of pl. de la République along r. du Château d'Eau.

ELEVENTH ARRONDISSEMENT

The 11ème is most famous for hosting the Revolutionary kickoff at the **Bastille** prison on July 14, 1789 (see **Life and Times,** p. 62). The French still storm this area nightly in search of the latest cocktail, culinary innovation, or up-and-coming artist. The 1989 opening of the glassy **Opéra Bastille** on the bicentennial of the Revolution breathed new life into the 11ème. In the early 1990s, the neighborhood near the opéra was touted as the next Montmartre, the next Montparnasse, and the next Latin Quarter: the city's latest Bohemia. Today, with its numerous bars along **rue de Lappe,** international dining options on **rue de la Roquette,** young designer boutiques, and avant-garde galleries, the Bastille is on its way to fulfilling these expectations. The area is still a little rough, however, and the wide commercial boulevards that run through Bastille lack the refined charm of so many Paris neighborhoods. North of the Bastille to **rue Oberkampf** and **rue Ménilmontant,** eclectic neighborhood bars provide the perfect end to an all-night bar crawl. Five metro lines converge at Ⓜ République and three at Ⓜ Bastille, making the 11ème a transport hub and mammoth center of action, the hangout of the young and fun. Budget accommodations also proliferate in the area.

see map p. 373

> **LET'S NOT GO.** While the area is generally safe during the day, pl. de la République and bd. Voltaire are best avoided after sunset.

TWELFTH ARRONDISSEMENT

The 12ème's **place de la Nation** was the setting for Louis XIV's wedding in 1660 and the site of revolutionary fervor in 1830 and 1848. The latest popular uprising has been in response to the construction of the controversial **Opéra Bastille** in 1989, but many protests and marches start here in reverence to the location's symbolism. Today, the 12ème borrows youthful momentum from the neighboring 4ème and 11ème. Its northwestern fringes are decidedly funky (the **Viaduc des Arts, rue de la Roquette,** and **rue du Faubourg St-Antoine** are lined with galleries and stores), and its core is working class, with a large immigrant population. The streets around the Bois de Vincennes offer some of the city's most pleasant places to stay, though they're slightly removed from the city center.

see map p. 371

> ❗ **LET'S NOT GO.** Be careful around Gare de Lyon, and avoid it altogether at night.

THIRTEENTH ARRONDISSEMENT

see map p. 374

Until the 20th century, the 13ème was one of Paris's poorest *arrondissements*, with conditions so terrible that Victor Hugo used parts of the neighborhood as a setting for *Les Misérables*. Traversed by the **Bièvre,** a stagnant stream clogged with industrial refuse, the 13ème was also the city's worst-smelling district. The 20th and 21st centuries have seen many changes to the 13ème, olfactory and otherwise. In 1910, the Bièvre was filled in. Environmentalists eventually won a campaign to close the neighborhood's tanneries and paper factories. The influx of construction that began with Mitterrand's ultra-modern **Bibliothèque de France** in 1996 has continued with the MK2 entertainment complex and other developments associated with **ZAC (Zone d'Aménagement Concerté),** a project that will make the *quai* banks of the 13ème into the largest cultural center in Paris. The area is also home to several immigrant communities residing in a thriving **Chinatown.**

> ❗ **LET'S NOT GO.** Be careful near the sleazy nightlife at av. du Maine's northern end.

FOURTEENTH ARRONDISSEMENT: MONTPARNASSE

see map p. 376

Montparnasse, one of the *quartiers* of Paris most imbued with the city's bohemian mythology, was named after the famous mountain of Greek lore (Mount Parnassus) by the students who gathered here in the 18th century. The first of many generations of immigrants to settle in the 14ème were Bretons who came to the neighborhood in the 19th century (Breton *crêperies*, handicraft shops, and cultural associations still line busy **rue du Montparnasse**). During the interwar period, the area became a haven for artists, writers, and political exiles, including Hemingway, Man Ray, Modigliani, and Henry Miller. The avant-garde set up studios in Montparnasse and talked, drank, and danced all night in cafes like **Le Select** and **Le Dôme.**

The Montparnasse area (which actually extends across the boulevard du Montparnasse into the 6ème) is no longer haunted by its legendary visitors, but the 14ème's continued affordability and well-entrenched cafe culture still attract young artists and students. Restaurants (of both the cheap and Lost Generation-chic varieties), cafes, and artists' havens make the 14ème worth a visit.

FIFTEENTH ARRONDISSEMENT

see map p. 375

Unlike its neighbors to the east, the Latin Quarter and Montparnasse, the 15ème has never been a legendary area. The 15ème today is the city's most populous *arrondissement,* and it has been predominantly middle-class for decades. The modern **Parc André Citroën** attracts families from all over Paris on weekends. Aside from the park, the 15ème doesn't have tourist sights to speak of, and the atmosphere is often crowded, busy, and—around Gare Montparnasse—very industrial. As a result, the 15ème is one of Paris's least touristed areas, and savvy travelers can benefit from low room rates and affordable restaurants. Locals have their pick among the many grocers on r.

du Commerce, the cafes at the corner of r. de la Convention and r. de Vaugirard, and the specialty shops along av. Emile Zola.

SIXTEENTH ARRONDISSEMENT

see map p. 378

When Notre Dame was under construction, this now-elegant suburb was little more than a cluster of tiny villages in the woods. So it remained for several centuries, as kings and nobles chased deer and boar through its forests. With the architectural revolution of Haussmann, however (see **Haussmania,** p. 273), the area was transformed. The villages of **Auteuil** to the south, **Passy** in the east, and northernmost **Chaillot** banded together, joining the city to form what is now the 16*ème*.

Today, the manicured, tree-lined streets of this elegant *quartier* provide a peaceful respite from the mobbed sidewalks of the neighboring 8*ème*. The 16*ème* offers some of the best views of the Eiffel Tower, framed by immaculate Art Nouveau and art deco architecture. There's also an impressive density of **museums** that showcase everything from cutting-edge contemporary art to 2nd-century Asian statuary. The upper 16*ème* is populated with mansions and townhouses, while the lower half of the *arrondissement* is more modest and commercial.

SEVENTEENTH ARRONDISSEMENT

see map p. 379

The 17*ème arrondissement* consisted of little more than farmers' fields until the mid-19th century, when Napoleon III incorporated it into the city. By the end of the century, the area had become a center for the **Impressionist** painters (see **Life and Times,** p. 80) who came for the cheap rent and stayed for the views. Today, the 17*ème* is a diverse district, where bourgeois turns working class and back again within a block. In general, the southern and eastern parts of the *arrondissement* share the aristocratic bearing of the neighboring 8*ème* and 16*ème*, while the western half resembles the more tawdry 18*ème* and Pigalle. Thanks in large part to its multicultural population, the 17*ème* offers a fabulous variety of restaurants across the spectrum of prices. The **Village Batignolles** is a nice change of pace from central Paris, and is a great place for a stroll (during daylight hours). Hip neighborhood bars like **L'Endroit** (see **Nightlife,** p. 319) cater to stylish young crowds, while the **Musée Jean-Jacques Henner** (see **Museums,** p. 269) affords art enthusiasts a stimulating afternoon.

LET'S NOT GO. Be careful where the 17*ème* borders the 18*ème* near pl. de Clichy.

EIGHTEENTH ARRONDISSEMENT: MONTMARTRE

see map p. 368-369

Like Montparnasse and the Latin Quarter, Montmartre still glows with the lustre of its bohemian past. Named "Mount of the Martyr" for St. Denis, who was beheaded there by the Romans in AD 260, the hill was for centuries a rural village covered with vineyards, wheat fields, windmills, and gypsum mines. In the late 19th and early 20th centuries, the area became a center of the city's rebellious artistic energies. During the Belle Epoque, its picturesque beauty and low rents attracted bohemians like painter Henri Toulouse-Lautrec and composer Erik Satie as well as performers and impresarios like Aristide Bruant. Toulouse-Lautrec, in particular, immortalized Montmartre with his paintings of life in disreputable nightspots like the (in)famous **Bal du Moulin Rouge.** Filled with cabarets like

DISCOVER

Le Chat Noir, satirical journals, and proto-Dada artist groups like *Les Incohérents* and *Les Hydropathes*, the whole *butte* (ridge) became the Parisian center of free love, fun, and *fumisme:* the satirical jabbing of social and political norms. A generation later, just before WWI smashed its spotlights and destroyed its crops, the *butte* welcomed eccentric innovators like Picasso, Modigliani, Utrillo, and Apollinaire into its artistic circle and its cabarets.

Nowadays, Montmartre is a mix of nostalgic history, pseudo-artistic schmaltz (pl. du Tertre), upscale bohemia (above r. des Abbesses), and sleaze (along bd. de Clichy). The rather strenuous climb (or relaxing ride on the furnicular) up to the **Basilique du Sacré-Coeur** is worth it for the incredible panoramas of the city. The northwestern part of the *butte* retains some village charm, with breezy, cobbled streets speckled with interesting shops and cafes. Cinephiles have been flocking recently to this area to spot different locations where the hit film *Amélie* was set. At dusk, gas lamps trace the stairways up the hillside to the basilica. Hotel rates rise as you climb the hill to Sacré-Coeur. Downhill and south at seedy pl. Pigalle, accommodations tend to rent by the hour.

> **!** **LET'S NOT GO.** At night, Ⓜ **Abesses** is safer than Ⓜ **Anvers**, Ⓜ **Pigalle**, and Ⓜ **Barbès-Rochechouart.** Always be careful in areas near the northern 9*ème*.

NINETEENTH ARRONDISSEMENT

see map p. 380

The 19*ème* never got the patronage of the artists that made its bohemian neighbor, Montmartre, so famous. Many of its landmarks were constructed without attention to building codes and were later replaced by housing projects. Like Paris's other peripheral *arrondissements*, the 19*ème* is predominantly working-class and far from most central sights. However, the *arrondissement* does boast a number of charming streets and two of Paris's finest parks: the romantic **Parc des Buttes-Chaumont** and the ultramodern **Parc de la Villette**. The area of **La Mouzaia** is very pleasant to wander around, with its tree-lined streets and charming villas, overflowing with greenery and bright colors. The 19*ème* is also home to a large Asian community, and full of excellent, inexpensive eateries.

> **!** **LET'S NOT GO.** Be careful at night, particularly in the more empty northwestern corner of the *arrondissement* as well as along r. David d'Angiers, bd. Indochine, av. Corentin Cariou, r. de Belleville, and by the "Portes" into the area.

TWENTIETH ARRONDISSEMENT

see map p. 381

As Haussmann's architectural reforms expelled many of Paris's workers from the central city in the mid-19th century, thousands migrated east to **Belleville** (the northern part of the 20*ème*), **Ménilmontant** (the southern), and **Charonne** (the southeastern). By the late Second Republic, the 20*ème* had come to be known as a "red" *arrondissement*, characterized as proletarian and radical. Some of the heaviest fighting during the suppression of the Commune took place in its streets, where the Communards made desperate last stands on their home turf. Caught between the Versaillais troops to the west and the Prussian lines outside the city walls, the Commune fortified the Parc des Buttes-Chaumont and the **Cimetière du Père Lachaise** but despite their heroic will to resist, they soon ran out of ammunition and *matériel*. On May 28, 1871, the Communards abandoned their last barricade and surrendered (see **Life and Times,** p. 63). The 20*ème* remained the fairly isolated home of those workers who survived the retributive massacres following the government's takeover.

Today, the *arrondissement* is still working-class, with busy residential areas and markets that cater to locals rather than visitors. The area is also home to sizable Greek, North African, Russian, and Asian communities.

BANLIEUE

The *banlieue* are the suburbs of Paris. They have recently gained international attention as sites of poverty and racism, though in fact they run the socioeconomic gamut from extremely wealthy to extremely depressed. The nearest suburbs, the *proche-banlieue*, are accessible by metro and bus lines from the city. These include the Vallé de Chevreuse towns to the south; St-Cloud, Neuilly, and Boulogne to the west; St-Mandé and Vincennes to the east; and to the north, the towns of housing projects known as *zones* or *cités*, Pantin, Aubervilliers, and La Courneuve, which have recently experienced high levels of crime and drug traffic. The *banlieue rouges* (red suburbs)—Montreuil, Bagnolet, Bobigny, and Kremlin-Bicêtre—are still run by communist governments. The *grandes banlieue* (Versailles, Chantilly, and St-Germain-en-Laye), farther afield and boasting some awesome sights (see **Daytrips**, p. 321), can be reached by RER or commuter train. The *banlieue* have also become sites of some of Paris's more exciting cultural productions. Every summer brings the annual *Banlieue Jazz* and *Banlieue Blues* festivals to the greater Paris area; throughout the year, artists' communes take advantage of government-controlled rents in the *banlieue rouges*. A radical artistic spirit continues to thrive at Parisian theater collectives. In the poorer suburbs, disaffection has in some cases been articulated as artistic expression; young people of Arab and North African descent in particular have been mixing their varied musical and cultural traditions to produce exciting, incendiary fusion music of all types.

✎ LET'S GO PICKS

BEST PLACE TO MEDITATE: The Japanese garden at **UNESCO** (p. 208).

BEST PLACE TO BE CAUGHT LOOKING FABULOUS: Anywhere in the Marais (p. 4)

BEST PLACE TO MOURN YOUR POVERTY: Avenue Montaigne in the 8ème, with the best clothes in Paris that you'll never afford.

BEST POT: Take your pick among the funky ceramic ware in the stellar **Musée Picasso** (p. 249).

BEST PLACE TO FEEL LIKE (AND MAYBE SEE) GERARD DEPARDIEU: Super-swanky **buddha-bar** (p. 311).

BEST PLACE TO FEIGN ARTSINESS: The *atelier* at **Musée Zadkine** (p. 255).

BEST PLACE TO SPEAK DRUNKEN FRENCH: The back of a taxi—the driver knows where you're going.

BEST BRIDGE BY NIGHT: The ornate **Pont Alexandre III** (p. 209) connects the Esplanade des Invalides to the Grand and Petit Palais. Built for the 1900 World's Fair, this bridge is a sight to behold when the Seine floodlights go on.

BEST PLACE TO SPEAK ENGLISH WITHOUT SHAME: O'Brien's in the 7ème. You'll feel right at home.

BEST PLACE TO LEARN ABOUT SEX: The **Musée de l'Erotisme** (p. 269), conveniently open until 2am.

MOST EXAGGERATED BREASTS: Madonna's "vast tracts of land," on display at the **Musée Grevin** (p. 263).

BEST PLACE TO EXHIBIT GRATUITOUS CANADIAN PRIDE: The friendly **Moose** bar and restaurant (p. 310).

THE MARAIS (6 DAYS)

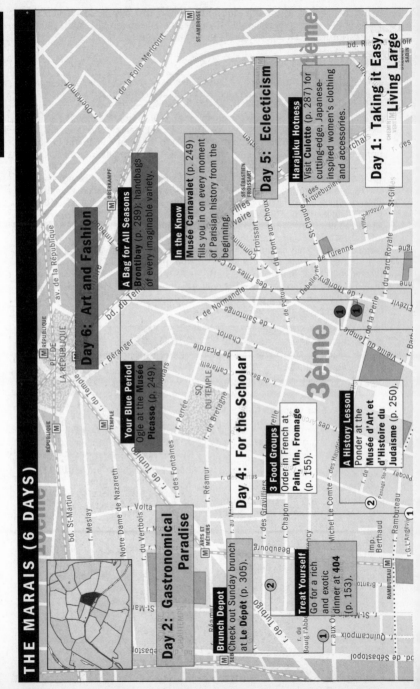

Day 1: Taking it Easy, Living Large

Harajuku Hotness Visit **Culotte** (p. 287) for cutting-edge, Japanese-inspired women's clothing and accessories.

Day 5: Eclecticism

In the Know **Musée Carnavalet** (p. 249) fills you in on every moment of Parisian history from the beginning.

Day 6: Art and Fashion

A Bag for All Seasons **Brontibay** (p. 289): handbags of every imaginable variety.

Your Blue Period Ogle at the **Musée Picasso** (p. 249).

Day 4: For the Scholar

3 Food Groups Order in French at **Pain, Vin, Fromage** (p. 155).

A History Lesson Ponder at the **Musée d'Art et d'Histoire du Judaisme** (p. 250).

Day 2: Gastronomical Paradise

Brunch Depot Check out Sunday brunch at **Le Dépôt** (p. 305).

Treat Yourself Go for a rich and exotic dinner at **404** (p. 153).

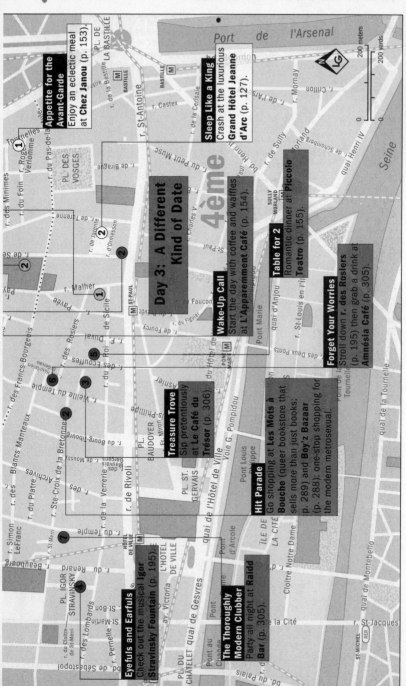

Port de l'Arsenal

Appetite for the Avant-Garde
Enjoy an eclectic meal at **Chez Janou** (p. 153).

Sleep Like a King
Crash at the luxurious **Grand Hôtel Jeanne d'Arc** (p. 127).

Day 3: A Different Kind of Date

4ème

Wake-Up Call
Start the day with coffee and waffles at **L'Apparemment Café** (p. 154).

Table for 2
Romantic dinner at **Piccolo Teatro** (p. 155).

Forget Your Worries
Stroll down r. des Rosiers (p. 195), then grab a drink at **Amnésia Café** (p. 305).

Treasure Trove
Sip pretentiously at **Le Café du Trésor** (p. 306).

Hit Parade
Go shopping at **Les Mots à Bouche** (queer bookstore that sells more than just books; p. 289) and **Boy'z Bazaar** (p. 288); one-stop shopping for the modern metrosexual.

Eyefuls and Earfuls
Check out the musical Igor (**Stravinsky Fountain**; p. 195).

The Thoroughly Modern Clubber
Party all night at **Raidd Bar** (p. 305).

THE VERY BEST OF THE LATIN QUARTER (5

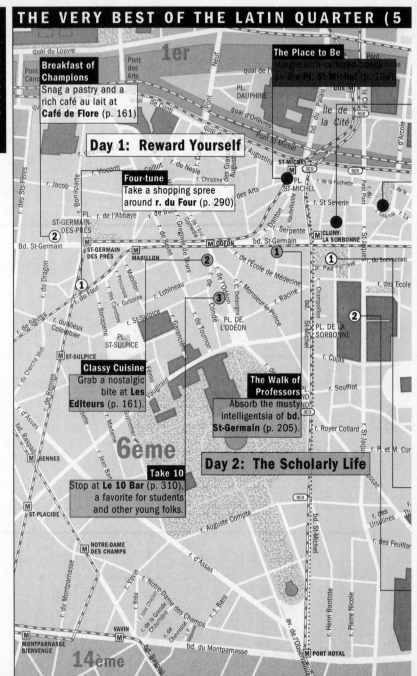

The Place to Be
Mingle with cultured coeds
on the Pl. St-Michel (p. 199).

Breakfast of Champions
Snag a pastry and a rich café au lait at **Café de Flore** (p. 161)

Day 1: Reward Yourself

Four-tune
Take a shopping spree around **r. du Four** (p. 290)

Classy Cuisine
Grab a nostalgic bite at **Les Editeurs** (p. 161).

The Walk of Professors
Absorb the musty intelligentsia of **bd. St-Germain** (p. 205).

Day 2: The Scholarly Life

Take 10
Stop at **Le 10 Bar** (p. 310), a favorite for students and other young folks.

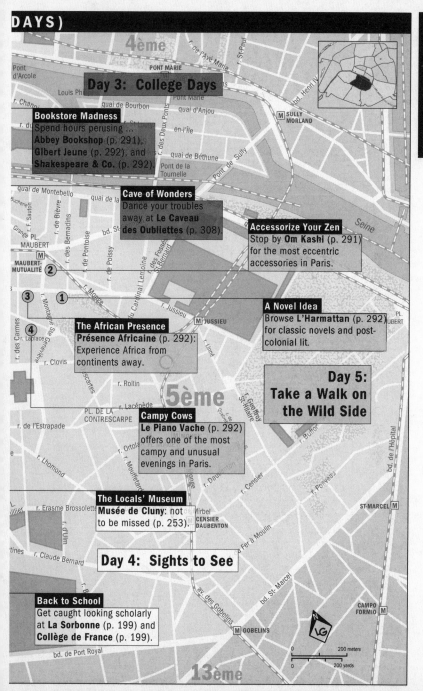

DAYS)

4ème

Day 3: College Days

Bookstore Madness
Spend hours perusing ...
Abbey Bookshop (p. 291),
Gibert Jeune (p. 292), and
Shakespeare & Co. (p. 292).

Cave of Wonders
Dance your troubles
away at **Le Caveau
des Oubliettes** (p. 308).

Accessorize Your Zen
Stop by **Om Kashi** (p. 291)
for the most eccentric
accessories in Paris.

A Novel Idea
Browse **L'Harmattan** (p. 292)
for classic novels and postcolonial lit.

The African Presence
Présence Africaine (p. 292):
Experience Africa from
continents away.

**Day 5:
Take a Walk on
the Wild Side**

5ème

Campy Cows
Le Piano Vache (p. 292)
offers one of the most
campy and unusual
evenings in Paris.

The Locals' Museum
Musée de Cluny: not
to be missed (p. 253).

Day 4: Sights to See

Back to School
Get caught looking scholarly
at **La Sorbonne** (p. 199) and
Collège de France (p. 199).

13ème

ESSENTIALS

PLANNING YOUR TRIP

ENTRANCE REQUIREMENTS

Passport (see p. 18). Required of non-EU citizens and citizens of Ireland and the United Kingdom. Passports that expire within three months of your planned departure date will not be accepted.

Visa (see p. 19). Required of non-EU citizens staying more than 90 days. A **short stay visa** is required of anyone planning to work or study in France for a period of less than 90 days. A **student visa** is required of anyone who wishes to study in France.

Work Permit (see p. 20). Required of all foreigners planning to work in France.

EMBASSIES AND CONSULATES

FRENCH CONSULAR SERVICES ABROAD

The website **www.embassyworld.com** has a complete, up-to-date list of consulates.

Australia, Consulate General, Level 26, St. Martin's Tower, 31 Market St., Sydney NSW 2000 (☎02 9261 5779; www.consulfrance-sydney.org). Open M-F 9am-1pm.

Canada, Consulat Général de France à Montréal, 1 pl. Ville-Marie, Montréal, QC H3B 4S3 (☎514-878-4385; www.consulfrance-montreal.org). Open M-F 8:30am-noon. Consulat Général de France à Québec, 25 r. St-Louis, Québec, QC G1R 3Y8 (☎418-694-2294; www.consulfrance-quebec.org). Open M-F 8:30am-noon, and 2-5pm by appointment only. Consulat Général de France à Toronto, 2 Bloor St. E, Ste. 2200, Toronto, ON M4W 1A8 (☎416-925-8041; www.consulfrance-toronto.org). Open M-F 9am-12:30pm by appointment only.

Ireland, French Embassy, Consulate Section, 36 Ailesbury Rd., Dublin 4 (☎01 277 5000; www.ambafrance.ie). Open M-F 9:30am-12:30pm.

New Zealand, New Zealand Embassy and Consulate, 34-42 Manners St., 12th Fl, P.O. Box 11-343, Wellington (☎04 384 2555; fax 04 384 2579). Open M-F 9:15am-1:15pm.

United Kingdom, Consulate General at London (for residents of England, Wales, and Northern Ireland), 58 Knightsbridge, London SW1X 7JT (☎020 7073 1000; www.ambafrance-uk.org). Open M 8:45am-2pm, Tu-Th 8:45am-noon, F 8:45-11:30am. Visa service: P.O. Box 57, 6a Cromwell Pl., London SW1X 7JT (☎020 7073 1250). Open M-F 8:45-11:30am.

United States, Consulate General, 4101 Reservoir Rd. NW, Washington, DC 20007 (☎202-944-6195, visa service 202-944-6200; www.ambafrance-us.org). Open M-F 8:45am-12:45pm. Consulates also located in Atlanta, Boston, Chicago, Houston, Los Angeles, Miami, New Orleans, New York, and San Francisco. See www.info-france-usa.org/intheus/consulates.asp for more info.

ESSENTIALS

CONSULAR SERVICES IN PARIS

In a dire situation, your country's embassy or consulate should be able to provide legal advice, and may be able to advance you some money. Dual citizens of France cannot call on the consular services of their second nationality for assistance. Call before visiting any of these embassies, as hours vary. Visa services tend to be available only in the morning.

Australia, Australian Embassy and Consulate, 4 r. Jean Rey, 75724 Paris, Cedex 15 (☎01 40 59 33 00, after-hours emergency 01 40 59 33 01; www.france.embassy.gov.au). Ⓜ Bir-Hakeim. Open M-F 9:15am-noon and 2-4:30pm.

Canada, Canadian Embassy and Consulate, 37 av. Montaigne, 75008 Paris (☎01 44 43 29 93, after-hours emergency assistance ☎01 44 43 29 00; www.dfait-maeci.gc.ca/canada-europa). Ⓜ Franklin Roosevelt. Open M-F 8:30am-11am; no appointments.

Ireland, Embassy of Ireland, 12 av. Foch, 75116 Paris (☎01 44 17 67 00, emergency 01 44 17 67 67; www.embassyofirelandparis.com). Open M-F 9:30am-noon.

New Zealand, New Zealand Embassy and Consulate, 7ter, r. Léonard de Vinci, 75116 Paris (☎01 45 01 43 43; www.nzembassy.com/france). Open July-Aug. M-Th 9am-1pm and 2-4:30pm, F 9am-2pm; Sept.-June M-Th 9am-1pm and 2-5:30pm, F 9am-1pm and 2-4pm.

United Kingdom, British Embassy, Consulate Section, 18bis, r. d'Anjou, 75008 Paris (☎01 44 51 31 02; www.amb-grandebretagne.fr). Open M and W-F 9:30am-12:30pm and 2:30-5pm, Tu 9:30am-4:30pm.

United States, Consulate General, 2 r. St-Florentin, 75382 Paris, Cedex 08 (☎01 43 12 22 22; france.usembassy.gov). Ⓜ Concorde. Open M-F 9am-noon. Notarial services Tu-F 9am-noon. Don't wait in the long line; go to the right and tell the guard that you are there for American services.

TOURIST OFFICES

The **French Government Tourist Office (FGTO)**, also known as Maison de la France, has branches throughout France and abroad. The FGTO's website, **www.franceguide.com,** offers very useful information on entry requirements and vacation packages for travelers from many countries. For Paris-specific information, visit the **Paris Office de Tourisme et des Congrès** online at www.paris-touristoffice.com or call ☎08 92 68 30 00 to consult an English-speaking representative. There are six branches of the tourist office in Paris; see the **Practical Information,** p. 116, for complete listings.

DOCUMENTS AND FORMALITIES

PASSPORTS

REQUIREMENTS
Citizens of Australia, Canada, New Zealand, Ireland, the UK, and the US need valid passports to enter France and to re-enter their home country. France does not allow entrance if the holder's passport expires within three months of the planned departure date; returning home with an expired passport is illegal and may result in a fine.

NEW PASSPORTS
Citizens of Australia, Canada, Ireland, New Zealand, the UK, and the US can apply for a passport at some post offices and at any passport office or court of law. Pass-

ports generally cost $60 for people over 16 or $40 for those younger. Applications for new passports or renewals take several months to process and should be filed well in advance of the departure date, although most passport offices can rush you a passport in two to three weeks for a very steep fee.

PASSPORT MAINTENANCE

Photocopy the page of your passport with your photo, as well as your visas, traveler's check serial numbers, and any other important documents. Carry one set of copies in a safe place, apart from the originals, and leave another set at home. Consulates also recommend that you carry an expired passport or an official copy of your birth certificate in a part of your baggage separate from other documents.

If you lose your passport, immediately notify the local police and the nearest embassy or consulate of your home government. To expedite its replacement, you will need to know all information previously recorded and show ID and proof of citizenship. In some cases, a replacement may take weeks to process, and it may be valid only for a limited time. Any visas stamped in your old passport will be irretrievably lost. In an emergency, ask for immediate temporary traveling papers that will permit you to re-enter your home country.

ONE EUROPE. European unity has come a long way since 1958, when the European Economic Community (EEC) was created to promote European solidarity and cooperation. Since then, the EEC has become the European Union (EU), a mighty political, legal, and economic institution. On May 1, 2004, 10 Southern, Central, and Eastern European countries—Cyprus, the Czech Republic, Estonia, Hungary, Latvia, Lithuania, Malta, Poland, the Slovak Republic, and Slovenia—were admitted to the EU, joining fifteen other member states: Austria, Belgium, Denmark, Finland, France, Germany, Greece, Ireland, Italy, Luxembourg, the Netherlands, Portugal, Spain, Sweden, and the UK.

What does this have to do with the average non-EU tourist? The EU's policy of **freedom of movement** means that border controls between the first fifteen member states (minus Ireland and the UK, but plus Norway and Iceland) have been abolished, and visa policies harmonized. While you're still required to carry a passport (or government-issued ID card for EU citizens) when crossing an internal border, once you've been admitted into one country, you're free to travel to other participating states. Britain and Ireland have also formed a **common travel area,** abolishing passport controls between the UK and the Republic of Ireland.

For more important consequences of the EU for travelers, see **The Euro** (p. 22), and **Customs in the EU** (p. 21).

VISAS AND WORK PERMITS

VISAS

In certain cases of travel or short residence, the government of France requires the traveler to obtain a visa. French visas are valid for travel in any of the states of the EU freedom of movement area(see **One Europe**, above), but if your primary destination is a country other than France, you should apply to that country's consulate for a visa. Before departure, check at the nearest French embassy or consulate (listed under **Embassies and Consulates**, p. 17) for up-to-date info on entry requirements. The website run by the French Government Tourist Office, www.franceguide.com, offers comprehensive and navigable visa information for citizens of most countries. US citizens can also consult the website www.pueblo.gsa.gov/cic_text/travel/foreign/foreignentryreqs.html.

VISITS OF UNDER 90 DAYS. Citizens of countries not in the EU or the European Economic Area (check www.egide.asso.fr for included countries) planning to work or study in France for a period of less than 90 days must apply for a short-stay visa *(visa court séjour)*. The fee for a short-stay visa is €35. See "Study and Work Permits," below.

VISITS OF OVER 90 DAYS. All citizens need a long-stay visa *(visa long séjour)* for stays of over 90 days. The visa can take two months to process and costs €99. US citizens can take advantage of the **Center for International Business and Travel** (**CIBT; ☎**800-925-2428; www.cibt.com), which secures visas for travel to almost all countries for a variable service charge. All foreigners (including EU citizens) who plan to stay in France for more than 90 days must apply for a temporary residence permit *(carte de séjour temporaire)* at the prefecture in their town of residence within eight days of their arrival in France. There are several types of long-stay student visas available; consult the French embassy in your home country for information, or for a supremely detailed French-language tutorial on the process, check www.service-public.fr.

STUDY AND WORK PERMITS

Admission as a visitor does not include the right to work, which is authorized only by a work permit. Entering France to study requires a special student visa. Foreign visitors are not permitted to enter France as a tourist and then change their status to that of a worker or student; they may be required to return to their home country to apply for the appropriate visas and permits. For more information, see **Beyond Tourism,** p. 105.

IDENTIFICATION

French law requires that all people carry a form of official identification at all times—either a passport or an EU government-issued identity card. The police have the right to demand to see identification at any time. Minority travelers, particularly black and Middle Eastern travelers, should be especially careful to carry proof that they are in France legally. Never carry all of your IDs together; split them up in case of theft or loss, and keep photocopies of them in your luggage and at home.

STUDENT, TEACHER, AND YOUTH IDENTIFICATION

The **International Student Identity Card (ISIC)**, the most widely accepted form of student ID, provides access to a 24hr. emergency helpline, insurance benefits for US cardholders (see **Insurance,** p. 29), and discounts on everything from airfare to museum admission to the cover charge at jazz clubs on r. de Lombards. Applicants must be full-time secondary or post-secondary school students at least 12 years of age. Because of the proliferation of fake ISICs, some services (particularly airlines) require additional proof of student identity.

The **International Teacher Identity Card (ITIC)** offers teachers the same insurance coverage as the ISIC and similar but limited discounts. For travelers who are 26 years old or under but are not students, the **International Youth Travel Card (IYTC)** also offers many of the same benefits as the ISIC.

Each of these identity cards costs US$22 or equivalent. ISIC and ITIC cards are valid for roughly one academic year; IYTC cards are valid for one year from the date of issue. Many student travel agencies (p. 32) issue the cards. For a list of issuing agencies or more information, see the **International Student Travel Confederation (ISTC)** website (www.istc.org).

The **International Student Exchange Card (ISE)** is a similar identification card available to students, faculty, and youth aged 12 to 26. The card provides discounts, medical benefits, access to a 24hr. emergency helpline, and the ability to purchase student airfares. The card costs US$25; call US ☎ 800-255-8000 for more info, or visit www.isecard.com.

CUSTOMS

Upon entering France, you must declare certain items from abroad and pay a duty on the value of those articles if they exceed the allowance established by France's customs service. Note that goods and gifts purchased at **duty-free** shops abroad are not exempt from duty or sales tax; "duty-free" merely means that you need not pay a tax in the country of purchase. Duty-free allowances were abolished for travel between EU member states on July 1, 1999, but still exist for those arriving from outside the EU. Upon returning home, you must likewise declare all articles acquired abroad and pay a duty on the value of articles in excess of your home country's allowance. In order to expedite your return, make a list of any valuables brought from home and register them with customs before traveling abroad, and be sure to keep receipts for all goods acquired abroad.

RECLAIMING VALUE-ADDED TAX. Most purchases in France include a 19.6% value-added tax (TVA). Non-EU residents (including EU citizens who reside outside the EU) can in principle reclaim the tax on purchases for export worth over €175 made in one store. Only certain stores participate in this *vente en détaxe* refund process; ask before you pay. You must show a non-EU passport or proof of non-EU residence at the time of purchase, and ask the vendor for a three-part form called a *bordereau de vente à l'exportation;* make sure that they fill it out, including your bank details. When leaving the country, present the receipt for the purchase together with the completed form to a French customs official. If you're at an airport, look for the window labeled *douane de détaxe,* and budget at least an hour for the intricacies of French bureaucracy. On a train, find an official or get off at a station close to the border. Once home, you must send a copy back to the vendor within six months; eventually the refunds will work their way into your account. Some shops exempt you from paying the tax at the time of purchase; you must still complete the above process. Food products, tobacco, medicine, firearms, unmounted precious stones, cars, means of transportation (e.g., bicycles and surfboards), and "cultural goods" do not qualify for a TVA refund. For more information, contact the Europe Tax-Free Shopping office in France, 4 pl. de l'Opéra, Paris 75002 (☎ 01 42 66 24 14).

 CUSTOMS IN THE EU. As well as freedom of movement of people within the EU (see p. 19), travelers in the 15 original EU member countries (Austria, Belgium, Denmark, Finland, France, Germany, Greece, Ireland, Italy, Luxembourg, the Netherlands, Portugal, Spain, Sweden, and the UK) can also take advantage of the freedom of movement of goods. This means that there are no customs controls at internal EU borders (i.e., you can take the blue customs channel at the airport), and travelers are free to transport whatever legal substances they like as long as it is for their own personal (non-commercial) use—up to 800 cigarettes, 10L of spirits, 90L of wine (60L of sparkling wine), and 110L of beer. You should also be aware that duty-free allowances were abolished on July 1, 1999 for travel between EU member states; however, travelers between the EU and the rest of the world still get a duty-free allowance when passing through customs.

ESSENTIALS

MONEY

CURRENCY AND EXCHANGE

The currency chart below is based on August 2006 exchange rates between local currency and Australian dollars (AUS$), Canadian dollars (CDN$), European Union Euros (€), New Zealand dollars (NZ$), British pounds (UK£), and US dollars (US$). Check the currency converter on websites like www.xe.com or www.bloomberg.com or a large newspaper for the latest exchange rates.

EUROS (€)		
AUS$ = €0.584		€1.712 = AUS$
CDN$ = €0.708		€1.411 = CDN$
NZ$ = €0.493		€2.028 = NZ$
UK£ = €1.457		€0.686 = UK£
US$ = €0.782		€1.300 = US$

As a general rule, it's cheaper to convert money in Paris than at home. While currency exchange will probably be available in your arrival airport, it's wise to bring enough foreign currency to last for the first 24 to 72 hours of your trip.

When changing money abroad, try to go only to banks or *bureaux de change* that have at most a 5% margin between their buy and sell prices. Since you lose money with every transaction, **convert large sums** (unless the currency is depreciating rapidly), **but no more than you'll need.**

If you use traveler's checks or bills, carry some in small denominations (the equivalent of US$50 or less) for times when you are forced to exchange money at disadvantageous rates, but bring a range of denominations since charges may be levied per check cashed. Store your money in a variety of forms; ideally, at any given time you will be carrying some cash, some traveler's checks, and an ATM and/or credit card.

THE EURO. The official currency of 12 members of the European Union—Austria, Belgium, Finland, France, Germany, Greece, Ireland, Italy, Luxembourg, the Netherlands, Portugal, and Spain—is now the euro.

The currency has some important—and positive—consequences for travelers hitting more than one euro-zone country. For one thing, money-changers across the euro-zone are obliged to exchange money at the official, fixed rate (see above), and at no commission (though they may still charge a small service fee). Second, euro-denominated traveler's checks can be used across the euro-zone, again at the official rate and commission-free.

TRAVELER'S CHECKS

Traveler's checks are one of the safest and least troublesome means of carrying funds. American Express and Visa are the most recognized brands. Many banks and agencies sell them for a small commission. Check issuers provide refunds if the checks are lost or stolen, and many provide additional services, such as toll-free refund hotlines abroad, emergency message services, and stolen credit card assistance. Some tourist-oriented businesses in Paris will accept traveler's checks in euros; few will accept checks in foreign currencies. Traveler's checks can be exchanged for cash at banks, post offices, or *bureaux de change*. Ask about toll-free refund hotlines and the location of refund centers when purchasing checks, and always carry emergency cash.

American Express: Checks available with commission at select banks, at all AmEx offices, and online (www.americanexpress.com; US residents only). American Express cardholders can also purchase checks by phone (☎800-721-9768). Checks available in Australian, Canadian, Euro, Japanese, British, and US currencies. For purchase locations or more information contact AmEx's service centers: in Australia ☎00 6129 18666, in New Zealand +649 367 4247, in the UK +44 1273 6969 33, in the US and Canada 800-221-7282, elsewhere, call the US collect at 801-964-6665.

Travelex: Thomas Cook MasterCard and Interpayment Visa traveler's checks available. For information about Thomas Cook MasterCard in Canada and the US call ☎800-223-7373, in the UK 0800 622 101; elsewhere call the UK collect at +44 1733 318 950. For information about Interpaymp Visa in the US and Canada call ☎800-732-1322, in the UK 0800 515 884; elsewhere call the UK collect at +44 1733 318 949. For more information, visit www.travelex.com.

Visa: Checks available (generally with commission) at banks worldwide. For the location of the nearest office, call the Visa Travelers Cheque Global Refund and Assistance Center: in the UK ☎0800 895 078, in the US 800-227-6811; elsewhere, call the UK collect at +44 2079 378 091. Checks available in British, Canadian, European, Japanese, and US currencies, among others. Visa also offers TravelMoney, a prepaid debit card that can be reloaded online or by phone. For more information on Visa travel services, see http://usa.visa.com/personal/using_visa/travel_with_visa.html.

CREDIT, ATM, AND DEBIT CARDS

Credit cards are widely accepted in Paris, though usually only for purchases of over €15. Major credit cards can be used to extract cash advances in euros from associated banks and cash machines throughout France. Credit card companies get the wholesale exchange rate, which is generally 5% better than the retail rate used by banks and other currency exchange establishments. The most commonly accepted cards, in both businesses and cash machines, are **Mastercard** (a.k.a. EuroCard) and **Visa** (a.k.a. Carte Bleue). **American Express** (US ☎800-639-1202) cards work in some ATMs, as well as at AmEx offices and major airports. Credit cards may also offer services such as insurance or emergency help, and are sometimes required in order to reserve hotel rooms or rental cars.

French-issued credit cards are fitted with a microchip (such cards are known as *cartes à puce*) rather than a magnetic strip (*cartes à piste magnétique*). Cashiers may attempt (and fail) to scan the card with a microchip reader. In such circumstances you should explain; say *"Ceci n'est pas une carte à puce, mais une carte à piste magnétique."* (This card doesn't have a chip, but a magnetic strip.)

Twenty-four hour **cash machines** are widespread in France. Depending on the system that your home bank uses, you can most likely access your personal bank account from abroad. ATMs get the same wholesale exchange rate as credit cards, but there is often a limit on the amount of money you can withdraw per day (usually around US$500). Depending upon your domestic bank, there may be a surcharge of $1-5 per withdrawal.

 BANKING ON IT. If you have a Bank of America account, you can withdraw euros with no extra charge directly from any BNP Paribas ATM.

Debit cards a are as convenient as credit cards but have a more immediate impact on your funds. A debit card can be used wherever its associated credit card company (usually Mastercard or Visa) is accepted, but the money is withdrawn directly from the holder's checking account. Debit cards often also function as ATM cards and can be used to withdraw cash from associated banks and ATMs in Paris.

The two major international money networks are **Cirrus** (US ☎800-622-7747; www.mastercard.com) and **Visa/PLUS** (US ☎800-847-2911; www.visa.com). Most ATMs charge a transaction fee that is paid to the bank that owns the ATM.

> **PINS AND ATMS.** To use a debit or credit card to withdraw money from a cash machine (ATM) in Europe, you must have a four-digit **Personal Identification Number (PIN).** If your PIN is longer than four digits, ask your bank whether you can just use the first four, or whether you'll need a new one. **Credit cards** don't usually come with PINs, so if you intend to use one at ATMs in Europe, call your credit card company before leaving to request one. Travelers with alphabetic, rather than numerical PINs may also be thrown off by the lack of letters on European cash machines. The following are the corresponding numbers to use: 1=QZ; 2=ABC; 3=DEF; 4=GHI; 5=JKL; 6=MNO; 7=PRS; 8=TUV; and 9=WXY. Note that if you mistakenly punch the wrong code into the machine three times, it will swallow your card for good.

GETTING MONEY FROM HOME

If you run out of money while traveling, the easiest and cheapest solution is to have someone back home make a deposit to your credit card or ATM card. Failing that, consider one of the following options.

WIRING MONEY

It is possible to arrange a **bank money transfer** *(un virement bancaire)*, which means asking a bank back home to wire money to a bank in Paris. This is the cheapest way to transfer cash, but it's also the slowest, taking anywhere from two days to two weeks. Note that some banks may only release your funds in local currency, potentially sticking you with a poor exchange rate; inquire about this in advance. Money transfer services like **Western Union** are faster and more convenient than bank transfers—but also much pricier. Western Union has many locations worldwide. To find one, visit www.westernunion.com, or call in Australia ☎800 173 833; in Canada 800-325-6000; in the UK 0800 83 38 33; in the US 800-325-6000; or in France 08 25 00 98 98. To wire money within the US using a credit card (Visa, MasterCard, Discover), call ☎800-225-5227. Money transfer services are also available at **American Express** and **Thomas Cook** offices. (See **Practical Information,** p. 115.)

US STATE DEPARTMENT (US CITIZENS ONLY)

In serious emergencies only, the US State Department will forward money within hours to the nearest consular office, which will then disburse it according to instructions for a US$30 fee. If you wish to use this service, you must contact the Overseas Citizens Service division of the US State Department (☎888-407-4747, or from overseas 202-501-4444).

COSTS

"Budget travel in Paris" is something of an oxymoron, but the cost of your trip will vary considerably depending on how you travel and where you stay. Before you go, work out a reasonable daily **budget** that will meet your needs.

STAYING ON A BUDGET

A modest daily budget (sleeping in hostels or budget hotels, eating one meal a day at a restaurant, going out at night) will probably fall between €45 and €50. If you stay in hostels and prepare your own food, you may be able to live on €35 per person per day. Don't forget to factor in emergency reserve funds (at least US$200) when planning how much money you'll need.

TIPS FOR SAVING MONEY

Some simpler ways include searching out opportunities for free entertainment, splitting accommodation and food costs with trustworthy fellow travelers, and buying food in supermarkets rather than eating out. Bring a sleepsack (p. 26) to save on sheet charges in European hostels, and do your **laundry** in the sink (unless you're explicitly prohibited from doing so). Museums often have certain days once a month or once a week when admission is free; plan accordingly. If you are eligible, consider getting an ISIC or an IYTC; many sights and museums offer reduced admission to students and youths. For getting around quickly, bikes are the most economical option. Renting a bike is cheaper than renting a moped or scooter. Don't forget about walking, though; you can learn a lot about a city by seeing it on foot. Drinking at bars and clubs quickly becomes expensive. It's cheaper to buy alcohol at a supermarket and imbibe before going out. That said, don't go overboard. Though staying within your budget is important, don't do so at the expense of your health or a great travel experience.

TIPPING AND BARGAINING

By law, service must be included at all **restaurants, bars,** and **cafes** in France. Look for the phrase *service compris* on the menu. If service is not included, tip 15%. If you are particularly pleased with the service, you may leave an additional *pourboire* at a cafe, bistro, restaurant, or bar, from half a euro to 5% of the bill. Concierges may expect to be tipped for services beyond the call of duty (never less than €1.50); tip porters €1-2 per bag and chambermaids €1-2 per day. Hairdressers are generally tipped 10%, assistants 5%. Taxi drivers expect 10-15% of the fare. It is polite to give €1 to cloakroom and washroom attendants and museum ushers and guides.

Though you should feel free to inquire about discounts and less pricey options, do not try to bargain at establishments like hotels, hostels, restaurants, cafes, museums, and nightclubs. Bargaining is acceptable, though not encouraged, at outdoor markets; haggling is standard, however, at flea markets like the Puces St-Ouen (see **Shopping,** p. 298).

TAXES

The **value-added tax (VAT)** is a general tax on doing business in France; it applies to a wide range of goods (entertainment, food, accommodations) and

---

10 7 4 2 6 5 3 1

TOP TEN LIST

TOP 10 WAYS TO SAVE IN PARIS

The City of Light is brimming with ways to experience its shimmering romance without breaking the bank, even despite the dollar's recent weakness overseas. Here are some tips to help you out.

1. Buy your food at grocery stores or an open-air markets instead of splurging at a restaurant.

2. Skip the costly museums and spend a day lounging in the gorgeous **Jardins de Luxembourg** (see **Sights,** p. 204).

3. Instead of springing for overpriced mixed drinks, buy your own liquor from the grocery store and drink it before going out.

4. In the summer, check out one of Paris's many **film festivals** (see **Life and Times,** p. 95). Most of them are free, and the **Fête du Cinéma** (p. 96) offers discounted rates at all major theaters.

5. Be on the lookout for days on which you can get into museums and sights for free.

6. Rent a bike, not a moped or a motorcycle.

7. Take the bus instead of the metro: it's cheaper, and you'll see more of Paris.

8. Find a hotel or hostel in the 17-20eme *arrondissements*, where rates are cheaper.

9. Guide yourself through a museum with an **audioguide** as an alternative to a guided tour.

10. Grab a *galette* as a hearty and inexpensive meal.

services. The tax can be up to 19.6% of the price of the good. Some of the VAT can be recovered (see **Reclaiming Value-Added Tax,** p. 21). There is also a tax on stays at hotels, hostels, and other accommodations *(taxe de séjour)*, which is typically included in the price of a stay and is the price quoted in *Let's Go Paris.*

PACKING

Even if Paris is the only stop on your travel itinerary, it's a good idea to pack lightly. Airports and train stations are more easily navigable with light luggage, and leaving your valuables at home lowers the risk of loss or theft. Lay out only what you absolutely need, then take half the clothes and twice the money. The Travelite FAQ (www.travelite.org) is a good resource for tips on traveling light. The online **Universal Packing List** (http://upl.codeq.info) will generate a customized list of suggested items based on your trip length, the expected climate, your planned activities, and other factors.

Clothing: The French tend to dress more conservatively than people in some other countries. They also live up to their reputation for being very stylish, so leave the shorts and t-shirts at home. Remember to dress modestly if you plan to visit any of the city's religious sights and centers like Notre Dame or la Mosqée de Paris. Flip-flops or waterproof sandals are must-haves for grubby hostel showers; a raincoat will be indispensible in winter and early spring.

Sleepsack: Some hostels require that you either rent sheets from them or provide your own linen. Save cash by making your own sleepsack: fold a full-size sheet in half the long way, then sew it closed along the long side and one of the short sides.

Converters and Adapters: In France, electricity is 220V AC, enough to fry any 120V North American appliance. 220/240V electrical appliances won't work with a 120V current, either. Americans and Canadians should buy an adapter (changes the shape of the plug; US$5) and a converter (changes the voltage; US$20). Don't make the mistake of using only an adapter (unless appliance instructions explicitly tell you to). New Zealanders and Australians (who use 230V at home) won't need a converter, but will need a set of adapters to use anything electrical. For more on adapters, check out http://kropla.com/electric.htm.

Contact lenses: It may be difficult to find your accustomed brand of contacts in Paris, so bring enough extra pairs and solution for your entire trip. Also bring your glasses and a copy of your prescription in case you need emergency replacements.

First-Aid Kit: For a basic first-aid kit, pack bandages, a pain reliever, antibiotic cream, a thermometer, a Swiss Army knife, tweezers, decongestant, diarrhea or upset-stomach medication (Pepto Bismol or Imodium), an antihistamine, and sunscreen.

Other Useful Items: Particularly if you're staying in a hostel, you might consider bringing a **money belt** and small **padlock** to protect your belongings. An **umbrella,** an **alarm clock,** and a small **calculator** are also helpful items to pack.

Important Documents: Don't forget your passport, traveler's checks, ATM and/or credit cards, adequate ID, and photocopies of all of the aforementioned in case these documents are lost or stolen (p. 20). Also check that you have any of the following that might apply to you: a hosteling membership card (p. 50); driver's license (p. 20); travel insurance forms (p. 29); ISIC card (p. 20); rail or bus pass (p. 38).

SAFETY AND HEALTH

GENERAL ADVICE

In any type of crisis situation, the most important thing to do is **stay calm.** Your country's embassy abroad (p. 18) is usually your best resource when things go wrong. The government offices listed in the **Travel Advisories** box can provide information on the services they offer their citizens in case of emergencies abroad.

SPECIFIC CONCERNS

DRUGS AND ALCOHOL
Possession of drugs in France can end your vacation abruptly; convicted offenders can expect a jail sentence and fines. Never bring any illegal drugs across a border. Trains from Amsterdam, especially, are often met by guard dogs ready to sniff out drugs. It is vital that **prescription drugs,** particularly insulin, syringes, or narcotics, be accompanied by their prescriptions and a statement from a doctor and left in original, labeled containers. In France, police may stop and search anyone on the street for no apparent reason. Also, a positive result of the gentlemanly drinking age (16) is that public drunkenness is virtually unseen, even in younger crowds.

DEMONSTRATIONS AND POLITICAL GATHERINGS
Paris has seen its share of strikes and demonstrations by students, labor groups, and other interests. While violent civil disorder is uncommon (though not unheard of; consider the race riots of 2005 and 2006), public protests always contain the threat of more dangerous confrontations among groups or with the police. Tourists are advised to avoid such demonstrations.

As in any big city, some neighborhoods of Paris experience unrest during sensitive political times. The most common form of violence is property damage, and tourists are unlikely targets. In general, use common sense in conversation and, as in dealing with any issues of a different culture, be respectful of locals' religious and political perspectives.

TERRORISM
Terrorism has not been a serious problem in France in recent years, but the country does contain cells of al Qaeda and other terrorist groups. After September 11, 2001, the French government heightened security at public places. Many train stations no longer permit luggage storage, for example. Many cities have recently experienced unrest, but conflict tends to center around immigrant conditions rather than terrorism. Since its colonial period, France has had a tense and often hostile relationship with Algeria. Anti-Semitic incidents in France have been in the international spotlight recently; several Jewish synagogues have been fire-bombed in the past few years. The box on **Travel Advisories** (p. 28) lists offices to contact and websites to visit to get the most up-to-date list of your home country government's warnings.

PERSONAL SAFETY

EXPLORING AND TRAVELING
To avoid unwanted attention, try to blend in as much as possible. Familiarize yourself with your surroundings before setting out, and carry yourself with confidence. Check maps in shops and restaurants rather than on the street. If you are traveling alone, be sure someone at home knows your itinerary, and *never admit to strangers that you're by yourself.* When walking at night, stick to busy, well-lit streets.

There is no sure-fire way to avoid all the threatening situations you might encounter while traveling, but a good **self-defense course** will give you concrete ways to react to unwanted advances. Impact, Prepare, and Model Mugging can

ESSENTIALS

TRAVEL ADVISORIES. The following government offices provide travel information and advisories by telephone, by fax, or via the web:

Australian Department of Foreign Affairs and Trade: ☎612 6261 1111; www.dfat.gov.au.

Canadian Department of Foreign Affairs and International Trade (DFAIT): Call ☎800-267-8376; www.dfait-maeci.gc.ca. Call for their free booklet, *Bon Voyage...But.*

New Zealand Ministry of Foreign Affairs: ☎044 398 000; www.mfat.govt.nz.

United Kingdom Foreign and Commonwealth Office: ☎020 7008 1500; www.fco.gov.uk.

US Department of State: ☎888-407-4747; http://travel.state.gov. Visit the website for the booklet *A Safe Trip Abroad.*

refer you to local self-defense courses in Australia, Canada, Switzerland and the US. Visit the website at www.modelmugging.org for a list of nearby chapters. Workshops (2-4hr.) start at US$50; full courses (20hr.) run US$350-500.

POSSESSIONS AND VALUABLES

RISKS

Tourists in Paris are often targets of petty crime. When traveling in Paris, **never let your passport or your bags out of your sight.** Bring your own **padlock** for hostel lockers, and never store valuables in any locker. Be vigilant with your baggage at **airports** and **train stations.** Take a **licensed taxi. Pickpockets** and **con artists** often work in groups, and children are among the most effective extortionists in Paris. Pickpocketing is common on the Paris metro, especially on line #1 and the RER B line to De Gaulle Airport, and at department stores, particularly on the escalators. Also be alert in public telephone booths: if you must say your calling card number, do so very quietly; if you punch it in, make sure no one can look over your shoulder. If you're driving in Paris, lock your doors and keep bags away from windows; scooter-borne thieves have been known to snatch purses and bags from cars stopped at lights.

PRECAUTIONS

There are a few steps you can take to minimize the financial risk associated with traveling. First, **bring as little with you as possible.** Second, buy a few combination **padlocks** to secure your belongings either in your pack or in a hostel locker. Third, **carry as little cash as possible.** Keep your traveler's checks and ATM/credit cards in a **money belt**—not a "fanny pack"—along with your passport and ID cards. Fourth, **keep a small cash reserve separate from your primary stash.** This should be about US$50 (US$ or euros are best) sewn into or stored in the depths of your luggage, along with your traveler's check numbers and important photocopies.

If you will be traveling with electronic devices, such as a laptop computer or a PDA, check whether your homeowner's insurance covers loss, theft, or damage when you travel. If not, you might consider purchasing a low-cost separate insurance policy. **Safeware** (☎US 800-800-1492; www.safeware.com) specializes in covering computers and charges $90 for 90-day comprehensive international travel coverage up to $4000.

PRE-DEPARTURE HEALTH

In your **passport,** write the names of any people you wish to be contacted in case of a medical emergency, and list any allergies or medical conditions you may have. Matching a prescription to a foreign equivalent is not always easy, so if you take prescription drugs, consider carrying up-to-date, legible prescriptions or a statement from your doctor stating the medication's trade name, manufacturer, chemical name, and dosage. While traveling, be sure to keep all medication with you in your carry-on luggage. For tips on packing a basic **first-aid kit** and other health essentials, see p. 26.

IMMUNIZATIONS AND PRECAUTIONS

Travelers over two years old should make sure that the following vaccines are up to date: MMR (for measles, mumps, and rubella); DTaP or Td (for diphtheria, tetanus, and pertussis); IPV (for polio); Hib (for *haemophilus* influenza B); and HepB (for Hepatitis B). For recommendations on immunizations and prophylaxis, consult the CDC (see below) in the US or the equivalent in your home country, and check with a doctor for guidance.

INSURANCE

Travel insurance covers four basic areas: medical/health problems, property loss, trip cancellation/interruption, and emergency evacuation. Though regular insurance policies may well extend to travel-related accidents, you may consider purchasing separate travel insurance if the cost of potential trip cancellation, interruption, or emergency medical evacuation is greater than you can absorb. Prices for travel insurance purchased separately generally run about US$50 per week for full coverage, while trip cancellation/interruption may be purchased separately at a rate of US$3-5 per day depending on length of stay.

Medical insurance (especially university policies) often covers costs incurred abroad; check with your provider. **US Medicare** does not cover foreign travel. **Canadian** provincial health insurance plans often do not cover foreign travel; check with the provincial Ministry of Health or Health Plan Headquarters for details. **Homeowners' insurance** (or your family's coverage) often covers theft during travel and loss of travel documents (passport, plane ticket, railpass, etc.) up to US$500.

ISIC and **ITIC** (see p. 20) provide basic insurance benefits to US cardholders, including US$165 per day of in-hospital sickness for up to 60 days and US$5000 of accident-related medical reimbursement (see www.isicus.com for details). Cardholders have access to a toll-free 24hr. helpline for medical, legal, and financial emergencies overseas. **American Express** (US ☎ 800-528-4800) grants most cardholders automatic collision and theft car rental insurance and ground travel accident coverage of US$100,000 on flight purchases made with the card.

INSURANCE PROVIDERS

STA (p. 32) offers a range of plans that can supplement your basic coverage. Other private insurance providers in the US and Canada include: **Access America** (☎ 800-729-6021; www.acessamerica.com); **Berkely Group** (☎ 800-797-4514; www.berkely.com); **CSA Travel Protection** (☎ 800-873-9855; www.csatravelprotection.com); **Travel Assistance International** (☎ 800-821-2828; www.europ-assistance.com); and **Travel Guard** (☎ 800-826-4919; www.travelguard.com). **Columbus Direct** (☎ 0870 033 9988; www.columbusdirect.co.uk) operates in the UK, and **AFTA** (☎ 02 9264 3299; www.afta.com.au) in Australia.

ESSENTIALS

USEFUL ORGANIZATIONS AND PUBLICATIONS

The American **Centers for Disease Control and Prevention** (**CDC**; ☎877-FYI-TRIP; www.cdc.gov/travel) maintains an international travelers' hotline and an informative website. Consult the appropriate government agency of your home country for consular information sheets on health, entry requirements, and other issues for various countries (see the listings in the box on **Travel Advisories**, p. 28). For quick information on health and other travel warnings, call the **Overseas Citizens Services** (M-F 8am-8pm from US ☎888-407-4747, from overseas 202-501-4444), or contact a passport agency, embassy, or consulate abroad. For information on medical evacuation services and travel insurance firms, see the US government's website at http://travel.state.gov/travel/abroad_health.html or the **British Foreign and Commonwealth Office** (www.fco.gov.uk). For general health info, contact the **American Red Cross** (☎202-303-4498; www.redcross.org).

STAYING HEALTHY IN PARIS

POTENTIAL AILMENTS

ASTHMA AND ALLERGIES

People with **asthma** or **allergies** should be aware that Paris has visibly high levels of air pollution, particularly during the summer, and that non-smoking areas are almost nonexistent. Call ☎01 44 59 47 64 for information on air quality in Paris. (Open M-F 9am-2:30pm and 3:30-5:45pm; operator speaks only French.) Consider bringing an over-the-counter antihistamine, decongestant, inhaler, etc., since there may not be a French equivalent with the correct dosage. Allergy sufferers might also want to obtain a full supply of necessary medication before the trip. Matching a prescription to a foreign equivalent is not always possible.

TRAVELER'S DIARRHEA

Results from drinking fecally contaminated water or eating uncooked and contaminated foods. Symptoms include nausea, bloating, and urgency. Try quick-energy, non-sugary foods with protein and carbohydrates to keep your strength up. Over-the-counter anti-diarrheals (e.g., Imodium) may counteract the problems. The most dangerous side effect is dehydration; drink 8 oz. of water with ½ tsp. of sugar or honey and a pinch of salt, try uncaffeinated soft drinks, or eat salted crackers. If you develop a fever or your symptoms don't go away after four to five days, consult a doctor. Consult a doctor immediately for treatment of diarrhea in children.

INFECTIOUS DISEASES

AIDS AND HIV. For detailed information on Acquired Immune Deficiency Syndrome (AIDS) in Paris, call the US Centers for Disease Control's 24hr. hotline at ☎800-342-2437. Note that France screens incoming travelers for AIDS, primarily those planning extended visits for work or study, and denies entrance to those who test HIV-positive. Contact the consulate of France for information.

HEPATITIS B. A viral infection of the liver transmitted via blood or other bodily fluids. Symptoms, which may not surface until years after infection, include jaundice, loss of appetite, fever, and joint pain. It is transmitted through activities like unprotected sex, injections of illegal drugs, and unprotected health work. A three-shot vaccination sequence is recommended for health-care workers, sexually active travelers, and anyone planning to seek medical treatment abroad; it must begin six months before traveling.

HEPATITIS C. Like Hepatitis B, but the mode of transmission differs. IV drug users, those with occupational exposure to blood, hemodialysis patients, and recipients of blood transfusions are at the highest risk, but the disease can also be spread through sexual contact or sharing items like razors and toothbrushes that may have traces of blood on them. No symptoms are usually exhibited, but if there are any, they can include loss of appetite, abdominal pain, fatigue, nausea, and jaundice. If untreated, Hepatitis C can lead to liver failure.

RABIES. Transmitted through the saliva of infected animals; fatal if untreated. By the time symptoms (thirst and muscle spasms) appear, the disease is in its terminal stage. If you are bitten, wash the wound thoroughly, seek immediate medical care, and try to have the animal located. Rabies is found all over the world, and it is often transmitted through dogs.

SEXUALLY TRANSMITTED INFECTIONS (STIS). Gonorrhea, chlamydia, genital warts, syphilis, herpes, and other STIs can be just as deadly as HIV. Hepatitis B and C can also be transmitted sexually. Though condoms may protect you from some STIs, oral or even tactile contact can lead to transmission. If you think you may have contracted an STI, see a doctor immediately.

MEDICAL CARE IN PARIS

France's socialized medical system provides care that is widely available and of high quality, but it may seem unfamiliar and intimidating to a foreigner, especially one who does not speak French fluently. **The American Hospital of Paris,** 63 bd. Victor Hugo (☎01 46 41 25 25) and **Hertford British Hospital,** 3, r. Barbes (☎01 46 39 22 22) are private hospitals staffed with English-speaking staff members. A visit to a doctor will cost around €20; if you go to a state hospital while in Paris, you will most likely have to pay in full and send in for reimbursement later on.

Pharmacies in Paris are ubiquitous and marked with a green cross. Almost every drug (including allergy medications and fever reducers) requires a prescription. The shelves of pharmacies display only skin care products and other ephemera; for non-prescription medications you'll have to ask the pharmacist. See **Practical Information,** p. 121, for a list of pharmacies.

If you are concerned about obtaining medical assistance while traveling, you may wish to employ special support services. The *MedPass* from GlobalCare, Inc., 6875 Shiloh Rd. East, Alpharetta, GA 30005, USA (☎800-860-1111; www.globalcare.net), provides 24hr. international medical assistance and support. The International Association for Medical Assistance to Travelers (IAMAT; US ☎716-754-4883, Canada 519-836-0102; www.cybermall.co.nz/NZ/IAMAT) has free membership, lists English-speaking doctors worldwide, and offers detailed info on immunization requirements and sanitation. If your regular **insurance** policy does not cover travel abroad, you may wish to purchase additional coverage.

Those with medical conditions (such as diabetes, allergies to antibiotics, epilepsy, heart conditions) may want to obtain a **Medic Alert** membership (first year US$35, annually thereafter US$20), which includes a stainless steel ID tag, among other benefits, like a 24hr. collect-call number. Contact the Medic Alert Foundation, 2323 Colorado Ave., Turlock, CA 95382, USA (☎888-633-4298, outside the US 209-668-3333; www.medicalert.org). For more on medical and emergency assistance, see the **Practical Information** (p. 121).

 AND YOU'LL FEEL BETTER FAST. Feeling a bit under the weather? Step into a *pharmacie* for all your basic cold and flu remedies. Regular stores aren't allowed to sell medicine in France, but there is a green-lighted *pharmacie* to be found on nearly every corner.

WOMEN'S HEALTH

All pharmacies in Paris carry **sanitary supplies,** though your favorite brand may not be stocked. **Condoms** can be purchased from pharmacies, supermarkets, and even vending machines in the metro; at a pharmacy ask for "*une boîte de préservatifs*" (oon BWAHT duh PREY-zehr-va-TEEF). You'll need a prescription for birth control pills *(la pillule),* but the morning-after pill is available without prescription at many pharmacies.

Surgical and pharmaceutical first-trimester **abortions** are legal in France. Minors need the permission of a legal adult. Contact the French branch of the International Planned Parenthood Federation, the **Mouvement Français pour le Planning Familial (MFPF),** which can supply the names of Paris hospitals and OB/GYN clinics performing abortions. (☎01 48 07 29 10. €550 if not covered by insurance.) More info about family planning centers can also be obtained through the **International Planned Parenthood Federation,** 120 Wall St., 9th fl., New York, NY 10005 (☎212 248 6400).

GETTING TO PARIS

BY PLANE

When it comes to airfare, a little effort can save you a bundle. If your plans are flexible enough to deal with the restrictions, courier fares are the cheapest. Tickets bought from consolidators and standby seating are also good deals, but last-minute specials, airfare wars, and charter flights often beat these fares. The key is to hunt around, to be flexible, and to ask persistently about discounts. Students, seniors, and those under 26 should never pay full price for a ticket.

AIRFARES

Airfares to Paris peak between June and September; holidays are also expensive. Mid-week (M-Th morning) round-trip flights run substantially cheaper than weekend flights, but they are generally more crowded and less likely to permit frequent-flier upgrades. Not fixing a return date (open return) or arriving in and departing from different cities (open-jaw) can be pricier than round-trip flights. Patching one-way flights together is the most expensive way to travel.

If Paris is only one stop on a more extensive globe-hop, consider a round-the-world (RTW) ticket. Tickets usually include at least five stops and are valid for about a year; prices range US$1200-5000. Try **Northwest Airlines/KLM** (US ☎800-225-2525; www.nwa.com) or **Star Alliance,** a consortium of 22 airlines including United Airlines (US ☎800-241-6522; www.staralliance.com).

Round-trip fares to Paris from the US range from US$250-500 (low season) to US$300-800 (high season); from Australia, AUS$1600-3000; from New Zealand, NZ$5000-9000; from Britain, UK$40-80; from Dublin to Paris, as little as €40.

BUDGET AND STUDENT TRAVEL AGENCIES

While knowledgeable agents specializing in flights to Paris can make your life easy and help you save, they may not spend the time to find you the lowest possible fare—they get paid on commission. Travelers holding **ISICs** and **IYTCs** (p. 20) qualify for big discounts from student travel agencies. Most flights from budget agencies are on major airlines, but in peak season some may sell seats on less reliable chartered aircraft.

CTS Travel, 30 Rathbone Pl., London W1T 1GQ, UK (☎020 7447 5000; www.ctstravel.co.uk). A British student travel agent with offices in 39 countries including the US, Empire State Building, 350 Fifth Ave., Suite 7813, New York, NY 10118 (☎877-287-6665; www.ctstravelusa.com).

STA Travel, 5900 Wilshire Blvd., Ste. 900, Los Angeles, CA 90036, USA (24hr. reservations and info ☎800-781-4040; www.statravel.com). A student and youth travel organization with over 150 offices worldwide (check their website for a listing of all their offices), including US offices in Boston, Chicago, L.A., New York, Seattle, San Francisco, and Washington, D.C. Ticket booking, travel insurance, railpasses, and more. Walk-in offices are located throughout Australia (☎03 9207 5900), New Zealand (☎09 309 9723), and the UK (☎08701 630 026).

Travel CUTS (Canadian Universities Travel Services Limited), 187 College St., Toronto, ON M5T 1P7, Canada (☎866-246-9762; www.travelcuts.com). Offices across Canada and the US including Los Angeles, New York, Seattle, and San Francisco.

USIT, 19-21 Aston Quay, Dublin 2, Ireland (☎01 602 1904; www.usit.ie), Ireland's leading student/budget travel agency has 20 offices throughout Northern Ireland and the Republic of Ireland. Offers programs to work, study, and volunteer worldwide.

Wasteels, Skoubogade 6, 1158 Copenhagen K., Denmark (☎3314 4633; www.wasteels.com). A huge chain with 180 locations across Europe. Sells Wasteels BIJ tickets discounted 30-45% off regular fare, 2nd-class international point-to-point train tickets with unlimited stopovers for those under 26 (sold only in Europe).

FLIGHT PLANNING ON THE INTERNET. The Internet may be the budget traveler's dream when it comes to finding and booking bargain fares, but the array of options can be overwhelming. **STA** (www.sta-travel.com) and **StudentUniverse** (www.studentuniverse.com) provide quotes on student tickets. **Orbitz** (www.orbitz.com), **Expedia** (www.expedia.com), and **Travelocity** (www.travelocity.com) offer full travel services, including flight and accommodations packages. **Priceline** (www.priceline.com) lets you specify a price, and obligates you to buy any ticket that meets or beats it; **Hotwire** (www.hotwire.com) also offers bargain fares. Other sites that compile deals for you include www.bestfares.com, www.flights.com, www.lowestfare.com, www.onetravel.com, and www.travelzoo.com.

Increasingly, there are online tools available to help sift through multiple offers. **SideStep** (www.sidestep.com; download required) and **Booking Buddy** (www.bookingbuddy.com) let you enter your trip information once and search multiple sites.

An indispensable resource on the Internet is the **Air Traveler's Handbook** (www.faqs.org/faqs/travel/air/handbook), a comprehensive listing of links to everything you need to know before you board a plane.

COMMERCIAL AIRLINES

The commercial airlines' lowest regular offer is the **APEX** (Advance Purchase Excursion) fare, which provides confirmed reservations and allows "open-jaw" tickets. Generally, reservations must be made seven to 21 days ahead of departure, with seven- to 14-day minimum-stay and up to 90-day maximum-stay restrictions. These fares carry hefty cancellation and change penalties (fees rise in summer). Book peak-season fares early. Use **Microsoft Expedia** (http://msn.expedia.com) or **Travelocity** (www.travelocity.com) to get an idea of the lowest published fares, then use the resources outlined here to try and beat those fares. Low-season fares should be appreciably cheaper than the **high-season** (mid-June through Aug.) ones listed here.

TRAVELING FROM NORTH AMERICA

Basic round-trip fares to Paris run about US$300-700. Standard commercial carriers like **American** (☎800-433-7300; www.aa.com), **United** (☎800-538-2929; www.ual.com), and **Northwest** (☎800-447-4747; www.nwa.com) will probably offer the most convenient flights, but they may not be the cheapest. Check **Lufthansa** (☎800-399-5838; www.lufthansa.com), **British Airways** (☎800-247-9297; www.britishairways.com), **Air France** (☎800-237-2747; www.airfrance.us), and **Alitalia** (☎800-223-5730; www.alitaliausa.com) for cheap tickets from destinations throughout the US to all over Europe. You might find an even better deal on one of the following airlines, if any of their limited departure points is convenient for you.

Icelandair: ☎800-223-5500; www.icelandair.com. Stopovers in Iceland for no extra cost on most transatlantic flights. New York to Paris May-Sept. US$500-1000; Oct.-May US$500-700. For last-minute offers, subscribe to their email Lucky Fares.

Finnair: ☎800-950-5000; www.finnair.com. Cheap round-trips from San Francisco, New York, and Toronto to Paris; connections throughout Europe.

TRAVELING FROM THE UK AND IRELAND

Because of the many carriers flying from the British Isles to the continent, we only include discount airlines or those with cheap specials here. The **Air Travel Advisory Bureau** in London (☎870 737 0021; www.atab.co.uk) provides referrals to travel agencies and consolidators that offer discounted airfares out of the UK. **Cheapflights** (www.cheapflights.co.uk) publishes airfare bargains.

Aer Lingus: Ireland ☎0818 365 000; www.aerlingus.ie. Return tickets from Dublin, Cork, Galway, Kerry, and Shannon to Paris (EUR€102-244).

bmibaby: UK ☎08702 642 229; www.bmibaby.com. Departures from throughout the UK. London to Paris (£35-75).

KLM: UK ☎08705 074 074; www.klmuk.com. Cheap return tickets from London and elsewhere to Paris.

Ryanair: Ireland ☎0818 303 030, UK 08712 460 000; www.ryanair.com. From Dublin, Glasgow, Liverpool, London, and Shannon to Paris.

TRAVELING FROM AUSTRALIA AND NEW ZEALAND

Air New Zealand: New Zealand ☎0800 73 70 00; www.airnz.co.nz. Auckland to Paris.

Qantas Air: Australia ☎13 13 13, New Zealand ☎0800 808 767; www.qantas.com.au. Flights from Australia and New Zealand to Paris for around AUS$2500-3000.

Singapore Air: Australia ☎13 10 11, New Zealand ☎0800 808 909; www.singaporeair.com. Flies from Auckland, Christchurch, Melbourne, Perth, and Sydney to Paris.

AIR COURIER FLIGHTS

Those who travel light should consider courier flights. Couriers help transport cargo on international flights by using their checked luggage space for freight. Generally, couriers must travel with carry-ons only and deal with complex flight restrictions. Most flights are round-trip only, with short fixed-length stays (usually one week) and a limit of a one ticket per issue. Most of these flights also operate only out of major gateway cities, mostly in North America. Round-trip courier fares from the US to Paris run about US$50-150. Most flights leave from Los Angeles, Miami, New York, or San Francisco in the US; and from Montreal, Toronto, or

Vancouver in Canada. Generally, you must be over 18 (in some cases 21). In sum-mer, the most popular destinations usually require an advance reservation of about two weeks (you can usually book up to two months ahead). Super-dis-counted fares are common for "last-minute" flights (three to 14 days ahead).

FROM NORTH AMERICA

Round-trip courier fares from the US to Paris run about US$100-500. Most flights leave from New York, Los Angeles, San Francisco, or Miami in the US; and from Montreal, Toronto, or Vancouver in Canada. The organizations below provide members with lists of opportunities and courier brokers for an annual fee. Prices quoted below are round-trip.

Air Courier Association, 1767 A Denver West Blvd., Golden, CO 80401 (☎800-211-5119; www.aircourier.org). Ten departure cities throughout the US and Canada to Paris, (high-season US$130-300). One-year membership US$49.

International Association of Air Travel Couriers (**IAATC;** www.courier.org). From 7 North American cities to Western European cities, including Paris. One-year membership US$45.

Courier Travel (www.couriertravel.org). Searchable online database. Multiple departure points in the US to Paris.

FROM THE UK, AUSTRALIA, AND NEW ZEALAND

The minimum age for couriers from the **UK** is usually 18. The **International Associa-tion of Air Travel Couriers** (www.courier.org; see above) often offers courier flights from London to Tokyo, Sydney, and Bangkok and from Auckland to Frankfurt and London. **Courier Travel** (see above) also offers flights from London and Sydney.

STANDBY FLIGHTS

Traveling standby requires considerable flexibility in arrival and departure dates and cities. Companies dealing in standby flights sell vouchers rather than tickets, along with the promise to get you to your destination (or near your destination) within a certain window of time (typically 1-5 days). Participants call in before their specific window of time to hear their flight options and the probability that they will be able to board each flight. You can then decide which flights you want to try to make, show up at the appropriate airport at the appropriate time, present your voucher, and board if space is available. Vouchers can usually be bought for both one-way and round-trip travel. You may receive a monetary refund only if every available flight within your date range is full; if you opt not to take an avail-able (but perhaps less convenient) flight, you can only get credit toward future travel. Carefully read agreements with any company offering standby flights, as tricky fine print can leave you in a lurch. To check on a company's service record in the US, call the Better Business Bureau (☎703-276-0100; www.bbb.org). It is dif-ficult to receive refunds, and clients' vouchers will not be honored when an airline fails to receive payment in time.

TICKET CONSOLIDATORS

Ticket consolidators, or **"bucket shops,"** buy unsold tickets in bulk from com-mercial airlines and sell them at discounted rates. The best place to find these deals is in the Sunday travel section of any major newspaper (such as *The New York Times*), where many bucket shops place tiny ads. Call quickly, as avail-ability is typically extremely limited. Not all bucket shops are reliable, so insist on a receipt that gives full details of restrictions, refunds, and tickets, and pay by credit card (in spite of the 2-5% fee) so you can stop payment if you never receive your tickets. For more info, see www.travel-library.com/air-travel/con-solidators.html.

TRAVELING FROM THE US AND CANADA

Some consolidators worth trying are **Rebel** (☎800-732-3588; www.rebel-tours.com), **Cheap Tickets** (www.cheaptickets.com), **Flights.com** (www.flights.com), and **TravelHUB** (www.travelhub.com). But these are just suggestions to get you started in your research. Let's Go does not endorse any of these agencies. As always, be cautious, and research companies before you hand over your credit card number.

BY TRAIN

THE REAL DEAL. A word on **safety:** each terminal shelters its chare of thieves. Gare du Nord and Gare d'Austerlitz are rough at night, when drugs and prostitution emerge. Official ciybters are the only safe (financially and other-wise) places to buy tickets. For the most current timetables and prices, consult the **SNCF** website at www.sncf.org.

If you're traveling to Paris from another European city, trains can be a scenic and inexpensive option. The prices below are the **undiscounted fares** for one-way, second-class tickets, unless otherwise noted. Prices and number of trips per day vary greatly according to the day of the week, season, and other criteria.

Gare du Nord: Trains to northern France, Britain, Belgium, the Netherlands, Scandinavia, Eastern Europe, and northern Germany (Cologne, Hamburg) all depart from this station. To: Amsterdam (4-5hr., €90); Brussels (1½hr., €68); London (by the Eurostar Chunnel; 3hr., up to €300).

Gare de l'Est: To eastern France (Champagne, Alsace, Lorraine, Strasbourg), Luxem-bourg, parts of Switzerland (Basel, Zürich, Lucerne), southern Germany (Frankfurt, Munich), Austria, Hungary, and Prague. To: Luxembourg (4-5hr., €45); Munich (9hr., €154); Prague (15hr., €152); Strasbourg (4hr., €50); Vienna (15hr., €154); Zürich (7hr., €73).

Gare de Lyon: To southern and southeastern France (Lyon, Provence, Riviera), parts of Switzerland (Geneva, Lausanne, Berne), Italy, and Greece. To: Florence (13hr., €120); Geneva (4hr., €97); Lyon (2hr., €55); Marseille (3-4hr., €70); Nice (6hr., €100); Rome (15hr., €176).

Gare d'Austerlitz: To the Loire Valley, southwestern France (Bordeaux, Pyrénées), Spain, and Portugal. (TGV to southwestern France leaves from Gare Montparnasse.) To Barce-lona (12hr., €140) and Madrid (12-13hr., €102).

Gare St-Lazare: To Normandy. To Caen (2hr., €28) and Rouen (1-2hr., 13 per day, €18).

Gare Montparnasse: To Brittany and southwestern France on the TGV. To Rennes (2hr., €48).

BY BUS

British travelers may find buses the cheapest (though slowest) way of getting to Paris, with round-trip fares starting around UK₤50. The journey by bus entails either a ferry trip or a descent into the Channel Tunnel; these extra trips are typically included in the price of a ticket. **Eurolines** is Europe's largest operator of international coach services; their return fares between London and Paris start at €40. They have offices in London (UK ☎ 0870 580 8080; www.eurolines.co.uk) and (☎ 01 49 72 57 80; www.eurolines.fr).

BY CHUNNEL FROM THE UK

Traversing 27 mi. under the sea, the Chunnel is undoubtedly the fastest, most convenient, and least scenic route from England to France.

BY TRAIN. Eurostar, Eurostar House, Waterloo Station, London SE1 8SE (UK ☎ 08705 186 186, elsewhere +44 1233 617 575; www.eurostar.com), runs frequent trains between London and the continent. Ten to 28 trains per day run to 100 destinations including Paris (4hr., US$75-400, 2nd class), Disneyland Paris, Brussels, Lille, and Calais. Book at major rail stations in the UK or at the office above.

BY CAR. Eurotunnel, UK Terminal, Ashford Rd., Folkestone, Kent, CT18 8XX (☎ 1303 28 22 22; www.eurotunnel.co.uk), shuttles cars and passengers between Kent and Nord-Pas-de-Calais. Round-trip fares for vehicles and all passengers range cost UK£223-317 with car. Same-day return costs UK£19-34, five-day return for either a car or a campervan UK£123-183. Book online or via phone. Travelers with cars can also look into sea crossings by ferry (see below).

BY BOAT

The fares below are **one-way** for **adult foot passengers** unless otherwise noted. Though standard return fares are usually just twice the one-way fare, **fixed-period returns** (usually within five days) are almost invariably cheaper. Ferries run **year-round** unless otherwise noted. **Bikes** are usually free, although you may have to pay up to UK£10 in high season. For a **camper/trailer** supplement, you will have to add UK£20-140 to the "with car" fare. If more than one price is quoted, the quote in UK£ is valid for departures from the UK, etc. A directory of ferries in this region can be found at www.seaview.co.uk/ferries.html.

Brittany Ferries: UK ☎ 08703 665 333, France ☎ 0033 298 800; www.brittany-ferries.com. **Plymouth** to **Roscoff, France** (6hr., in summer 1-3 per day, off-season 1 per week, UK£20-58 or €21-46) and **Santander, Spain** (18hr., 2 per week, return UK£80-145). **Portsmouth** to **St-Malo** (10¾hr., 1 per day, €23-49) and **Caen, France** (5¾hr., 2-4 per day, €21-44). **Poole** to **Cherbourg** (4¼hr., 2-3 per day, €21-44). **Cork** to **Roscoff, France** (14hr., mid-Mar. to early Nov. 1 per week, €52-99).

DFDS Seaways: UK ☎ 08702 520 524; www.dfdsseaways.co.uk. **Harwich** to **Cuxhaven** (19½hr., UK£29-49) and **Esbjerg, Denmark** (18hr., UK£29-49). **Newcastle** to **Amsterdam** (16hr., UK£19-39); **Kristiansand, Norway** (18¼hr., UK£19-59); and **Gothenburg, Sweden** (26hr., UK£19-59).

Fjord Line: UK ☎ 08701 439 669; www.fjordline.no. **Newcastle, England** to **Stavanger** (19½hr., UK£30-40) and **Bergen, Norway** (26hr., UK£30-40).

Irish Ferries: France ☎ 1 56 93 43 40; Ireland ☎ 353 818 300 400; UK ☎ 8705 17 17 17; www.irishferries.ie. **Rosslare** to **Cherbourg** and **Roscoff** (18hr., €49-99); and **Pembroke, UK** (3¾hr., €26-54). **Holyhead, UK** to **Dublin** (2-3hr., €24-40).

P&O Ferries: UK ☎08705 980 333; www.posl.com. **Dover** to **Calais** (1¼hr., every 40min.-1hr., 50 per day; from UK£10). Daily ferries from **Hull** to **Rotterdam, Netherlands** (10hr.) and **Zeebrugge, Belgium** (12½hr.). Both from UK£100.

SeaFrance: France ☎08 25 08 25 05; www.seafrance.com. **Dover** to **Calais** (1½hr., 15 per day, UK£7-11).

Stena Line: UK ☎ 08705 707 070; www.stenaline.co.uk. **Harwich** to **Hook of Holland** (3½hr., €31). **Fishguard** to **Rosslare** (1¾hr., €32). **Holyhead** to **Dublin** or **Dún Laoghaire** (1¾hr., €32). **Stranraer** to **Belfast** (3¼hr., €30).

GETTING INTO PARIS

AIRPORTS

ROISSY-CHARLES DE GAULLE (ROISSY-CDG)

Most transatlantic flights land at **Aéroport Roissy-CDG**, 23km northeast of Paris. For info, call the 24hr. English-speaking information center (☎01 48 62 22 80) or look it up on the web at www.adp.fr. The two cheapest and fastest ways to get into the city from Roissy-CDG are by RER and by bus.

RER

The RER train from Roissy-CDG to Paris leaves from the Roissy train station, which is in Terminal 2. To get to the station from Terminal 1, take the Red Line of the Navette, a free shuttle bus that leaves every 6-10 min. From there, the RER B (one of the Parisian commuter rail lines) will transport you to central Paris. To transfer to the metro, get off at Gare du Nord, Châtelet-Les-Halles, or St-Michel, all of which are RER and metro stops. You will need a ticket covering five zones to travel between Paris and Roissy-CDG. To get to the airport from central Paris, take the RER B to Roissy, which is the end of the line. Get on the free shuttle bus if you need to get to Terminal 1. The trip should take 30-35 minutes in either direction (RER every 15min. 5am-midnight; €7.75, children €5.50).

BUS

Taking a shuttle bus the whole distance from the airport to Paris is much simpler than the RER, and it takes about the same amount of time. The ☒**Roissybus** (☎01 49 25 61 87) leaves from r. Scribe at Place de l'Opéra every 15min. during the day (5:45am-7pm) then every 20min. at night (7-11pm). You can catch the Roissybus from Terminals 1, 2, and 3, from 6am to 11pm (adults €8.20, children under 5 free). Roissybus is not wheelchair accessible.

The **Daily Air France Buses** (recorded info available in English ☎08 92 35 08 20) are faster and more expensive than the Roissybus and run to two areas of the city. Tickets can be purchased on the bus. **Line 2** runs to and from the Arc de Triomphe (Ⓜ Charles de Gaulle-Etoile) at 1 av. Carnot (35min.; every 15min. 5:45am-11pm; one-way €10, round-trip €17, children one-way €5; 15% group discount), and to and from the pl. de la Porte de Maillot/Palais des Congrès (Ⓜ Porte de Maillot) on bd. Gouvion St-Cyr, opposite the Hôtel Méridien (same schedule and prices). **Line 4** runs to and from r. du Commandant Mouchette opposite the Hôtel Méridien (Ⓜ Montparnasse-Bienvenüe; to airport every 30min. 7am-9pm; one-way €11.50, round-trip €19.55, children one-way €5.75; 15% group discount); and to and from Gare de Lyon, at 20bis, bd. Diderot (same schedule and prices). The shuttle stops are at or between Terminals 2A-D and F and at Terminal 1 on the departures level of the airport. The Air France buses are not wheelchair accessible.

DOOR-TO-DOOR SERVICE
While the RER B and buses are the cheapest means of transportation to and from the airport, it can be pretty harrowing to navigate the train and metro stations when you're loaded down with luggage. As taxis are exorbitantly expensive (€40-50 to the center of Paris), **shuttle vans** are the best option for door-to-door service. Several companies run shuttles to and from both airports; prices range from €15 to €30. See **Practical Information,** p. 116, for services and phone numbers.

For the motion-impaired, **Airhop** (☎01 41 29 01 29; reserve 48hr. in advance) and **GIHP** (☎01 41 83 15 15) offer transport to and from the airport.

ORLY
Aéroport d'Orly (☎01 49 75 15 15 for info in English; 6am-11:45pm), 18km south of the city, is used by charters and many continental flights.

RER
From Orly Sud gate G or gate I, platform 1, or Orly Ouest level G, gate F, take the **Orly-Rail** shuttle bus (every 15min. 6am-11pm; €5.15, children €3.55) to the **Pont de Rungis/Aéroport d'Orly** train stop, where you can board the **RER C2** for a number of destinations in Paris. (35min.; every 15min. 6am-11pm; adults €5.35, children €3.75.) The **Jetbus** (every 15min. 6:20am-10:50pm, €5.15) provides a quick connection between Orly Sud, gate H, platform 2, or Orly Ouest level 0, gate C and Ⓜ Villejuif-Louis Aragon on line 7 of the metro.

BUS
Another option is the RATP ▇**Orlybus** (☎08 36 68 77 14), which runs between metro and RER stop Denfert-Rochereau in the 14*ème* and Orly's south terminal. (25min.; every 15-20min. 6am-11:30pm from Orly to Denfert-Rochereau, 5:35am-11pm from Denfert-Rochereau to Orly; €5.70.) You can also board the Orlybus at Dareau-St-Jacques, Glacière-Tolbiac, and Porte de Gentilly.

Air France Buses run between Orly and **Gare Montparnasse,** near the Hôtel Méridien, 6*ème* (Ⓜ Montparnasse-Bienvenüe), and the Invalides Air France agency, pl. des Invalides (30min.; every 15min. 6am-11:30pm; one-way €7.50, round-trip €12.75). Air France shuttles stop at Orly Ouest and then Orly Sud, at the departure levels.

ORLYVAL
RATP also runs **Orlyval** (☎01 69 93 53 00)—a combination of metro, RER, and VAL rail shuttle—which is probably your fastest option. The VAL shuttle goes from Antony (a stop on the RER line B) to Orly Ouest and Sud. You can either get a ticket just for the VAL (€7), or combination VAL-RER tickets (€8.80). Buy tickets at any RATP booth in the city, or from the Orlyval agencies at Orly Ouest, Orly Sud, and Antony. **To Orly:** Be careful when taking the RER B from Paris to Orly, because it splits into 2 lines right before the Antony stop. Get on the train that says "St-Rémy-Les-Chevreuse" or just look for the track that has a lit-up sign saying "Antony-Orly." (35min. from Châtelet; every 10min. M-Sa 6am-

10:30pm, Su and holidays 7am-11pm.) **From Orly:** Trains arrive at Orly Ouest 2min. after reaching Orly Sud. (32min. to Châtelet, every 10min. M-Sa 6am-10:30pm, Su 7am-11pm.)

DOOR-TO-DOOR SERVICE

See **Practical Information,** p. 116, for information on **shuttle van service. Taxis** from Orly to town cost around €25. Allow at least 30min.; traffic can make the trip much longer.

BEAUVAIS

Ryanair, easyJet, and other intercontinental airlines often fly into and depart from **Aéroport Beauvais.** Buses run between the airport and bd. Pershing in the 17*ème*, near the hotel Concorde Lafayette (Ⓜ Porte Maillot). Tickets are €13 and can be purchased in the arrivals lounge of the airport or on board the bus. Call ☎ 03 44 11 46 86 or consult www.aeroportbeauvais.com for bus schedules and other information.

TRAIN STATIONS

GENERAL INFORMATION

Each of Paris's six train stations is a veritable community of its own, with resident street people and police, cafés, *tabacs*, banks, and shops. Locate the ticket counters (*guichets*), the platforms (*quais*), and the tracks (*voies*), and you will be ready to roll. Each terminal has two divisions: the suburbs (*banlieue*) and the destinations outside the metropolitan area (*grandes lignes*). Some cities can be accessed by both regular trains and **trains à grande vitesse** (**TGV**; high speed trains). TGVs are more expensive, much faster, and require reservations that cost a small fee. For **train information** or to make reservations, contact SNCF (☎ 08 90 36 10 10, €0.23 per min.; www.sncf.fr). Yellow **ticket machines** (*billetteries*) at every train station sell tickets. You'll need to have a Master-Card, Visa, or American Express card and know your PIN (only MC/V accat ticket booths). **SNCF** offers discounted round-trip tickets for travelers in France, which go under the name **Tarifs Découvertes**—you should rarely have to pay full price.

    Travelers should exercise caution in train stations at night; Gare du Nord and Gare d'Austerlitz, in particular, are home to after-hours drug traffic and prostitution. Also, it is not advisable to buy tickets anywhere in the stations except at official counters. The SNCF doesn't have any outfits in refrigerator boxes, no matter what you're told.

 COMPOSTEZ! Before boarding a train, you must **validate** (*composter*) your ticket at one of the orange machines on the platform, which will stamp it with the date and time. If you fail to *composter,* the *contrôleur* will severely reprimand you in fast-paced French, and could slap you with a heavy fine.

BUS STATIONS

International buses arrive in Paris at **Gare Routière Internationale du Paris-Gallieni** (Ⓜ Gallieni), just outside Paris at 28 av. du Général de Gaulle, Bagnolet 93170.

ESSENTIALS

Eurolines (☎08 92 89 90 91, €0.34 per min.; www.eurolines.com) sells tickets to most destinations in France and neighboring countries.

GETTING AROUND PARIS

BY PUBLIC TRANSPORTATION

The **RATP (Régie Autonome des Transports Parisiens)** coordinates a network of sub-ways, buses, and commuter trains in and around Paris. For info, contact **La Maison de la RATP**, right across the street from Ⓜ Gare de Lyon (190 r. de Bercy) or the **Bureau de Tourisme RATP**, pl. de la Madeleine, 8ème (☎01 40 06 71 45; Ⓜ Madeleine; open daily 8:30am-6pm).

ESSENTIALS

FARES

Individual tickets for the RATP cost €1.30 each, or €9.60 for a *carnet* of 10. Say, *"Un ticket, s'il vous plaît"* (UHN ti-KAY…), or *"Un carnet…"* (UHN car-NAY…), to the ticket vendor. Each metro ride takes one ticket. The bus takes at least one, sometimes more, depending on connections you make and the time of day. For directions on using the tickets, see **Metro,** below.

▨ PASSES

If you're staying in Paris for several days or weeks, a **carte orange** can be very economical. Bring an ID photo (taken by machines in most major stations for €3.81) to the ticket counter and ask for a weekly *carte orange hebdomadaire* (€14.50) or the equally swank monthly *carte orange mensuelle* (€48.60). These cards have specific start and end dates (the weekly pass runs M-Su, and the monthly starts at the beginning of the month). Prices quoted here are for passes in Zones 1 and 2 (the metro and RER in Paris and suburbs), and work on all metro, bus, and RER modes of transport. If you intend to travel to the suburbs, you'll need to buy RER passes for more zones (they go up to 5). If you're only in town for a day or two, a cheap option is the **carte mobilis** (€5.20 for a 1–day pass in Zones 1 and 2; available in metro stations; ☎08 91 36 20 20), which provides unlimited metro, bus, and RER transportation within Paris.

Paris Visite tickets are valid for unlimited travel on bus, metro, and RER, as well as discounts on sightseeing trips, museum admission, and shopping at stores like Galeries Lafayette. These passes can be purchased at the airport or at metro and RER stations. The passes are available for one day (€8.35), two days (€13.70), three days (€18.25), or five days (€26.65). The discounts you receive do not nec-essarily outweigh the extra cost.

METRO

In general, the metro system is easy to navigate (pick up a colorful map at any sta-tion or use the one in the front of this book), and trains run swiftly and frequently. Metro stations, in themselves a distinctive part of the Paris landscape, are marked with an "M" or with the *"Métropolitain"* lettering designed by Art Nou-veau legend Hector Guimard.

GETTING AROUND

The earliest trains of the day start running around 5:30am, and the last ones leave the end-of-the-line stations (the *portes de Paris*) for the center of the city at about 12:15am. For the exact departure times of the last trains, check the poster in the center of each station marked *Principes de Tarification* (fare guidelines), the white sign with the platform's number and direction, or the monitors above the platform. Transport maps are posted on platforms and near turnstiles; all have a *plan du quartier* (map of the neighborhood). Connections to other lines are indicated by orange *correspondance* signs, exits indicated by blue *sortie* signs. Transfers are free if made within a station, but it is not always possible to reverse direction on the same line without exiting the station.

USING TICKETS

To pass through the turnstiles, insert your ticket into the small slot in the metal divider just to your right as you approach the turnstile. It disappears for a moment, then pops out about a foot farther along, and a little green or white circle lights up, reminding you to retrieve the ticket. If the turnstile makes a peevish whining sound and a little red circle lights up, your ticket is not valid; take it back and try another. When you have the right light, push through the gate and retrieve your ticket. **Hold onto your ticket** until you exit the metro, and pass the point marked **Limite de Validité des Billets;** a uniformed RATP *contrôleur* (inspector) may request to see it on any train. If caught without one, you must pay a hefty fine. Also, any *correspondances* (transfers) to the RER require you to put your validated (and uncrumpled) ticket into a turnstile in order to exit.

LATE AT NIGHT

Do not count on buying a metro ticket home late at night. Some ticket windows close as early as 10pm, and many close before the last train is due to arrive. It is a good idea to carry **one ticket more than you need,** although large stations have ticket machines that accept coins. Avoid the most **dangerous stations** (Barbès-Rochechouart, Pigalle, Anvers, Châtelet-Les-Halles, Gare du Nord, Gare de l'Est) after dark. Remain vigilant, as the stations are frequented by criminals looking to prey on tourists. When in doubt, take a bus or taxi.

RER

The RER (Réseau Express Régional) is the RATP's suburban train system, which passes through central Paris. The RER travels much faster than the metro. There are five RER lines, marked A-E, with different branches designated by a number: for example, the C5 line services Versailles-Rive Gauche. The newest line, the E, is called the Eole (Est-Ouest Liaison Express), and links Gare Magenta to Gare St-Lazare. Within Paris, the RER works exactly the same as the metro, requiring the same ticket. The principal stops within the city, which link the RER to the metro system, are **Gare du Nord, Nation, Charles de Gaulle-Etoile, Gare de Lyon,** and **Châtelet-Les-Halles** on the Right Bank and **St-Michel** and **Denfert-Rochereau** on the Left Bank. The electric signboards next to each track list all the possible stops for trains running on that track. Be sure that the little square next to your destination is lit up. Trips to the suburbs require special tickets. You'll need your ticket to exit RER stations. Insert your ticket just as you did to enter, and pass through. Like the metro, the RER runs 5:30am-12:30am.

BUS

Although slower and often costlier than the metro, a bus ride can be a cheap sightseeing tour and a helpful introductions to the city's layout.

HIT THE ROAD. In the summer, take the bus instead of the metro. You'll see more of Paris, and avoid the jostling, sweaty metro crowd. Those handy little purple tickets can be used on the metro and the bus.

TICKETS

Bus tickets are the same as those used in the metro, and they can be purchased either in metro stations or on the bus from the driver. Enter the bus through the front door and punch your ticket by pushing it into the machine by the driver's seat. If you have a *carte orange* or other transport pass, simply flash it at the driver. Inspectors may ask to see your ticket, so hold onto it until you get off. Should you wish to leave the earthly paradise that is the RATP autobus, just press the red button and the *arrêt demandé* sign will magically light up.

ROUTES

The RATP's *Grand Plan de Paris* includes a map (free at metro stations) of the bus lines for day, evening, and nighttime. The free bus map *Autobus Paris-Plan du Réseau* is available at tourist offices, metro information booths, and online at www.ratp.com. Buses with **three-digit numbers** travel to and from the suburbs, while buses with **two-digit numbers** travel exclusively within Paris.

NIGHT BUSES

Most buses run daily 7am-8:30pm, although those marked **Autobus du nuit** continue until 1:30am. Still others, ominously named **Noctambus,** run all night. Night buses (€2.50) run from Châtelet to the *portes* of the city every hour on the half hour from 1-5:30am (1-6am from the *portes* into the city). Noctambuses I-M, R, and S have routes along the Left Bank en route to the southern suburbs. Those marked A-H, P, T, or V have routes on the Right Bank going north. Look for bus stops marked with a bug-eyed moon sign. Ask at a major metro station or at Gare de l'Est for more information on Noctambuses.

TOUR BUSES

The RATP's **Balabus** (☎01 44 68 43 35) stops at virtually every major sight in Paris (Bastille, St-Michel, Louvre, Musée d'Orsay, Concorde, Champs-Elysées, Charles de Gaulle-Etoile; whole loop takes 1¼hr.). The circuit requires three standard bus tickets and starts at the Grande Arche de La Défense or Gare de Lyon.

BY TAXI

For taxi companies, see **Practical Information,** p. 116. If you have a complaint, or have left personal belongings behind, contact the taxi company, or write to **Service des Taxis de la Préfecture de Police**, 36 r. des Morillons, 75015 (☎01 55 76 20 00; ⓜ Convention). Ask for a receipt; if you want to file a complaint, record and include the driver's license number.

RATES

Tarif A, the basic rate, is in effect in Paris 7am-7pm (€0.62 per km). **Tarif B** is in effect Monday through Saturday 7pm-7am, all day Sunday, and during the day from the airports and immediate suburbs (€1.06 per km). **Tarif C,** the highest, is

ESSENTIALS

ESSENTIALS

in effect from the airports 7pm-7am (€1.24 per km). In addition, there is a *prix en charge* (base fee) of €2, and a minimum charge of €5. You should wait for taxis at the nearest **taxi stand;** oftentimes, taxis will not stop if you attempt to flag them down on the street. Lines at taxi stands can get long in the late afternoon during the week and on weekend nights. Should you call a taxi rather than hail one at a taxi stand, the base fee will increase according to how far away you are and how long it takes the driver to get there. For all cabs, stationary time (at traffic lights and in traffic jams) costs €26.23 per hour. Additional charges (€0.90) are added for luggage over 5kg. Taxis take three passengers; there is a €2.60 charge for a fourth. Some take credit cards (AmEx/MC/V).

BY CAR

Traveling by car in Paris is only convenient if your plans include significant travel outside the city. Parisian drivers are merciless. **Priorité à droite** gives the right of way to the car approaching from the right, regardless of the size of the streets, and Parisian drivers exercise this right even in the face of grave danger. Technically, drivers are not allowed to honk their horns within city limits unless they are about to hit a pedestrian, but this rule is often broken. The legal way to show discontent is to flash your headlights. A map of Paris marked with one-way streets is indispensible for drivers. Parking is expensive and hard to find.

FINDING YOUR WHEELS

Expect to pay at least €200 per week, plus 19.6% tax, for a very small car; you'll probably be asked to purchase **insurance** as well. Automatic transmission is often unavailable on cheaper cars. Reserve well before leaving for France and pay in advance if at all possible; it's always significantly less expensive to reserve a car from home. Check if prices quoted include tax, unlimited mileage, and collision insurance; some credit card companies will cover this automatically. Ask about discounts and check the terms of insurance, particularly the size of the deductible. Non-Europeans should check with their national motoring organization (e.g., AAA) for international coverage. Airlines sometimes offer special fly-and-drive packages, with up to a week of free or discounted rental. The minimum rental age in France is 21; those under 25 will often have to pay a surcharge. At most agencies, all that's needed to rent is a valid driver's license and proof that you've had it for a year; bring your passport just in case. For agencies, see **Practical Information,** p. 115.

INTERNATIONAL DRIVING PERMIT (IDP)

Those with an EU-issued driving license are entitled to drive in France with no further ado. While others may be legally able to drive in France on the strength of their national licenses for a few months, it's safest to get an International Driving Permit (IDP), a translation of your regular license into 10 languages, including French. The IDP, valid for one year, must be issued in your own country before you depart. You must be 18 years old to receive the IDP. The IDP is in addition to—not a replacement for—your home license, and it is not valid without it. An application for an IDP usually includes one or two photos, a current local license, and an additional form of ID; it also requires a fee. To apply, contact the local branch of your home country's automobile association.

CAR INSURANCE

EU residents driving their own cars do not need extra insurance coverage in France. For those renting, paying with a gold credit card usually covers standard insurance. If your home car insurance covers you for liability, make sure you get a **green card,** or **International Insurance Certificate,** to prove it. If you have an accident abroad, it will show up on your domestic records if you report it to your insurance company. Also, be prepared to pay US$8-10 per day for rental car insurance. Leasing should include insurance and the green card in the price. Some travel agents offer the card; it may also be available at border crossings.

BY THUMB

 Let's Go never recommends hitchhiking as a safe means of transportation, and none of the information presented here is intended to do so.

Let's Go strongly urges you to consider the risks before you choose to hitchhike (*faire l'autostop*). **Hitching puts you at risk for theft, assault, sexual harassment, and more.** If you're a woman traveling alone, don't hitch, period.

France is the hardest country in Europe in which to get a lift. If you do decide to chance it, remember that hitching (or even standing) on *autoroutes* is illegal and thumbing is generally permissible only at rest stops, tollbooths, and highway entrance ramps.

BY TWO-WHEELER

BICYCLES

During metro strike after Parisian metro strike, bike shops have come to the rescue of stranded citizens, and an emergent cycling community has approached its dream of an auto-free Paris. If you have never ridden a bike in heavy traffic, however, don't use central Paris as a testing ground. Safer, shaded bike paths wind through the Bois de Boulogne and the Bois de Vincennes, on the city's periphery. Bicycles can be transported on all RER lines anytime except rush hour (M-F 6:30-9am and 4:30-7pm) and on metro line 1 Sunday before 4:30pm. Ask for a helmet (not legally required, but always a good idea) and inquire about insurance. For bike rental listings, see **Practical Information,** p. 115.

SCOOTERS

Motorized two-wheelers, called *motos* or *mobylettes*, are everywhere in Paris. Everyone seems to own one, and just as many seem to have been injured on one. If you want to sacrifice safety for the speed and style that only a scooter can provide, you can rent one; no special license is required, though a helmet most definitely is. See **Practical Information,** p. 115.

KEEPING IN TOUCH

BY EMAIL AND INTERNET

As in most other European destinations, Internet is easy and usually cheap (sometimes free) to access in Paris. Internet cafes exist on practically every street corner, and many hotels and hostels offer an Internet connection for a small fee. Occasionally, wireless Internet (known in France as WiFi) is available in certain hotels and cafes.

FRENCH CONNECTION

f you choose to stay in Paris for longer than a few days, it can become inconvenient (and expensive) to have to trek to the nearest internet cafe to get your fix of Ebay and Google. While investing in wireless for your apartment is only really advisable for those who, well, have an apartment, there are ways to avoid spending exorbitant amounts just to stay in touch.

Those in the know bring their laptops to certain cafes and restaurants. Many cafes, including the trendy Le Sancerre in the 18ème (see **Food**, p. 178) offer "free" WiFi (wireless) with the condition that you buy something to eat or drink. In theory, you could try to sit unnoticed and covertly connect, but some places guard against this by requiring you to buy a card to gain access. Check out www.hotcafe.fr for more information.

An even better option is to find one of the many McDonalds that offer a great deal: absolutely free wireless inside the restaurant. Look for the wireless sticker on the window (or just go in and try, and if it doesn't work, just pretend you came for the atmosphere). No purchase is necessary.

If you are without a laptop, you can find hostels that have free internet. It is important to check before you book, however, as some cheaper hostels charge rather high rates for a connection, whereas others provide it for free.

Though in some places it's possible to forge a remote link with your home server, in most cases this is a much slower (and thus more expensive) option than taking advantage of free **web-based email accounts** (e.g., www.hotmail.com and www.yahoo.com). **Internet cafes** and the occasional free Internet terminal at a public library or university are listed in the **Practical Information** sections of major cities.

Increasingly, travelers find that taking their **laptop computers** on the road with them can be a convenient option for staying connected. Laptop users can call an Internet service provider via a modem using long-distance phone cards specifically intended for such calls. They may also find Internet cafes that allow them to connect their laptops to the Internet. And most excitingly, travelers with wireless-enabled computers may be able to take advantage of an increasing number of Internet "hotspots," where they can get online for free or for a small fee. Newer computers can detect these hotspots automatically; otherwise, websites like www.jiwire.com, www.wififreespot.com, and www.wi-fihotspotlist.com can help you find them. For information on insuring your laptop while traveling, see p. 29.

BY TELEPHONE

CALLING HOME FROM PARIS

You can usually make direct international calls from pay phones, but if you aren't using a phone card, you may need to drop your coins as quickly as your words. Prepaid phone cards are a common and relatively inexpensive means of calling abroad. Each one comes with a Personal Identification Number (PIN) and a toll-free access number. You call the access number and then follow the directions for dialing your PIN. To purchase prepaid phone cards, check online for the best rates; www.callingcards.com is a good place to start. Online providers generally send your access number and PIN via email, with no actual "card" involved. You can also call home with prepaid phone cards purchased in Paris (see Calling Within Paris, below).

Another option is to purchase a **calling card,** linked to a major national telecommunications service in your home country. Calls are billed collect or to your account. To obtain a calling card, contact the appropriate company listed below. Where available, there are often advantages to purchasing

PLACING INTERNATIONAL CALLS. To call Paris from home or to call home from Paris, dial:

1. The **international dialing prefix.** To call from **Australia**, dial 0011; **Canada** or the **US**, 011; **Ireland, New Zealand,** or the **UK,** 00; **France** 00.

2. The **country code** of the country you want to call. To call **Australia,** dial 61; **Canada** or the **US,** 1; **Ireland,** 353; **New Zealand,** 64; the **UK,** 44; **France,** 33.

3. The **city/area code.** If the first digit in the *Let's Go* phone listing a zero (e.g., 020 for London), omit the zero when calling from abroad (e.g., dial 20 from Canada to reach London).

4. The **local number.**

calling cards online, including better rates and immediate access to your account. To call home with a calling card, contact the operator for your service provider in Paris by dialing the appropriate toll-free access number (listed below in the third column).

COMPANY	TO OBTAIN A CARD:	TO CALL ABROAD:
AT&T (US)	800-364-9292 or www.att.com	0 800 99 00 11
Canada Direct	800-561-8868 or www.infocanadadirect.com	0 800 99 00 16 or 0 800 99 02 16
MCI (US)	800-777-5000 or www.minutepass.com	0 800 99 00 19
Telstra Australia	1800 676 638 or www.telstra.com	0 800 99 00 61

Placing a collect call through an international operator can be quite expensive, but may be necessary in case of an emergency. You can frequently call collect without even possessing a company's calling card just by calling its access number and following the instructions.

CALLING WITHIN PARIS

The simplest way to call within the country is to use a coin-operated phone. **Prepaid phone cards** (available at newspaper kiosks and tabacs), which carry a certain amount of phone time depending on the card's denomination, usually save time and money in the long run. The computerized phone will tell you how much time, in units, you have left on your card. Another kind of prepaid telephone card comes with a PIN and a toll-free access number. Instead of inserting the card into the phone, you call the access number and follow the directions on the card. These cards can be used to make international as well as domestic calls. Phone rates typically tend to be highest in the morning, lower in the evening, and lowest on Sunday and late at night.

CELLULAR PHONES

Most international (non-EU) cell phones do not work in France. Check with you service provider to see if your phone's band can be switched to 900/1800/ Switching bands will automatically register your phone with one of the three French cell phone servers: **Bouygue** (www.bouygtel.com), **Itineris** (www.i-france.com/binto/itineris.htm), or **France Télécom** (www.francetelecom.com/

fr). If you plan to stay in France for several months, buy a French cell phone. In France, incoming calls to cell phones are free (even from abroad), local calls are charged the local rate, and cell phone service is free. Cell phone calls are paid for with a **Mobicarte**, a prepaid card. Mobicartes are available in denominations of €15, €25, or €35. An easy, inexpensive option is to rent a cellular phone.

The international standard for cell phones is **Global System for Mobile Communication (GSM).** To make and receive calls in Paris, you will need a **GSM-compatible phone** and a **SIM (Subscriber Identity Module) card,** a country-specific, thumbnail-sized chip that gives you a local phone number and plugs you into the local network. Many SIM cards are **prepaid,** meaning that they come with calling time included and you don't need to sign up for a monthly service plan. Incoming calls are frequently free. When you use up the prepaid time, you can buy additional cards or vouchers (usually available at convenience stores) to get more. For more information on GSM phones, check out www.telestial.com, www.orange.co.uk, www.roadpost.com, or www.planetomni.com. Companies like **Cellular Abroad** (www.cellularabroad.com) rent cell phones that work in a variety of destinations around the world, providing a simpler option than picking up a phone in-country.

GSM PHONES. Just having a GSM phone doesn't mean you're necessarily good to go when you travel abroad. The majority of GSM phones sold in the United States operate on a different **frequency** (1900) than international phones (900/1800) and will not work abroad. Tri-band phones work on all three frequencies (900/1800/1900) and will operate through most of the world. As well, some GSM phones are **SIM-locked** and will only accept SIM cards from a single carrier. You'll need a **SIM-unlocked** phone to use a SIM card from a local carrier when you travel.

TIME DIFFERENCES

Paris is 6hr. ahead of Greenwich Mean Time (GMT), and observes Daylight Saving Time.

BY MAIL

SENDING MAIL HOME FROM PARIS

Airmail is the best way to send mail home from Paris. **Aerogrammes,** printed sheets that fold into envelopes and travel via airmail, are available at post offices. Write "airmail," or "par avion" on the front. Most post offices will charge exorbitant fees or simply refuse to send aerogrammes with enclosures. **Surface mail** is by far the cheapest and slowest way to send mail. It takes one to two months to cross the Atlantic and one to three to cross the Pacific—good for heavy items you won't need for a while, such as souvenirs or other articles you've acquired along the way that are weighing down your pack.

SENDING MAIL TO PARIS

To ensure timely delivery, mark envelopes "airmail" or "par avion."In addition to the standard postage system whose rates are listed below, **Federal Express** (Australia ☎ 13 26 10, Canada and the US 800-463-3339, Ireland 1800 535 800, New Zealand

0800 733 339, the UK 08456 070 809; www.fedex.com) handles express mail services from most countries to France.

There are several ways to arrange pick up of letters sent to you while you are abroad. Mail can be sent via **Poste Restante** (General Delivery) to almost any city or town in France with a post office, and it is very reliable. Address *Poste Restante* letters like so:

Napoleon BONAPARTE

Poste Restante

Paris, FRANCE

The mail will go to a special desk in the central post office, unless you specify a post office by street address or postal code. It's best to use the largest post office, since mail may be sent there regardless. It is usually safer and quicker, though more expensive, to send mail express or registered. Bring your passport (or other photo ID) for pick up; there may be a small fee. If the clerks insist that there is nothing for you, have them check under your first name as well. *Let's Go* lists post offices in the **Practical Information** section for each city and most towns.

American Express's travel offices throughout the world offer a free Client Letter Service (mail held up to 30 days and forwarded upon request) for cardholders who contact them in advance. Some offices provide these services to non-cardholders (especially AmEx Travelers Cheque holders), but call ahead to make sure. Let's Go lists AmEx locations for most large cities in Practical Information sections; for a complete list, call ☎800-528-4800 or visit www.americanexpress.com/travel.

ACCOMMODATIONS

HOTELS

Small hotels have long been an institution in Paris, and most proudly flaunt their eccentric character. They offer considerable privacy and are often family-run enterprises with friendly managers. Most importantly, they routinely accept advance reservations. Groups of two or more may find it more economical to stay in a hotel than a hostel, since hotels charge by the room and not by the body. Double rooms can often be made into triples with the use of a *lit supplementaire* (pull-out bed; €10-25 extra)—especially useful for families with small children. *Mansarde* rooms are on the top floor; they have sloping ceilings and more space for extra beds.

The French government rates hotels with zero to four stars depending on the services offered, the percentage of rooms with bath and other amenities. Most hotels listed here are zero-, one-, or two-star hotels, with a smattering of inexpensive three-stars. At the absolute minimum, expect to pay €25 for a single room and €35 for a double.

If you want a room with twin beds, make sure to ask for *une chambre avec deux lits* (a room with two beds); otherwise you may find yourself in *une chambre avec un grand lit* (a room with a double bed). In our listings, the term "doubles" refers to rooms with one full-size bed; "two-bed doubles" or "twins" refer to the rare room with two separate (usually twin) beds. The cheapest hotel rooms normally don't have private showers or toilets, but share both with other guests on the same floor. In these cases, you will likely pay extra for a hot shower (€2-4). Otherwise, hotel rooms may come with a variety of add-ons: *avec bidet-lavabo* means a sink and a bidet, but no toilet; *avec WC* or *avec cabinet* means with sink and toilet; *avec douche* means with shower; and *avec salle de bain* is with a full bathroom. All French hotels display a list on the back of each room's door of the prices of rooms, breakfast, and any residency tax. It is illegal for a hotel to charge a guest more than is shown on this list, although you can try to bargain for a lower rate if you are staying in the hotel for more than a few days.

HOSTELS AND FOYERS

Many of Paris's **hostels** don't bother with the restrictions that characterize most international hostels, such as sleepsheets. They do have maximum stays, age restrictions, and lockouts, but these are often flexible. According to French law, all hostels must have a curfew of 2am, although some are more flexible than others. Accommodations in hostels usually consist of single-sex rooms with two to eight beds, but you may be asked whether or not you are willing to stay in a co-ed room. Most rooms are simply furnished with metal- or wood-frame bunkbeds, thin sheets, and cheap blankets. Most hostel rooms have sinks and mirrors; showers and toilets are in a courtyard or communal hallway.

Foyers are simple accommodations intended for university students or workers during the academic year and are available for short- or long-term stays during the summer. They offer the security and privacy of a hotel and the lower prices and camaraderie of a hostel.

Hostels of Europe cards cost €15, and many independent hostels are members. These cards are not obligatory, but usually offer 5% off your bill; you can order online at www.hostelseurope.com. Despite the hype, there are only three official **Hostelling International (HI)** hostels in Paris. Most of the hostels and *foyers* in the city are privately run organizations, usually with services comparable to those at HI and often preferable to the HI hostels because of their more central locations. To stay in a HI hostel, you must be a member.

RESERVATIONS

A good rule of thumb is to make hotel reservations two weeks ahead of time, up to two months ahead in summer and early fall. The staff at smaller hotels may not speak English, but most proprietors are used to receiving calls from non-French-speakers. *Let's Go* has tried to include useful phrases for getting around the language barrier (see **Appendix**, p. 348). In order to reserve a room you may be asked to either read your credit card number over the phone, or to fax it to the hotel. Ask about your hotel's cancellation policy before giving out your credit card number, and find out if your credit card is going to be billed. If you can, avoid leaving a credit card number; either say you don't have a credit card or ask to send written confirmation instead. If you decide to leave Paris early, or if you want to switch hotels, don't expect to get back all of your deposit. Most hotels don't hold rooms without prior notice, so if you plan to arrive late, call and ask a hotel to hold your room. For last-minute accommodations, outposts of the **Office du Tourisme** (see **tourist offices**, p. 116) should be able to find you a room, although the lines at such offices may extend to the horizon and the selections are not necessarily the cheapest. For accommodation agencies, see **Practical Information**, p. 115.

LONG-TERM ACCOMMODATIONS

Almost every *arrondissement* in Paris contains some form of affordable housing and is well connected to the city by the extensive public transportation system. You will probably find the cheapest housing in peripheral *arrondissements*. If you are set on a central location, the more commercial parts of the 2*ème* may have something within your price range. During August, even ritzier locales can provide affordable housing, as the entire city empties out for the *grandes vacances*.

STUDENTS

For travelers planning a summer, semester, or academic year visit to Paris, student housing is available in the dormitories of most French universities. Contact the **Centre Régional des Oeuvres Universitaires (CROUS)** for more information (see **Practical Information,** p. 115). Lodging is available on a month-to-month basis at the **Cité Universitaire,** 17, bd. Jourdain, 14*ème*. (☎01 44 16 64 48; www.ciup.fr. Ⓜ Cité Universitaire. For information, write to M. le Délégué Général de Cité Universitaire de Paris, 19, bd. Jourdain, 75690 Paris Cedex 14. Over 30 different nations maintain dormitories at the Cité Universitaire, where they board their citizens studying in Paris. In summer, dorms lodge students and academics in Paris for short-term stays; an application is required. Some kitchens are available. To stay in the **American House,** write to Fondation des Etats-Unis, 15, bd. Jourdain, 75690 Paris Cedex 14. (☎01 53 80 68 80, fax 01 53 80 68 99. Rates vary according to demand: summer €440 per month; cheaper low season. Office open M-F 9am-5pm.)

RENTING AN APARTMENT

For help renting an apartment in France, call, fax, write, or visit **Allô Logement Temporaire** (see **Practical Information,** p. 115). This helpful, English-speaking association charges a membership fee of €50 if they succeed in finding an apartment for you, which is followed by an additional charge of €35 per month up to a year, with a maximum fee of €470. The company suggests writing or calling before you leave for France.

Alternatively, the French Department at local universities may be able to connect you with students abroad who want to sublet their apartments. Short-term rentals, more expensive per month than longer rentals, are difficult to procure, especially in winter months. There are dozens of rental agencies in Paris that cater to out-of-town visitors, but they are often expensive or unreliable.

If possible, stay in a hotel or hostel your first week in Paris and find an apartment while you're there. Among the best places to look are the bulletin boards in the **American Church** (see **Practical Information,** p. 120). Those upstairs tend to advertise long-term rentals, while those downstairs list short-term, cheaper arrangements. A smaller list of apartments to rent or share can be found at the bookstore **Shakespeare & Co.** (see **Shopping,** p. 292). Check listings in any of the English-French newsletters like **Paris Free Voice** or **France-USA Contacts (FUSAC),** a free publication found in English bookstores and restaurants throughout Paris. FUSAC is also distributed in the US. (FUSAC, P.O. Box 115, Cooper Station, New York, NY 10276; ☎212-777-5553; www.fusac.com. In Paris, 26, r. Bernard, 75014 Paris; ☎01 56 53 54 54; www.fusac.fr. Ⓜ Pernety.) It includes classified ads, in which Anglophones offer apartments for rent or sublet. The Paris office also has a bulletin board with apartment and job listings.

De Particulier à Particulier is a French publication that comes out on Thursdays with listings, as does the **Le Figaro** on Tuesdays. *De Particulier à Particulier* also has an excellent website with a number of apartment listings in Paris (www.pap.fr).

Subletting is legal and fairly common; however, marking up the price above what the tenant is currently paying is a technical violation of the law. Subletters should work out a written agreement, defining all of their mutual expectations. The original renter may require cash payments to avoid paying heavy taxes, and the utilities and mailbox are likely to remain under the renter's name. The subletter may need to tell the building superintendent or concierge that he or she is a guest of the renter. Your best bet to find an apartment in Paris is a service website like Craigslist (www.craigslist.com), where you can post your criteria for accommodations and link directly to the proprietors. If you are in Paris, it is a good idea to check the place out before making any final decisions.

SPECIFIC CONCERNS

TRAVELING ALONE

There are many benefits to traveling alone, including independence and greater interaction with locals. On the other hand, any solo traveler is a more vulnerable target of harassment and street theft. As a lone traveler, try not to stand out as a tourist: look confident, and be especially careful in deserted or very crowded areas. **If questioned, never admit that you are traveling alone.** Maintain regular contact with someone at home who knows your itinerary. For more tips, pick up *Traveling Solo* by Eleanor Berman (Globe Pequot Press, US$12.50), visit www.travelaloneandloveit.com, or subscribe to **Connecting: Solo Travel Network,** 689 Park Rd., Unit 6, Gibsons, BC V0N 1V7, Canada. (☎604-886-9099; www.cstn.org. Membership US$30-48.)

WOMEN TRAVELERS

Women exploring on their own inevitably face some additional safety concerns, but it's easy to be adventurous without taking undue risks. If you are concerned, consider staying in hostels offering single rooms that lock from the inside or in religious organizations with rooms for women only. Stick to centrally located accommodations and avoid solitary late-night treks or metro rides.

Always carry extra money for a phone call, bus, or taxi. **Hitchhiking** is **never safe** for lone women, or even for two women traveling together. Look as if you know where you're going and approach older women or couples for directions if you're lost. Generally, the less you look like a tourist, the better off you'll be. Wearing a conspicuous **wedding band** sometimes helps to prevent unwanted overtures.

Your best answer to verbal harassment is no answer at all; feigning deafness, sitting motionless, and staring straight ahead at nothing in particular will do a world of good that reactions usually don't achieve. The extremely persistent can sometimes be dissuaded by a firm, loud, and very public *"laissez-moi tranquille!"* ("leave me alone!"). Don't hesitate to seek out a police officer or a passerby if you are being harassed. A self-defense course will both prepare you for a potential attack and raise your level of awareness of your surroundings (see **Self Defense,** p. 28).

GLBT TRAVELERS

Next to Berlin, London, and Amsterdam, Paris has one of the largest gay populations in Europe. Paris's queer communities are vibrant, politically active, and full of opportunities for fun (see **Festivals**, p. 95 and **Nightlife**, p. 301). The website **www.paris-gay.com**, in French and English, is an extraordinarily hip and helpful guide for gay (particularly male) visitors. The Paris Tourist Office's website (www.paris-touristoffice.com) is also furnished with a list of Internet resources for GLBT travelers. Listed below are contact organizations, mail-order bookstores, and publishers that offer materials addressing some specific concerns. **Out and About** (www.outandabout.com) offers a bi-weekly newsletter addressing travel concerns. The online newspaper **365gay.com** also has a travel section (www.365gay.com/travel/travelchannel.htm). See **Practical Information** (p. 118) for resources in Paris.

Listed below are contact organizations, mail-order catalogs, and publishers that offer materials addressing some specific concerns. **Out and About** (www.planetout.com) offers a weekly newsletter addressing travel concerns and a comprehensive site addressing gay travel concerns. The online newspaper **365gay.com** also has a travel section (www.365gay.com/travel/travelchannel.htm).

Gay's the Word, 66 Marchmont St., London WC1N 1AB, UK (☎44 020 7278 7654; http://freespace.virgin.net/gays.theword/). The largest gay and lesbian bookshop in the UK, with both fiction and non-fiction titles. Mail-order service available.

Giovanni's Room, 345 South 12th St., Philadelphia, PA 19107, USA (☎215-923-2960; www.queerbooks.com). An international lesbian/feminist and gay bookstore with mail-order service (carries many of the publications listed below).

International Lesbian and Gay Association (ILGA), Avenue des Villas 34, 1060 Brussels, Belgium (☎32 2 502 2471; www.ilga.org). Provides political information, such as homosexuality laws of individual countries.

ADDITIONAL RESOURCES: GLBT

Spartacus 2005-2006: International Gay Guide. Bruno Gmunder Verlag (US$33).

Damron Men's Travel Guide, Damron Accommodations Guide, Damron City Guide, and *Damron Women's Traveller.* Damron Travel Guides (US$18-24). For info, call ☎800-462-6654 or visit www.damron.com.

The Gay Vacation Guide: The Best Trips and How to Plan Them, Mark Chesnut. Kensington Books (US$15).

Gayellow Pages USA/Canada, Frances Green. Gayellow Pages (US$20). They also publish smaller regional editions.

TRAVELERS WITH DISABILITIES

Many of Paris's museums and sights are fully accessible to wheelchairs, and some provide guided tours in sign language. Unfortunately, budget hotels and restaurants are generally ill-equipped to handle the needs of disabled visitors. Wheelchair-accessible bathrooms are virtually non-existent among hotels in the one- to two-star range, and many elevators could double as shoeboxes. *Let's Go: Paris* tries to list at least one wheelchair-accessible hotel in each *arrondissement*. Note that the hotels described as such are those with reasonably wide elevators or with ground-floor rooms wide enough for wheelchair entry. To ask restaurants, hotels, railways, and airlines if they are accessible, say: *"Etes-vous accessible aux fauteuils roulants?"* Many establishments can provide a ramp if you ask for one. If transporting a **seeing-eye dog** to France, you will need a rabies vaccination certificate issued from home.

The RATP and its personnel are generally well-equipped to assist blind or deaf passengers. Very few metro stations are wheelchair accessible, but RER lines A and B are. For a guide to metro accessibility, pick up a free copy of the RATP's brochure, *Lignes et stations équipées pour Personnes à Besoins Spécifiques* (information regarding wheelchair-accessible stations ☎01 45 83 67 77, for help in English 08 36 68 41 14), which provide a list of stations equipped with escalators, elevators, and moving walkways. Public buses are not yet wheelchair accessible except for line 20, which runs from Gare de Lyon to Gare St-Lazare. Taxis are required by law to take passengers in wheelchairs. **Airhop** (☎01 41 29 01 29; reserve 48hr. in advance) and **GIHP** (☎01 41 83 15 15) offer transport to and from the airport for the motion impaired (see **Practical Information,** p. 117).

USEFUL ORGANIZATIONS

Access Abroad, www.umabroad.umn.edu/access. A website devoted to making study abroad available to students with disabilities. The site is maintained by Disability Services, University of Minnesota, 230 Heller Hall, 271 19th Ave. S., Minneapolis, MN 55455, USA (☎612-626-7379).

Accessible Journeys, 35 West Sellers Ave., Ridley Park, PA 19078, USA (☎800-846-4537; www.disabilitytravel.com). Designs tours for wheelchair users and slow walkers. The site has tips and forums for all travelers.

Flying Wheels, 143 W. Bridge St., P.O. Box 382, Owatonna, MN 55060, USA (☎507-451-5005; www.flyingwheelstravel.com). Specializes in escorted trips to Europe for people with physical disabilities; plans custom trips worldwide.

Mobility International USA (MIUSA), P.O. Box 10767, Eugene, OR 97440, USA (☎541-343-1284; www.miusa.org). Provides a variety of books and other publications containing information for travelers with disabilities.

Society for Accessible Travel and Hospitality (SATH), 347 Fifth Ave., Ste. 610, New York, NY 10016, USA (☎212-447-7284; www.sath.org). An advocacy group that publishes free online travel information and the travel magazine *OPEN WORLD* (annual subscription US$13, free for members). Annual membership US$45, students and seniors US$30.

MINORITY TRAVELERS

Despite Paris's extraordinary diversity and its wealth of multi-ethnic restaurants and cultural events, racism is a serious problem here; France's postcolonial legacy is not, predictably, a happy one. Travelers of Arab, North African, or West African descent are more likely than Caucasians to be stopped by the police and may be met with suspicious or derogatory glances from passersby. In addition, incidents of anti-Semitism have become both more frequent and more violent in the last few years. While anti-Semitic sentiment is by no means the norm in Paris (which, after all, is home to half of France's nearly 600,000 Jews), Jewish visitors should be aware that religious tension is a current issue in Paris and throughout France.

Should you confront race-based exclusion or violence, you should make a formal complaint to the police. It is also a good idea to work through either SOS Racisme or MRAP in order to facilitate your progress through a confusing foreign bureaucracy. (For additional listings consult **Minority Resources** in **Practical Information,** p. 119.)

SOS Racisme, 28 r. des Petites Ecuries, 10ème (☎01 40 35 36 55; www.sos-racisme.org). Primarily helps illegal immigrants and people whose documentation is irregular. They provide legal services and are used to negotiating with police. Open M-F 9:30am-6pm.

MRAP (Mouvement contre le racisme et pour l'amitié entre les peuples), 43 bd. Magenta, 10ème (☎01 53 38 99 99; www.mrap.asso.fr). Handles immigration issues and monitors racist publications and propaganda. Open M-Sa 9am-noon and 2-6pm.

DIETARY CONCERNS

Paris has traditionally been unaccommodating to those with special dietary requirements, but the number of restaurants with **vegetarian** and **vegan** options is increasing. *Let's Go* has tried to list as many vegetarian- and vegan-friendly restaurants as possible (see **Food,** p. 147). For more info on vegetarian travel, visit your local bookstore or health food store, and consult *The Vegetarian Traveler: Where to Stay if You're Vegetarian, Vegan, Environmentally Sensitive,* by Jed and Susan Civic (Larson Publications; US$16). Also available is *Vegetarian France* (US $8; www.vegetarianguides.com). Vegetarians will also find numerous resources on the web; try www.vegdining.com, www.happycow.net, and www.vegetariansabroad.com, for starters.

Kosher delis, restaurants, and bakeries abound in the *3ème* and *4ème arrondissements,* particularly on r. des Rosiers and r. des Ecouffes. Contact the **Union Libéral Israélite de France Synagogue** (see **Religious Services** in **Practical Information,** p. 120) for more information on kosher restaurants. Travelers looking for **halal** restaurants may find www.zabihah.com a useful resource.

OTHER RESOURCES

Let's Go tries to cover all aspects of budget travel, but we can't put *everything* in our guides. Listed below are books and websites that can serve as jumping-off points for your own research.

BOOKS

A Traveller's Wine Guide to France, Christopher Fielden. Traveller's Wine Guides, 1999. (US$15). Exactly what it says it is, by a well-known oenophile.

Cultural Misunderstandings: The French-American Experience, Raymonde Carroll, trans. Carol Volk. University of Chicago Press, 1990 (US$14). An interesting academic examination of cross-cultural communication; useful for Americans baffled by the French outlook on life.

Culture Shock! France: A Guide To Customs and Etiquette, Sally Adamson Taylor. Graphic Arts Center Publishing Company, 1991 (US$12). Tips and warnings.

ESSENTIALS

Fragile Glory: A Portrait of France and the French, Richard Bernstein. Plume, 1991 (US$15). A witty, nuanced look by the former Paris bureau chief of *The New York Times.*

French or Foe? Getting the Most Out of Visiting, Living and Working in France, Polly Platt. Distribooks Intl., 1998 (US$11). A popular guide to getting by in France.

The Food Lover's Guide to Paris, Patricia Wells. Workman, 1999 (US$50). A fabulous guide to all things culinary by the food critic for the *International Herald Tribune.*

Wicked French, Howard Tomb. Workman, 1989 (US$5). A hilarious guide to everything you really didn't need to know how to say in French.

WORLD WIDE WEB

The web offers a wealth of information on all aspects of budget travel. In 10min. at the keyboard, you can make a hostel reservation, get advice on travel hotspots from other travelers, or find fares for a train ride from Paris to Rome.

Listed here are some regional and travel-related sites to start off your surfing; other relevant web sites are listed throughout the book. Because website turnover is high, use search engines (such as www.google.com) to strike out on your own.

 WWW.LETSGO.COM. Let's Go's website features a wealth of information and valuable advice at your fingertips. It offers excerpts from all our guides as well as monthly features on new hot spots in the most popular destinations. In addition to our online bookstore, we have great deals on everything from airfares to cell phones. Our resources section is full of information you'll need before you hit the road, and our forums are buzzing with advice from other travelers. Check back often to see constant updates, exciting new tips, and prize giveaways. See you soon!

THE ART OF TRAVEL

Backpacker's Ultimate Guide: www.bugeurope.com. Tips on packing, transportation, and where to go. Also tons of country-specific travel information.

BootsnAll.com: www.bootsnall.com. Numerous resources for independent travelers, from planning your trip to reporting on it when you get back.

How to See the World: www.artoftravel.com. A compendium of great travel tips, from cheap flights to self defense to interacting with local culture.

Travel Intelligence: www.travelintelligence.net. A large collection of travel writing by distinguished travel writers.

Travel Library: www.travel-library.com. A fantastic set of links for general information and personal travelogues.

World Hum: www.worldhum.com. An independently produced collection of "travel dispatches from a shrinking planet."

INFORMATION ON PARIS

France Diplomatie (www.france.diplomatie.fr) is the French Department of Foreign Affairs site, with information on visas and other official matters, as well as comprehensive info on French history, culture, geography, politics, and current affairs. English version available.

Maison de France (www.franceguide.com) is the main government tourist site. Up-to-date information on tourism in France, including a calendar of festivals and major events, regional info with links to local servers, and a host of tips on everything from accommodation to smoking laws. English version available.

Météo-France (www.meteo.fr) has 2-day weather forecasts and maps for France. In French.

Paris Tourist Office (www.paris-touristoffice.com) has information on everything from baby-sitting agencies to hotel reservations in Paris. In French and English.

Secretariat for Tourism (www.tourisme.gouv.fr) has a number of government documents and press releases relating to the state of tourism in France, plus links to all the national, regional, and departmental tourist authorities. In French.

TF1 (www.tf1.com) is the home page of France's most popular TV station, with news, popular culture, and weather and traffic reports. In French.

ESSENTIALS

LIFE AND TIMES

HISTORY

ANCIENT PARIS

ROMAN BEGINNINGS. Paris was first settled around 300 BC by the Parisîi, a clan of Celtic Gauls who set up camp on the Île de la Cité. The Parisîi were successful fishermen and traders, and their settlement thrived until **Julius Caesar's** troops arrived in 52 BC. According to Caesar's *Commentaries*, the Parisîi resisted fiercely, but they eventually succumbed, initiating a two-millennium tradition of French military defeats. The Romans named the new colony **Lutetia Parisiorum** (Latin for "the Mid-water-Dwelling of the Parisîi") and expanded the city, building new roads (including **rue St-Jacques,** in the 5*ème*), public baths (now the **Musée de Cluny,** p. 253), and gladiatorial arenas (like the **Arènes de Lutèce,** p. 203). A temple to Jupiter stood on the present-day site of the **Cathédrale Notre Dame** (p. 183), and Roman ruins are still on display in the cathedral's crypt. By AD 360, the Romans had fortified the Île de la Cité and shortened its name to "Paris."

CHRISTIANITY AND CHARLEMAGNE. After three centuries of Roman prosperity, Paris was beseiged by a series of assaults from Vandals and Visigoths. Attila and the Huns tried to take the city in AD 450 and were supposedly thwarted by the prayers of St. Genevieve, henceforth the patron saint of Paris. Meanwhile, the arrival of Christianity in the 3rd century threatened to erode Roman rule from within: when St. Denis appeared in Paris with orders from Pope Fabian to convert the population, he was beheaded by a mob of obdurate citizens (**Basilique de St-Denis,** p. 242). The overstretched Roman empire was losing its grasp on Paris.

In AD 476, the year that saw the fall of the Roman empire, **King Clovis** of the Franks defeated the Gallo-Romans in Paris. Clovis founded France's first royal house, he named Paris the capital of France, and he declared the entire city a Christian territory. The brutal **Merovingian Dynasty** (481-751) of Clovis's descendants ruled France for almost 300 years and was suceeded by the more sophisticated (read: less likely to dismiss Roman law in favor of military rule) **Carolingian Dynasty** (751-987).

Charlemagne, the second Carolingian king, took power in 768. Paris lost some influence under Charlemagne, as he took the title Holy Roman Emperor, expanded his territorial claims, and moved his capital to Aix-la-Chapelle (now Aachen, in Germany). Charlemagne's fascination with classical art and literature sparked the **Carolingian Renaissance.** When invading **Normans** (Vikings) and **Saracens** (people of the Arab world) menaced Europe in the 9th and 10th centuries, Charlemagne's empire fell and France crumbled into fragments.

MIDDLE AGES TO THE RENAISSANCE

MEDIEVAL PARIS. By the end of the first millennium AD, France was a decentralized collection of feudal kingdoms with their own languages and traditions. In 987,

c. 300 BC
The Parisii settle on
Île de la Cité.

52 BC
Julius Caesar con-
quers Paris, offi-
cially beginning of
Roman rule.

AD 260
St. Denis is
beheaded by the
Romans for
attempting to
Christianize Paris.

476
Fall of the Roman
Empire; King Clovis
comes to power.

800
Charlemagne is
named Holy
Roman Emperor.

987
Hugh Capet
elected to the
throne.

1163
Construction of
Notre Dame Cathe-
dral begins.

1170
French literature is
born with *Chanson
de Roland*
(*Roland's Song*)
and Marie de
France's *Lais*.

1215
The University of
Paris is founded.

1337-1453
The Hundred Years'
War: England vs.
France. France
wins, naturally.

Hugh Capet, the Count of Paris, was crowned King of France. Capet made Paris his capital, and under the 350-year rule of the **Capetian Dynasty** (987-1328), the city gradually consolidated power. The Capetians' most famous king, **Philippe-Auguste** (1179-1223), expanded the city and oversaw the construction of **Notre Dame** (p. 183) and **Les Halles** (p. 191).

With the establishment of the University of Paris in 1215 and the **Sorbonne** in 1253 (p. 199), Paris was reorganized into two parts: the commercial Rive Droite (Right Bank) and the academic Rive Gauche (Left Bank).

PLAGUE AND WAR IN THE LATE MIDDLE AGES. The 14th century was a dark time for Europe. Three hundred years of rapid population growth had overcrowded cities and depleted food resources, and a **mini ice age** (1150-1450) had cooled and dampened Europe's climate. These trends culminated in a widespread explosion of violence and disease: the **Black Death,** which ravaged Paris from 1348-49, killed more than a third of the city's population; hundreds more died in peasant uprisings.

FRANCE AND ENGLAND DUKE IT OUT. When the last Capetian died in 1328, England's Edward III tried to claim the throne of France. In retaliation, the French Philippe de Valois (later King Phillip III) encroached upon English-owned Aquitaine, in what is now southwestern France. Edward III responded by landing his troops in Normandy, and the **Hundred Years' War** (1337-1453) began. The French took some serious battering over the course of the war. When the English crowned their own Henri VI king of France in 1418, salvation arrived in the form of a 17-year-old peasant girl. Legend has it that **Joan of Arc** was inspired by a choir of angels to save France from British conquest. Joan led the Valois troops to victory at the Battle of Orléans before being captured by the English and burned at the stake in 1431 for heresy. In 1437, Charles VII reclaimed Paris and drove the English back to Calais. The Valois Dynasty took over where the Capetians left off and moved toward securing a unified France.

THE RENAISSANCE. In the early 16th century, the imported ideals of the Italian Renaissance sparked interest in literature, art, and architecture in Paris. The printing press was introduced in the 1460s, and the universities on the Left Bank were flourishing. An unprecedented percentage of the population had access to literature, and writers like Montaigne, Rabelais, and Ronsard embodied the era's increasingly secular humanism. The 16th century also saw the strengthening of the monarchy as the French rallied around the Valois king **François I,** a popular patron of the arts and sciences.

In 1527 François I had the **Louvre** rebuilt in the style of the Renaissance (p. 245) and moved the royal residence there. Under François's successor, **Henri II,** the **place Royale** (now called **place des Vosges;** p. 198) became a masterpiece of French Renaissance architecture. When Henri died in the *place* after a jousting accident, his wife, **Catherine de Médicis,** ordered it destroyed and began work on the **Tuileries Palace and Garden** and **Pont Neuf** (p. 188).

RELIGIOUS BLOODSHED. Paris's budding religious tension, sparked by the Protestant Reformation, played itself out brutally in the **Wars of Religion** (1562-98). The conflict unfolded in a series of military faceoffs and civilian clashes, fought between the **Huguenots** (French Protestants) and the Catholics. Catherine de Médicis, effective ruler of France after her husband's death, was particularly ruthless toward the Huguenots from the southwestern kingdom of Navarre. **Henri de Navarre** agreed to marry Catherine's daughter, **Margeurite de Valois** (Queen Margot) as a peace-making gesture. Catherine played along, but when France's most prominent Protestants had assembled in Paris for the royal union, Catherine had 2000 of them slaughtered in the **St. Bartholomew's Day Massacre** (Apr. 24, 1572). Henri saved his life and his throne with a strategically convenient conversion to Catholicism. In 1589, he ascended to the throne as **Henri IV de Bourbon,** uniting France and establishing the last of France's royal houses, the **Bourbons.** Upon his coronation, Henri IV made light of his sudden change of spiritual conviction with the remark, "Paris vaut bien une messe" (Paris is well worth a mass). His heart still lay with the Huguenots, though: in 1598, he issued the **Edict of Nantes,** which granted tolerance for French Protestants and quelled religious wars for almost a century.

THE 17TH CENTURY

LOUIS XIII AND RICHELIEU. The French monarchy reached its height of power, opulence, and egomania in the 17th century. Henri IV was assassinated in 1610 and succeeded by Louis XIII. Louis's capable and ruthless minister, Cardinal Richelieu, consolidated political power in the hands of the monarch and created the centralized, bureaucratic administration characteristic of France to this day. He expanded Paris and built the **Palais du Luxembourg** (p. 204) for the Queen Mother, **Marie de Médicis,** and the Palais Cardinal (today the **Palais-Royal;** p. 189) for himself. Richelieu manipulated the nobility and tantalized the bourgeoisie with promises of social advancement, tightening the monarchy's hold over the state.

HERE COMES THE SUN KING. Proving their commitment to one another for eternity, Richelieu and Louis XIII died within months of each other in 1642 and were replaced by **Louis XIV** and his minister **Cardinal Mazarin.** Since Louis was only five years old at the time, the cardinal took charge, but by 1661 the precocious 23-year-old was ready to rule alone. Louis adopted the title "Sun King" and took the motto, "L'état, c'est moi" (I am the state). He lent a personal touch to national affairs, moving the government to his new 14,000-room palace, the flamboyant and extravagant **Château de Versailles** (p. 321). The court at Versailles was a spectacle of regal opulence and noble privilege, where the king himself

1348-49
The Paris leg of the Black Death world tour, 1347-51.

1430
Joan of Arc is burned at the stake for heresy after leading the French troops to victory.

1461
François Villon writes *Le Grand Testament,* beginning France's tradition of political parody.

1527
François I sets up royal residence in the Louvre.

1532
François Rabelais writes *Gargantua,* a creatively titled story about a giant.

c. 1558
Margeurite de Navarre writes *Héptameron,* introducing the frame novel to France.

1562-98
The Wars of Religion: Huguenots vs. Catholics.

1572
St. Bartholemew's Day Massacre.

1580
Michel de Montaigne writes *Essais.*

1598
Henri V de Bourbon issues the Edict of Nantes, proclaiming religious tolerance.

LIFE AND TIMES

62 ■ HISTORY

LIFE AND TIMES

1610 Beginning of the reign of Louis XIII and Cardinal Richelieu.

1637 René Descartes writes *Discours de la Méthode.*

1642 Five-year-old Louis XIV comes to the throne.

1648 The Académie Française is founded under the direction of Charles le Brun.

1658 Blaise Pascale writes *Pensées.*

1661 Louis XIV, the Sun King, moves the court to his new chateau at Versailles.

1664 Molière writes *Tartuffe.*

1667 Jean Racine writes *Phèdre.*

1701- 13 War of Spanish Succession.

1715 Louis XIV dies and is succeeded by Louis XV.

1752 Denis Diderot and Jean D'Alembert write *Encyclopédie.*

1758 Voltaire writes *Candide.*

was on display: favored subjects could observe him and his queen as they rose in the morning, groomed, and dined. The king kept the nobility under a close watch at Versailles to avoid challenges to his rule; the nobles, caught up in the elaborate choreography of the court, suffered a complete loss of political power.

Louis XIV reigned for 72 years by the principle of "un roi, une loi, une foi" (one king, one law, one faith). He revoked the Edict of Nantes in 1685 at the behest of his mistress and initiated the ruinous **War of the Spanish Succession** (1701-13). From Versailles, he commissioned the **avenue des Champs-Elysées** (p. 212) and the **place Vendôme** (p. 188). His daughter, the Duchesse de Bourbon, commissioned the **Palais Bourbon,** today home to the **Assemblée Nationale** (p. 210).

Louis XIV finally died in 1715 and was succeeded by the two-year-old **Louis XV.** The light that had once radiated from the French throne could no longer eclipse the country's ruinous domestic problems. The lavish expenditures of the Sun King left France in debt, and, after his death, the weakened nobility began to resent the monarchy.

THE FRENCH REVOLUTION

BOURBON ON THE ROCKS. When Louis XVI ascended to the throne in 1774, the country was in desperate financial straits. Civilians blamed the monarchy for their mounting debts, while aristocrats detested the king for his gestures toward reform. In 1789, Louis XVI called a meeting of the Estates General, an assembly of delegates from three classes of society: aristocrats, clergy, and the bourgeois-dominated Third Estate. On June 17, after weeks of wrangling over voting procedures, the Third Estate declared itself the independent National Assembly and was promptly expelled from the convention chamber. The National Assembly then reconvened on the Versailles tennis greens, and on June 20, they swore the Oath of the Tennis Court, promising not to disband until the king had recognized their proposed constitution. The king did not dismiss the Assembly; instead he sent in troops to intimidate it and received a haughty response: "the assembled nation cannot receive orders." As rumors of revolution multiplied, the initiative passed to the panicked Parisian masses, alarmed by astronomical bread prices and the tottering government.

STORMING OF THE BASTILLE. When a mob of almost 1000 citizens stormed the old fortress of the Bastille (p. 218) on July 14, peasants across France burned the records of their debts. **Le quatorze juillet** is now the Fête Nationale (p. 95), the equivalent of America's Independence Day. The Assembly joined the Revolution in August with the abolition of feudal law and the Declaration of the Rights of Man, which embodied the principles **liberté, égalité,** and **fraternité.** On October 5, a crowd of revolutionaries descended on Versailles, seized the king and queen, and brought them back to Paris.

REIGN OF TERROR. When the petrified Louis XVI, under virtual house arrest in the Tuileries Palace, tried to flee the country in 1791, he was apprehended and imprisoned. Meanwhile, a number of aristocrats and other counter-revolutionaries had fled the country to seek help from other European powers. Partly in response to the pleas of these *émigrés*, Austria and Prussia mobilized and prepared to stamp out the democratic disease. In 1793, the revolutionary armies miraculously defeated the invaders, and the radical **Jacobin** faction, led by **Maximilien Robespierre** and his **Committee of Public Safety**, took over the National Assembly. The period of suppression and mass execution under the Committee of Public Safety is known as the Reign of Terror. In January, the Jacobins guillotined Louis XVI and Queen **Marie-Antoinette.** By the end of the Reign of Terror, the ironically named **place de la Concorde** (p. 31) had been the site of more than 1300 beheadings.

With a republic declared, the *ancien régime* was history. The Revolution had taken a radical turn. The Church refused to submit to the National Assembly and so was replaced by the **Cult of Reason,** which renamed and renumbered the calendar and invented the metric system. As counter-revolutionary paranoia set in, power lay with Robespierre and his Committee of Public Safety. Even the slightest suspicion of royalist sympathy led to the block; Dr. Guillotine himself did not escape the vengeance of his invention. By 1794, Robespierre was physically exhausted and frustrated by divisions in the forces behind the Revolution. Like any egomaniacal autocrat, he faced heavy criticism from both the left and the right as his intimidation factor stagnated. Loyalists attacked Robespierre for his democratic ideals, while radicals criticized his leniency. On July 28, members of the National Assembly felt strongly enough in favor of a regime change that they beheaded Robespierre and all of his closest supporters. The terror was over, and power was entrusted to a five-man **Directory.**

NAPOLEON AND EMPIRE

THE RISE OF NAPOLEON... As wars raged on throughout Western Europe, an ambitious young Corsican general swept through northern Italy and into Austria. **Napoleon Bonaparte** returned to Paris from the wars in 1799. Riding a wave of public support, he deposed the Directory and declared himself First Consul of a triumvirate. In an 1802 fit of ego, Napoleon changed that title to Consul for Life, and ultimately to **Emperor** in 1804. In just one decade, Napoleon expanded France's empire, unified its people, and centralized its government. Portions of his **Napoleonic Code** still exist today, although it outlined an oppressively autocratic approach to life, re-establishing slavery and requiring wives to show unwavering obedience to their husbands.

Paris benefited from Napoleon's international booty. His interest in ancient and classical civilizations brought sculptures from Alexandria and Rome into Paris, including the Lou-

1766
Jean-Jaques Rousseau writes *Confessions.*

1774
Louis XVI and Marie Antoinette take the throne.

1778
France allies with the United States in the American Revolution.

1784
Caron de Beaumarchais writes *Le Mariage de Figaro.*

1789
The French Revolution begins with the Oath of the Tennis Court and the equally dramatic storming of the Bastille.

1793-4
Thousands are beheaded during the Reign of Terror.

1793
Jean-Paul Marat, publisher of revolutionary newspaper *L'Ami du Peuple*, is assassinated in his bathtub by Charlotte Corday, beginning the trendy Parisian bathtub death movement.

1793
Jacques-Louis David writes *Marat Assassiné.*

LIFE AND TIMES

vre's *Dying Gladiator* and *Discus Thrower* (p. 245). He ordered the constructions of two Roman arches, the **Arc de Triomphe** (p. 211) and the **Arc du Carrousel** (p. 245), topping the latter with a gladiatorial sculpture stolen from St. Mark's Cathedral in Venice. Napoleon's many new bridges, including the **Pont d'Austerlitz,** the **Pont Iéna,** and the **Pont des Arts** (p. 206) spanned the Seine in style. He ordered the construction of a neo-Greco-Roman temple, the **Madeleine** (p. 213), and he finished the Cour Carrée of the Louvre, originally ordered by Louis XIV. Meanwhile, when his wife Josephine failed to produce an heir, she and Napoleon amicably annulled their marriage. The Emperor was re-married to **Marie Louise d'Autriche,** and his armies pushed east to Moscow.

...AND HIS DOWNFALL. In the winter of 1812, after occupying a deserted Moscow, Napoleon was forced to withdraw. The freezing cold decimated the sensitive and pampered French ranks, and of the 700,000 men Napoleon had led into Russia, barely 200,000 returned. Having lost the support of a war-weary nation, Napoleon abdicated in 1814. He retired to the Mediterranean island of **Elba,** and the monarchy was reinstated under **Louis XVIII,** brother of the unfortunate Louis XVI.

Fortunately or unfortunately, the French had not seen the last of Napoleon. In a final spurt of delusional grandeur, he left Elba and landed near Cannes on March 26, 1815. As Napoleon marched north, the king fled to England. The adventures of the ensuing **Hundred Days' War** ended on the field of **Waterloo** in Flanders, Belgium, where the **Duke of Wellington** triumphed over Napoleon's army. Napoleon threw himself on the mercy of the English, who banished him to remote **St. Helena** in the south Atlantic, where he died in 1821. Oddly enough, Napoleon is popularly regarded as a hero in France; thousands still pay their respects at his tomb at **Les Invalides** (p. 259). After his death, the **Restoration** of the monarchy brought Louis XVIII to the helm, and the **Bourbon** dynasty went on...and on...and on...

RESTORATION AND MORE REVOLUTION

THE JULY REVOLUTION. Although initially forced to recognize the achievements of the Revolution, the reinstated monarchy soon (as monarchies are wont to do) reverted to its tyrannical ways. But the precedent for rebellion had been set: when **Charles X** restricted the press and limited the electorate to the landed classes in 1830, the people launched the July Revolution. Remembering the fate of his brother, Charles quickly abdicated. A constitutional monarchy was instated under **Louis-Philippe,** Duke of Orléans, whose more modest bourgeois lifestyle garnered him the name **"Citizen King."** The middle classes prospered under Louis-Philippe, but industrialization created a class of urban poor, who were receptive to the ideas of **socialism.**

LIKE JULY, ONLY EFFECTIVE: THE FEBRUARY REVOLUTION.
When the king's bourgeois government refused to oblige the demands of the working class, the people were well practiced: there followed the February Revolution of 1848, the declaration of the **Second Republic,** and France's first universal male suffrage. The late emperor's nephew, **Louis Napoleon,** was elected president. The constitution barred him from seeking a second term, but he ignored it and seized power in a coup in 1851, proving that megalomania must have some basis in genetics. Following a referendum in 1852, he declared himself **Emperor Napoleon III,** to popular acclaim. Napoleon III's reign saw the industrialization of Paris, the rise of urban pollution, and the abject poverty described in novels by Balzac and Victor Hugo (p. 74). Still, France's prestige was restored during his reign: factories hummed, and **Baron Georges Haussmann** replaced Paris's medieval street plan (too conducive to demonstrations) with *grand boulevards* along which an army could be deployed (p. 82).

FRANCO-PRUSSIAN WAR. Napoleon III's downfall came in July 1870 with France's defeat in the **Franco-Prussian War.** The confident French didn't notice the storm clouds gathering across the Rhine, where **Otto von Bismarck** had almost completed the unification of Germany. The Iron Chancellor's troops swiftly overran France and captured the emperor. Paris held out for four months, with residents so desperate for food that they devoured most of the animals in the zoo, sparking the Parisian reputation for cutting-edge cuisine (p. 238).

PARIS COMMUNE. When the government admitted defeat, placing a conservative regime led by Adolphe Thiers in power, the Parisian mob revolted again, and in 1871, they declared the Paris Commune. For four months, a committee of leftists known as the *communards* assumed power and rejected the Thiers government, throwing up barricades and declaring the city a free Commune. When French troops were sent in to recapture the city, the *communards* burned the Hôtel-de-Ville, the Palais-Royal, and Catherine de Médicis's Tuileries Palace before retreating to their last stand, Père Lachaise Cemetery (p. 232). The crushing of the Commune, like a good beheading, was quick and bloody. Many estimate that over 20,000 Parisians died, slaughtered by their compatriots in about a week. The last of the *communards* were shot against Père Lachaise's **Mur des Fédérés** (now a site of pilgrimage for radical leftists everywhere) on May 21, 1871. The defeat broke both the power of Paris over the provinces and that of the Parisian proletariat over the city.

BELLE EPOQUE

ART AND INDUSTRIALIZATION. After more than 80 years of violence and political instability, Paris finally took a hiatus from chaos with a period of peace and stability aptly titled the *Belle Epoque* (Beautiful Time). The colors of the **Impression-**

1830
Eugene Delacroix writes *La Liberté Guidant la Peuple* (*Liberty Guiding the People*).

1831
Victor Hugo writes *Notre Dame de Paris* (*The Hunchback of Notre Dame*).

1832
George Sand writes *Valentine.*

1848
The February Revolution and the declaration of the Second Republic; Baron Georges Haussmann begins redesigning Paris.

1848
French conquest of Vietnam begins.

1852
Louis Napoleon declares himself emperor.

1856
Gustave Flaubert writes *Madame Bovary.*

1857
Charles Baudelaire writes *Les Fleurs du Mal* (*The Flowers of Evil*).

1861
Construction begins on the Opéra Garnier.

ists (p. 83), the novels of **Marcel Proust** (p. 76), and the **Expositions Universelles** (World's Fairs) of 1889 and 1900 reflected the optimism and energy of the Belle Epoque. The expositions gave Paris the **Eiffel Tower** (p. 207), the **Pont Alexandre III**, the **Grand** and **Petit Palais** (see Sights, p. 213), and the first line of the *Métropolitain*, the Paris metro. At the same time, industrialization introduced many new social problems to the Third Republic. While the government's reforms laid the foundation for the contemporary social welfare state, class-related tensions continued to grow.

DREYFUS AFFAIR. The Third Republic was further undermined by the **Dreyfus Affair.** Alfred Dreyfus was a Jewish army captain convicted and exiled in 1894 on dubious-at-best charges of treason. When the army refused to consider the case even after proof of Dreyfus's innocence was uncovered, France became polarized between the *Dreyfusards*—who argued for his release—and the reactionary, right-wing *anti-Dreyfusards*, to whom Dreyfus was an unpatriotic traitor, regardless of the evidence. These ethnic tensions foreshadowed the conflicts that France would later confront in its colonial territories.

WORLD WAR I

After centuries of antagonism, the **Entente Cordiale** brought the British and the French into cooperation in 1904. Together with czarist Russia, this **Triple Entente** faced the **Triple Alliance** of Germany, Italy, and the Austro-Hungarian Empire. Tensions exploded in 1914, when a Serbian nationalist assassinated the heir to the Austrian throne, **Archduke Franz-Ferdinand.** Austria marched on Serbia, Russia responded, and suddenly almost all of Europe was at war. Paris itself survived the war unscathed, but close to 1,400,000 French soldiers had died by the time fighting stopped in November of 1918.

TREATY OF VERSAILLES. The Germans were forced to sign the Treaty of Versailles in the Hall of Mirrors, where Prussian King Wilhelm I had been crowned Kaiser of the German Reich in 1870 at the end of the Franco-Prussian War. The treaty contained a clause that blamed Germany for the war—the great resentment that would aid Hitler's rise to power was born in the Sun King's fabulous chateau.

ROARING 20s AND 30s DEPRESSION

IMPORTED ARTS AND LETTERS. Parisians danced in the streets with British, Canadian, and American soldiers at the end of WWI. The party continued into the **Roaring 20s,** when expatriate artists like **Picasso, Chagall,** and **Man Ray** and American writers like **Gertrude Stein, Ernest Hemingway, Ezra Pound,** and **F. Scott Fitzgerald** (p. 76) flooded Paris's cafes and salons. Black American artists like **Josephine Baker,** faced with discrimination back home, found recognition in Paris. France's long-standing love affair with jazz began in the interwar period.

RISE OF FASCISM. The experimental, artistic, and wild 20s eventually succumbed to the more practical and sober 30s. The era ended with the **Great Depression,** and Paris was rocked by a political crisis as well as an economic one: in the violent right-wing **fascist demonstrations,** thousands of Parisians marched on pl. de la Concorde and stormed the Assemblée Nationale. To combat the fascists, socialists and communists united under **Léon Blum's** left-wing **Front Populaire,** seeking better wages, unionization, and vacation benefits. The Popular Front split over the Spanish Civil War, when Blum decided not to aid the Republicans against the fascist General Franco. Tensions between left and right made France ill-equipped to deal with Hitler's rapid rise to power and his impending mobilization on the opposite shores of the Rhine.

WORLD WAR II

NAZI OCCUPATION. After invading Austria, Czechoslovakia, Poland, Norway, and Denmark, Adolf Hitler's armies swept through the Ardennes in Luxembourg and blitzkrieged across Belgium and the Netherlands before entering Paris on June 13, 1940. Curators at the Louvre, sensing the inevitable Nazi occupation, removed many works of art, including the *Mona Lisa*, and placed them in hiding. Stunned Parisians lined up along the Champs-Elysées to watch Nazi foot soldiers and SS troops goosestep through the Arc de Triomphe. The French signed a truce with the Germans, ceding the northern third of the country to the Nazis and designating the lower two-thirds to a collaborating government set up in Vichy. The puppet Vichy government under **Maréchal Pétain** cooperated with Nazi policy, including the **deportation** of over 120,000 French and foreign Jews to **Nazi concentration camps** between 1942 and 1944.

DEPORTATION OF THE JEWS. Soldiers broke down doors in the largely Jewish neighborhoods of the Marais in the *3ème* and *4ème arrondissements* and relocated Jewish families to the Vélodrome d'Hiver, an indoor winter cycling stadium. Here, Jews awaited transportation to concentration camps like **Drancy,** in the northeastern industrial suburb of Paris near St-Denis, or to camps in Poland and Germany (the **Mémorial de la Déportation** on the Île de la Cité honors those who perished in the Holocaust; p. 186). France was plagued by many profiteering and anti-Semitic **collaborators** *(collabos)* who aided the Gestapo. Recently, the French government and the Roman Catholic Church in France have acknowledged some responsibility for the deportations and for their moral apathy, but the issue remains a controversial one.

REPERCUSSIONS OF OCCUPATION-PERIOD CULTURE.
Paris's theaters, cinemas, music halls, and cafes continued to operate for the Nazi soldiers and officers who flocked to Paris

1913-27
Marcel Proust writes *A la Recherche du Temps Perdu.*

1914
WWI begins.

1917
Marcel Duchamp overturns a urinal, signs it, and calls it *La Fontaine.* Priceless.

1918
WWI ends with victory for France and its allies; the Treaty of Versailles is signed

1920s
American expat culture in Paris has its heyday.

1924
André Breton writes *The Surrealist Manifesto.*

1938
Jean-Paul Sartre writes *La Nausée (Nausea),* whose title aptly anticipated its critical reviews.

1940-44
Nazis occupy Paris.

1942-44
Deportation and murder of thousands of French Jews.

1942
Albert Camus writes *L'Etranger (The Stranger).*

LIFE AND TIMES

1944
Liberation of Paris and declaration of the Fourth Republic under Charles de Gaulle.

1946
French women win the right to vote.

1949
Simone de Beauvoir writes *La Deuxième Sexe* (*The Second Sex*).

1953
Samuel Beckett writes *On Attend Godot* (*Waiting for Godot*).

1954
Vietnam is liberated from colonial rule at Dien Bien Phu.

1957
A good year for writing. Roland Barthes: *Mythologies*, Jean Genet: *Le Balcon* (*The Balcony*).

1958
The Fourth Republic ends and de Gaulle is voted back into power.

1954-1962
The Algerian War

1961
Police kill hundreds of peaceful protestors in Paris.

1967
Jacques Derrida writes *De la Grammatologie.*

1968
Student revolution of May 1968.

for recreation. Many of the establishments and individuals that the Nazis patronized for food and entertainment, including the **Moulin Rouge, Maxim's, Yves Montand, Maurice Chevalier,** and **Edith Piaf,** were maligned as traitors at the end of the war. Women who had taken German lovers had their heads shaved after the war and were forced to walk in the streets amid spitting and jeering.

RESISTANCE. Today, France prefers to commemorate the brave men and women of the Resistance, who fought in secret against the Nazis throughout the occupation. In Paris, the Resistance fighters *(maquis)* set up headquarters below the boulevards, in the **sewers** (p. 260) and **catacombs** (p. 222). In London, **Général Charles de Gaulle** established the **Forces Françaises Libres** (Free French Forces), declared his **Comité National Français** the government-in-exile, and broadcast inspirational messages to his countrymen on the BBC (the first of which is now engraved above the **Tomb of the Unknown Soldier** under the Arc de Triomphe).

LIBERATION AND RECOVERY. On June 6, 1944, British, American, and Canadian troops launched the D-Day invasion on the Normandy coast. On August 25, after four years of occupation, Paris was free. Again, Parisian civilians and Resistance fighters danced and drank with the American, Canadian, and British soldiers. De Gaulle evaded sniper fire to attend mass at Notre Dame and give thanks for the **Liberation of Paris.** His procession down the Champs-Elysées was met with the cheers of thousands of elated Parisians. After the war, as monuments to French bravery were established in the Musée de l'Armée and the Musée de l'Ordre de la Libération (p. 260), and as thousands of French Jewish survivors began to arrive at the main Repatriation Center in the **Gare d'Orsay** (p. 258), there was a move to initiate change and avoid returning to the stagnation of the prewar years. De Gaulle promised new elections once deportees and exiled citizens had been repatriated, and France drafted a new constitution. In 1946, French women finally gained the right to vote.

POSTCOLONIAL PARIS: 50s AND 60s

FOURTH REPUBLIC. The Fourth Republic was proclaimed in 1944, but de Gaulle, its provisional president, denounced the decentralizing agenda of the new constitution and resigned in 1946. The Fourth lacked a strong replacement for de Gaulle, and in the following 14 years, France went through an astounding 25 different governments. Despite these problems, the Fourth Republic presided over an economically resurgent country.

COLONIAL INDEPENDENCE. The end of the war also signaled great change in France's residual 19th-century **colonial empire.** France's defeat in 1954 at the Vietnamese liberation of **Dien**

LIFE AND TIMES

Bien Phu inspired the colonized peoples of France's other protectorates and colonies, which all gained their independence in rapid succession: Morocco and Tunisia in 1956, Mali, Senegal, and the Ivory Coast in 1960. But in Algeria, France drew the line when Algerian nationalists, backed by the resistance efforts of the **FLN (Front Libération National)**, moved for independence. With a population of over one million French *colons*, or **pieds-noirs** (literally "black feet" in French), who were either born in or had immigrated to Algeria, France was reluctant to give up a colony that it had come to regard as an extension of the French *hexagone*.

ALGERIAN WAR. Fighting in Algeria lasted from 1954 to 1962. The Fourth Republic came to an end in the midst of this chaos overseas. De Gaulle was called out of retirement to deal with the crisis and voted into power by the National Assembly in 1958. Later that year, with a new **constitution** in hand, the nation declared itself the **Fifth Republic.** This, unsurprisingly, did nothing to resolve the Algerian conflict. Terrorist attacks in Paris by desperate members of the FLN were met by curfews for African immigrants. At a peaceful demonstration against these restrictions in 1961, police opened fire on the largely North African crowd, killing hundreds. Amid the violence in Paris and the war in Algeria, a 1962 referendum granted Algeria independence. A century of French rule in Algeria came to an end, and the colonial empire crumbled in its wake.

The repercussions of colonial exploitation continue to haunt Paris, where racial tensions exist today between the French and Arab North Africans, Black West Africans, and Caribbeans, many of whom are second- and third-generation citizens.

REVOLUTION OF 1968. De Gaulle's foreign policy was a success, but his ideological conservatism spurred growing domestic problems. In May 1968, what started as a student protest against the university system rapidly grew into a full-scale revolt, as workers went on strike in support of social reform. Frustrated by racism, sexism, capitalism, an outdated curriculum, and the threat of a reduction in the number of students allowed to matriculate, students seized the **Sorbonne.** Barricades were erected in the **Latin Quarter,** and an all-out riot began. Students dislodged cobblestones to hurl at riot police, and their slogan, "Sous les pierres, la plage" (Under the pavement, the beach), symbolized the freedom of shifting sand that lay beneath the rock-hard bureaucracy of French institutions. The situation escalated over the next several weeks. Police used tear gas and clubs to storm the barricades, while students fought back by throwing Molotov cocktails and lighting cars on fire. When 10 million state workers went on **strike** in support of the students, the government deployed tank and commando units.

Once the riot was quelled, the Parisian university system was almost immediately decentralized, with various campuses scattered throughout the city and the nation so that student power

1975
Hélène Cixous writes *La Rire de la Méduse (The Laugh of the Medusa)*.

1976
Michel Foucault writes *Histoire de la Secualité (The History of Sexuality, Volume I)*.

1977
Jacques Lacan elaborates on Freud in *Écrits*.

1981
Socialist François Mitterand's presidency begins.

1984
Margeurite Duras writes *L'Aimant (The Lover)*.

1986
Trouble ahead. In the parliamentary elections, the Socialists suffer major losses, and the far-right wins 10% of the vote.

1991
The Maastricht treaty and the formation of the European Union

1993
The Law Pasqua gives police greater freedom to interrogate immigrants.

1995
Jacques Chirac is elected president.

LIFE AND TIMES

1996
Mitterrand dies; Chirac criticized for nuclear weapons tests.

1996
Disney releases *The Hunchback of Notre Dame*; Victor Hugo rolls over in grave.

1999
Border controls abolished for the entire EU; the PACS extends benefits to same-sex couples.

2002
The euro replaces the franc as France's official currency; far-right nationalist Jean-Marie Le Pen wins a shocking number of votes in the presidential election.

2003
France comes into conflict with the United States over the war in Iraq.

2003
Etienne Balibar writes *Nous, Citoyens d'Europe? Les Frontières, l'Etat, le Peuple* (*We, Citizens of Europe? The Borders, the State, the People*).

2003
French workers strike in protest of Prime Minister Raffarin's pension reforms.

could never again come together so explosively. The aging General de Gaulle resigned following a referendum in 1969.

80s AND 90s

POMPIDOU AND D'ESTAING. Four parties have dominated French politics since the era of de Gaulle. When de Gaulle's allies split in 1974, they formed two right-of-center camps: the Union pour la Démocratie Française (UDF), led by **Valéry Giscard d'Estaing,** and the Rassemblement pour la République (RPR), led by **Jacques Chirac.** In 2002, The RPR merged with the UDF to form the Union pour un Mouvement Populaire (UMP), now the dominant party in the French government. On the left is the Parti Socialiste (PS)—in power throughout the 1980s under **François Mitterrand**—and the Parti Communiste Français (PCF), which currently holds few seats and little power.

After de Gaulle's resignation, many feared that the Fifth Republic would collapse. It has endured, but with substantial change. De Gaulle's prime minister, **Georges Pompidou,** was elected president in 1969. The years under Pompidou were fairly uneventful; he held a *laissez-faire* position toward business and a less assertive foreign policy than de Gaulle. He died suddenly in 1974 from Kahler's Disease, and was suceeded by conservative **Valéry Giscard d'Estaing.** D'Estaing's term saw the construction of the **Centre Pompidou** (p. 195), famous for its controversial architecture and excellent collection of modern art. D'Estaing carried on de Gaulle's legacy by concentrating on economic development and strengthening French presence in international affairs.

MITTERRAND AND COHABITATION. Ending a lengthy period of conservative leadership, Socialist **François Mitterrand** took over the presidency in 1981, and the Socialists gained a majority in the National Assembly. Within weeks they had raised the minimum wage and added a fifth week to the French worker's annual vacation. Though workers' rights and social justice had begun to burgeon under Mitterrand's leadership, a widespread financial crisis soon after his election drove the political left to tatters, forcing Mitterrand to compromise with politicians on the right. Mitterrand began his term with widespread nationalization, but the international climate could not support a socialist economy. In the wake of the 1983 recession, the Socialists met with serious losses in the **1986 parliamentary elections.** The right gained control of parliament, and Mitterrand had to appoint the conservative **Jacques Chirac** as prime minister.

Meanwhile, in an unprecedented power-sharing relationship known as "cohabitation," Mitterrand withdrew from the domestic sphere to control only foreign affairs, allowing Chirac to assume power over all in-country business. To the right's delight, Chirac privatized many industries, but widespread terrorism and a large-scale transportation strike hurt conservatives, allowing Mitterrand to win a second term in 1988. He proceeded to preside over a series of unpopular Socialist governments, one led briefly by **Edith Cresson,** France's first female prime minister.

GRANDS PROJETS. Mitterrand's Grands Projets (p. 84) transformed the architectural landscape of Paris. Seeking immortality in stone, steel, and concrete, Mitterrand was responsible for the **Musée d'Orsay** (p. 258), the **Parc de la Villette** (p. 231) the **Institut du Monde Arabe** (p. 254), the **Louvre Pyramid** (p. 245), the **Opéra Bastille** (p. 219), the **Grande Arche de la Défense** (p. 240), and the new **Bibliothèque Nationale** (p. 221). Although expensive and at times as controversial as was the construction of the Eiffel Tower in 1889, Mitterrand's vision for a 21st-century Paris has produced some of the city's most breathtaking new architecture. Mitterrand's other great legacy was his Socialist project to decentralize financial and political power, shifting it from Paris to local governments outside the Île de France. Unfortunately, the people of France were more concerned with scandals involving Mitterrand's ministers than his grand plans. Contributing to the level of intrigue, Mitterrand revealed two startling facts in the mid-90s—that he had worked with the Vichy government in WWII before joining the Resistance and that he had been seriously ill with cancer since the beginning of his presidency.

CHIRAC TAKES OVER. In 1995, Mitterrand chose not to run again because of his failing health, and Chirac was elected president. With unemployment at 12.2% at the time of the election, Chirac faced a difficult year. The crisis ended in a prolonged **Winter Strike** by students, bus drivers, subway operators, electricians, and postal workers, who protested against budget and benefit cuts proposed by Chirac and his unpopular prime minister, **Alain Juppé.** For weeks, Paris was paralyzed. Stores kept reduced hours, mail delivery came to a halt, and occasional blackouts and traffic jams plagued the city. Despite hardships, many Parisians were glad to see the revived spirit of 1968 and to rediscover some of the neighborhoods' local treasures that were taken for granted before the transportation strikes. The following year proved to be an equally difficult one for Chirac and France. The nation mourned the loss of Mitterrand, who died in early January, and later that year, Chirac was denounced around the globe for conducting underground **nuclear weapons tests** in the South Pacific.

With crises looming from every angle, the ascendancy of the right was short-lived; the 1997 elections reinstated a Socialist government. Chirac was forced to accept his one-time presidential rival, majority leader **Lionel Jospin,** as prime minister.

EUROPEAN UNION. One of the most important challenges for the Western world in the 80s and 90s was the question of

2003
Hundreds of Parisians die in a devastating August heat wave.

2004
Chirac approves ban forbidding Muslim women to wear headscarves in French schools.

2004
Socialists gain majority in March elections.

2005
A series of race- and class-inspired riots shake Paris in October and November.

2006
Edourad Michelin, CEO of the multinational company that bears his name, dies at age 43.

LIFE AND TIMES

European integration. Despite France's support of the creation of the **European Economic Community (EEC)** in 1957, the idea of a unified Europe has met with considerable resistance among the French and others. Since the inception of the 1991 **Maastricht Treaty,** which significantly strengthened economic integration by expanding the 13-nation EEC to the European Union (EU), the French have manifested fear of a loss of French national character and autonomy. Hoping that a united Europe would strengthen cooperation between France and Germany, Mitterrand led the campaign for a "Oui" vote in France's 1992 referendum on the treaty. This position lost him prestige, and the referendum scraped past with a 51% approval rating. The **Schengen Agreement** of 1995 created a six-nation zone without border controls. This zone extended to the entire EU and some other countries in 1999 (barring the UK, Ireland, and Denmark), as well as the birth of the European single currency, the **euro,** which in 2002 superceded the franc as France's official currency.

PARIS TODAY

2004 ELECTIONS. President Chirac's center-right suffered its worst defeat in years in the elections of March of 2004, with the Greens and Socialists gaining control of all but two regions of France. While Chirac's party, the Union for a Popular Movement (UMP), has traditionally rallied around the president, its support has been waning. Most of the party was quite displeased with Chirac's reappointment of unpopular Prime Minister Jean-Pierre Raffarin. Meanwhile, Alain Juppé, an intimate ally of Chirac, resigned as head of the UMP in 2004 after being convicted for corrupt dealings. He was replaced by Dominique de Villepin, whose demeaning remarks about members of his own party have garnered him a mixed reputation. Rumor has it that Chirac has his eye on Villepin as a possible successor, if he chooses not to run in 2007.

IRAQ AND AMERICA... In early 2003, France joined with Germany and Russia to voice opposition to the US-led **Iraq War,** insisting on the use of political and diplomatic means to disarm Iraq. A breach in US-France relations opened as France criticized American unilateralism and defended a multi-polar world and a cohesive, unified Europe. Since the June 2003 **G-8 summit,** Presidents Bush and Chirac have made public displays of reconciliation, but tensions still exist. At the D-Day 60th anniversary ceremonies in June of 2004, President Bush's attempt to draw a correlation between the WWII liberation of France and the Iraq takeover and was met with a stiff dismissal from the French president.

...AND ITS ASSOCIATED SOAP OPERA. Exactly two years later, when Franco-American tensions seemed somewhat subsided and "freedom fries" had sunk deep into the memories of most Americans, the death toll in Iraq approached 200,000. With American opinion increasingly divided on the subject of war, France seemed slowly to be regaining favor in the American eye. Meanwhile, Chirac appeared to be falling out of favor with French citizens, as his stance regarding pre-emptive nuclear attack had begun to resemble that of US President George W. Bush. As of June 2006, Chirac has not made a statement about re-election in 2007, but analysts have cited his ailing health and general unpopularity as reasons why he may abstain from the race.

THE FRENCH ECONOMY. For most of the 21st century, events such as the terrorist attacks of September 11, 2001 and the war in Iraq have consistently damaged France's economy, in particular the tourism and airline industries. The situation was aggravated by months-long strikes that occurred in protest of Prime Minister Raffarin's **plan Fillon,** a series of pension reforms. Beginning in April 2003, thousands of public workers went on strike, including garbage collectors, train conductors, tax officials, airport workers, teachers, electricity board workers, postal workers, and emergency doctors. The train and airline industries both lost millions of dollars. Shrugging off angry, inconvenienced tourists and French workers disgruntled about having to walk to work in the heat, strikers pulled through for one major event: the *baccalauréat* exam. On the day of the high school graduation exams, trains throughout the country ran flawlessly.

The French government had not heard the last of the transportation workers, though. In the spring of 2006, workers joined forces with students to demonstrate for a living wage and higher employment throughout the country. As a result of nationwide protests and rallies, public transportation in France remained unreliable throughout the late spring, and student takeovers forced the Sorbonne to close for six weeks.

SARKO AND CHIRAC: A TUMULTOUS AFFAIR. The 2004 elections installed Nicolas Sarkozy as Finance Minister, and many looked to the energetic young politican for a solution to France's economic problems. In the fall of 2003, Sarkozy was one of the primary advocates of state investment in France's high-speed train company, Alstom, which found itself in dire financial straits. France was greatly criticized for the proposed bail-out, which was perceived as going against EU free-market principles. In May, France reached a compromise with the EU by which Alstom would have to sell only a small portion of the company to private investors.

Meanwhile, tensions between Sarkozy and Chirac continue to heighten as the 2007 election draws near. Considering himself the darling of the conservative party, Sarkozy was extremely offended by Chirac's decision to appoint Villepin as the head of the UMP in 2004, and rumors of his botched affair with one of the president's daughters blazed through France shortly thereafter. In 2005, however, Sarkozy got his wish and was elected president of the UMP by an astounding 85% margin. But the politician has recently set his sights even higher: when asked by a Parisian newspaper whether he thinks about the upcoming presidential election while he shaves in the morning, Sarkozy responded, "Not just when I shave."

THE HEADSCARF DEBACLE. One of the biggest political controversies of the past 10 years has had to do with the wearing of Muslim headscarves (*hijab*) in public schools. Chirac approved a ban on the headscarves, arguing that the garments erode the principle of separation of church and state. The issue has been hotly contested throughout the nation, with some viewing it as the infiltration of far-right discrimination into educational policy.

ANTI-SEMITISM. Since early in the decade, anti-Semitic violence in France has been on the rise. France has the third largest Jewish population in Europe, including large numbers of Eastern European and North African Sephardic immigrants. There have been particularly harrowing conflicts between Jewish and Muslim North Africans in the Paris *banlieu*, but recent events have suggested that religious tensions penetrate all classes. There were 970 documented acts of anti-Semitic hatred in France in 2004, including cases of harassment and vandalism in synagogues and Jewish cemeteries. In July of 2004, Israeli Prime Minister Ariel Sharon urged French Jews to immigrate to Israel, citing France as unsafe because of its rampant anti-Semitism. President Chirac responded furiously to the accusation, defending his country's commitment to protecting its Jewish citizens, and while Sharon maintained that his comments had been misinterpreted, the incident brought France's racial and religious tensions into the international spotlight. In 2005, three reporters for Paris's *Le Monde* newspaper were found guilty of conscious anti-Semitism in their columns, and France still wrestles with its anti-Jewish reputation to this day.

GLBT RIGHTS. In 1999, France became the first traditionally Catholic country in the world to legally recognize same-sex unions. The **Pacte Civil de Solidarité,** known by its acronym **PACS,** was designed to extend to both same-sex and unmarried opposite-sex couples greater welfare, tax and inheritance rights. While PACS is now such a common term that it is used as both a verb *(pacser)* and an adjective *(pacsé)*, it is has faced serious detractors. For many French people, official gay partnership is still an unwelcome concept; for others, PACS is an inadequate conciliatory gesture, designed to patch over the fact that gay marriage is still illegal. GLBT activists are currently struggling to attain the same parenting rights that heterosexual married couples enjoy.

Polls have indicated that an increasing number (65% in 2005) of French citizens support gay marriage, but legalization may be slow in coming. In the summer of 2004, a French court annulled the country's first gay marriage, performed by the mayor of Bègles, in the southwest. The controversy over "Le Mariage de Bègles" proved difficult for Paris mayor Bertrand Delanoë, the only openly queer mayor of a major world city and one of France's few gay senior politicians. While Delanoë has been a determined advocate for GLBT rights, he supported the annulment and has declined to conduct same-sex marriages in Paris until they are sanctioned by French law.

THE ARTS

LITERATURE AND PHILOSOPHY

MEDIEVAL CHANSONS AND FABLIAUX. Medieval France produced an extraordinary number of literary texts. Popular **chansons de geste** were epics in verse that recounted tales of 8th-century crusades and conquests. The most famous of these, the **Chanson de Roland** (1170), dramatizes the heroism of Roland, one of Charlemagne's *chevaliers.* While *chansons de geste* entertained 12th-century masses, the aristocracy enjoyed more refined tales of knightly honor and courtly love, such as the *Lais* (narrative songs) of **Marie de France,** the romances of **Chrétien de Troyes,** and Béroul's adaptation of the Irish legend of **Tristan et Iseult.**

During the 13th century, popular satirical stories called fabliaux celebrated the bawdy and the scatological. The 14th and 15th centuries produced the protofeminist writings of **Christine de Pizan,** who actively challenged the male-dominated literary aristocracy by debating the merit of many so-called classics. The era also saw the ballads of **François Villon** and the birth of comic theater, with pieces like the *Farce de Maître Pathelin,* which is now a popular choice for children's school plays.

RENAISSANCE INNOVATION. Renaissance literature in France challenged medieval notions of courtly love and Christian thought. Inspired by Boccaccio's *Decameron,* Marguerite de Navarre's *Héptaméron* used pilgrim stories to explore humanist ideas. Frenchman **John Calvin's** treatises criticized the Church and opened the road to the Protestant Reformation in France. With Jacques Cartier's founding of Nouvelle France (Québec) in 1534, French writers began to expand their perspectives on themselves and the world. **Rabelais's** fantastical *Gargantua and Pantagruel* explored (and satirized) the world from a giant's point of view, and **Montaigne's** *Essais* pushed the boundaries of individual intellectual thought. While the poetry of **Ronsard** and **Du Bellay,** the memoirs of **Marguerite de Valois,** and the sonnets of **Louise Labé** contributed to the Renaissance's spirit of optimism and change, they also expressed anxiety over the atrocities of the 16th-century Wars of Religion.

RATIONALISM AND THE ENLIGHTENMENT. The **Académie Française** (p. 204) was founded in 1635 to regulate and codify French literature and language, and has since served as the holy ground of French letters. There and elsewhere, French philosophers reacted to the musings of the Humanists with Rationalism, a school of thought that, somewhat intuitively, championed logic and order. In his *Discourse on Method,* **René Descartes** proved his own existence with the famously catchy deduction, "I think, therefore I am." **Blaise Pascal** misspent his youth inventing the mechanical calculator and the science of probabilities. He later became a devotee of Jansenism—an extremist sect of Catholicism that emphasized Augustinian teachings—and retired from public life to write about the virtues of solitude in his *Pensées* (1658). **Jean-Baptiste Molière,** the era's comic relief, used his plays to satirize the social pretensions of the bourgeoisie. Molière founded the **Comédie Française**—the world's oldest national theater company—which still produces top-notch versions of French classics at its theater in Paris (p. 275).

In the 18th century, the Enlightenment sought to promote reason and a definitive social code. **Denis Diderot** and **Jean D'Alembert's** *Encyclopédie* (1752-1780) was the ultimate compendium of Enlightenment thought, containing entries by philosophers **Jean-Jacques Rousseau** and **Voltaire.** Voltaire's famous satire *Candide* (1758) refuted the claim that "all is for the best in the best of all possible worlds," while Rousseau's *Confessions* (1766-1769) and novels like *Emile* (1762) and *Julie, ou La Nouvelle Héloïse* (1761), argued that leaving society behind is better than living in a corrupt world. Playwright **Beaumarchais's** incendiary comic masterpieces *Le Barbier de Seville* (1775) and *Le Mariage de Figaro* (1784) were banned by Louis XVI for their criticisms of the aristocracy.

SEX AND REVOLUTION. The traumas of the era surrounding the French Revolution are perhaps best represented in literature by the works of the **Marquis de Sade.** In libertine novels like *Philosophy in the Bedroom* (1795) and *Justine* (1791), de Sade attacked hypocrisy and repression and dealt with what he perceived to be a mad world through the violently excessive representation of the sexual practice that now bears his name.

ROMANTICISM AND REALISM. During the 19th century the expressive ideals of Romanticism, which first came to prominence in Britain and Germany, found their way to analytically minded France. **François-René de Chateaubriand** drew inspiration for his novel *Atala* from his experiences with Native Americans near Niagara Falls. **Henri Stendhal** *(Le Rouge et le Noir)* and **Honoré de Balzac** *(La Comédie Humaine)* helped to establish the novel as the new pre-eminent literary medium, but finally it was **Victor Hugo's** *The Hunchback of Notre Dame* (1831) that dominated the Romantic age. In the same period, the young Aurore Dupin left her husband and childhood home, took the *nom de plume* of **George Sand,** and published passionate novels condemning sexist social conventions. Sand was as famous for her scandalous lifestyle as for her prose, with a tendency to cross-dress and a string of high-profile relationships including a 10-year dalliance with **Frédéric Chopin** (p. 85). The heroine of **Gustave Flaubert's** *Madame Bovary* (1856) spurned provincial life for romantic, adulterous daydreams in his famous realist novel. Flaubert was prosecuted for immorality in 1857 and was only narrowly acquitted. Poet **Charles Baudelaire** was not so lucky; the same tribunal fined him 50 francs. Although Baudelaire gained a reputation for obscenity during his own lifetime, today his *Fleurs du Mal (Flowers of Evil)* is considered the most influential piece of 19th-century French poetry.

SOCIALISM AND SCIENCE. Baudelaire participated in the 1848 revolution, and his radical political views closely resembled those of the anarcho-socialist innovator **Pierre-Joseph Proudhon.** Born into poverty and luckily brilliant, Proudhon received a scholarship to college at Besançon and then at Paris where, in 1840, he published the leaflet, *What is Property?* His inflammatory thesis stated that "property is theft." Put on trial in 1842, he escaped punishment only because the jury refused to condemn ideas it could not understand. A pivotal figure in the history of socialism, Proudhon inspired the *syndicaliste* trade-union movement of the 1890s. A more optimistic philosophy was provided by the **positivism** of **Auguste Comte,** which anticipated that science would give way to a fully rational explanation of nature.

NATURALISM AND SYMBOLISM. Like its artistic counterpart, Impressionism, literary Symbolism reacted against stale conventions and used new techniques to capture instants of perception. Led by **Stéphane Mallarmé** and **Paul Verlaine,** the movement was instrumental in the creation of modern poetry as we understand it, particularly through the work of the precocious **Arthur Rimbaud.** Naturalism, an outgrowth of Realism conceived around 1880, uses a scientific, analytic approach to dissect and reconstruct reality; the genre is represented by writers as diverse as **Emile Zola** and **Guy de Maupassant.**

BELLE EPOQUE. Works that confronted the anti-Semitism of the **Dreyfus Affair,** like Zola's *J'Accuse,* laid the foundation for a whole new literature that would explore issues of individual identity—including sexuality, gender, and ethnicity—in 20th-century France. **Marcel Proust's** seven-volume *Remembrance of Things Past* (1913-1927) captured the social snobbery of the turn of the century and inquired into the nature of time, memory, and love. Like most serious French authors of the time, Proust was published in the influential *Nouvelle Revue Française.* Founded in Paris in 1909, the journal rose to prominence under the guidance of **André Gide,** who won the Nobel Prize in 1947 for morally provocative novels like *The Counterfeiters* (1924). Throughout his career, Gide was engaged in a rivalry with Catholic revivalist **Paul Claudel.** Claudel struggled unsuccessfully to persuade Gide that divine grace would eventually overcome greed and lust, the basic theme behind plays such as *The Satin Slipper* (1924).

QUEER MODERNISM. Proust, Gide, and novelist/playwright **Colette** wrote frankly about homosexuality. Proust's portraits of *Belle Epoque* Parisians in *Sodom and Gomorrah,* Gide's homoerotic novels like *l'Immoraliste,* and Colette's sensual descriptions of the opium dens of the 1920s and cabarets of the 1930s in *Le Pur et l'Impur* and *La Vagabonde* inspired later feminist and homoerotic writing. Authors who continued to explore these novel themes include **Jean Genet** in *Funeral Rites* (1949), **Monique Wittig** in *Les Guerillères* (1967), and **Hervé Guibert** in *Fou de Vincent (Crazy about Vincent).* The sexual freedom that seems to characterize Paris in the artistic imagination was also represented by American and British expatriate writers like **Gertrude Stein, Djuna Barnes, F. Scott Fitzgerald,** and **Henry Miller.**

DADAISM AND SURREALISM. Like contemporary art, film, dance, and music, 20th-century French literature moved increasingly toward abstraction. Inspired by the nonsensical art movement called Dadaism, the theatrical collaborations of choreographer Serge Diaghilev, set-designer Pablo Picasso, composer Erik Satie, and writer **Jean Cocteau** during WWI laid the foundation for even further abstraction following the war. In France, Dadaism took a literary bent under the influence of Romanian-born **Tristan Tzara,** whose poems of nonsensically scrambled words attacked the structure of language. Tzara's colleagues **André Breton** and **Louis Aragon** soon became dissatisfied with the anarchy of Dadaism and set about developing a more organized protest, which exploded in 1924 with the publication of Breton's first *Surrealist Manifesto*, a proclamation of the artistic supremacy of the subconscious. But what is not created consciously is difficult to understand consciously—most Surrealist poetry defies analysis. Surrealism later influenced absurdist French theater, such as **Eugène Ionesco's** *Rhinocéros*, expatriate **Samuel Beckett's** *Waiting for Godot*, and **Sartre's** *Huis Clos (No Exit)*. Meanwhile, the rising threat of Nazi Germany spurred a literary call to arms, led by the indomitable **André Malraux.** Malraux drew inspiration from his experience in the Chinese civil war for his masterpiece, *The Human Condition* (1933). Another adventurer, **Antoine de St-Exupéry,** used his experiences as an early aviation pioneer to create classics such as *The Little Prince* (1943).

EXISTENTIALISM. The period following the war was intellectually dominated by **Jean-Paul Sartre,** the undisputed guru of Existentialism. His philosphy held that life, as an independent entity, is meaningless; only by choosing and then committing oneself to a cause can existence take on a purpose. Though **Albert Camus** is often grouped with Sartre, his brand of existentialism differs from Sartre's in its morality: Camus mainained that mere commitment was not enough to give life meaning if it was unfair to others. He achieved fame with his debut novel *L'Étranger* (1942), which tells the story of a dispassionate social misfit condemned to death for a cold-blooded murder. Both Camus and Sartre used the stage as a vehicle for their ideas.

FEMINISM. Existentialist and acclaimed feminist, Sartre's companion **Simone de Beauvoir** made waves with *The Second Sex* (1949), an essay attacking the myth of femininity. Its famous statement, "One is not born, but becomes a woman" planted the roots of the French second-wave feminism that would last through the 70s. With their exploration of gender identity, writers like **Marguerite Duras** *(L'Amant)*, **Nathalie Sarraute** *(Tropismes)*, **Marie Cardinal** *(Les Mots Pour le Dire)*, **Christine Rochefort** *(Les Stances à Sophie)*, **Hélène Cixous** *(Le Rire de la Méduse)*, **Luce Irigaray** *(Ce Sexe Qui n'en est Pas Un)*, and **Marguerite Yourcenar** *(Le Coup de Grace)* carried the feminist torch worldwide. While American feminist literature emphasized practical action, French feminism tended to be more theoretical, influenced by **Jacques Lacan's** psychoanalytic writings and concerned with the structure of language. Specifically, French second-wave feminists advocated *femme écriture*, the philosophy of "writing the body" that inspired such sentiments as "deflating the phallus." The founding of the publishing house *Des Femmes* in the 70s ensured that French women writers would continue to have a means of expressing themselves in print.

The Postwar Years

World War II and the Nazi occupation of France between 1940 and 1944 polarized Parisian intellectuals. While some (Robert Brasillach [1909-1945], Pierre Drieu La Rochelle [1893-1945]) chose to collaborate with the enemy, most joined the Resistance to fight actively or by writing, often at the price of their lives, clandestine tracts that denounced the enemy and urged the population to resist. With the liberation of Paris in August 1944, intellectual freedom returned. The postwar years were under the sign of hope associated with ideals from the Resistance and soon of decolonization. Most postwar intellectuals tended to the left. The Communist Party had organized much of the Resistance during the war. After Liberation, it retained its influence through the "Comité national des écrivains" (National Committee of Writers), founded in 1942 and composed of writers and artists of different political stripes. With the escalation of the Cold War and the rise of McCarthyism in the US, many intellectuals turned to the Soviet Union, which since the 30s had been a symbol of peace. Dominated by the fear of nuclear war, the late 1940s and early 50s were for intellectuals a time of mass manifestations and international peace movements. Writers and artists signed countless appeals. They defended Henri Martin, a French sailor condemned for distributing anti-colonialist tracts (1951) and the Rosenbergs, a Jewish-American couple executed in the US for supposedly selling atomic secrets to Russia (1952-53). These years of militancy coincided with political, economic, and social instability in France. The death of Stalin (1952), revelations about gulags and repression in satellite states like Hungary (1945), and growing economic prosperity in France led to the loss of unity among intellectuals.

The postwar Parisian intellectual scene was dominated by a neo-Hegelianism of Marxist and existential signature. While intellectuals who stayed with the Communist Party lost influence amid ebbing postwar euphoria, existentialisms centered around various philosopher-writers thrived. Jean-Paul Sartre (1905-1980) and Simone de Beauvoir (1908-1986) were known for their writings and anti-bourgeois "bohemian lifestyle." It was rumored that they wrote treatises on tables at the Café de Flore and frequented dimly lit jazz cellars in hip areas of St-Germain. Sartre's pronouncement on the importance of existence above and beyond human essence, his insistence on the necessity of action, personal responsibility, and *engagement* (commitment) not only in life but in writing, molded a generation. Next to his arduous *L'Être et le Néant* (1943; *Being and Nothingness*, 1956), Sartre popularized his thought in novels, short stories, and plays. He drew readers and viewers into existential experiences (*La Nausée* [1938; *Nausea*, 1939]), made them ponder the mixtures of courage, chance, and fate in war times (*Le Mur* [1939; *The Wall*, 1948]), and reflect on human self-deception and fear of action (*Huis Clos* [1945; *No Exit*, 1946]).

Simone de Beauvoir quit teaching to further her career as a writer. In *Le Deuxieme Sexe* (1949; *The Second Sex*, 1953), a book taking on the condition of women, she coined the famous aphorism "one is not born woman, one becomes woman." Her novels (*Le Sang des autres*, [1945; *The Blood of Others*, 1948]), plays, and autobiographies (*Memoires d'une fille rangée* [1958; *Memoires of a Dutiful Daughter*, 1958]) address the question of our responsibility to others and of living one's life in an open-ended way without accepting the living death imposed by institutional norms (family, church, or schools).

Born in Algeria, Albert Camus (1913-1960) represented another strain of existentialism. *L'étranger* (1942; *The Stranger*, 1946) became influential in the postwar era. Camus's critique of bourgeois institutions, insistence on living according to one's bodily rhythms and pleasures, and his will to reject false moral values engaged debate. His theater of the absurd dealt with life's unexpected twists, with misunderstandings, impossible situations, chance, fate, and power (*Le Malentendu* [1944; *Cross Purpose*, 1947]; *Caligula* [1944; 1947]). In his Nobel Prize (1957) acceptance speech, he declared that the artist needed to be "in the arena," involved in universal human dilemmas but without realism or dogmatism. He intrigued the public with his brooding image of a solitary soul wearing a trench coat à la Humphrey Bogart, an omnipresent cigarette hanging from his lips. In 1960, Camus was the victim of an accident that took place when the car driven by his editor smashed into a tree. When it was revealed that Camus had a train ticket in his pocket, his untimely and absurd death seemed to come out of one of his own plays.

Yet the 1950s were for Camus not only a time of hedonism, existential humanism, and the absurd, but also a time of politics. While he lived in Algeria, Camus had worked as a journalist. Early on, he had decried the human misery of a mountainous region of Algeria known as Kabylia ("Chroniques algériennes, 1939-1958" in *Actuelles* III, 1958). Though appalled by the poverty of the indigenous population, Camus took on the subject of Algeria a position opposed to the position of Sartre, which led to a permanent rift between the two. Until his death, two years before Algerian independence, Camus was convinced compromise was possible, with French settlers—"pied-noirs"—remaining side-by-side with natives in an independent Algeria. Sartre, as shown in his preface to Frantz Fanon's *Les Damnés de la terre* (1961; *The Wretched of the Earth*, 1963) took a far more radical stand, arguing for independence and an evacuation of all settlers from native soil.

Slightly older, André Malraux (1901-1976) had been known for dramatic pre-war novels about life in a transforming world, be it that of the Chinese revolution (*La condition humaine* [1933; *Man's Fate*, 1938]) or the Spanish civil war (*L'espoir* [1938; *Man's Hope*, 1953]). After the war, he wrote about art (*Les Voix du Silence* [1951; *The Voices of Silence*, 1953]) and became Minister of Culture (1959) under de Gaulle. He brought art to the people by building *Maisons de la Culture* (Houses of Culture) all over France and ordered the preservation and restoration of Paris's historic buildings. Malraux's elegance and good looks—whether in aviator garb or black-tie—were legendary. As a cultural envoy, he traveled to India, China, and to the US on the invitation of Jackie Kennedy (1963), who was charmed by Malraux's talent for furthering the arts.

If the postwar years were the time when tourists hoped to find a quaint Paris of painters, writers, and musicians (as romanticized in Vincent Minelli's musical *An American in Paris*; 1951), major changes were under way. With the Marshall Plan, industrialization and "Americanization" of both the city and the country took place. In the films of Jacques Tati (1909-1982), Paris was seen losing its gallic quaintness (*Mon Oncle*, 1958), becoming a postmodern nightmare or simulacrum for tourists (*Playtime*, 1967). Intellectuals saw their lives threatened by consumerism. Despite rising consumer culture, the intellectual aura of Sartre, Beauvoir, Camus, and Malraux continued to radiate beyond the City of Lights.

The late 1950s and 60s, marked by prosperity, the Algerian War's end and decolonization, the waning of Resistance memories, and a lessening of Cold War tensions, saw the rise of a new intellectual breed. "New novelists" like Michel Butor (1926-) and Alain Robbe-Grillet (1922-) launch experimental writings. A young generation of intellectual, poetic "new wave" filmmakers defied studio rules to deal with human dilemmas in a modernizing city (François Truf-faut, *Les Quatre Centes Coups* [1959; 400 Blows]); Jean-Luc Godard, *A Bout de soufflé* [1961; *Breathless*]; *Deux ou trois choses que je sais d'elle* [1967; *Two or Three Things I Know About Her*]).

In 1960, criticizing their elders for militant leftism and concepts of historical self, Philippe Sollers (1936-) and others founded interdisciplinary journal *Tel Quel*. Editors touted textual Marxism based on psychoanalysis and argued that true liberation is that of desire. The journal published rising stars like Julia Kristeva (1941-)—soon to be Sollers' wife—and Jacques Derrida (1930-). A decade of intellectual effervescence under the aegis of structuralism and, later, poststructuralism culminated with the 1968 uprisings. From Claude Lévi-Strauss's (1908-) "savage thought," to Louis Althusser's (1918-1990) reading of Marx, Michel Foucault's (1925-1984) history as discourse, Jacques Lacan's (1901-1981) French Freud, Gilles Deleuzes (1925-1995) and Félix Guattari's (1930-1992) rhizomes, Derrida's (1930-) deconstruction of oppositions and Hélène Cixous's (1937-) textual feminism, the sixties are rife with talent. Tourists report sightings at the Coupole and the Hotel Lutetia.

After 1968, the values inherited from the Resistance were resolutely passé. Decolonization had been largely achieved and new problems arose in its wake. The ideals of 1968—promising transformations of oppositions into an endless play of sexual, racial, and cultural differences—ran afoul when a rising market economy, a sense of acceleration under the impact of new technologies, and massive migrations transformed Paris and France. With the disappearance of the countryside, the gentrification of old neighborhoods, and the emergence of squalid suburban living conditions, the very concept of the city was re-evaluated (Henri Lefebvre, *La Révolution Urbaine* [1970; The Urban Revolution, 2003]). Paris is now comprised of many histories and cultures. New intellectuals, writers, and artists are re-evaluating the recent past and discussing a present (Étienne Balibar, *Nous, citoyens d'Europe? Les frontières, l'Etat, le peuple* [2001; *We, Citizens of Europe? Borders, the State, the People*]) that, with the arrival in Paris of people from all over the world, promises to be increasingly diverse.

Verena Andermatt Conley teaches Romance Languages and Literatures at Harvard University. She has published extensively; a book on postwar Parisian intellectuals is forthcoming.

POSTCOLONIAL VOICES. In the 20th century, many voices emerged from France's former colonies and protectorates in the **Antilles** (Martinique and Guadeloupe), the **Caribbean** (Haiti), **North America** (Québec), **North Africa** (Algeria, Tunisia, and Morocco, known as the Maghreb), and **West Africa** (Senegal, Mali, Côte d'Ivoire, Congo, and Cameroon). Much of this literature speaks out against France's colonial exploitation and deals with the trauma of the decolonization process (p. 68). In Paris in the 1920s, intellectuals **Aimé Césaire** (Martinique) and **Léopold Sédar Senghor** (Senegal) founded the **Négritude** movement, which emphasized the shared history and identity of black Francophones. Their work and the subsequent founding of the press **Présence Africaine** on the Left Bank (p. 292) inspired generations of Francophone intellectuals on both sides of the Atlantic, the most celebrated of whom is Antillean writer **Frantz Fanon** (*Les Damnées de la Terre*).

Since the atrocities of the Algerian War in the 1960s (p. 69), much Maghrébin literature has been characterized by a search for cultural identity, subjectivity, and the conflicts between colonial and postcolonial history. Some of the most prolific writers of the movement are **Assia Djébar** (*Les Femmes d'Alger Dans Leur Appartement*) from Algeria; **Driss Charibi** (*La Civilisation...Ma Mère!*) from Morocco; and **Albert Memmi** (*La Statue de Sel*) from Tunisia. North African immigration to France in the 70s, 80s, and 90s has had a profound impact on French language, culture, and politics. Many second- and third-generation Maghrébin writers in France, such as **Mehdi Charef** (*Le Thé au Harem d'Archi Ahmed*), have written about French-Arab culture and the difficulties of assimilation.

POSTMODERN -ISMS. From the 70s to the present day, postmodernism, a diverse confederation of ideas that reject the possibility of stable meaning and identity, has exerted a great influence over literary, political, and intellectual life worldwide. In *The Postmodern Condition: A Report on Knowledge* (1979), **Jean François Lyotard** turned a routine report commissioned by the Canadian government into a postmodernist manifesto. Among the most important postmodern thinkers are structuralist **Ferdinand de Saussure**, historical "archaeologist" **Michel Foucault** (*Discipline and Punish, The History of Sexuality*), psychoanalyst **Jacques Lacan,** poststructural feminist **Hélène Cixous,** and cultural critic **Jean Baudrillard.** Theory and literary criticism, both in France and in the United States, were transformed by **deconstruction,** a practice founded by **Jacques Derrida,** whereby a text's inherent oppositions are examined through careful analysis of language and form. Lyotard, Saussure, Lacan, Cixous, Baudrillard, and Derrida all spent most of their lives in Paris. The hugely popular public seminars given by Foucault, Lacan, and other thinkers are indicative of Paris's intellectual tenor: it seems that in Paris, literature and public life are more closely related than anywhere else in the world. For more on postwar French intellectuals and writers, see **Parisian Intellectuals Abuzz,** p. 78.

FINE ARTS AND ARCHITECTURE

ROMAN STONES. Paris's first achievements in architecture were the baths, arenas, and roads built by the Romans, which include the partially reconstructed Arènes de Lutèce and the baths preserved in the **Musée de Cluny** (p. 253). Though few of the ruins still remain intact, prominent figures throughout Paris's history have looked fondly back to Parisian classical architecture as a model for more recent construction.

GOTHIC CATHEDRALS. Most **Medieval art** aimed to instruct the average 12th- and 13th-century churchgoer on religious themes: as most commoners were illiterate, stained glass and intricate stone facades, like those at **Chartres** (p. 329), **Ste-Chapelle** (p. 186), and **Notre Dame** (p. 183), served as large, pictoral reproductions of the Bible. The churches that contain these Biblical works are themselves stunning examples of Gothic architecture, characterized by flying buttresses that allow for high ceilings and enormous stained-glass windows. Monastic industry brought the art of illumination to its height, as monks added ornate illustrations to manuscripts. The **Cluny** and the **Chantilly** museums (p. 335) display some of these manuscripts, including the illuminated *Très Riches Heures du Duc de Berry*.

THE RENAISSANCE. Inspired by the painting, sculpture, and architecture of the Italian Renaissance, 16th-century France imported much of its style from its boot-shaped neighbor to the east. François I had viewed such re-born art during his Italian campaigns, and when he inherited France in 1515, he decided that the time had come to put his country, artistically, on the map. The king implored friends in Italy to send him works by **Titian** and **Bronzino**. He also imported the artists themselves to create **Fontainebleau** (p. 333), the most perfect example of French Renaissance architecture. **Leonardo da Vinci** appeared soon after, with the **Mona Lisa** in tow as a gift to the French monarch (p. 245).

BAROQUE EXCESS. In the 17th century under Louis XIV, the delightfully excessive Baroque movement swept up from Italy to France. The architecture of **Versailles** (p. 321) benefited greatly from this Italian infusion. The palace, first built over a period of three years (1631-34), was extravagantly re-imagined by Louis XIV during the second half of the century. The Sun King drew inspiration from the chateau of **Vaux-le-Vicomte** (p. 339), the 1657 accomplishment of the architect-artist-landscaper triumvirate of **Louis Le Vau, Charles Le Brun,** and **André Le Nôtre** (see **Garden Party,** p. 326). But the Baroque period had room for realism, even as it indulged a monarch's penchant for gilt and high heels—the brothers **Le Nain** (who worked together on all their canvases) and **Georges de La Tour** (1593-1652) produced representations of everyday life.

ACADÉMIE ROYALE. Baroque exuberance was subdued by the more serious and classical works of painter **Nicolas Poussin** (1594-1665). Poussin believed that reason should be the guiding principle of art and was fortunate enough to promulgate these views with the endorsement of the **Académie Royale.** Under director **Charles Le Brun** (1619-90), the traditionalist Academy, founded in 1648, became the sole arbiter of taste in all matters artistic. It held annual **salons**—"official" art exhibitions held in vacant halls of the Louvre—and it set strict, conservative guidelines for artistic technique and subject matter.

ROCOCO. The early 18th century brought on the playful **Rococo** style. Its asymmetrical curves and profusion of ornamentation were far more conducive (read: less nauseating) to **Louis XV's** interior design than to architecture itself. **Antoine Watteau** (1684-1721) captured the secret *rendez-vous* of the aristocracy and **François Boucher** (1703-70) painted landscapes and scenes from courtly life.

NEOCLASSICISM AND REVOLUTIONARY ART. After the Revolution wreaked havoc on symbolic strongholds of the aristocracy like Versailles and Notre Dame the reign of Napoleon I saw the emergence of Neoclassicism, exemplified architecturally by the **Eglise de la Madeleine** (p. 213)—a giant imitation of a Greco-Roman temple—and the imposing **Arc de Triomphe** (p. 211), both begun in 1806. The influence of painter **Jacques-Louis David** (1748-1825) spanned the period from revolution to empire; his *Death of Marat* (1793) was a rallying point for revolutionaries and is considered by some critics to mark the onset of "modernity"; later, he created giant canvases on Classical themes and facilitated the emergence of

Empire style in fine and decorative art and fashion, which exploited the Greek and Roman iconography so admired by Napoleon. The French Revolution had inspired painters to create heroic depictions of scenes from their own time. Following David, and encouraged by the deep pockets of Napoleon, painters created large, dramatic pictures, often of the emperor as Romantic hero and god, all rolled into one *petit* package. But after Napoleon's fall, few artists painted nationalistic *tableaux*. One exception was **Théodore Géricault** (1791-1824), whose *Raft of the Medusa* (1819) can be seen in the Louvre (p. 245).

ROMANTICISM AND ORIENTALISM. Nineteenth-century France was ready to settle into respectable, bourgeois ways after several awkward years of transitioning from Republic to Empire. The paintings of **Eugène Delacroix** (1798-1863) were a shock to salons of the 1820s and 1830s. The *Massacre at Chios* (1824) and *The Death of Sardanapalus* (1827) both display an extraordinary sense of color and a penchant for melodrama. Delacroix went on to do a series of "Moroccan" paintings; he shared this Orientalist tendency with **Jean-Auguste-Dominique Ingres** (1780-1867), among others. Ingres's most famous representation of the sexual and racial otherness that so fascinated the Romantic imagination is the nearly liquid reclining nude, *La grande odalisque*. Another influential Romantic, **Paul Delaroche** (1797-1859) created charged narratives on large canvases (*The Young Martyr*, 1855).

CLASSICISM AND THE INFLUENCE OF HAUSSMAN. Aside from a romantically inspired **Gothic revival** led by the so-called "great restorer" **Viollet-le-Duc,** Neoclassicism reigned in 19th-century architecture, supported by the strictly classical curriculum of the dominant Ecole des Beaux-Arts. The ultimate expression of 19th-century classicism is **Charles Garnier's** Paris **Opéra** house, built 1862-75 (**Sights,** p. 215). More influential to the face of today's Paris, however, was the direction of **Baron Georges Haussmann.** From 1852 to 1870, Haussmann transformed Paris from a medieval city to a modern metropolis. Commissioned by Napoleon III to modernize the city, Haussmann tore long, straight boulevards through the tangled clutter and narrow alleys of old Paris, creating a unified network of **grands boulevards.**

REALISM. The late 19th and early 20th centuries saw the reinvention of painting in France: first, a shift of subject matter to everyday life, and then a radical change in technique. **Impressionism** found its beginnings in the mid-19th century with **Théodore Rousseau** (1812-67) and **Jean-François Millet** (1814-75), who were leaders of the **Ecole de Barbizon,** a group of artists who painted nature for its own sake. Landscape paintings capturing a "slice of life" paved the way for Realism. The Realists were led by **Gustave Courbet** (1819-77), who focused on everyday subjects but portrayed them magnified many times on tremendous canvases.

MANET'S MODERNITY. Edouard Manet (1832-83) facilitated the transition from the Realism of Courbet to what we now consider **Impressionism;** in the 1860s, he began to shift the focus of his work to color and texture. Manet's *Déjeuner Sur l'Herbe* was refused by the Salon of 1863 due to its less-than-kosher Naked Lunch theme (two suited men and a naked woman are shown picnicking in the forest, in a formation taken from Raimondi's *Judgement of Paris*) and revolutionary technique; it was later shown proudly at the Salon des Refusés, along with 7000 other rejected salon works. In the equally scandalous *Olympia* (1862), appropriating the form of Titian's *Venus of Urbino*, Manet boldly re-imagined the classically idealized female nude. He depicted a distinctly contemporary Parisian prostitute, wearing only a shoe and staring unapologetically at the viewer. This display of fleshy modernity, inserted into the grand Western tradition, disconcerted viewers, earned accusations of pornography, and inspired numerous caricatures—and, later, iconic status. Both works can be seen at Paris's fantastic Musée d'Orsay (p. 258).

IMPRESSIONISM AND POST-IMPRESSIONISM. By the late 1860s Manet's new aesthetic had set the stage for **Claude Monet** (1840-1926), **Camille Pissarro** (1830-1903), and **Pierre-Auguste Renoir** (1841-1919), who began further to explore new techniques. They strove to attain a sense of immediacy; colors were used to capture visual impressions as they appeared to the eye, and light became subject matter in itself. In 1874, these revolutionary artists had their first collective exhibition, and one critic snidely labeled the group "Impressionists." The artists themselves found the label accurate, and their Impressionists' show became an annual event for the next seven years. In the late 1880s, the group inspired **Edgar Degas** (1834-1917), **Gustave Caillebotte** (1848-94), **Berthe Morisot** (1841-95), and **Henri Fantin-Latour** (1836-1904).

The Post-Impressionists, also called **Neo-Impressionists,** were for the most part loners. **Paul Cézanne** (1839-1906) painted landscapes using an early Cubist technique while in isolation at Aix-en-Provence; **Paul Gauguin** (1848-1903) took up a solitary residence in Tahiti, where he painted in sensuous color; **Vincent van Gogh** (1853-90) projected his tortured emotions onto the countryside at Auvers-sur-Oise (p. 341). **Georges Seurat** (1859-91), something less of a social outcast, revealed his **Pointillist** technique at the Salon des Indépendants of 1884. Sculptor **Auguste Rodin** (1840-1917) focused on the energetic, muscular shaping of bronze (p. 257).

BOHEMIA AND ART NOUVEAU. As the 19th century drew to a close, Bohemia had moved its center to the cabarets and cafes of Montmartre, a refuge from the chaos of the modern city below. **Henri de Toulouse-Lautrec** (1864-1901) captured the spirit of the Belle Epoque in vibrant silkscreen posters that covered Paris, as well as in his paintings of brothels, circuses, and can-can cabarets. The curves of Art Nouveau transformed architecture, furniture, lamps, jewelry, fashion, and even the entrances to the Paris **Métropolitain.** The World's Fairs of 1889 and 1900 led to the construction of the **Grand** and **Petit Palais** and the **Eiffel Tower,** which, over a century after its controversial construction, remains the best loved landmark in France. Meanwhile, **Charles Frederick Worth** opened Paris's first house of *haute couture*, turning fashion into a sort of commodified art form (p. 283).

CUBISM AND FAUVISM. Pablo Picasso, one of the most prolific artists of the 20th century, first arrived in Paris from Spain in 1900 and made a reputation for himself with collectors like writer **Gertrude Stein.** Together with fellow painter **Georges Braques** (1882-1963), Picasso patented **Cubism,** a radical movement de-emphasizing an object's form by showing all its sides at once. The word "Cubism" was coined by **Henri Matisse** (1869-1964) as he described one of Braque's landscapes. Matisse, who was engaged in a lifelong battle between rivalry and inspiration with Picasso, chose to squeeze paint from the tube directly onto canvas. This aggressive style earned the name **Fauvism** (from *fauves*, or wild animals).

DADAISM AND SURREALISM. Marcel Duchamp (1887-1968) put Cubism in motion with his *Nude Descending a Staircase* (1912). **Marc Chagall** (1887-1985) moved to Paris from Russia and found himself in La Ruche, or "The Beehive" (an artists' colony on the outskirts of Montparnasse; p. 224) with artists like **Fernand Léger** (1881-1955) and **Jacques Lipchitz** (1891-1973). The disillusionment that pervaded Europe after WWI kindled Duchamp's leadership of the **Dada** movement in Paris. The production of "non-art" was for Dadaists a rejection of artistic conventions and traditions. This movement culminated in the exhibition of Duchamp's *La Fontaine* (*The Fountain*, 1917), a urinal that the the guerilla artist turned upside-down and signed.

Surrealism's goal was a union of dream and fantasy with the everyday to form "an absolute reality, a surreality," according to poet and leader of the movement, **André Breton.** The bowler-hatted men of **René Magritte** (1898-1967), the dreamscapes of **Joan Miró** (1893-1983), the patterns of **Max Ernst** (1891-1976), and the infamous melting timepieces of **Salvador Dalí** (1904-1989) all arose from time spent in Paris.

1930S PHOTOGRAPHY AND ARCHITECTURE. During the 30s, photographers like **Georges Brassaï** (1889-1984), **André Kertész** (1894-1985), and **Henri Cartier-Bresson** began using small cameras to record the streets and *quartiers* of Paris in black and white. Meanwhile, architects began to incorporate new building materials in their designs. A Swiss citizen by the name of Charles-Edouard Jeanneret, known to Parisian citizens simply as **Le Corbusier,** pioneered the use of reinforced **concrete** in the city's modern architecture. A prominent member of the legendary **International School,** Le Corbusier dominated his field from the 1930s until his death in 1965, and is famous for such buildings as the Villas La Roche and Jeanneret, today preserved by the **Fondation Le Corbusier** (p. 268).

NAZI DESTRUCTION AND THEFT. The arrival of WWII forced many artists working in Paris to move across the continent or the ocean, and, as the Nazis advanced, the Louvre's treasures were hidden in the basements of Paris. On May 27, 1943, hundreds of "degenerate" paintings by Picasso, Ernst, Klee, Léger, and Miró were destroyed in a bonfire in the garden of the Jeu de Paume. Tens of thousands of masterpieces belonging to Jewish collectors were appropriated by the Germans, most of which were retained for several decades or destroyed.

GRANDS PROJETS. The 80s and 90s produced some of Paris's most controversial architectural masterpieces. Inspired by President Giscard d'Estaing's daring **Centre Pompidou** in the late 70s, President Mitterrand initiated his famous 15-billion-franc *Grands Projets* program to provide a series of modern monuments at the dawn of the 21st century (p. 70). New projects such as the **ZAC (Zone d'Aménagement Concerté),** which plans to build a new university, sports complex, public garden, and metro in the 13*ème,* continue to transform the city. Museums, theaters, and cathedrals throughout Paris are under constant renovation, both fortifying antiquated architecture and adding modern flare to stagnated designs.

CONTEMPORARY ART. Later 20th- and early 21st-century experiments in photography, installation art, video, and sculpture can be seen in the collections and temporary exhibitions of the **Centre Pompidou** (p. 252) and the **Fondation Cartier pour l'Art Contemporain** (p. 265), as well as in numerous galleries throughout the city, evidence of the continuing vibrancy and creativity of the Parisian art scene (p. 272).

MUSIC

EARLY MUSIC TO THE REVOLUTION. The early years of music in Paris date back to the Gregorian chant of 12th-century monks in Notre Dame. Other early highlights include the ballads of medieval troubadours, the Renaissance masses of **Josquin des Prez** (c. 1440-1521) and the Versailles court opera of **Jean-Baptise Lully** (1632-87).

During the reign of **Robespierre,** Parisians rallied to the strains of revolutionary music, such as **Rouget de Lisle's** *War Song of the Army of the Rhine.* Composed in 1792, it was taken up with gusto by volunteers from Marseille; renamed *La Marseillaise,* it became the French national anthem in 1795.

GRAND AND COMIC OPERA. With the rise of the middle class in the early part of the 19th century came the spectacle of grand opera, as well as the simpler opéra comique. These styles later merged and culminated in the Romantic **lyric**

opera, a mix of soaring arias, exotic flavor, and tragedy; examples include **St-Saëns's** *Samson et Dalila* (1877), **Bizet's** *Carmen* (1875), and **Berlioz's** *Les Troyens* (1856-58).

ROMANTICISM TO THE BEGINNINGS OF MODERNISM. Paris served as a musical epicenter for foreign composers during the Romantic period. The half-French, half-Polish **Frédéric Chopin** (1810-49) started composing at the age of seven, and his mature works went on to transcend the Romantic style. In Paris, Chopin mingled with the Hungarian **Franz Liszt,** the Austrian **Félix Mendelssohn,** and the French **Hector Berlioz.**

Music at the turn of the 20th century began a new period of intense, often abstract invention. **Impressionist Claude Débussy** (1862-1918) used tone color and nontraditional scales in his instrumental works, *Prélude à l'Après-midi d'un Faune* (1894) and *La Mer* (1905). Such technique also influenced his opera, *Pelléas et Mélisande* (1902). **Ravel's** use of Spanish rhythm betrayed his Basque origins. When a listener screamed "but he is mad!" at the 1928 premiere of his *Boléro,* the composer retorted, "Aha! She has understood." The music of **Igor Stravinsky,** whose ballet, *The Rite of Spring,* caused a riot at its 1913 premiere at the Théâtre des Champs-Elysées (p. 212), was violently dissonant and rhythmic, and effectively began the Modernist movement.

KLEIN AND NEOSERIALISM. Already famous for his monochromatic *Blue* paintings, **Yves Klein** presented to the world in 1960 *The Monotone Symphony:* three naked models painted a wall blue with their bodies, while the artist conducted an orchestra on one note for 20 minutes. Composer **Pierre Boulez** (born 1925) was an adept student of the Neo-serialist school, which uses the 12-tone system developed in the 1920s by Austrian Arnold Schönberg. Always innovative, Boulez's work includes aleatory music and partial compositions, but his greatest influence on modern music has been as director of the **IRCAM** institute in the Centre Pompidou (p. 252).

JAZZ AND CHANSONS. France recognized the artistic integrity of American jazz sooner than most Americans did. In the 1930s, French musicians copied the swing they heard on early Louis Armstrong records, but the 1934 Club Hot pair of violinist **Stéphane Grapelli** and stylish Belgian-Romany guitarist **Django Reinhardt** needed no help with their innovative style. After WWII, American musicians streamed into Paris. A jazz festival in 1949 brought the young **Miles Davis**

MAKE SOME NOISE

When France was inhabited by the ancient Gauls, the summer solstice was celebrated with feasting, dancing, and human sacrifice, as any reader of the French comic book *Astérix* knows. These days, thanks to former Culture Minister Jack Lang, the country enjoys a raucous music festival instead.

The **Fête de la Musique** takes place every June 21. In Paris, official concerts in major squares combine with impromptu jam sessions to make sweet sounds all over the city. While you can catch a few acts as early as noon, things don't get humming until about 8pm. A gigantic show on the Champ de Mars features big international musicians.

There's no real center of festivities—the fête extends all over the city. Cafes and bars stay open through the night, pumping music into the street. Everything is free—including entry into normally pricey venues—and vendors blanket the city with cheap beer and *merguez.* Some subway lines stay open late, and night buses run regularly. For €2.50 you can buy an unlimited metro pass good from the evening of June 21 through the next morning, but you'll have a tough time getting home between midnight and 6am. Do what the Parisians do—stay out until the sun comes up. See p. 96 for details.

across the pond for a dreamy April in the City of Love. Pianist **Bud Powell,** drummer **Kenny Clarke,** and others stayed in Paris for the respect, dignity, and gigs that their race denied them in the United States. **Duke Ellington** and others played clubs like the Left Bank hot spot, **Le Caveau de la Huchette** (p. 310), and before long, the city's rain-slicked streets took on a saxophonic gloss.

While American standards are known and loved throughout France, the Parisian public has been happiest with the songs of crooner **Charles Aznavour** and the unforgettable **Edith Piaf. Jacques Brel** and **Juliette Gréco's** popular *chansons* charmed smoky cabarets in the 1960s. Recent hit albums from **Francis Cabrel, Benjamin Biolay,** and **Isabelle Boulay** have resuscitated the genre, celebrated by the French as *Nouvelle Chanson Française.*

For those with a big travel budget (or a corporate credit card), Paris is a great place to see jazz. Nearly every type of jazz is represented here, from New Orleans to cool, from acid to hip-hop and fusion. Brazilian samba and bossa nova are steadily growing in popularity together with music from the West Indies and Francophone Africa. Paris's jazz clubs charge either through inflated drink prices or a cover charge. Once you have paid your cover, you are not required to drink, though you should brace yourself for a disapproving look every time the server passes your table. You will probably not be disturbed if you choose to nurse one drink for the rest of the night. Frequent summer festivals sponsor free or nearly free jazz concerts. The **Fête du Marais** often features Big Band, while the **Villette Jazz Festival** has very big names and a few free shows (see **Festivals,** p. 95). In the fall, the **Jazz Festival of Paris** comes to town as venues open their doors to celebrity and up-and-coming artists. *Jazz Hot* (€7) and *Jazz Magazine* (€5.50) are great sources, as is the bimonthly LYLO (Les Yeux, Les Oreilles; free). *Pariscope* and *Figaroscope* (both available at any tabac) also have jazz listings.

THE ROCKSTARS. British and American rock 'n roll swept through France in the early 60s, inspiring the imitative *yéyé* craze. France's answer to Elvis was—and is to this day—**Johnny Halliday.** In 1960 he released his first album, "Hello! Johnny," and headlined France's first rock festival at the Palais des Sports, in the 15*ème.* Over the past forty years, Johnny's fans have matured from screaming teenage girls into swooning middle-aged women; at age 61, the alive-and-kicking teen idol continues to make the charts by recording American rock hits in French.

France's legitimate pop icon is the inimitable **Serge Gainsbourg,** a blackguard as famous for his public sex life and hard partying as for his commitment to musical innovation. As a musician, he bounced all over the spectrum, from rock to jazz to reggae, always astonishing fans with his newest inspiration. Gainsbourg also wrote songs for a wide range of artists, recorded his own albums, and penned more than 40 film soundtracks over the course of his career. He recorded his steamiest hit, *"Je t'aime...moi non plus,"* with lover Brigitte Bardot in 1968, and again several months later with wife Jane Birkin.

WORLD MUSIC. A vibrant music scene also emerged from the immigrant communities of the *banlieue* in the 80s and 90s, combining rap, hip hop, and the sounds of African, Arab, and French traditions. **Cheb Khaled** brought traditional Algerian *raï* to the mainstream dance floor with his 1996 hit, *Aïcha,* which remains popular over a decade later. The most well-loved French rapper throughout the 90s, **MC Solaar,** was born in Senegal. Some claim that the artistic output of the *banlieue,* including this music and its often caustic lyrics exploring the tensions of racism and ethnic identities, is the where the most important and exciting possibilities for the present and future of French culture lie.

FILM

FRENCH CINEMA. Not long after he and his brother Louis presented the world's first paid screening in a Paris cafe in 1895, **Auguste Lumière** remarked, "The cinema is a medium without a future." In defiance of this statement, the French have consistently sought to reveal the broadest possibilities of film and have always remained on the edge of celluloid innovation. The French government subsidizes the film industry, and American studios, which dominate the French market, generally think this policy unfair. But Paris wins in the end, retaining a vibrant film culture and ample funds to expand it.

BEGINNINGS AND SURREALISM. The trick cinema of magician-turned-filmmaker **Georges Méliès** astounded audiences with "disappearing" objects, but gave way by 1908 to an emphasis on narrative. At 14 minutes in length, Méliès's *Journey to the Moon* (1902) was the first motion picture to realize the story-telling possibilities of the medium. Paris was the Hollywood of the early days of cinema, dominating production worldwide. New movements in art engaged filmmakers and yielded the slapstick *Entr'acte* (1924) by **René Clair,** starring that grand-Dada of impertinence, **Marcel Duchamp.** Meanwhile, **Luis Buñuel's** *Un Chien Andalou* (1928) offered audiences a marvel of jarring associations featuring the work of Salvador Dalí. The Dane **Carl Dreyer's** *Passion of Joan of Arc* (1928) exhibits a notable fetish for close-ups.

THE 20S AND 30S. Although WWI allowed Hollywood to wrest celluloid dominance from a shattered Europe, in the 1920s and 1930s French cinema was the most critically acclaimed in the world under such great directors as **Jean Renoir,** son of the Impressionist painter. *La Grande Illusion*, which he directed in 1937, is a powerful anti-war statement, set in the POW camps of WWI. His *Les Règles du Jeu* (1939) reveals the erosion of the French bourgeoisie and his country's malaise at the doorstep of another world-altering war. The 1930s brought sound, crowned by **Jean Vigo's** *Zero for Conduct* (1933), which prefigured the growth of **Poetic Realism** under **Marcel Carné** and writer **Jacques Prévert** (*Daybreak*, 1939). Censorship during the Occupation led to a move from political films to nostalgia and escapist cinema. Carné and Prévert's epic *Children of Paradise* (1943-45) finds the indomitable spirit of the French in 1840s Paris.

NEW WAVE AUTHORS. Jean Cocteau carried the poetic into fantasy with *Beauty and the Beast* (1946) and *Orphée* (1950). The Surrealist *Beauty and the Beast* featured an early use of special effects. On the other end of the ideological spectrum, a group of young intellectuals gathered by critic **André Bazin** took issue with the "cinema of quality" that had dominated the French screen since WWII. Encouraged by government subsidies, they swapped the pen for the camera in 1959. **François Truffaut's** *The 400 Blows* and **Jean-Luc Godard's** *A Bout du Souffle (Breathless)* were joined the same year by **Alain Resnais's** *Hiroshima, Mon Amour* (written by Marguerite Duras) and together, the canon heralded the French New Wave *(Nouvelle Vague)*. Aznavour starred in Truffaut's *Shoot the Piano Player* (1960). Three years earlier, a star was born when **Jean Vadim** sent the incomparable **Brigitte Bardot** shimmying naked across the stage in *And God Created Woman*. Other directors of the New Wave are **Jean Rouch** (*Chronicle of a Summer*, 1961), **Louis Malle** (*The Lovers*, 1958), **Eric Rohmer** (*My Night with Maud*, 1969), **Agnès Varda** (*Cléo from 5 to 7*, 1961), and **Chris Marker** (*La Jetée;* 1962). These visionaries are unified by their interest in off-beat fiction and documentary, the fragmentation of linear time, and the thrill of youth. Their fascination with speed, cars, noise, and Hitchcock and Lang's American films garnered them infinite popularity with teens and twentysomethings of the era. The filmmaker as *auteur* (author) remains a concept crucial to French film, as does the term "*Art et Essai*," used to describe what Anglophones call "Art Cinema." Godard emerged as the New Wave oracle of the 60s. His collaborations with actors **Jean-Paul Belmondo** and **Anna Karina,** including *Vivre Sa Vie* (1962) and *Pierrot le Fou* (1965), inspired a generation of filmmakers.

NEW CLASSICS. The world impact of French cinema in the 60s led to wider recognition of French film stars in the 70s and 80s. The stunning **Catherine Deneuve** *(Belle de Jour, Les Parapluies de Cherbourg)*, **Gerard Depardieu** *(Danton, 1492, Camille Claudel)*, and, more recently, **Juliette Binoche** *(Blue)* and **Julie Delpy** *(Europa, Europa)* have become faces almost as famous worldwide as they are in Paris. **Jean-Jacques Beineix's** *Betty Blue* (1985), **Claude Berri's** *Jean de Florette* (1986) and sequel *Manon des Sources* (1986), **Louis Malle's** heart-wrenching WWII drama *Au Revoir les Enfants* (1987), **Marc Caro** and **Jean-Pierre Jeunet's** dystopic *Delicatessen* (1991), and Polish **Krzysztof Kieslowski's** three colors trilogy, *Blue* (1993), *White* (1994), and *Red* (1994), have all become classics of 20th-century French cinema. Several recent French films explore the issue of sexual identity, including Belgian **Alain Berliner's** transgender tragicomedy *Ma vie en rose* (1997). Explicitly artistic cinema now prospers under **Marcel Hanoun** *(Bruit d'Amour et de Guerre,* 1997) and **Jacques Doillon** *(Ponette,* 1997). A group of incendiary young directors like **Gaspar Noe** *(Irreversible,* 2003), **Catherine Breillat** *(Romance,* 1999), and **Claire Denis** *(Trouble Every Day,* 2002) have stirred controversy in their attempts to blur the boundaries between pornography and art while exploring some pretty heavy themes and proving that the French tradition of embracing content and technique far too provocative for Hollywood is alive and well. In 2001, **Jean-Pierre Feunet's** international hit *Le Fabuleux Destin d'Amélie Poulain (Amélie)* was the highest grossing film of the decade in France.

SPORTS AND RECREATION

There are really only two sports of any importance in France: football and cycling. The others are just pleasant diversions.

FOOTBALL

The French take *le foot* very seriously. Their national team, *Les Bleus,* emerged in the late 90s from a half-century of mediocrity to perform spectacularly in recent years. They captured the 1998 **World Cup,** schooling perennial favorite Brazil 3-0 in the newly built Stade de France, outside Paris. The victory ignited celebrations from the Champs-Elysées to the Pyrénées. In the 2000 European Championship, *Les Bleus* took the trophy in an upset against Italy, and in the 2001 *Coupe des Confederations,* France completed the Triple Crown of *football.* The charismatic star of the team, **Zinedine Zidane,** has attained a hero status second only to de Gaulle. The son of an Algerian immigrant, "Zizou" has helped unite a country divided by tension over immigration. Sadly, France failed to make it past the qualifying round of the 2002 *Cup Mondiale,* finishing even behind Uruguay. So shocking was the failure that President Chirac issued a message of condolence. This left the French eagerly awaiting their team's next shot at glory in the 2004 European Cup, but much to fans' disappointment they fell to Greece in the quarterfinals. In 2006, the team came close to winning the World Cup, but the season ultimately distinguished itself to fans everywhere for Zidane's excruciating headbutt to Italian player Marco Materazzi during their July 8th game. Zidane refused to apologize for his actions, citing a racist remark by Materazzi as his provocation. Despite the fiasco, he remains a French football hero, and *Les Bleus* made a great showing at the Cup before finally losing to Italy.

CYCLING

Cycling is another national obsession with an equally ardent following. France annually hosts the only cycling event anyone can name: the grueling three-week, 3500km **Tour de France,** which celebrated its 100-year anniversary in 2003. Unfortunately, competitors from the host country have not fared well in the competition lately, as American **Lance Armstrong** has triumphed over the rest of the field to capture the last seven championships.

OTHER ACTIVITIES

For those who prefer a bit less exertion, the game of **pétanque,** once dominated by old men, has been gaining popularity in younger age brackets. The basic premise of *pétanque*, also known as *boules* or *bocce*, is to throw a large metal ball as close as possible to a small metal ball. Pickup games of *pétanque* are a common sight in the parks around Paris.

Despite the objections of French traditionalists, sports from other continents are also gaining a foothold in France, particularly **rugby, golf,** and even the heresy that is **American football.**

CULTURE

FOOD AND DRINK

A BRIEF HISTORY. In the 16th century, Catherine de Médicis, disgusted with bland and dull French dishes, imported master chefs from her native Florence to spice things up. They taught the French to appreciate the finer aspects of sauces and seasonings, a culinary development elaborated upon by the great 19th-century chef Antoine Carême, acknowledged as the father of haute cuisine, the elegantly prepared foods now thought of as typically "French." He and others such as George August Escoffier made fine food an essential art of civilized life, and much of their wisdom on sauces and glazes is collected in the voluminous *Larousse*

THE LOCAL STORY

LIFE'S A BEACH

In 2001, the inauguration of the super-fast TGV line to the Mediterranean brought Paris closer to the beach. In 2002, Mayor Bertrand Delanoë did even better: he came up with **Paris Plage,** an annual event that turns the banks of the Seine into a sun-splashed summer paradise.

From the mid-July to mid-August, kilometers of quayside are covered with sand and planted with palm trees. The beaches are free and open to all, and Parisians come in droves to sunbathe by the lapping of the Seine. The city provides hammocks, deckchairs, and beach umbrellas, and ice cream carts are everywhere.

The festival was such a success in its first two years that in 2004, a 20m open-air bathing pool was thrown into the mix. The pool held morning aquagym classes for adults and afternoon free-swim for kids. Add to that a paddling pool, changing rooms, and a humidifed solarium, and Paris felt about as posh as St. Tropez. Other facilities included numerous volleyball courts, a *boulodrome* for *pétanque*-players, a climbing wall by Pont Neuf, trampolines near the Pont de Sully, and a concert stage for beach-side entertainment. See p. 98 for details.

Gastronomique, a standard reference for French chefs today. The style made famous in the US by Julia Child is cuisine bourgeoise, quality home-cooking. A glance through her *Mastering the Art of French Cooking I & II* will give you ideas for dishes to try in France. Both *haute cuisine* and *cuisine bourgeoise* rely heavily on local specialties that make up the cuisine de province (provincial cuisine), also called *cuisine campagnarde*. Trendy and health-conscious nouvelle cuisine—tiny portions of delicately cooked, artfully arranged ingredients with light sauces—was made popular in the 1970s by the celebrated Paul Bocuse. Immigrant communities have shaken up the traditional French culinary scene: in addition to ubiquitous Greek *gyros*, there are outstanding Moroccan, Algerian, Tunisian, Senegalese, Ivorian, and Caribbean restaurants in Paris. Chinese, Thai, Vietnamese, Cambodian, Korean, Tibetan, Japanese, Indian, and Pakistani restaurants, especially in the "Chinatowns" of the *9ème*, *13ème*, and *19ème*, have brought vegetarian options to the traditionally meat-heavy Paris dining experience.

MEALTIMES. *Le petit déjeuner* (breakfast) is usually light, consisting of bread, croissants, or *brioches* (buttery breads) with jam and butter, plus an espresso with hot milk or cream (*café au lait* or the more trendy *café crème*) or a hot chocolate (*chocolat chaud*, often served in a bowl). *Le déjeuner* (lunch) is served between noon and 2:30pm, although some cafes and restaurants in tourist areas stay open throughout the day. Restaurants are most crowded from 1-3pm, when much of Paris takes a lengthy lunch break. During lunch, some shops, businesses, and government offices close; linger over a 2hr. lunch a few times and you'll be hooked, too. *Le dîner* (dinner) begins quite late. Most restaurants open at 7pm, but business really picks up around 8-9pm. *Bon vivants* sometimes extend their meals into the early morning. A complete French dinner includes an *apéritif*, an *entrée* (appetizer), a *plat* (main course), salad, cheese, dessert, fruit, *café*, and a *digestif* (after-dinner drink, typically a cognac or other local brandy). However, the large majority of diners content themselves with a three-course meal or less. Most Parisians drink wine with dinner.

HOW TO ORDER. Greet your server politely by looking him or her in the eye and saying, *"Bonjour."* In the evening, bring out your smartest *"Bonsoir."* Starting your dining experience without a friendly greeting is impolite by French standards, so be sure to do so. The French are very polite to waiters, and visitors would do well to follow their lead. It is uncommon for French diners to ask to take home any unfinished food or to split dishes with dining partners, so avoid those practices if you can. The bill rarely comes without your requesting it, so simply say *"L'addition, s'il vous plaît"* when you are ready to pay.

THE MENU. Most restaurants offer *un menu à prix fixe* (fixed-price meal) that is less expensive than ordering *à la carte* (when you pick individual items out). Importantly, lunch *menus* are often cheaper than dinner *menus*—if there is a pricier restaurant that you particularly want to try, consider going for lunch. A *menu* will usually include an appetizer *(entrée)*, a main course *(plat)*, cheese *(fromage)*, or dessert. Some also include wine or coffee. For lighter fare, try a *brasserie*, which has a fuller menu than a cafe but is more casual than a restaurant.

DRINKS. Mineral water is everywhere; order sparkling water (*eau pétillante* or *eau gazeuse*) or flat mineral water *(eau plate)*. Ice cubes *(glaçons)* won't come with your drink; you'll have to ask for them. To order a pitcher of tap water, ask for *une carafe d'eau*. *Kir*, a blend of white wine and *cassis* (black currant liqueur), and *kir royale* (substitutes champagne for the wine) are popular pre-meal *apéritifs*. Others include *pastis*, a licorice liqueur; *suze*, made from fermented *gentiane* (a sweet-smelling mountain flower that yields a wickedly bitter brew); *picon-bière*, beer mixed with a sweet liqueur; and the classic martini. Finish the meal with an espresso *(un café)*, which comes in lethal little cups with blocks of sugar. *Café au lait* and *café crème* are generally considered breakfast drinks, so if you prefer your nighttime coffee with milk, try a *noisette*, which is espresso with just a dash of milk. When *boisson compris* is written on the menu, you will receive a free drink (most often wine) with the meal. In cafes, drinks are usually cheaper at the counter than seated.

WINE

In France, wine is not a luxury; it is a staple. During WWI, French infantrymen pinned down in the trenches by heavy shell-fire subsisted on the barest of rations: bread and wine. The first French citizen to orbit the Earth brought along the indispensable beverage with him.

WINE-PRODUCING REGIONS. The **Loire Valley** of France produces a number of whites, with the major vineyards at Angers, Chinon, Saumur, Anjou, Tours, and Sancerre. **Cognac,** farther south on the Atlantic coast, is famous for the double-distilled spirit that carries the same name. Centered on the Dordogne and Garonne Rivers, the classic **Bordeaux** region produces red and white Pomerol, Graves, and sweet Sauternes. The spirit *armagnac*, similar to cognac, comes from **Gascony,** while Jurançon wines come from vineyards higher up the slopes of the **Pyrénées.** Southern wines include those of **Languedoc and Roussillon** on the coast and **Limoux and Gaillac** inland. The vineyards of **Provence** on the coast near Toulon are recognized for their rosés. The **Côtes du Rhône** from Valence to Lyon in the Rhône Valley are home to some of the most celebrated wines produced in France, including Beaujolais. **Burgundy** is especially renowned for its reds, from the wines of Chablis and the Côte d'Or in the north to the Mâconnais in the south. The white wines produced in **Alsace** tend to be much spicier and more pungent than others. Many areas of France produce sparkling wines, but the only one that can legally be called "Champagne" is distilled in the **Champagne** region of the country, surrounding Reims.

SELECTING WINE. There are specific wines for every occasion and every type of meal, with pairings dictated by draconian rules. These rules, however, are not as hard and fast as they once were, so don't worry too much about them and feel free to go with your gut. **White wines** are lighter, drier, and fruitier. They go with fish, and many of the white dessert wines, like Barsac, Sauternes, or Coteaux du Layon, are great with fruit. **Red wines** tend to be heavier, more fragrant, and considerably older. Red meat and red wine is a fine combination. When confused about which wine to choose, just ask. Most waiters in restaurants and employees in wine shops will be more than happy to recommend their favorites to you. Or, fall back on the *vin de maison* (house wine), served in pitchers at reduced prices.

FOOD SHOPS AND MARKETS

SPECIALTY SHOPS. Restaurants and cafes are well and good, but you will not have had a complete French eating experience if you don't forego fine dining at least once and strike out on your own. Trust us, Parisians can often be found with hamper and *baguette*, munching in parks or crunching on *quais*. One tour of some choice food stores, and you'll be ready to join them; picnic ingredients are generally cheap and always delectable. Here's a guide to the different types of specialty shops around Paris.

A **charcuterie** is the French version of a delicatessen, a **crémerie** sells dairy products, and the corner **fromagerie** may stock over 100 kinds of cheese. **Boulangeries** will supply you with your daily bread—they're usually best visited in the early morning or right before mealtimes, when the *baguettes* are steaming hot. **Pâtisseries** sell pastries, and **confiseries** sell candy; both often vend ice cream as well. You can buy your produce at a **primeur,** your meat and poultry at a **boucherie,** and all manner of prepared foods at a **traiteur. Epiceries** (grocery stores) have staples, wine, and produce. A **marché,** an open-air market (held weekly), is the best place to buy fresh produce, fish, and meat. Finally, you can grab an array of simple food items, cigarettes, and lotto tickets at any corner **alimentation** (convenience store).

Supermarchés (supermarkets) are, of course, also an option, but they're no fun. Do capitalize on the one-stop shopping at the **Monoprix** and **Prisunics** that litter the city (48 in all). They carry men's and women's clothing and have photocopiers, telephone cards, and a supermarket. They are usually open during the week until 9pm; the Prisunic at 52, av. Champs-Elysées is open until midnight. Starving students swear by the ubiquitous **Ed l'Epicier** and **Leader Price.** At both you can buy in bulk and save a good amount of money. **Picard Surgelés,** with 50 locations in the city, stocks every food ever frozen—from *crêpes* to calamari.

MARKETS. In the 5th century, ancient Lutèce held the first market on what is now Île de la Cité. More than a millennium and a half later, markets exude conviviality and neighborliness in every *arrondissement,* despite the ongoing growth of the *supermarché.* Most are open two to six days per week (always on Sunday). The freshest products are often sold by noon, when many stalls start to close. Quality and price can vary significantly from one stall to the next, making it a good idea to stroll through the entire market before buying.

SALONS DE THÉ. Parisian *salons de thé* (tea rooms) fall into three categories: stately salons straight out of the last century and piled high with macaroons, Seattle-style joints for pseudo-intellectuals, and cafes that simply want to signal that they also serve tea. For *salon de thé* culture at its best, enjoy delicate sandwiches and pastries at Sunday brunch—but be sure to reserve ahead, as lines often stretch out the door at the larger salons.

ETIQUETTE

BLENDING IN. It's a good rule of thumb in Paris (and anywhere, really) to avoid fitting the stereotype of the American tourist. The more of an effort that you make to blend in, the better your Parisian experience will be. For dress, what may look perfectly innocuous in Peoria will mark you out instantly in Paris. The French are known for their conservative stylishness: go for restrained sneakers or closed-toe shoes, solid-color pants or jeans, and plain T-shirts or button-down shirts, rather than Teva sandals (again, a horror no matter where they're worn), baggy pants, or cutoffs. Parisians rarely wear shorts, even in warm weather. Trying to blend in is also great excuse to shop for French clothes. If you're traveling in January or August, be sure to take advantage of massive sales *(les soldes)*—prices are often slashed as much as 75%.

CHURCHES. "Cutoff," "tight," "short," "bare-shouldered," "sloppy," and "dirty" should not enter into your vocabulary for church-going clothes. Do not walk into the middle of a mass or other service unless you plan to give an impromptu homily. Do not take flash photographs or walk directly in front of the altar.

ETAGES (FLOORS). In French, the ground floor is called the *rez-de-chaussée;* numbers begin with the first floor above the ground floor *(premier étage)*. In an elevator or call-box, the button labeled "R" and not "1" is typically the ground floor.

GREETINGS AND SALUTATIONS. Although customer service in Paris is a bit more brusque than in the US or the UK, the French consider polite greetings to be essential. Always say *"Bonjour, madame/monsieur"* when entering an establishment and *"au revoir"* when leaving. If you bump into someone on the street or the metro, it is polite to say *"pardon"* (Excuse me). The proper way to answer the telephone is *"âllo,"* but if you use this on the street as a personal greeting, you'll immediately blow your cover as a tourist.

HOURS. Most restaurants open at noon for lunch and then close for some portion of the afternoon before re-opening for dinner, while some bistros and most cafes remain open throughout the afternoon. Small businesses, as well as banks and post offices, close for "lunch," which often lasts for two or three hours.

LANGUAGE. Even if your French is near-perfect, waiters and salespeople who detect the slightest accent will often respond in English. This can be frustrating, especially if you came to Paris to practice your French, or if the Parisian in question speaks poor English. If your language skills are good, continue to speak in French. More often than not, they will both respect and appreciate your fortitude, and speak to you, in turn, in French.

POCKET CHANGE. Cashiers and tellers will constantly ask you *"Avez-vous de la monnaie?"* (Do you have change?) as they would rather not break your €20 note for a pack of gum. If you don't have it, say *"Non, désolée,"* and a nasty look is the worst you will get in return.

POLITESSE. Parisians are polite, especially to older people. In Paris, the difference between getting good and bad service is often the difference between a little *politesse* and careless rudeness. Tone and facial expressions are important. Maintain composure and act like you mean business; speak softly and politely (*do* employ the standard *"monsieur/madame"* and *"s'il vous plaît"*) to Parisians in official positions, especially if they are older than you.

PUBLIC RESTROOMS. The streetside public restrooms *(pissoirs)* in Paris are worth the €0.30 they require. These magic machines are self-cleaning after each use, so you're guaranteed a clean restroom. Toilets in train stations, major metro stops, and public gardens are tended to by *gardiens* and generally cost €0.40. In your average cafe, on the other hand, cleanliness should not be expected, as they tend to have squat toilets. Most cafes reserve restrooms for their clients only.

SERVICE. There is no assumption in Paris that "the customer is always right," and complaining to managers about poor service is rarely worth your while. Your best bet is to take your business elsewhere. When engaged in any official process (e.g., opening a bank account, purchasing insurance, etc.), don't fret if you get shuffled from one desk to another. Hold your ground, patiently explain your situation as many times as necessary, and you'll probably get the service you need.

SMOKING. A very large number of Parisians smoke cigarettes, and they do not appreciate anti-tobacco evangelism. Although some restrictions have been placed on smoking in public areas (such as metro platforms), and eating establishments are technically required to have a clearly marked non-smoking section, these laws are not strictly enforced. Tourists who smoke will find this atmosphere liberating; those who do not may find themselves constantly coughing in smoky restaurants, bars, and cafes—those with asthma will find themselves particularly frustrated and should ask *maître d's* if their restaurants have specifically *"non-fumeurs"* sections.

SUNDAY. Paris (non-Marais Paris, at least) appears to shut down entirely on Sundays. Minimarkets, supermarkets, shops, and restaurants will generally be closed, though some services may be available in the morning. Do as Parisians do, and head for open-air markets to pack a picnic. Many establishments and most museums are closed on Mondays, and other hours vary: calling ahead is always a good idea.

TIPPING. Service is almost always included in meal prices in restaurants and cafes, and in drink prices at bars; look for the phrase *service compris* on the menu or just ask. If service is not included, tip 15-20%. If you're excpetionally pleased with the service at a cafe, bistro, restaurant, or bar, you can leave a *pourboire* of a euro or two. Tip your hairdresser well; do not tip taxis more than 15% of the metered charge.

MEDIA

TELEVISION AND RADIO

French television, in the hands of a state-run monopoly until the 1980s, is notoriously bad. **TF1** is the most popular station in France. The public channel **ARTE** appeals to more intellectual tastes. Cable TV is also available; the pay channel **Canal Plus** shows recent films and live sporting events. TV guides are the most popular publications in France, with **Télé 7 jours** leading the pack. Second in line is **Télérama,** which provides commentary not only on TV but also on culture in general. French **radio** went commercial in 1984, although the success of large conglomerates means that few stations remain independent. National stations include **Fun Radio** for teens; **RTL2,** a pop rock station; **Skyrock,** a noisy and provocative rock station; and **Nostalgie,** an adult-oriented station with quiz shows and easy-listening music. **Radio FG,** once Paris's queer wavelength, has become the city's primary source for house, techno, dance, and R&B. Public stations include **France-Inter**—a quality general interest station—and **France Info,** an all-news station.

NEWSPAPERS AND OTHER PUBLICATIONS

NEWSPAPERS. The French are bombarded with many different views from just as many newspapers (and the various political factions that they represent). On the left are **Libération** (€1.20), a socialist newspaper that offers comprehensive news coverage of world events, and **L'Humanité** (€1.99), produced by the communist party. More to the middle (though sometimes with a socialist streak) is the widely read **Le Monde** (€1.20), which offers especially thorough political coverage. To the right are **Le Figaro** (€1) and **La Tribune,** the latter of which is France's version of the *Wall Street Journal,* providing international financial coverage.

MAGAZINES. Magazines offer more in-depth coverage of news and culture. **Le Nouvel Observateur** (€3) proffers an inquisitive take on French culture and society; the cultural magazine **Nova** (€7) has a special summer guide to Parisian cultural events; **L'Express** (€2.30) is a weekly publication similar to *Time* magazine, with coverage of national and international news; **Marianne** (€2.50) resembles a French *Vanity Fair,* filled with gossip and world news; **Tetu** (€5) has the latest in queer politics, fashion and events; and **Technikart** (€3.50) is a monthly communique for the Parisian hipster. **Paris Match** (€2.20) dishes up the latest dirt on European royals and socialites as well as internationally known celebrities. For the best selection of English-language magazines, as well as copies of the Sunday edition of the *New York Times* (after noon on Mondays) try **W.H. Smith** (see **Shopping**, p. 286). Of course, if you are after cultural listings and reviews, you need only venture as far as the nearest *tabac*, as all carry the vital publications.

GOINGS-ON. Pariscope (€0.40) and **Officiel des Spectacles** (€0.35), both published Wednesdays, have the most comprehensive listings of movies, plays, exhibits, festivals, clubs, and bars. *Pariscope* may well be worth the extra €0.05; it has an English-language section called **Time Out Paris** and an easy-to-use (free) online counterpart at **www.pariscope.fr.** Also free is the tourist office monthly **Where: Paris,** which highlights exhibits, concerts, walking tours, and events, and the Mairie de Paris's monthly **Paris le Journal,** which has articles about what's going on around the city. For other listings, check **Figaroscope,** a Wednesday supplement to **Le Figaro,** which lists happenings about Paris; **Free Voice,** a monthly English-language newspaper published by the American Church; and the bi-weekly **France-USA Contacts (FUSAC)** both of which provide job and housing listings, as well as general information for English speakers and are available for free from English-speaking bookstores, restaurants, and travel agencies throughout Paris.

FESTIVALS

For information on festivals, the Paris Tourist Office (see p. 115) has a home page (www.paris-touristoffice.com) and a pricey info line (☎08 92 68 30 00). You can also get a listing of festivals before you leave home by writing the French Government Tourist Office. *Let's Go* lists its favorite **Festivals** below. This isn't all of them—just the ones that promise to keep you fat, happy, or drunk (or all three). Be sure to check listings in *Time Out* and *Pariscope* (€0.40 at any newsstand) a week or more ahead of time for updates and details on all events.

SPRING

Foire du Trône, Apr.-May (☎01 46 27 52 29; www.foiredutrone.com). ⓜ Porte Dorée. On Reuilly Lawn, Bois de Vincennes, 12ème. A 1063-year-old fair complete with carnival rides (€2-5), *barbe à papa* (cotton candy), and a freak show. Free *navette* (shuttle) from from Nation to Pelouse de Reuilly. Open M-F and Su noon-midnight, Sa noon-1am.

Portes Ouvertes des Ateliers d'Artistes, May-June. Call tourist office or check *Pariscope* for details. For selected days during the year, each *quartier*'s resident artists open their workshops to the public; the majority of expositions are in the 13ème.

SUMMER

Grandes Eaux Musicales de Versailles, early Apr. to early Oct. (info ☎01 30 83 78 88, tickets 01 30 83 78 89; www.chateauversailles-spectacles.fr). RER C7. Outdoor concerts of period music and fountain displays every Sa and Su at Parc du Château de Versailles. A magical event that displays Versailles's gardens in all their excess and glory. Tickets €7, concessions €5.50, under 10 free. For reservations through FNAC, call ☎08 92 68 36 22 or go to www.fnac.com.

Paris Jazz Festival, June-July (☎01 43 41 16 26; www.parcfloraldeparis.com). Excellent jazz artists from Europe and beyond play every Sa and Su afternoon in the Parc Floral.

GAY PAH-REE!

Boasting the first openly gay mayor of a major European city and a substantial GLBT population, Paris is a queer-friendly city bursting at the seams with entertainment and resources. Most notably, the City of Lights participates in a campaign of marches across France from mid-May to the end of June to celebrate and raise awareness of queer communities. The highlight of this month is the fantastic annual Gay Pride Festival, held on the last Saturday of June.

Nearly all of Paris's vibrant queer communities turn out for this infectiously exuberant parade, which changes location yearly. The festive din can be heard from several metro stops away, and a sort of fabulous Carnaval scene greets visitors as they reach the Festival. Drag queens in bejewelled and feathered costumes pose daintily next to scantily clad dancers shimmying on floats.

This might be the only time the Communist Party, the Socialist Party, and the UMP (Union pour un Mouvement Populaire, Chirac's right-wing party) root cheek to cheek for the same-cause. A sense of organized chaos ensues as crowds march from Montparnasse to the Bastille, dancing, chanting and waving banners proclaiming, among other messages, the poignant "I love my two mothers." *Gay Pride Paris, last weekend in June (www.gaypride.fr).*

The park holds several other festivals throughout the summer, including children's theater events and classical concerts. All shows free with €3 park entrance, under 25 €1.50, under 7 free. Schedules at the tourist office and in *Pariscope.*

Festival Chopin, mid-June to mid-July (☎01 45 00 22 19; www.frederic-chopin.com). Route de la Reine Marguerite. From Ⓜ Porte Maillot, take bus #244 to Pré Catelan, stop #12. Concerts and recitals held at the Orangerie du Parc de Bagatelle in the Bois de Boulogne. Not all Chopin, but all piano, arranged each year around a different aspect of the master's *oeuvre.* Prices vary: €17-34, concessions only for afternoon concerts.

Gay Pride, last Sa in June (www.gaypride.fr). For additional information on dates and events, call the **Centre Gai et Lesbien** (☎01 43 57 21 47), **Le Duplex bar** (☎01 42 72 80 86), or **Les Mots à la Bouche bookstore** (☎01 42 78 88 30; www.motsbouche.com). Or check bars and cafes in the Marais for posters.

Fête de la Musique, June 21 (☎01 40 03 94 70). Also called "Faîtes de la Musique" ("Make Music"), this summer solstice celebration gives everyone the chance to make as much racket as possible, as Paris's usual noise laws don't apply for the duration of the festival. The metro runs all night to transport tired revelers home.

Feux de la St-Jean Baptiste (Fête Nationale du Québec), June 24 (☎01 45 08 55 61 or 01 45 08 55 25). Magnificent fireworks in the Jardin de Tino Rossi at quai St-Bernard, 5*ème*, honoring the Feast of St. John the Baptist. Sacré-Coeur offers a spectacular bird's-eye view. The festival also includes an elaborate display at the Canal de l'Ourcq in the Parc de la Villette. In addition, Québec's National Holiday is celebrated by Paris's Québecois community with dancing, *drapeaux fleurs-de-lys,* and music at various spots throughout Paris, including: the Délégation Générale du Québec, 66, r. Pergolèse, 16*ème* (☎01 40 67 85 00); the Association Paris-Québec, 5, r. de la Boule Rouge, 9*ème*; and the Centre Culturel Québécois, 5, r. de Constantine, 7*ème* (Ⓜ Invalides).

Fête du Cinéma, late June (www.feteducinema.com). Started in 1984, this festival aims to bring cheaper movies to all Parisians. Purchase 1 ticket at regular movie price (€6-8) and receive a passport for unlimited showings (during the 3-day festival) of participating films for €2 each. Arrive early for popular favorites, and expect long lines. Full listings of movies and events can be found online, at theaters, or in metro advertisements. Don't miss this opportunity to join the millions of movie-goers who relish the blockbusters, the indie flicks, the imports, and the ever-enduring classics that make the Parisian cinema scene one of the most diverse and enjoyable in the world.

Fête des Tuileries, late June to late Aug. (☎01 20 00 75 75). ⓜ Tuileries. A large, spunky fair held on the terrace of the Jardin des Tuileries. The huge ferris wheel with views of nighttime Paris offers decisive proof that the carnival ethos is the same the world over. A mix of tame rides suitable for children and even some high-speed ones for thrill-seekers. The festival also somehow manages to fit a water-flume ride in the Jardin des Tuileries. Open M-Th 11am-midnight, F-Sa 11am-1am. Free entrance; ferris wheel €5, under 10 €3.

▨ **Bastille Day (Fête Nationale),** July 14. France's independence day. Festivities begin the night before, with traditional street dances at the tip of Île St-Louis. The free Bals des Pompiers (Firemen's Balls) take place inside every Parisian fire station the night of July 13 and/or 14th from 9pm-4am, with DJs, bands, and cheap alcohol (€5). These balls are the best of Paris's Bastille Day celebrations. The fire stations on r. Blanche, bd. du Port-Royal, r. des Vieux-Colombiers, and the Gay Ball near quai de la Tournelle in the 5*ème* are probably your best bets. For information on the *Bals,* call the **Sapeurs Pompiers** (☎01 47 54 68 22) or visit them at 1, pl. Jules Renard in the 17*ème*. There is dancing at pl. de la Bastille with a concert, but be careful as young kids sometimes throw fireworks into the crowd. July 14 begins with the army parading down the Champs-Elysées at 10:30am (be prepared to get in place by 8 or 9am) and ends with fireworks at 10:30-11pm. The fireworks can be seen from any bridge on the Seine or from the Champs de Mars (get there as early as 3-4hr. beforehand to snag a decent spot). Be aware that for the parade and fireworks the metro stations along the Champs and at the Trocadéro are closed. Groups also gather in the 19*ème* and 20*ème* (especially in the Parc de Belleville) where the hilly topography allows a long-distance view to the Trocadéro. Unfortunately, the entire city also becomes a nightmarish combat zone with firecrackers underfoot; avoid the metro and deserted areas if possible. *Vive la France!*

Paris, Quartier d'Eté, mid-July to mid-Aug. (☎01 44 94 98 00; www.quartierdete.com). This city-wide, multifaceted festival features dance, music from around the world, and a giant parade. Locations vary, but many events are held in the Jardin des Tuileries, Grand Palais, and Parc de la Villette. This is one of Paris's largest festivals and includes both world-class (i.e., international ballet companies and top-10 rock bands) and local artists, musicians, and performers. Prices vary, but much is free. Pick up a brochure at the tourist office.

Tour de France, enters Paris the 3rd or 4th Su in July (☎01 41 33 15 00; www.letour.fr). The Tour de France, the world's premier long-distance bicycling event, ends

FROLICSOME FIREMEN

You know Bastille Day is approaching when two things occur: French flags go up around the city, and all Parisians leave town. The weekend is the most extravagant and fun of the year, but expats in Paris will find themselves enjoying the festivities with a large proportion of other tourists, as many French natives prefer to escape to the countryside for the long weekend. Despite the prevalence of the English language, Bastille "Day" provides an action-packed weekend of fun. For a truly unusual patriotic experience, be sure not to miss *Les Saupeurs Pompiers.*

Paris celebrates the night of July 13th with huge parties in fire stations called "Fireman's Balls." Makes sense right? *Les Saupeurs Pompiers* open the courtyards of their stations to the public for a night of flowing alcohol, loud music, and, yes, firemen. Those less than smitten with the idea of partying in a sea of beefy *pompiers* should not be put off—these balls are fun for everyone. Doors open at around 9pm, depending on the station, and lines can be very long. Show up early or late for shorter queues. The parties go on until 4am, but time flies by as you dance, drink, and are entertained by shows put on by the pompiers. Entrance is free and drinks are cheap, usually between €2 and €5.

in Paris and thousands turn out at the finish line to see who will win the *chemise d'or.* Expect huge crowds at pl. de la Concorde as well as along the av. des Champs-Elysées.

■ **Paris Plages,** late July to late Aug. (☎08 20 00 75 75; www.paris.fr). For 4 weeks at the end of the summer, the banks of the Seine are decked out like St. Tropez, with white sand, deck chairs, cabanas, and swimming pools.

■ **Le Festival de Cinema en Plein Air,** early July to mid-Aug. (www.cinema.arbo.com). Ⓜ Porte de Pantin. At the Parc de la Villette. Families, couples, and large groups lounge on the grass and enjoy some of the greatest movies ever made. A limited number of lounge chairs are provided, so many people bring their own picnic blankets. Films start at nightfall—usually around 10:30pm—but arrive early to get a good spot on the grass.

Cinema au Clair de Lune, first 3 weeks in Aug. (☎01 44 76 63 00; www.clairdelune.forum-desimages.net). Classic French films projected on a giant screen that moves all over Paris, from the Hôtel de Ville to the Parc Choisy. Shows start around 9:30pm. Free.

FALL

■ **Jazz à la Villette,** early Sept. (☎01 40 03 75 75 or 01 44 84 44 84; www.villette.com). Ⓜ Porte de Pantin. At Parc de la Villette. A week-long celebration of jazz from big bands to new international talents, as well as seminars, films, and sculptural exhibits. Past performers have included Herbie Hancock, Ravi Coltrane, Taj Mahal, and B.B. King. Marching bands parade every day, and an enormous picnic closes the festival. Concerts €18, under 26 €15. For reduced price tickets, you must call ahead.

Fête de l'Humanité, 2nd weekend of Sept. (☎01 49 22 73 86; www.humanite.fr). At the Parc de la Courneuve. Take the metro to Porte de la Villette and then bus #177 or one of the buses reserved especially for the festival. The annual fair of the French Communist Party. Charles Mingus, Marcel Marceau, the Bolshoi Ballet, and radical theater troupes have appeared. 3-day pass €15, under 12 free.

Festival d'Automne, Sept. 14-Dec. 19 (☎01 53 45 17 17; www.festival-automne.com). Notoriously highbrow and avant-garde drama, ballet, cinema, and music arranged around a different theme each year. Many events held at the Théâtre du Châtelet, 1er; the Théâtre de la Ville, 4ème; even some in the auditorium of the Louvre and in the Centre Pompidou. Ticket prices vary according to venue.

Journées du Patrimoine, 3rd weekend of Sept. (☎01 40 15 37 37; www.journeesdupatrimoine.culture.fr). The few days each year when certain ministries, monuments, and palaces are opened to the public. The Hôtel-de-Ville should be on your list, as well as the Palais de l'Elysée and the Palais Luxembourg. Offerings vary from year to year; check with the tourist office 2-3 days in advance. Free.

Fête des Vendanges de Montmartre, 2nd weekend in Oct. R. des Saules, 18ème (☎01 46 06 00 32; www.fetedesvendangesdemontmartre.com). Ⓜ Lamarck-Caulaincourt. A celebration of the harvest from Montmartre's vineyards. Folk songs, parades, and the picking and stomping of grapes. Much wine is consumed.

WINTER

Christmas (Noël), Dec. 24-25. At midnight on Christmas Eve, Notre Dame becomes what it only claims to be the rest of the year: the cathedral of the city of Paris. Midnight mass is celebrated with pomp and incense. Get there early to get a seat. Christmas Eve is more important than Christmas Day in France. Families gather to exchange gifts and eat Christmas food, including *bûche de Noël* (Yule Log), a rich chocolate cake. During Advent, the city illuminates the major boulevards with holiday lights and decorations. A huge *crèche* (nativity scene) is displayed on pl. Hôtel-de-Ville. Restaurants offer Christmas specialties and special *menus.*

New Year's Eve and Day, Dec. 31-Jan. 1. Young punks and tons of tourists throng the Champs-Elysées to set off fireworks, while restaurants host pricey evenings of *foie gras* and champagne galore. On New Year's Day, there is a parade with floats and dolled-up *dames* from pl. Pigalle to pl. Jules-Joffrin.

NATIONAL HOLIDAYS

When a holiday falls on a Tuesday or Thursday, the French often take Monday or Friday off, a practice known as *faire le pont* (to make a bridge). Banks and public offices close at noon on the nearest working day before a public holiday.

DATE	HOLIDAY	
January 1	Le Jour de l'An	New Year's Day
March 28	Le Lundi de Pâques	Easter Monday
May 1	La Fête du Travail	Labor Day
May 5	L'Ascension	Ascension Day
May 8	L'Anniversaire de la Libération	Anniversary of the Liberation of Europe
May 16	Le Lundi de Pentecôte	Whit Monday
July 14	La Fête Nationale	Bastille Day
August 15	L'Assomption	Feast of the Assumption
November 1	La Toussaint	All Saints' Day
November 11	L'Armistice 1918	Armistice Day
December 25	Le Noël	Christmas

LIFE AND TIMES

BEYOND TOURISM

A PHILOSOPHY FOR TRAVELERS

HIGHLIGHTS OF BEYOND TOURISM IN PARIS

FIGHT AIDS as a volunteer for one of Paris's many awareness and prevention programs (p. 105).

HELP needy families in Paris and beyond with the Action Contre la Faim (p. 103).

BECOME the next Julia Child after a term at the famous Cordon Bleu cooking school (p. 109).

CHANGE the life of a child by doing au pair work (p. 111).

With so many different ways to experience a foreign place, it is essential to consider your options before setting out on your trip. Hostel-hopping and sightseeing can be great fun, but you may want to consider going Beyond Tourism. *Let's Go* believes that travelers can have a positive influence on the natural and cultural environments they visit. With this Beyond Tourism chapter, *Let's Go* hopes to promote a better understanding of Paris and enhance your experience there.

There are several options for those who seek to participate in Beyond Tourism activities. Opportunities for **volunteering** abound, both with local and international organizations. **Studying** can also be very fulfilling, whether through direct enrollment in a local university or with an independent research project. **Working** is a way to immerse yourself in the local culture and finance your travels.

As a **volunteer** in Paris, you can participate in projects from tutoring prisoners to fighting homophobia, either on a short-term basis or as the main component of your trip. Paris may be one of the world's wealthiest cities, but it certainly harbors its fair share of economic and social unrest, as well as a plethora of organizations that work to confront these issues. A favorite project of Parisian philanthropists in recent years has been activism concerning AIDS, a scourge that affects Europe as well as many French-speaking areas in Africa. Paris is also home to a wealth of organizations that deal with the city's impoverished population as well as needy families around the globe. Recently, unemployment in France has spiked, leaving much of its citizenry with a reinvigorated interest (and a personal stake) in contributing to this cause. Later in this chapter, we recommend organizations that can help you find the opportunities that best suit your interests, whether you're looking to pitch in for a day or a year.

Studying at a college or in a language program is another option. Paris offers excellent programs in both language and cultural immersion, and its culinary institutes are known to be among the world's finest. Any trip can be enhanced by deepening one's knowledge of a destination's history and customs, and the best way to immerse oneself in Paris is to take a course or two there. Whether you're interested in fine-tuning your understanding of existentialist literature or the perfect *crêpe suzette*, you will find an outlet for your passion in the City of Love.

Many travelers also structure their trips by the **work** that they can do along the way—either odd jobs as they go, or full-time stints in cities where they plan to stay for some time. Those looking for short-term employment in Paris will have no trouble finding local (usually English-speaking) employers, while travelers in search of a steadier source of income will be incredibly fulfilled with a job as an *au pair*, an English teacher, or an intern at a local business.

 Start your search at ■ www.beyondtourism.com, *Let's Go*'s brand-new search able database of alternatives to tourism, where you can find exciting feature articles and helpful program listings divided by country, continent, and program type.

VOLUNTEERING

 WHY PAY MONEY TO VOLUNTEER?

Many volunteers are surprised to learn that some organizations require large fees or "donations." While this may seem ridiculous at first glance, such fees often keep the organization afloat, in addition to covering airfare, room, board, and administrative expenses for the volunteers. (Other organizations must rely on private donations and government subsidies.) If you're concerned about how a program spends its fees, request an annual report or finance account. A reputable organization won't refuse to inform you of how volunteer money is spent.

Pay-to-volunteer programs might be a good idea for young travelers who are looking for more support and structure (such as pre-arranged transportation and housing), or anyone who would rather not deal with the uncertainty implicit in creating a volunteer experience from scratch.

Volunteering can be one of the most fulfilling experiences you have in life, especially if you combine it with the thrill of traveling in a new place. Particularly in a city like Paris that presents itself to the world as a tourist's paradise, having an experience that wanders off the beaten path can be uniquely valuable. Nothing beats the satisfaction of knowing that you have left your travel destination in better condition than it was when you arrived, and Paris is bursting at the seams with opportunities to do just that.

Most people who volunteer in Paris do so on a short-term basis, at organizations that make use of drop-in or once-a-week volunteers. The best way to find opportunities that match up with your interests and schedule may be to check with an **International Service Database,** such as **Concordia International Volunteer Programs,** Heversham House, 20-22 Boundary Rd., Hove BN34ET, England (☎+12 73 42 22 18), **University of California at Irvine's International Service Database** (www.cie.uci.edu/iop/voluntee.html), or **Jeunesse et Reconstruction** (☎01 47 70 15 88; www.volontariat.org). Some of the most popular forms of short-term volunteering in Paris are working at drop-in medical centers for the indigent, spending a week or two restoring damaged architecture, or assisting activist organizations with causes such as the living wage or AIDS awareness.

Those looking for longer, more intensive volunteer opportunities usually choose to go through a parent organization that takes care of logistical details and often provides a group environment and support system—for a fee. There are two main types of organizations—religious and non-sectarian—although there are rarely restrictions on participation for either.

HISTORICAL RESTORATION

For centuries, Paris has attempted to strike a delicate balance between maintaining its architecture's rich history and paving the way for new and innovative methods of viewing and constructing the urban world. As much as Paris would like to place itself in the center of the modern architectural revolution, its allegiances remain close to its historical monuments, and rightly so. Many restoration programs accept volunteers; for a modest fee, you could find yourself working on stained-glass windows shattered in the 2004 riots or marble statues smashed during the time of the Crusades.

Archaeological Institute of America, 656 Beacon St. Boston, MA 02215, USA (☎617-353-9361; www.archaeological.org). The *Archaeological Fieldwork Opportunities Bulletin*, available on the organization's website, lists field sites throughout Europe (including France) at which you can volunteer.

Association CHAM, 5 et 7 r. Guilleminot, 75014 (☎01 43 35 15 51; www.cham.asso.fr). Organizes groups to restore medieval French landmarks. Open M-F 8:30am-12:30pm and 1:30-6pm, Sa 9am-12:30pm and 1:30-4pm.

Club du Vieux Manoir, Ancienne Abbaye du Moncel, 60700 Pontpoint (☎03 44 72 33 98; cvmclubduvieuxmanoir.free.fr). Year-long and summer work restoring castles and churches. €14 membership. Insurance fee €16 per day, including food and tent.

REMPART, 1 r. des Guillemites, 75004 Paris (☎01 42 71 96 55; www.rempart.com). Offers summer and year-long programs for the restoration of monuments. Anyone 13 or over is eligible. Membership fee €17; most projects charge €6-8 per day.

URBAN ISSUES

Many people think of Paris as the land of wine, flamboyant monarchs, and a veritable universe of fragrant cheese. But holding up a post as the City of Intrigue comes at a price for France's capital: increased unemployment in recent years has impoverished many Parisian families. Children and the elderly also suffer from Paris's newly depressed economy, as health care and education are becoming ever less accessible. Organizations dedicated to charitable work are scattered throughout the city, and all are more than happy to accept volunteers on a short- or long-term basis.

Care France, CAP 19, 13 rue de Georfes Auric, 75019 (☎01 53 19 89 89; www.care.org). An international humanitarian organization providing volunteer opportunities in 6000 locations throughout France, doing activities such as combating AIDS, supporting urban development, and promoting education.

France Bénévolat, 127 r. Falguière 75015 Paris (☎01 40 61 01 61; www.globenet.org/CNV). 70 offices in France help people find the volunteer associations in which they would be most helpful, based on their wishes, skills, and availability.

International Volunteer Program, 678 13th St., Ste. 100, Oakland, CA 94612, USA (☎510-433-0414; www.ivpsf.org). 6-week programs in France ranging from aiding recovering alcoholics to elderly assistance. Fee of US$1800 includes in-country transportation, room, and meals. Intermediate knowledge of French required.

Action Contre la Faim, 4 r. Niepce, 75014 Paris (☎01 43 35 88 88; www.actioncontrelafaim.org). As an international organization combating hunger, Action Contre la Faim can always use the help of volunteers. The Race Against Hunger, a running competition that raises money for the cause, always requires a good deal of assistance.

Fédération Familles de France, 28 pl. St-Georges, 75009 Paris (☎01 44 53 45 90, www.familles-de-france.org). Supports families in need by offering grants, providing assistance with education and résumés, and giving access to social organizations.

Fondation Claude Pompidou, 42 rue du Louvre, 75001 Paris (☎01 40 13 75 00; www.fondationclaudepompidou.asso.fr). The Fondation Claude Pompidou is a charitable organization that aids the sick, elderly, and disabled by providing support, homecare, and companionship for them. Volunteers are generally expected to commit a full year of service.

GENEPI, 12 rue Charles Fourier, 75013 Paris (☎01 45 88 37 00; www.genepi.fr). GENEPI promotes the social rehabilitation of those in prison in France by creating relationships between students and prisoners. All volunteers are students.

Les Papillons Blancs de Paris—APEI, 44 rue Blanche, 75009 (☎01 42 80 44 43; www.apei75.org). An NGO that aids the mentally handicapped and their families by providing transportation, assistance, homecare, and friendship.

Secours Catholique: Delegation de Paris, 106 rue du Bac, 75007 Paris (☎01 45 49 73 00; www.secours-catholique.asso.fr). Works to support the poor, the unemployed, children, immigrants, and other marginalized groups.

Secours Populaire Français, 9/11 rue Froissart, 75140 Paris (☎01 44 78 21 00; www.secourspopulaire.asso.fr). Secours is a nonprofit organization that provides support for poor children and families through food and clothing provisions, as well as offering sports activities and social interactions, all done with a commitment to human rights.

WICE, 20 bd. du Montparnasse, 75015 (☎01 45 66 75 50; www.wice-paris.org). Founded in 1978 as a part of the American College of Paris, WICE is an organization dedicated to helping English-speakers transition into life in France. It is run almost entirely by volunteers and offers support and resources of various kinds, including courses on topics from art history to business strategies, opportunities for artists to show their work, social gatherings, a library, and information on health care. As a volunteer, you can either help with day-to-day operations or plan and lead your own course. Closed July-Aug.

SOCIAL ACTIVISM

From the decline of the Roman Empire to the recent influx of post-colonial and political refugees, Paris has been home to a diverse collection of the world's cultural, ethnic, and social groups. Occasionally, however, this metropolitan melting pot boils over into a haven of racism, hate crimes, and acts of violence. Organizations located throughout the city accept volunteers to speak up on behalf of marginalized communities, fighting for the rights of ethnic and social minorities in an ever-changing political landscape.

ACT-UP Paris, 45 rue de Sedene (☎01 48 06 13 89; www.actupparis.org). Organization devoted to education and health care within Paris's GLBT communities as well as awareness and activism nationwide. Provides opportunities to get involved with AIDS treatment and prevention as well as anti-homophobia campaigns, support groups, and trans rights issues.

Movement Against Racism and for Friendship Between Peoples (MRAP), 43 bd. Magenta, 75010 (☎01 53 38 99 99; www.mrap.asso.fr). Campaigns for diversity and tolerance in Paris and beyond. Provides counseling and support for victims of racism and discrimination; assists people experiencing difficulty in obtaining proper immigration documents. Opportunities for political action as well as for service.

Ni Putes Ni Soumises, 70 rue des Rigoles, 75020 (☎01 53 46 63 00; www.niputesni-soumises.com). The Ni Putes Ni Soumises (Neither Whores Nor Doormats) movement began in April of 2003 in response to violent acts against women in ghettos in the Paris *banlieus* (suburbs). NPNS campaigns against racism, sexism, and homophobia by organizing marches, petitions, and publications. The movement is popular and highly publicized; it's a great opportunity for social action.

Simon Wiesenthal Center, 64 av. Marceau, 75008 Paris (☎01 47 23 76 37; www.wiesenthal.org). Fights anti-Semitism and Holocaust denial throughout Europe. Small, variable donation required for membership.

MEDICAL OUTREACH AND AIDS AWARENESS

With more of Europe's HIV-positive population than any other major city on the continent, Paris has pioneered an agenda of AIDS awareness and prevention that it hopes will spread throughout the EU. Opportunities for volunteering abound and are especially popular with young people. AIDS work in Paris can either be political or completely charity-based, depending upon the organization. Medical outreach opportunities unrelated to AIDS have also been more active lately, given the recent strain on France's socialized health care system.

Arcat-Sida, 94-102 rue de Buzneval, 75020 (☎01 44 93 29 29; www.arcat-sida.org). Association of doctors, journalists, sociologists, and volunteers offering information and support on HIV/AIDS as well as promoting AIDS research.

AIDES, 119 rue des Pyrenées, 75020 (☎01 53 27 63 00; www.aides.org). AIDES is one of Europe's largest community-based organizations for people living with AIDS, providing education, support, and access to treatment. In France, 350 staff members and 800 AIDES volunteers are active in 80 cities.

Médecins Sans Frontières (Doctors Without Borders), 8 rue St-Sabin, 75011 (☎01 40 21 29 29; www.msf.fr). The French branch of this international organization coordinates volunteers aged 18+ to provide health care for immigrants and asylum seekers. Around 25,000 volunteers help out each year. Interview required.

Sol En Si (Solidarité Enfants Sida), 9 bis, rue Léon Giraud, 75019 (☎01 44 52 78 78; www.solensi.asso.fr). Sol En Si's mission is to support the children of AIDS victims and to preserve families in the face of illness. Volunteering for Sol En Si may not be feasible if you're only in Paris for a short time, but for those who can make a longer-term commitment, service opportunities include working at Sol En Si's daycare center, providing at-home childcare when a parent is struggling with illness.

STUDYING

VISA INFORMATION

Any study-abroad program lasting more than a few weeks will likely require visas of its students. Before your departure, check the nearest French embassy or consulate (see **Embassies and Consulates**, p.23).

Study-abroad programs range from basic language and culture courses to college-level classes, often for credit. In order to choose a program that best fits your needs, research as much as you can before making your decision—determine costs and duration, as well as what kind of students participate in the program and what sort of accommodations are provided. If you're considering culinary or art school, keep in mind that these facilities rarely offer the same amenities (housing, etc.) as standard universities because they cater to the settled adult population as much as to college-age people in transit.

In programs that have large groups of students who speak your native language, there is a trade-off. You may feel more comfortable in the community, but you will not have the same opportunity to practice your French or to befriend other international students. For accommodations, dorm life provides a better opportunity to mingle with fellow students, but there is less of a chance to experience the local scene. If you live with a family, there is a potential to build lifelong friendships with natives and to experience day-to-day life in more depth, but conditions can vary greatly from family to family.

UNIVERSITIES

Most university-level study-abroad programs are conducted in French, although many programs offer a limited selection of classes in English. Those relatively fluent in French may find it cheaper to enroll directly in a Parisian university, although getting college credit may be more difficult if you employ this plan. You can search **www.studyabroad.com** for various semester-abroad programs that meet your criteria, including your desired location and focus of study. The following is a list of organizations that can help place students in university programs abroad, or those that have their own branch in Paris.

AMERICAN PROGRAMS

American Institute for Foreign Study, College Division, River Plaza, 9 West Broad St., Stamford, CT 06902, USA (☎800-727-2437; www.aifsabroad.com). Organizes programs for high school and college study in universities in Paris.

Council on International Educational Exchange (CIEE), 7 Custom House St., 3rd fl., Portland, ME 01401, USA (☎800-407-8839; www.ciee.org/study). Sponsors work, volunteer, academic, and internship programs in Paris.

Cultural Experiences Abroad, France, (☎800-266-4441; www.gowithcea.com). Programs in Aix-en-Provence, the French Alps, and Paris. Tuition US$10,000-12,000 per term.

International Association for the Exchange of Students for Technical Experience (IAESTE), 10400 Little Patuxent Pkwy. Ste 250, Columbia, MD 21044, USA (☎410-997-3069; www.aipt.org/subpages/iaeste_us/index.php). Offers 8- to 12-week internships in Paris for college students ages of 19-30 who have completed 2 years of technical study. US$50 application fee and US$500 program fee.

School for International Training, College Semester Abroad, Kipling Rd., P.O. Box 676, Brattleboro, VT 05302, USA (☎888-272-7881 or 802-257-7751; www.sit.edu/study-abroad). Semester-long programs in Paris run US$12,900-16,000. Also runs **The Experiment in International Living,** 1 Kipling Rd., Brattleboro, VT 05301, USA (☎800-345-2929; www.usexperiment.org), 3- to 5-week summer programs that offer high-school students cross-cultural homestays, community service, ecological adventure, and language training in Paris and cost around US$5000.

FRENCH PROGRAMS

Students who apply directly to French universities should be prepared for earlier application dates (fall or early spring) and a required French language exam. Higher education in France is divided into three categories: *première* cycle (first two years of undergraduate study), *deuxième* cycle (second two years of undergraduate study, culminating in a *maîtrise*, or masters), and *troisième* cycle (graduate studies). French universities (except for the Grandes Écoles; see below) must admit anyone holding a **baccalauréat** (French high-school diploma) or a recognized equivalent to their first year of courses (British A-levels or two years of college in the US). French competency or other testing may be required for non-native speakers. The more selective and more demanding **Grandes Écoles** cover specializations from physics to photography to veterinary medicine. These have notoriously difficult entrance examinations that require a year of preparatory schooling to pass. For more information on programs of study, requirements, and grants or scholarships, visit **www.egide.asso.fr.**

EU citizens studying in France can take advantage of the three- to twelve-month **ERASMUS-SOCRATRES** program (www.psed.duth.gr/ENGLERAS-MUS.html), which offers grants to support intra-European educational exchanges. Most UK and Irish universities will have details regarding the grants available and the application procedures required. EU law dictates that educational qualifications be recognized across the Union (with the exception of some professional subjects).

As a student at a French university, you will receive a student card *(carte d'étudiant)* upon presentation of a residency permit and a receipt for your university fees. The Centre Régional des Oeuvres Universitaires et Scolaires (CROUS) offers several student benefits and discounts, including cheap meals. The brochure *Le CROUS et Moi* lists addresses and info on student life. Pick up their free guidebook, *Je Vais en France*, in French or English from any French embassy.

Agence EduFrance (www.edufrance.fr). A comprehensive, one-stop resource for North Americans thinking about studying for a degree in France. Info on courses, costs, and grant opportunities are all available (in French) on the website.

American University of Paris, 31 av. Bosquet, 75343 Paris, Cédex 07 (☎01 40 62 06 00; www.aup.fr.). Offers US-accredited degrees and summer programs taught in English at its Paris campus. Tuition US$10,470 per semester, not including living expenses. US$50 application fee.

Université Paris-Sorbonne, 1 rue Victor Cousin, 75005 Paris, Cédex 05 (☎01 40 46 22 11; www.paris4.sorbonne.fr). In 1968, the Université de Paris split into 10 independent universities, each at a different site offering a different program. The **Sorbonne,** or the Université de Paris IV, devotes itself to the humanities and is considered the granddaddy of French universities (it was founded in 1253). Inscription into degree courses costs about €400 per year. Also offers 3- to 9-month-long programs for American students.

LANGUAGE SCHOOLS

Language schools can be independently run international or local organizations or divisions of foreign universities. They rarely offer college credit, but are a good alternative to university study if you desire a deeper focus on the language or a slightly less rigorous courseload. These programs are also good for younger high school students who might not feel comfortable surrounded by college-age classmates. Some worthwhile programs include:

BEYOND TOURISM

Alliance Française, École Internationale de Langue et de Civilisation Française, 101 bd. Raspail, 75270 Paris, Cédex 6 (☎01 42 84 90 00; www.alliancefr.org). Instruction at all levels, with courses in legal and business French. Courses are 1-4 months in length, costing €267 for 16 2hr. sessions and €534 for 16 4hr. sessions.

AmeriSpan, 117 S 17th St., Ste. 1401, Philadelphia, PA 19103 (In US and Canada ☎1-800-879-6640, elsewhere 215-751-1100; www.amerispan.com). Offers French courses in Paris with the option of a homestay. Draws an international mix of participants. Prices range from US$700-2400, depending on length of stay. US$100 registration fee.

Cours de Civilisation Française de la Sorbonne, 47 rue des Ecoles, 75005 (☎01 40 46 22 11; www.ccfs-sorbonne.fr). French-language courses at all levels; also a comprehensive lecture program on French cultural studies taught by Sorbonne professors. Must be at least 18 and at *baccalauréat* level to enroll. Semester- and year-long courses during the year (from €450) and 4-, 6-, 8-, and 11-week programs in the summer.

Eurocentres, Seestr. 247, CH-8038 Zurich, Switzerland (☎41 1 485 50 40; www.eurocentres.com). Language programs for beginning to advanced students with homestays in Paris.

French Language Learning Vacations, French-American Exchange, 3213 Duke St. #620, Alexandria, VA 22314, USA (☎800-995-5087; www.frenchamericanexchange.com). French-language programs in Paris. 2-week sessions US$1250-2300.

Institut de Langue Française, 3 av. Bertie-Albrecht, 75008 (☎01 45 63 24 00; www.inst-langue-fr.com). Language, civilization, and literature courses. Offers 4-week-to year-long programs, 6-20 hr. per week, starting at €185.

Institut Parisien de Langue et de Civilisation Française, 29 r. de Lisbonne, 75008 (☎01 40 56 09 53; www.institut-parisien.com). French language, fashion, culinary arts, and cinema courses. Intensive language courses 10-25 hr. per week, starting at €107 per week.

Language Immersion Institute, WSB 03D, State University of New York at New Paltz, 1 Hawk Dr., New Paltz, NY 12561, USA (☎845-257-3500; www.newpaltz.edu/lii). 2-week summer language courses and some overseas courses in French. Program fees start around US$670 for a 2-week course, not including accommodations.

Langue Onze Paris, 10 r. Gambey, 70511 (☎01 43 38 22 87; www.langueonze-paris.com). Part of the Tandem International association of language schools (see www.tandem-schools.com/index.html). Offers French-language courses and homestays in Paris. Costs for the program average €150-595, depending on course intensity and length of stay.

CULTURAL STUDIES

One final—and pricier—study abroad option for students and amateurs of all ages is enrollment in a French culinary institute or art school. While the very best of France's trade schools are oriented toward pre-professionals, many programs offer day- or week-long workshops to budding gourmands and closet Van Goghs. Museums like the Louvre and Musée D'Orsay frequently hold educational workshops; the Musée Rodin even offers a scultpture class for children. To find out more, just ask for a brochure at the information desk of any of these museums. If you're looking for informal, private classes, check the classified ads on **www.expatriates.com**—they post lessons in everything from candle-making to *kama sutra*. Cooking workshops are by far the most common educational opportunity open to English speakers, and they can be a fabulous introduction to French culture.

> **Cordon Bleu Paris Culinary Arts Institute,** 8 r. Léon Delhomm, 75015 (☎01 53 68 22 50; www.cordonbleu.edu). The *crème de la crème* of French cooking schools. Offers a plethora of tourist-friendly tours and workshops (€39 per day for lessons in "cooking for friends").

> **Françoise Meunier's Cours de Cuisine,** 7 r. Paul-Lelong, 75002 (☎01 40 26 14 00; www.fmeunier.com). €100 for a 3hr. class in which you'll cook and then share a 3-course meal. Typical class has 8-10 students; private lessons are available, as well as youth workshops for children ages 10-12. Classes taught in French, but *cuisinière* Meunier is also glad to speak English and limited Spanish.

> **Promenades Gourmandes,** 187 r. du Temple, 75003 (☎01 48 04 56 84; www.promenadesgourmandes.com). Offers fabulous walking tours of culinary Paris and cooking classes in the intimate, top-of-the-line kitchen of Paule Caillat. Walking tours €100 per person. Cooking classes €240 per person for a half-day. English speakers welcome.

WORKING

As with volunteering, work opportunities tend to fall into two categories. Some travelers want long-term jobs that allow them to get to know another part of the world as a member of the community, while others seek out short-term jobs to finance the next leg of their travels. In France, unemployment rates hovering near 10.5% mean that job-seeking expats are likely to meet with little sympathy from employers. In general, the French tend to be conservative about their job choices, and there is a much slower turnover in terms of job openings. Those who find work can take comfort in government regulations that limit the work week to a leisurely 35-39 hours, a measure intended to encourage hiring. **Non-EU citizens** will find it nearly impossible to get a work permit without a concrete job offer. To hire a non-EU expat legally in France, the employer must prove that the hiree can perform a task that cannot be performed by a French person. For a frequently updated international internship and job database, try **www.jobsabroad.com.**

Those looking for work can also check **help-wanted columns** in French newspapers and the English-language *International Herald Tribune*, as well as **France-USA Contacts (FUSAC)**, a free weekly circular filled with classified ads that is available at anglophone hangouts. Many of the jobs offered are "unofficial" and therefore illegal (the penalty is deportation), but many people find them convenient because they don't often require work permits. Youth hostels sometimes provide room and board to travelers in exchange for work. Those seeking more permanent employment should have a **résumé** in both English and French. Type up your résumé for a prospective employer, but write the cover letter by hand. Handwriting is considered an important indicator of your character among French employees. Be aware of your rights as an employee, and always get written confirmation of your agreements, including job offers. Note that working abroad (legally) often requires a special work visa.

VISA INFORMATION

EU citizens have the right to work and study in France without a visa, but they are required to have a **residency permit** *(carte de séjour)*. Those without an offer of employment have a grace period of three months in which to seek work; they are eiligible for social security benefits during this time. In order to receive benefits, you must make arrangements with your local social security office before leaving France. Be aware that the French bureaucracy often takes three months just to process the paperwork. If you do not succeed in finding work within the grace period, you must return home unless you can prove your financial independence. By law, all EU citizens must be given equality of opportunity when applying to jobs not directly related to national security. **Non-EU citizens** will find it much more difficult to obtain permission to work in France. In addition to a residency permit, non-EU citizens must have a firm offer of employment approved by the French Ministry of Labor before applying for a long-stay visa (€99) through a French consulate. International students looking for part-time work (up to 20hr. per week) can apply for a provisional work authorization upon completing their first academic year in a French university. For **au-pairs, scientific researchers,** and **teaching assistants,** special rules apply; check with your local consulate.

FINDING A JOB

The organizations listed below will help expats navigate the difficult process of finding a job in Paris.

American Church, 65 quai d'Orsay, 75007 (☎01 40 62 05 00; www.acparis.org). Posts a bulletin board full of job and housing opportunities targeting Americans and other Anglophones. Open M-Sa 9am-7:30pm.

Centre d'Information et de Documentation Jeunesse (CIDJ), 101 quai Branly, 75015 (☎01 44 49 12 00; www.cidj.asso.fr). An invaluable state-run youth center that provides info on education, résumés, employment, and careers. English spoken. Jobs are posted on the bulletin boards outside. Open M-W and F 10am-6pm, Th 1-6pm, Sa 9:30am-1pm.

Chamber of Commerce in France, 156 bd. Haussmann, 75008 Paris (☎01 56 43 45 67; www.amchamfrance.org). An association of American businesses in France. Keeps résumés on file for two months and places them at the disposal of French and American companies. Open M-Th 9:30am-1pm and 2-5pm.

LONG-TERM WORK

If you're planning on spending a substantial amount of time (more than three months) working in Paris, search for a job well in advance. International placement agencies are often the easiest way to find employment abroad, especially for those interested in teaching English. **Internships,** usually for college students, are a good way to segue into working abroad; although they are often unpaid or poorly paid, many say the experience is well worth it. Be wary of advertisements for companies claiming the ability to get you a job abroad for a fee—often the same listings are available online or in newspapers. Some reputable organizations include:

French-American Chamber of Commerce (FACC), 122 E 42nd St., Ste. 2015, New York, NY 10168 (☎212-867-0123; www.faccnyc.org). Offers work programs, internships, and teaching opportunities.

Paris-Anglo (www.paris-anglo.com). A community for anglophone expats in Paris offering jobs, housing, food, and study-abroad opportunities. The site provides a comprehensive listing of openings in every field imaginable, as well as a plethora of recruiting agencies and tips on how to beat the bureaucracy.

TEACHING ENGLISH

Teaching jobs in Paris are rarely well paid, although some elite private American schools offer competitive salaries. Volunteering as a teacher in lieu of getting paid is a popular option; even then, teachers often receive some sort of a daily stipend to help with living expenses. In almost all cases, you must have at least a bachelor's degree to be a full-fledged teacher, although college undergraduates can often get summer positions teaching or tutoring. The Fulbright Teaching Assistantship and and French Teaching Assistantship programs through the French Ministry of Education are the best options for students and recent grads with little experience teaching. Another alternative is to make contacts directly with schools; the best time to do so is several weeks before the start of the academic year.

Many schools require teachers to have a **Teaching English as a Foreign Language (TEFL)** certificate. Not having this certification does not necessarily exclude you from finding a teaching job, but certified teachers often find higher-paying jobs. Native English speakers working in private schools are most often hired for English-immersion classrooms where no French is spoken. Those volunteering or teaching in public, poorer schools are more likely to be working in both English and French. Placement agencies or university fellowship programs are the best resources for finding teaching jobs. The alternative is to make contact directly with schools or just to try your luck once you get there. If you are going to try the latter, start looking for positions in mid to late July. The following organizations are extremely helpful in placing teachers in Paris.

French Ministry of Education Teaching Assistantship in France, Cultural Service of the French Embassy, 972 Fifth Ave., New York, NY 10021 (☎212-439-1407; www.french-culture.org/education). This program designed for US citizens sends 1500 college students and recent grads to teach English part-time in France.

Fulbright English Teaching Assistantship, US Programs Division, Institute of International Education, 809 United Nations Plaza, New York, NY 10017 (☎212-984-5400; www.iie.org). Competitive program sends college graduates to teach in France.

Office of Overseas Schools, 2201 C St. NW, Washington, DC 20520 (☎202-647-4000; www.state.gov/m/a/os). Keeps a list of schools abroad and agencies that arrange placement for Americans to teach abroad.

AU PAIR WORK

Au pairs are typically women (although sometimes men), aged 18-27, who work as live-in nannies, caring for children and doing light housework in foreign countries in exchange for room, board, and a small spending allowance or stipend. Most former au pairs speak favorably of their experiences. One perk of the job is that it allows you to really get to know the country without the high expenses of traveling. Drawbacks, however, often include mediocre pay and long hours of constantly being on duty. Much of the au pair experience depends on the family with whom you're placed. The agencies below are a good starting point for looking for employment as an au pair.

Au Pair Homestay, World Learning, Inc., 1015 15th St. NW, Ste. 750, Washington, DC 20005, USA (☎800-287-2477; fax 202-408-5397).

> ### FURTHER READING ON BEYOND TOURISM
> *Alternatives to the Peace Corps: A Directory of Third World and U.S. Volunteer Opportunities,* by Jennifer S. Willsea. Food First Books, 2003 (US$10, or US$1 used).
>
> *Back Door Guide to Short-Term Job Adventures: Internships, Extraordinary Experiences, Seasonal Jobs, Volunteering, Working Abroad,* by Michael Landes. Ten Speed Press, 2002 (US$22, or US$1.50 used).
>
> *Green Volunteers: The World Guide to Voluntary Work in Nature,* by Ausenda and McCloskey. Universe, 2003 (US$15).
>
> *How to Get a Job in Europe,* by Sanborn and Matherly. Planning Communications, 2003 (US$15).
>
> *How to Live Your Dream of Volunteering Overseas,* by Collins, DeZerega, and Heckscher. Penguin Books, 2002 (US$12).
>
> *International Directory of Voluntary Work,* by Whetter and Pybus. Peterson's Guides and Vacation Work, 2000 (US$14).
>
> *International Job Finder: Where the Jobs Are Worldwide,* by Daniel Lauber. Planning Communications, 2002 (US$13).
>
> *Invest Yourself: The Catalogue of Volunteer Opportunities,* published by the Commission on Voluntary Service and Action (US$17, ☎646-486-2446).
>
> *Live and Work Abroad: A Guide for Modern Nomads,* by Francis and Callan. Vacation-Work Publications, 2001 (US$17).
>
> *Summer Jobs Abroad 2003 (Overseas Summer Jobs),* byJames and Woodworth. Vacation and Work Publications, 2003 (US$18, or US$1 used).
>
> *Volunteer Vacations: Short-term Adventures That Will Benefit You and Others,* by Cutchins and Geissinger. Chicago Review Press, 2003 (US$18 or US$1 used).
>
> *Work Abroad: The Complete Guide to Finding a Job Overseas,* by Hubbs, Griffith, and Nolting. Transitions Abroad Publishing, 2002 (US$16).
>
> *Work Your Way Around the World,* by Susan Griffith. Vacation Work Publications, 2003 (US$15).

Au Pair in Europe, P.O. Box 68056, Blakely Postal Outlet, Hamilton, Ontario, Canada L8M 3M7 (☎905-545-6305; www.princeent.com).

Childcare International, Ltd., Trafalgar House, Grenville Pl., London NW7 3SA (☎+44 020 8906-3116; www.childint.co.uk).

InterExchange, 161 Sixth Ave., New York, NY 10013, USA (☎212-924-0446; www.interexchange.org).

SHORT-TERM WORK

Traveling for long periods of time can get expensive; therefore, many travelers try their hand at odd jobs for a few weeks at a time to help finance another month or two of touring around. While such jobs are relatively accessible in Paris through anglophone newspapers and friendly hostel owners, they are technically illegal and can result in deportation. For those who wish to take the plunge, some opportunities include translating for French professionals, giving informal English lessons, or babysitting. Another popular option is to work several hours a day at a hostel in exchange for free or discounted room and/or board. Most often, these short-term jobs are found by word of mouth, or by simply talking to the owner of a hostel or restaurant. Due to the high turnover in the tourism industry, many places are eager for help, even if it is only temporary. *Let's Go* tries to list temporary jobs like these whenever possible; check out the list below for some of the available short-term jobs in Paris.

Paris-Anglo (www.paris-anglo.com). See "Long-Term Work" p. 110.

Transitions Abroad, P.O. Box 3000, Denville, NJ 07834 (☎866-760-5340; www.transitionsabroad.com/listings/work). Provides accurate and up-to-date information about everything from au-pairing to farm jobs. Subscribe to the monthly magazine for tips on how best to live (and make money) like a local while traveling and to get some extensive resources for doing so. Website offers a comprehensive database of opportunities for short-term employment abroad, sorted by location and the type of job desired.

Easy Expat (www.easyexpat.com/paris_en). Provides a wealth of opportunities for those seeking summer, seasonal, or short-term jobs in Paris. The website lists positions in everything from teaching ski lessons to working at Disneyland Paris. Also has information about discount cards and student benefits.

BEYOND TOURISM

PRACTICAL INFORMATION

TOURIST AND FINANCIAL SERVICES

ACCOMMODATION AGENCIES

Allô Logement Temporaire, 64, r. du Temple, 3ème (☎01 42 72 00 06; www.allo-loge-ment-temporaire.asso.fr). Ⓜ Hôtel-de-Ville. Open M-F noon-8pm.

Centre Régional des Oeuvres Universitaires (CROUS), 39, av. Georges Bernanos, 5ème (☎01 40 51 36 00, lodging 01 40 51 55 55; www.crous-paris.fr). RER: Port-Royal.

OTU-Voyage (Office du Tourisme Universitaire), 119, r. St-Martin, 4ème (☎08 20 81 78 17 or 01 49 72 57 19 for groups; www.otu.fr). Levies a €1.53 service charge. Open M-F 9:30am-7pm, Sa 10am-noon and 1:30-5pm. Another branch at 2, r. Malus, 5ème (☎01 44 41 74 74). Ⓜ Place Monge. Open M-Sa 9-6pm.

BIKE AND SCOOTER RENTAL

Paris à velo, c'est sympa!, 22, r. Alphonse Baudin, 11ème (☎01 48 87 60 01; www.parisvelosympa.com). Ⓜ St-Richard Lenoir. Rentals available with a €200 (or credit card) deposit. 24hr. rental €16; 9am-7pm €12.50; half day (9am-2pm or 2-7pm) €9.50. Open daily 9am-1pm and 2-6pm.

Paris-Vélo, 2, r. de Fer-à-Moulin, 5ème (☎01 43 37 59 22). Ⓜ Censier-Daubenton. Bike rental €14 per day. Open M-Sa 10am-7pm, Su 10am-2pm and 5-7pm.

Roulez Champions, 5, r. Humblot, 15ème (☎01 40 58 12 22; www.roulezchampi-ons.com). Bike rental from €15 per day. Also rents in-line skates. Open Apr.-Oct. daily 10am-8pm; Nov.-Mar. Tu-Su 11am-8pm.

SEJEM, 144, bd. Voltaire, 11ème (☎01 44 93 04 03; www.sejem.com). Rents bikes and scooters. Open M-F 9am-1pm and 2-7pm, Sa 10am-1pm and 2-6pm.

CAR RENTAL

Autorent, 98, r. de la Convention, 15ème (☎01 45 54 22 45, fax 01 45 54 39 69; autorent@wanadoo.fr). Ⓜ Boucicaut. Also at 36, r. Fabert, 7ème (☎01 45 55 12 54, fax 01 45 55 14 00). Ⓜ Invalides. Open M-F 8am-7pm, Sa 8:30am-noon. AmEx/MC/V.

Hertz, Carrousel de Louvre (☎01 47 03 49 12). Ⓜ Louvre. Open M-Th 8am-7pm, Sa 8am-1pm and 2-4pm, Su 8am-1pm. AmEx/MC/V.

Rent-a-Car, 79, r. de Bercy, 12ème (☎01 43 45 98 99; www.rentacar.fr). Open M-Sa 8:30am-noon and 2-6:30pm. AmEx/MC/V.

CELL PHONE RENTAL

Call'Phone, CDG Terminal 2F (☎01 48 62 37 53; www.callphone.com). Free cell phone rental. 5min. minimum charge daily (outgoing calls €0.70 per min.). Incoming calls free. MC/V.

CURRENCY EXCHANGE

American Express, 11, r. Scribe, 9ème (☎01 47 77 79 28). Ⓜ Opéra or Auber. Open M-Sa 9am-6:30pm; exchange counters also open Su 10am-5pm.

Thomas Cook, 26, av. de l'Opéra, 1er (☎01 53 29 40 00, fax 01 47 03 32 13). Ⓜ Georges V. Open M-Sa 9am-10:55pm, Su 8am-6pm.

TAXIS

Alpha Taxis, ☎01 45 85 85 85.

Taxis Bleus, ☎01 49 36 10 10.

Taxis G7, ☎01 47 39 47 39.

TOURIST OFFICES

Bureau Gare d'Austerlitz, 13ème (☎01 45 84 91 70). Ⓜ Gare d'Austerlitz. Open M-Sa 8am-6pm.

Bureau Gare de Lyon, 12ème (☎01 43 43 33 24). Ⓜ Gare de Lyon. Open M-Sa 8am-6pm.

Bureau Tour Eiffel, Champs de Mars, 7ème (☎08 92 68 31 12). Ⓜ Champs de Mars. Open daily May-Sept. 11am-6:40pm.

Montmartre Tourist Office, 21, pl. dy Tertre, 18ème (☎01 42 62 21 21). Ⓜ Anvers. Open daily 10am-7pm.

TOURS

Bateaux-Mouches, ☎01 42 25 96 10, info 01 40 76 99 99; www.bateaux-mouches.fr. Ⓜ Alma-Marceau. 70min. tours in English. Departures every 30min. 10:15am-10:40pm (no boats 1-2pm) from the Right Bank pier near Pont d'Alma.

City Segway Tours, ☎01 56 58 10 54; www.citysegwaytours.com. See Paris from a Segway Human Transporter electric scooter. 4-5hr. tours leave at 10:30am and 6:30pm Mar.-Nov. from beneath the Eiffel Tower. €70 per person. Reserve by phone or Internet.

Mike's Bullfrog Bike Tours, ☎01 56 58 10 54; www.mikesbiketours.com. New Segway tours! Tours meet by the south leg (Pilier Sud) of the Eiffel Tower. Tours depart every F from Place d'Italie, 10pm (return 12:30am). Tickets €30, students €28.

Canauxrama, 13, quai de la Loire, 19ème ☎01 42 39 15 00, fax 01 42 39 11 24. Reservations required. Departures either from Port de l'Arsenal (Ⓜ Gaures) or La Villette (Ⓜ Bastille) at 9:45am and 2:45pm. €15, students €12 except on weekends and holidays. Call ahead for departure point.

Paris à velo, c'est sympa!, 37, bd. Bourdon, 4ème (☎01 48 87 60 01). Ⓜ Bastille. 3hr. tours 10am and 3pm. €30, under 26 €26. See **Bike and Scooter Rental.**

Paristoric, 11bis, r. Scribe, 9ème (☎01 42 66 62 06; www.paris-story.com). Ⓜ Opéra. Shows daily on the hr. Nov.-Mar. 9am-6pm; Apr.-Oct. 10am-8pm. €8, students and children under 18 €5, under 6 and second child in a family free.

Paris-Vélo, 2, r. de Fer-à-Moulin, 5ème (☎01 43 37 59 22). Ⓜ Censier-Daubenton. Call for group tours (6-8 people).

Vedette Pont Neuf Boats, ☎01 46 33 98 38. Ⓜ Pont Neuf or Louvre. Departures daily 10:30, 11:15am, noon, every 30min. 1:30-6:30, 7, 8pm, and every 30min. 9-10:30pm. 1hr. Leave from the Pont Neuf landing near the Eiffel Tower. €9, under 12 €4.50, under 4 free.

TRANSPORTATION

Aeroports de Paris, ☎01 48 62 22 80; www.adp.fr. One stop for all info related to Charles de Gaulle and Orly Airports—ground transportation, flight times, delays, etc. 24hr. English hotline.

Aéroport d'Orly, info ☎8 92 68 15 15. Open 6am-11:45pm.

Air France Buses, ☎08 92 35 08 20; www.cars-airfrance.com. Between Orly and Charles de Gualle and major metro stops in Paris. Daily 6am-11pm. €11

Airport Shuttle (to both airports), ☎01 30 11 11 90. Door-to-door service. €29, smaller additional fee for each person going to same destination.

Eurolines, ☎08 92 69 52 52. Intercity and international buses.

Paris Airports Service (to both airports), ☎01 55 98 10 80 or 01 55 98 10 89.

Paris Shuttle, ☎01 43 90 91 91. Serves both airports. Door-to-door service. €25 for one person. €15 person for groups of two people or more.

Régie Autonome des Transports Parisiens (RATP), ☎08 92 68 77 14, €0.34 per min. Includes info on the **Roissybus** and **Orlybus,** RATP-run shuttles to both airports.

LOCAL SERVICES

CHUNNEL RESERVATIONS
Eurostar, reservation ☎01 49 70 01 75; www.eurostar.co.uk.

Eurotunnel, ☎03 21 00 61 00; www.eurotunnel.com.

DENTISTS AND DOCTORS
Centre Médicale Europe, 44 r. d'Amsterdam, 9ème (☎01 42 81 93 33). Ⓜ St-Lazare. Open M-F 8am-7pm, Sa 8am-6pm.

SOS Dentaire, 87 bd. Port-Royal (☎01 40 21 82 88). RER: Port-Royal. Open daily 9am-6pm and 8:30-11:45pm. No walk-ins.

SOS Médecins, ☎01 48 07 77 77. Makes house calls.

SOS Oeil, ☎01 40 92 93 94. Open daily 6am-11pm.

SOS Optique Lunettes, ☎01 48 07 22 00. Open 24hr.

Urgences Médicales de Paris, ☎01 53 94 94 94. Makes house calls.

DISABILITY RESOURCES
L'Association des Paralysées de France, Délégation de Paris, 13, pl. de Rungis, 13ème (☎01 53 80 92 99; www.apf.asso.fr). Ⓜ Place d'Italie. Open M-F 9am-12:30pm and 2-5:30pm.

Comité National Français de Liaison pour la Réadaption des Handicapés (CNFLRH), 236bis, r. de Tolbiac, 13ème (☎01 53 80 66 66, fax 01 53 80 66 67; www.handi-tel.org). Open daily 9am-1pm and 2-5:30pm.

DRY CLEANING
Arc en Ciel, 62, r. Arbre Sec, 1er (☎01 42 41 39 39). Ⓜ Louvre. Open M-F 8am-1:15pm and 2:30-7pm, Sa 8:30am-1:15pm.

Belnet Pressing, 140, r. Belleville, 20ème (☎01 46 36 65 51). Ⓜ Jourdain. Open M-Sa 8am-1pm and 2-7:30pm. MC/V.

Buci Pressing, 7, r. Ancienne Comédie, 6ème (☎01 43 29 49 92). Ⓜ Odéon. Open M-Sa 8am-7pm. MC (for over €13).

Home Pressing, 140, r. Lamartine, 14ème (☎01 48 83 05 05; www.homepress-ing.com). Pick-up and delivery services provided. Open M-F 7:30am-5:30pm. AmEx/V.

Pressing de Seine, 67, r. de Seine, 6ème (☎01 43 25 74 94). Ⓜ Odéon. Open M-Sa 8am-7pm. Hours vary in Aug. MC/V

Pressing Villiers, 93, r. de Rocher, 8ème (☎01 45 22 75 48). Ⓜ Villiers. Open M-F 8am-7:30pm. MC/V.

ENTERTAINMENT INFO
Info-Loisirs, ☎08 92 68 31 12; €0.34 per min.

FITNESS CLUBS

The following listings of fitness clubs are by *arrondissement*.

Centre Sivananda de Yoga Vedanta, 123, bd. de Sébastopol, 2ème (☎01 40 26 77 49). ⓜ Réaumur-Sébastopol.

Club Med Gym, 10, pl. de la République, 3ème (☎01 47 00 69 98; www.clubmedgym.com). Membership €140 per month. 36 locations throughout Paris.

Espace Vit'Halles, 48, r. Rambuteau, 3ème (☎01 42 77 21 71). Membership €149 per month, students €119.20.

Centre de Danse du Marais, 41, r. du Temple, 4ème (☎01 42 77 71 57). ⓜ Hôtel-de-Ville.

Squash Club Quartier Latin, 19, r. de Pontoise, 5ème (☎01 55 42 77 88). ⓜ Maubert-Mutualité or Jussieu. Gym, weight room, pool, martial arts, squash, sauna, and jacuzzi. Open M-F 8am-midnight, Sa-Su 9:30am-7pm.

Club Med Gym Montparnasse, 149 r. de Rennes, 6ème (☎01 45 44 24 35). Membership €140 per month.

Club Med Gym Champs Elysées, 26, r. Berri, 8ème (☎01 43 59 04 58). Membership €140 per month.

Les Cercles de la Forme, 11, r. de Malte, 11ème (☎01 47 00 80 95). Membership €307 for 3 months (min.).

Anthony's Studio Gym Club, 16, r. Louis Braille, 12ème (☎01 43 43 67 67). Annual membership €610, students €460.

Club Energym, 6, r. Lalande, 14ème (☎01 43 22 12 02). Membership €99 per month.

Jeu de Paume de Paris, 74, r. Lauriston, 16ème (☎01 47 27 46 86). ⓜ Charles de Gaulle-Etoile. Squash and handball courts. Yearly membership required. Open M-F 9am-10pm and Sa-Su 9am-8pm.

GBLT RESOURCES

ACT-UP Paris, 45, r. de Sedene, 11ème (☎01 48 06 13 89). ⓜ Bréguet-Sabin.

Boobs Bourg, 26, r. de Montmorency, 3ème (☎01 42 72 80 86). Sign up at this bar to join a Paris-wide lesbian email list with information on lectures and social events.

Centre du Christ Libérateur (Metropolitan Community Church), 5, r. Crussol, 11ème (☎01 48 05 24 48 or 01 39 83 13 44). ⓜ Oberkampf.

Centre Gai et Lesbien, 3, r. Keller, 11ème (☎01 43 57 21 47; fax 01 43 57 27 93). ⓜ Ledru-Rollin or Bastille. Open M-F 4-8pm.

Ecoute Gaie, ☎01 44 93 01 02. Crisis hotline. Open M-Tu and F evenings; if no one answers, a message will give the hours for the next 2 weeks.

SOSS Homophobie, ☎01 48 06 42 41. Takes calls M-F 8-10pm.

HAIR SALONS

Planet Hair, 26, r. Beaubourg, 4ème (☎01 48 87 38 86). ⓜ Rambuteau. Women's cut and style €42, men's €26; student discount 20%. Open Tu-W and F-Sa 10am-8pm, Th noon-9pm.

Space Hair, 10, r. Rambuteau, 3ème (☎01 48 87 28 51). ⓜ Rambuteau. Women's cut and style €37-46, men's €24; 15% student discount. Open M noon-10pm, Tu-Sa noon-8pm.

INTERNET ACCESS

Listings are by *arrondissement*.

easyInternetCafé, 31, bd. de Sébastopol, 1er (☎ 01 40 41 09 10). ⓜ Les Halles. €3 per hr. Open daily 7:30am-midnight.

Internet Café, 30, Grenier St-Lazare, 3ème (☎01 42 77 12 21). ⓜ Rambuteau. €3 per hr. Open M-F 10am-11pm, Sa noon-11pm.

Web Bar, 32, r. de Picardie, 3ème (☎01 42 72 66 55). Ⓜ Temple. €3 per hr. Open M-F 8:30am-2am, Sa-Su 10:30am-2am.

Akyrion Net Center, 19, r. Charlemagne, 4ème (☎01 40 27 92 07). €2.80 per hr. Open M-Th 11am-10:30pm, F-Sa 11am-11pm, Su 2-9:30pm.

Clickside, 14, r. Domat, 5ème (☎01 56 81 03 00). Ⓜ Maubert-Mutualité. €3 per hr. Open M-F noon-11pm, Sa-Su 2pm-11pm.

EasyInternetCafé, 6, r. de la Harpe, 5ème (☎01 55 42 55 42). Ⓜ St-Michel. €3 per hr. Open daily 7:30am-midnight.

Cyber Cube, 5, r. Mignon, 6ème (☎01 53 10 30 50). Ⓜ St-Michel or Odéon. €0.15 per min., €30 for 5hr., €40 for 10hr. Open M-Sa 10am-10pm.

Cyber Cube, 12, r. Daval, 11ème (☎01 49 29 67 67). Ⓜ Bastille. Prices, hours as above.

Le Sputnik, 14-16, r. de la Butte-aux-Cailles, 13ème (☎01 45 65 19 82). Ⓜ Place d'Italie. €1 for 15min., €4 for 1hr.

Care Photo, 5, r. Liard, 14ème (☎01 45 89 12 97). Ⓜ Cité Universitaire. €5 per hr. Open M-Sa 9am-12:30pm and 2-7pm.

Taxiphone, 6, r. Polonceau, 18ème (☎01 53 09 95 12). Ⓜ Anvers. €3 per hr. Open daily noon-10pm.

LIBRARIES

The American Library, 10, r. Général Camou, 7ème (☎01 53 59 12 60; www.american-libraryinparis.org). Ⓜ Ecole Militaire. Short-term and annual memberships available, check website for details. Open Tu-Sa 10am-7pm.

Bibliothèque Marguerite Duras, 79, r. Nationale, 13ème (☎01 45 70 80 30). Ⓜ Nationale. Open Tu-Su 10am-7pm.

Bibliothèque Nationale de France includes **Mitterrand** branch at 11, quai François Mauriac, 13ème (☎01 53 79 59 59). Ⓜ Quai de la Gare or Bibliothèque. Reading rooms open Tu-Sa 10am-8pm, Su noon-7pm. Branches at 66-68, r. de Richelieu, 2ème (☎01 47 03 81 26). Ⓜ Bourse. Bibliothèque de l'Opéra, 8, r. Scribe, 9ème (☎01 47 42 07 02), Ⓜ Opéra. Reader's card €3 per day, €30.50 per year, students €15.25.

Bibliothèque Publique, in the Centre Pompidou, 4ème (☎01 44 78 12 33). Ⓜ Rambuteau. Open M and W-F 11am-9pm, Sa-Su 11am-10pm.

MINORITY RESOURCES

Agence Pour le Développement des Relations Interculturelles, 4, r. Réne-Villermé, 11ème (☎01 40 09 69 19; www.adri.fr). Ⓜ Père Lachaise. Open M-Th 9:30am-1pm and 2-6pm, F 9:30am-1pm and 2-5pm.

Association des Trois Mondes, 63bis, r. du Cardinal Lemoine, 5ème (☎01 42 34 99 09; www.cine-3mondes.fr). Ⓜ Cardinal Lemoine.

Centre Culturel Algérien, 171, r. de la Croix-Nivert, 15ème (☎01 45 54 95 31). Ⓜ Boucicault. Open M-F 9am-5:30pm.

Centre Culturel Coréen, 2, av. d'Iéna, 16ème (☎01 47 20 84 15; www.coree-culture.org). Ⓜ Iéna. Open M-F 9:30am-6pm.

Centre Culturel Egyptien, 111, bd. St Michel, 5ème (☎01 46 33 75 67). Ⓜ Luxembourg. Open M-F 10am-7pm.

Maison de l'Asie, 48, av. Parmentier, 11ème (☎01 48 06 01 36). Ⓜ Parmentier. Open M-F 9am-6pm.

MRAP (Mouvement contre le racisme et pour l'amitié entre les peuples), 43, bd. Magenta, 10ème (☎01 53 38 99 99). Open M-F 9am-12:30pm.

SOS Racisme, 51, av. Flandre, 19ème (☎01 40 35 36 55). Open M-F 10:30am-6pm.

Pharmacie Les Champs, in the Galerie des Champs, 84, av. des Champs-Elysées, 8ème (☎ 01 45 62 02 41). Ⓜ George V. Open 24hr.

British and American Pharmacy, 1, r. Auber, 9ème (☎01 42 65 88 29 or 01 47 42 49 40). Ⓜ Auber or Opéra. Open daily 8am-8:30pm.

Pharmacie Gacha, 361, r. des Pyrénées, 20ème (☎01 46 36 59 10). Ⓜ Pyrénées or Jourdain. Open M-Sa 10am-7pm.

RELIGIOUS SERVICES

American Cathedral (Anglican and Episcopalian), 23, av. George V, 8ème (☎01 53 23 84 00). Ⓜ George V. English services winter Su 9am, summer 9 and 11am. Open M-F 9am-5pm.

American Church in Paris, 65, quai d'Orsay, 7ème (☎01 40 62 05 00). Ⓜ Invalides or Alma-Marceau. Service in English Su 9 and 11am. Open M-Sa 9am-10:30pm.

Buddhist Temple, Centre de Kazyn Dzong, route de la ceinture du Lac Daumesnil, 12ème (☎01 40 04 98 06). Ⓜ Porte Dorée. Buddhist temple and meditation center. Meditations Tu-F 9:30am, 6, and 7:30pm; Sa-Su 10am-noon and 2:30-5:30pm.

Eglise Russe (Russian Eastern Orthodox), also known as **Cathédrale Alexandre-Nevski,** 12, r. Daru, 8ème (☎01 42 27 37 34). Ⓜ Ternes. Open Tu, F, Su 3-5pm. Services (in French and Russian) Su 10:30am.

Mosquée de Paris, Institut Musulman, pl. de l'Ermite, 5ème (☎01 45 35 97 33). Ⓜ Place Monge. Open M-Th and Sa-Su 9am-noon and 2-6pm.

St. Joseph's Church (Catholic), 50, av. Hoche, 8ème (☎01 42 27 28 56). Ⓜ Charles de Gaulle-Etoile. English mass Su 11am and 6:30pm. Phone for other service times following renovations.

St. Michael's Church (Anglican and Episcopalian), 5, r. d'Aguesseau, 8ème (☎01 47 42 70 88). Ⓜ Concorde. Services in English Su 9:30, 11:15am, and 6:30pm. Open M-Tu and Th-F 10am-1pm and 2-5:30pm.

Union Libérale Israélite de France (Jewish), 24, r. Copernic, 16ème (☎01 47 04 37 27). Ⓜ Victor Hugo. Services F 6-7pm, Sa 10:30am-noon, mostly in Hebrew with a little French. Services in the evenings and mornings of High Holy Days; call for info. Open M-F 9am-noon and 2-6pm, Sa 9am-5:30pm.

TICKET SERVICES

FNAC, 74, av. des Champs-Elysées, 8ème (☎01 53 53 64 64; www.fnac.fr). Ⓜ F. D. Roosevelt.

Kiosque Info Jeune, 25, bd. Bourdon, 4ème (☎01 42 76 22 60). Ⓜ Bastille. Open M-F 10am-7pm.

Virgin Megastore, 52, av. des Champs-Elysées, 8ème (☎01 49 53 50 00; www.virgin-mega.fr). Ⓜ F. D. Roosevelt. Open M-Sa 10am-midnight, Su noon-midnight.

WOMEN'S RESOURCES

Bibliothèque Marguerite Duras, 79, r. Nationale, 13ème (☎01 45 70 80 30). Ⓜ Nationale. Open Tu-Sa 2-6pm.

Centre de Planification et d'Education Familiale, 27, r. Curnonsky, 17ème (☎01 48 88 07 28). Ⓜ Porte de Champerret. Open M-F 9am-5pm.

Mouvement Français pour le Planning Familial (MFPF), 10, r. Vivienne, 2ème (☎01 42 60 93 20). Ⓜ Bourse. Open for calls M-F 9:30am-5:30pm. On F, the clinic is held at 94, bd. Massanna, on the 1st fl. of the Tour Mantoue, door code 38145, 13ème (☎01 45 84 28 25); F 10am-4pm call ahead. Ⓜ Porte d'Ivry.

EMERGENCY AND COMMUNICATIONS

EMERGENCY

Ambulance (SAMU), ☎15.

Fire, ☎18.

Poison, ☎01 40 05 48 48. In French, but some English assistance is available.

Police, ☎17. **For emergencies only.**

Rape: SOS Viol (☎08 00 05 95 95). Open M-F 10am-7pm.

SOS Help!, ☎01 46 21 46 46. An anonymous, confidential hotline for English speakers in crisis. Open daily (including holidays) 3-11pm.

HOSPITALS

American Hospital of Paris, 63, bd. Hugo, Neuilly (☎01 46 41 25 25). Ⓜ Port Maillot, then bus #82 to the end of the line.

Hôpital Bichat, 46, r. Henri Buchard, 18ème (☎01 40 25 80 80). Ⓜ Port St-Ouen. Emergency services.

Hertford British Hospital (Hôpital Franco-Britannique de Paris), 3, r. Barbès, in the Parisian suburb of Levallois-Perret (☎01 46 39 22 22). Ⓜ Anatole France. Has some English speakers, but don't count on finding one.

HOTLINES AND SUPPORT CENTERS

AIDES, ☎0 800 84 08 00. Open 24hr.

Alcoholics Anonymous (AA), ☎01 43 25 75 00; www.aaparis.org. Holds both English and French meetings.

Free Anglo-American Counseling Treatment and Support (FACTS), HIV/AIDS information line ☎01 44 93 16 69. Open M-F 11am-2pm.

HIV, 43 r. de Valois, 1er (☎01 42 61 30 04). Ⓜ Palais-Royal or Bourse. Open M-W 9am-5pm. HIV testing at 218, r. de Belleville, 20ème (☎01 40 33 52 00). Ⓜ Télégraphe. Open M-F 1-6pm. 3-5, r. de Ridder, 14ème (☎01 58 14 30 30). Ⓜ Plaisance. Testing M-F noon-6:30pm, Sa 9:30am-noon.

International Counseling Service (ICS), ☎01 45 50 26 49. Open M-F 8am-8pm, Sa 8am-2pm.

SOS Crisis Help Line Friendship, ☎01 46 21 46 46. English spoken. Open M-F 3-11pm.

MAIL

Federal Express, ☎01 40 06 90 16. Call M-F before 5pm for pick up. Or, drop off at 63, bd. Haussmann, 8ème. Open M-Sa 9am-7pm, drop off by 4:45pm.

Poste du Louvre, 52, r. du Louvre, 1er (postal info ☎01 40 28 20 40). Ⓜ Louvre. Open daily 24hr.

PHARMACIES

Listings by *arrondissement*.

Pharmacie des Halles, 10, bd. de Sébastopol, 1er (☎01 42 72 03 23). Ⓜ Châtelet-Les Halles. Open M-Sa 9am-midnight, Su 9am-10pm.

Pharmacie Beaubourg, 50, r. Rambuteau, 3ème (☎01 48 87 86 37). Ⓜ Rambuteau. Open M-Sa 8am-8pm, Su 10am-8pm. MC/V

Pharmacie de l'Hôtel de Ville, 4, r. Bourg Tibourg, 4ème (☎01 48 87 60 92). Ⓜ Hôtel de Ville. Open daily 10am-8pm. AmEx/MC/V.

ACCOMMODATIONS

BY PRICE

UNDER €31 (❶)

Aloha Hostel (139)	15ème
Aub. de Jeun. "Le D'Artagnan" (143)	20ème
Aub. de Jeun. "Jules Ferry" (135)	11ème
Ctr. Internt'l CISP "Kellerman" (138)	13ème
Ctr. Internt'l CISP "Ravel" (137)	12ème
Ctr. Internt'l (BVJ) Paris Louvre (124)	1er
Foyer de Chaillot (133)	8ème
Foyer Internt'l des Etudiants (129)	5ème
Foyer des Jeunes Filles (138)	13ème
Hôtel Henri IV (124)	Île de la Cité
Hôtel de la Herse d'Or (128)	4ème
Hôtel des Jeunes (MIJE) (127)	4ème
Hôtel des Médicis (129)	5ème
Hôtel du Marais (127)	3ème
Hôtel Palace (134)	10ème
Hôtel Tiquetonne (125)	2ème
Three Ducks Hostel (139)	15ème
Union Chrétienne de Jne. Filles (133)	8ème
Le Village Hostel (141)	18ème
Woodstock Hostel (134)	9ème
Young & Happy Hostel (129)	5ème

€31-50 (❷)

Cambrai Hôtel (134)	10ème
Ctr. Internt'l (BVJ) Quartier Latin (129)	5ème
Eden Hôtel (143)	20ème
FIAP Jean-Monnet (138)	14ème
Hôtel André Gill (141)	18ème
Hôtel des Argonauts (129)	5ème
Hôtel de l'Aveyron (137)	12ème
Hôtel Belidor (141)	17ème
Hôtel de Blois (138)	14ème
Hôtel le Central (129)	5ème
Hôtel Caulaincourt (141)	18ème
Hôtel Ermitage (143)	20ème
Hôtel Esmeralda (129)	5ème
Hôtel Gay-Lussac (129)	5ème
Hôtel Marignan (128)	5ème
Hôtel La Marmotte (126)	2ème
Hôtel de Milan (134)	10ème
Hôtel Montana La Fayette (134)	10ème
Hôtel Montebello (131)	7ème
Hôtel Notre-Dame (135)	11ème
Hôtel Picard (126)	3ème
Hôtel Printania (137)	12ème
Hôtel Printemps (139)	15ème
Hôtel de Reims (137)	12ème
Hôtel Rhetia (135)	11ème

€31-50 (❷), CONT'D.

Hôtel Ribera (140)	16ème
Hôtel Riviera (140)	17ème
Hôtel Rivoli (128)	4ème
Hôtel du Séjour (126)	3ème
Hôtel Stella (130)	6ème
Mistral Hôtel (137)	12ème
Nièvre-Hôtel (137)	12ème
Perfect Hôtel (133)	9ème
La Perdrix Rouge (143)	19ème
Plessis Hôtel (135)	11ème
Ouest Hôtel (139)	14ème
Rhin et Danube (141)	19ème
Style Hôtel (141)	18ème
Villa d'Auteuil (140)	16ème

€51-75 (❸)

Crimée Hôtel (143)	19ème
Delhy's Hôtel (130)	6ème
Grand Hôtel Lévêque (131)	7ème
Hôtel Andréa Rivoli (128)	4ème
Hôtel de Belfort (135)	11ème
Hôtel Boileau (140)	16ème
Hôtel des Boulevards (126)	2ème
Hôtel Camélia (139)	15ème
Hôtel Champerret Héliopolis (140)	17ème
Hôtel de Chevreuse (130)	6ème
Hôtel Chopin (133)	9ème
Hôtel Europe-Liège (133)	8ème
Hôtel Lion d'Or (124)	1er
Hôtel Louvre-Richelieu (125)	1er
Hôtel Montpensier (124)	1er
Hôtel de Nesle (130)	6ème
Hôtel du Parc (139)	14ème
Hôtel Paris France (127)	3ème
Hôtel Practic (128)	4ème
Hôtel Prince Albert Wagram (140)	17ème
Hôtel de Roubaix (126)	3ème
Hôtel St-André des Arts (130)	6ème
Hôtel St-Honoré (124)	1er
Hôtel St-Jacques (128)	5ème
Hôtel de Turenne (131)	7ème
Modern Hôtel (135)	11ème
Modial Hôtel Européen (134)	9ème
Nouvel Hôtel (137)	12ème
Pacific Hôtel (139)	15ème
Paris Nord Hôtel (134)	10ème
Touring Hotel Magendie (138)	13ème

C76-95 (●)		**C76-95 (●), CONT'D.**	
Castex Hôtel (128)	4ème	Hôtel du Lys (130)	6ème
☒ Grand Hôtel Jeanne d'Arc (127)	4ème	☒ Hôtel Vivienne (126)	2ème
Hôtel Amélie (131)	7ème	Practic Hôtel (139)	15ème
☒ Hôtel Beaumarchais (135)	11ème		
Hôt'l Bellevue & du Chariot d'Or (126)	3ème	**C96 AND UP (●)**	
Hôtel du Champs de Mars (131)	7ème	Hôtel Madeleine Haussmann (133)	8ème
☒ Hôtel Eiffel Rive Gauche (131)	7ème	Hôtel du Midi (138)	14ème
Hôtel de France (131)	7ème	Timhotel Le Louvre (125)	1er
Hôtel de Nice (127)	4ème		

BY NEIGHBORHOOD

ÎLE DE LA CITÉ

☒ **Hôtel Henri IV,** 25, pl. Dauphine (☎01 43 54 44 53). ⓜ Pont Neuf. Henri IV is one of Paris's best located and least expensive hotels. Named in honor of Henri IV's printing presses, which once occupied the 400-year-old building, this hotel has big windows and charming views of the tranquil pl. Dauphine. The spacious rooms have sturdy, mismatched furnishings and clean bathrooms. Breakfast included. Showers €2.50. Reserve one month in advance, earlier in the summer. Singles €29-34, €48 with shower; doubles €38-48, with shower and toilet €58; triples €72. MC/V. ●

FIRST ARRONDISSEMENT

Because the 1er is one of Paris's more heavily touristed areas, high-quality budget accommodations can be somewhat sparse. There is, however, a wide variety of mid-priced hotels and hostels whose locations can't be beat.

☒ **Hôtel Montpensier,** 12, r. de Richelieu (☎01 42 96 28 50, fax 01 42 86 02 70). ⓜ Palais-Royal. Walk around the left side of the Palais Royal to r. de Richelieu. Clean rooms, lofty ceilings, bright decor. Its good taste distinguishes it from most hotels in the area and price range. English-speaking staff. Great location. TVs in rooms with shower or bath. Breakfast €8. Shower €4. Internet €10 for 2hr.; wireless €30 for 24hr. Reserve 1 month in advance in high season. Singles and doubles with toilet €66, with toilet and shower €86, with toilet, bath, and sink €99. AmEx/MC/V. ●

☒ **Centre International de Paris (BVJ): Paris Louvre,** 20, r. Jean-Jacques Rousseau (☎01 53 00 90 90). ⓜ Louvre or Palais-Royal. From ⓜ Louvre, take r. du Louvre away from the river, turn left on r. St-Honoré and right on r. Jean-Jacques Rousseau. Large hostel that draws a very international crowd. Courtyard hung with brass lanterns and strewn with *brasserie* chairs. Bright, dorm-style rooms with 2-10 beds per room. English spoken. Breakfast and showers included. Lockers €2. Internet €1 per 10min. Reception 24hr. Weekend reservations up to 1 week in advance; reserve by phone only. Rooms held for only 5-10min. after your expected check-in time; call if you'll be late. Dorms €26, doubles €29. ●

Hôtel du Lion d'Or, 5, r. de la Sourdière (☎01 42 60 79 04; www.hotelduliondor.com). ⓜ Tuileries or Pyramides. From ⓜ Tuileries, walk down r. du 29 Juillet away from the park and turn right on r. St-Honoré, then left on r. de la Sourdière. Clean and carpeted, in a quiet area. Phone and TV in most rooms. English-speaking staff. Breakfast €6. Reserve 1 month in advance in high season. Singles with shower and toilet €65; doubles €85; triples €115. 5% discount for stays of more than 3 nights. AmEx/MC/V. ●

Hôtel St-Honoré, 85, r. St-Honoré (☎01 42 36 20 38 or 01 42 21 46 96; paris@hotel-sainthonore.com). ⓜ Louvre, Palais Royal, or Les Halles. From ⓜ Louvre, cross r. de Rivoli onto r. du Louvre and turn right on r. St-Honoré. Friendly, English-speaking staff

and 30-something clientele. Recently renovated, with breakfast area and sizable modern rooms. Refrigerator access. Breakfast €5. All rooms have shower, toilet, and TV. Internet €7 per hr. Reserve by phone or email 3 weeks ahead. Singles €59; 1-bed doubles from €74; triples and quads €92. AmEx/MC/V. ❸

Hôtel Louvre-Richelieu, 51, r. de Richelieu (☎01 42 97 46 20; www.louvre-richelieu.com). Ⓜ Palais-Royal or Pyramides. See directions for Hôtel Montpensier, above. 14 simple but large, comfortable, clean rooms. English spoken. Breakfast €6. Internet access €2 per 15min., €5 a day for wireless. Reserve 2 weeks ahead in high season. Singles €65, with shower €90; doubles €78/94; triples with shower and toilet €117. MC/V. ❸

Timhotel Le Louvre, 4, r. Croix des Petits-Champs (☎01 42 60 34 86; www.timhotel.com). Ⓜ Palais-Royal. Cross r. de Rivoli to r. St-Honoré and take a left onto r. Croix des Petits-Champs. Although more expensive, this recently renovated 2-star chain hotel has the only wheelchair-accessible rooms at reasonable prices in the 1er. Clean, modern rooms with bath, shower, and cable TV. Great location next to the Louvre. Small garden. Breakfast €10. Singles and doubles €109-190; 1 triple €190; 1 quad suite €210. AmEx/MC/V. ❺

SECOND ARRONDISSEMENT

The accommodations offered in the *2ème* are as diverse and quirky as the *arrondissement*'s attractions. Take your pick from among the many budget locations.

▨ **Hôtel Tiquetonne,** 6, r. Tiquetonne (☎01 42 36 94 58, fax 01 42 36 02 94). Ⓜ Etienne-Marcel. Walk against traffic on r. de Turbigo; turn left on r. Tiquetonne. Near Marché Montorgueil, some tasty eateries on r. Tiquetonne, the rowdy English bars near Etienne-Marcel, and r. St-Denis's sex shops—what more could you want in a location? An elevator. Breakfast €6. Hall showers €6. Closed Aug. and 1 week at Christmas. Reserve 2 weeks in advance. Singles €30, with shower €36; doubles with shower and toilet €50. AmEx/MC/V. ❶

🏨 **Hôtel Vivienne,** 40, r. Vivienne (☎01 42 33 13 26; paris@hotel-vivienne.com). Ⓜ Grands Boulevards. Follow the traffic on bd. Montmartre, pass the Théâtre des Variétés, and turn left on r. Vivienne. From the hardwood floors and square tiles in the reception area to the spacious rooms complete with *armoires,* Hôtel Vivienne adds a touch of refinement to budget digs. This place is worth the extra money; most rooms are spacious, and some have balconies. Rooms with toilet and shower on the courtyard are smaller. Breakfast €7; room service €9. Singles with shower €56, with shower/bath and toilet €83-86; doubles €71-110, 3rd person add 30%. MC/V. ❹

Hôtel des Boulevards, 10, r. de la Ville Neuve (☎01 42 36 02 29, fax 01 42 36 15 39). Ⓜ Bonne Nouvelle. Walk down bd. de Bonne Nouvelle and turn down r. de la Ville Neuve. In a funky but slightly run-down neighborhood, this hotel features quiet, simple rooms with TV, phone, wooden wardrobe, and new carpets. Higher rooms are brighter. Breakfast included. Friendly reception. Singles and doubles €40, with shower €52, with bath €57. Extra bed €10. 10% *Let's Go* discount. AmEx/MC/V. ❸

Hôtel La Marmotte, 6, r. Léopold Bellan (☎01 40 26 26 51; www.hotelmarmotte.fr). Ⓜ Sentier. From r. Petit Carreaux (the street market), turn right at r. Léopold Bellan. Reception is located in the cheerful ground-floor bar. Rooms are quiet and come with TVs, phones, and free safe-deposit boxes. Breakfast €4. Shower €3. Reserve at least 2 weeks in advance. Singles and 1-bed doubles €32-36, with shower €49-56; 2-bed doubles €61. Extra bed €12. ❷

THIRD ARRONDISSEMENT

This part of the Marais offers several quality accommodations, many of which are also friendly on the wallet.

🏨 **Hôtel du Séjour,** 36, r. du Grenier St-Lazare (☎01 48 87 40 36). From Ⓜ Etienne-Marcel, follow traffic on r. Etienne-Marcel, which becomes r. du Grenier St-Lazare. 1 block from Les Halles and the Centre Pompidou, this family-run hotel offers 20 clean, bright rooms and a warm welcome. Showers €4. Reception 7:30am-10:30pm. Reserve 2-3 weeks in advance. Singles €35; doubles €47, with shower and toilet €58; third person €22. ❷

Hôtel de Roubaix, 6, r. Greneta (☎01 42 72 89 91). From Ⓜ Réaumur-Sébastopol, walk opposite traffic on bd. de Sébastopol; turn left on r. Greneta. Helpful staff, clean rooms with flowered wallpaper, soundproof windows, and pristine, lovely new baths. All rooms have shower, toilet, phone, locker, and satellite TV. Some with balconies. Breakfast included. Reserve 1-2 weeks ahead. Singles €57-63; doubles €65-73; triples €78-88; quads €94; quints €100. MC/V. ❸

Hôtel Bellevue et du Chariot d'Or, 39, r. de Turbigo (☎01 48 87 45 60; chariot-dor@wanadoo.fr). Ⓜ Etienne-Marcel. A handsomely and generously furnished Belle Epoque lobby with bar and breakfast room. Clean, basic rooms with phone, TV, and spacious full bathrooms. Some rooms with balcony. Quiet courtyard. Breakfast €5.25. Reserve 3 weeks in advance. Singles €60; doubles €68; triples €78-90; quads €95. 5% discount for *Let's Go* users. AmEx/MC/V. ❹

Hôtel Picard, 26, r. de Picardie (☎01 48 87 53 82; fax 01 48 57 62 56). Ⓜ République. Follow bd. du Temple and turn right on r. Charlot. Take the first right on r. de Franche Comte, which becomes r. de Picardie. Superb location; helpful staff and a well-behaved parrot named Johnny. TVs in rooms with showers. Breakfast €4.50. Hall showers €3. Reserve 1 week ahead during summer and 2 weeks ahead the rest of the year. Singles €37, with shower €56, with shower and toilet €64; doubles €47/72/94; triples €94-114. 5% discount if you flash your *Let's Go.* MC/V. ❷

Hôtel du Marais, 16, r. de Beauce (☎01 42 72 30 26; hotelmarais@voila.fr). ⓜ Temple or Filles du Calvaire. From ⓜ Temple, follow r. du Temple south; take a left on r. de Bretagne and a right on r. de Beauce. Dirt cheap without the dirt. This small hotel offers very simple but adequate rooms in a great location near an open-air market. Ideal for students and backpackers. Take the small stairs above the cafe owned by the same friendly man. 3rd fl. showers €3. Curfew 2am. Singles with sink €25; doubles €35-38. Cash only. ❶

Hôtel Paris France, 72, r. de Turbigo (☎01 42 78 00 04; resa@paris-france-hotel.com). ⓜ République or Temple. From ⓜ République, take r. de Turbigo. Clean, bright, and welcoming, this hotel has a lovely cafe-style breakfast room and an 18th-century-style lobby with leather sofas, mosaic-tiled floors, chandeliers, and a big TV. All rooms have TV, phone, hair dryer, shower, and locker. Breakfast €6. Reserve 2-4 weeks in advance. Singles €62-72; doubles €76-109; triples with bath €109-146; extra bed €25. AmEx/MC/V. ❸

FOURTH ARRONDISSEMENT

The trendy-yet-down-to-earth 4*ème* is home to some of the best deals and most worth-it accommodation splurges in the city. Take your pick from among numerous hotels, hostels, and foyers in the area.

▨ **Hôtel des Jeunes** (MIJE; ☎01 42 74 23 45; www.mije.com). Books beds in Le Fourcy, Le Fauconnier, and Maubuisson (see below), 3 small hostels on cobblestone streets in beautiful old Marais residences recognized as historical 17th-century monuments. No smoking. English spoken. The restaurant (at Le Fourcy) offers a main course with drink (€8.50, lunch only) and 3-course "hosteler special" (€10.50). Breakfast, in-room shower, and sheets (no towels) included. Internet €0.10 per min. with €0.50 initial connection fee. Public phones and free lockers (with a €1 deposit). Under 18 need signed parental consent. 7-day max. stay. Reception 7am-1am. Lockout noon-3pm. Curfew 1am; notify in advance if coming back after this time. Quiet after 10pm. Arrive before noon the first day of reservation (call in advance if you'll be late). Groups of 10 or more may reserve a year in advance. Individuals can reserve months ahead online and 2-3 weeks ahead by phone. MIJE membership required (€2.50). 4- to 9- bed dorms €28; singles €43; doubles €33; triples €29; quads €27. Cash only. ❶

Le Fourcy, 6, r. de Fourcy. ⓜ St-Paul or Pont Marie. From ⓜ St-Paul, walk opposite the traffic for a few meters down r. St-Antoine and turn left on r. de Fourcy. Hostel surrounds a large courtyard ideal for meeting travelers or for open-air picnicking. Light sleepers should avoid rooms on the social courtyard.

Le Fauconnier, 11, r. du Fauconnier. ⓜ St-Paul or Pont Marie. From ⓜ St-Paul, take r. du Prevôt, turn left on r. Charlemagne, and turn right on r. du Fauconnier. Ivy-covered, sun-drenched building steps away from the Seine and Île St-Louis.

Maubuisson, 12, r. des Barres. ⓜ Hôtel de Ville or Pont Marie. From ⓜ Pont Marie, walk opposite traffic on r. de l'Hôtel-de-Ville and turn right on r. des Barres. A half-timbered former girls' convent on a silent street by the St. Gervais monastery. Accommodates more individual travelers rather than groups, so it has a quieter atmosphere.

▨ **Grand Hôtel Jeanne d'Arc,** 3, r. de Jarente (☎01 48 87 62 11; www.hoteljeanne-darc.com). From ⓜ St-Paul, walk against traffic on r. de Rivoli and turn left on r. de Sévigné, then right on r. de Jarente. This bright, clean hotel on a quiet side street features a pleasant lounge and breakfast area. Pleasant, cozy rooms with shower, toilet, and TV. 1 wheelchair-accessible room on the ground floor. English spoken. Breakfast €6. Reserve 2-3 months in advance (longer if for stays in Sept.-Oct.) by emailing or calling with credit card. Singles €60-84; doubles €84-97; triples €116; quads €146. MC/V. ❹

Hôtel de Nice, 42bis, r. de Rivoli (☎01 42 78 55 29; www.hoteldenice.com). ⓜ Hôtel de Ville. Walk opposite traffic on r. de Rivoli for about 4 blocks; the hotel is on the left. Extravagantly wallpapered and painted rooms featuring vintage prints, TV, toilet, shower, hair dryer and phone. A few have balconies with great views. Hot in the summer (fans provided). Breakfast €7. Reserve as far ahead as possible (2-4 weeks) by fax or phone with credit card. Singles €75; doubles €105; triples €130; quads €145. Extra bed €25. MC/V. ❹

Hôtel Andréa Rivoli, 3, r. St-Bon (☎01 42 78 43 93; fax 01 44 61 28 36). ⓜ Hôtel de Ville. Follow traffic down r. de Rivoli and then turn right on r. St-Bon. This hotel is on a quiet street 2 blocks from Châtelet. Clean rooms come with comfortable mattresses, plus phone, toilet, shower, TV, and A/C. Top floor rooms have balconies. Breakfast €7. Internet available, €5 for 45min. Reserve at least 1 month in advance with a credit card. Singles €62-110; doubles €78-110; triples €100-130. MC/V. ❸

Hôtel Pratic, 9, r. d'Ormesson (☎01 48 87 80 47; www.hotelpratic.com). ⓜ St-Paul. Walk opposite traffic on r. de Rivoli, turn left on r. de Sévigné and right on r. d'Ormesson. A clean hotel on a leafy cobblestone square in the heart of the Marais; plenty of restaurants nearby. Rooms are modest but bright, and all have TVs, direct-dial phones, and hair dryers. English spoken. Breakfast included for long stays, €6 for stays less than 5 days. Reserve online or by phone 2-3 weeks in advance. Book online for a discount. Doubles €89-129; triples €98-149. MC/V. ❸

Hôtel de la Herse d'Or, 20, r. St-Antoine (☎01 48 87 84 09; fax 01 48 87 94 01). ⓜ Bastille. Take r. St-Antoine from the metro; the hotel will be about a block down on the right. The rooms are small but clean and pleasant. All rooms with TV. Breakfast €5. Internet in lobby. Singles with toilet €40, with full bath €62; doubles with toilet €55, with full bath €68. Extra bed €21. MC/V. ❶

Hôtel Rivoli, 44, r. de Rivoli/2, r. des Mauvais Garçons (☎01 42 72 08 41). ⓜ Hôtel de Ville. Walk against traffic on r. de Rivoli. Small with basic rooms, but extremely well situated. Breakfast €4. Lockout 2-7am. Reserve 2-4 weeks in advance. Singles €30, with shower €42; doubles €40, with shower €47, with bath and toilet €50; triples €60. Extra bed €10. ❷

Castex Hôtel, 5, r. Castex (☎01 42 72 31 52; www.castexhotel.com). ⓜ Bastille or Sully-Morland. Exit ⓜ Bastille on bd. Henri IV and take the 3rd right on r. Castex. This comfortable hotel boasts A/C, cable TV, and full bath in 30 sizable rooms. Fabulous complimentary toiletries. Attractively decorated in "Louis XIII style." Breakfast €10. Reserve by sending a fax, calling, or reserving online with a credit card 2-4 weeks in advance. Singles €95-115; doubles €120-140; triples and quads €190-220. Discounts available for online reservation; see website for details. AmEx/MC/V. ❹

FIFTH ARRONDISSEMENT

To stay in the 5ème, **reserve well in advance**—from one week in the winter to two months in the summer. If foresight eludes you, don't despair: you may find same-day vacancies at even the most popular hotels. In the fall, the return of students means more competition for *foyers.*

🏨 **Hôtel St-Jacques,** 35, r. des Ecoles (☎01 44 07 45 45; www.paris-hotel-stjacques.com). ⓜ Maubert-Mutualité. Turn left on r. des Carmes, then left on r. des Ecoles and cross the road. Jim Morrison may have bummed around Hôtel de Médicis, but Cary Grant filmed *Charade* here—a telling difference. Spacious, faux-elegant rooms at reasonable rates, with balcony, renovated bath, and TV. Chandeliers and walls decorated with *trompe-l'oeil* designs give it a regal feel. English spoken. Breakfast €8.50-10. Internet. Singles €55-84; doubles €95-124; triples €152. AmEx/MC/V. ❸

🏨 **Hôtel Marignan,** 13, r. du Sommerard (☎01 43 54 63 81; www.hotel-marignan.com). From ⓜ Maubert-Mutualité, turn left on r. des Carmes, then right on r. du Sommerard. Clean, freshly decorated, amenable rooms that can sleep up to 5—almost an impossibility in the rest of Paris. Over half of the hotel is set up to sleep 3-4 people, in various combinations of double and twin beds. English-speaking owner welcomes backpackers and families to a place with the privacy of a hotel and the friendliness of a hostel. TV (upon request). Breakfast included. Hall showers open until 10:45pm. Free laundry and kitchen access. Internet. Reserve in advance. Singles €49-60; doubles €65, with shower and toilet €90; triples €90/110; quads €105/130; quints €120/150. Discount from Aug.-Mar. AmEx/MC/V. €400 credit card min. ❷

Young and Happy (Y&H) Hostel, 80, r. Mouffetard (☎01 47 07 47 07; www.youngandhappy.fr). ⓜ Monge. Cross r. Gracieuse and take r. Ortolan to r. Mouffetard. A funky, lively hostel located on r. Mouffetard. The laid-back staff and clean rooms make this a perfect place for college-age and 20-something adventurers to crash for a few weeks. 21 rooms, a few with showers and toilets. English spoken. Breakfast included. Kitchen. Sheets €2.50, towels €1. Laundry nearby. Internet €2 per 30min. Lockout 11am-4pm. Curfew 2am. Dorms €23; doubles €26 per person. Jan.-Mar. €2 discount per night. ❶

Hôtel Esmeralda, 4, r. St-Julien-le-Pauvre (☎01 43 54 19 20; fax 01 40 51 00 68). ⓜ St-Michel. Walk along the Seine on quai St-Michel toward Notre Dame, then turn right at Parc Viviani. Rooms here are clean and tend to have an ancient, professional feel about them. Antique wallpapers, ceiling beams, and red velvet. Great location near a small park, within sight of the Seine and earshot of Notre Dame's bells. Breakfast €6. Singles €35, with shower and toilet €65; doubles €85-95; triples €110; quads €120. ❷

Hôtel des Argonauts, 12, r. de la Huchette (☎01 43 54 09 82; fax 01 44 07 18 84). ⓜ St-Michel. With your back to the Seine, take the first left off bd. St-Michel onto r. de la Huchette. Above a Greek restaurant of the same name. Ideally located in a bustling, antique pedestrian quarter (a stone's throw from the Seine), this hotel's clean rooms flaunt a cheerful Mediterranean motif. Leopard-print chairs in the lobby bar, photographs of idyllic Greek islands, and mirrors on every floor. Breakfast €4. Reserve 3-4 weeks in advance in high season. Singles with shower €50; doubles with bath or shower and toilet €70-80. AmEx/MC/V. ❷

Hôtel Gay-Lussac, 29, r. Gay-Lussac (☎01 43 54 23 96; fax 01 40 51 79 49). ⓜ Luxembourg. Friendly owner and clean, stately old rooms, some with fireplace. It can get a bit noisy from neighborhood traffic, but the peaceful shade of the Luxembourg gardens is just a few blocks away. Breakfast included. Reserve at least 2 weeks in advance. Winter discounts. Singles €65; doubles €75; triples €95; quads €110, all with shower and toilet. ❷

Centre International de Paris (BVJ): Paris Quartier Latin, 44, r. des Bernardins (☎01 43 29 34 80; fax 01 53 00 90 91). ⓜ Maubert-Mutualité. Walk with traffic on bd. St-Germain and turn right on r. des Bernardins. A boisterous, generic, and only slightly dingy hostel with a large cafeteria. 100 beds. English spoken. Breakfast included. Showers in rooms. Lockers €2. Microwave, TV, and message service. Internet €1 per 10min. Reception 24hr. Reserve at least 1 week in advance or arrive at 9am to check for availability. 10-person dorms €27; singles €40; doubles and quads €29 per person. ❷

Foyer International des Etudiantes, 93, bd. St-Michel (☎01 43 54 49 63). RER: Luxembourg. Across from the Jardin du Luxembourg. Rooms are elegant (if faintly musty smelling), with wood paneling and furnishings. Some rooms have balconies. Breakfast included in summer. Kitchenettes, showers, and toilets on hallways. Marbled reception area, library, laundry facilities, and TV lounge. 2-night min. July-Sept. foyer is coed and open 24hr. Oct.-June foyer is women only, and rooms are available for rent by the month (inquire at desk for prices). Reserve in writing as early as Jan. for summer months; €35 deposit. Singles €30; 2-bed dorms €22 per person; doubles €16. ❶

Hôtel des Médicis, 214, r. St-Jacques (☎01 43 54 14 66). RER Luxembourg. Turn right on r. Gay-Lussac and left on r. St-Jacques. Old place that shuns right-angle geometry; perhaps that's why Jim Morrison slummed here (room #4) for 3 weeks in 1971. You get what you pay for here, and this could be the least expensive place in the *arrondissement*. English spoken. 1 shower and toilet per floor. Reception 9am-11pm. Singles €16, larger singles €20; doubles €31-35; triples €45-50, some rooms with balcony. ❶

Hôtel le Central, 6, r. Descartes (☎01 46 33 57 93). ⓜ Maubert-Mutualité. Walk up r. de la Montagne Ste-Geneviève. Great location near r. Mouffetard and the Panthéon.

Carpeted but uneven stairs (watch out!) lead to well-priced, unpretentious rooms. Views of the Right Bank. All rooms have shower. Rooms €36-49. Cash and checks only. ❷

SIXTH ARRONDISSEMENT

The 6ème is a frugal traveler's dream, offering some of the most elegant budget accommodations in the city.

■ **Hôtel de Nesle,** 7, r. du Nesle (☎01 43 54 62 41; www.hoteldenesleparis.com). Ⓜ Odéon. Walk up r. de l'Ancienne Comédie, take a right onto r. Dauphine and then take a left on r. du Nesle. Fantastic, friendly, and absolutely sparkling, the Nesle (pronounced "Nell") stands out in a sea of nondescript budget hotels. Every room is unique, representing a particular time period or locale. There is, for instance, a Molière room and an African room. The lobby's ceiling is made of bouquets of dried flowers. Garden with terrace and duck pond. Laundry room. Reserve by telephone; confirm 2 days in advance with arrival time. Singles €55-65; doubles €75-100, extra bed €15. AmEx/MC/V. ❸

■ **Hôtel St-André des Arts,** 66, r. St-André-des-Arts (☎01 43 26 96 16; hsaintand@wanadoo.fr). Ⓜ Odéon. Take r. de l'Ancienne Comédie, then turn right on r. St-André-des-Arts. Stone walls, high ceilings, and exposed beams give this hotel a country inn feeling, though it's in the heart of St-Germain. Free breakfast, new bathrooms (all have showers or baths, sinks, and toilets), and friendly owner. Reservations recommended. Singles €66; doubles €85-90; triples €108; quads €119. MC/V. ❸

■ **Hôtel Stella,** 41, r. Monsieur-le-Prince (☎01 40 51 00 25; http://site.voila.fr/hotel-stella). Ⓜ Odéon. Walk against traffic on bd. St-Germain and make a left onto r. Monsieur-le-Prince. Takes the exposed-beam look to a whole new level, with centuries-old woodwork. Gigantic triples have pianos. Reserve in advance. Singles €30, with shower/bath €35, with shower/bath and WC €45; doubles €35/40/55; triples €75; quads €85. Closed Aug. ❷

Hôtel du Lys, 23, r. Serpente (☎01 43 26 97 57; www.hoteldulys.com). Ⓜ Odéon or St-Michel. From Odéon, turn left onto r. Danton and then right onto r. Serpente. This splurge is well worth it. Floral wall-prints, rustic beams, and antique porcelain tiles give this spotless hotel a sublime country feel. All rooms have bath or shower, TV, phone, and hair dryer. Breakfast and tax included. Reserve 1 month in advance in summer. Singles €95; doubles €110-115; triples €130. MC/V. ❹

Delhy's Hôtel, 22, r. de l'Hirondelle (☎01 43 26 58 25; delhys@wanadoo.fr). Ⓜ St-Michel. Just steps from pl. St-Michel and the Seine on a cobblestone way. Wood paneling, flower boxes, modern facilities, and quiet location. TV with satellite dish and phone in rooms. Breakfast included. Hall showers €4. Toilets in the hallways. Each night must be paid in advance. Reserve 10 days ahead. Singles €52, with shower €73; doubles €64/79; triples €116, extra bed €15. MC/V. ❸

Hôtel de Chevreuse, 3, r. de Chevreuse (☎01 43 20 93 16; fax 01 43 21 43 72). Ⓜ Vavin. Walk up bd. du Montparnasse away from the Tour and turn left on r. de Chevreuse. Small, clean, quiet rooms with TV and Ikea-style furniture. Breakfast €6. Reserve 2 weeks in advance. Singles €43, with shower and toilet €68, with bath €73; triples with shower, TV, and toilet €93. MC/V. ❸

TIP **PAY FOR WHAT YOU GET...** You should be aware that the city of Paris has a **Taxe de Séjour** of approximately €1.50 flat-rate per person per night: this does not have to be included in advertised or quoted prices, but must be listed along with the room price on the price list posted on the back of the hotel room door. It is advisable to check for other add-on expenses such as **direct telephone service** (some hotels will even charge you for collect calls) before making your reservation. Also, **always insist on seeing a room** before you settle in, even if the proprietor is not amenable to the request.

SEVENTH ARRONDISSEMENT

The elegant environs and convenient location of the 7ème means there are few budget accommodations to be found in the area. However, it abounds with charming little hotels that often have English-speaking staff, and it's one of the safest areas in Paris.

🏨 **Hôtel Eiffel Rive Gauche,** 6, r. du Gros Caillou (☎01 45 51 24 56; www.hotel-eiffel.com). Ⓜ Ecole Militaire. Walk up av. de la Bourdonnais, turn right onto r. de Grenelle, then left onto r. du Gros Caillou. Located on a quiet street, this family-run hotel is a favorite of Anglophone travelers. Hôtel Eiffel's bright courtyard is a cozy yellow, and it's as welcoming as the cheeful staff. Rooms have cable TV, phone, Internet jack, and full bath; some have Eiffel Tower views. Breakfast buffet €9. Safe deposit box €3. On average, singles €75; doubles and twins €85; triples €105; quads €125. Extra bed €10. MC/V. ❹

🏨 **Hôtel Montebello,** 18, r. Pierre Leroux (☎01 47 34 41 18; hmontebello@aol.com). Ⓜ Vaneau. A bit far from the sights of the 7ème, but unbeatable rates for this upscale neighborhood. Clean, cheery rooms. Breakfast served 7:30-9:30am, €4. Reserve at least 2 weeks in advance. Singles €35-42; doubles €40-49. Extra bed € 10. ❷

Hôtel de France, 102, bd. de la Tour Maubourg (☎01 47 05 40 49; www.hoteldefrance.com). Ⓜ Ecole Militaire. Directly across from the Hôtel des Invalides. Sparkling clean rooms and amazing views of the gold-domed Invalides, particularly from 5th fl. balconies. Staff gives advice on Paris in English, Spanish, German, and Italian. 2 wheelchair-accessible rooms (€95). Buffet breakfast €9. Rooms with phone, cable TV, minibar, hair dryer, Internet jacks, and full bath. Reserve 1 month in advance. Singles €78; doubles €95; twins €98; triples €110; connecting rooms for families available from €151. AmEx/MC/V. ❹

Hôtel du Champs de Mars, 7, r. du Champ de Mars (☎01 45 51 52 30; www.hotel-du-champs-de-mars.com). Ⓜ Ecole Militaire. Cottage chic rooms, each named after a particular flower and decorated accordingly, have phone and satellite TV. Continental breakfast €7. Reserve 1 month ahead by fax or email and confirm with credit card and expiration date. Singles with shower €78; doubles with bath €84; twins with bath €88; triples with bath €105. MC/V. ❹

Grand Hôtel Lévêque, 29, r. Cler (☎01 47 05 49 15; www.hotel-leveque.com). Ⓜ Ecole Militaire. Take av. de la Motte-Picquet to cobbled and colorful r. Cler. Clean and modern. Luggage storage. English spoken. Buffet breakfast in bistro-style dining room €8. Showers for singles on the 5th fl. Satellite TV, safe deposit box (€5), telephone, A/C, and ceiling fan in all rooms. Reserve at least 2 months ahead, and longer for Sept.-Oct. Singles €57; doubles with shower and toilet €87-93; twins with shower and toilet €87-110; triples with shower and toilet €125. AmEx/MC/V. ❸

Hôtel de Turenne, 20, av. de Tourville (☎01 47 05 99 92; hotel.turenne.paris7@wanadoo.fr). Ⓜ Ecole Militaire. 34 rooms with A/C, full bath, and satellite TV. Spotless bathrooms and convenient location. Breakfast €7.50. Reserve 1-2 months ahead for Sept.-Oct., 2 weeks otherwise. Singles €64; doubles €74-82; triples €104. Extra bed €9.50. AmEx/MC/V. ❸

Hôtel Amélie, 5, r. Amélie (☎01 45 51 74 75; www.123france.com). Ⓜ La Tour-Maubourg. Walk in the direction of traffic on bd. de la Tour Maubourg, make a left onto r. de Grenelle, then a right onto r. Amélie. On a picturesque back street, Amélie is tiny but charmingly decorated, with a friendly owner and staff. Mini-bar, TV, and full bath in all rooms. Breakfast €8. Prices depend on season. Reserve 1 month ahead Apr. to mid-Jul., 1 week otherwise. Singles €65-90; doubles with shower €75-100, with bath €80-110; triples €90-120. AmEx/MC/V. ❹

EIGHTH ARRONDISSEMENT

As with everything in the posh 8ème, accommodations tend to be pricey but generally worth it. For those not looking to break the bank, a few quality hostels present a more accessible option.

▨ **Hôtel Europe-Liège,** 8, r. de Moscou (☎01 42 94 01 51, fax 01 43 87 42 18). ⓜ Liège. Turn left onto r. de Moscou and the hotel is on your right. Cheerful, quiet, and reasonably priced (for the 8ème). Sparkling clean rooms and a lovely interior courtyard. Many restaurants nearby. All rooms have TV, hair dryer, phone, and shower or bath. Breakfast €7. Suggested reservations 3-4 weeks in advance, especially July-Aug. Singles €68; doubles €84. AmEx/MC/V. ❸

▨ **Foyer de Chaillot,** 28, av. George V (☎01 47 23 35 32; www.ufjt.org). ⓜ George V. Turn right onto av. George V and walk about 3 blocks until you reach a high-rise silver office building called Eurosite George V. Take the elevator to the foyer on the 3rd fl. Well-equipped rooms in an upscale dorm-like environment; **for women only.** Dinner included M-F. Full kitchen. Singles each have a sink, while doubles have shower and sink. Toilets and additional showers in each hall. Large common rooms equipped with stereo and TV. Full *salle informatique* with Internet. Residents must be working or holding an internship and be between the ages of 18-25; 3-month min. stay, 1-year max. stay. Guests permitted until 9pm. Bulletin boards advertise apartments for rent, theater outings, and other activities. €350 deposit required to reserve a room; request an application by contacting hebergement.chaillot@wanadoo.fr. Reserve 1-2 months ahead, especially for Sept.-Nov. €40 application/booking fee. Doubles €530 per month per person; singles available for €600 per month. ❶

Hôtel Madeleine Haussmann, 10, r. Pasquier (☎01 42 65 90 11; www.hotels-emeraude.com). ⓜ Madeleine. Walk up bd. Malesherbes and turn right on r. Pasquier. Among the luxury hotels in the poshest part of town, Hôtel Madeleine Haussmann is the best value. Comfortable and professional, with a bathroom, hair dryer, TV, safe deposit box, and minibar in every room. 1 small room on the ground floor is wheelchair accessible. Breakfast €12. Reserve 2 weeks in advance, 1-2 months in advance during high season (Sept.-Nov.). Singles from €140; doubles from €160. Discounts of 15-25% available with advance reservation outside of high season, making this splurge a little more reasonable. AmEx/MC/V. ❺

Union Chrétienne de Jeunes Filles (UCJF/YWCA), 22, r. de Naples (☎01 53 04 37 47; fax 01 53 04 37 54). ⓜ Europe. Take r. de Constantinople and turn left onto r. de Naples. Second location at 168, r. Blomet, 15ème (☎01 56 56 63 00; fax 01 56 56 63 12). ⓜ Convention. For **women only;** men should contact the YMCA Foyer **Union Chrétienne de Jeunes Gens,** 14, r. de Trévise, 9ème (☎01 47 70 90 94; fax 01 44 79 09 29). The UCJF has spacious and quiet (if a bit worn) rooms with hardwood floors, sinks, and desks. Large oak-paneled common room with fireplace, TV, VCR, books, theater space, and family-style dining room. Kitchen, laundry. Free Internet in the lobby. 1-month min. stay; 1-year max. stay. Reception M-F 8am-12:25am, Sa 8:30am-12:25pm, Su 9am-12:25pm and 1:30pm-12:30am. Guests permitted until 10pm; men not allowed in bedrooms. No curfew, but ask for key ahead of time. 1 month rent deposit required, which includes processing and membership fees. Singles, doubles and dorm rooms €372-488 per month. ❶

NINTH ARRONDISSEMENT

Unless you reserve one of the more popular hotels along the southern border, staying in the 9ème will provide for a relatively quiet stay.

▨ **Hôtel Chopin,** 10, bd. Montmartre or 46, passage Jouffroy (☎01 47 70 58 10, fax 01 42 47 00 70). ⓜ Grands Boulevards. Walk west on bd. Montmartre and make a right into passage Jouffroy. At the end of a spectacular old passage lined with shops. Rooms are new, very clean, and tastefully decorated. Some rooms have views of the Musée Grévin's wax studio (see **Museums,** p. 245). Breakfast €7. TVs, phones, and fans by request. Book 2-3 months in advance. Singles with toilet €59, with shower or bath €66-74; doubles with shower or bath €77-88; triples €103. AmEx/MC/V. ❸

▨ **Perfect Hôtel,** 39, r. Rodier (☎01 42 81 18 86 or 01 42 81 26 19; www.paris-hostel.biz). ⓜ Anvers. Across from the Woodstock Hostel. This hotel lives up to its name with hotel-quality rooms at hostel prices. Some have balconies, and the upper floors have a beautiful view. Fun atmosphere. English-speaking staff. Breakfast free for *Let's Go* users. Phones, communal refrigerator and kitchen access, free coffee, beer vending machine (€1.50). Book a month or so in advance. Singles €38, with toilet €58; doubles €50/58. MC/V. ❷

■ **Woodstock Hostel,** 48, r. Rodier (☎01 48 78 87 76; www.woodstock.fr). Ⓜ Anvers. From the metro, walk against traffic on pl. Anvers, turn right on av. Trudaine and left on r. Rodier. With ubiquitous incense, reggae music, tie-dyed paraphernalia, and a Beatles-decorated VW Bug hanging from the ceiling. The nicest rooms are off the courtyard. International staff; English spoken. Breakfast included. Showers on every floor are free. Sheets €2.50; towels €1, each with deposit. Communal kitchen, safe deposit box, Internet access (€2 for 30min.), and fax. 1-week max stay. Lockout 11am-3pm. Curfew 2am. Call ahead to reserve a room. 4- or 6-person dorms €21; doubles €24. For cheapest deals, book online at www.hostelbookers.com. ❶

Modial Hôtel Européen, 21, r. Notre Dame de Lorette (☎01 48 78 60 47; www.hotelmodial.fr). Ⓜ St-Georges. Safely removed from the grimy debauchery of Pigalle, this charming hotel has spotless and comfortable rooms. All come with direct telephone line, color TV, and either bath and toilet or shower and toilet. Reservations recommended 2 weeks in advance. Singles €73.50; doubles €81.50; twins €96; triples €115. MC/V. ❸

TENTH ARRONDISSEMENT

The 10ème is great for budget accommodations. There is a glut of cheap hotels around the Gares du Nord and de l'Est. If the ones listed below are full, there is probably an adequate one nearby.

■ **Cambrai Hôtel,** 129bis, bd. Magenta (☎01 48 78 32 13; www.hotel-cambrai.com). Ⓜ Gare du Nord. Follow traffic on r. de Dunkerque to pl. de Roubaix and turn right on bd. de Magenta. A family-owned hotel close to the Gare du Nord. Bright, 50s-style rooms with high ceilings and TVs. Breakfast €5.50. All rooms come with shower. Singles €46, with toilet €48, with bath €54; doubles €50/54/60; twin with toilet €60, with full bath €75; triples €80/90. Quads €120. Extra bed €10. AmEx/MC/V. ❷

Hôtel Palace, 9, r. Bouchardon (☎01 40 40 09 45). Ⓜ Strasbourg-St-Denis. Walk against traffic on bd. St-Denis until the small arch; follow r. René Boulanger on the left, then turn left on r. Bouchardon. A clean, centrally located (for the 10ème) hotel with the rates of a hostel. Breakfast €3.50. Shower €3.50. Laundromat next door and supermarket across the street. Reserve 2 weeks ahead. Singles €19-25, with shower €33; doubles €25-28/38; triples €51; quads €61-71. AmEx/MC/V. ❶

Paris Nord Hôtel, 4, r. de Dunkerque (☎01 40 35 81 70; fax 01 40 35 09 30). Ⓜ Gare du Nord. Facing the Gare du Nord, take r. Dunkerque to the right. Conveniently located between the 2 train stations. Clean rooms with hardwood floors and walls. Be sure not to confuse it with the nearby Nord Hotel, which is significantly more expensive. All rooms have double beds and full bathrooms. Breakfast €5. Reserve 1 week in advance. €60 for 1 person, €65 for 2 people. AmEx/MC/V. ❸

Hôtel de Milan, 17, r. de St-Quentin (☎01 40 37 88 50; fax 01 46 07 89 48). Ⓜ Gare du Nord. Follow r. de St-Quentin from outside Gare du Nord; the hotel is on the right-hand corner of the 3rd block. This hotel's location is very well-suited for access to the nearby *gares*, and the concierge is extremely friendly. Breakfast €5. Hall showers €4. Singles €27-30; doubles €34-41, with shower or bath €47-53. with twin beds and full bath €59; triples with full bath €69. MC/V. ❷

Hôtel Montana La Fayette, 164, r. la Fayette (☎01 40 35 80 80; fax 01 40 35 08 73). Ⓜ Gare du Nord. Conveniently close to the Gare du Nord, yet still quiet. Some cracks in the walls, but clean rooms with generous bathrooms, all with shower, toilet, and TV. Breakfast €5. Internet €2 per hr. Singles €46; doubles €68; triples €80. AmEx/MC/V. ❷

ELEVENTH ARRONDISSEMENT

The 11ème houses a wide range of accommodations, with ample options for budget travelers and big spenders alike.

■ **Modern Hôtel,** 121, r. de Chemin-Vert (☎01 47 00 54 05; www.modern-hotel.fr). ⓜ Père Lachaise. A few blocks from the metro on r. de Chemin-Vert, on the right. Modern furnishings, pastel color scheme, and spotless marble bathrooms. 6 floors of rooms but no elevator. Breakfast free. All rooms have a hair dryer, modem connection, and safe-deposit box. Reserve 2-4 weeks ahead. Singles €51-77; doubles €61-85; triples €91. Extra bed €15. AmEx/DC/MC/V. ❸

■ **Hôtel Beaumarchais,** 3, r. Oberkampf (☎01 53 36 86 86; www.hotelbeaumarchais.com). ⓜ Oberkampf. Exit on r. de Malte and turn right on r. Oberkampf. This spacious hotel is worth the extra money. Elegantly decorated with colorful, modern furniture, clean baths, and cable TVs. Each room is decorated in the style of a different artist, like Kandinsky or Gaudi. Suites include TV room with desk and breakfast table. A/C. Buffet breakfast €10. Reserve 2 weeks in advance. Singles €75-90; doubles €110; suites €150. Baby beds €16. No adult-sized extra beds. AmEx/MC/V. ❹

Plessis Hôtel, 25, r. du Grand Prieuré (☎01 47 00 13 38). ⓜ Oberkampf. Walk north on r. du Grand Prieuré. 6 floors of clean, bright rooms. Windows on the higher floors look out over the rooftops of Paris. Rooms with shower have hair dryer, fan, TV, and balcony. Breakfast €6.50. Lounge with TV, vending machines, and free Internet. Open Sept.-July. Singles or doubles with sink, €49; singles or doubles with shower €74, with bath €76. AmEx/MC/V. ❷

Hôtel Rhetia, 3, r. du Général Blaise (☎01 47 00 47 18; fax 01 48 06 01 73). ⓜ Voltaire or St-Ambroise. From the Voltaire metro, take av. Parmentier and turn right on r. Rochebrune, then left on r. du Général Blaise. In a calm, out-of-the-way neighborhood. Moderately clean, with simple furnishings and narrow single beds. Small public garden across the street. TV in all rooms. Breakfast €3. Reception 7:30am-9:30pm. Reserve at least 15 days in advance. Singles with shower €35, with shower and toilet €40; doubles €37/45; twins €46; triples €55. ❷

Hôtel Notre-Dame, 51, r. de Malte (☎01 47 00 78 76; www.hotel-notredame.com). ⓜ République. Walk down av. de la République and go right on r. de Malte. Nowhere near Notre Dame. Rooms are basic but upbeat; those facing the street have big windows. Breakfast €6.50. Showers €3.50. Reserve 10 days ahead. Requires credit card and email or fax to hold reservation. Singles with sink €39, with shower, €46.50, with shower and TV €56.50, with bath and TV €60; doubles with shower and TV €61.50, with bath and TV €69; twins €74.50; triples €83.50-88.50. MC/V. ❷

Hôtel de Belfort, 37, r. Servan (☎01 47 00 67 33; fax 01 43 57 97 98). ⓜ Père-Lachaise, St-Maur, or Voltaire. From ⓜ Père-Lachaise, take r. de Chemin-Vert and turn left on r. Servan. 15min. from Bastille. Dim corridors and clean, functional rooms. English spoken. Draws a young crowd; popular with schools and tour groups, but the layout prevents noise from resonating throughout. All rooms with shower, toilet, TV, and phone. Breakfast €6. Reserve 1 week in advance, 1 month in advance Mar.-June and Sept.-Oct. Singles €55; doubles €65; twins €75; triples €90. MC/V. ❸

Auberge de Jeunesse "Jules Ferry" (HI), 8, bd. Jules Ferry (☎01 43 57 55 60; auberge@micronet.fr). ⓜ République. Walk east on r. du Faubourg du Temple and turn right on the far side of bd. Jules Ferry. Wonderful location in front of a park and next to pl. de la République. 100 beds. Modern, clean rooms with sinks, mirrors, and tiled floors. Doubles with big beds. Party atmosphere. Breakfast and showers included. Sheets free. Laundry €3 wash, €2 dry. Lockers €2. Internet in lobby €1 for 10min. 1-week max. stay. Reception and dining room 24hr. Lockout 10:30am-2pm. No reservations; arrive between 8am and 11am to ensure a room. If there are no vacancies, the staff will try to book you in one of the other nearby hostels. 4- to 6-bed dorms and doubles €20.50 per person. MC/V. ❶

TWELFTH ARRONDISSEMENT

The 12*ème* offers relatively inexpensive and simple accommodations, with a good smattering of budget hotels around the Gare de Lyon. As usual, be sure to book considerably in advance in September and October.

▨ Hôtel Printania, 91, av. du Dr. A. Netter (☎01 43 07 65 13; fax 01 43 43 56 84). Ⓜ Porte de Vincennes. Walk west on the cours de Vincennes and turn left on av. du Dr. A. Netter. 25 rooms with mini-fridge, large soundproof windows, and faux-marble floors. Breakfast €4.50. Reserve 1 month in advance for Sept.-Oct., otherwise 1-2 weeks. Confirm by fax in high season; you may need a credit card for deposit. Doubles with shower €50, with shower and toilet €58, with shower, toilet, and TV €65-76. Extra bed €15. AmEx/MC/V. ●

Hôtel de l'Aveyron, 5, r. d'Austerlitz (☎01 43 07 86 86; fax 01 43 07 85 20). Ⓜ Gare de Lyon. Walk away from the train station on r. de Bercy and take a right on r. d'Austerlitz. On a quiet street, with clean, unostentatious rooms. Downstairs lounge and bar with TV. English-speaking staff is eager to make suggestions. 26 rooms. Breakfast €5. Reserve 2-3 months in advance for Sept.-Oct. and Mar.-Apr., 1 week ahead otherwise. Singles or doubles with shower €55. Singles or doubles with bath €60; triples with shower €65, with bath €70; quads €90. Possibility of 1 wheelchair-accessible room. MC/V. ●

Mistral Hôtel, 3, r. Chaligny (☎01 46 28 10 20; www.parishotelmistral.com). Ⓜ Reuilly-Diderot. Walk west on bd. Diderot and turn left onto r. Chaligny. Clean and reasonably priced. All rooms have TV and phone. Breakfast €5.50. Hall showers €2.50. Reserve 1 month in advance via telephone, fax, or email. Free storage. Singles €45; doubles €48; twins €50; and triples €58. Extra bed €8. MC/V. ●

Hôtel de Reims, 26, r. Hector Malot (☎01 43 07 46 18; fax 01 43 07 56 62). Ⓜ Gare de Lyon. Take bd. Diderot away from the tall buildings and make a left onto r. Hector Malot. Stay at this hotel for its central location, just off av. Daumesnil near Opéra Bastille and the Gare de Lyon. 24 clean rooms. English spoken. Breakfast €4. Reserve by phone 1 week in advance and confirm in writing or by fax. Singles €43, doubles €45; triples €48. Closed late July to late Aug. MC/V. ●

Nièvre-Hôtel, 18, r. d'Austerlitz (☎01 43 43 81 51; fax 01 43 43 81 86). Ⓜ Gare de Lyon or Quai de la Rapée. From Gare de Lyon, walk away from the train station on r. de Bercy and turn right on r. d'Austerlitz. Centrally located but quiet, the hotel has a friendly atmosphere and rooms with high ceilings and spotless baths. Breakfast €4. Reserve 1-2 months ahead for Sept.-Oct., otherwise 1-2 weeks. Singles €34; doubles with sink and bidet €39, with shower or toilet €56. MC/V. ●

Nouvel Hôtel, 9, r. d'Austerlitz (☎01 43 42 15 79; fax 01 43 42 31 11). Ⓜ Gare de Lyon. Walk away from the train station on r. de Bercy and take a right on r. d'Austerlitz. Basic, clean rooms with big windows, big bath, and TV. Newly renovated, with sparkling bathrooms and calm, neutral decor. Breakfast €5.50. Singles €80; doubles €84; twins €90; triples €105. Extra bed €15. AmEx/MC/V. ●

Centre International du Séjour de Paris: CISP "Ravel," 6, av. Maurice Ravel (☎01 44 75 60 00; www.cisp.asso.fr). Ⓜ Porte de Vincennes. Walk east on cours de Vincennes then take the 1st right on bd. Soult, left on r. Jules Lemaître, and right on av. Maurice Ravel. Large, clean rooms (most with fewer than 4 beds), art displays, auditorium, and outdoor public pool (€3-4). Attracts a diverse group of travelers, both individuals and groups. Cafeteria open daily 7:30-9:30am, noon-1:30pm, and 7-10:30pm (full meal €10.50). Restaurant open noon-3pm (lunch €15.50). Breakfast, sheets, and towels included. Free Internet. 24hr. reception; doors close at 1:30am, so arrange to have the night guard let you in after that. Reserve at least 1-2 months-ahead by phone or email. 8-bed dorm with shower and toilet in hall €18.50; 2-to 4-bed dorm €22.50; singles with shower and toilet €30; doubles with shower and toilet €24 per person. AmEx/MC/V. ●

THIRTEENTH ARRONDISSEMENT

The relative lack of tourism in the 13ème means less expensive accommodations, although the location is a bit far from central Paris. Nevertheless, you might find it refreshing to stay here, away from the mad throngs of the 5ème and 6ème.

Touring Hôtel Magendie, 2, r. Magendie (☎01 43 36 13 61; www.touring-hotel.com). From ⓜ Glacière, follow r. de la Glacière to r. Magendie. Offers a quiet stay in a bustling area. Basic but pristine rooms in a modern complex. 4 wheelchair-accessible rooms on the ground floor. Breakfast buffet €6.50. Reserve at least 2 weeks in advance. Singles €65; doubles €76; triples €95. Special weekend rates for 2-night min. stay (€52-83, breakfast included). AmEx/MC/V. ❸

Centre International du Séjour de Paris: CISP "Kellerman," 17, bd. Kellerman (☎01 44 16 37 38; www.cisp.asso.fr). ⓜ Porte d'Italie. Cross the street and turn right onto bd. Kellerman. This large, 396-bed hostel resembles a retro spaceship on stilts but is surprisingly modern inside. Rooms are clean and adequate. Breakfast included (7-9am). Free showers on floors with dorms. TV room, laundry, meeting rooms, Internet, and cafeteria (open daily noon-1:30pm and 6:30-9:30pm). No reception 1:30-6:30am. Reserve 1 month in advance. 8-bed dorms €18.50; 2- to 4-bed dorms €22.50; singles with shower and toilet €34; doubles with shower and toilet €25. Wheelchair accessible. AmEx/MC/V. ❶

Association des Foyers de Jeunes: Foyer des Jeunes Filles, 234, r. de Tolbiac (☎01 44 16 22 22; www.foyer-tolbiac.com). ⓜ Glacière. Walk east on bd. Auguste Blanqui, turn right on r. de Glacière, then left on r. de Tolbiac. Unfortunately, it's the salmon-and-white building. Large, modern foyer **for women** ages 18-25 from outside of France, with an emphasis on non-students (the number of students is kept down by a quota). 278 rooms. Linens €6 for short-term stays. Facilities include kitchen, TV, laundry, gym, library, cafeteria, and free Internet. Reserve as far in advance as possible (2-3 months), especially for June and July. Deposit €46 for stays under 1 month, one month's rent for longer stays. Mandatory €4.50 registration fee (good for 1 year) and €46 application fee. Sunny singles €405 per month; doubles €295 per month. MC/V. ❶

FOURTEENTH ARRONDISSEMENT

🏨 **Hôtel de Blois,** 5, r. des Plantes (☎01 45 40 99 48; www.hoteldeblois.com). ⓜ Mouton-Duvernet. Turn left on r. Mouton Duvernet, then left on r. des Plantes. One of the best deals in Paris. Each room has a slightly different feel, with colorful wallpaper, ornate ceiling carvings, and velvet chairs. Send the very welcoming owner a thank-you note and she'll put it in the scrapbook that she proudly displays at the reception desk. TVs, phones, hair dryers, and big, clean bathrooms. Laundromat across the street, public pool nearby. 26 rooms on 5 floors, but no elevator. Breakfast €6.30. Free hall showers. Reserve ahead for rooms on lower floors. Singles €45, with shower and toilet €51, with bath and toilet €56; doubles €49/55/62; triples €55, with bath and toilet €72. AmEx/MC/V. ❷

🏨 **FIAP Jean-Monnet,** 30, r. Cabanis (☎01 43 13 17 00, reservations 01 43 13 17 17; www.fiap.asso.fr). ⓜ Glacière. From the metro, walk straight down bd. Auguste-Blanqui, turn left on r. de la Santé, then right on r. Cabanis. With a high-end, pre-fab feel, this 500-bed student center offers spotless rooms with phone, toilet, and shower. The fabulous concrete complex has a ping-pong table, TV rooms, 2 restaurants, an outdoor terrace, and a disco. Breakfast included; €1.50 extra for buffet. Wheelchair accessible. 3-month max. stay. Check-in 2:30pm. Check-out 9am. Curfew 2am. Reserve 2-4 weeks in advance; often, the hostel is booked for the entire summer by the end of May. Be sure to specify if you want a dorm bed, or you will be booked for a single. Payment made on arrival for duration of stay. Singles €30; doubles €34.20; 3- to 4-bed rooms €30.90; 5- to 6-bed rooms €23.90 MC/V. ❷

Hôtel du Midi, 4, av. René Coty (☎01 43 27 23 25; fax 01 43 21 24 58). ⓜ Denfert-Rochereau. From the metro, take the av. du G. Leclerc côté du Nos Impairs exit; turn right at the corner onto av. René Coty. Popular with families, but also attracts other travelers looking for a few extra amenities. Rooms have showers and toilets, and are bright and pleasantly decorated. If you have some extra cash, this is a nice place to spend it and relax. Breakfast €10. Parking €10. Reserve at least a month in advance for summer bookings. Room with shower and toilet €68-98, with bath and toilet €88-118. ❺

Hôtel du Parc, 6, r. Jolivet (☎01 43 20 95 54; www.hotelduparc-paris.com). ⓜ Edgar Quinet. From the metro turn left on r. de la Gaîté, right on r. du Maine, then right on r. Jolivet. Well-lit rooms with cable TV, phone, hair dryer. Breakfast €6. Internet access €5 per hr., or €5 a night if you use your own computer in your room. Book at least a month in advance for the summer season. Singles €55, with shower €74; doubles €78; triples €85. Prices vary with seasons. AmEx/DC/MC/V. ❸

Ouest Hôtel, 27, r. de Gergovie (☎01 45 42 64 99; fax 01 45 42 46 65). ⓜ Pernety. Walk against traffic on r. Raymond Losserand and turn right on r. de Gergovie. A clean hotel with modest prices and correspondingly modest furnishings. This place is not for those who prioritize aesthetics, although the owner is friendly and has even started a collection of books to borrow, left by previous guests. Breakfast €5. Hall shower €5. 1-bed doubles €28 (without toilet), with shower €37. MC/V. ❷

FIFTEENTH ARRONDISSEMENT

▨ **Hôtel Camélia,** 24, bd. Pasteur (☎01 47 83 76 35 or 01 47 83 69 91; www.hotelcameliaparis15.com). ⓜ Pasteur. Conveniently located next to the metro and surrounded by shops and cafes. Small, comfortable rooms, with windows that block the noise of the bustle below. Breakfast €5. Doubles €65; twins €70, extra bed €15. AmEx/MC/V. ❸

▨ **Aloha Hostel,** 1, r. Borromée (☎01 42 73 03 03; www.aloha.fr). ⓜ Volontaires. Walk against traffic on bd. de Vaugirard then turn right on r. Borromée. More tranquil than the nearby Three Ducks (see below), but still a lively mix of international backpackers. Music and drinks in the cafe. No outside alcohol on premises. Breakfast included. Sheets €3; towels €3 to rent, groups should bring their own. Internet €2 for 30mins. Safety deposit boxes and security cameras. No groups in Aug. Reception 8am-2am. Lockout 11am-5pm. Curfew 2am. Reserve 1 week ahead. Apr. to late Oct. dorms €22; doubles €25. Mid-Sept. to Apr. €17/23. ❶

▨ **Hôtel Printemps,** 31, r. du Commerce (☎01 45 79 83 36; hotel.printemps.15e@wanadoo.fr). ⓜ La Motte-Picquet-Grenelle. In a busy neighborhood, surrounded by shops (including Monoprix) and budget restaurants, this 53-room hotel is pleasant, clean, and cheap. Breakfast €4. Hall showers €3. Reserve ahead if possible. Singles and doubles with sink €34, with shower €40, with shower and toilet €43; twins with shower and toilet €47. MC/V. ❷

Pratic Hôtel, 20, r. de l'Ingénieur Robert Keller (☎01 45 77 70 58; www.pratichotel.fr). ⓜ Charles Michels. From pl. Charles Michels, walk up r. Linois (by the McDonalds), turn left on r. des 4-Frères Peignot, then turn right on r. de l'Ingénieur Keller. Small hotel run by a meticulous owner. Very clean, with spacious bathrooms and a delightful breakfast nook. Close to movie theaters, shopping, and the metro. Breakfast €7.50. Singles or doubles with toilet €55, with shower or bath €75; twins with shower or bath €95; triples and quads €120-140. MC/V. ❹

Pacific Hôtel, 11, r. Fondary (☎01 45 75 20 49; www.pacifichotelparis.com). ⓜ Dupleix or av. Emile Zola. A little bit out of the way, but easily the most elegant of the 15ème's budget offerings. Spacious rooms with desks. Breakfast €7 (or €0.80 for a croissant from the bakery down the street). Reserve at least 2 weeks in advance. Singles with shower €59; doubles €68. MC/V. ❸

Three Ducks Hostel, 6, pl. Etienne Pernet (☎01 48 42 04 05; www.3ducks.fr). ⓜ Félix Faure. Head toward the church from the metro and walk against traffic on the left side of the church; the hostel is on the left. With palm trees in the courtyard and bizarre beach-style shower shacks, this hostel is aimed at Anglo fun-seekers. Shower and breakfast included. Sheets €3.50; towels €1. Both require a deposit. Free Internet access in lobby. 1-week max. stay. Reception daily 8am-2am. Enjoy the in-house bar until the 2am curfew, as everyone else will and sleep might be difficult. Lockout daily noon-4pm. Kitchen, lockers, and small 4- to 12-bed dorm rooms. 2 twin rooms available but must be reserved far in advance. Reserve with credit card 1 week ahead. Mar.-Oct. dorm beds €23; doubles €26 per person. Special low-season rates Nov.-Feb. MC/V. ❶

SIXTEENTH ARRONDISSEMENT

Affordable accommodations are difficult to find in the upper 16*ème*. The less posh but still genteel lower area has a smattering of inexpensive lodgings in a very safe area, albeit one that's far from the city center.

▨ **Villa d'Auteuil,** 28, r. Poussin (☎01 42 88 30 37; villaaut@aol.com). ⓜ Michel-Ange Auteuil. Walk up r. Girodet and turn left on r. Poussin. At the edge of the Bois de Boulogne, this delightful, family-run hotel offers pastel-hued rooms with wood-frame beds, shower, toilet, phone, and TV. Free wireless Internet. Friendly staff members work alongside a parrot named Oscar who bursts out snippets of the *Marseillaise* in the reception area. Breakfast €5.50. Reserve 1 month ahead during high season (Feb., July-Aug.). Singles €56-60; doubles €64-68; triples €78. AmEx/MC/V. ❷

▨ **Hôtel Boileau,** 81, r. Boileau (☎01 42 88 83 74; www.hotel-boileau.com). ⓜ Exelmans. Walk down bd. Exelmans away from its curving corner and turn right on r. Boileau. Features marble busts, Tuscan tiling, Oriental rugs, vintage cashboxes and a sunny breakfast room complete with fishtank. The spotless rooms all have a toilet, shower, cable TV, and a telephone. Breakfast €8.50-10. Internet. Reserve 1 month ahead in high season (Sept.-Dec., Mar.-June). Singles €70-79; doubles €80-98; triples €125-130. AmEx/MC/V. ❸

Hôtel Ribera, 66, r. la Fontaine (☎01 42 88 29 50; www.hotelribera-paris.com). ⓜ Jasmin. Walk down r. Ribera to its intersection with r. La Fontaine; hotel is on your left. The cheerful, colorful rooms overlook the Art Nouveau ornamentation of the historic r. la Fontaine. Some rooms are aptly decorated with flamboyant faux sculpture and marble fireplaces to match the surrounds. Pull-out beds in doubles are perfect for a small child. Safe deposit box and television in every room. Spacious bathrooms. Breakfast €6. Free wireless Internet. Not all rooms come with both shower and sink; specify when reserving. Singles, doubles and triples €51-70. 10% discount July-Aug. AmEx/MC/V. ❷

SEVENTEENTH ARRONDISSEMENT

Because of its location on Paris's outskirts, the 17*ème* offers more budget options than areas closer to the city's center.

Hôtel Champerret Héliopolis, 13, r. d'Héliopolis (☎01 47 64 92 56; www.champerret-heliopolis-paris-hotel.com). ⓜ Porte de Champerret. Turn left off av. de Villiers. 22 brilliant blue-and-white rooms, some with little wooden balconies opening onto a sunny palm-lined terrace. In a beautiful location close to the metro and several pleasant eateries. Welcoming and helpful staff. All rooms have shower, TV, phone, and hair dryer. 1 wheelchair-accessible room. Breakfast €9. Reserve 3 weeks in advance with credit card via fax, email, or phone. Singles €72; doubles €85, with bath €93; twins €93; triples with bath €100. Check website for discounts of up to 15%. AmEx/MC/V. ❸

Hôtel Riviera, 55, r. des Acacias (☎01 43 80 45 31; fax 01 40 54 84 08). ⓜ Charles de Gaulle-Etoile. Walk north on av. MacMahon, then turn left on r. des Acacias. Close to the Arc de Triomphe, this hotel wins on location. Modern, quiet, and prettily decorated rooms have comfortable bed, TV, telephone, and hair dryer. Some have A/C. Breakfast €6.50. Reservations 1 month in advance. Singles with shower €51, with toilet and bath or shower €65-82; doubles with toilet and bath or shower €72-90; triples with toilet and bath or shower €100-106; quads €106-115. AmEx/MC/V. ❷

Hôtel Prince Albert Wagram, 28, passage Cardinet (☎01 47 54 06 00; www.hotel-princealbert.com). ⓜ Malesherbes. Follow r. Cardinet across bd. Malesherbes and r. de

Tocqueville and turn left into passage Cardinet. In a quiet neighborhood; a 10min. walk from the metro. Entirely renovated in a fresh mint-green color scheme, with clean, quiet rooms and an elevator. Dogs allowed with owner's assumption of responsibility. All rooms with shower, toilet, TV, and safe deposit box. Breakfast €6. Reserve 1-2 weeks ahead, 2-3 months ahead for Sept.-Oct. Singles €75; doubles €90. Extra bed €16. AmEx/MC/V. ❸

Hôtel Belidor, 5, r. Belidor (☎01 45 74 49 91; fax 01 45 72 54 22). Ⓜ Porte Maillot. Go north on bd. Gouvion St-Cyr and turn right on r. Belidor. Clean, spacious rooms, some with bathtubs. Most rooms face a quiet, tiled courtyard. Breakfast included. Reserve 10-15 days in advance. Open Sept.-July. Singles €43, with shower €54, with shower and toilet €61; doubles €66; 2-bed doubles with toilet €84. MC/V. ❷

EIGHTEENTH ARRONDISSEMENT

Staying in the bustling 18*ème* usually promises noisy quarters at rock-bottom prices. While it's easy to find a deal here, it's harder to spot a location where you'll actually be able to sleep.

▨ Hôtel Caulaincourt, 2, sq. Caulaincourt (☎01 46 06 46 06; www.caulaincourt.com). Ⓜ Lamarck-Caulaincourt. Walk up the stairs to r. Caulaincourt and proceed to your right, between no. 65 and 67. This student-friendly establishment is located in a quiet area of picturesque Montmartre. Formerly used as artists' studios, the simple rooms have great light and wonderful views of Montmartre and the Paris skyline. One of the best values around. TVs and phones in every room. Breakfast €5.50. Free Internet. Reserve up to 1 month in advance for your pick of rooms. Singles €38, with shower €48, with shower and toilet €58, with bath and toilet €68; doubles €52-79; twins €56-83; triples with shower €70-86. MC/V. ❷

Style Hôtel, 8, r. Ganneron (☎01 45 22 37 59; fax 01 45 22 81 03). Ⓜ Place de Clichy. Walk up av. de Clichy and turn right onto r. Ganneron. Next to the cemetery. Two buildings: the newer is decorated in Art Deco style, with large rooms and wood floors; the older is quieter and slightly worn, but charming. No TVs. Breakfast €6. Reserve at least 3 weeks in advance. Singles €45; doubles €50; triples €57; quads €67. Extra bed €6. AmEx/MC/V. ❷

Hôtel André Gill, 4, r. André Gill (☎01 42 62 48 48; fax 01 42 62 77 92). Ⓜ Abbesses. Walk downhill on r. des Abbesses; turn right on r. des Martyrs and left on r. André Gill. In a cul-de-sac, André Gill provides refuge from the noise and seediness of bd. de Clichy. Breakfast €4. Hall showers €4. Internet available. Reserve 1 week in advance. Dorms (breakfast included) €25; singles €50; doubles with shower or bath €89. MC/V. ❷

Le Village Hostel, 20, r. d'Orsel (☎01 42 64 22 02; www.villiagehostel.fr). Ⓜ Anvers. Go uphill on r. Steinkerque and turn right on r. d'Orsel. In the midst of the Sacré-Coeur tourist traffic, but clean and cheap. Doubles, triples, and 4- to 8-bed dorms, some with a view of Sacré-Coeur, some off a spacious patio, and some facing the noisy street (make sure to specify). Breakfast included. Toilet and shower in every room. Sheets €2.50; towel €1. Kitchen, beer dispenser, TV, stereo, telephones, and Internet in the lounge. Lockout 11am-4pm. 7-day max. stay. Online reservation. For same-day phone reservations, call at 8am when reception opens. 4-, 6-, or 8-bed dorms €23; doubles €50; triples €81. ❶

NINETEENTH ARRONDISSEMENT

A quieter alternative than the neighboring 18*ème* arrondissement, the 19*ème* offers similar deals with less hustle and bustle.

▨ Rhin et Danube, 3, pl. de Rhin et Danube (☎01 42 45 10 13; fax 01 42 06 88 82). Ⓜ Danube; or bus #75 from Ⓜ Châtelet (30min.). Just steps from the metro, the R&D is a real deal for the budget traveler. The suites are not fancy, but they are spacious, and many look onto a quaint *place*. Each room has kitchen, fridge, dishes, coffeemaker,

Hotel
ARMSTRONG
Paris

The Armstrong offers excellent value and is a favourite for back-packers. It has a direct metro to the Eiffel Tower and the Champs-Elysées, and there is a fast train service to Disneyland Paris.

With its multi-lingual staff, cosy fully licensed bar, 24-hour in-house internet café, sauna and private car park, the Hotel Armstrong is an ideal choice for visiting the City of Lights.

36 rue de la Croix Saint Simon
75020 PARIS

Tel. :33 (0) 1 - 43 70 53 65
Fax :33 (0) 1- 43 70 63 31

www.hotelarmstrong.com
info@hotelarmstrong.com

hair dryer, shower, toilet, direct phone, and color TV with satellite. Book a month in advance. Singles €46; doubles €61; triples €73; quads €83; quints €92. MC/V. ❷

Crimée Hôtel, 188, r. de Crimée (☎01 40 36 75 29; fax 01 40 36 29 57). ⓜ Crimée. Walk down av. de Flandre and turn right onto r. de Crimée. In the northern, commercial 19ème, relatively close to La Villette. This place has a business-conference feel. The rooms, though a bit sterile, are spotless. Some rooms have hair dryer, TV, A/C, toilet, and shower. Breakfast €6.50. Reserve at least 2 weeks in advance. Singles €62-64; doubles €64-68; triples €78. AmEx/MC/V. ❸

La Perdrix Rouge, 5, r. Lassus (☎01 42 06 09 53; fax 01 42 06 88 70). ⓜ Jourdain. Facing a gorgeous church and steps from the metro, a bank, a grocery store, a laundromat, and a few restaurants, this is a great spot for a little peace away from the clamor of central Paris. Simple, pleasant rooms, each with TV, toilet, and bath or shower. Breakfast €7.50. Reserve by phone. Singles €61; doubles €65-75, extra bed €16. If you stay more than several nights you can negotiate a discounted price. MC/V. ❷

TWENTIETH ARRONDISSEMENT

While not the budget accommodation capital of Paris, the 20ème offers a high-quality selection of reasonable hotels and hostels.

🎖 **Eden Hôtel**, 7, r. Jean-Baptiste Dumay (☎01 46 36 64 22, fax 01 46 36 01 11). ⓜ Pyrénées. When facing the church outside the metro, turn left down r. de Belleville; r. Jean-Baptiste Dumay is on the left. An oasis of hospitality with good value for its 2 stars. Clean rooms with TVs and toilets. Breakfast €5. Bath or shower €4. Reserve rooms 1 week in advance. Singles €40-47, with shower €53-55; doubles with shower/bath €55-58. MC/V. ❷

Auberge de Jeunesse "Le D'Artagnan" (HI), 80, r. Vitruve (☎01 40 32 34 56; www.hostels-in.com). ⓜ Porte de Bagnolet or Porte de Montreuil. From Porte de Bagnolet, walk south on bd. Davout and make a right on r. Vitruve. An enormous backpacker's colony, making sure that the 20ème doesn't feel left out of the action. Neon lights and funky decorations in every color welcome legions of boisterous young people as well as older single travelers and families. 435 beds. Breakfast served 7am-11am. Sheets included. Lockers €2-4 per day. Laundry €3 per wash, €1 per dry. Restaurant (open noon-2pm and 6:30-9:30pm; *plat* €4.50), bar (open 9pm-2am; happy hour 9-10pm), and a small cinema (free films, usually nightly at 6:30pm). 6-night max. stay. Reception 8am-1am. Lockout noon-3pm. Reservations by fax or email a must. 2-, 3-, 4-, 5-, and 9-bed dorms €21.50 per person with the *carte des auberges de jeunesse* (international hostel card), €24.40 per person without. Children under 10 half-price, under 5 free. ❶

Hôtel Ermitage, 42bis, r. de l'Ermitage (☎01 46 36 23 44; hotelermitage@aol.com). ⓜ Jourdain. Walk down r. Jourdain, turn left onto r. des Pyrénées, and left on r. de l'Ermitage. Welcoming, family-run establishment with clean, simple rooms. Breakfast €4.50 in the nearby cafe. Singles €30, with TV and shower €45; doubles with TV and shower €53. AmEx/MC/V. ❷

FOOD

French cooking is universally renowned and has influenced cuisine from around the world. The preparation and consumption of food are integral to French daily life, and food establishments of all kinds—elegant restaurants with six-course meals and as many forks; street markets where old women haggle for fresh produce; sidewalk cafes where intellectuals brood, sip espresso, and smoke endless cigarettes; and *pâtisseries* displaying artfully conceived desserts provide the setting for scenes of Parisian life imagined, filmed, written, touristed, and lived.

Don't approach French dining with the assumption that chic equals *cher;* while world-famous chefs and their three-star restaurants are a valued Parisian institution, you don't have to pay their prices for excellent cuisine, either classic or adventurous. Join locals at a bistro, a more informal, and often less expensive type of restaurant. Even more casual are *brasseries*, often crowded and convivial, best for large groups and high spirits. The least expensive option is usually a *crêperie*, a restaurant specializing in thin Breton pancakes filled with meats, vegetables, cheeses, chocolates, or fruits, where you can often eat for less than you would pay at McDo. The offerings of specialty food shops, including *boulangeries* (bakeries), *pâtisseries* (pastry shops), and *traiteurs* (prepared food shops), make delicious, inexpensive picnic supplies and cheap meals on the go. A number of North African and Middle Eastern restaurants serve affordable international dishes. At *nouveaux bistros*, French, Mediterranean, Asian, and Spanish flavors converge in a setting that is usually modern and artsy. Eating and drinking can easily be the most memorable part of any visit to Paris. *Bon appetit!*

BY TYPE

AFRICAN

Babylone Bis (153)	2ème ❸
⚑ 404 (153)	3ème ❸
⚑ Café de la Mosquée (158)	5ème ❷
La Banane Iviorienne (169)	11ème ❷
Djerba Cacher Chez Guichi (179)	18ème ❷
⚑ Café Flèche d'Or (180)	20ème ❷

ALL-YOU-CAN-EAT

Restaurant Natacha (177)	17ème ❸

AMERICAN

Café du Marché (163)	7ème ❷
⚑ Chez Haynes (166)	9ème ❸

BASQUE

⚑ Le Caveau du Palais (148)	Île de la Cité ❸
Chez Gladines (172)	13ème ❷
Le Troquet (175)	15ème ❹

BISTRO

Les Fous de l'Île (149)	Île St-Louis ❸
Café Med (149)	Île St-Louis ❷
⚑ Le Carré Blanc (150)	1er ❸
Au Père Fouettard (150)	1er ❸
Au Vieux Comptoir	1er ❹
⚑ Les Noces de Jeannette (152)	2ème ❹
⚑ Le Petite Pamphlet	3ème ❸

Le Grizzli (156)	4ème ❷
Le Divin (155)	4ème ❸
Le Perraudin (158)	5ème ❸
Le "Relais de l'Entercôte" (161)	6ème ❸
Le Bistro Ernest (161)	6ème ❸
Au Pied de Fouet (163)	7ème ❷
⚑ Chez Paul (168)	11ème ❷
Juan et Juanita (169)	11ème ❷
Le Bistrot du Peintre (169)	11ème ❷
⚑ Le Dix Vins (174)	15ème ❸
Le Bistro de Théo (177)	17ème ❹
Le Zéphyr (181)	20ème ❹

BRUNCH

⚑ Le Fumoir (151)	1er ❸
Le Loup Blanc (152)	2ème ❸
L'Apparement Café (154)	3ème ❸
Café Beaubourg (156)	4ème ❹
⚑ Café des Lettres (163)	7ème ❷
Le Troisième Bureau (169)	11ème ❸
Café du Commerce (172)	13ème ❸
⚑ L'Endroit (177)	17ème ❷
⚑ The James Joyce Pub (177)	17ème ❷
Le Niv's (177)	17ème ❷
⚑ Le Sancerre (178)	18ème ❶
La Mer à Boire (181)	20ème ❷

CLASSIC CAFÉ

Place Numéro Thé (148)	Île de la Cité ❷	
🖼 Café Vavin (160)	6ème ❷	
Café Parisien (159)	6ème ❷	
Café de Flore (161)	6ème ❸	
Les Deux Magots (161)	6ème ❸	
Le Paris (165)	8ème ❸	
Café de la Paix (167)	9ème ❹	
Au Général La Fayette (167)	9ème ❷	
🖼 No Stress Café (167)	9ème ❸	
Les Hortensias (178)	17ème ❷	
La Maison Rose (179)	18ème ❸	
La Kaskad' (180)	19ème ❷	

CRÊPERIE

La Crêpe Rit du Clown (160)	6ème ❶
Crêperie Saint Germain (160)	6ème ❶
Ty Yann (165)	8ème ❷
Des Crêpres et des Cailles (172)	13ème ❶
Ty Breiz (175)	15ème ❶
La Bolée Belgrand (181)	20ème ❷

FUSION/ECLECTIC

Babylone Bis (153)	2ème ❸
Le Réconfort (154)	3ème ❸
Grannie (163)	7ème ❹
🖼 Mood (165)	8ème ❸
Toi (165)	8ème ❹

HISTORIC

Le Sélect (162)	6ème ❸
Café de Flore (161)	6ème ❸
Les Deux Magots (161)	6ème ❸
Le Procope (162)	6ème ❹
Fouquet's (165)	8ème ❹
Café de la Paix (167)	9ème ❹
La Coupole (174)	14ème ❹

ICE CREAM

🖼 Amorino (149)	Île St-Louis ❶
🖼 Berthillon (149)	Île St-Louis ❶
Octave (158)	5ème ❶

INDIAN

Anarkali Sarangui (166)	9ème ❸
Pooja (168)	10ème ❷

IRISH

🖼 The James Joyce Pub (177)	17ème ❷

ITALIAN

Little Italy Trattoria (155)	4ème ❷
Le Jardin des Pâtes (158)	5ème ❷
Les Grandes Marchés (171)	12ème ❹

JAPANESE

Kintaro (153)	2ème ❷

KOSHER

Resto-Flash (168)	10ème ❸

LATE NIGHT FOOD (1AM OR LATER)

Brasserie de l'Île St-Louis (149)	Île St-Louis ❷
Au Père Fouettard (150)	1er ❸
🖼 Le Fumoir (151)	1er ❸
Le Café Marly (151)	1er ❹
Babylone Bis (153)	2ème ❸
🖼 Au Petit Fer à Cheval (155)	4ème ❷
Café Beaubourg (156)	4ème ❹
Café Delmas (158)	5ème ❷
Les Editeurs (161)	6ème ❷
Café de Flore (161)	6ème ❸
Les Deux Magots (161)	6ème ❸
Le Sélect (162)	6ème ❸
Fouquet's (165)	8ème ❹
Le Paris (165)	8ème ❸
Toi (165)	8ème ❹
Au Général La Fayette (167)	9ème ❷
Café de la Paix (167)	9ème ❹
Le Bistrot du Peintre (169)	11ème ❷
Café de l'Industrie (169)	11ème ❶
Pause Café (169)	11ème ❷
Le Troisième Bureau (169)	11ème ❷
Papagallo (172)	13ème ❷
🖼 Chez Papa (173)	14ème ❷
La Coupole (174)	14ème ❹
Casa Tina (176)	16ème ❸
🖼 L'Endroit (177)	17ème ❸
Chez Ginette (179)	18ème ❸
🖼 Refuge des Fondues (178)	18ème ❷
🖼 Le Sancerre (178)	18ème ❶

MEXICAN

La Cucaracha (152)	2ème ❷
Ay, Caramba! (180)	19ème ❸

MIDDLE EASTERN

🖼 L'As du Falafel (155)	4ème ❶
Chez Omar (154)	3ème ❸
Comptoir Méditerranée (157)	5ème ❶
Savannah Café (157)	5ème ❸
Samaya (175)	15ème ❷
🖼 Byblos Café (176)	16ème ❷

PROVENÇALE

Le Divin (155)	4ème ❸
L'Aimant du Sud (172)	13ème ❸
Le Troquet (175)	15ème ❹
🖼 Le Patio Provençal (177)	17ème ❷
🖼 Le Soleil Gourmand (178)	18ème ❷
Aux Arts et Sciences Réunis (180)	19ème ❸

SANDWICHERIE/DELI

Cosí (159)	6ème ❶
Guen-maï (160)	6ème ❷
Bagel & Co. (165)	8ème ❶
Comme Par Hasard (167)	9ème ❶

SCANDINAVIAN

☒ Café des Lettres (163)   7ème ❷

SOUTHEAST ASIAN

Le Lotus Blanc (163)   7ème ❸
Thabthim Siam (165)   8ème ❷
☒ Tricotin (171)   13ème ❶
Chez Fung (175)   15ème ❷
☒ Thai Phetburi (174)   15ème ❷
☒ Lao Siam (180)   19ème ❷

SPANISH

Caves St-Gilles (153)   3ème ❷
Papagallo (172)   13ème ❷
☒ Rosimar (175)   16ème❹
Casa Tina (176)   16ème ❸
La Bodega (179)   18ème ❶

TRADITIONAL AND MODERN FRENCH

Au Rendez-Vous des
Camionneurs (148)   Île de la Cité ❸
Auberge de la
Reine Blanche (149)   Île St-Louis ❸
Au Chien qui Fume (150)   1er ❹
☒ Jules (150)   1er ❹
Le Grillardin (150)   1er ❸
☒ Les Noces de Jeannette (152)   2ème ❹
Taxi Jaune (153)   3ème ❹
☒ Au Petit Fer à Cheval (155)   4ème ❷
Bistrôt du Dome (156)   4ème ❸
☒ Pain, Vin, Fromage (155)   4ème ❷
Petit Bofinger (163)   4ème ❸
Au Port Salut (158)   5ème ❷
L'Auberge Bressane (163)   7ème ❺
☒ Le 36 (164)   8ème ❸
Fouqeut's (165)   8ème ❹
Chartier (166)   9ème ❷
La 25ème Image (168)   10ème ❷
Au Bon Café (168)   10ème ❷
Les Broches à l'Ancienne (171)   12ème ❷
La Connivence (170)   12ème ❸
☒ L'Ebauchoir (170)   12ème ❸
Les Grandes Marchés (171)   12ème ❷
Café du Commerce (172)   13ème ❸
Le Temps des Cerises (172)   13ème ❷
L'Amuse Bouche (173)   14ème ❹
☒ Chez Papa (173)   14ème ❷
Au Rendez-Vous
Des Camionneurs (174)   14ème ❷
L'Encens (174)   14ème ❸
Aux Artistes (175)   15ème ❷
Le Tire Bouchon (174)   15ème ❸
Le Troquet (175)   15ème ❹
Au Vieux Logis (177)   17ème ❷
Chez Ginette (179)   18ème ❸

TRADITIONAL AND MODERN FRENCH (CONT'D)

☒ Refuge des Fondues (178)   18ème ❷
La Kaskad' (180)   19ème ❷
☒ Café Flèche d'Or (180)   20ème ❷

TRENDY/INTELLIGENTSIA

Le Café Marly (151)   1er ❹
☒ Le Fumoir (151)   1er ❸
Chez Omar (154)   3ème ❸
L'Apparemment Café (154)   3ème ❸
☒ Chez Janou (153)   3ème ❷
Les Arts et Métiers (154)   3ème ❸
☒ Georges (156)   4ème ❹
Café Beaubourg (156)   4ème ❹
Curieux Spaghetti Bar (155)   4ème ❷
Café de Flore (161)   6ème ❸
Le Sélect (162)   6ème ❸
Les Editeurs (161)   6ème ❷
☒ Chez Paul (168)   11ème ❷
Café de l'Industrie (169)   11ème ❶
Pause Café (169)   11ème ❷
Le Troisième Bureau (169)   11ème ❷
Polichinelle (170)   11ème ❷
Aux Artistes (175)   15ème ❷
La Rotunde (176)   16ème ❷
☒ L'Endroit (177)   17ème ❷
☒ Le Sancerre (178)   18ème ❶
☒ Café Flèche d'Or (180)   20ème ❷

TURKISH

Restaurant Assoce (169)   11ème ❷
Le Cheval de Troie (171)   12ème ❷

VEGETARIAN AND VEGAN/ DETOX

☒ La Victoire Suprême
du Coeur (150)   1er ❷
☒ Piccolo Teatro (155)   4ème ❷
Le Jardin des Pâtés (158)   5ème ❷
Le Grenier de Notre-Dame (157)   5ème ❷
Guen-maï (160)   6ème ❷
Le Lotus Blanc (163)   7ème ❸
☒ Le 36 (164)   8ème ❸❷
Aquarius Café (174)   14ème ❷
Au Grain de Folie (179)   18ème ❷
☒ Le Soleil Gourmand (178) 1   8ème ❷

SALONS DE THÉ

Angelina's (151)   1er
Muscade (151)   1er
☒ Mariage Frères (156)   4ème
L'Heure Gourmande (162)   6ème
☒ Ladurée (166)   8ème

FOOD

SPECIALTY SHOPS				
O&CO (149)	Throughout Paris	Poujauran (163)	7ème
▨ L'Epicerie (149)	Ile St-Louis	Debauve et Gallais (164)	7ème
La Petite Scierie (149)	Île St-Louis	Barthélémy (164)	7ème
Julien (152)	1er	Fromage Rouge (164)	7ème
Nicolas (152)	1er	Fauchon (166)	8ème
La Cure Gourmande (154)	3ème	La Maison du Chocolat (167)	9ème
Jadis et Gourmande (157)	4ème	Marché St-Quentin	10ème
Izrael (157)	4ème	Marché Bastille (170)	11ème
▨ Marché Monge (158)	5ème	Marché Popincourt (170)	11ème
Marché Port Royal (159)	5ème	Marché Beauvau St-Antoine (171)	12ème
Marché Mouffetard	5ème	Tang Frères (172)	13ème
Poilâne (162)	6ème	Au Coin du Pétrin (175)	15ème
Gérard Mulot (162)	6ème	Marché Président-Wilson (176)	16ème
Marché Biologique (162)	6ème	Marché Berthier	17ème

BY NEIGHBORHOOD

The *arrondissement* listings rank restaurants in order of value; the top entry may not be the cheapest, but it will be the best value in its price range and area.

SEINE ISLANDS

The islands are crowded with tiny, traditional French restaurants with wood-panelled dining rooms and old-world charm. Be warned, however, that these restaurants, particularly on the Ile St-Louis, cater mostly to tourists, so you should expect to pay more than you would for an equivalent meal on the mainland.

ÎLE DE LA CITÉ

Elegant, occasionally pricey dining characterizes the restaurant scene of Île de la Cité. A wonderful traditional French meal can be found, though, at one of any moderately priced restaurant-cafes in the area.

▨ **Le Caveau du Palais,** 19, pl. Dauphine (☎01 43 26 04 28). Ⓜ Cité. Le Caveau serves up traditional, hearty French fare in a warm, casual ambience of timbered ceilings and rough-hewn stone walls. A favorite with locals, who crowd the terrace in the summertime. The meat-heavy menu is pricy, but worth the splurge. Appetizers €9.50-15. Main dishes €18-28. Desserts €8-9. Reservations necessary for dinner and encouraged for lunch. Open daily noon-2:30pm and 7-10:30pm. AmEx/MC/V. ❸

Place Numéro Thé, 20, pl. Dauphine (☎01 44 07 28 17). Ⓜ Cité. A tiny, tastefully casual restaurant-cafe tucked into a corner of the tree-lined pl. Dauphine. The pleasant staff serve light lunch fare and noteworthy desserts such as the *coulis* with *fromage blanc* (€5). Also has an array of exotic teas (€5). Outdoor seating in summer is delightful. Open M-Tu and Th-F noon-5:30pm. MC/V. ❷

Au Rendez-Vous des Camionneurs, 72, quai d'Orfèvres (☎01 43 54 88 74). Ⓜ Cité. Outside corner of pl. Dauphine facing the Left Bank. Italian decorations, French food, scores of recommendations, and an €18 lunch *menu* (M-Sa). *Formule* meal €26. Friendly, English-speaking staff. Open M-F noon-11pm. AmEx/MC/V. ❸

ÎLE ST-LOUIS

Île St-Louis is perhaps the best place in Paris to stop for a *crêpe*, a Greek *gyro*, or some ice cream while strolling along the Seine. Those in search of something a little more formal may be disappointed, but this is a snacker's heaven.

🍨 **Amorino,** 47, r. St-Louis-en-l'Île (☎01 44 07 48 08). Ⓜ Pont Marie. Cross the Pont Marie and turn right on r. St-Louis-en-l'Île. With a selection of 20 *gelati* and *sorbetti* (more in summer) flavors, Amorino serves amazing concoctions in your choice of combination and more generous servings than its more famous neighbor, Berthillon. Your cone (€4) will look like a work of art. ❶

🍨 **Berthillon,** 31, r. St-Louis-en-l'Île (☎01 43 54 31 61). Ⓜ Cité or Pont Marie. Reputed to have the best ice cream and sorbet in Paris. Choose from dozens of *parfums,* ranging from blood orange to gingerbread to the house specialty, *nougat miel* (honey nougat). Look for stores nearby that sell Berthillon indulgences; the wait is shorter, they usually offer a wider selection of flavors, and they're open in late July and Aug., when the main outfit is closed. Single scoop €2; double €3; triple €4. Open Sept.-July 14. Store and tea room open W-Su 10am-8pm. Closed 2 weeks in Feb. and Apr. ❶

Brasserie de l'Île St-Louis, 55, quai de Bourbon (☎01 43 54 02 59). Ⓜ Pont Marie. Cross the Pont Marie and turn right on r. St-Louis-en-l'Île; continue to the end of the island. This old-fashioned *brasserie* is known for its delectable Alsatian specialties, such as *choucroute garnie* (sausages and pork on a bed of sauerkraut; €17). Also features an array of omelettes and other typical cafe fare (€7-15). Outdoor seating with a view of the Pantheon through the Left Bank rooftops. Open M-Tu and Th-Su noon-midnight. No reservations accepted. AmEx/MC/V. ❷

Les Fous de l'Île, 33, r. des Deux Ponts (☎01 43 25 76 67). Ⓜ Pont Marie. A mellow, dimly-lit bistro for the neighborhood crowd with friendly servers. Displays the work of local artists and has evening concerts (jazz, pop, piano, rock) every Th except in Aug. Appetizers €6.50-10. *Plats* €11-14. Delicious €15 and €19 lunch *menus* with changing specials of traditional French cuisine with a twist. Open W noon-3pm and Th-Sa noon-11pm. ❸

Café Med, 79, r. St-Louis-en-l'Île (☎01 43 29 73 17). Ⓜ Pont Marie. Cross the Pont Marie and make a right on r. St-Louis-en-l'Île; the restaurant is on the left. Small, bustling bistro serves up both French and Italian food in a blue and yellow room right on the island's main street. Its prices are hard to beat on either island, as are its bargain-friendly 3-course *menus* at €10/10.50/12.50. Generous salads (€9-10) could easily serve as meals in themselves. MC/V. ❷

Auberge de la Reine Blanche, 30, r. St-Louis-en-l'Île (☎01 46 33 07 87). Ⓜ Pont Marie. Cross Pont Marie and make a left on r. St-Louis-en-l'Île. Miniature doll furniture and burnished copper pots adorn the walls of this cozily dim restaurant. Accolades posted on the front window attest to the friendliness of the establishment. *Plat du jour* €12 lunch, €15 dinner. Lunch *menu* €15.50 and dinner *menu* €19.50. Open daily noon-2:30pm and 6-10:30pm. MC/V. ❸

SPECIALTY SHOPS

🛍 **L'Epicerie,** 51, r. St-Louis-en-l'Île(☎01 43 25 20 14). Elegantly creative concoctions line the walls of this tiny store. Perfumed sugars (€5), infused olive oils (€7.50), and jams such as the sweet orange with *curaçao* and vodka (€7.50) make perfect presents. Open daily 11am-8pm. MC/V.

La Petite Scierie, 60, r. St-Louis-en-l'Île (☎01 55 42 14 88). *Foie gras, rilettes,* quail's eggs, and other meat-based house specialties and preserves are naturally prepared from a local farm. You can also try before you buy, with a lunch deal of *foie gras* on a baguette with a glass of white wine (€8). AmEx/MC/V.

O&CO, locations throughout Paris. Sells high-quality olive oils made in France. Olives are harvested from farms in Provence and other regions throughout the Mediterranean, like Italy, Spain, and Tunisia. Gifts can be wrapped to make it safely home. Bottles range from

FOOD

€6-12. Also sells olive, fruit, and herb spreads, along with other gourmet food products and olive oil-related cooking accessories. Most branches open M-Sa 10am-8pm.

FIRST ARRONDISSEMENT

The arcades overlooking the Louvre along **rue de Rivoli** are filled with everything chic and expensive, but visitors can enjoy the surroundings while sipping a tea or *chocolat chaud* at one of the many *salons de thé* without breaking the bank. **Les Halles** has louder, more crowded eateries, serving everything from fast food to four-course Italian feasts. Diverse lunch and dinner options are also available along **rue Jean-Jacques Rousseau**. Those in search of a quieter meal should head to the many restaurants located along **rue St-Honoré** or behind the **Palais Royal**.

■ **Le Carré Blanc,** 62, r. Jean-Jacques Rousseau (☎ 01 40·28 99 04). Ⓜ Les Halles. Take the r. Rambuteau exit and walk toward St-Eustache, then turn left onto r. Coquillère and right on r. Jean-Jacques Rousseau. *Menu "Les Petits Sabots"* offers small plates to share (or keep all to yourself). Reminiscent of tapas, these dishes are petite, and it will probably take 3 of them to fill you up (€7; 3 for €18). Choices include lamb skewers flavored with oregano and coriander, and roasted aubergine *millefeuille*. This small restaurant has a great ambience and simple but classy decor. Desserts (€6) are an eclectic mix just like the food. Lunch *menus* €7-15. Open M-Sa noon-2:30pm and 7:45-10:30pm, until 11pm Sa. AmEx/MC/V. ❸

■ **La Victoire Suprême du Coeur,** 41, r. des Bourdonnais (☎01 40 41 93 95). Ⓜ Châtelet. Walk down r. de Rivoli and turn right onto r. des Bourdonnais. Run by the devotees of Sri Chinmoy, who have both body and soul in mind when creating dishes like *escalope de seitan à la sauce champignon* (€14). Never mind the weird photos of their Yul Brynner-esque guru up to his elbows in dough. The cuisine is all vegetarian and very tasty. Meals marked with a "V" can be made vegan. 2-course *menu* (€15.50). Smoothies made daily from fresh fruit. Open M-F 11:45am-10pm, Sa noon-10pm. AmEx/MC/V. ❷

Le Grillardin, 52, r. de Richelieu (☎01 42 97 54 40). Ⓜ Louvre. This French restaurant has been serving customers since 1827. In an excellent location (behind the Palais-Royal) for those needing rest after the Louvre. *Menu* (lunch €15-18; dinner €25) includes roasted duck leg with *herbes de Provence* gravy. Start with the homemade *terrine de foie gras* or a dozen snails in garlic butter. Open Tu-Sa noon-3pm and 7-11pm. AmEx/MC/V. ❸

Au Chien qui Fume, 33, r. du Pont Neuf (☎01 42 36 07 42; www.au-chien-qui-fume.com). Ⓜ Châtelet or Les Halles. Even passersby who aren't hungry stop at this popular restaurant just to see the cooks arrange beautiful plates of shellfish at its famous oyster bar. The Saint-Malo *menu* (€39), named after the fabled port, includes a tray of shellfish. Bazil's *menu* (€29) offers more of a selection, including steak and duck for those uninterested in seafood. Excellent starters (à la carte; €7.50-17). Pictures of dogs dancing, eating, and, of course, smoking, appear almost every wall, and statues of dogs sit on every countertop. Open daily noon-2am. ❹

Au Père Fouettard, 9, r. Pierre Lescot (☎01 42 33 74 17; www.paris-zoom.com). Ⓜ Les Halles. Serves very typical (but tasty) bistro fare with some more inventive specials (change daily). Great terrace sheltered from the busy street by carefully placed foliage. *Entrées* €6-15. Salads €12-14. *Plats* €12-21. Lunch *menu* M-F €13. Brunch €17.50, served Sa-Su and holidays 11:30am-4:30pm. Open daily 7:30am-2am. V. ❸

Au Vieux Comptoir, 17, r. des Lavandières (☎01 45 08 53 08 www.au-vieux-comptoir.com). Ⓜ Châtelet. An extensive wine list accompanies delicious *plats* in this great little French bistro. The *coquilles St-Jaques* (scallops in a cream sauce) is to die for, but somewhat of a splurge. The beef dishes, a more reasonably-priced choice, come highly recommended. Desserts €8. Seating inside or outside under an awning. Tu-Sa noon-10:30pm; cold cuts and salads until 11:30pm. MC/V. ❹

CAFES

🔲 **Le Fumoir,** 6, r. de l'Amiral Coligny (☎01 42 92 00 24; www.lefumoir.com). Ⓜ Louvre. As you cross r. de Rivoli on r. du Louvre, it becomes r. de l'Amiral Coligny. Although you may hear as much English as French while you sip a beverage in their deep leather sofas, Le Fumoir is authentically Parisian in style. It's part bar, part tea house, and it serves one of the best brunches in Paris (€21), Su noon-3pm. Coffee €2.50. Open daily 11am-2am. AmEx/MC/V. ❸

Le Café Marly, 9, r. de Rivoli (☎01 49 26 06 60). Ⓜ Palais-Royal. One of Paris's classiest cafes; located in the Richelieu wing of the Louvre. With one terrace facing the famed I.M. Pei pyramids and others overlooking the Louvre's Cour Napoléon, this is a prime spot for tourists and locals alike. Enjoy a full meal or sit back with a glass of wine and watch the sunset. Breakfast (pastry, toast, jam, juice, and coffee, tea, or hot chocolate; €13) served all morning. Main dishes €19-29. Omelettes €10. Open daily 8am-2am. AmEx/MC/V. ❹

Bioboa, 3, r. Danielle Casanova (☎01 42 61 17 67). Ⓜ Pyramides. Follow Av. de l'Opéra towards the Opéra itself and turn left on r. Danielle Casanova. A small, stylish "food spa" just down the road from the Opéra Garnier. Bioboa offers soups, salads, sandwiches, paninis, desserts and pastries; almost all ingredients are organic (organic lychees are apparently very hard to find). Delicious smoothies (€5-5.90). Decor as simple and chic as the menu. Open M-Sa 11am-6pm. MC/V. ❷

SALONS DE THÉ

Angelina's, 226, r. de Rivoli (☎01 42 60 82 00). Ⓜ Concorde or Tuileries. Audrey Hepburn's old favorite. Little has changed here since the *salon*'s 1903 opening; the frescoes, mirrored walls, and marble tables are all original. *Chocolat africain* (hot chocolate; €6.50) and *Mont Blanc* (meringue with chestnut nougat; €6) are the tantalizing house specialties. Tea €6. Open daily 9am-7pm. AmEx/MC/V.

Muscade, 36, r. de Montpensier (☎01 42 97 51 36). Ⓜ Palais-Royal. In the Palais-Royal's northwest corner. Muscade's walls are adorned with mirrors and art by Jean Cocteau, but in summer the terrace is more pleasant. *Le Chocolat a l'Ancienne* (€6) is a melted chocolate bar parading as a liquid. An assortment of pastries (€7) and 23 kinds of tea (€5-5.50). Reservations recommended, especially for terrace seats. Open Tu-Su for tea 10-11:30am and 3-6pm; lunch 12:15-3pm; dinner 7:15-10:30pm. Closes 7pm Su. AmEx/MC/V.

ON THE MENU

YOUR DAILY BREAD

Bread is one of those Paris icons that, like the sidewalk cafe, is as present on the living city streets as in the imagination. Though the average Parisian today consumes only around 160g of bread per day, down from around 1kg in 1900, it is still eaten with almost every meal, and you'll rarely walk down a street without seeing a few people sneaking bites of their dinner loaves.

But with 1300 *boulangeries* in Paris to choose from, how do you separate the wheat from the chaff? Start with the definition. According to the craft, a baguette must weigh 250-300g, measuring about 70cm in length and 6cm in diameter. The crust must be smooth and golden, ready to crackle under moderate finger pressure (ask for it *"bien cuit"*). The underside, or "sole," should never be charred; beware a honeycomb imprint, which indicates accelerated cooking in a rotating oven—the taste will be cut short. The inside (*mie*) should be light with large air holes. The bread should have a full, salty taste and a subtly doughy texture.

Each February, city hall holds a cut-throat competition: the Grand Prix de la Baguette. The winner becomes the official baguette of the Elysée Palace for the next year. Current resident Jacques Chirac takes his bread seriously: he has dismissed supermarket baguettes as "not even a Christian food."

THE CAMEMBERT AFFAIR

According to legend, the creation of Camembert cheese coincides with that of the French Republic. In 1791, a milkmaid from Normandy combined a local recipe with the process used to make brie and *voilà:* a new national symbol.

But while the French still consume more cheese than any other nation—25kg per person annually—Camembert is no longer the nation's *fromage préféré.* From 1997 to 2001, Camembert sales fell 5.5%, now accounting for a mere 10% of French cheese sales.

Producers blame the decline on a subjection to the rules of the EU. Farmers now sell their cheeses to large industrial groups rather than directly to picky *fromageries.* Additionally, the EU's obsession with cleanliness has led to stringent regulations, forcing cheese makers to leave behind their stone-walled buildings and the natural yeasts that accumulated on their walls and equipment and gave Camembert its distinctive flavor. Producers also claim that ultra-clean milk demanded by the EU leads to tasteless cheese.

Camembert is also falling victim to supermarket culture. Less pungent, pre-wrapped cheeses are taking up more shelf space. For Camembert, made from full-fat milk, convenience has begun to replace convention.

SPECIALTY SHOPS

Julien, 75 r. St-Honoré, (☎01 42 36 24 83). The best of everything: breads, sandwiches, pastries, cakes. For an indulgent breakfast, try the *pain au chocolat* (a flaky, buttery chocolate croissant; €1) or the very different but equally delicious *pain chocolat* (a small loaf of bread with chocolate chips; €1.50). Long lines at lunch.

Nicolas, 142, r. de Rivoli (☎01 42 33 58 45). Locations throughout Paris. Super-friendly English-speaking staff will help you pick the perfect Burgundy. They'll even pack it up in a sturdy travel box with handles. Most branches open M-F 10am-8pm. AmEx/MC/V.

SECOND ARRONDISSEMENT

The *2ème* has many inexpensive dining options. **Rue Montorgueil** is lined with excellent bakeries, fruit stands, cafe-bars, and specialty stores. Side streets like **rue Marie Stuart** and **rue Mandar** are also worthwhile. You'll find fast, cheap food on **passage des Panoramas** and **passage des Italiens**.

■ **Les Noces de Jeannette,** 14, r. Favart and 9, r. d'Amboise (☎01 42 96 36 89). ⓜ Richelieu-Drouot. Exit onto bd. des Italiens, then turn left onto r. Favart. Named after a 19th-century *opéra comique* playing across the street at the time of its opening, this elegant and diverse restaurant will certainly impress your date (or your mother). *Menu du Jeanette* (€27) includes salad *entrées;* grilled meat, and roasted fish and duck *plats;* and fabulous desserts. *Kir* included with meal. *Menu Bistro* is €3 more and includes a half-bottle of Bordeaux. Reservations recommended. Open daily noon-1:30pm and 7-9:30pm. ❹

Le Loup Blanc, 42, r. Tiquetonne (☎01 40 13 08 35). ⓜ Etienne-Marcel. Walk against traffic on r. de Turbigo and go left on r. Tiquetonne. *Mixed Grille* samples 4 kinds of meat or seafood and sides. Depending on the meat and the number of sides, a plate will run €14-17.50. Vegetarian option of 4-6 sides (€12.50-14.50), including quinoa tabbouleh. Open M-Th and Su 7:30pm-midnight, F 7:30pm-12:30am, Sa 7:30pm-1am. MC/V. ❸

La Cucaracha, 31, r. Tiquetonne (☎01 40 26 68 36). ⓜ Etienne-Marcel. Walk against traffic on r. de Turbigo and go left on r. Tiquetonne. At this small Mexican restaurant, dishes like *enchiladas verde* or fajitas run a reasonable €12-15. The *mole* sauce used in a number of dishes is made with 39 different spices. The flavors are intense (but not too hot), the crowd mostly French (and very hot). If you can't get a table outside on the pedestrian-packed r. Tiquetonne, you'll be subjected to the Mexican kitsch decor inside. Open daily 7-11:30pm. MC/V. ❷

Babylone Bis, 34, r. Tiquetonne (☎01 42 33 48 35). ⓜ Etienne-Marcel. Walk against traffic on r. de Turbigo and turn left onto r. Tiquetonne. On a road where one restaurant celebrates Halloween year-round, it's hardly surprising to find an establishment with zebra skin on the walls, banana leaves on the ceiling, and incredibly loud *zouk* music blasting from the speakers. Serving Antillean and African cuisine, this place cooks up such sumptuous specialties as *aloko* (flambéed bananas; €5.50) and *poulet braisé* (lime-marinated chicken; €15). Dinner served all night. Open daily 8pm-8am. MC/V. ❸

Kintaro, 24, r. St-Augustin (☎01 47 42 13 14). ⓜ Opéra. Walk down av. de l'Opéra and turn left on r. St-Augustin. Delicious and popular Japanese restaurant with everything but sushi. Kintaro instead offers great noodle bowls (€6.80-8.50) and an array of menu combinations (€8-18). Sapporo €4.60. Open M-Sa 11:30am-10pm. MC/V. ❷

THIRD ARRONDISSEMENT

The restaurants of the upper Marais serve an array of international and traditionally French cuisine. Dozens of charming bistros line r. St-Martin, and a number of kosher food stands and restaurants are located around r. du Vertbois and r. Volta. Dinner in the Marais can be pricey, but lunchtime *menus* often offer good deals. Reservations are strongly recommended in the evening.

🏅 **Chez Janou,** 2, r. Roger Verlomme (☎01 42 72 28 41). ⓜ Chemin-Vert. From the metro, take r. St-Gilles and turn left almost immediately on r. des Tournelles. The restaurant is on the corner of r. Roger Verlomme. Tucked into a quiet corner of the 3ème, this is a bustling, classic Parisian bistro lauded for its inexpensive gourmet food. No menus; the dishes are listed on blackboards scattered throughout the restaurant. There is a new *plat du jour* (€13.50) every day. The *ratatouille* and the goat cheese and spinach salad are both €9 and delicious. Desserts €7-8. The shady terrace is superb for dining *al fresco* during the summer. Reservations always recommended, as this local favorite is packed every night of the week. Open M-F noon-3pm and 7:45pm-midnight, Sa-Su noon-4pm and 7:45pm-midnight. ❷

🏅 **404,** 69, r. des Gravilliers (☎01 42 74 57 81). ⓜ Arts et Métiers. Walk down r. Beaubourg and take a right on r. des Gravilliers. The plain stone facade masks an intimate, rich decor of deep red curtains and dark carved wood. Seating in the airy, casual terrace in the back during lunchtime is a must. Features mouth-watering couscous (€14-24) and *tagines* (€14-18), with plenty of vegetarian options marked on the menu. Lunch *menu* €17, M-F only. Open M-F noon-2:30pm and 8pm-midnight, Sa-Su noon-4pm and 8pm-midnight. AmEx/MC/V. ❹

🏅 **Le Petit Pamphlet,** 15, r. St-Gilles (☎01 42 71 22 21). ⓜ Chemin Vert. This casually elegant and cozy new bistro in the Bastille is hard to beat for prices and excellence in cuisine. Creatively and exquisitely plated dishes delight both sight and taste, and offer a lighter take on classic French favorites. The menu uses only fresh, available ingredients, and changes weekly, but the service is always attentive and discreet. Delightful complimentary *amuse-bouche* to begin your meal, and a tidbit to finish the meal in sweetness. Appetizers €9, *plats* €12-15, and desserts €7. Reservations suggested. Open M-Su noon-2pm and 7-10:30pm. MC/V. ❸

🏅 **Caves St-Gilles,** 4, r. St-Gilles (☎ 01 48 87 22 62). ⓜ Chemin Vert. Take r. St-Gilles exit. This Spanish-style bistro is cheerily decorated with a mosaic tile floor, small wooden tables, and checkered tablecloths. An obliging and super-friendly waitstaff brings generous, filling portions of tapas to satisfied customers, many of whom are Spanish. The cold or hot tapas plate combinations are a good deal at €14.50. The multilingual staff speaks French, Spanish and English. Open M-Th noon-3pm and 8-11pm, F noon-3pm and 7:30-11:45pm, Sa-Su noon-4pm and 7:30-11:45pm. MC/V. ❷

Taxi Jaune, 13, r. Chapon (☎01 42 76 00 40). ⓜ Arts et Métiers. Walk along r. Beaubourg and turn left onto r. Chapon. The soft-spoken owner personally hand-picks ingredients and designs the menus to reflect the change in seasonal produce. A casual, intimate and convivial atmosphere redolent of a 1930s French diner brings a devoted regular crowd who delight in the creative and original dishes prepared by the owner himself. Appetizers €8. *Plats* €17. Lunch *menu* €14. Open M-F 9am-1am. Food served noon-3pm and 8-10:30pm. Closed 3 weeks in Aug and winter holidays. Reservations strongly recommended. V. ❸

Le Réconfort, 37, r. de Poitou (☎01 49 96 09 60). ⓂSt-Sébastien-Froissart. Walk along r. du Point-Aux-Choux to r. de Poitou. Plush red velvet French salon decor with an elegant but not intimidating vibe. The food is a delightful melange of cuisines, featuring coconut-lemon king prawns and pork filet mignon with balsamic sauce. Lunch *menu* €14-18. Main courses €16-21. The lunchtime *plat du jour* is a steal at €10. Open M-F noon-2pm and 8-11pm, Sa-Su 8-11:30pm. Reservations recommended for dinner. MC/V. ❸

Chez Omar, 47, r. de Bretagne (☎01 42 72 36 26). ⓂArts et Métiers. Walk along r. Réamur, away from r. St-Martin. R. Réamur turns into r. de Bretagne. One of the better Middle Eastern places in town, featuring airy and bright decor; packed past 8:30pm. Come at 7:30pm for peace and quiet, later to see the local intelligentsia in action. Couscous with vegetables €12. The *steak au poivre* (€16) is served in a spectacular sauce. Other specialties like *brochettes* and *ratatouille* €13-16. Vegetarian options available. Open M-Sa noon-2:30pm and 7-11pm, Su 7-11pm. Cash only. ❸

CAFES

L'Apparement Café, 18, r. des Coutures St-Gervais (☎01 48 87 12 22). ⓂSt-Paul. Behind the Picasso Museum, this cafe serves coffee (€2), make-your-own salads (€11-16), and choose-your-own Su brunch (€15.50-20) to trendy young things in cushioned chairs. Come to chat or to play ping-pong or Scrabble in the game room (see **Nightlife,** p. 304). Open M-Sa noon-2am, Su 12:30pm-midnight. Reservations recommended for brunch. MC/V. ❸

Les Arts et Métiers, 51, r. de Turbigo (☎01 48 87 83 25). ⓂArts et Métiers. A hip cafe overlooking a busy intersection and a favorite with locals of all stripes. The terrace is lovely, but somewhat noisy from the passing traffic; the sleek and chic interior offers jazz, blues and rock concerts F-Sa 7:45pm and Su 5:30pm. Delicious milkshakes €6.50. Sandwiches €3.50-9.50. Happy hour (6-9pm) features beers and mixed drinks for only €5. Open daily 7am-2am. MC/V *with* €15 min. charge. ❶

SPECIALTY SHOPS

🏠 **La Cure Gourmande,** 88, r. St-Martin (☎01 42 71 26 18; www.la-cure-gourmande.com). ⓂRambuteau. This one-of-a-kind candy shop prepares its original treats using only natural ingredients. Indulge in the amazing almond-olive chocolates (€7 per *sachet*) and the scrumptious traditional caramels (€4.50 for 100g), or play it cheap with €1 lollipops. Feast your eyes on the plump marzipan sweets and delightfully decorated tins. All sweets are displayed in bulk for customers to serve themselves. Open M-Sa 10am-6:30pm. MC/V.

FOURTH ARRONDISSEMENT

In the 4*ème*, dining is more about where you're eating and how good you look doing it than about food. Dining in the 4*ème* isn't cheap, but living off salads and sandwiches from the many cafe/bar/restaurants or grabbing an Eastern European snack *à emporter* from **rue des Rosiers** can get you through the day without breaking the bank. Sunday brunch is your chance to eat as much as you can at one of the many buffets. So splurge: go somewhere happening, get as little food as possible, and revel in the chic Marais atmosphere.

■ **L'As du Falafel,** 34, r. des Rosiers (☎01 48 87 63 60). ⓂSt-Paul. This kosher falafel stand and restaurant displays pictures of Lenny Kravitz, who credited it as "the best falafel in the world, particularly the special eggplant falafel with hot sauce." The falafel special is incredible in taste and price (€6, takeout €4). Thimble-sized (but damn good) lemonade, €3.50 per glass. Open M-Th and Su noon-midnight, F noon-6pm. MC/V. ❶

■ **Pain, Vin, Fromage,** 3, r. Geoffrey L'Angevin (☎01 42 74 07 52). ⓂRambuteau or Hôtel de Ville. On a small side street right near the Centre Pompidou, this cozy Parisian classic (complete with seating in the rustic basement wine cellar) serves France's 3 basic food groups in original combinations. Fondues (€13.50-16) and salads (€7.50-9) are accompanied by a winning wine list. Try the tasting platters of regional cheese, complete with little name tag flags. Open M-Sa 7-11:30pm. Reservations recommended. AmEx/MC/V. ❷

■ **Piccolo Teatro,** 6, r. des Ecouffes (☎01 42 72 17 79). ⓂSt-Paul. Walk with the traffic down r. de Rivoli and take a right on r. des Ecouffes. A romantic vegetarian hideout draped in red velvet. Weekday lunch *menus* €9, €10.50, and €14.50. Appetizers €4-7.50. *Plats* €8-12. Open daily noon-3pm and 7-11pm. AmEx/MC/V. ❷

■ **Au Petit Fer à Cheval,** 30, r. Vieille-du-Temple (☎01 42 72 47 47). ⓂHôtel de Ville or St-Paul. From Ⓜ St-Paul, go with the traffic on r. de Rivoli and turn right; the restaurant will be on your right. An oasis of *chèvre, kir,* and *Gauloises,* graced by a crowd of low-key sophisticates. Hidden behind the bar are a few tables where you can order *filet mignon de veau* (€16) or any of the excellent house salads (€10-12). Delicious *tarte tatin,* €7.50. Open daily 9am-2am; food served noon-1:15am. MC/V. ❷

AN EPICUREAN EMPIRE. The same charming fellow who owns Au Petit Fer à Cheval also has two equally fantastic restaurants nearby–**Les Philosophes** and **La Chaise au Plafond,** which are a great alternative if Au Petit Fer is crowded.

Petit Bofinger, 6, r. de la Bastille (☎01 42 72 05 23). ⓂBastille. R. de la Bastille runs directly off pl. de la Bastille. Totally classic cuisine in a relaxed yet refined atmosphere. Worth-the-splurge *prix fixe* (€20/28.50) includes wine and all the greatest hits of fine French cooking. Kids menu €8.50. Across the street, the original **Bofinger** attracts an older crowd dressed to the nines (dinner *menu* €30). Open daily noon-3pm and 7pm-midnight. AmEx/MC/V. ❸

Le Divin, 41, r. Ste-Croix-de-la-Bretonnerie (☎01 42 77 10 20). ⓂHôtel de Ville. Walk away from Hôtel de Ville on r. Vieille-du-Temple and go right on r. Ste-Croix-de-la-Bretonnerie. Go South, where sun and cheer (in the form of friendly service and vintage beach prints) bounce off the sun-kissed yellow walls. Country-style Provençal fare. Plenty of vegetarian options available. *Menus* €16 and €21. Open Tu-Su 7-11:30pm. Reservations suggested for the weekend. AmEx/MC/V. ❸

Little Italy Trattoria, 13, r. Rambuteau (☎01 42 74 32 46). ⓂRambuteau. Walk along r. Rambuteau in the direction of traffic; it's on the right, you'll see people waiting outside. An enticing *salumeria* with tables both indoors and out. Amazing *antipasti* selection for 2 €21; delicate, fresh pastas €8-14. Pitcher of wine €7-7.50. Open daily 8:30am-11:30pm. Food served noon-3:30pm and 7:30-11pm. MC/V. ❷

Curieux Spaghetti Bar, 14, r. St.-Martin (☎01 42 72 75 97; www.curieuxspag.com). ⓂRambuteau or Hotel de Ville. A storefront spraying light mist welcomes you into this trendy cafe-restaurant. Self-consciously hip, the walls are decorated with pixelated, multicolored graphics, and clients dine to strains of techno and hip-hop. A fashionable serving staff busily caters to a youngish clientele, who smoke chains of cigarettes

F O O D

UNIVERSITY RESTAURANTS

For students, university restaurants can provide some of the cheapest eats and best company in Paris. When school is in session (Sept.-June), Paris's 17 *restos U'* serve ample fare to crowds of hungry students. A three-course meal (€2.40 with student ID) generally includes a cafeteria-style choice of sandwiches, regional and international dishes, and grilled meats. All *restos* are open for lunch; Bullier, Châtelet, Citeaux, Mabillon, and Dauphine are also open for dinner. For hours, contact the Centre Régional des Oeuvres Universitaires et Scolaires (CROUS; ☎01 40 51 55 55; www.crous-paris.fr).

Bullier, 39, av. Georges Bernanos, 5ème (RER: Port-Royal); **Cuvier-Jussieu,** 8bis, r. Cuvier, 5ème (Ⓜ Cuvier-Jussieu); **Censier,** 31, r. Geoffroy St-Hilaire, 5ème (Ⓜ Censier-Daubenton); **Châtelet,** 10, r. Jean Calvin, 5ème (Ⓜ Censier-Daubenton); **Assas,** 92, r. d'Assas, 6ème (Ⓜ Notre-Dame-des-Champs); **Mabillon,** 3, r. Mabillon, 6ème (Ⓜ Mabillon); **Citeaux,** 45, bd. Diderot, 12ème (Ⓜ Gare de Lyon); **Tolbiac,** 17, r. de Tolbiac, 13ème; **Dareau,** 13-17, r. Dareau, 14ème (Ⓜ St-Jacques); **Necker,** 156, r. de Vaugirard, 15ème (Ⓜ Pasteur); **Dauphine,** av. de Pologne, 16ème (Ⓜ Porte Dauphine); **Bichat,** 16, r. Henri Huchard, 18ème (Ⓜ Porte de St-Ouen).

while dining on generous helpings of pasta (€9-18). Share a pot of noodles for 2, perhaps the gorgonzola spaghetti or the classic meatball. Daily special €10, lunch *menu* €12. Also doubles as a cafe-bar with a happy hour from 4-8pm. Try the specialty shots of perfumed vodka in fanciful flavors such as bubble gum and mojito. Open M-W and Su noon-2am and Th-Sa noon-4am. MC/V. ❷

Bistrot du Dome, 2, r. de la Bastille (☎01 43 21 40 64). Ⓜ Bastille. R. de la Bastille runs directly off pl. de la Bastille. The fresh fish at this refined restaurant is a cut above the fast-food fare that dominates the Bastille area. Light, simple main courses (€20-27) are composed of fish and vegetables. A variety of desserts, such as cherry *clafouti* (€7). Open daily 12:30-2:30pm and 7:30-11pm. AmEx/MC/V. ❸

Le Grizzli, 7, r. St-Martin (☎01 48 87 77 56). Ⓜ Châtelet or Hôtel de Ville. Walk along quai de Gesvres and turn left onto r. St-Martin. This cool bistro near the Centre Pompidou serves meticulously prepared salads (€14) and pastas (€11-12). Outdoor seating on a pleasant terrace. Su brunch €21. Open daily noon-2am. Food served noon-2:30pm and 7:30-11pm. AmEx/MC/V. ❷

CAFES

🏛 **Georges,** Centre Pompidou, 6th fl. (☎01 44 78 47 99). Enter via the centre or the elevator to the left of the Pompidou's r. Beaubourg entrance. Ⓜ Rambuteau or Hôtel de Ville. Even if you miss the museum, stop by this ultra-sleek cafe, if only for the terrace. Its minimalist design draws tourists and locals alike, and the rooftop view is magnificent. Come for a glass of wine or champagne (€8-10) or a snack (gazpacho €10, fruit salad €9.50); splurge on a *plat* (lobster macaroni €29, *mandarina* crispy duck €27); or just to take a peek at the menu, supposedly designed by Dior menswear creator Hedi Slimane. Reservations suggested for dinner. Open M and W-Su noon-2am. AmEx/MC/V. ❸

Café Beaubourg, 100, r. St-Merri (☎01 48 87 63 96). Ⓜ Rambuteau or Hôtel de Ville. Facing Centre Pompidou. Clientele wears everything from the newest Lagerfeld to Dockers to nose piercings. This is the spot to see and be seen during the day. Coffee €2.50. Steamed vanilla milk €5. Mixed drinks €9. Grog with rum or honey €6. 3-course brunch €22-25. Open M-Tu and Su 8am-1am, and W-Sa 8am-2am. AmEx/MC/V. ❹

SALONS DE THÉ

🏛 **Mariage Frères,** 30, r. du Bourg-Tibourg, 4ème (☎01 42 72 28 11). Ⓜ Hôtel-de-Ville. Started by 2 brothers who found British tea shoddy, this salon offers 500 varieties of tea (€7-15) and an in-house book detailing the history and uses of each variety. The subtle, white-suited waiters and the sophisticated clientele make this a classic French institution. Tea *menu* includes sandwich, pastry, and tea (€25). Classic brunch *menu* is excellent (bri-oche, eggs, tea, cakes; €25), as is the decadent Snob Salad (€21) which comes piled high with foie gras and smoked salmon. Reserve for brunch. After eating, exit through the impressive tea store which sells a wide variety of books (such as *The Art of French Tea*), pots of tea, and tea kettles. Open daily 10:30am-7:30pm; lunch M-Sa noon-3pm; afternoon tea 3-6:30pm; Su brunch 12:30-6:30pm. AmEx/MC/V. Also at 13, r. des Grands Augustins, 6ème (☎01 40 51 82 50); and at 260, r. du Faubourg St-Honoré, 8ème (☎01 46 22 18 54).

SPECIALTY SHOPS

Jadis et Gourmande, 39, r. des Archives, (☎01 48 04 08 03). Ⓜ Rambuteau. Choco-late's equivalent to a flower shop. Violet perfumed chocolates, candy arrangements tucked into bamboo cases. Custom-order chocolate messages. Rich chocolate ice cream €2.50 for 1 scoop. Open M 1-7:30pm, Tu-F 10am-7:30pm, Sa 10:30am-7:30pm. AmEx/MC/V.

Izrael, 30, r. François Miron(☎01 42 72 66 23). Ⓜ St-Paul. Barrels and bins flowing with orange lentils, brazil nuts, candied cherries, couscous, and other delicacies. Nar-row shelves of Hershey's syrup and peanut butter jostle a large selection of curries and specialty alcohols. Best known for its pungent, aromatic spices from all over the world sold from huge sacks. Open Tu-F 9:30am-1pm and 2:30-7pm, Sa 9am-7pm.

FIFTH ARRONDISSEMENT

A particularly diverse area of Paris, the 5ème is home to a score of inexpensive bis-tros as well as Tibetan, Vietnamese, and Middle Eastern restaurants. All along **rue Mouffetard**, back-to-back restaurants serve high-quality food at surpassingly low prices (expect a *menu* from €9.50-14). Hordes of sidewalk bistros crowd **rue de la Montagne Ste-Geneviève** and continue north of the Panthéon onto **rue Descartes** and into **place de la Contrescarpe**. Cheap, touristy Greek and Middle Eastern establish-ments line **rue de la Huchette** and **rue Galande**. **Mavrommatis,** 47-49, r. Censier, comes highly recommended as one of the best Greek restaurants in Paris (☎01 43 31 17 17).

Savannah Café, 27, r. Descartes (☎01 43 29 45 77). Ⓜ Cardinal Lemoine. Follow r. du Cardinal Lemoine uphill, turn right on r. Clovis, and walk 1 block to r. Descartes. Decorated with eclectic knick-knacks, this cheerful restaurant serves Lebanese food and other "selections from around the world." Dishes include eggplant caviar, taboule, and a selection of pasta dishes (€12.50). Try the perfectly composed starter sampler (€16), 6 choices to share between 2 diners. *Plats* €12.50-14.50. Open M-Sa 7-11pm. MC/V. ❸

Comptoir Méditerranée, 42, r. du Cardinal Lemoine (☎01 43 25 29 08). Savannah Café's little sister, run by the same welcoming owner. Tastes from Lebanon and else-where presented in a fresh and colorful array of ingredients. Select from 20 hot and cold dishes to make your own plate (€6). Open M-Sa 11am-10pm. ❶

Le Grenier de Notre-Dame, 18, r. de la Bucherie (☎01 43 29 98 29; www.legrenierde-notredame.net). Ⓜ St-Michel. Walk along quai St-Michel to quai de Montebello; turn right on r. Lagrange and left on r. de la Bucherie. Sunflowers and organic plants deco-rate the patio and interior of this eclectic cafe. Macrobiotic and vegetarian specialties with a contemporary French spin. A haven for vegans in this *fromage*-loving city. *La formule* is 3 courses for €17.50, or €12.50 at lunch. Salads €8.50-13.50. Open daily noon-11pm. MC/V. ❷

Le Perraudin, 157, r. St-Jacques (☎01 46 33 15 75). ⓜ Cluny-La Sorbonne, RER Luxembourg. From Cluny, walk down bd. St-Michel, turn left on r. Soufflot, then right on r. St-Jacques; the restaurant is on the corner across the street. Simple, elegant, and *pas trop cher*, Le Perraudin has a deep red exterior, an intimate garden, and traditional "French" red-and-white checked tablecloths. Serves Parisian favorites like *confit de canard* and *boeuf bourguignon* to a boisterous crowd, mostly students and locals. *Plats à la carte* €16-29. *Menu* €28. Open M-F noon-2:30pm and 7-10:30pm. ❸

Le Jardin des Pâtes, 4, r. Lacépède (☎01 43 31 50 71). ⓜ Jussieu. Walk up r. Linné and turn right on r. Lacépède. As calming and pleasant as the Jardin des Plantes around the corner. Le Jardin's menu of organic food emphasizes fresh *pâtes* (pasta; €8-14). Appetizers €4.50-9. Open daily noon-2:30pm and 7-11pm. AmEx/MC/V. ❷

Au Port Salut, 163bis, r. St-Jacques (☎01 46 33 63 21). RER Luxembourg. Down the road from Le Perraudin; follow directions and then continue along r. St-Jacques. Behind its iron portcullis, this old stone building (once a cabaret with the same name) houses 3 floors of traditional French gastronomy. Upstairs is a non-smoking dining room, the *rez-de-chaussée* is a boisterous bar with a piano, and the cabaret downstairs is decorated with Romanesque frescoes. Seasonal 3-course *menus* (lunch or dinner €15.60 or €27). Salads €12-16.50. Open Tu-Sa noon-2:30pm and 7-11pm. MC/V. ❸

CAFES

▨ **Café de la Mosquée,** 39, r. Geoffrey St-Hilaire (☎01 43 31 38 20). ⓜ Censier-Daubenton. In the Mosquée de Paris. With fountains, white marble floors, and an exquisite multi-level terrace, this cafe deserves a visit whether a trip to the Mosquée is on your itinerary or not. Rest under the shady fig and olive trees and savor Persian mint tea (€2.50) and *maghrebain* pastries (€2.50), or sit inside in the beautifully decorated dining room. Restaurant serves couscous (€9-25) on gorgeous copper tabletops. For dessert, the Coupe Orientale is very tasty, with 2 scoops of mint tea ice cream and 1 scoop of honey nougat. Tea room and restaurant open daily 9am-11pm. MC/V. ❷

Café Delmas, 2-4, pl. de la Contrescarpe (☎01 43 26 51 26). ⓜ Cardinal Lemoine. Walk up r. du Cardinal Lemoine straight into pl. de la Contreescarpe. In this happening area, Delmas is the place to while away the hours in style. Black-clad waiters serve trendy food like Chinese chicken salad (€12) and mixed drinks from a lengthy drinks menu to glamorous people-watchers. *Café* €2.50. Happy hour 7-9pm. Open M-Th and Su 7am-2am, F-Sa 7am-5am. MC/V. ❷

Octave, 136, r. Mouffetard (☎01 45 35 20 56). ⓜ Censier-Daubenton. If heaven ever froze over, it would be served in a cone at Octave. With no preservatives or coloring (unlike rival Berthillon), all this ice cream delivers with each scoop is fresh melon, rich chocolate, or soothing cinnamon. Ingredients are held to such high standards that Octave doesn't serve strawberry or raspberry ice cream in winter—when berries are out of season. Unfortunately, Octave has a weak price-to-volume ratio: the servings are tiny compared to those at Amorino (p. 149). 1 scoop €2, 2 scoops €3.50, a whopping 5 scoops €7. Open M 2-8:30pm, Tu 10:30am-10:30pm, W-Th and Su 10:30am-11pm, F-Sa 10:30am-11:30pm. ❶

SPECIALTY SHOPS

▨ **Marché Monge,** ⓜ Monge. In pl. Monge at the metro exit. A bustling, friendly, and easy-to-navigate market. You'll find everything from cheese to shoes to jewelry and flowers in these stalls. Look for the very popular prepared foods (perfect for a lunch picnic at the Arènes de Lutèce). Open W, F, and Su 8am-1pm.

Marché Port Royal, Ⓜ Les Gobelins. Walk downhill to the major intersection, turn left onto bd. de Port Royal, look for the stalls in front of the hospital (about 10min.). Sells mostly fresh vegetables, fruit, meat, and cheese. Primarily local patrons. Some clothes and housewares also for sale. Open Tu, Th, and Sa 7am-2:30pm.

Marché Mouffetard, Ⓜ Monge. Walk through pl. Monge and follow r. Ortolan to r. Mouffetard. Cheese, meat, fish, produce, and housewares sold here. Great fruit selection, and the bakeries are reputed to be some of the best of all the markets. Don't miss the ice cream at Octave near the far end of the market. Open Tu-Sa 10am-1pm and 4-7pm, Su 10am-1pm.

SIXTH ARRONDISSEMENT

Any restaurants with rock-bottom prices vie for space and customers in the streets enclosed by **boulevard St-Germain, boulevard St-Michel, rue de Seine,** and the river. Within the tangle, **rue de Buci** harbors bargain Greek restaurants and a rambling street market, while **rue Grégoire de Tours** has the highest density of cheap, greasy tourist joints. **Rue St-Andre-des-Arts** is lined with *crêperies* and panini purveyors. Around Odéon, the **Carrefour d'Odéon** has several traditional bistros, and **rue Princesse, rue Guisarde,** and **rue des Canettes** are jam-packed with cheap and pedestrian-friendly eateries.

Café Parisien, 15, r. d'Assas (☎01 45 44 41 44). Ⓜ Sèvres Babylone or Rennes. You'll hear nothing but French spoken in this small cafe on the west side of the 6ème. Café Parisien serves up some delicious dishes, like *espadon* in a basil sauce (€14), on stylish square plates. Menu changes with the weather, but everything is of the highest quality. Salads €8.50-10. Coffee €2.50. Reservations recommended. Open daily noon-3pm and 8-11pm. Sa-Su brunch is served, with some American brunch options. MC/V. ❷

Le Bistro d'Henri, 16, r. Princesse (☎01 46 33 51 12). Ⓜ Mabillon. Walk down r. du Four and left onto r. Princesse. This Left Bank bistro serves classic (read: delicious but heavy) food, prepared with fresh ingredients. Appetizers €6-7. Plats €12-18. Open daily noon-2:30pm and 7-11pm. MC/V. Around the corner is **Le Machon d'Henri,** 8, r. Guisarde (☎01 43 29 08 70), with the same menu in a smaller, white-stone alcove. ❹

Cosi, 54, r. de Seine (☎01 46 33 35 36). Ⓜ Mabillon. Walk down bd. St-Germain and make a left onto r. de Seine. Enormous, tasty, inexpensive sandwiches on fresh, brick-oven bread. Sandwiches €5-8. Desserts €3-4. Open daily noon-11pm. ❶

THE HIDDEN DEAL

SPRING FOR A ROLL

In an area known for its cheap food, good value is no guarantee of popularity. The prospect of a fresh spring roll for €0.35, however, is enough to stop even the most frugal shoppers in their tracks. Hoa Nam, a Vietnamese *traiteur* in the heart of Chinatown, is in the business of seriously budget eats. You can get a dense and delicious vermicelli and beef salad packaged to go for €3.80, and chunky, ready-to-eat ravioli for €0.40 a piece.

The specialty of this tiny corner shop, jam-packed with food and customers, is the Vietnamese baguette. The Vietnamese baguette is more than just a sandwich. It's any number of tantalizing combinations of cold cut meats, vegetables, and pâté, doused liberally in Hoa Nam's tangy house sauce, from just €2.30 to go.

To make a meal of it, grab a Vietnamese baguette and head to Parc Choisy, a short walk away from the controlled chaos of Chinatown. Hoa Nam also sells frozen goods, made on the premises, to take home—the dumplings are renowned. The enthusiastic staff will help out with cooking instructions and serving suggestions.

Hoa Nam, 51, av. d'Ivry, 13ème. ☎01 45 82 66 66. × Porte d'Italie.

ON THE MENU

GETTING THE SKINNY

Many theories have been put forward to explain the widely observed yet narrowly understood phenomenon of the slimness of the French, especially of French women. There seems to be no evidence of French cuisine's passion for cream and oil in the svelte hips of young Parisians. Just looking at clothing sizes in upscale boutiques, one can see that obesity is simply a rarity in Paris. But how can this be, in a country famous for its cheese and *pâté*?

A popular theory maintains that French women smoke constantly and drink copious amounts of coffee, thereby reducing their appetites and occupying their mouths in one unhealthy stroke. Smokers do indeed seem ever-present in Paris, but whether or not this prevents them getting hungry, many French can be seen in local cafes indulging in two- or three-course meals at lunchtime. A more convincing theory, and one that has been put forward on the basis of much research and many time-consuming studies, is that the French... wait for it... eat less than Americans and Brits. Genius.

Portion size is America's greatest weakness. Ever since McDonald's began offering to Super-Size your meal, it's been a slippery slope. The French, on the other hand, seem to have an ingrained Weight Watchers-style mentality of moderation. Although

Guen-maï, 2bis, r. de l'Abbaye, entrance at 6, r. Cardinale (☎01 43 26 03 24). ⓜ Mabillon. Walk against traffic on bd. St-Germain and go right on r. de la Petite Boucherie, then left on r. de l'Abbaye. This healthy-living oasis might have more appeal for vegetarians and vegans than for carnivores (though they do have fish); anyone who craves seitan and soy will find a little piece of macrobiotic heaven here. The lunch counter doubles as a *salon de thé* and bookstore, as well as a vitamin boutique. Choices include miso soup (€4.50), agar fruit salad (€5), *poisson crudités* (€10.50), and daily specials (€11.50). Lunch served M-Sa 11:45am-3:30pm. Store open M-Sa 9am-8:30pm. MC/V. ❷

Crêperie Saint Germain, 33, r. St-André-des-Arts (☎01 43 54 24 41). ⓜ St-Michel. Cross pl. St-Michel and walk down r. St-André-des-Arts. Serves filling wheat-flour *crêpes noirs*, like the Chihuahua (chicken cooked with peppers, tomatoes, and onions; €9) or the Lolita (asparagus, ham, cheese and nuts; €8.50). Sweet dessert *crêpes* like the Zanzibar (pear ice cream, raspberries, chocolate sauce, and chantilly). Colorful lighting. €9 *menu* (M-F noon-3pm) includes 2 *crêpes* and a *cidre* or a soda. Open daily noon-midnight. AmEx/MC/V. ❶

La Crêpe Rit du Clown, 6, r. des Canettes (☎01 46 34 01 02). ⓜ Mabillon. Walk down r. du Four and turn left on r. des Canettes. The clown figure greeting patrons at the door may smack of an unfortunate horror movie, but the food is tasty and cheap. Lunchtime *formule* €10.50. Savory *crêpes* €7-9. *Kir* €4 a glass. Open M-Sa noon-11:30pm. MC/V. ❶

CAFES

Forget fine dining; cafes are the heart (and stomach) of the 6ème. Ordering a *café express* will guarantee you a seat and a place to while away the hours with your friends. While historic establishments like **Le Sélect** and **Café de Flore** still hold court along the **boulevard Montparnasse** and **boulevard St-Germain-des-Prés**, newer cafes cluster around **Carrefour d'Odéon** and north of bd. St-Germain near the galleries. This area contains many brasseries and is probably your best bet for eating cheap in Paris.

🕮 **Café Vavin,** 18, r. Vavin (☎01 43 26 67 47). ⓜ Vavin. The elusive creature: a cafe with personality, location, and delicious food. Vavin inhabits the part of Montparnasse that spills over into the 6ème and is surrounded by small boutiques. Funky tiling on the walls completes a trendy, bohemian look for this corner cafe. *Entrecôte* and fries €13. Salads €9.50-12. Open 8am-1am, Su until 8:30pm. MC/V. ❷

Le "Relais de l'Entrecôte", 20, r. St-Benoit (☎01 45 49 16 00). Ⓜ Odéon. This restaurant serves up the French bourgeois version of fast food, and it's a far cry from your average McDonald's. Patrons sit down and are never presented with a menu (how environmentally friendly!); they're simply asked how they would like their meat. For €21.90, you can enjoy a salad with walnuts to start, followed by steak and fries in their inimitable sauce (don't be fooled; other chains' versions are simply inferior). Possibly the most delicious meal you will have in Paris, unless you're a vegetarian. Friendly wait staff refills your plate, so don't fret if your portion seems small. For dessert, there is a choice of profeteroles, fruit tarts, or sorbet. Cash only. ❸

Le Bistro Ernest, 21, r. de Seine (☎01 56 24 47 47). Gallery owners, artists, students, filmmakers, musicians, and other Left Bank riff-raff gather in this small cafe-bar lined with gallery posters and manned by a friendly bartender from Martinique. A calm alternative to the bustle of St-Germain. Jazz music plays in the background of the tiny cafe, a nice soundtrack for a cup of coffee in the heart of the gallery district. *Café* €1.50 at the bar. Beer €2.50. Prices increase with table service. MC/V. ❷

Les Editeurs, 4, carrefour de l'Odéon (☎01 43 26 67 76). Les Editeurs pays homage to St-Germain's literary pedigree with a small library containing books on everything from Marilyn Monroe to Brassaï. The best thing about this cafe, however, is its masterfully prepared food. The seared tuna on aubergine and courgettes (€22) is sumptuous, as is the steak with *bernaise* sauce (€20). Coffee €3. Beer €4.50-5. Mixed drinks €9-9.50. Ice creams like *mandarine des montagnes* €8. Open daily 8am-2am. AmEx/MC/V. ❸

Café de Flore, 172, bd. St-Germain (☎01 45 48 55 26). Ⓜ St-Germain-des-Prés. Walk against traffic on bd. St-Germain. Sartre composed *Being and Nothingness* here; Apollinaire, Camus, Artaud, Picasso, Breton, and Thurber sipped brew; and in the contemporary feud between Café de Flore and Les Deux Magots, Flore reportedly snags more local intellectuals—possibly by offering a well-respected literary prize. While Brigitte Bardot used to drink tea on the terrace, the Art Deco seating upstairs is still the coolest (check out Sartre and de Beauvoir's booth on the left). *Café* €5.50. Pastries €5-10. *Salade flore* €14.50. Open daily 7:30am-1:30am. AmEx/MC/V. ❸

Les Deux Magots, 6, pl. St-Germain-des-Prés (☎01 45 48 55 25). Ⓜ St-Germain-des-Prés. Just across the street from the Eglise St-Germain-des-Prés. The cloistered area behind the famous high hedges has been

going to the gym is about as popular as the Atkins Diet in the country that invented the *baguette*, portion control seems to compensate entirely for the lack of exercise, speaking strictly in terms of slimness. If you do not consume so many calories, there's no need to sweat for an hour while reading Cosmo on the elliptical at your local gym.

Americans and other non-French who seek advice on how to achieve the svelte French figure have had their prayers answered by the book *French Women Don't Get Fat.* Author (and slim Frenchwoman) Mireille Guiliano has made a fortune from this book, which aims to enlighten the world as to how the French can stay so slim without cultivating a diet nation similar to that in the US (and England to a certain extent). Guiliano advocates savoring your food by turning off your television and focusing on what you are consuming. This way you can enjoy the taste and realize when you are full.

However, with the rise of McDonalds-style fast food and delivery pizza, who knows how long the French will stay ahead in the slimming game (only until 2020 according to BBC news)? So instead of trying to emulate the French, the United States et al could just sit tight and wait for them to catch up...and for the release of the next book, *Whoops, French Women Got Fat.*

home to literati (from Mallarmé to Hemingway) since 1885, but is now favored mostly by Left Bank residents and tourists. The cafe is named for 2 Chinese porcelain figures (the originals are still inside), not for fly larvae. Sandwiches €6.80-12.50. Pastries from €8.50. Coffee €4. Hot chocolate €6.50. Breakfast *menu* €18. Open daily 7:30am-1am. AmEx/MC/V. ❸

Le Sélect, 99, bd. du Montparnasse (☎01 45 48 38 24). Ⓜ Vavin. Walk west on bd. du Montparnasse; across the street from La Coupole. An "American" bar of the Lost Generation once frequented by Trotsky, Satie, Breton, Cocteau, Picasso, and of course, Hemingway. Have the bartender mix you a classic mixed drink (€12), and enjoy it in the company of a surprisingly local crowd. Go at teatime and enjoy a *café au lait* (€4). Dinner *plats* start at €11. Simpler offerings like a *croque-monsieur* start at €7. Open daily 7am-3am. MC/V. ❸

Le Procope, 13, r. de l'Ancienne Comédie (☎01 40 46 79 00). Ⓜ Odéon. Walk against traffic on bd. St-Germain and go right on r. de l'Ancienne Comédie. Founded in 1686, making it the first cafe in the world. Voltaire drank 40 cups a day here while writing *Candide;* his table remains what the owners call "a testimony of permanence." Marat came here to plot the Revolution. Now a seafood restaurant, or history with a price, if you will: dinner *menu* €30, lunch *menus* €19 and €24. Coffee (€3) and beer (€6.50) are slightly more affordable. Open daily noon-2am. AmEx/MC/V. ❹

SALONS DE THÉ

L'Heure Gourmand, 22, passage Dauphine (☎01 46 34 00 40). Ⓜ Odéon. Walk up r. de l'Ancienne Comédie and turn right onto the passage Dauphine after the Carrefour Buci. A classy, quiet *salon de thé* with a terrace on a beautiful side street. The inside has magenta carpets and a romantic balcony upstairs. All teas €5-6. Berthillon ice cream €3-4 per *boule*. Pastries and desserts €6-8. Open M-Sa 11:30am-7:30pm, Su noon-7pm. MC/V.

SPECIALTY SHOPS

Poilâne, 8, r. Cherche Midi (☎01 45 48 42 59; www.poilane.fr). Widely regarded as one of the best bread-makers in Paris, Poilâne has lines out the door every morning—and they don't even sell *baguettes!* Try the famous sourdough loaf (€3.80), which is very dense, but infused with a smoky, rich flavor. For dessert, pick up a melt-in-your-mouth apple tart filled with great gobs of brown sugar (€2). Visitors can observe all baking processes done by hand in the cellar. Order online for international delivery, but beware of much higher prices. Open M-Sa 7:15am-8:15pm.

Gérard Mulot, 76, r. de Seine (☎01 43 26 85 77). Ⓜ Odéon or St-Sulpice. Outrageous selection of painstakingly crafted pastries, from flan to marzipan with virtually any kind of fruit. The *macaron* is heaven on earth (€3). Tarts around €3.50. Eclairs €2.50. Délicieux (which it is!) €3.10. Open M-Tu and Th-Su 6:45am-8pm.

Marché Biologique, on bd. Raspail between r. du Cherche-Midi and r. de Rennes. Ⓜ Rennes. French new-agers peddle everything from organic produce to 7-grain bread and tofu patties. Open Su 7am-1:30pm.

SEVENTH ARRONDISSEMENT

The 7*ème* is not budget-friendly, but ubiquitous bakeries and markets sell sandwiches and quiche at reasonable prices. **La Grande Epicierie de Paris,** the immense gourmet food hall annex of the department store Au Bon Marché, is pricey, but it's fun to marvel at the presentation and immense array of produce (see **Shopping,** p. 294). The restaurants below are worth the splurge.

L'Auberge Bressane, 16, av. de la Motte Picquet (☎01 47 05 98 37; www.auberge-bressane.com). ⓜ Ecole Militaire or Tour Mauberg. This small and luxuriously decorated restaurant is bouncing with regular patrons enjoying dishes like butter-soft artichoke hearts in a light vinaigrette (€9) and their famous *poulet à la crème et aux morilles* (€22). Order one of the famous house *soufflés* (*Grand Marnier* or chocolate) at the start of your meal to ensure a fine finale (€9). *Menus* €20 and €25; add €5 for a half bottle of wine. Reservations are a must. Open daily noon-2:30pm and 8-10:45pm (closed Sa lunch), but patrons stay as late as 2am, drinking and chatting with the friendly, multilingual waitstaff. Closed in Aug. AmEx/MC/V. ❸

Le Lotus Blanc, 45, r. de Bourgogne (☎01 45 55 18 89). ⓜ Varenne. Walk on bd. des Invalides, toward the Invalides; turn left onto r. de Varenne and onto r. de Bourgogne. Chef Pham-Nam Nghia has been perfecting Vietnamese dishes for over 25 years. The specialties *à la vapeur* (€7-15) are excellent. Lunch and all-day *menus* €11-33. Great vegetarian and vegan dishes (€7.50-9.50). Reservations for the tiny dining room are encouraged. Open M-Sa noon-2:30pm and 7:30-11pm. Closed in Aug. AmEx/MC/V. ❹

Grannie, 27, r. Pierre Leroux (☎01 43 34 94 14). ⓜ Vaneau. Walk west on r. de Sèvres and make a right onto r. Pierre Leroux. French fare with a subtle Japanese twist served in a cozy and classy atmosphere. Specialties include roast pigeon and other creatively prepared meat dishes. *Menus* €23 (lunch only) or €30. Appetizers and desserts €8. Open M-F noon-2:30pm and 7:30-10:30pm, Sa 7:30-10:30pm. MC/V. ❹

Au Pied de Fouet, 45, r. de Babylone (☎01 47 05 12 27). ⓜ Vaneau. Take r. Vaneau and turn left onto r. de Babylone. Small, bustling, and friendly bistro that attracts both cigarette-puffing locals and tourists. Straightforward French home cooking at bargain prices. Cheeses, wines, and dishes change regularly. Appetizers €3-5. Main dishes €8-11. Desserts (try the *crème caramel*) €3-4. Open M-Sa noon-2:30pm and 7-11pm. ❷

CAFES

▦ **Café des Lettres,** 53, r. de Verneuil (☎01 42 22 52 17). ⓜ Solférino. Exit the metro onto r. de Solférino, turn right on r. de l'Université, left on r. de Poitiers, and right on r. Verneuil. Enter the open arch; the cafe is to your left. Hidden in the side streets of the 7*ème*, this Scandinavian cafe located in the same sunny courtyard as the Maison des Ecrivains touts fresh, healthy fare. Enjoy platters of smoked salmon and *blinis* (€21) and other Danish seafood dishes (€10.50-24). Su Scandinavian-style brunch buffet (€28); reservations strongly recommended. Coffee €2.50. Beer €5. Open M noon-3pm, Tu-F noon-11pm, Sa noon-7pm. ❷

Café du Marché, 38, r. Cler. ⓜ Ecole Militaire. Walk up r. de la Motte Picquet and turn left onto r. Cler. Frequented by the chic residents of this picturesque Anglophone corner and American tourists. Serves up surprisingly delicious and generous salads, like the Indian-inspired tandoori chicken caesar salad (€9.50). Also serves hearty and traditional French standbys such as beef tartare (€10.50). Coffee €1.50. Open M-Sa 7am-midnight. MC/V. ❷

SPECIALTY SHOPS

Poujauran, 20, r. Jean-Nicot (☎01 47 05 80 88). ⓜ La Tour-Maubourg. The bakery and adjacent pastry shop are now under the direction of the accomplished Stéphane Secco and remain a taster's delight, selling a wide range of *petit pains* (miniature breads) alongside their bigger brothers (€3.50-9.50). Try bread studded with olives, herbs, figs, or apricots, or dive right into dessert with a rich *macaron* (€2). Open Tu-Sa 8am-8:30pm.

ON THE MENU

DON'T CALL THEM PANCAKES

'o someone who's just arrived in ⁾aris, the *crêpe* will seem like an ncredibly cheap meal substitute. ¯he ubiquitous *crêpe* stand ꞈerves up sweet delights from ꞈround €2, but be warned: a ꞈtomach can only take so much nutella and *confiture*. When ꞈou've reached your limit, *gal- ꞈttes* will come to the rescue.

The more sophisticated sibling n the *crêpe* family, *galettes* are ꞈften advertised as *crêpes sar- ꞈassins*. The *galette* is made from nutritious buckwheat (*sarrassin*) ꞈatter, which has a nutty, savory aste. It is cooked in the same nanner as the *crêpe*, but ends up ꞈ darker, crispier masterpiece.

Galettes are no paltry excuse ꞈor a meal; they are a feast in ꞈhemselves, and many restau- ants specialize in them. The clas- ꞈic *galette* is filled with ham and ꞈheese, often with an egg cracked ꞈver the top during the final stage ꞈf cooking. They can be filled with ꞈbsolutely anything, though, from ꞈpinach and *chèvre* to scallops ꞈnd leeks to peas and potatoes.

Cooked on a round *billig*, with ꞈ *rozell* twisted deftly in the ꞈhef's hand, *galettes* were con- ꞈumed in place of bread in ꞈncient Brittany. The first *crêpe* ꞈecipe in France dates to about ꞈ390, and hungry late-night club- ꞈers and budget travelers have ꞈenefited from it ever since.

Debauve et Gallais, 30, r. des Saints-Pères (☎01 45 48 54 67; www.debauve-et-gallais.com). In 1800, a chocolate factory was founded near the Abbey St-Germain-des-Près by the official pharmacist of Louis XVI. The dark, unsweetened chocolate soon became the favorite of Louis XVIII, and then later Charles X and Louis-Philippe. Debauve et Gallais is still steeped in tradition: this flagship store is housed in a historic building designed by Napolean's choice of architects for Malmaison, and the chocolates themselves continue to be produced without additives, dyes, or sweeteners of any sort. Customers can pick and choose individual chocolates with flavors like peach and almond, nougat, and Earl Grey tea, or pick up a pack of golf-ball shaped pralines (300g, €33). Try the velvety bars of chocolate, €5. Open M-Sa 9am-7pm. Second location in the 2ème at 33, r. Vivienne (☎01 40 39 05 50).

Barthélémy, 51, r. de Grenelle (☎01 45 48 56 75). A cluttered, old-fashioned storefront showcasing adorable livestock and poultry figurines; inside, the finest cheese in Paris. President Chirac has been known to stop in. Open Tu-F 8am-1pm and 4-7:15pm, Sa 8am-1:30pm and 3:30-7:15pm.

Fromage Rouge, 83, r. St-Dominique (☎01 45 50 45 75). The pleasantly pungent aroma of Livarot and its other savory cousins greet customers at the shop formerly known as Androuët's. Features a wide and carefully selected array of cheese, some molded with ingenious patterns. Open Tu-Sa 9am-1pm and 4-8pm. Closed Aug. AmEx/MC/V. 2 additional locations in the 14ème: 8, r. Delambre (☎01 42 79 00 40) and 19, r. Daguerre (☎01 43 21 19 09).

EIGHTH ARRONDISSEMENT

The 8ème has traditionally been Paris's center of glamorous dining and world-class cuisine. There are still plenty of extravagant establishments in the *arrondissement*, particularly south of the Champs-Elysées, but lately the area has been losing importance as a culinary center. The best affordable restaurants are on side streets around **rue la Boétie** and **place de Dublin.**

▨ **Le 36,** 36, r. du Colisée (☎01 45 62 94 00). Ⓜ Franklin D. Roosevelt. Take av. Franklin D. Roosevelt and turn right on r. du Colisée. Formerly Escrouzailles, this restaurant has kept its family-style cuisine delicious, and the proprietress, Valerie, is warm and accommodating. An intimate establishment with dusty rose-colored dining rooms, it is perhaps the best place to enjoy

fine yet relaxed dining after a day wandering the Champs. Try the house specialties, such as the *feuilleté de canard* (€18) and *cassoulet* (€20). Vegetarian and child-friendly dishes upon request. Smoking and non-smoking rooms. Open M-Sa 11am-3pm and 7-11pm. MC/V. ❸

■ **Mood,** 114, av. des Champs-Elysées and 1, r. Washington (☎01 42 89 98 89). Ⓜ George V. Walk down the bamboo-lined entrance hall from the clamorous Champs into the gorgeous Mood. A sophisticated restaurant-lounge presides over the former Latina Café nightclub. A sensuously elegant melange of Western contemporary decor with delicate Japanese accents reflects the fusion cuisine. Dine on the fixed-price lunch (a great value at €20) in the upper dining room with stylized geisha prints, or indulge your hedonistic side on the plush, deep red beds of the lower level lounge at night. Appetizers €9-17.50, *plats* €16-22. A fanciful drink list with poetic mixed drinks (€9-11) such as *l'ombre d'une rose* (shadow of a rose). Live music and DJ in the evening. Reservations recommended, and required for the lounge beds. Open daily 10am-4am (lounge open after 10pm). AmEx/MC/V. ❸

Thabthim Siam, 28, r. de Moscou (☎01 43 87 62 56). Ⓜ Rome. From the metro, take a right onto r. de Moscou. Local favorite, with embroidered tapestries, silk-draped chairs and bronze statues. An intimate restaurant wtih a romantic ambience, excellent curry dishes, and a rotating menu. All appetizers €8, main dishes €13. The €14-lunch *menu* is a great option, and it includes choice of appetizer, *plat,* and drink. Open M-Sa noon-3pm and 7-11pm. MC/V. ❷

Ty Yann, 10, r. de Constantinople (☎01 40 08 00 17). Ⓜ Europe. Turn right onto r. de Rome and take a left onto r. de Constantinople. Meaning "House of Yann" in the Brittany dialect, this rustic and warm *crêperie* serves up delicious *crêpes* with a dash of creativity. The welcoming chef-owner, M. Yann, cheerfully prepares *galettes* (€7-10) and *crêpes* in the tiny restaurant decorated with his mother's pastoral paintings. House specialties include *la Saint-Brieuc* (€10) with scallops, leeks, and *crème fraiche* in a cider sauce. Create your own *crêpe* (€5.50-6.50) for lunch. Takeout available for 15% less. Open M-F noon-2:30pm and 7-10:30pm, Sa 7-10:30pm. MC/V. ❷

Toi, 27, r. Colisée (☎ 01 42 56 56 58). Ⓜ Franklin D. Roosevelt. Walk toward the arch on the Champs-Elysée and take the first street on the right. Deep red sofas; warm, dim lighting; and artfully black-clad waitstaff. A favorite hangout for the young and chic locals (who prefer the retro upper level), Toi is all about tantalizing and beautiful visual presentation. Evenings feature themed *soirées* beginning 9pm. M Jazz Night, Tu Magic Night, Th Ladies' Night. The experimental cuisine menu rotates each season, with appetizers €8-19, *plats* €14-25, and desserts €7-12. €17 lunch *menu* and €22 dinner *menu* (both M-F only). Open M-Sa noon-2am. AmEx/V. ❹

CAFES

Le Paris, 93, av. des Champs-Elysées (☎01 47 23 54 37). Ⓜ George V. Trendy and upmarket, but more reasonably priced than many of the cafes on the Champs. Le Paris is outfitted in deep purple and turquoise, with plasma screens above the bar playing anime. The terrace is ideal for people-watching and sipping tea, but ensconce yourself inside to experience the cool smoke machine's swirling vapors. At night, the cafe turns into a bar with a live DJ. Coffee €3.50-6.50. Tea €6.50. Glass of wine €6-7. Oreo smoothie €8.50. Sandwiches from €12. Full breakfast €12-25. Add €1.50 to drinks after 9pm. Open daily 8am-6am. ❸

Fouquet's, 99, av. des Champs-Elysées (☎01 47 23 50 00). Ⓜ George V. Decorated with sumptuous, red velvet upholstery and gilded fittings, Fouquet's is an experience of quintessential old-time Parisian glamor (see **Sights,** p. 212). Easy on the eye but dev-

FOOD

astating for the bank balance. Coffee €6. Club sandwiches from €18. Nordic caviar €90 for 30g. Open daily 8am-2am. Food served all day in the cafe; 7:30am-10am noon-3pm and 7pm-midnight in the restaurant. AmEx/MC/V. ❹

SALONS DE THÉ

▨ **Ladurée,** 16, r. Royale (☎01 42 60 21 79). Ⓜ Concorde. Ever wondered what it would be like to dine inside a Fabergé egg? The rococo decor of this classic tea salon attracts the well-groomed shoppers who frequent the boutiques in the area. Famous for the mini macaroons stacked in the window (€3, in 9 different varieties). Pastry counter for take-away. Pretty sampler tea packs (from €19) and chocolate boxes (from €12). Specialty tea *Ladurée mélange* €6.50. House-branded champagne €5.50 a glass. Su brunch €29. Open daily 8:30am-7pm; lunch served until 3pm. AmEx/MC/V. Also at 75, av. des Champs-Elysées, 8ème (☎01 40 75 08 75). Ⓜ FDR.

SPECIALTY SHOPS

Fauchon, 26-30, pl. de la Madeleine (☎01 47 42 60 11; www.fauchon.com). Ⓜ Madeleine. Paris's favorite gourmet food shop (complete with gourmet prices), this *traiteur/pâtisserie/épicerie/charcuterie* has it all. Go home with a pretty tin of *madeleines,* or browse their wine cellar, one of the finest in Paris. Excellent selection of specialty teas, €10-50 for 100g. Market open M-Sa 9:30am-8pm, *boulangerie* 8am-9pm, *traiteur/pâtisserie* 9am-9pm, tea room 9am-7pm. AmEx/MC/V.

NINTH ARRONDISSEMENT

Except for a few gems, restaurants and eateries close to the Opéra cater to the after-theater and movie crowd; meals here can be quite expensive. For cheaper deals, head farther north in the 9ème. **Rue du Faubourg-Montmartre** is crammed with all sorts of restaurants, including those serving Mexican, Japanese, Chinese, and French food. It is lined with cafes, *salons de thé,* fast-food joints, and specialty shops, which are usually cheap, although perhaps not of the highest quality.

▨ **Chez Haynes,** 3, r. Clauzel (☎01 48 78 40 63). Ⓜ St-Georges. Head uphill on r. Notre Dame de Lorette and turn right on r. H. Monnier, then right on r. Clauzel to the end of the block. Opened in 1949, this was the first African American-owned restaurant in Paris, although it is now run by a Portuguese and Brazilian couple. This place was also a former hangout of Louis Armstrong, James Baldwin, and Richard Wright. Haynes is famous for its New Orleans soul food and its complimentary cornbread with meat sauce. There is no other place like this in Paris. The portions are very generous, and most of them are under €16. Ma Sutton's fried chicken with honey €14. Sister Lena's BBQ spare ribs €14. Live music F-Sa nights; €5 cover. Chez Haynes's soul food menu Tu-Sa, Brazilian food Su. Open Tu-Su 7pm-midnight. AmEx/MC/V. ❸

Anarkali Sarangui, 4, pl. Gustave Toudouze (☎01 48 78 39 84). Ⓜ St-Georges. Walk uphill on r. Notre Dame de Lorette and turn right onto r. H. Monnier. A rare North Indian restaurant with pleasant outdoor seating and a thoughtful interior. Tandoori and curries €7.50-12.50. Open Tu-Su 11am-2:30pm and 7-11pm. MC/V. ❸

Chartier, 7, r. du Faubourg-Montmartre (☎01 47 70 86 29; www.restaurant-chartier.com). Ⓜ Grands Boulevards. This Parisian fixture, tucked away through a covered passageway off the busy road, has been serving well-priced French cuisine since 1896. Come for the classic Parisian atmosphere more than the diner-style food. As tradition dictates, the waitstaff add up the bill on the paper tablecloth at your table. Traditional main dishes like *steak au poivre* run €7.50-10.50. Side dishes €2.50. Open daily 11:30am-3pm and 6-10pm. AmEx/MC/V. ❷

Comme Par Hasard, 48, r. Notre Dame de Lorette (☎01 42 80 45 09). ⓂSt-Georges. The *9ème* has many *sandwicheries*, but this one stands out from the crowd, proving that a sandwich joint can truly be hip. The sandwiches are delicious and more interesting than the standard *jambon beurre*. Although it is small, patrons can sit inside or out, or take a sandwich away to eat on the go. Try the €6.50 *menu* (sandwich, drink, and dessert) for a great value. Open 10am-8pm. ❶

CAFES

🔲 **No Stress Café,** 2, pl. Gustave Toudouze (☎01 48 78 00 27). ⓂSt-Georges. Walk uphill on r. Notre Dame de Lorette and turn right onto r. H. Monnier. A funky place with a holistic approach to dining: after 9pm (W-Sa), massages are available as a side to the tasty, healthful food. Although you may have some trouble attracting the attention of the too-cool-for-school waitstaff, a meal in this colorful cafe is worth your persistence. Try the *wok*, a sizable stir-fry with noodles and vegetables from €13, with meat from €16. Vegetarian options abound. Open Tu-Su 11am-2am. Su brunch noon-3:30pm. MC/V. ❸

Au Général La Fayette, 52, r. la Fayette (☎01 47 70 59 08). ⓂLe Peletier. With Art Nouveau lamps and mirrors and Klimt-esque decor from floor to ceiling, Au Général is one of the few classy cafe-bars in the area. Features a newspaper and magazine reading room and a laid-back atmosphere. *Galettes* €10-11. Salads €4-12. Large selection of beer, both on tap (€4.50-6.50 at the bar), and bottled (€5-11). Mixed drinks €9. Open daily 10am-4am. Food served noon-3am. AmEx/MC/V. ❷

Café de la Paix, 12, bd. des Capucines (☎01 40 07 36 36). ⓂOpéra. On the left as you face the Opéra. The most expensive property on French Monopoly, Café de la Paix has drawn a classy crowd since it opened in 1862. Oscar Wilde was a regular; now the clientele are mostly tourists. Expensive coffee €6. Sandwiches €13-14. Desserts €11 (the mille-feuille comes highly recommended). Croissants €2. Soft drinks €6. Open daily 8am-11:30pm. AmEx/MC/V. ❹

SPECIALTY SHOPS

La Maison du Chocolat, 8, bd. de la Madeleine (☎01 47 42 86 52; www.lamaisonduchocolat.com). Ⓜ Madeleine. A chain store now with branches in New York, London, and Tokyo, this delightful emporium offers a range of exquisite chocolates, from milk to dark; and for those tired of solid chocolates, a mysteri-

THE HIDDEN DEAL

BUCK-A-BRICK

For one shiny euro, **Du Pain et des Idées,** an ambitiously named bakery in the 10*ème*, will furnish you with perhaps the tastiest and certainly the most practical snack in Paris: a *pavé garné* (brick). Flavors include blue cheese with dried apricots, bell peppers with goat cheese, *lardon et reblochon* (ham and cheese), and, for your sweet tooth, banana and chocolate. The ingredients are folded into the center of the dough then baked (think Italian calzone minus the grease), producing a light snack you can throw in your backpack and forget about until it's time for a *pause*. Two or three of them make a meal.

The bakery has been open continuously since 1889, and the new, young, English-speaking owners are dedicated to offering a *boulangerie* experience *à l'ancienne*. Their baguettes (€0.90) are made the old-fashioned way—without yeast—producing a unique taste and longer freshness. Don't miss the heirloom ceiling decorations.

Du Pain et des Idées, 34, r. Yves Toudic, 10ème (☎01 42 40 44 52). Ⓜ République. Walk against traffic on r. du Fauborg du Temple then left on r. Yves Toudic. Bricks €1, tartelettes €2.10. Open M-F 7:30am-2:30pm and 3:30-8pm.

ous distilled chocolate essence drink. Box of 2 chocolates €3.50. Mouth-watering chocolate eclairs €4. Other locations include 19, r. de Sèvres, 6ème (☎01 45 44 20 40).
Open M-Sa 10am-7:30pm, Su 10am-2pm. MC/V.

TENTH ARRONDISSEMENT

While many tourists never see more of the 10ème than their Gare du Nord layover
allows, those who venture out will find French, Indian, and African restaurants with
reasonable prices, as well as neighborhood cafes and brasseries on every corner.

■ **La 25ème Image**, 9, r. des Récollets (☎01 40 35 80 88). Ⓜ Gare de l'Est. Go down r. du
Faubourg St-Martin and make a left on r. des Récollets. Right near the Canal St-Martin, this
funky cafe, with colorful walls and patrons, offers a lovely selection of light food. Try one of
the salads, or feast on a *plat* like roast duck breast and fries (€10). *Plats* change regularly.
Make sure to leave room for dessert–the berry-centric tarts and crumbles are divine (€4-
4.50). Dinner is slightly more elaborate and pricy. M-F 10am-3pm and 5:30pm-12:30am,
Sa 5pm-12:30am. MC/V. ❷

Au Bon Café, 2, bd. St-Martin (☎01 42 02 14 57). Ⓜ République. The cafe is just off
pl. de la République. A haven from the frenzy of the pl. de la République, and a nice
alternative to the *place*'s McDonald's and pizza chain stores. Patrons can grab one of
its wooden tables and try a crisp salad with creative ingredients like *coquilles,* grapefruit, pear, avocado, and tomato. Salads €10-12. *Assiettes* €10-12, including an *assiette* with salmon prepared in 3 different ways. AmEx/MC/V. ❷

Pooja, 91, passage Brady (☎01 48 24 00 83; www.poojarestaurant.com). Ⓜ Strasbourg-St-Denis. Passage Brady is located at no. 46 r. du Faubourg St-Denis. Pooja's
Indian cuisine is best enjoyed at night, when the *passage* (which also houses many
other Indian restaurants) is lit with hanging lanterns. Don't have too many of the delicious green *cocktail Poojas* (€4) before you depart, or you'll have to navigate the noc-
turnal 10ème slightly tipsy. Lunch *menu* €12. Several vegetarian options. Open daily
noon-3pm and 7-11pm. ❷

Resto-Flash, 10, r. Lucien Sampaix (☎01 42 45 03 30). Ⓜ Jacques Bonsergent. A rare
find in Paris, Resto-Flash is a kosher restaurant tucked away in the less-than-spotless
10ème. Serving standards like *côte de veau* (€17) and house couscous (€20) at
slightly elevated prices, this restaurant offers the primary attraction of kosher food reg-
ulated by the Beth-Din of Paris. Takeaway sandwiches €6. Open M-F noon-3:30pm. ❸

SPECIALTY SHOPS

Marché St-Quentin, 85bis, bd. de Magenta. Ⓜ Gare de l'Est or Gare du Nord. Outside:
a massive construction of iron and glass, built in the 1880s, renovated in 1982, and
covered by a glorious glass ceiling. Inside: stalls of all varieties of produce, meat,
cheese, seafood, and wine. A small bar in the center for those in need of a break. Open
Tu-Sa 8am-1pm and 2:30-7:30pm, Su 8am-1pm.

ELEVENTH ARRONDISSEMENT

Although Bastille swells with fast-food joints, this increasingly diverse neighborhood offers Spanish, African, and Asian cuisines, among others. The most popular
haunts line the bustling **rues de Charonne, Keller, de Lappe,** and **Oberkampf.**

■ **Chez Paul**, 13, r. de Charonne (☎01 47 00 34 57). Ⓜ Bastille. Go east on r. du Faubourg St-Antoine and turn left on r. de Charonne. Downstairs has a classic bistro feel;
upstairs has a cozy, romantic atmosphere. Paul's fun, witty staff serves a menu of farm-
style favorites. Regulars go for the house specialty *steak tartare* (€15), while the very

brave can give in to St. Antoine's Temptation (€17.50), a dish of pig ear, foot, tail, and groin. Reservations suggested and are a must for dinner. Open daily noon-2:30pm and 7pm-2am. Food served until 12:30am. AmEx/MC/V. ❷

Juan et Juanita, 82, r. Jean-Pierre Timbaud (☎ 01 43 57 60 15). ⓜ Couronnes. A leather-and-lace style interior with embossed black walls and stylishly chipped pink tables reflect this small restaurant's funky-elegant atmosphere. Sit back in the delightfully mismatched chairs as the helpful server presents the daily specialties on a huge blackboard. The house special, braised pork with honey and spices (€16), is intensely flavored and beautifully plated. The lunch special is an excellent value at €12. Appetizers €5.50-10, main courses €14-16. Reservations suggested. Open daily noon-2am. AmEx/MC/V. ❷

La Banane Ivoirienne, 10, r. de la Forge-Royale (☎01 43 70 49 90). ⓜ Faidherbe-Chaligny. Walk west on r. du Faubourg St-Antoine and turn right on r. de la Forge-Royale. Ivorian prints, palm trees, and African cuisine like *brochettes* of shrimp (€16) and cooked plantains (for parties of 3 or more; €16 per person). Come for the upbeat ambience as much as for the food. *Plats* €10-16. Veggie *menu* €11. Live African music F 10pm; enjoy with Ivorian specialty drinks, €5-6. Reservations recommended. Open Tu-Sa 7pm-midnight. AmEx/MC/V. ❷

Restaurant Assoce, 48bis, r. St-Maur (☎01 43 55 73 82). ⓜ St-Maur. This restaurant serves excellent, inexpensive Turkish cuisine. Try lamb with garlic yogurt and tomato sauce or the chef's specialty, sauteed Turkish sausage with legumes (€10). Lunch *menu* is a steal at €9.50; dinner *menu* €19.50. Main dishes €9-11.50. Lots of veggie options. Open M-F 11am-3pm and 6-11:30pm, Sa-Su 6-11:30pm. MC/V. ❷

Le Bistrot du Peintre, 116, av. Ledru-Rollin (☎01 47 00 34 39). ⓜ Ledru-Rollin. Walk up av. Ledru-Rollin directly from the metro. Le Bistrot du Peintre sticks to its Art Nouveau roots, sporting rich dark wood, curvy mirrors, and ornate floral tiles. An outdoor table here is just the place to watch the 11*ème* whirl, clang, and honk by. The classic menu includes *charcuterie* platters (€4.50-11.50) and *confit de canard* (€13.50). Main dishes €13-15. Desserts €4-5.50, including delectable Berthillon sundaes. Open daily 8am-2am. MC/V. ❷

CAFES

Café de l'Industrie, 15-17, r. St-Sabin (☎01 47 00 13 53). ⓜ Breguet-Sabin. Happening cafe frequented by funky 20-somethings; dining area decorated with palm trees and framed by huge windows. With the recent acquisition of a neighbor, l'Industrie may be the only restaurant in Paris to straddle a street. Both sides serve the same quality food, including a €10.50 lunch *menu* M-F. Coffee €2.50. *Vin chaud* €4.50. Popular fruit-filled brunch Sa-Su €18. Salads €7.50-9. Open daily 10am-2am. Lunch served noon-2pm. MC/V. ❶

Pause Café, 41, r. de Charonne (☎01 48 06 80 33). ⓜ Ledru-Rollin. Walk along av. Ledru-Rollin and turn left onto r. de Charonne. Long the coffee spot of choice for a hip crowd, Pause is now all the cooler for having starred in the film *Chacun Cherche Son Chat*. Generous portions. Goat cheese salad €8. Beer €3.50-4.50. Mixed drinks €6-7.50. The menu changes regularly—trust the fresh daily chalkboard specials. Sun-soaked and spacious outdoor seating area. Open M-Sa 7:30am-2am, food served noon-midnight; Su 9am-8pm, food served noon-5pm. MC/V. ❷

Le Troisième Bureau, 74, r. de la Folie-Méricourt (☎01 43 55 87 65). ⓜ Oberkampf. Take r. de Crussol across bd. Richard Lenoir and turn left on r. de la Folie-Méricourt. A trendy cafe-bar with a pared-down artistic aesthetic and a substantial wine list. Gets lively in the evenings to the sound of drum and bass and acid funk. Coffee €2. Try the

FOOD

ON THE MENU

THE RAW DEAL

Meat-eating travelers in France will commonly encounter the "undercooked" steak problem. It's a cultural shock to realize just how rare the French like their meat, and those accustomed to dining on medium-rare or rare steak might want to reconsider when ordering red meat in France.

Some helpful vocabulary: *bien cuit* is well done, *à point* is medium-rare, *saignant* is rare (literally "bleeding"), and *bleu* is very, very rare. Expect meat to come less cooked than you imagined—"well done" in a French restaurant is like medium-rare. Only the daring would order their beef *saignant*, while truly adventurous diners might try the slightly warmed-over *bleu*.

Those who develop a taste for moist red meat might delve into *steak tartare*, a raw ground beef kneaded with onions, capers, and herbs, and topped with raw egg. If planning to dine on *tartare*, choose a reputable restaurant (some prepare it at your table)— these chefs will have their hands all over your raw meat.

So how French is this recipe? It's said that the dish actually comes from the ancient clans of the Baltic states, but don't tell that to any of the Parisian restaurants that proudly list their range of *tartares* on their chalkboard menus.

ginger-, rose-, or chocolate-flavored Absolut shots (€5.50). 2-course *menu* €13, main dishes €13-19. Su brunch. Open daily 10am-2am. Lunch served noon-3pm; dinner served 7pm-midnight. MC/V. ❷

Polichinelle, 64-66 r. de Charonne (☎01 58 30 63 52). Ⓜ Ledru-Rollin. Take av. Ledru-Rollin and turn right at r. de Charonne. Look past the unflattering yellow paint job and make yourself at home in the comfortably aged, colorful interior. Crowded late at night with chattering friends, the cafe serves classics such as *magret de canard* and other meat- and fish-based dishes. Main dishes €10.50-15.50. The outdoor terrace is located on a tranquil corner and is great for drinking coffee (€2) or sipping a mixed drink (€5-7). Open daily 10am-2am; 4pm-2am in the summer. MC/V. ❷

SPECIALTY SHOPS

Marché Bastille, on bd. Richard-Lenoir from pl. de la Bastille north to r. St-Sabin. Ⓜ Bastille. Produce, cheese, exotic mushrooms, bread, meat, flowers, second-hand clothing, and housewares stretch all the way from Ⓜ Richard Lenoir to Ⓜ Bastille. Popular Su morning family outing. Open Th and Su 7am-1:30pm.

Marché Popincourt, on bd. Richard-Lenoir between r. Oberkampf and r. de Jean-Pierre Timbaud. Ⓜ Oberkampf. Fresh, well-priced fruits, vegetables, meat and fish. A smattering of vendors selling essentials you may need to restock before your next European stop— socks, sunglasses, shoes, shirts and underwear. A DJ in the center of the market announces special deals while he spins all the latest Edith Piaf jams. Open Tu and F 7am-2:30pm.

TWELFTH ARRONDISSEMENT

There are many cafes and cheap fast-food joints along the r. du Faubourg St-Antoine. The 12*ème* in general is a culinarily affordable *arrondissement*, with an abundance of casual neighborhood joints that serves a wide variety of cuisines from North African to Middle Eastern to traditional French.

🍽 **L'Ebauchoir**, 45, r. de Citeaux (☎01 43 42 49 31). Ⓜ Faidherbe-Chaligny. Walk down r. du Faubourg St-Antoine, turn left on r. de Citeaux. L'Ebauchoir feels something like a funky, dressed-up diner. €13.50 lunch *menu* includes a drink, and à la carte *plats* start at €15. All-day *menu* €23. Open M 8-11pm and Tu-Sa noon-11pm. Food served noon-2:30pm and 8-11pm. MC/V. ❸

La Connivence, 1, r. de Cotte (☎01 46 28 49 01). Ⓜ Ledru-Rollin. Take r. Rollin to r. de Charenton and turn left. R. de Cotte is on your left. An elegant, intimate restaurant with deep orange walls and mint-green tablecloths. Lunch *menus* €14-17. Dinner *menus* €20-25. Very professional chef-owner uses only market-fresh ingredients to make her traditional cuisine with a twist, devising dishes such as iced fennel soup and marinated duck carpaccio. Appetizers €9.50, main dishes €14, and desserts €6.50 (try the *Grand Marnier* and raspberry *crêpes*). Vegetarian options. Wine €18-24.50 per bottle. Open Tu-Sa noon-2:40pm and 8-11pm. Closed 3rd week of Aug. MC/V. ❸

Le Cheval de Troie, 71, r. de Charenton (☎01 43 44 24 44; www.chevaltroie.com). ⓜ Bastille. As you're facing the opera, r. de Charenton is the street just to the left; the restaurant is on your left. Savory Turkish food in an appealing setting populated with locals. Lunch *formule* €10-11. Feast on generous appetizers (€5-9.50) and main courses (€10-13.40). Emphasis on kebabs and grilled meats, although vegetarian options are available. Light and refreshing desserts like balli yogurt (the house yogurt with honey and almonds; €4). Asian dancers Sa night at 9:30pm. Dinner *menu* €18.50, or splurge on the 5-course *menu gourmand* with *aperitif* and *digestif*. Open M-Sa noon-2:30pm and 7-11:30pm, Su 7-11:30pm. MC/V. 10% student discount. ❷

Les Broches à l'Ancienne, 21, r. St-Nicolas (☎01 43 43 26 16). ⓜ Ledru-Rollin. Walk along r. du Faubourg St-Antoine away from the Bastille column and turn right onto r. St-Nicolas. Follow your nose: the meats here are slow-cooked over flames in a stone oven. Dark wood and crimson leather upholstery set the tone for serious, high-minded food at surprisingly low prices. Succulent shoulder of lamb with *frites* €18.50. Appetizers €5-12.50. Photography displays in basement. Jazz F nights starting at 8pm; dinner and performance €25 on average; reservations recommended. Open M-Sa noon-2:30pm and 7-10:30pm. Closed 2nd and 3rd weeks of Aug. AmEx/MC/V. ❷

Les Grandes Marchés, 6, pl. de la Bastille (☎01 43 42 90 32; www.lesgrandsmarches.com). ⓜ Bastille. Adjacent to the opera. Sleek, air-conditioned, and expensive (but worth it), this is among the area's nicest restaurants. An elegant, older clientele dines on the ample €23.50 and €30.50 lunch *menus*. Feast on delicious, Italian-influenced appetizers like creamy risotto with truffles (€18.50; appetizers €8.50-18) before savoring one of the countless meat or fish dishes (€15-29). Outdoor seating overlooks the bustling pl. de la Bastille. Open daily noon-midnight. AmEx/MC/V. ❹

SPECIALTY SHOPS

Marché Beauvau St-Antoine, on pl. d'Aligre between r. de Charenton and r. Crozatier. ⓜ Ledru-Rollin. One of the largest and most diverse Parisian markets, lined with Muslim *halal* butcher shops, florists, and delis. Quality of produce varies between stands. Produce market open Tu-Sa 8:30am-1pm and 4-7:30pm, Su 8am-1pm.

THIRTEENTH ARRONDISSEMENT

The 13*ème* is a budget gourmand's dream. The **Butte-aux-Cailles's** high-spirited restaurants and bars fill to capacity with locals most nights of the week. Scores of Asian restaurants cluster in Paris's **Chinatown,** located just south of pl. d'Italie on av. de Choisy, and a number of North African restaurants crowd in near ⓜ St-Marcel.

▩ **Tricotin,** 15, av. de Choisy (☎01 45 84 74 44). ⓜ Porte de Choisy. 6 chefs prepare delicious food from Cambodia, Thailand, and Vietnam, which is served in 2 large, cafeteria-style rooms. Try the famed Cambodian fried rice with beef (€7) or any of the dim sum (called *vapeur* in French) foods, such as the steamed shrimp ravioli (€3.40). Always busy, but Tricotin has quick and diligent service. Open daily 9:30am-11:30pm. MC/V. ❶

Le Temps des Cerises, 18, r. de la Butte-aux-Cailles (☎01 45 89 69 48). Ⓜ Place d'Italie. Take r. Bobillot and turn right on r. de la Butte-aux-Cailles. A local restaurant cooperative, Le Temps has been in shared ownership between all its workers, from cook to bartender, since 1976. Classic French dishes like *andouillette* (€14) are house specialties; also try the *assiette Grècque,* piled high with cold cuts (€14), or the excellent *magret de canard* (€18). Lunch *menu* €9.50, anytime *menus* €14.50 and €22.50. Open M-F 11:45am-2:15pm and 7:30-11:45pm, Sa 11:45am-2:15pm. Reservations recommended for dinner. AmEx/MC/V. ❷

L'Aimant du Sud, 40, bd. Arago (☎01 47 07 33 57). Ⓜ Les Gobelins. Walk down av. des Gobelins, then turn right onto bd. Arago. This delightful restaurant—with many sunny accolades posted in the window—serves tasty food from the South of France. Main dishes emphasize steak and fish. Pleasant, leafy outdoor seating. Lunch *menu* €13-16, dinner *menu* €17-20. Open M noon-2:30pm, Tu-F noon-2:30pm and 7:30-10:30pm. AmEx/MC/V. ❸

Chez Gladines, 30, r. des Cinq Diamants (☎01 45 80 70 10). Ⓜ Place d'Italie. Take bd. Auguste Blanqui and turn left onto r. des Cinq Diamants; on the corner of r. Jonas. Serves southwestern French and Basque specialties (€7-11) to carnivorous locals with whom you may find yourself getting cozy, given the intimate seating. 3-course lunch *menu* €10. Popular large salads (featuring lots of intestine and liver morsels) €6.50-9. Wines by the glass €2.50-3. Open daily M-Tu noon-3pm and 7pm-midnight; W-F noon-3pm and 7pm-1am; Sa noon-2pm and 7pm-1am; Su noon-2pm and 7pm-midnight. ❷

Des Crêpes et des Cailles, 13, r. de la Butte-aux-Cailles (☎01 45 81 68 69). Ⓜ Place d'Italie. Take r. Bobillot and turn right on r. de la Butte-aux-Cailles. Well-known in Paris, this tiny, nautical-themed *crêperie* is a favorite haunt of local intellectuals. Jazz music and cheery gingham curtains float in the 2-room restaurant, where service is brisk, and food is cheap but good. *Galettes* €2.50-8. *Crêpes* €2-7. Cider €3. Open daily noon-3:30pm and 5:30-11:30pm. ❶

Café du Commerce, 39, r. des Cinq Diamants (☎01 53 62 91 04). Ⓜ Place d'Italie. Take bd. Auguste Blanqui and turn left onto r. des Cinq Diamants; it will be on your left. This funky establishment serves traditional food with a twist. Dinner (€16-22) and lunch (€10.50) *menus* both feature options like *boudin antillais* (spiced bloodwurst) and smoked haddock with blinis. Happy hour *menu* 6-7:45pm (€14). Open M-F 11am-3pm and 6pm-1am, Sa-Su 11am-1am. Jazz performances every Su at 4pm. Free wireless Internet. Reservations recommended for dinner and weekends. ❸

Papagallo, 25, r. des Cinq Diamants (☎01 45 80 53 20; www.restaurant-papa-gallo.com). Ⓜ Place d'Italie. Take bd. Auguste Blanqui and turn left onto r. des Cinq Diamants. The flower-covered facade and Spanish menu barely prepare you for the reggae ambience of this tiny restaurant/bar. Small assortment of tapas like guacamole or eggplant caviar (€5-8), main dishes such as *chili con carne* €8.50-12, and a *menu* for €12, but the locals come for the rum-infused mixed drinks (€6). Open M-F noon-2:30pm and 7pm-midnight; Sa-Su 7pm-midnight. Reservations for dinner. MC/V. ❷

SPECIALTY SHOPS

Tang Frères, 48, av. d'Ivry (☎01 45 70 80 00). Ⓜ Porte d'Ivry. Look for no. 44 and go down a few steps, or look for no. 48 and follow the sign through a parking lot. Also at 174, r. de Choisy. Ⓜ Place d'Italie. This huge shopping center in the heart of Chinatown contains a grocery store, flower store, bakery, *charcuterie,* and porcelain shop. Rice, spices, teas, soups, and noodles in bulk. Exotic fruits (*durian* €5 per kg), cheap Asian beers (Sapporo and Kirin €1.19), rice wines, and sake. Open Tu-F 9am-7:30pm, Sa-Su 8:30am-7:30pm. Paris Store, right next door, is also excellent.

FOURTEENTH ARRONDISSEMENT

The 14ème is bordered at the top by the busy **boulevard du Montparnasse,** which is lined with various restaurants, ranging from Tex-Mex chains to classic Parisian cafes. **Rue du Montparnasse,** which intersects with the boulevard, teems with delicious and reasonably priced Breton *crêperies.* The central **rue Daguerre** is a haven of vegetarian-friendly establishments. Inexpensive restaurants cluster on **rue Didot** and **rue Raymond Losserand,** and fabulously priced ethnic takeout spots and couscous restaurants line **avenue du Maine.**

Chez Papa, 6, r. Gassendi (☎01 43 22 41 19). Ⓜ Denfert-Rochereau. Walk down Froidevaux along the cemetery; the restaurant will be on the left at the intersection with r. Gassendi. Many of Chez Papa's delicious, generous dishes are served straight from the cooking pot. The hearty lunch *menu* (served M-F) is a very good deal, with 2 courses and a coffee for €9.55. Alternatively, try one of a large choice of hot dishes and salads, including the massive *salade boyarde,* which consists of lettuce, potatoes, cantal, ham, and *bleu de brebis* (€7.45). Add 2 eggs for just €0.90 more. This place is one of the rare Parisian gems with a non-smoking section, so sensitive-lunged visitors should take note. Open daily 9am-2am. AmEx/MC/V. Additional locations in the 8ème (29, r. de l'Arcade; ☎01 42 65 43 68), 10ème (206, r. Lafayette; ☎01 42 09 53 87), and 15ème (101, r. de la Croix Nivert; ☎01 48 28 31 88). ❷

L'Amuse Bouche, 186, r. du Château (☎01 43 35 31 61). Ⓜ Alésia. Take av. du Maine to r. du Château. Classy and welcoming, in a nice neighborhood just away from the bustle of the main drag. Traditional French cuisine prepared to perfection. The €30.50 dinner *menu* offers 3 courses with options including escargots with mushrooms and tuna steak with honey and soy sauce. Reservations recommended. Open Tu-Sa noon-2pm and 7:30-10:30pm. MC/V. ❹

Au Rendez-Vous Des Camionneurs, 34, r. des Plantes (☎01 45 40 43 36). Ⓜ Alésia. Walk up av. du Maine with the church St-Pierre de Montrouge to your right, turn left onto r. du Moulin Vert and right onto r. des Plantes. Bottlecaps line the bar and red lights decorate the facade of this vibrant local spot, whose patrons have included cartoonist Reiser, artist Giacommetti (a drawing of whose hangs proudly on the back wall), and a bevy of local models who flock here every weekday from a nearby modeling agency for lunch. The *menus* consist of simple, country-style

THE BIG SPLURGE

THE ENCHANTED ISLAND

Once upon a time, on an island in the tranquil outskirts of the Bois de Boulogne, there was a little Swiss *châlet* that Napoleon III offered to his beloved empress Eugenie. The *châlet* later became a literary cafe, and after burning down in the early 1900's, was rebuilt as a lakeside restaurant. A little boat picks up diners at the far shore and skims across the water to dock at the *châlet.* The interior is decorated with elegant French country-style furniture, but the real treat is the spectacular outdoor seating. The terrace is interspersed with trellises covered in vines and blossoms, offering an unobstructed view of the lake. Take in the romantic setting with a fresh appetizer: the soft, mild chevre in mango coulis with balsamic vinegar (€10) dissolves tenderly on the palate. For main courses, choose from an extensive seafood menu featuring the house specialty prawns with basmati rice (€23), or from an array of land-based delicacies, like the crunchy and tender almond-covered duck brochettes with red risotto (€22). Finish with a classic dessert—chocolate eclairs or strawberry tart—or sip a *digestif* under the moonlight. Reservations always a must, especially for dinner. Call ahead at least one day for weekends.

Le Châlet des Îles, Carrefour des Cascades, lac inférieur du Bois de Boulogne (☎01 42 88 04 69; www.lechaletdesiles.net). Ⓜ *Rue de la Pompe or RER Henri Martin.* Open T-F noon-2:30pm and 8-10pm; Sa noon-3:30pm and 8-10:30pm; Su noon-3:30pm.

dishes (€14.50). Reservations reccommended. Open M-Sa noon-2:30pm and 7:30-10:30pm. Closed first 3 weeks of Aug. ❷

Aquarius Café, 40, r. de Gergovie (☎01 45 41 36 88). ⓜ Pernety. Walk against traffic on r. Raymond Losserand and turn right on r. de Gergovie. A celebrated local favorite, Aquarius Café offers a wide selection of entirely vegetarian dishes, with moderately priced *menus* for lunch (€11) and dinner (€15). You can finish your meal with a slice of homemade cake, displayed next to the tables to ensure continual salivation. Open M-Sa noon-2:30pm and 7-10:30pm. MC/V. Additional location in the 4ème (54, r. St-Croix de la Bretonnerie. ☎01 48 87 48 71). ❷

L'Encens, 84, bd. du Montparnasse (☎01 43 35 36 12). ⓜ Montparnasse-Bienvenüe. Take the r. d'Odessa exit and head straight down bd. du Montparnasse to the corner of r. du Montparnasse. This new restaurant and bar is a classy alternative to some of the other options on bd. Montparnasse. While the food is reasonably priced, the mixed drinks aren't, so you may end up paying more for your beverages than your meal. Main courses come for €11-17; try the delicious *coupe encens* (lychee sorbet, *sake*, and fresh fruit; €6.50) for dessert. Drinks range from €7 beers to the €12 Long Island Ice Tea. Stick to the restaurant, because visits to the bar and DJ booth (Th-Sa nights) might leave you more than slightly out of pocket. ❸

CAFES

La Coupole, 102, bd. du Montparnasse (☎01 43 20 14 20). ⓜ Vavin. La Coupole's Art Deco chambers have hosted the likes of Stravinsky, Hemingway, and Einstein. Though the trendy cafe is touristy and unabashedly overpriced, it's still worth the nostalgic splurge on coffee (€3), hot chocolate (€4), or a *croque monsieur* (€5). The cuisine is considered to be among the best in Paris, including an impressive seafood selection. Sadly, however, La Coupole offers only 1 vegetarian choice. Dancing Tu, Fr, and Sa (salsa and Latin) 7:30pm-5am. Cover from €10. Open M-F 8:30am-1am, Sa-Su 8:30am-1:30am. AmEx/MC/V. ❹

FIFTEENTH ARRONDISSEMENT

The 15ème offers a diverse selection of restaurants, with traditional French cuisine alongside Middle Eastern and Asian specialties. Cheap eateries crowd **rue du Commerce, rue de Vaugirard, boulevard de Grenelle,** and **Gare Montparnasse.**

▧ **Thai Phetburi,** 31, bd. de Grenelle (☎01 40 58 14 88; www.phetburi-paris.com). ⓜ Bir-Hakeim. Head away from the river on bd. de Grenelle; the restaurant is on your left. Award-winning food, friendly service, and low prices, just minutes from the Eiffel Tower. The *tom yam koung* (shrimp soup flavored with lemongrass; €7.30) and the *lab kai* (chicken in thai grass; €9.10) are both favorites. A multitude of vegetarian options available. Open M-Sa noon-2:30pm and 7-10:30pm. AmEx/MC/V. ❷

▧ **Le Dix Vins,** 57, r. Falguière (☎01 43 20 91 77; www.le-dix-vins.com). ⓜ Pasteur. Follow Pasteur away from the rails and make a left onto r. Falguière. This outstanding bistro, in typical French fashion, has a pun for a name. The pun is appropriate, as both the meals and the wines (fortunately numbering more than 10) are indeed divine. The *menu*, while not exactly cheap (€24), offers diners a classic meal with a *nouvelle cuisine* twist. Large and varied wine menu with some out-of-the-ordinary options.Open M-F noon-2:30pm and 7:30-11pm. MC/V. ❸

Le Tire Bouchon, 62, r. des Entrepreneurs (☎01 40 59 09 27). ⓜ Charles Michels. Run by a charming couple, Le Tire Bouchon serves classic French cuisine to a mixed crowd of Parisians and Americans. Their selection of surprisingly original desserts includes carrot sticks cooked in vanilla sauce with a caramel mousse (€7). €22 *menu* (M-Th nights), or order à la carte (starters €7; main dishes €18.50). Open M and Sa 7:30-11pm, Tu-F noon-2:30pm and 7:30-11pm. MC/V. ❸

Chez Fung, 32, r. Frémicourt (☎01 45 67 36 99). ⓜ Cambronne. Walk across pl. Cambronne, then turn left onto r. Frémicourt. Authentic, absolutely superb Malaysian cuisine, though the small portions may leave you hungry. 3-course lunch *menu* €9.90; M-F dinner *menu* €14.50. *Menus* include delicacies cooked in banana leaves and unique combinations of sweet and salty, like the *rojak* Malaysian salad. Open M-Sa noon-2:30pm and 7-10:30pm. MC/V for purchases over €15. ❷

Samaya, 31, bd. de Grenelle (☎01 45 77 44 44). ⓜ Bir-Hakeim. Head away from the river on bd. de Grenelle; adjacent to Thai Phetburi (see above). Samaya serves traditional Lebanese food at reasonable prices. Dinner *menu* €18. Lunch €13. Takeout sandwiches €4-4.50. Vegetarians rejoice: falafel for €3.80. Open daily until 11pm. ❷

Le Troquet, 21, r. François Bonvin (☎01 45 66 89 00). ⓜ Sèvres-Lecourbe. Take r. Lecourbe and turn right on r. François Bonvin. Run by a husband-and-wife team, this hidden-away restaurant serves an enticing blend of Basque, Provençal, and Parisian flavors. *Menu* (3 plates for €28—lots of money but well spent; 6 plates for the table for €38) changes daily. Open Tu-Sa noon-2pm and 7:30-10pm. MC/V. ❹

Ty Breiz, 52, bd. de Vaugirard (☎01 43 20 83 72). ⓜ Pasteur. Walk out of the metro and up the hill and turn left onto bd. de Vaugirard. This classic Breton *crêperie* brings a taste of Northern France to Paris (satisfying crêpes, wooden clogs on the wall). Particularly appropriate given the historic Breton presence in the area. One of the nicer crêperies in Paris, this is a great place to try your first. *Crêpes salées* €3.50-9.50. *Crêpes sucrées* €3.50-10. Open Tu-Sa 11:45am-2:30pm and 7-11pm. MC/V. ❶

CAFES

Aux Artistes, 63, r. Falguière (☎01 43 22 05 39). ⓜ Pasteur. Walk up the hill and then turn right onto r. Falguière. One of the 15*ème*'s cooler spots, this lively cafe draws a mix of professionals, students, and artists. Modigliani was supposedly a regular. Don't be put off by the surf board and American license plates on the wall; the food is traditional French cafe style. Lunch *menu* €10. Dinner *menu* €13. Open M-F noon-2:30pm and 7:30pm-midnight, Sa 7:30pm-midnight. ❷

SPECIALTY SHOPS

Au Coin du Pétrin, 96, r. des Entrepreneurs (☎01 45 79 36 67). ⓜ Felix Faure. Walk against traffic on the left side of the church; turn left onto r. des Entrepreneurs. Devotees gladly make the trek to this bakery, home to an award-winning *baguette traditionnelle* and a hard-working staff. One bite of your favorite indulgence will have you coming back for more. Sandwich and drink for €5 (M-F only). Open M-Sa 7am-9pm.

SIXTEENTH ARRONDISSEMENT

There is high-quality fare to be had in the 16*ème*, if you have a deep pocket. For those who don't (or who just want an alternative to *foie gras*), budget-friendly ethnic restaurants crowd **rue de Lauriston**. Excellent picnic fare can be purchased from *traiteurs* on **rue Passy** and **avenue Mozart**, at the *marchés* on av. du Président Wilson, r. St-Didier, along r. d'Auteuil and at the intersection of r. Gros and r. la Fontaine.

▨ Rosimar, 26, r. Poussin (☎01 45 27 74 91). ⓜ Michel Ange Auteuil. Walk up r. Girodet and turn left on r. Poussin. This small, intimate Spanish restaurant with Catalan specialties draws a devoted local crowd. Wall-to-wall mirrors, pink tablecloths and a polite, attentive staff create an unpretentious and charming dining experience. The food is undoubtedly the best and most authentic Spanish cuisine in the area, with a focus on seafood. Try the €32 *menu* with a delicious starter of *moules* (mussels) or the generous €34 paella *menu*. Vegetarian options. Reservations suggested. Open M-F 12pm-2pm and 7-10pm. AmEx/MC/V. ❹

THE HIDDEN DEAL

PITCHER THIS

Foreign visitors to France have an understandable fear of ordering the cheapest wine on the menu. In many countries, the cheapest wine is cheap for a reason: it is grainy and has a faint hint of vinegar, better suited for putting on a salad than in a glass. The same cannot be said of the lower-priced wines you find on menus in Paris, including the cheapest of the cheap—*vin en pichet*. Often poured straight from the barrel into the *pichet* brought to your table, these wines offer great taste at significant savings compared to bottled wine. The only true sacrifice is the loss of the *presentation du vin*, but unless you are trying to impress a date with your oenophilic savvy, this isn't much of a sacrifice at all. And whereas soft drinks are the beverage of choice for those on a budget in the US, in Paris splitting a half carafe of wine between a few people can be much cheaper than four Cokes. Restaurants make it easy for you, carrying one red, one white, and one rosé in pitchers. The most common sizes you'll see on the menu are 12cl (1 glass), 50cl (4 glasses), and 1L (a party).

If you want to live large and sample expensive wines without breaking your budget, head to a wine bar, where they are available by the glass for remarkably low prices. For a list of wine bars, see **Nightlife**, p. 301.

Byblos Café, 6, r. Guichard (☎01 42 30 99 99). ⓜ La Muette. Walk down r. Passy 1 block and turn left on r. Guichard. This airy, modern Lebanese restaurant, decked out in polished timber and stainless steel, serves cold *mezzes* (think Middle Eastern tapas) that are good for pita-dipping: taboulé, moutabal, moussaka, and a variety of hummus dishes, all €5.50-9. Various 2-person meal combinations starting at €34. Great vegetarian options. Takeout 15-20% less. Open M-Sa 11am-10:30pm, Su noon-3pm. AmEx/MC/V. ❷

Casa Tina, 18, r. Lauriston (☎01 40 67 19 24; www.casa-tina.com). ⓜ Kléber. Walk down av. Victor Hugo toward the Arc de Triomphe, turn left on r. Presbourg and right on r. Lauriston going uphill. Spanish tiles, edge-to-edge tables, and dried peppers hanging from the ceiling create an authentic ambience. The food and the sangria (€5) are both divine, but expect to sacrifice leg and elbow room. Tapas *menu* €19; other *menus* starting at €35. Open daily noon-2:30pm and 7-11:30pm. Reservations recommended. AmEx/MC/V. ❸

CAFES

La Rotonde, 12, Chaussée de la Muette (☎01 45 24 45 45). ⓜ La Muette. 2min. from the metro down Chaussée de la Muette; head toward the Jardin de Ranelagh. Located in a beautiful *fin-de-siècle* building overlooking the tree-lined Chaussée de la Muette, this cafe draws a mostly local crowd. Indoors, the stylish red and yellow lamps, hip music, and plush burgundy seats take a sleek spin on the patio's classic feel—but the outdoor seating is the best. A good place for a sandwich (€4-11), salad (€5.50-13.50), or the tart of the day (€6) before heading to the excellent Musée Marmottan. Beer, mixed drinks, and wine available (€5-10). Open daily 7am-midnight. AmEx/MC/V. ❷

SPECIALTY SHOPS

Marché Président-Wilson, on av. du Président Wilson between r. Debrousse and pl. d'Iéna. ⓜ Iéna or Alma-Marceau. The smart alternative to the 16ème's exorbitantly priced restaurants. Agricultural and dairy products, meat, fish, exotic breads, rich pastries and ready-to-eat Chinese and Middle Eastern fare. Flower stalls, clothing, table linens, and other household goods can all be found here. Open W and Sa 8am-2pm.

SEVENTEENTH ARRONDISSEMENT

The 17*ème* is far away from tourist attractions, so its restaurants depend on local support. Fortunately, the variety of classes and ethnicities in the district means variety in cuisine. The best place to look for cheap, high-quality, country-style eats is in the **Village Batignolles,** around r. des Batignolles, north of r. des Dames.

▓ **Le Patio Provençal,** 116, r. des Dames (☎01 42 93 73 73). Ⓜ Villiers. Follow r. de Lévis away from the intersection and go right onto r. des Dames. Le Patio Provençal is an airy, rustic restaurant that serves staples of southern French fare, such as *ravioles de Royans*. Glass of wine €2.50. 3-course *formule* €24. Appetizers €8, *plats* €11-14.50, and desserts €7. Often super-busy, making service a bit slow and reservations a must. Open M-Sa noon-2:30pm and 7-11pm. MC/V. ❷

▓ **The James Joyce Pub,** 71, bd. Gouvion St-Cyr (☎01 44 09 70 32; www.kittyosheas.com). Ⓜ Porte Maillot (exit at Palais de Congrès). Take bd. Gouvion St-Cyr past Palais de Congrès. Upstairs from the pub is a friendly restaurant with stained-glass windows depicting scenes from Joyce's novels. Downstairs, the pub pulls pints of what Joyce called "...Ghinis. Foamous bomely brew bebattled by bottle gagerne de guergerre..." An informal tourist office for middle-aged and younger Anglophone expats. Televised sporting events are posted outside the pub. Traditional Irish meals like stew with bacon and cabbage or ham with spuds and cheese (from €9.50). F nights live Irish rock music from 9:30pm on, except in summer. Open daily 11am-2am. Food served until 9pm. AmEx/MC/V. ❷

Le Bistrot de Théo, 90, r. des Dames (☎01 43 87 08 08). Ⓜ Villiers. From r. de Lévis, turn right on r. des Dames. This classy bistro serves cuisine as quirky and offbeat as its minimalist-with-a-twist decor of artful bric-a-brac. Rich, delicious *foie gras plats* (€11-21) are a must-try. Changing menu with dishes like roasted lamb with sweet spices and duck carpaccio with pesto and parmesan. *Plats* €13.50-17 and desserts €6.50. Lunch *menu* €14; all-day *menu* €25. Open M-Sa noon-2:30pm and 7:30-11:30pm. AmEx/MC/V. ❹

Restaurant Natacha, 35, r. Guersant (☎01 45 74 23 86). Ⓜ Porte Maillot. Take bd. Gouvion St-Cyr past the Palais de Congrès and turn right on r. Guersant. This always-bustling, traditional French country-style *grillade* prides itself on its *pavé de boeuf* and is especially great for lunch, with a buffet for €13.50. Dinner *menu* €20. Open M-Sa noon-2:30pm and 8-10:30pm. Reservations recommended. MC/V. ❸

Au Vieux Logis, 68, r. des Dames (☎01 43 87 77 27). Ⓜ Rome. Take r. Boursault to r. des Dames; the restaurant is on the corner. An acclaimed but friendly local spot, this provincial bar-restaurant features a simple and traditional 3-course *menu* (€19) that changes daily. *Plats* €11.50-15.50. Open M-F noon-2:45pm and 8-10:45pm, Sa 8-10:45pm. MC/V. ❷

Le Niv's, 8, r. des Batignolles (☎01 45 22 54 22). Ⓜ Rome. On the corner of r. des Batignolles and r. Caroline. Located in the heart of the Village Batignolles, this charming sidewalk bistro serves up fruity salads (€10.50-11.50) with ingredients like chicken, mango, and pineapple. Hearty, generous dishes with daily specials like fried chicken. *Plats* €14-17, desserts like vanilla and strawberry pannacotta €6-7. Lunch *formules* €15-17. Open M-Sa 8:30am-2am. Food served noon-3pm and 7-10:30pm. MC/V. ❷

CAFES

▓ **L'Endroit,** 67, pl. du Dr. Félix Lobligeois (☎01 42 29 50 00). Ⓜ Rome. Follow r. Boursault to r. Legendre, and turn right. Look for the blue exterior and cutting-edge haircuts on the waitstaff. As cool during the day as it is at night, L'Endroit is the place to be seen in the 17ème—especially if you snag an outdoor table. 4-course Su brunch (noon-3:30pm; €20, €6 children's brunch) headlines a long menu packed with an array of big salads (€10.50-16) and toasted sandwiches (€11.50). Open daily 10am-2am (open later during the weekend). MC/V. ❷

F O O D

Les Hortensias, 4, pl. du Maréchal de Juin (☎01 47 63 43 39 or 01 46 22 69 84). Ⓜ Pereire. Simple, summery fare is served to an opulent crowd of locals in a sprawling and airy rotunda. Menu includes the *croque monsieur* (€5.50), gazpacho (€7), salads (€9.50), and fish- and meat-based main dishes starting at €14. Coffee €2.50. Open M-F 9am-1am, Sa-Su 8am-1am. Food served 11am-11pm. MC/V. ❷

SPECIALTY SHOPS

Marché Berthier, on bd. de Reims between r. de Courcelles and r. du Marquis d'Arlandes, along pl. Ulmann. Ⓜ Porte de Champerret. Turn left off bd. Berthier onto r. de Courcelles, then right on bd. de Reims. Follow the scent of produce—the cheapest in Paris. North African and Middle Eastern specialties like fresh mint, Turkish bread, and baklava. Open W and Sa 7am-2:30pm.

EIGHTEENTH ARRONDISSEMENT

When Napoleon was defeated by the Sixth Coalition in 1814, the victorious European powers of Austria, Prussia, Russia, Sweden, the United Kingdom, and some German states occupied Paris. The heights of Montmartre, in particular, were the headquarters of the Russian Cossacks. The Cossacks, like many visitors to Paris, were dissatisfied with the speed of service of Parisian waiters. Unlike modern visitors, however, they had massive weaponry to back up their complaints. So when they yelled "bistro!" (faster!), waiters promptly complied. Fortunately, the Prussian soldiers of von Blücher were much better behaved, otherwise a French restaurant would be called a *schnell* instead of a *bistro*. The Russian soldiers are gone, but the tourists are here in full force, particularly around the kitschy pl. du Tertre and pl. St-Pierre. Lovely bistros and cafes are common between **rue des Abbesses** and **rue Lepic** and along **rue des Trois Frères,** and touristy piano bars can be found around **Place du Tertre.** In addition to the listings below, **Chez Louisette** and **Au Baryton,** within the **Puces de St-Ouen** just north of the 18*ème,* offer *moules marinière, frites,* and live entertainment (see **Shopping,** p. 283).

🍴 **Le Soleil Gourmand,** 10, r. Ravignan (☎01 42 51 00 50). Ⓜ Abbesses. Facing the church in pl. des Abbesses, head right down r. des Abbesses and go right (uphill) on r. Ravignan. Local favorite with funky artistic flare serves refreshing, light *Provençale* fare. Try the specialty *bricks* (grilled stuffed filo dough; €11), the 5-cheese *tartes* with salad (€10.50), and the delicious homemade cakes (around €5). The menu is rounded out with vegetarian options like the *assiette sud* (€12.50), a generous collection of grilled and marinated vegetables. Water is flavored with fresh mint. Anything and everything you see in the restaurant is available for purchase, from jams to magazines to the dishes off of which you eat. Evening reservations advised. Open daily 12:30-2:30pm and 7:30-11pm. ❷

🍴 **Refuge des Fondues,** 17, r. des Trois Frères (☎01 42 55 22 65). Ⓜ Abbesses. Walk down r. Yvonne le Tac and take a left on r. des Trois Frères. Only 2 main dishes: *fondue bourguignonne* (meat fondue) and *fondue savoyarde* (cheese fondue). The wine (2 choices: red or white) is served in baby bottles with rubber nipples. Leave your Freudian hang-ups at home, and join the family-style party at the 2 long tables. *Menu* with wine, *amuse-gueule* (a light appetizer), fondue, and dessert €16. Reserve a table or show up early. Open daily 5pm-2am, food from 7pm. Doesn't accept new diners after 12:30am. Closed Aug. ❷

🍴 **Le Sancerre,** 35, r. des Abbesses (☎01 42 58 08 20). Ⓜ Abbesses. Facing the church in pl. des Abbesses; head right on r. des Abbesses. A modernized Montmartre cafe with a topless mermaid on the ceiling and simple but delicious dishes like tomato-mozza-

With Cellular Abroad, talk is not only cheap, *it's free.*

Unlimited FREE incoming calls and no bills or contracts for overseas use!

1-800-287-5072
www.cellularabroad.com

Otel.com

Are you aiming for a budget vacation**?**

US & CANADA
1-800-820-4171 OR 1-212-594-8045
EUROPE
00-800-468-35482 OR 44-207-099-2035

DO NOT
DISTURB

rella salad (€7). Hip 20-somethings congregate on the terrace for mixed drinks and a relaxing place to while the evening away. Beer €3.50-5.50. *Apéritifs* €3.50-8. Wines €3-5. Open daily 7am-2am. MC/V. ❶

La Bodega, 54, r. Ordener. Ⓜ Jules Joffrin. Facing the *mairie*, turn left on r. Ordener. This informal bar/restaurant specializes in Latin American cuisine with a Spanish influence. Patrons can order a sandwich (€2.30-4.50) or an *assiette* of the day in one of 3 sizes. Limited seating outside or bar-style inside. Mixed drinks €5. Soft drinks €1.50. Open Tu-Su noon-2am. ❶

Chez Ginette, 101, r. Caulaincourt (☎01 46 06 01 49). Ⓜ Lamarck-Caulaincourt. Upstairs from the metro. This popular, modern bistro caters both to locals and tourists with tasty French dishes like leg of lamb flavored with rosemary and vegetables (€17), as well as a few less traditional dishes. Homesick, rich Americans can have the €15.50 cheeseburger, or possibly the world's only cooked steak tartare (€16). Open daily 9am-midnight. AmEx/MC/V. ❸

Djerba Cacher Chez Guichi, 76, r. Myrha (☎01 42 23 77 99). Ⓜ Barbès-Rochechouart. From the metro, walk up bd. Barbès and turn right onto r. Myrha. Guichi's owners opened this watering hole in order to provide cheap North African cuisine to local merchants. Parisians come from all over the city to sample Guichi's specialty, *brochette foie gras* (€10). Sandwiches €4-7.50. *Plats* €7-11.50. Open M-Th and Su noon-4pm and 7-11pm, F noon-4pm. ❷

Wassana, 10, r. Ganneron (☎01 44 70 08 54). Ⓜ Place de Clichy. Walk up av. de Clichy and turn right onto r. Ganneron. Stylishly decorated dining room and delicious Thai food 5min. from the corpse of Stendhal (in the Cimitière Montmartre). Lunch *menu* (€12) includes Thai chicken curry in coconut milk or beef in Thai herbs. Vegetarian options available. Appetizers €6.50-12.50. *Plats* €7-17.50. Open M-F noon-2:30pm and 7-11:30pm, Sa 7-11:30pm. AmEx/MC/V. ❷

Au Grain de Folie, 24, r. Lavieuville (☎01 42 58 15 57). Ⓜ Abbesses. Near the intersection with r. des Trois Frères. A great refuge for vegetarians and vegans. *Grain de folie* plate (€12) includes goat cheese, lentils, grains, grilled vegetables, and fresh salad. Dessert is a vegan apple crumble (€6). Vegan meal options also available. Coffee €2.50. Wine €3. Open M-Sa 12:30-2:30pm and 7:30-11pm, Su 12:30-11pm. ❷

La Maison Rose, 2, r. de l'Abreuvoir (☎01 42 57 66 75). Ⓜ Lamarck-Caulaincourt. Walk right on r. Lamarck and then right on r. des Saules. The restaurant is on the

ON THE MENU

PRESSÉ PASS

When you sit down in any cafe or restaurant in Paris, you will probably come across a strange assortment of drinks on the menu, including unknowns such as *citron pressé* and *orange pressé*. These are the French versions of the "freshly squeezed" genre of juice so popular in the United States.

On ordering a *citron pressé* (the classic lemon-flavored *pressé*), you will be presented with several elements: a tall glass about 1/3 to 2/3 full of pure lemon juice with ice, a little jug of water, and a seemingly irrational quantity of sugar. All three ingredients are essential to make the traditional drink. Add the sugar and water to the juice to taste, but be warned, the lemon can be strong; you might have to postpone your diet plans as you add the sugar.

This childhood favorite can be a wonderfully refreshing drink on a hot day. It usually costs around €4, but the price depends on the restaurant. For those who can handle it, the sour *citron pressé* is the quintessential *jus pressé*, but the orange version provides a sweeter alternative. Some restaurants are even more adventurous, offering other flavors such as grapefruit. Beware of errant seeds among the pulp as you sip your cool *boisson*.

corner with r. de l'Abreuvoir. As its name implies, this restaurant/cafe is in a small pink house on a corner in historic Montmartre. *Menu* for €17.50 includes appetizer, *plat*, and dessert. Here you can try the ultimate French delicacy—*escargots* (snails, 12 for €13)—while relaxing outside on the quiet *terrasse*. Open M-Sa noon-3pm and 7-10pm. MC/V. ❸

NINETEENTH ARRONDISSEMENT

The finest budget dining in the ethnically diverse 19*ème* is in **Little Chinatown,** where Chinese, Vietnamese, Thai, and Malaysian restaurants cluster along **rue de Belleville** (Ⓜ Belleville). Greek sandwich shops line **avenue Jean Jaurès** and **rue de Crimée.** The **Parc des Buttes-Chaumont** is a winning spot for a picnic.

▨ **Lao Siam,** 49, r. de Belleville (☎01 40 40 09 68). Ⓜ Belleville. Even before your food arrives, you'll be impressed by this Chinese and Thai favorite (where else can you order something in a hip-hop sauce?), or at least amused by the wall of articles singing the eatery's praises (in case you weren't sure what to think of it). A unique Thai-dried calamari salad (€6.30) makes for a light preamble to the *poulet royal au curry* (€8.40) or *filet du poisson "hip-hop"* (€8.60). Wash it down with a *citron pressé* (€2.30), finish it off with kumquats (€2.80), and you'll forget that you came so far out of your way to get it. Non-smokers get the front of the restaurant. Open daily noon-3pm and 7-11:30pm. MC/V. ❷

Aux Arts et Sciences Réunis, 161, av. Jean-Jaurès (☎01 42 40 53 18). Ⓜ Ourcq. On the corner right by the metro, and a short stroll away after a day at La Villette. Serving up hearty southwestern French meals family-style, Aux Arts brings in a local crowd. *Plats*, like salmon with a choice of sauces, €13-18. Lunch *menu* (M-F), €12 for a starter, *plat*, and dessert. French piano music Sa during dinner. Open M-Sa 7:30am-10:30pm. Food served noon-2:30pm and 7:30-10:30pm. MC/V. ❸

Ay, Caramba!, 59, r. de Mouzaïa (☎01 42 41 23 80). Ⓜ Pré-St-Gervais. From the metro, turn directly onto r. de Mouzaïa. With nightly *mariachi* music and sombreros on the wall, this Tex-Mex joint stands out in a quiet, residential neighborhood. Pricey but generous fajitas and tacos (€18). *Nachos rancheros* €7. Margaritas €7. Open daily 7:30pm-11pm, open for lunch F-Su noon-2:30pm. AmEx/MC/V. ❸

CAFES

La Kaskad', 2, pl. Armand-Carrel (☎01 40 40 08 10). Ⓜ Laumière. Facing the imposing Mairie, La Kaskad' offers a wonderful terrace at which to relax after a morning in the Parc des Buttes-Chaumont. The cuisine is varied and delicious. Big salad €13-14.50. Dessert €7.50. Coffee €2.50. Open daily 8am-11:30pm. MC/V. ❷

TWENTIETH ARRONDISSEMENT

A traditional meal amid Belleville's cobblestones is a breath of fresh air after spending time in Paris's crowded center. A number of trendy cafes and bistros line **rue St-Blaise** in the south. Come for lunch if you're in the neighborhood, or are just plain lost.

▨ **Café Flèche d'Or,** 102bis, r. de Bagnolet (☎01 44 64 01 02; www.flechedor.fr). Ⓜ Alexandre Dumas. Follow r. de Bagnolet until it crosses r. des Pyrénées; the cafe is on the right. Near Porte de la Réunion at Père Lachaise. In a defunct train station, this bar/cafe/performance space serves dishes inspired by various countries around the world and by New York, which apparently deserved its own dish despite being only a city. There is also nightly entertainment, usually in the form of live bands (see **Nightlife,** p. 319). Dinner *menus* €12-14.50. Bar/cafe open daily 10am-2am. Dinner served daily 8pm-1am. MC/V. ❷

La Bolée Belgrand, 19, r. Belgrand (☎01 43 64 04 03). ⓜ Porte de Bagnolet. Take the Hôpital Tenon exit; the restaurant will be across the street. In cramped but friendly quarters, this *petite crêperie* serves up delicious *crêpes* to a local crowd of families and couples. Order half a pitcher of *cidre* (€5) with your meal. Lunch *menu* €10.50. *Crêpes* €3-6.50. *Galettes* €6-9. Open Tu-Su noon-2:30pm and 7-10:30pm. MC/V. ❷

Le Zéphyr, 1, r. Jourdain (☎01 46 36 65 81). ⓜ Jourdain. Take the r. Jourdain exit and walk downhill to the end of the road. A classic Parisian bistro with unique dishes and 1930s decor. 4-course dinner *menu* €28. Limited lunch *menu* €13.50. Reservations recommended for dinner. Open daily 9am-2am. MC/V. ❹

CAFES

La Mer à Boire, 1-3, r. des Envierges (☎01 43 58 29 43). ⓜ Pyrénées. Walk down the sloping r. de Belleville, turn left on r. Piat and left on r. des Envierges. This multi-purpose cafe/bar on a corner across from Parc de Belleville offers spectacular views and simple but delicious food. Hosts art exhibitions and occasional concerts. *Assiettes* €10. Small tapas selection €5 each. Open daily in summer noon-1am, closed F from 6pm in winter. ❷

FOOD

SIGHTS

ÎLE DE LA CITÉ

see map p. 362-363

If you're looking to be humbled by magnificent architecture and hundreds of years of history, Île de la Cité is a wonderful place to start. Here lies the renowned **Nôtre Dame Cathedral** as well as a multitude of lesser-known but equally awe-inspiring locations such as **Ste-Chapelle.**

NOTRE DAME

Ⓜ *Cité.* ☎*01 42 34 56 10; crypt 01 55 42 50 10. Cathedral open daily 7:45am-7pm. Towers open Jan.-Mar. and Oct.-Dec. 10am-5:30pm, Apr.-Sept. 10am-6:30pm, June-Aug. Sa-Su until 11pm. €7.50, ages 18-25 €5, under 18 free. Audioguides €5. Tours begin at the booth to the right as you enter. In French M-F 2 and 3pm; call ahead for English-language tours. Free. Mass M-F 8, 9am (except July-Aug.), noon, 6:15pm; Sa 6:30pm; Su 8:30am, 10am High Mass with Gregorian chant, music at 11:30am, 12:45, and 6:30pm. Free recital by one of the cathedral organists at 4:30pm. Vespers sung 5:30pm. Treasury open M-F 9:30am-6pm, Sa 9:30am-5pm, and Su 1-1:30pm and 6-6:30pm, last entry 15min. before closing. €3, under 26 €2, children €1. Crypt open Tu-Su 10am-6pm, last entry 5:30pm. €3.50, over 60 €2.50, under 27 €1.50, under 13 free. MC/V with €15 min. charge.*

Once the site of a Roman temple to Jupiter, the ground upon which Notre Dame stands witnessed three previous churches before Maurice de Sully began construction of the cathedral in 1163. De Sully, the bishop of Paris under King Philip II, was anxious to avoid the poor interior design that characterized Notre Dame's dark and cramped predecessor. He aimed to create an edifice filled with air and light, in a style that would later be dubbed **Gothic** (see **Life and Times,** p. 80). De Sully died before his ambitious plan was completed, but the cathedral was reworked over several centuries into the composite masterpiece that stands today. Royals used Notre Dame for marriage ceremonies, most notably that of **Henri of Navarre** to Marguerite de Valois (see **Life and Times,** p. 61). While royal burials were performed at the St-Denis cathedral, coronations took place at Reims (with the exception of **Henri VI's,** performed at Notre Dame in 1431), and relics went to Ste-Chapelle (p. 186), Notre Dame had an unrivaled hold on the public's attention from the beginning.

In addition to its royal functions, the cathedral was also the setting for notable events like **Joan of Arc's** trial for heresy in 1455. During the Revolution, secularists renamed the cathedral *The Temple of Reason* and encased its Gothic arches in Neoclassical plaster moldings. The church was reconsecrated after the Revolution and was the site of **Napoleon's** coronation in 1804. However, the building soon fell into disrepair, and for two decades, it was used to shelter livestock, until **Victor Hugo's** 1831 novel *Notre-Dame de Paris* (The Hunchback of Notre Dame). This novel revived the cathedral's popularity and inspired Napoleon III and Haussmann to devote finances and attention to its restoration. Modifications by **Eugène Viollet-le-Duc** (including a new spire, gargoyles, and a statue of himself admiring his own work) reinvigorated the cathedral's image in the public consciousness, and Notre Dame once again became a valued symbol of civic unity. Indeed, in 1870 and again in 1940 thousands of Parisians attended masses in the church to pray for deliverance from the invading Germans. On August 26, 1944, **Charles de Gaulle** braved Nazi sniper fire to come here and give thanks for the imminent liberation of Paris.

All of these upheavals (not to mention the herds of tourists who invade its portals every day or the equally sacrilegious 1996 Disney movie of Hugo's novel) seem to have left the cathedral unscarred.

EXTERIOR. Notre Dame is still in the throes of a massive cleaning project, and has been for several years, but at least now its newly glittering **West Facade** has been set free from scaffolding. Such restorative efforts are in line with tradition: work on the exterior started in the 12th century and continued into the 17th, when artists were still adding Baroque statues. The oldest work is found above the **Porte de Ste-Anne** (on the right), mostly dating from 1165-1175. The **Porte de la Vierge** (on the left), which relates the life of the Virgin Mary, dates from the 13th century. The central **Porte du Jugement** was almost entirely redone in the 19th century; the figure of Christ dates from 1885. Revolutionaries wreaked havoc on the facade during the frenzied rioting of the 1790s. Not content with decapitating Louis XVI, they attacked the statues of the Kings of Judah above the doors, thinking that they represented the monarch's ancestors. The heads were found in the basement of the Banque Française du Commerce in 1977 and were installed in the Musée de Cluny (see **Museums,** p. 254).

TOWERS. The two towers—home to the cathedral's fictional resident, Quasimodo the Hunchback—stare with gray solemnity across the square below. Streaked with black soot, the twin towers of Notre Dame were an imposing shadow on the Paris skyline for years. Now, after several years of sandblasting, the blackened exterior has been brightened, once again revealing the rose windows and rows of saints and gargoyles that adorn the cathedral. There's always a considerable line to make the 422-step climb (look for the crowd of people to the left of the cathedral entrance), but it's well worth it (20 visitors are let in every 10min.). The narrow staircase emerges onto a spectacular perch, where rows of gargoyles survey the heart of the city, notably the Left Bank's Latin Quarter and the Marais on the Right Bank. In the South Tower, a tiny door opens onto the 13-ton bell that even Quasimodo couldn't ring: it requires the force of eight people to move. For a striking view of the cathedral, cross Pont St-Louis (behind the cathedral) to Île St-Louis and turn right on quai d'Orléans. At night, the cathedral's buttresses are lit, and the sight is truly awe-inspiring. The Pont de Sully, at the far side of Île St-Louis, also affords an impressive view of the cathedral.

INTERIOR. Notre Dame cathedral can seat over 10,000 people. From the inside, it seems to be constructed of soaring, weightless walls. This effect is achieved by the spidery **flying buttresses** that support the vaults of the ceiling from outside, allowing light to fill the cathedral through delicate stained-glass windows. Walk down the **nave** (the long, open part of the church) to arrive at the **transept** and an unforgettable view of the **rose windows.** The north window (to the left) is still almost entirely 13th-century glass, and the south and west windows are equally enchanting, though they contain more modern glass. At the center of the 21m north window is the Virgin, depicted as the descendent of the Old Testament kings and judges who surround her. The base of the south window shows Matthew, Mark, Luke, and John on the shoulders of Old Testament prophets, and in the central window, Christ is surrounded by the 12 apostles. The cathedral's **treasury,** south of the choir, contains an assortment of glittering robes, sacramental cutlery, and other gilded artifacts from the cathedral's past. The Crown of Thorns, believed to have been worn by Christ is reverentially presented only on the first Friday of every month at 3pm.

Far below the cathedral towers, beneath the pavement of the square in front of the cathedral, the **Crypte Archéologique,** pl. du Parvis du Notre Dame, houses artifacts that were unearthed in the construction of a parking garage. The crypt is a virtual tour of the history of Île de la Cité; it houses architectural fragments from various eras throughout Paris's history—from Roman Lutèce up through the 19th-century sewers—as well as temporary art exhibits.

ELSEWHERE ON THE ÎLE DE LA CITÉ

PALAIS DE LA CITÉ. The Palais de la Cité houses the infamous **Conciergerie**, a Revolutionary prison, and **Ste-Chapelle**, the private chapel of St. Louis. Both are remnants from St. Louis's 13th-century palace. Most of the complex is occupied by the **Palais de Justice**, which was built after the great fire of 1776 and is now home to the district courts of Paris. *(4, bd. du Palais. ⓜ Cité.)*

■ **STE-CHAPELLE.** Ste-Chapelle remains the foremost example of Flamboyant Gothic architecture and a tribute to the craft of medieval stained glass. The chapel was constructed in 1241 to house King Louis IX's most precious possession: the Crown of Thorns from Christ's Passion. Bought along with a section of the Cross by the Emperor of Constantinople in 1239 for the ungodly sum of £135,000, the crown required an equally princely home. Although the crown itself—minus a few thorns that St-Louis gave away in exchange for political favors—has been moved to Notre Dame, Ste-Chapelle is still a wonder for the eyes. The Lower Chapel has a blue vaulted ceiling dotted with golden *fleurs-de-lis* and contains a few "treasures," platter-sized portraits of saints. While a gift shop detracts from the sanctity of the lower level, the real star of the building is the Upper Chapel. When light pours through its stained glass windows on sunny days, illuminating frescoes of saints and martyrs, it's one of the most breathtaking sights in Paris. Read from bottom to top, left to right, the windows, dating from 1136, narrate the Bible from Genesis to the Apocalypse. *(6, bd. du Palais. ⓜ Cité. Within Palais de la Cité. ☎01 53 73 78 50; www.monum.fr. Open daily Nov.-Feb. 9am-5pm and Mar.-Oct. 9:30am-6pm, last entry 30min. before closing. €6.50, seniors and ages 18-25 €4.50, under 18 free. Twin ticket with Conciergerie €9.50, seniors and ages 18-25 €7, under 18 free if accompanied by parent. Cash only. Occasional candlelit classical music concerts (€16-25) held in the Upper Chapel Mar.-Nov. Check FNAC (www.fnac.fr) or the booth to the left of the ticket-taker for details.)*

PALAIS DE JUSTICE. Enter through the Ste-Chapelle entrance, go down the hallway after the security check and turn right onto a double-level courtroom area. To go in the main entrance, turn right into the courtyard after the security check. A wide set of stone steps at the main entrance of the Palais de Justice leads to three doorways: you have your choice of entering through one marked *Liberté*, *Egalité*, or *Fraternité—*

TOP TEN LIST

TOP TEN SIGHTS

1. The Seine. The perfect backdrop to absolutely any Parisian experience and a gorgeous place to spend the day.

2. Musée du Louvre. Once a palace of kings and now the home of Mona Lisa (p. 245).

3. Notre Dame Cathedral. The famous home of the hunchback and the many fabled gargoyles, historical anecdotes, and stained-glass windows (p. 183).

4. Musée Rodin. Locals don't hesitate to call this the best museum in Paris (p. 257).

5. Place des Vosges. Paris's oldest public square is one of the city's loveliest spots to spend an afternoon reading in the sun (p. 198).

6. The Marais. A confluence of classy cuisine, cafes, carousal, and cruising. Plan on making it a late night (p. 4).

7. St-Germain-des-Prés. This charming historic area boasts exciting galleries, upscale boutiques, and legendary cafes.

8. Jardin du Luxembourg. Pitch *boules*, see the *grand guignol*, and sail a toy boat in the most popular of Paris's formal gardens (p. 204).

9. Centre Pompidou. Plumbing on the outside, contemporary art on the inside, and a squiggly fountain to boot (p. 252).

10. The Eiffel Tower. No matter how many desk-sized reproductions you may have seen, nothing can prepare you for the grace of this iron lady (p. 207).

words that once signified revolution and now serve as the bedrock of French tradition. All trials are open to the public, and even if your French is not up to legalese, the theatrical sobriety of the interior is worth a quick glance. Choose a door, turn right down the hallway and present yourself to a guard or the information desk. *(Within Palais de la Cité, 4, bd. du Palais; use the entrance for Ste-Chapelle at 6, bd. du Palais. ⓂCité. ☎01 44 32 51 51. Courtrooms open M-F 9am-noon and 1:30-end of last trial. Free.)*

CONCIERGERIE. The effect of walking into this dark, historically rich monument to the Revolution is a far cry from that of entering its neighbor, Ste-Chapelle. Built by Philip the Fair in the 14th century, the Conciergerie is a good example of secular medieval architecture. The name Conciergerie refers to the administrative officer of the Crown who acted as the king's steward, the *Concierge* (Keeper). When Charles V moved the seat of royal power from Île de la Cité to the Hôtel St-Pol and then to the Louvre, he left the *Concierge* in charge of the Parliament, Chancery, and Audit Office on the island. Later, this edifice became a royal prison and was taken over by the Revolutionary Tribunal after 1793. The northern facade, blackened by auto exhaust, casts an appropriate gloom over the building: 2780 people were sentenced to death here between 1792 and 1794. Among its most famous prisoners were Marie-Antoinette, Robespierre, and 21 Girondins. At the farthest corner on the right, a stepped parapet marks the oldest tower, the **Tour Bonbec,** which once housed torture chambers. The modern entrance lies between the **Tour d'Argent,** stronghold of the royal treasury, and the **Tour de César,** used by the Revolutionary Tribunal.

Past the entrance hall, stairs lead to rows of cells complete with replicas of prisoners and prison conditions. Plaques explain how, in a bit of opportunism on the part of the Revolutionary leaders, the rich and famous could buy themselves private cells with cots and tables for writing while the poor slept on straw in pestilential cells. Marie-Antoinette was imprisoned in the Conciergerie for five weeks, and the model of her room is one of the most crowded spots on the touring circuit. To escape the crowds, follow the corridor named for "Monsieur de Paris," the executioner during the Revolution; you'll be tracing the final footsteps of Marie-Antoinette as she awaited decapitation on October 16, 1793. Other exhibits tell the stories of the conflicting Revolutionary factions. In 1914, the Conciergerie ceased to be used as a prison. Occasional concerts and wine tastings in the Salle des Gens d'Armes have, happily, replaced torture and beheadings. *(1, quai de l'Horloge, entrance on bd. du Palais, to the right of Palais de Justice. Ⓜ Cité. ☎01 53 40 60 93; www.monum.fr. Open daily Mar.-Oct. 9:30am-6pm and Nov.-Feb. 9am-5pm; last entry 30min. before closing. €6.50, students €4.50, under 18 free. Includes tour in French, 11am and 3pm. For English tours, call in advance.)*

MÉMORIAL DE LA DÉPORTATION. This haunting memorial commemorates the 200,000 French victims of Nazi concentration camps. Inside the high concrete walls, the focal point is a tunnel lined with 200,000 quartz pebbles, reflecting the Jewish custom of placing stones on the graves of the deceased. To the sides are empty cells and wall carvings of concentration camp names and humanitarian quotations. Near the exit is the simplest and most arresting of these, the injunction, "*Pardonne. N'Oublie Pas*" (Forgive. Do Not Forget). Walking through the memorial is a claustrophobia-inducing experience, with narrow staircases, spiked gates, and restricted views. Also featured are numerous references to triangles, the mark of the deported, in the memorial's design. *(Ⓜ Cité. At the very tip of the island on pl. de l'Île de France, a 5min. walk from the back of the cathedral, and down a narrow flight of steps. Open daily Apr.-Sept. 10am-noon and 2-7pm; Oct.-Mar. 10am-noon and 2-5pm. Free.)*

HÔTEL DIEU. A hospital was first founded on this site in AD 651 by Bishop St. Landry. In the middle ages, the Hôtel Dieu was built to confine the sick rather than to cure them. Guards were posted to keep the patients from infesting and infecting the city. More recently, Louis Pasteur conducted much of his pioneering research inside (see **Life and Times,** p. 76). In 1871, the hospital's proximity to Notre Dame saved the cathedral—Communards were dissuaded from burning the church for fear that the flames would engulf their hospitalized comrades. Today, the serene inner courtyard gardens of the city's oldest hospital regularly feature sculpture exhibits. *(1, pl. du Paris, to the side of Notre Dame. Ⓜ Cité. ☎ 01 42 34 82 34. Open daily, 7am-8pm. Free.)*

PONT NEUF. Leave Île de la Cité by Paris's oldest bridge, the Pont Neuf (New Bridge), behind pl. Dauphine. Completed in 1607, the bridge was considered quite innovative because its sides were not lined with houses. Before the construction of the Champs-Elysées, the bridge was Paris's most popular thoroughfare, attracting peddlers, performers, and thieves. More recently, Bulgarian artist Christo wrapped the bridge in 44,000 sq. m of nylon. You can see the comic gargoyle faces carved into the supports from a Bâteau-Mouche (see **Practical Information,** p. 116) or from the park at the base of the bridge, Square du Vert-Galant. Visiting around sunset is one of the most romantic experiences in Paris: just ask the innumerable couples lip-locked along its sides. *(Ⓜ Pont Neuf.)*

ÎLE ST-LOUIS

see map p. 362-363

The true gems of Île St-Louis are its many *quais,* or riverside piers perfect for a stroll or an afternoon of people-watching. It's truly the area of the city for a promenade; come here with comfortable walking shoes.

QUAI DE BOURBON. Sculptor **Camille Claudel** lived and worked at **no. 19** from 1899 until 1913. Claudel was the protegé and lover of sculptor Auguste Rodin, and her most striking work is displayed in the Musée Rodin (see **Museums,** p. 252). She spent her years on the quai de Bourbon wavering between prolific artistic brilliance and insanity provoked by her love for Rodin, until her brother had her incarcerated in an asylum. The wrought-iron and grilled facade of the cafe **Au Franc-Pinot,** at the intersection of the quai and r. des Deux Ponts, is almost as old as the island itself. The grapes that decorate the ironwork gave the cafe its name; the pinot is a grape from Burgundy used for making wines such as pinot noir. Closed in 1716 after authorities found a basement stash of anti-government tracts, the cafe-cabaret re-emerged as a treasonous address during the Revolution. Cécile Renault, daughter of the proprietor, mounted an unsuccessful attempt on Robespierre's life in 1794 and was guillotined the following year. Today the Pinot houses a mediocre jazz club (live music most nights of the week) and serves lunch and dinner in its vaulted basement. *(Visible immediately to the left after crossing the Pont St-Louis, the quai de Bourbon wraps around the northwest edge of the island.)*

QUAI D'ANJOU. Some of the island's most beautiful old *hôtels particuliers* line quai d'Anjou, between Pont Marie and Pont de Sully. **No. 37** was home to writer John Dos Passos; **No. 29** housed the Three Mountains Press, which published books by Hemingway and Ford Maddox Ford and was edited by Ezra Pound; and **no. 9** was the address of Honoré Daumier, realist painter and caricaturist, from 1846 to 1863, during which time he painted, among other works, *La Blanchisseuse (The Washer Woman),* now hanging in the Louvre. The **Hôtel Lambert,** at **no. 2,** was designed by Le Vau in 1640 for Lambert le Riche and was home to Voltaire and Mme. de Châtelet, his mathematician mistress. *(The quai wraps around the northeast edge of the island to the left after the Pont Marie.)*

RUE ST-LOUIS-EN-L'ÎLE. The main thoroughfare of Île St-Louis, the narrow, cobblestoned r. St-Louis-en-l'Île, is home to an enticing collection of clothing boutiques, gourmet food stores, galleries, and ice cream shops, including the famous Berthillon glacerie (see **Shopping**, p. 284; **Food**, p. 148). *(This street bisects the island lengthwise.)*

EGLISE ST-LOUIS-EN-L'ÎLE. Built by Le Vau in 1726 and vandalized during the Revolution, this church has more to offer than initially meets the eye. Beyond the building's sooty, humdrum facade, you'll find an ostentatious Rococo interior lit by more windows than appear to exist from the outside. Gilded carvings and paintings are well-labeled in all of the chapels. Legendary for its acoustics, the church hosts concerts (usually classical) throughout the year. *(19bis, r. St-Louis-en-l'Île. ☎01 46 34 11 60; www.saintlouisenlile.com. Open Tu-Su 9am-noon and 3-7pm. Mass M-Sa 6:30pm and Su 11am. Check with FNAC (www.fnac.com) or call the church for concert details; ticket prices vary, around €20, students €15)*

QUAI DE BÉTHUNE. **Marie Curie** lived at **no. 36,** quai de Béthune, until she died of radiation-induced cancer in 1934. French President **Georges Pompidou** died just a few doors down at **no. 24.** *(The quai is on the southeast side of the island.)*

FIRST ARRONDISSEMENT

The 1*er* should be, as its name suggests, one of the first stops visitors make upon reaching Paris. It is home to some of the city's most important and beautiful sights, not to mention the best shopping.

see map p. 356-357

EAST OF THE LOUVRE

JARDIN DES TUILERIES. Sweeping down from the Louvre to the pl. de la Concorde, the Jardin des Tuileries was built by Catherine de Médicis in 1564 in order to assuage her longing for the promenades of her native Florence. In 1649, André Le Nôtre (gardener for Louis XIV and designer of the gardens at Versailles) imposed his preference for straight lines and sculpted trees upon the landscape of the Tuileries. The elevated terrace by the Seine affords remarkable views, including some of the **Arc de Triomphe du Carrousel** and the **glass pyramid** of the Louvre's Cour Napoléon. Sculptures by Rodin and others stand amid the garden's cafes and courts. In the summer, the r. de Rivoli terrace becomes an amusement park with children's rides, food stands, and a huge ferris wheel. (Ⓜ *Tuileries.* ☎01 40 20 90 43. *Open daily Apr.-Sept. 7am-11pm; Oct.-Mar. 7:30am-7:30pm. English tours from the Arc de Triomphe du Carrousel. Amusement park open July to mid-Aug.)*

JEU DE PAUME AND L'ORANGERIE. Flanking the pathway at the Concorde end of the Tuileries are the Jeu de Paume and the Musée de l'Orangerie (see **Museums**, p. 248).

PLACE VENDÔME. The stately pl. Vendôme, three blocks north of the Tuileries along r. de Castiglione, was begun in 1687 by Louis XIV. The square was designed by Jules Hardouin-Mansart and was intended to house embassies, but bankers built lavish private homes for themselves here instead. Today, the smell of money is still in the air: bankers, perfumers, and jewelers (including Cartier, at no. 7) line the square.

In the center of pl. Vendôme, Napoleon stands atop a large column dressed as Caesar. In 1805, Napoleon erected the work, modeled after Trajan's Column in Rome and fashioned out of the bronze from the 1250 cannons he captured at the Battle of Austerlitz. After Napoleon's exile, the Royalist government arrested the sculptor and forced him, on pain of death, to get rid of the statue. For all the government's pains, the return of Napoleon from Elba soon brought the original statue back to its perch. Over the next 60 years, it would be replaced by the white flag of the monarchy, a renewed Napoleon in military garb, and a classical Napoleon modeled after the original. During the Commune, a group led by uppity artist Gustave Courbet toppled the entire column, planning to replace it with a monument to the "Federation of Nations and the Universal Republic." The original column was recreated with new bronze reliefs, at Courbet's expense. The painter was subsequently jailed and sent to Switzerland, where he died a few years later (see **Life and Times,** p. 82.)

PALAIS-ROYAL AND SURROUNDINGS

PALAIS-ROYAL. One block north of the Louvre along r. St-Honoré lies the once regal and racy Palais-Royal. Today, the palace houses a handful of government offices and is not open to the public, but visitors are free to enjoy the palace from the outside. In summer, the fountain in the palace garden is a popular foot-bath destination. Futuristic metal sculptures by Arnaldo Pomodoro on the sides of the garden attract almost as much attention as the palace itself. In the central court-yard, the **Colonnes de Buren**—a set of black-and-white striped pillars—have inspired controversy *ever* since artist Daniel Buren installed them in 1986. m
    The Palais-Royal was constructed for Richelieu between 1628 and 1642 by Jacques Lemercier. After Richelieu's death in 1642, Queen Anne d'Autriche moved in, preferring the Cardinal's palace to the Louvre. She brought with her the young Louis XIV. Louis was the first king to inhabit the palace, but he fled during the Fronde uprising. In 1781, a broke Duc d'Orléans rented out the buildings around the palace's formal garden, turning the complex into an 18th-century shopping mall with boutiques, restaurants, theaters, wax museums, and gambling joints. (Its covered arcades were a favorite of local prostitutes.) On July 12, 1789, 26-year-old Camille Desmoulins leapt onto a cafe table here and urged his fellow citizens to arm themselves, shouting, "I would rather die than submit to servitude." The crowd filed out and was soon skirmishing with cavalry in the Jardin des Tuileries. *(Palace closed to the public. Fountain and garden open daily June-Aug. 7am-11pm; Sept. 7am-9:30pm; Oct.-Mar. 7:30am-8:30pm; Apr.-May 7am-10:15pm. Free.)*

COMÉDIE FRANÇAISE. Located on the southwestern corner of the Palais-Royal is the Comédie Française, home of France's leading dramatic troupe (see **Entertainment,** p. 275). Built in 1790 by architect Victor Louis, the theater was the first permanent home for the Comédie Française troupe, created by Louis XIV in 1680. The entrance displays several busts of famous actors crafted by equally famous sculptors. Visitors can peruse Rodin's *Mirabeau* or David d'Angers's *Talma* as they pass through to watch the show. Molière, the company's founder, took ill here on stage while playing the role of the Imaginary Invalid. The chair onto which he collapsed is still on display. At the corner of r. Molière and r. Richelieu, Visconti's **Fontaine de Molière** is only a few steps from where Molière died at no. 40.

LES HALLES AND SURROUNDINGS

EGLISE DE ST-EUSTACHE. There is a reason why Richelieu, Molière, and Mme. de Pompadour were all baptized in the Eglise de St-Eustache, and it's probably the same reason why Louis XIV received communion in its sanctuary, and why Mozart chose to have his mother's funeral here: the church is magnificent. Eustache (Eustatius) was a Roman general who adopted Christianity upon seeing the sign of a cross between the antlers of a deer. As punishment for converting, the Romans locked him and his family into a brass bull that was placed over a fire until it became white-hot. Construction of the church in his honor began in 1532 and dragged on for over a century. In 1754, the unfinished facade was demolished and replaced with the Romanesque one that stands today—incongruous with the rest of the Gothic building but appropriate for its Roman namesake. The chapels con-

1 MUSÉE PICASSO. This museum traces Picasso's life and work chronologically, all the way from Paris to the Riviera, from blue to pink, from first mistress to last (5, r. de Thorigny; see p. 249).

2 PLACE DES VOSGES. The exquisite manicured grass of Paris's oldest public square has been tread by the likes of Molière and Victor Hugo (no. 6 is a museum of his life and work), not to mention a good number of royals. An arcade runs around all four of its sides and houses restaurants, art galleries, and shops (p. 198).

3 EGLISE ST-PAUL-ST-LOUIS. This Jesuit cathedral dominates r. St-Antoine and offers the weary traveler a break from the heat and car exhaust on the *rue*. The church's Baroque interior houses Eugène Delacroix's 1826 *Christ in the Garden of Olives* (p. 197).

4 RUE DES ROSIERS. This quintessential Marais street is filled with bakeries, off-beat boutiques, and kosher restaurants. For lunch, enjoy a delicious falafel sandwich at the perpetually crowded **L'As du Falafel**, no. 34 (p. 195).

5 MARIAGE FRÈRES. This classic and classy *salon de thé* has 500 varieties of tea to choose from (30, r. du Bourg-Tibourg; p. 156).

6 SAMARITAINE. Eleven floors of shopping for him, her, and home are topped off with an unbeatable panoramic view of the city. Markers name every dot on the horizon, making this Art Deco department store worth a visit even if shopping isn't on the agenda (67, r. de Rivoli; p. 192).

7 PONT NEUF. By way of the very long, very straight, r. de Rivoli and the scenic quai du Louvre, make your way to the Pont Neuf, Paris's oldest bridge (c. 1607). Its gargoyles have seen peddlers and pickpockets, and a whole lot of bubble wrap (p. 187).

8 RUE ST-LOUIS-EN-ÎLE. Wander down the charming 17th-century main street of the Île St-Louis and pop into **Berthillon** (no. 34) or **Amorino** (no. 47) for ice cream (p. 187).

START: Ⓜ Chemin-Vert

FINISH: Ⓜ Ile St-Louis

DURATION: 3-4hr.

WHEN TO GO: Start in the late morning

tain paintings by Rubens, as well as the British artist Raymond Mason's bizarre relief *Departure of the Fruits and Vegetables from the Heart of Paris*, commemorating the closing of the market at Les Halles in February 1969. In the summertime, organ concerts commemorate St-Eustache's premieres of Berlioz's *Te Deum* and Liszt's *Messiah* in 1886. Outside the church, Henri de Miller's 1986 sculpture *The Listener* depicts a huge stone human head and hand. (Ⓜ *Les Halles. Above r. Rambuteau. ☎01 42 36 31 05; www.saint-eustache.org. Open M-F 9:30am-7pm, Sa 10am-7pm, Su 9am-7:15pm. Mass M-F 12:30, 6pm; Su 9:30, 11am, 6pm; Sa 6pm.)*

LES HALLES. Emile Zola called Les Halles "le ventre de Paris" (the belly of Paris). The metro station Les Halles exits directly into the underground mall. To see the gardens above, use one of the four "Portes" and ride the escalators up towards daylight. A sprawling food market since 1135, Les Halles received a much-needed facelift in the 1850s with the construction of large iron-and-glass pavilions to shelter the vendors' stalls. Designed by Victor Baltard, the pavilions resembled the one that still stands over the small market at the Carreau du Temple in the 3*ème*. In 1970, authorities moved the old market to a suburb near Orly. Politicians and city planners debated next how to fill "le trou des Halles" (the hole of Les Halles), 106 open acres that presented Paris with the largest urban redesign opportunity since Haussmann's overhaul. Most of the city adored the elegant pavilions and wanted to see them preserved, but planners destroyed the pavilions to build a subterranean transfer point between the metro and the new commuter rail, the RER. The city retained architects Claude Vasconti and Georges Penreach to replace the pavilions with a subterranean shopping mall, the **Forum des Halles** (see **Shopping**, p. 285). Descend from one of the four main entrances to discover over 200 boutiques and three movie theaters. Putting the mall underground allowed designers to landscape the vast Les Halles quadrangle with greenery, statues, and fountains. The forum and gardens attract a large crowd, especially during the summer months and winter holiday season. Like in any crowded space, watch out for pickpockets. (Ⓜ *Les Halles.)*

BOURSE DU COMMERCE. Between r. du Louvre and the Forum des Halles, the round Bourse du Commerce brokers commodities trading. The beautiful interior makes paying a visit worthwhile for more than just the business-minded. Inside, the iron-and-glass cupola forms a tremendous skylight, and the room is surrounded by frescoes. In the Middle Ages, a convent of repentant sinners occupied the site. Catherine de Médicis threw them out in 1572, when a horoscope convinced her that she should abandon construction of the Tuileries and build her palace here instead. Most of the palace was demolished in 1763, leaving only the observation tower of her personal astrologer, as a memorial to her superstition. Louis XV later replaced the structure with a grain market. In 1889, it was transformed into the commodities market that it is today. (Ⓜ *Louvre-Rivoli. ☎01 55 65 55 65; www.ccip.fr. Open M-F 9am-5:30pm. Free.)*

FONTAINE DES INNOCENTS. Built in 1548 and designed by Pierre Lescot, the Fontaine des Innocents is the last trace of the Eglise and Cimetière des Sts-Innocents, which once bordered Les Halles. Until its demolition in the 1780s, the cemetery's edges were crowded by merchants selling produce amid the smell of rotting corpses. The cemetery closed during the Enlightenment's hygienic reforms, and the corpses moved to the catacombs (p. 222). (Ⓜ *Châtelet, RER Châtelet-Les Halles.)*

EGLISE ST-GERMAIN L'AUXERROIS. Tucked directly behind the Louvre along r. de l'Amiral de Coligny is the Gothic Eglise St-Germain l'Auxerrois. On August 24, 1572, the church's bell sounded the signal for the St. Bartholomew's Day Massacre. Thousands of Huguenots were hacked to death by a mob of Catholic Parisians and the troops of the counter-reformist Duc de Guise, while King Charles IX shot at the survivors from the palace window (see **Life and Times**, p. 61). Visitors are allowed inside to view the violet windows or listen to Sunday evening vespers before mass. *(2, pl. du Louvre.* Ⓜ *Louvre-Rivoli.* ☎*01 42 60 13 96. Open weekdays 9am-7pm, 9am-8pm. Su mass 11am, 5:30, and 7pm; Sa 6pm. Free.)*

SAMARITAINE. Samaritaine, one of the oldest department stores in Paris, spans a total of three blocks. Founded in 1869, it helped to usher in the age of conspicuous consumption. The building began as a delicate iron and steel construction in 1906 and was revamped in Art Deco style in 1928. The roof, accessible by a quick elevator ride, has a fantastic, free view of the city. Unfortunately, the complex is closed indefinitely as of summer 2006 for security renovations. Check online for progress. *(Starting at 67, r. de Rivoli,* ☎*0800 010 015; www.lasamaritaine.com.)*

SECOND ARRONDISSEMENT

More than any other *arrondissement*, the 2*ème* immerses visitors in the the institutionalization of some of Paris's pet vices: money perfumes the air around the Bourse de Valeurs, and the world's oldest profession reigns supreme along the curbs of r. St-Denis. For those who wish to keep their hands a bit cleaner, the Bibliothèque Nationale is guaranteed to please.

see map p. 356-357

TO THE WEST

🏛**PASSAGES AND GALERIES.** Paris's *passages* might be considered the world's first shopping malls. In the early 19th century—the dawn of *haute bourgeois* consumer culture—speculators built shopping arcades in alleyways all over central Paris. They designed panes of glass, held in place by lightweight iron rods, to attract window shoppers. This innovation let daylight into their shops, while gas lamps and electric heating made for comfortable browsing. Most of these arcades have disappeared over centuries of urban development, but the 20 or so that remain have been restored and are perfect for a nostalgic rainy-day stroll. Today, the *passages* (and their posh siblings, the *galeries*) are home to upscale clothing boutiques, cafes, food shops, and gift shops (look for the several that sell antique postcards).

BIBLIOTHÈQUE NATIONALE: SITE RICHELIEU. The Site Richelieu was the main branch of the **Bibliothèque Nationale de France** (National Library) until 1998, when most of the collection was moved to the new Site Mitterrand in the the 13*ème arrondissement* (p. 221). Richelieu still holds collections of stamps, money, photography, medals, and maps, as well as original manuscripts written on everything from papyrus to parchment. Scholars must pass through a strict screening process to gain access to the main reading room of the library.

For the viewing of the general public, the **Galerie Mazarin** and **Galerie de photographie** host excellent temporary exhibits of books, prints, lithographs, and photographs taken from the collection. Upstairs, the **Cabinet des Médailles** displays coins, medallions, and objets d'art confiscated from the French Revolution. Across from the library's main entrance is the **place Louvois**. This place's sculpted fountain personifies the four great rivers of France—the Seine, the Saône, the Loire, and the Garonne—as heroic women. *(58, r. de Richelieu.* Ⓜ *Bourse. Just north of the Galeries Vivienne and Colbert, across r. Vivienne. Info line* ☎*01 53 79 87 93; www.bnf.fr. Library open M-F 9am-6pm, Sa 9am-5pm. Books available only to researchers who prove they need access to the collection with a letter of introduction from their university, research advisor, or editor. Tours of the former reading room (through a window), La Salle Labrouste, first Tu of the month 2:30pm in English and French; €7. Book ahead;* ☎*01 53 79 86 87. Galleries open Tu-Sa*

10am-7pm, Su noon-7pm, only when there are exhibits. Admission depends on the exhibit, but is usually €5-7, students €4-5. Cabinet des Médailles open M-Sa 1-5pm, Su noon-6pm. Free.)

BOURSE DES VALEURS. The Bourse des Valeurs (Paris's stock exchange) was founded in 1724 so that the monarchy could raise money by issuing bonds. The Jacobins closed the exchange during the Revolution to fend off war profiteers. It was re-opened under Napoleon, who relocated it to its current building with his typical Neoclassical panache. Computers have diminished the significance of the building, but many still work here. The Bourse houses a museum that explains its history and ambiguous present function. *(r. Vivienne. ⓜ Bourse. ☎01 49 27 55 55 or 01 49 27 55 50. Open to the public for tours Sept.-July M-F 9am-4pm; call ahead. 1 1/2hr. €8.50, students €5.50.)*

THÉÂTRE MUSICAL POPULAIRE (OPÉRA COMIQUE). The Opéra Comique has resounded with laughs and sobs for over two centuries. Originally built as the Comédie Italienne, it burned down twice in the 1840s and was rebuilt for good in 1898. It was here that Bizet's Carmen first hitched up her skirts and seduced Don José. Under new management, the opera has changed its name and expanded to embrace all kinds of musical theater, including Broadway musicals and operettas. *(ⓜ Richelieu-Drouot. ☎01 42 44 45 46. pl. Boieldieu. To the west of the Bourse, between r. Favart and r. Marivaux. For performance info, see **Entertainment**, p. 280. Ticket office open M-Sa 9am-9pm. Tickets €7-100. €7 tickets usually available at the door. For tours, reserve ahead.)*

TO THE EAST

RUE SAINT-DENIS. In the mid-1970s, Paris's sex workers demonstrated in churches, monuments, and public squares, demanding unionization. They marched down r. St-Denis— the central artery of the city's prostitution district—to picket for equal rights and protection under the law. Their campaign was successful, and prostitution is now legal in France. While sex workers are still not allowed to work the streets, the protest did garner them a few legal protections. For example, only sex workers themselves can use the money they earn on the job. However, this law can create problems for workers using their earnings to support a family— their partners can be prosecuted as procurers. Despite its legalization, prostitution is far less common in France than it is in other countries, like the Netherlands. You might think otherwise along r. St-Denis, an enclave of debauchery, sex shops, and sketchy clubs in the otherwise G-rated *2ème*. *(ⓜ Strasbourg-St-Denis.)*

THIRD ARRONDISSEMENT

The *3ème* offers a collection of sights and attractions as diverse as the crowd that visits them. Don't miss the **Archives Nationales** or **rue Vieille-du-Temple**.

see map p. 358-359

CONSERVATOIRE NATIONAL DES ARTS ET MÉTIERS. Formerly the Abbey St-Martin-des-Champs, this flamboyant Gothic structure became the National Conservatory of Art and Mechanics in 1794, with the goal of showcasing the finest in French industry. Its collection of over 80,000 scientific and mechanical objects and nearly 15,000 detailed scientific drawings is now gathered in the informative, if rather dry, **Musée des Arts et Métiers.** The first floor exhibition space is free, as is the Merovingian-era former chapel that houses historical scientific instruments and a 1/16-size copper model of the Statue of Liberty. The conservatory's developing design ideas don't stop within its walls; the Arts et Métiers metro station that serves the area is entirely covered in copper tiling in homage to the museum and the conservatory. *(60, r.*

SIGHTS

Réaumur. On the corner of r. St-Martin and r. Réaumur. ⓜ *Arts et Métiers or Réaumur-Sébastopol.* ☎ *01 53 01 82 00; www.arts-et-metiers.net. Wheelchair accessible. Open Tu-Su 10am-6pm, Th 10am-9:30pm. €6.50, students €4.50, under 18 free. Special exhibits €3/2; combined ticket €7.50/5.50/2. Audioguide €2.50. Daily guided visits in French.)*

RUE VIEILLE DU TEMPLE. R. Vieille du Temple is lined with many stately residences, including the 18th-century **Hôtel de la Tour du Pin** (no. 75) and the more famous **Hôtel de Rohan** (no. 87). The latter was built between 1705 and 1708 for Armand-Gaston de Rohan, Bishop of Strasbourg and alleged lovechild of Louis XIV. Frequent temporary exhibits allow access to the interior *Cabinet des Singes* and its original decorations. Now a part of the National Archives, the Hôtel de Rohan also boasts a grand courtyard and fragrant rose garden (see **Museums,** p. 250). Equally engaging are the numerous art galleries that have settled on the street (see **Museums,** p. 248, for gallery listings in this area). At the corner of r. des Francs-Bourgeois and r. Vieille du Temple are the Gothic turrets of the **Hôtel Hérouët,** built in 1528 for Louis XII's treasurer. *(*ⓜ *Filles du Calvaire or St-Paul.* ☎ *01 40 27 63 94 for info on guided tours of Hôtel de Rohan.)*

ARCHIVES NATIONALES. The most famous documents of the National Archives are on display in the **Musée de l'Histoire de France** (see **Museums,** p. 250), ensconced in the plush 18th-century Hôtel de Soubise. The Treaty of Westphalia, the Edict of Nantes, the Declaration of the Rights of Man, Marie-Antoinette's last letter, Louis XVI's diary, letters between Benjamin Franklin and George Washington, and Napoleon's will are all preserved here. Louis XVI's entry for July 14, 1789, the day the Bastille was stormed, reads simply "Rien" (Nothing). His Majesty, of course, was referring to the unproductive hunting expedition at Versailles, far from the riotous uprising in Paris. In recent summers, excellent performances by foreign dance companies have graced the Hôtel de Soubise—you can buy tickets at the box office to the left of the main entrance. *(60, r. des Francs-Bourgeois.* ⓜ *Rambuteau.* ☎ *01 40 27 60 00.)*

MÉMORIAL DU MARTYR JUIF INCONNU. The Memorial to the Unknown Jewish Martyr was created in 1956 by a committee that included Charles de Gaulle, Winston Churchill, and David Ben-Gurion. The memorial features a poignant wall carved with the names of 76,000 Jews who were deported from France to Nazi death camps with the collaboration of the puppet Vichy government. Only 2500 of those deported ultimately survived. *(17, r. Geoffroy l'Asnier. From the metro, walk down r. St-Antoine, which becomes r. François Miron; turn left onto r. Geoffroy l'Asnier.* ⓜ *St-Paul.* ☎ *01 42 77 44 72; www.memorialdelashoah.org. Wheelchair accessible. Open M-W and Su 10am-6pm, Th 10am-10pm. Free.)*

OTHER SIGHTS. The **Eglise St-Denys du St-Sacrement** (68bis, r. de Turenne; ⓜ Chemin Vert or St-Sébastien-Froissart) houses a dark, well-hidden Delacroix fresco (open M-Sa 8:30am-noon and 4:30-7pm; Su 9am-noon.) Farther east is **L'Auberge Nicolas Flamel** (51, r. de Montmorency; ⓜ Etienne-Marcel), the oldest remaining house in all of Paris, built in 1407. The inscription on the building's facade, "Here, one eats and drinks," still holds true: the ground floor of the home remains a working bistro, though the passage of time has added some weight to its prices.

FOURTH ARRONDISSEMENT

see map p. 359-359

The *4ème* mixes modern and old, and you are likely to see Jewish rabbis walking just feet away from trendy fashionistas tottering on stilettos. Although the historical Marais sprawls over a considerable portion of the *4ème*, bold and quirky architecture sprouts to the west of the *arrondissement* in the form of the Centre Pompidou. The central *4ème*, home to the Marais, is crammed with small streets housing a smattering of churches and some of Paris's most beautiful *hôtels particuliers* (particularly around the pl. des Vosges).

TO THE NORTH: BEAUBOURG

CENTRE POMPIDOU. One of the most visible examples of renovation in the 4*ème* is the Centre Pompidou, the ultra-modern exhibition, performance, and research space that houses the **Musée National d'Art Moderne** (see **Museums,** p. 252). Erected in Beaubourg, a former slum *quartier* whose high rate of tuberculosis earned it classification as an *îlot insalubre* (unhealthy block) in the 1930s, the Pompidou shocked Parisians when it opened in 1977. The building is considered alternately an innovation and an eyesore. The design, pioneered by architects Richard Rogers, Gianfranco Franchini, and Renzo Piano, features color-coded electrical tubes (yellow), water pipes (green), and ventilation ducts (blue) along the exterior of the building. It was engineered to accommodate 5000 visitors a day, but today, the center attracts more than 20,000. More people visit the Pompidou every year than visit the Louvre. Don't miss the spectacular view from the top of the escalators, which can be reached only after purchasing a museum ticket. The cobblestone square out front collects artists, musicians, punks, and passersby. As in all crowded spaces, keep an eye on your belongings. *(Ⓜ Rambuteau or Hôtel de Ville.)*

IGOR STRAVINSKY FOUNTAIN. This novel installation features irreverent mobile sculptures by Niki de St. Phalle and Jean Tinguely. The sculptures—of elephants, lips, and bowler hats—are inspired by Stravinsky's works, and have been known to squirt water at unsuspecting bystanders. While the fountain's colorful whimsy is in keeping with the bold lines of the Centre Pompidou, it stands in intriguing contrast with the nearby historic r. Brisemiche and Eglise de St-Merri. *(In pl. Igor Stravinsky, adjacent to the Centre Pompidou on r. de Renard. Ⓜ Hôtel de Ville.)*

RUE DES ROSIERS. At the heart of the Jewish community of the Marais, the r. des Rosiers is packed with kosher shops, butchers, bakeries, and falafel counters (see **Food,** p. 154). Until the 13th century, Paris's Jewish community was concentrated in front of Notre Dame. When Philippe-Auguste expelled the Jewish population from the city limits, many families moved to the Marais, just outside the walls. Since then, the r. des Rosiers has been Paris's Jewish center, taking in the influx of Russian Jews in the 19th century and new waves of North African Sephardim fleeing Algeria in the 1960s. During WWII, many who had fled to France to escape the pogroms of Eastern Europe were murdered by the Nazis. Assisted by French police, Nazi soldiers stormed the Marais and hauled Jewish families to the Vélodrome d'Hiver, an indoor cycling stadium. Here, French Jews awaited deportation to work camps like Drancy, in a northeastern suburb of Paris, or to camps farther east in Poland and Germany. **The Mémorial de la Déportation** on the Île de la Cité commemorates these victims (p. 186). Today, the Jewish community thrives in the Marais, with two synagogues (at 25, r. des Rosiers and 10, r. Pavée) designed by Art Nouveau architect Hector Guimard. The mix of Mediterranean and Eastern European Jewish cultures gives the area a unique flavor, with *kugel* and falafel served side by side. The GLBT community also flourishes here, with heavy traffic especially around r. Vieille-du-Temple and r. Ste-Croix de la Bretonnerie. *(4 blocks east of Beaubourg, parallel to r. des Francs-Bourgeois. Ⓜ St-Paul.)*

RUE VIEILLE-DU-TEMPLE AND RUE STE-CROIX DE LA BRETTONERIE. Winter, spring, summer, fall—the intersection of r. Vieille-du-Temple and r. Ste-Croix de la Brettonerie is always hot. The epicenter of Paris's thriving GLBT community, these streets boast beautiful boys in tight pants and super-stylish girls walking hand-in-hand. Although many establishments fly the rainbow flag, queer and straight go together: women of all stripes wander through trendy boutiques while intellectuals sip merlot at **La Belle Hortense,** a bookish oasis in this on-the-move enclave (see **Nightlife,** p. 308). *(Ⓜ St-Paul or Hôtel de Ville. 1 block north of r. de Rivoli, runs the parallel r. du Roi de Sicile (which becomes r. de la Verrerie); r. Vieille du Temple meets it and then, 1 block north, crosses r. Ste-Croix de la Brettonerie.)*

HÔTEL DE VILLE AND SURROUNDINGS

HÔTEL DE VILLE. Paris's grandiose city hall dominates the **Place Hôtel de Ville,** a large square dotted with fountains and Belle Epoque lampposts. The present structure is the second incarnation of the original edifice, built during medieval times. The first building served as a meeting hall for merchants who controlled traffic on the Seine. In 1533, King François I appointed Domenica da Cortona, known as Boccador, to expand and renovate the structure into a city hall worthy of Paris. The result was an impressive building in the Renaissance style of the Loire Valley châteaux. The building was witness to municipal executions on the *place*: in 1610, Henri IV's assassin was quartered alive here by four horses bolting in opposite directions.

On May 24, 1871, the Communards (see **Life and Times,** p. 65) doused the building with gasoline and set it afire. Lasting a full eight days, the blaze spared nothing but the frame. The Third Republic built a virtually identical structure on the ruins, with a few significant changes. The Republicans integrated statues of their own heroes into the facade: historian Jules Michelet graces the right side of the building while author Eugène Sue surveys the r. de Rivoli. They also installed crystal chandeliers, gilded every interior surface, and created a Hall of Mirrors in emulation of the original at Versailles. When Manet, Monet, Renoir, and Cézanne offered their services, they were all turned down in favor of the ponderous, didactic artists whose work decorates the Salon des Lettres, the Salon des Arts, the Salon des Sciences, and the Salon Laurens. The Information Office holds exhibits on Paris in the lobby off the r. de Lobau.

Originally called pl. de Grève, the pl. Hôtel de Ville made a vital contribution to the French language. Poised on a marshy embankment *(grève)* of the Seine, the medieval square served as a meeting ground for angry workers, giving France the useful phrase *en grève* (on strike). Strikers still gather here amid riot police. Less frequently, the square hosts concerts, TV broadcasts, and light shows against the backdrop of the Hôtel de Ville. During major football tournaments, fans watch *Les Bleus* on huge screens erected in the square. *(Information office, 29, r. de Rivoli. Ⓜ Hôtel de Ville. ☎01 42 76 43 43. Open M-F 9am-7pm when there is an exhibit; until 6pm otherwise. Group tours available with advance reservations, call for available dates. Special exhibit entry on r. de Lobau.)*

TOUR ST-JACQUES. This Flamboyant Gothic tower, the only remnant of the 16th-century Eglise St-Jacques-la-Boucherie, stands in its own park. The 52m tower's meteorological station and the statue of Pascal at its base commemorate Pascal's experiments on the weight of air, performed here in 1648. The tower also marks Haussmann's *grande croisée* of r. de Rivoli and the bd. Sébastopol, the intersection of his east-west and north-south axes for the city. *(39-41, r. de Rivoli. Ⓜ Hôtel de Ville. 2 blocks west of the Hôtel de Ville.)*

SOUTH OF RUE ST-ANTOINE AND RUE DE RIVOLI

EGLISE ST-GERVAIS-ST-PROTAIS. St-Gervais-St-Protais was named after Gervase and Protase, two Romans martyred during Nero's reign. The Classical facade, Flamboyant Gothic vaulting, stained glass, and Baroque wooden Christ by Préault are part of a working convent. The exterior of the church dates to the end of the 15th century, while the parish, going back to the 6th century, is thought to be one of the oldest on the Right Bank. *(R. François-Miron. Ⓜ Hôtel de Ville. Gregorian chant at matins (Tu-Sa 7am, Su 8am), vespers (Tu-Sa 6pm), and high mass (Su 11am).)*

HÔTEL DE BEAUVAIS. The Hôtel de Beauvais was built in 1654 for Catherine Bellier, wife of merchant Pierre de Beauvais, and chambermaid and intimate of Anne d'Autriche. After the 40-year-old Mme. Bellier sexually initiated the Queen's son, the 16-year-old Louis XIV, her husband was promoted as a royal advisor. In 1660, from the balcony of the *hôtel*, Anne d'Autriche and Cardinal Mazarin watched the entry of Louis XIV and his bride, the Spanish princess Marie-Thérèse, into Paris. A century later, Mozart played his first piano recital here as a guest of the Bavarian ambassador. Restored in 1967 and home to the Administrative Court of Appeals since 1995, it is open to the public only through tours given by Paris Historique. *(Hôtel de Beauvais: 68, r. François-Miron. ⓜ Hôtel de Ville. Paris Historique: 44-46, r. François Miron. ☎01 48 87 74 31. Open M-Sa 11am-6pm, Su 2-5pm.)*

HÔTEL DE SENS. One of the city's few surviving examples of medieval residential architecture and older than the Hotel de Cluny, the Hôtel de Sens was built in 1474 for Tristan de Salazar, the Archbishop of Sens. Its military features reflect the violence of the day: the turrets were designed to survey the streets outside, and the square tower served as a dungeon. An enormous Gothic arch entrance—complete with chutes for pouring boiling water on invaders—makes the mansion all the more intimidating. The former residence of Henri IV's first wife Marguerite de Valois, infamously known as Queen Margot, the Hôtel de Sens has witnessed some of Paris's most daring romantic escapades. In 1606, the 55-year-old queen drove up to the door of her home, in front of which her two current lovers were arguing. One opened the lady's carriage door, and the other shot him dead. Unfazed, the queen demanded the execution of the other, which she watched from a window the next day. The hôtel now houses the **Bibliothèque Forney,** a reference library for the fine arts open to the public, and a beautiful courtyard with an ornately designed garden. Special exhibits are held four times a year; call for schedule. *(1, r. du Figuier. ⓜ Pont Marie. ☎01 42 78 14 60. Open Tu-Sa 1:30-7pm. Special exhibits €4, seniors and under 26 €3.)*

LA MAISON EUROPÉENNE DE LA PHOTOGRAPHIE. The **Hôtel Hénault de Cantobre** houses rotating galleries, an excellent library, and a *vidéothèque* with almost 600 films by photographers. La Maison hosts both temporary exhibits featuring international contemporary photography and works from its permanent collection. *(5-7, r. de Fourcy. ⓜ St-Paul. ☎01 44 78 75 00; www.mep-fr.org. Wheelchair accessible. Open W-Su 11am-8pm; last entry at 7:30pm. Admission €6, under 26 and seniors €3, under 8 free, W 5-8pm free. MC/V with €9 minimum charge. Tours ☎01 44 78 75 30 or 01 44 78 75 24.)*

EGLISE ST-PAUL-ST-LOUIS. Dating from 1627 (when Louis XIII placed its first stone), the Eglise St-Paul dominates r. St-Antoine. Its large dome—a trademark of Jesuit architecture—is visible from afar, but hidden by ornamentation on the facade. Paintings inside the dome depict four French kings: Clovis, Charlemagne, Robert the Pious, and St. Louis. The embalmed hearts of Louis XIII and Louis XIV were kept here in vermeil boxes carried by silver angels before they were destroyed during the Revolution. The church's Baroque interior is graced with three 17th-century paintings of the life of St. Louis and Eugène Delacroix's dramatic *Christ in the Garden of Olives* (1826). The holy-water vessels were gifts from Victor Hugo. *(99, r. St-Antoine. ⓜ St-Paul. ☎01 42 72 30 32. Open M-Sa 9am-10pm, Su 9am-8:30pm. Free tours in French at 3pm every 2nd Su of the month, or call to arrange special visits. Mass M 7pm; Tu, W, F 9am and 10pm; Th 9am, 7, 10pm; Sa 6pm; Su 9:30, 11am, 7pm.)*

17, RUE BEAUTREILLIS. Jim Morrison died here in his bathtub on the third floor, allegedly of a heart attack. There is no commemorative plaque, and today the building houses a massage parlor. In memoriam, visit his grave at the Cimetière Père Lachaise (p. 232). *(ⓜ Bastille.)*

SIGHTS

PLACE DES VOSGES AND SURROUNDINGS

PLACE DES VOSGES. At the end of r. des Francs-Bourgeois sits the magnificent pl. des Vosges, Paris's oldest public square and one of its best spots for a picnic or an afternoon siesta. The central park (Sq. Louis XIII), lined with manicured trees and centered around four fountains, is surrounded by 17th-century Renaissance townhouses. Kings built several mansions on this site, including the Palais de Tournelles, which Catherine de Médicis ordered destroyed after her husband Henri II died there in a jousting tournament in 1563. Henri IV later ordered the construction of a new public square.

Each of the 36 buildings that line the square has arcades on the street level, two stories of pink brick, and a slate-covered roof. The largest townhouse, which forms the square's main entrance, was the king's pavilion; opposite is the smaller pavilion of the queen. Originally intended for merchants, the pl. Royale, as it was known, attracted nobility such as Mme de Sevigné and Cardinal Richelieu. In the 18th century, Molière, Racine, and Voltaire filled the grand parlors with their *bon mots*, and Mozart played a concert here at the age of seven. Even when the city's nobility moved across the river to the Faubourg St-Germain, pl. Royale remained among the most elegant spots in Paris. During the Revolution, however, the statue of Louis XIII in the center of the park was destroyed (the current statue is a copy), and the park was renamed pl. des Vosges in 1800, after the first *departement* in France to pay its taxes. Follow the arcades around the perimeter of pl. des Vosges for an elegant promenade, window shopping, and a glimpse of the plaques that mark the homes of famous residents. **Théophile Gautier** and **Alphonse Daudet** lived at no. 8. **Victor Hugo** lived at no. 6, now a museum of his life and work (See **Museums,** p. 252). The corner door at the right of the south face of the *place* (near no. 5) leads into the garden of the Hôtel de Sully. (Ⓜ *Chemin Vert or St-Paul.*)

HÔTEL DE SULLY. Built in 1624, the Hôtel de Sully, was acquired by the Duc de Sully, minister to Henri IV. Often cuckolded by his young wife, Sully would say when giving her money, *"Voici tant pour la maison, tant pour vous, et tant pour vos amants"* (Here's some for the house, some for you, and some for your lovers). The classical composition of the building is adorned with elaborate, sculpted decoration representing the elements and the seasons. The inner courtyard accommodates fatigued tourists with benches and a formal garden. The building houses both an annex of the Musée de Jeu de Paume and the **Centre d'Information des Monuments Nationaux,** which distributes free maps and brochures on Paris monuments and museums. The back garden contains an entrance into the pl. des Vosges. (*62, r. St-Antoine.* Ⓜ *St-Paul. Centre d'Information des Monuments Nationaux* ☎ *01 44 61 20 00. Open M-Th 9am-12:45pm and 2-6pm, F 9am-12:45pm and 2-5pm.*)

HÔTEL DE LAMOIGNON. Built in 1584 for Henri II's daughter, Diane de France, the Hôtel de Lamoignon is one of the finest *hôtels particuliers* in the Marais. The facade's Colossal style was copied later in the Louvre. Lamoignon and the adjacent buildings now house the **Bibliothèque Historique de la Ville de Paris,** a non-circulating library of Parisian history with 800,000 volumes. An exhibition hall next door hosts rotating exhibits. A quiet courtyard on the r. des Francs-Bourgeois is great for picnicking or sunbathing. (*22, r. Malher.* Ⓜ *St-Paul. Exhibition hall* ☎ *01 44 59 29 60. Open Tu-Su 11am-7pm. €4, students and seniors €2. Bibliothèque open M-Sa 9am-6pm.*)

FIFTH ARRONDISSEMENT

Undisputedly Paris's intellectual epicenter, the 5*ème* brims with university campuses, musty bookstores, and cozy cafes for the curious traveler. History buffs will adore the epic Panthéon, and those looking for a place to relax should not miss the steam baths in the Mosquée de Paris.

TO THE WEST: LATIN QUARTER

see map p. 362-363

PLACE ST-MICHEL. The busiest spot in the Latin Quarter, pl. St-Michel is rich in political history: the 1871 Paris Commune and the 1968 student uprising both began here. One of the *5ème*'s great meeting places is Davioud's **St-Michel Fountain,** a bronze rendering of archangel St. Michel slaying a dragon. Plaques around the square commemorate the citizens of the neighborhood who died during the August 1944 Liberation of Paris. The academic history of the *place* also manifests itself readily. Several branches of the **Gibert Joseph/Jeune** bookstore are located along the beginning of bd. St-Michel, welcoming visitors to the home of one of the oldest universities in the world. There are scores of antiquarian booksellers and university presses around the *place*, ready to indulge even the most arcane of literary appetites (see **Shopping,** p. 286). For those more interested in feeding their stomachs than their minds, there are an overwhelming number of *crêpe* stands and gyro counters along the twisting **rue St-Séverin** and **rue de la Huchette.** Watch your belongings, as pickpockets like to operate in the busy *place.*

The huge Gothic complex of nearby **Eglise St-Séverin** is decorated with spiraling columns and modern stained glass (follow r. de la Harpe away from the *place* and turn left on r. St-Séverin). **Eglise St-Julien-le-Pauvre,** across bd. St-Jacques from St-Séverin, is one of the oldest churches in Paris, dating to 1170. The **Musée de Cluny,** at the intersection of bd. St-Germain and bd. St-Michel, houses an extraordinary collection of medieval art, tapestries, and illuminated manuscripts (see **Museums,** p. 254). A major tourist and student thoroughfare, **boulevard St-Michel** (or boul' Mich') doesn't have a lot of flavor these days—for that, visitors should check out the many traditional bistros on nearby **rue Soufflot** and **rue des Fossés St-Jacques.** (Ⓜ St-Michel.)

LA SORBONNE. Founded in 1253 by Robert de Sorbon as a dormitory for 16 poor theology students, the Sorbonne is one of Europe's oldest universities. Soon after its founding, it became the administrative base for the University of Paris and the site of France's first printing house, opened in 1469. As it grew in power and size, the Sorbonne often defied the French throne, even siding with England during the Hundred Years' War (to be fair to the old alma mater, the English *did* occupy Paris at the time). Today, the university is safely in the folds of governmental administration, officially known as Paris IV, the fourth of the University of Paris's 13 campuses. Its main building, **Ste-Ursule de la Sorbonne** (closed to the public), was commissioned in 1642 by Cardinal Richelieu and is located on r. des Ecoles. Visitors can stroll through the **Chapelle de la Sorbonne** (entrance off of pl. de la Sorbonne), which houses temporary exhibits on the arts and letters. Nearby **place de la Sorbonne,** off bd. St-Michel, boasts a flavorful assortment of cafes, bookstores, and—during term-time—students. *(45-47, r. des Ecoles. Ⓜ Cluny-La Sorbonne or RER: Luxembourg. Walk away from the Seine on bd. St-Michel and turn left on r. des Ecoles to see the main building.)*

COLLÈGE DE FRANCE. Created by François I in 1530 to contest the university's authority, the prestigious Collège de France stands immediately behind the Sorbonne. The humanist motto "Doce Omnia" (Teach Everything) is emblazoned in mosaics in the interior courtyard. Courses at the Collège—given in the past by such luminaries as Henri Bergson, Pierre Boulez, Paul Valéry, and Milan Kundera—are free and open to all. Lecture schedules are posted around the courtyard. *(11, pl. Marcelin-Berthelot. Ⓜ Maubert-Mutualité. Walk against traffic on bd. St-Germain, turn left on r. Thenard; the entrance to the Collège is at the end of the road, across r. des Ecoles and up the steps.* ☎01 44 27 12 11 or 01 44 27 11 47; www.college-de-france.fr. Courses Oct.-May. Closed Aug.)

PANTHÉON. The Panthéon is one of the most impressive buildings in Paris. Unreal airiness and geometric grandeur are its architectural claims to fame, but it's what's

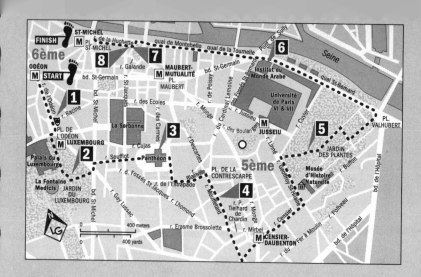

1 THÉÂTRE DE L'ODÉON. When you get off the metro, take a look at the impressive facade of the Odéon, Paris's oldest and largest theater (p. 276).

2 JARDIN DU LUXEMBOURG. Architectural excesses, beautiful lawns, miniature sailboats, and plenty of shady spots make this garden a favorite. On your left before you mount the stairs around the lake is the famous **Fontaine des Médicis,** a beautiful, tranquil, shaded spot with a fantastic art installation in the middle (see **Sights,** p. 204).

START: Ⓜ Odéon

FINISH: Ⓜ St-Michel

DISTANCE: 6.1km (3¾ mi.)

DURATION: 3-4hr.

WHEN TO GO: Start in the afternoon

3 PANTHÉON. The inscription reads: "To great men from a grateful fatherland." The Panthéon indeed houses some great men (and women): its crypt contains the remains of Emile Zola, Marie Curie, Victor Hugo, and others. And the fatherland must have been grateful, to have laid them to rest in a building as beautiful as this one (p. 199).

4 RUE MOUFFETARD. The Mouff' has held onto its charm since the 2nd century. Paul Verlaine and Ernest Hemingway both came to stay. Pause for dinner at one of the numerous traditional bistros that line the *rue*. Afterwards, head over to **Octave,** at no. 138, for some of (arguably) the best ice cream in Paris (p. 158).

5 JARDIN DES PLANTES. The Jardin's rare plants and exquisite *roserie* draw visitors. The **Grand Galerie de l'Evolution** is the star of the garden's several museums (p. 254).

6 INSTITUT DU MONDE ARABE. This modern building has excellent exhibits, striking architecture, and a great (free!) view of the city (p. 254).

7 SHAKESPEARE & CO. Stroll along the Seine until you reach Shakespeare & Co. No visit to the Latin Quarter would be complete without a stop in at this famed bookstore. (37, r. de la Boucherie; see p. 292.)

8 LE CAVEAU DE LA HUCHETTE. This club serves refreshing *digestifs* upstairs and great jazz downstairs. (5, r. de la Huchette; see p. 310.)

below the building that garners the real renown. Some of France's greatest citizens are buried in the Panthéon's crypt. Marie and Pierre Curie, Jean Jaurès, Louis Braille, Voltaire, Jean-Jacques Rousseau, Emile Zola, and Victor Hugo are just a few of the luminaries whose remains rest here. At Hugo's burial in 1885, two million mourners escorted his coffin to its resting place while an orchestra played Chopin's *Marche Funèbre*. Fans of *Le Petit Prince* can pay homage to Antoine de St-Exupéry in the main rotunda. The crypt's most recent addition, interred in November 2002, was Alexandre Dumas.

The inscription in stone across the front of the Panthéon proudly declares, *"Aux Grands Hommes La Patrie Reconnaisante"* (To the great men, a grateful fatherland). Originally, however, the Panthéon was one man's gift to his wife. In AD 507, King Clovis converted to Christianity and had a basilica designed to accommodate his tomb and that of his wife, Clotilde. In 512, **St. Geneviève,** believed to have saved Paris from the marauding Huns, was buried alongside the king and queen. Her tomb immediately became a pilgrimage site, and so many people came to visit that a set of worshippers dedicated themselves to the preservation of her relics and remains, calling themselves *Génovéfains.*

It was Louis XV who transformed the basilica into the awesome monument it is today. Ascribing his recovery from a grave illness in 1744 to the powers of St. Geneviève, he vowed to build a memorial to the saint and entrusted its design to architect Jacques-Germain Soufflot. Louis laid the first stone himself in 1764. After Soufflot's death, construction of the Neoclassical basilica was continued by architect Jean-Baptiste Rondelet and completed in 1790. The walls of the interior were redesigned in 1874 when the director of the Musée des Beaux-Arts commissioned some of the finest artists of the time to depict the saint's story.

On April 4, 1791, in the midst of the Revolution, the Panthéon was converted into a mausoleum of heroes. The first nominated for burial there was the Compte de Mirabeau, the great orator of the Revolution. Mirabeau was interred, only to have his ashes expelled the next year when his counter-revolutionary correspondence with Louis XVI was revealed to the public. In 1806, Napoleon reserved the crypt for those who had given "great service to the State."

The Panthéon's other main attraction is a famous science experiment: **Foucault's Pendulum.** The pendulum's plane of oscillation stays fixed as the Earth rotates around it. The rotation of the pendulum confirms the rotation of the Earth. Louis Napoleon Bonaparte (later Napoleon III) was among those present at its unveiling in 1851. *(pl. du Panthéon.* ⓜ *Cardinal Lemoine or RER Luxembourg. From r. Cardinal Lemoine, turn right on r. Clovis; walk around to the front of the building to enter.* ☎ *01 44 32 18 04. Open daily 10am-6:30pm; last admission 5:45pm. €7.50, ages 18-25 €5, under 18 free. Free 1st Su of the month Oct.-Mar. Guided tours in French, English, Spanish, and German leave from inside the main door; call ahead for times. The Panthéon is tenue correcte; visitors must dress conservatively.)*

EGLISE ST-ETIENNE DU MONT. While everyone's dying to get in, not all of France's legends are buried in the Panthéon. Pascal and Racine are buried next door in the Eglise St-Etienne du Mont, whose facade takes a lot of artistic license, blending Gothic windows, an ancient belfry, and a Renaissance dome. Inside, the central attraction of the sanctuary is the outrageous **rood-screen** made of ornate stone fretwork and flanked by spiral staircases. It is the very last of its kind in Paris, after the other screens used to separate the priest from his congregation were removed to make way for an altar. To the right of the nave, check out a Herculean Samson holding up the wood-carved pulpit. *(Pl. de l'Abbé Basset, just east of the Panthéon.* ⓜ *Cardinal Lemoine. Follow directions to the Panthéon; the church is to the right. Closed M and lunchtime (until 4pm) in summer, open all day in winter.)*

ECOLE NORMALE SUPÉRIEURE. France's premier university, the Ecole Normale Supérieure is located southeast of the Sorbonne and is part of the *Grands*

Ecoles, a consortium of prestigious French schools. *Normale Sup'* (as its students, the *normaliens,* call it) has programs in literature, philosophy, and the natural sciences. Its graduates include Jean-Paul Sartre, Michel Foucault, and Louis Pasteur. *(45, r. d'Ulm. Closed to the public.)*

TO THE EAST: PLACE DE LA CONTRESCARPE

RUE MOUFFETARD. South of pl. de la Contrescarpe, **rue Mouffetard** is home to one of the liveliest street markets in Paris (see **Food,** p. 157) and is generally crowded with a friendly mix of Parisians and visitors. Along with **rue Monge,** the Mouff' is the spirit of the Latin Quarter's tourist and student social life. The street began as a Roman road. It was the main thoroughfare of a wealthy estate from the second century until the 13th century; some current buildings date back to the 12th century. It holds the distinction of having been the most barricaded street in Paris— no mean feat in the capital of revolution. Perfect for an afternoon stroll is the winding stretch up r. Mouffetard past pl. de la Contrescarpe, and onto **rue Descartes** and **rue de la Montagne Ste-Geneviève.** Poet Paul Verlaine died at no. 39, r. Descartes in 1844. (Ⓜ *Cardinal Lemoine, Place Monge, or Censier Daubenton.)*

JARDIN DES PLANTES. In the eastern corner of the 5*ème* is the Jardin des Plantes, a 45,000 sq.m stretch of carefully tended flowers and lush greenery. Created in 1635 by Louis XIII's doctor, the gardens originally grew medicinal plants to promote His Majesty's health. Today they are a destination for sunbathers, families, and the occasional jogger. The gardens are also a sanctuary for the natural sciences, surrounded on both sides by a score of museums, research institutions, and scientific libraries.

If you want to stick to greenery, start in the center, where the charming, rustic **Jardin Alpin** contains more than 2000 plant species, including flora from the Alps, the Pyrenees, and the Himalayas. The **Ecole de Botanique** is a landscaped botanical garden tended by students, horticulturists, and amateur botanists. The **Roserie** is filled with roses from all over the world (in full bloom mid-June). On the southern side, the **Grandes Serres** (Big Greenhouses, due to re-open in 2007) enclose two climates: the *serre mexicaine* has desert-dwelling flora, and the *serre tropicale* simulates a humid rain forest with banana trees, orchids, and a few carnivorous plants. The gardens also include the fantastic **Musée d'Histoire Naturelle** (see **Museums,** p. 254) and the **Ménagerie Zoo.** Although no match for the Parc Zoologique in the Bois de Vincennes (p. 238), the zoo is home to 240 mammals, 500 birds, and 130 reptiles. During the siege of Paris in 1871, starving Parisians martyred some of the elephants for the cause. (Ⓜ *Gare d'Austerlitz, Jussieu, or Censier-Daubenton.* ☎*01 40 79 37 94. Jardin des Plantes, Ecole de Botanique, Jardin Alpin, and Roserie open daily in summer 7:30am-8pm, in winter 8am-5:30pm. Free. Grandes Serres, 57, r. Cuvier. Due to re-open in 2007. Ménagerie Zoo, 3, quai St-Bernard and 57, r. Cuvier. Open daily Apr.-Sept. 10am-6pm, Oct.-Mar. 10am-5:30pm. Last entrance 30min. before closing. €6, students €4.)*

MOSQUÉE DE PARIS. The Institut Musulman houses the beautiful Persian gardens, elaborate minaret, and shady porticoes of the Mosquée de Paris, constructed in 1920 by French architects to honor the role played by North African countries in WWI. The cedar doors open onto an oasis of blue and white where Muslims from around the world meet by the fountains and pray in the carpeted prayer rooms (visible from the courtyard but closed to the public). All visitors can relax in the steam baths of the exquisite *hammam* or sip mint tea at the soothing cafe (see **Food,** p. 158). Please dress appropriately; bare shoulders and legs are discouraged. *(39, r. St-Hilaire. Behind the Jardin des Plantes at pl. du Puits de l'Ermite.* Ⓜ *Censier Daubenton. Walk down r. Daubenton and turn left at the end of the street onto r. Georges Desplas; the mosque is on the right.* ☎*01 43 31 38 20. www.la-mosquee.com. Open daily 10am-noon and 2-5:30pm. Guided tour €3, reduced €2. Hammam open for men Tu 2-9pm, Su 10am-9pm; women*

M, W-Th, and Sa 10am-9pm, F 2-9pm; €15. Massage €10 for 10min., €30 per 30min. Bikini wax €11. MC/V.)

ARÈNES DE LUTÈCE. Once an outdoor theater, now a glorified sand-pit (used for pick-up games of soccer or *boules* and amateur theatricals), the Arènes de Lutèce were built by the Romans in the first century AD to accommodate 10,000 spectators. Similar to the remains of oval amphitheaters in Rome and southern France, the ruins were unearthed in 1869 and restored in 1910; all the seats are reconstructions. Ⓜ *Place Monge or Jussieu. At the intersection of r. de Navarre and r. des Arènes.*

ALONG THE SEINE

SHAKESPEARE & CO. BOOKSTORE. Sylvia Beach's original Shakespeare and Co., at 8, r. Dupuytren (later at 12, r. de l'Odéon), is legendary among Parisian Anglophones. It was a gathering place for expats in the 20s, described memorably by Hemingway in *A Moveable Feast*. The shop is most famous for publishing James Joyce's *Ulysses* in 1922 when it was deemed too obscene to print in England and America. The original shop closed in 1941, and George Whitman (alleged grandson of Walt) opened the current, rag-tag bookstore in 1951. Frequented by Allen Ginsberg and Lawrence Ferlinghetti, Shakespeare hosts poetry readings, Sunday evening tea parties, a literary festival, and other funky events. No traces of the Lost Generation remain, but there are plenty of lost boys and girls who call its burlap couches home. See also **Shopping,** p. 292. *(37, r. de la Bucherie. Ⓜ St-Michel. Open daily noon-midnight.)*

JARDIN DES SCULPTURES EN PLEIN AIR. The Jardin's collection of modern sculpture, including works by Zadkine and Brancusi, is scattered over a long, thin stretch of green along the Seine. It's a nice place to read and relax by the river, although in recent years the beauty of the embankments has been marred by graffiti. *(Ⓜ Jussieu or Gare d'Austerlitz. From either station, head toward the Seine; the garden stretches along quai St-Bernard.)*

SIXTH ARRONDISSEMENT

The 6ème's grandest attraction is the big and beautiful Jardin de Luxembourg and the palace within it. The Eglise de St-Sulpice is also a significant site, and one that has much increased in popularity thanks to Dan Brown's imagination and Tom Hanks's acting.

see map p. 362-363

PISCINE THE DAY AWAY

If you're feeling worn down by the hectic pace of sightseeing, take a break in one of the many pools (*piscines*) sprinkled around the city. One of the most popular is **Club Quartier Latin,** which offers its guests a unique, reasonably priced experience. For €4 you can take a dip in the 33m pool with lap lanes for those in search of a workout as well as space for just relaxing. The building, erected in the 1930s by the Swimming Pool Society of France, truly merits its status as a historical monument. The entrance is decorated with mosaics. Above the giant pool are two tiers of colonnaded galleries lined with bright blue changing-room doors. The high glass roof lets in all the sunlight but none of the unpredictable Paris weather. For €0.50 you get your own private changing room; for another €12 you can use their individual and group fitness rooms. For other fitness clubs in Paris, see **Practical Information,** p. 342.

19, r. de Pontoise, 5ème (☎01 55 42 77 88; www.club-quartierlatin.com). Ⓜ Maubert-Mutualite. Pool open June-Aug. M-F 7-8:30am and 11:30am-8:45pm, Sa 10am-7pm, Su 8am-7pm; Sept.-May same hours except also closed M-Tu and Th-F 1:30-4:30pm. Gym open M-F 9am-midnight, Sa-Su 9:30am-midnight.

JARDIN DU LUXEMBOURG AND ODÉON

■ JARDIN DU LUXEMBOURG. "There is nothing more charming, which invites one more enticingly to idleness, reverie, and young love, than a soft spring morning or a beautiful summer dusk at the Jardin du Luxembourg," wrote Léon Daudet in an absolute fit of sentimentality in 1928. Parisians flock to these sculpted gardens to sunbathe, stroll, and read by the rose gardens and central pool. Beware of ostentatious PDAs, though: kissing and touching in public is very *à la mode* in Paris. The gardens themselves have been through many eras and uses; a residential area in Roman Paris, the site of a medieval monastery, and later the home of 17th-century French royalty, they were liberated during the Revolution and are now open to all. Children can sail toy boats in the fountain, ride ponies, and see the grand guignol (puppet show; see **Entertainment**, p. 281) while their granddads pitch *boules*. Visitors saunter through the park's sandy paths, passing sculptures of France's queens, poets, and heroes. The best and the brightest come to challenge the local cadre of aged chessmasters to a game under the shady chestnut trees, or sit and nap by the Renaissance facade of the **Palais du Luxembourg.** One of the loveliest spots in the Jardin is the **Fontaine des Médicis,** just east of the Palais, a vine-covered grotto complete with a murky fish pond and Baroque fountain sculptures. In 2005, a Swedish artist added a new touch to the ancient fountain: a giant nose. The sculpture is in complete contrast to the surroundings and well worth a visit. A mammoth task force of gardeners tends the grounds—each spring they plant or transplant 350,000 flowers and move 150 palm and orange trees out of winter storage. As in most public parks, you'll notice "Pelouse Interdite" signs forbidding you to sit on the grass; use the benches or find the areas of grass where lounging is permitted. (*Ⓜ Odéon or RER Luxembourg. The wrought-iron gates of the main entrance are on bd. St-Michel. Open daily dawn-dusk. Free. Guided tours in French first W of the month, Apr.-Oct. at 9:30am; depart from pl. André Honorat in front of the observatory—but it's very pleasant to wander on your own as well.*)

MUSÉE DU LUXEMBOURG. Run by the Ministère de la Culture et la Communication, the Musée du Luxembourg is housed in the historic Palais du Luxembourg and offers rotating art exhibitions featuring everything from classical to contemporary artists. (*19, r. de Vaugirard. Ⓜ Odéon. Walk through the Carrefour de l'Odéon and down r. de Conde; turn right on r. Vaugirard; the museum entrance is on the left. €10, ages 10-25 €8. Open M-Th 11am-7pm, F 11am-10pm, Sa-Su 9am-7pm. Last entry 45min. before closing. Wheelchair accessible.*)

PALAIS DE L'INSTITUT DE FRANCE. The Palais de l'Institut de France broods over the Seine from beneath its famous black-and-gold dome. Designed by Le Vau to lodge a college established in Cardinal Mazarin's will, it has served as a school (1688-1793), a prison (1793-1805), and is now home to the **Académie Française,** devoted to the patronage of the arts, letters, and sciences. The académiciens, who rather hopefully call themselves "The Immortals," were symbolically militarized by Napoleon and thus get to wear snazzy green jackets and carry swords—very useful to them in their task of regulating the French language. The glorious building has housed the Académie since 1806 and also contains the **Bibliothèque Mazarine,** founded in 1643. The Palais is not open to the public, but peek inside the courtyard to the right (if the doors are open) to catch a glimpse of Mazarin's funeral sculpture. The grounds are frequently open for historical seminars and conferences. (*Pl. de l'Institut. Ⓜ Pont Neuf. Walk west on quai du Louvre and cross the Seine on the Pont des Arts. 1 block to the east of the ENSB-A on quai Malaquai. Check Pariscope or Figaroscope for listings of frequent seminars, lectures, and openings.*)

THÉÂTRE DE L'ODÉON. The Théâtre de l'Odéon is Paris's oldest and largest theater (see **Entertainment,** p. 276). Upon its completion in 1782, it was purchased by Louis XVI and Marie-Antoinette for the Comédie Française, Molière's celebrated theater troupe. Beaumarchais's *Marriage of Figaro,* nearly banned by Louis XVI for its attacks on the nobility, premiered here in 1784 before delighted aristocrats. As the Revolution approached, the Comédie Française splintered over political loyalties. Republican members moved to the Right Bank, settling into the company's current location near the Louvre. The actors who remained behind were jailed under the Terror and the theater closed. It later earned the name *théâtre maudit* (cursed theater) after two fires and a chain of flops left it nearly bankrupt. The Odéon's fortunes changed after WWII, when it became a venue for experimental theater. (Ⓜ *Odéon. Walk down r. de l'Odéon to the pl. de l'Odéon.)*

EGLISE ST-SULPICE. The gigantic facade of Eglise St-Sulpice dominates the large square of the same name, home to children, street vendors, and a lovely fountain. The building, designed by Servadoni in 1733, remains unfinished. While the outside itself is beautiful, the interior is even more magnificent. The first chapel on the right contains a set of fierce, gestural Delacroix frescoes (Jacob Wrestling with the Angel and Heliodorus Driven from the Temple). The rear chapel boasts a Virgin and Child by Jean-Baptiste Pigalle, and an enormous organ. In the transept, an inlaid copper band runs along the floor from north to south, connecting a plaque in the south to an obelisk in the north. A ray of sunshine passes through a hole in the upper window of the south transept during the winter solstice, striking a marked point on the obelisk at midday. A beam of sunlight falls on the copper plaque during the summer solstice, and behind the communion table during the spring and autumn equinoxes. Da Vinci Code fans may remember this church from the scene in which Silas digs "under the rose" in his quest for the Holy Grail. (Ⓜ *St-Sulpice or Mabillon. From* Ⓜ *Mabillon, walk down r. du Four and make a left onto r. Mabillon. R. Mabillon intersects r. St-Sulpice at the entrance to the church.* ☎*01 42 34 59 60; www.paroisse-saint-sulpice-paris.org. Open daily 7:30am-7:30pm. Guided tour in French every Su 3pm.)*

ST-GERMAIN-DES-PRÉS

Known as *le village de St-Germain-des-Prés*, the area around **boulevard St-Germain** between St-Sulpice and the Seine is packed with cafes, restaurants, galleries, cinemas, and expensive boutiques.

BOULEVARD ST-GERMAIN. Most famous as the former literati hangout of Existentialists (who frequented the Café de Flore, p. 161) and Surrealists (who preferred Deux Magots, p. 161), the bd. St-Germain is torn between nostalgia for its smoky, intellectual past and unabashed delight with all things fashionable and cutting-edge. It is home to scores of cafes, both new and old, where expensive coffee is de rigeur. The boulevard and the many sidestreets around **rue de Rennes** have become a serious shopping area (see **Shopping,** p. 290), filled with designer boutiques from Armani to Louis Vuitton. (Ⓜ *St-Germain-des-Prés.)*

EGLISE ST-GERMAIN-DES-PRÉS. The Eglise St-Germain-des-Prés is the oldest standing church in Paris, and it shows: the only decorations on the church's exterior are pink and white hollyhocks growing on one side. King Childebert I commissioned a church on this site to hold relics he had looted from the Holy Land. Completed in AD 558, it was consecrated by Germain, Bishop of Paris, on the very day of King Childebert's death—the king was buried inside the church's walls.

The rest of the church's history reads like an architectural Book of Job. Sacked by the Normans and rebuilt three times, the present-day church dates from the 11th century. On June 30, 1789, precocious revolutionaries seized the church two weeks before the storming of the Bastille. The church then did a brief stint as a saltpeter mill, and in 1794, 15 tons of gunpowder that had been stored in the abbey exploded. The ensuing fire devastated the church's artwork and treasures, including much of its monastic library. Baron Haussmann destroyed the last remains of the deteriorating abbey walls and gates when he extended r. de Rennes to the front of the church and created pl. St-Germain-des-Prés.

Completely redone in the 19th century, the magnificent interior is painted in shades of maroon, deep green, and gold—enough regal grandeur to counteract the building's modest exterior. Especially striking are the royal blue and gold-starred ceiling, frescoes (by a pupil of Ingres) depicting the life of Jesus, and decorative mosaics along the archways. In the second chapel—on the right after the apse—a stone marks the interred heart of 17th-century philosopher René Descartes, who died of pneumonia at the frigid court of Queen Christina of Sweden. Here, visitors can also find an altar dedicated to the victims of the September 1792 massacre, in which 186 refractory priests were slaughtered in the courtyard. *(3, pl. St-Germain-des-Prés. ⓜ St-Germain-des-Prés. Walk into pl. St-Germain-des-Prés to enter the church from the front. ☎01 55 42 81 18. Open daily 8am-7:45pm. Info office open M-F 10am-noon and 2-7pm. Mass in Spanish Su 5pm. €0.10 maps available at the entrance to the church. Info window has a schedule of frequent concerts: see Entertainment, p. 278.)*

ECOLE NATIONALE SUPÉRIEURE DES BEAUX-ARTS. France's most acclaimed art school, the Ecole Nationale Supérieure des Beaux-Arts was founded by Napoleon in 1811 and soon became the stronghold of French academic painting and sculpture. Its current building, the Palais des Etudes, was finished in 1838 and represents a mix of architectural styles. Though the public is not normally permitted to tour the building itself, you may be able to prowl around its gated courtyard. The best shot at a glimpse of the lifeblood of the Ecole des Beaux-Arts, however, is the **Exhibition Hall** at no. 13, quai Malaquais, where you can get a look at the painting, photography, and installation work of an exciting new generation of Parisian artistes. *(14, r. Bonaparte, at quai Malaquais. ⓜ St-Germain-des-Prés. ☎01 47 03 50 00; www.ensba.fr. Tours by reservation; call ahead. Open Tu-Su 1-7pm. €4, students €2.50. 2 "open days" each year allow the public to peruse studios and teaching areas. Call for schedule and info.)*

ODÉON. Cour du Commerce St-André, branching off bd. St-Germain to the north, is one of the most picturesque walking areas in the 6ème, with cobblestone streets and centuries-old cafes (including Le Procope; see **Food,** p. 162). Beyond the arch at the north end of the Cour du Commerce stands the **Relais Odéon,** a bistro whose stylish exterior, decked with floral mosaics and a hanging sign, is a fine example of Art Nouveau (see **Life and Times,** p. 83). The doorway of no. 7, r. Mazarine, several blocks north, is decorated in the same Belle Epoque style. Farther down this passageway, on the top floor of the building on the left, is the site where a Revolutionary-era clandestine press published Marat's *L'Ami du Peuple.* Jean-Paul Marat was assassinated by Charlotte Corday in the bathtub of his home, which once stood at the spot where the *cours* meets r. de l'Ancienne Comédie.

Just to the south of bd. St-Germain is the **Carrefour de l'Odéon,** a bustling square filled with bistros, cafes, and cinemas. The cafes here are a little calmer than their counterparts on the bd. St-Germain, perhaps because their denizens are thinking and scribbling—there is a nascent wave of literary life here, evidenced by the occasional laptop.

PONT DES ARTS. The footbridge across from the Institut de France, appropriately called the Pont des Arts, is one of the best bridges in Paris. It is celebrated by poets and artists for its delicate ironwork, its beautiful views of the Seine, and its spiritual locus at the heart of France's Academy of Arts and Letters. Built as a toll bridge in 1803, it was the first bridge to be made of iron. On the day it opened, 65,000 Parisians paid to walk across it; today, it is less crowded, free, and perfect for a picnic dinner, a view of the sunset, and a little romancing.

SEVENTH ARRONDISSEMENT

The 7ème's undisputed hub is the famous Eiffel Tower, but the arrondissement boasts plenty of other magnificent sights. The physical seat of the French national government and a good smattering of embassies, the 7ème contains appropriately grandoise and imposing architecture. While the neighborhood has recently been accused of lacking a soul, it is extremely pleasing to the eyes.

see map p. 364-365

TO THE WEST

EIFFEL TOWER

Ⓜ *Bir-Hakeim or Trocadéro. ☎01 44 11 23 23; www.tour-eiffel.fr. Open daily Jan. to mid-June and Sept.-Dec., elevator 9:30am-11:45pm (last access 11pm), stairs 9:30am-6:30pm (last access 6pm); mid-June to Aug., elevator 9am-12:45am (last access 11pm), stairs 9am-12:45am (last access midnight). Elevator to 1st fl. €4.50, under 12 €2.50; 2nd fl. €8/4.50; summit €11. Stairs to 1st and 2nd fl. €4, under 25 €3. Under 3 free.*

Gustave Eiffel, who also engineered the Statue of Liberty, wrote of his tower: "France is the only country in the world with a 300m flagpole." The Eiffel Tower was designed in 1889 as the tallest structure in the world—a monument to engineering that would surpass the Egyptian pyramids in size and notoriety. But before construction had even begun, shocks of dismay reverberated through Paris. Critics dubbed it a "metal asparagus" and a Parisian Tower of Babel. After the tower's completion, writer Guy de Maupassant ate lunch every day at its ground-floor restaurant—the only place in Paris, he claimed, from which he couldn't see the offensive thing.

Nevertheless, when the tower was inaugurated in March 1889 as the centerpiece of the World's Fair, Paris was won over. Nearly two million people ascended it during the event. Numbers dwindled over the following decades, and as the 20-year property lease approached expiration, Eiffel faced the imminent destruction of his masterpiece. The structure survived due to its importance as a communications tower, a function Eiffel had helped cultivate in the 1890s. During WWI, the radio-telegraphic center atop the tower intercepted enemy messages, including the one that led to the arrest of Mata Hari, the Danish dancer accused of being a German spy.

With the 1937 World's Fair, the Eiffel Tower again became a showpiece. Eiffel himself walked humbly before it, remarking: "I ought to be jealous of that tower. She is more famous than I am." Luckily, the gold bust of Eiffel at the base of the tower is hard to miss. Since the expo, Parisians and tourists alike have reclaimed the monument in over 150 million visits. An icon of Paris represented on everything from postcards to neckties and umbrellas, Eiffel's wonder still takes heat from some who see it as Maupassant did: an "excruciating nightmare" overrun with tourists and their trinkets. Don't believe the anti-hype, though. The tower is a wonder of design and engineering, and is surprisingly beautiful up close. The top floor, with its unparalleled view, is especially deserving of a visit. And despite the 7000 tons of metal and 2.5 million rivets that hold together its 12,000 parts, the tower appears light and elegant, especially at night. The distinctive bronze color is repainted every seven years and is graduated from a lighter tone at the summit to a darker one at the base to highlight the elegant line of perspective.

The cheapest way to ascend the tower is by walking up the first two floors. The third floor, however, is only accessible by elevator, so if you plan to go all the way to the top, you'll have to pay for the lift. It's a good idea to wait until nightfall to make your ascent, as lines tend to be shorter after dark. The **Cinémax** on the first floor, which shows films about the tower, is a good excuse to catch your breath. At

PRINCE OF HEARTS

The mystery of the "lost dauphin" has captivated wistful monarchists since the dying days of the French Revolution. Following his parents' grisly end at the Bastille, the 10-year-old heir to the throne, Louis XVII, was kept in solitary confinement for three years before dying alone in his prison cell.

At least that was the official story. Rumors that the heir had actually been spirited away from the prison and a commoner left in his place spread quickly. With the restoration of the monarchy in 1814, over 100 people stepped forth to claim his identity. Claimants were recorded as far away as the Seychelles and Wisconsin.

The myth has recently been shattered, thanks to modern science. The boy's heart had been removed before the body was dumped in a common grave, according to tradition. The doctor who performed the operation kept the organ as a curiosity before relinquishing it to the Spanish royal family. DNA testing on the heart in June of 2004 compared it to hair trimmed from Marie Antoinette during her childhood. The tests indicated that the heart was "almost certainly" that of Louis XVII. Once the results were known, a mass was held for the young prince at the Basilique de St. Denis, where the heart is on view for visitors today. The lost dauphin has finally been found.

the top, captioned aerial photographs help you locate landmarks. On a clear day it is possible to see Chartres Cathedral, 88km away. From nightfall until 2am (1am in winter), the tower sparkles and scintillates for 10min. on the hour.

NEAR THE TOWER

CHAMPS DE MARS. The Champs de Mars (Field of Mars) is a tree-lined expanse that stretches from the Ecole Militaire to the Eiffel Tower. The field is close to the 7ème's military monuments and museums, and its history suggests a number of reasons why it should celebrate the Roman god of war. The name comes from the days of Napoleon's Empire, when the field was used as a drill ground for the adjacent Ecole Militaire. In 1780, Charles Montgolfier launched the first hydrogen balloon from this site. During the Revolution, the park witnessed civilian massacres and political demonstrations. Today, the park is a series of daisy-strewn lawns filled with hordes of tourists and playgrounds overflowing with rambunctious children. The glass monument to international peace was erected at the end of the Champs in 2000. Named the **Mur pour la Paix** (Wall for Peace), the structure consists of two large glass walls covered from top to bottom with the word "peace" written in 32 languages. It stands in quiet defiance of the formidable Ecole Militaire directly across the way. A choice picnicking spot—after a few glasses of cheap wine in front of the Eiffel Tower, you'll reach Parisian nirvana. (Ⓜ *La Motte Picquet-Grenelle or Ecole Militaire. From the av. de la Motte-Picquet, walk towards Ecole Militaire.*)

ECOLE MILITAIRE. In 1751, Louis XV founded the Ecole Militaire at the urging of his mistress, Mme. de Pompadour, who hoped to make officers of "poor gentlemen." In 1784, 15-year-old Napoleon Bonaparte enrolled. A few weeks later, he presented administrators with a comprehensive plan for the school's reorganization. By the time he graduated three years later, he was a lieutenant in the artillery. Teachers foretold he would "go far in favorable circumstances." Louis XVI made the building into a barracks for the Swiss Guard, but it was converted back into a military school in 1848. Today, French and foreign officers attend the Ecole's School of Advanced War Studies. (*1, pl. Joffre.* Ⓜ *Ecole Militaire.*)

UNESCO. The Ecole Militaire's architectural and spiritual antithesis, UNESCO (United Nations Educational, Scientific, and Cultural Organization), occupies the Y-shaped, concrete-and-glass building across the road. Established in 1958 to foster science and culture throughout the world, the organization built this major international monument in Paris to represent its 188 member nations. The design itself is the work of three international architects: American **Marcel Breuer**, Italian **Luigi Nervi,** and Frenchman **Bernard Zehrfuss.** Don't be deterred by the institutional exterior: the organization welcomes visitors, and the exhibits and permanent pieces are worth the hassle of navigating the entrance. The bookshop, just inside on your right, sells everything from United Nations publications to educational computer games, as well as folk music and literature. Temporary exhibits often have unique pieces of art for sale, while bulletin boards around the elevators list upcoming events; language, music, and dance classes; and even apartments for rent.

In the outer courtyard, a huge sculpture by **Henri Moore** called *Figure in Repose* is joined by a mobile by the American **Alexander Calder** and a walking man by Swiss sculptor **Alberto Giacometti.** The large framework globe by Danish artist **Erik Reitzel** is eyecatching amongst the hedges. Two murals by **Joán Miró** and **Josep Llorens Artigas,** *The Wall of the Sun* and *The Wall of the Moon,* reside in the Miró Halles. Inside the foyer of Room I is **Picasso's** *Fall of Icarus,* and next door in the Salle des Actes is a tapestry by architect **Le Corbusier.** Behind Ségur Hall there is a lovely Japanese garden of peace—a serene oasis filled with goldfish and turtles. By the garden are a set of metal sculptures by **Vassilakis Takis** and an angel from the facade of a Nagasaki church destroyed by the atomic bomb during WWII. *(7, pl. de Fontenoy.* ⓜ *Ségur.* ☎ *01 45 68 16 42 or 01 45 68 03 59; www.unesco.org. Bookshop open M-F 9am-noon and 2:30-5:15pm; exhibits open M-F 9am-6pm. Tours M-F 10am or 3pm. Free, but reservations necessary; bring some form of identification. Pick up a map of the building at the information desk to your left, beyond the elevators after you enter.)*

AMERICAN CHURCH IN PARIS. The first American church founded on foreign soil has become an interdenominational meeting-place for expats and travelers. Besides being a good place for visitor information (such as job and apartment listings and language courses), the church hosts concerts—usually chamber music and solo classical performances—September through May on Sundays at 6pm. The brick and stone Gothic structure surrounds a charming courtyard. *(65, quai d'Orsay, at the corner of quai d'Orsay and r. A. Moissan.* ⓜ *Invalides.* ☎ *01 40 62 05 00; www.acparis.org. Services Su at 11am.)*

TO THE EAST

INVALIDES. The gold-leaf dome of the **Hôtel des Invalides** shines conspicuously at the center of the 7ème. Originally founded by Louis XVI in 1671 as a home for disabled soldiers, it is now the headquarters of the military governor of Paris and continues to serve, on a small scale, as a military hospital. The tree-lined **Esplanade des Invalides** runs from the *hôtel* to the **Pont Alexandre III,** an ornate bridge with gilded lampposts where you can catch a great view of the Invalides and the buildings along the Seine. The **Musée de l'Armée, Musée des Plans-Reliefs, Musée des Deux Guerres Mondiales,** and **Musée de l'Ordre de la Libération** are housed within the Invalides museum complex (see **Museums,** p. 259), as is **Napoleon's tomb,** in the **Eglise St-Louis.** To the left of the Tourville entrance, the **Jardin de l'Intendant** is strewn with benches and impeccably groomed trees and bushes, for those who've had their fill of guns and emperors. A ditch lined with foreign cannons runs around the Invalides area where a moat used to be, making it impossible to leave by any but the two official entrances. Be aware that certain areas are blocked to tourists in order to respect the privacy of the war veterans who still live in the hospital. *(127, r. de Grenelle.* ⓜ *Invalides. Enter from either pl. des Invalides or pl. Vauban and av. de Tourville.)*

ASSEMBLÉE NATIONALE. The Palais Bourbon's original occupants probably would not recognize their former home. Built in 1722 for the Duchesse de Bourbon, the spunky daughter of the autocratic Louis XIV and his mistress, Mme de Montespan, the palace is now the home of the French parliament. Open only to French civil servants. *(33, quai d'Orsay.* ⓜ *Assemblée Nationale.* ☎ *01 40 63 60 00; www.assemblee-nat.fr.)*

PALAIS DE LA LÉGION D'HONNEUR. Once the elegant **Hôtel de Salm,** the Palais de la Légion d'Honneur was built in 1786 by architect Pierre Rousseau for the Prince de Salm-Kyrburgh. The mansion came into Napoleon's hands in 1804. It burned down during the Commune of 1871, but the members of the Légion rebuilt it soon after, using the original plans. It now houses the **Musée National de la Légion d'Honneur** (see **Museums,** p. 260). Both the Palais and the museum re-opened in November 2006 after extensive renovations. *(At the corner of r. de Lille and r. de Belle-chasse.* ⓜ *Solférino. Walk up r. Solférino and turn right onto r. de Lille; the short r. de la Légion d'Honneur will be on your left.* ☎ *01 40 62 84 25.)*

QUAI VOLTAIRE. The quai Voltaire, known for its views of the monuments along the Seine, boasts an artistic heritage more distinguished than any other block in the city. Voltaire himself spent his last days at no. 27. No. 19 was home to Baudelaire while he wrote *Les Fleurs du Mal (Flowers of Evil)* from 1856 to 1858, to Richard Wagner as he composed *Die Meistersinger* between 1861 and 1862, and to Oscar Wilde while he was in exile. Eugène Delacroix lived at no. 13 from 1829 to 1836, followed by Jean-Baptiste-Camille Corot. Jean-Auguste-Dominique Ingres died at no. 11 in 1867. The Russian ballet dancer Rudolf Nureyev lived at no. 23 from 1981 until his death in 1993. *(Along the Seine between Pont Royal and Pont du Carrou-sel.* ⓜ *rue du Bac. Walk up r. du Bac to the river.)*

LA PAGODE. A Japanese pagoda built in 1895 by the Bon Marché department store magnate M. Morin as a gift to his wife, La Pagode endures as an artifact of the Orientalist craze that swept France in the 19th century. When Mme. Morin left her husband for his associate's son just prior to WWI, the building became the scene of Sino-Japanese *soirées,* despite the tension between the two countries. In 1931, La Pagode opened its doors to the public, becoming a cinema and swank cafe where the likes of silent screen-star Gloria Swanson were known to raise a glass. The theater closed during the Nazi occupation, re-opened in 1945, and closed again in 1998 due to a lack of funding, despite having been declared a historic monument by the Ministry of Culture in 1982. It was re-opened under private ownership in November 2000. The two-screen cinema continues to show smaller, independent films (see **Entertainment,** p. 278). *(57bis, r. de Babylone.* ⓜ *St-François-Xavier.* ☎ *01 45 55 48 48. Cafe open daily between shows.)*

HÔTEL MATIGNON. Once owned by the royal family of Monaco and Talleyrand, Hôtel Matignon is now the official residence of the prime minister. It is considered one of the most stunning *hôtels particuliers* in Paris. Visitors are not permitted. Nearby, at 53, r. Varenne, a plaque commemorates American novelist Edith Wharton, one of the first of the early 20th-century expats. She lived at this address from 1910 to 1920. *(57, r. de Varenne.* ⓜ *Varenne.)*

EGLISE ST-THOMAS D'AQUIN. The 17th-century Eglise St-Thomas d'Aquin was originally dedicated to St. Dominique but was reconsecrated by revolutionaries as the Temple of Peace. While the church facade is an unassuming continuation of the city block, the interior is fantastically decorated with wall and ceiling murals, particularly behind the altar. The church holds occasional organ concerts. Information about group pilgrimages within Europe can be found on the bulletin boards inside the main entrance. *(On r. de Gribeauval, off r. du Bac.* ⓜ *Rue du*

Bac. ☎01 49 24 11 43. Open in winter M-F and Su 9am-noon and 4-7pm, Sa 10am-noon and 4-7:30pm; in summer daily 9am-noon and 4-7pm.)

EGLISE ST-FRANÇOIS-XAVIER. This beautiful church, with its blue-and-red stained-glass windows, provides sanctuary from the endless noise and chaos of city streets. Its strategic location near the Invalides and ministerial buildings is reflected in its distinguished parishioners. Built between 1861 and 1874, its grand size provides much room for reflection, and candles may be lit for an offering. *(12, pl. du Président Mithouard, on bd. des Invalides. ⓜ St-François-Xavier. ☎01 44 49 62 62; www.paroisse-sfx-paris.org. Open summer M-F 8:15am-noon and 3:30-7:30pm, Sa 8:45am-noon and 3:30-7:45pm, Su 9am-12:45pm and 3:30-8pm. Winter hours begin later and end earlier; check website for precise times and for mass schedules.)*

EIGHTH ARRONDISSEMENT

There's a reason that the 8*ème* remains Paris's most touristed *arrondissement* long after the Champs Elysées has ceased to be posh. With more architectural diversity, historical significance, and bustling commerce than many other areas in the city, it's a great (if hectic) place to spend a day.

see map pp. 366-367 ## ALONG THE CHAMPS-ELYSÉES

ARC DE TRIOMPHE. It's hard to believe that the majestic Arc de Triomphe was first designed as a huge, bejeweled elephant. The arch is situated at the top of a hill with a view down the Champs-Elysées to the Tuileries, and in 1758, architect Charles François Ribart envisaged the spot as the perfect setting for a gargantuan monument to France's military prowess. Fortunately for France, construction of the monument was not actually undertaken until 1806, when Napoleon imagined a more decorous monolith with which to welcome his troops home. Napoleon was exiled before the arch was completed, and Louis XVIII took over construction in 1823. He dedicated the arch to the war in Spain and its commander, the Duc d'Angoulême, and placed its design in the hands of Jean-François-Thérèse Chalgrin. The Arc de Triomphe was consecrated in 1836. The names of Napoleon's generals and battles are engraved inside.

Since the days of Napoleon, the arch has been a magnet for various triumphant armies. After the Prussians marched through in 1871, the mortified Parisians purified the ground with fire. On July 14, 1919, the Arc provided the backdrop for an Allied victory parade headed by Maréchal Foch. During WWII, Frenchmen were reduced to tears as the Nazis goose-stepped through their beloved monument. After the demeaning years of German occupation, a sympathetic Allied army made sure that a French general would be the first to drive under the arch.

The **Tomb of the Unknown Soldier** has lain under the arch since November 11, 1920. Its marker bears the inscription, "Here lies a French soldier who died for his country, 1914-1918" and represents the 1,500,000 Frenchmen who died during WWI. There is a daily remembrance ceremony at the tomb at 6:30pm. Inside the arch, visitors can climb 205 steps up a winding staircase to the *entresol* between the arch's two supports, and 29 steps farther to a museum that documents the Arc's construction. There is an elevator for the less athletic; the lines for it are always long. Forty-six steps beyond the museum, the **terrasse** observation deck provides a brilliant view of the Champs-Elysées and the tree-lined av. Foch. You can also clearly mark the "Historic Axis" from the Arc de Triomphe du Carrousel and the Louvre Pyramid (p. 245) at one end to the Grande Arche de la Défense (p. 240) at the other. *(ⓜ Charles de Gaulle-Etoile. Open daily Apr.-Sept. 10am-11pm; Oct.-Mar. 10am-10:30pm. Last entry 30min. before closing. €8, ages 18-25 €5, under 17 free. Wheelchair accessible. Expect lines even on*

SIGHTS

weekdays, although you can escape the crowds if you go before noon. You will kill yourself trying to dodge the 10 "lane" merry-go-round of cars (and face a hefty fine), so use the pedestrian underpass on the right side of the Champs-Elysées facing the arch. Buy your ticket in the pedestrian underpass before going up to the ground level. MC/V.)

AVENUE DES CHAMPS-ELYSÉES. The Champs-Elysées, one of the 12 symmetrical avenues radiating from the huge rotary of pl. Charles de Gaulle-Etoile, is a legendary epicenter of chic. The avenue was born in 1616 when Marie de Médicis ploughed the Cours-la-Reine through the fields and marshland west of the Louvre. It remained an unkempt thoroughfare until the early 19th century, when the city built sidewalks and installed gas lighting. The height of the Champs was during the Second Empire, when elegant mansions sprang up along the avenue and splashy cafes catered to the *beau monde*. The infamous Bal Mabille opened in 1840 at no. 51. At no. 25, visitors can catch a glimpse of a Second Empire *hôtel particulier*. Here, the Marquise de Paiva, adventuress, famous courtesan, and spy, entertained the luminaries of the era.

In recent years, commercial encroachment has diluted the romantic glamor of the Champs-Elysées. The shops along the avenue range from the behemoth Louis Vuitton flagship store to the low-budget Monoprix. Overpriced cafes compete with fast-food outlets for the patronage of swarming tourists. Glitzy nightclubs and multiplex cinemas draw large crowds well into the evening.

Successive governments have made an effort to resurrect the avenue by widening the sidewalks, planting more trees, and building underground parking lots. Standing at either end of the bustling boulevard, one can see that the restoration efforts have paid off: from a distance, the Champs-Elysées is a magnificent vista of pomp and glory. The streets merge with park space just past av. Franklin D. Roosevelt, one of the six avenues that radiate from the Rond Point des Champs-Elysées. Av. Montaigne, lined with Paris's finest houses of *haute couture*, runs southwest. (Ⓜ *Charles de Gaulle-Etoile. The Champs runs from the pl. Charles de Gaulle-Etoile southeast to the pl. de la Concorde.)*

FOUQUET'S. Fouquet's is a living monument to the Champs's glorious past. Once a favorite with French film stars, this outrageously expensive cafe/restaurant now boasts more stars in picture frames than in clientele. Open since 1899 and a designated historical monument, the red-awninged eatery hosts the annual César awards, the French answer to the Oscars (see **Food,** p. 165). *(99, av. des Champs-Elysées. Ⓜ George V. ☎ 01 47 23 70 60.)*

THÉÂTRE DES CHAMPS-ELYSÉES. Built by the Perret brothers in 1912 with bas-reliefs by Bourdelle, the Théâtre des Champs-Elysées is best known for staging the controversial premiere of Stravinsky's ballet *Le Sacre du Printemps*. The score, conducted by Pierre Monteux, was dissonant and arhythmic, and Vaslav Nijinsky's choreography had the dancers dressed in feathers and rags, hopping about pigeon-toed to evoke primitivism. The spectacle provoked the most famous riot in music history—the audience jeered and shouted so loudly that the dancers couldn't hear the orchestra. The theater's three *salles* still host operatic, orchestral, and dance performances (see **Entertainment,** p. 280). *(15, av. Montaigne. Ⓜ Alma-Marceau. ☎ 01 49 52 50 50, tours 01 44 54 19 30. €4.)*

PALAIS DE L'ELYSÉE. The guards pacing around the corner of av. de Marigny and r. du Faubourg St-Honoré are protecting the Palais de l'Elysée, the state residence for French presidents since 1870. The Palais was built in 1718 and later served as home to Louis XV's celebrated mistress Madame de Pompadour. Other residents have included Josephine Bonaparte and Napoleon III. Entrance requires a personal invitation. (Ⓜ *Champs-Elysées-Clemenceau.)*

GRAND AND PETIT PALAIS. The Grand and Petit Palais face each other on av. Winston Churchill at the foot of the Champs-Elysées. Built for the 1900 World's Fair, they were lauded as a dazzling combination of "banking and dreaming" and exemplify ornate Art Nouveau architecture. While the Petit Palais houses an eclectic mix of artwork, its big brother has been turned into a space for temporary exhibits on architecture, painting, sculpture, and French history. The Grand Palais also houses the **Palais de la Découverte,** a science museum/playground for children (see **Museums,** p. 262). The Palais is most beautiful at night, when its statues are backlit and the glass-and-steel dome glows greenly from within. *(⓶ Champs-Elysées-Clemenceau.)*

AROUND PLACE DE LA CONCORDE

PLACE DE LA CONCORDE. Paris's largest and most infamous public square is the eastern terminus of the Champs-Elysées. If you stand between the Champs-Elysées and the Tuileries Gardens, the *place* affords a fine view of the gold-domed Invalides, the columns of the Assemblée Nationale (across the river to your right), and the Madeleine (to your left). In the center of the *place* is the monumental **Obélisque de Luxor.** The spot was originally occupied by a statue of Louis XV (after whom the square was originally named) that was destroyed in 1748 by an angry mob. King Louis-Philippe, anxious to avoid revolutionary rancor, opted for a less contentious symbol—the hieroglyphic-covered obelisk presented to Charles X from the Viceroy of Egypt in 1829. Getting the obelisk to Paris was no simple task—it traveled by sea and up the Seine in a specially built boat. Erected in 1836, Paris's oldest monument dates back to the 13th century BC and recalls the royal accomplishments of Ramses II. Reproductions of Guillaume Coustou's **Cheveaux de Marly** flank the Champs-Elysées at pl. de la Concorde. Also known as *Africans Mastering the Numidian Horses,* the original sculptures are now in the Louvre to protect them from pollution. Perfect replicas graciously hold their places on the Concorde. Eight large statues representing France's major cities also stand in the *place.*

Constructed between 1757 and 1777 by Louis XV, the *place* soon became an epicenter of public grievance against the monarchy. It eventually became pl. de la Révolution, the site of the guillotine that severed 1343 aristocratic heads. In 1793, Louis XVI was beheaded by guillotine on a site near where the statue representing the city of Brest now stands. The heads of Marie-Antoinette, Charlotte Corday (Marat's assassin), Lavoisier, Danton, Robespierre, and others rolled into baskets here and were held up to the cheering crowds who packed the pavement.

After the Reign of Terror, the square was optimistically renamed **place de la Concorde,** though the noise of the cars zooming through this busy intersection today hardly makes for a harmonious visit. With its monumental scale and heavy traffic, the *place* is not pedestrian-friendly. At night, the ambience softens as the obelisk, fountains, and lamps are lit to create a romantic glow. On Bastille Day, a military parade led by the President of the Republic marches through pl. de la Concorde (usually around 10am) and down the Champs-Elysées to the Arc de Triomphe (see **Life and Times,** p. 97). In the evening, an impressive fireworks display lights up the sky over pl. de la Concorde. At the end of July, the Tour de France finalists pull into the home stretch on the Champs-Elysées and the pl. de la Concorde. *(⓶ Concorde.)*

MADELEINE. Mirrored by the Assemblée Nationale across the Seine, the Madeleine—formally called Eglise Ste-Marie-Madeleine (Mary Magdalene Church)—was built to look like a Greek temple. Construction, overseen by Louis XV, began in 1764 and was halted during the Revolution, when the Cult of Reason proposed transforming the building into a bank, a theater, or a courthouse. Napoleon, of course, decreed that it should be a temple to the greatness of his army, while Louis XVIII shouted, "It shall be a church!" Finally completed in 1842, the structure stands alone amongst Parisian churches, distinguished by its gigantic pediment, four ceiling domes, 52 66-foot exterior Corinthian columns, and a curious altarpiece adorned by an immense sculpture of the ascension of Mary Magdalene, the church's namesake. The reliefs on the impressive bronze doors depict the 10 commandments. A colorful flower market thrives on the east side of the church. **Marcel Proust** spent most of his childhood nearby at no. 9, bd. Malesherbes, which might explain his penchant for his aunt Léonie's *madeleines* with tea. You, too, can enjoy a few *madeleines* or pick up some chocolate *macarons* at the world-famous **Fauchon**, 24-30, pl. de la Madeleine, behind the church (see **Food**, p. 166). Today, expensive clothing and food shops line the surrounding square. *(pl. de la Madeleine. ⓜ Madeleine. ☎01 44 51 69 00; www.eglise-lamadeleine.com. Open daily for visiting 9:30am-7pm. Regular organ and chamber concerts; contact the church for a schedule and come to the church or call Virgin or FNAC for tickets (commission fee). Mass M-F 7:45am, 12:30, and 6:30pm (crypt); Sa 11am and 6pm; Su 9:30, 11am, 12:30, and 6pm.)*

OTHER SIGHTS. On either side of the r. de Royal, directly north of pl. de la Concorde stand the **Hôtel de Crillon** (on the left) and the **Hôtel de la Marine** (on the right). Architect Jacques-Ange Gabriel built the impressive colonnaded facades between 1757 and 1770. The Crillon, originally home to noblemen, now houses the world-famous Hôtel de Crillon. The Marine served as furniture storage for the Louvre palace and is today the headquarters of the French national marines. On February 6, 1778, France became the first European country to recognize the independence of the United States of America, after the Treaty of Friendship and Trade was signed here by Louis XVI and American statesmen, including Benjamin Franklin. World-renowned **Maxim's** restaurant, 3, r. de Royale, once home to Cardinal Richelieu, stands nearby. A meal at this historic house may be beyond the budgets of most, but the souvenir shop and Cafe Minim's next door offer a more affordable slice of celebrity.

TO THE NORTH

CHAPELLE EXPIATOIRE. Pl. Louis XVI is comprised of the immense Chapelle Expiatoire, monuments to Marie-Antoinette and Louis XVI, and a lovely, quiet park excellent for picnicking. During the Revolution, when burial sites were in high demand, lime-filled trenches were dug here to accommodate piles of bodies. Louis XVIII had his brother's and sister-in-law's remains removed to St-Denis in 1815, and there are no graves remaining, despite rumors of Marat's assassin Charlotte Corday being buried here. Statues of the expiatory king and queen stand inside the Chapelle, symbolically guarding a tomb-shaped altar. Their touching final letters are engraved in French on the base of the sculptures. *(29, r. Pasquier, inside pl. Louis XVI, just below bd. Haussmann. ⓜ Madeleine, Havre-Caumartin or St.-Lazare. ☎01 44 32 18 00. Open Th-Sa 1-5pm. €3, under 18 free. Tours in French available every Fr in June at 1:30 and 3:30pm. English-language pamphlets available at information desk. 30min. tours in French each afternoon in summer.)*

■ **PARC MONCEAU.** The signs say *"Pelouse interdite"* (keep off the lawn), but on a sunny day, no one's listening. Lying behind gold-tipped, wrought-iron gates, the Parc Monceau is an expansive urban oasis especially popular with families. There's plenty of shade, courtesy of the largest tree in the capital: an oriental platane, 7m thick and two centuries old. It's not just a formal garden, since the park also features a number of architectural *folies*, including a pyramid, a covered bridge, an East Asian pagoda, Dutch windmills, and Roman ruins. The park was designed by painter Carmontelle for the Duc d'Orléans and completed by Haussmann in 1862. The well-stocked park *chalet* (open daily 10am-7pm; sandwiches €2.50-5, *crêpes* €2.80-5.50) is great for a quick bite to eat. Year-round pony rides (€2.50) near the av. Velazquez entrance. *(ⓜ Monceau or Courcelles. Open daily Apr.-Oct. 7am-10pm; Nov.-Mar. 7am-8pm; last entry 15min. before closing.)*

CATHÉDRALE ALEXANDRE-NEVSKI. The Cathédrale Orthodoxe Russe, or Cathédrale Alexandre-Nevski, was built in 1860. Its domes, designed by artists from St. Petersburg, are intricately painted in gold, deep reds, blues and greens. Recently restored, they are spectacular from both outside and in. Today, the cathedral is the center of the Constantinople jurisdiction of the Russian Orthodox faith, and Russian restaurants spangle the surrounding streets. Be sure to dress appropriately; no shorts or uncovered shoulders are allowed in the cathedral. *(12, r. Daru.* Ⓜ *Ternes.* ☎ *01 42 27 37 34. Open Tu, F, and Su 3-5pm. Services in French and Russian, Sa 6-8pm, Su 10am-12:30pm,, other times posted on church calendar.)*

NINTH ARRONDISSEMENT

The *9ème* offers visitors a grand lesson in contrast: from the serenely gorgeous frescoes of the Opéra Garnier to the seedy pockets of the Pigalle, this *arrondissement* perfectly exemplifies the distinctly Parisian cohabitation of vice and virtue.

see map p. 368-369

OPÉRA AND SURROUNDINGS

The area around the southernmost border of the *9ème* is known simply as *l'Opéra* after the area's incomparable landmark: the **Opéra Garnier.** Opéra and its surrounding *grands boulevards* are the *9ème*'s busiest and most prosperous areas, touched by spill-over glamour from the ritzy *8ème.* Those who aren't interested in the world-class ballet at the Garnier can walk down the road to **L'Olympia** (see **Entertainment,** p. 279), one of Paris's leading venues for American, European, and Brazilian pop, jazz, and rock concerts. Just to the north of the Opéra is the most crowded and bustling area in the *9ème.* Here you can find the city's enormous department stores, **Galeries Lafayette** and **Au Printemps** (see **Shopping,** p. 296), which offer some of the best shopping in Paris. Look out for the sale seasons—crowded but fabulous—in July and January.

OPÉRA GARNIER. The exterior of the Opéra Garnier—with its newly restored multi-colored marble facade, sculpted golden goddesses, and ornate columns and friezes—is one of Paris's most impressive sights. On bright days, its recently renovated exterior shimmers like gold. It's no wonder that Oscar Wilde once swore he saw an angel floating on the sidewalk while he was sitting next door at the Café de la Paix.

Designed by Charles Garnier in the style of the Second Empire, the eclectic Opéra emphasizes both the ostentation and the ideological rootlessness of the era. Asked whether his building was in the style of Louis XIV, Louis XV, or Louis XVI, Garnier responded that his creation belonged only to Napoleon III, who financed the project. Garnier was 35 and unknown when he won the Opéra commission in a contest among Paris's top architects; the building made him a superstar. After 15 years of construction, the Opéra opened its doors in 1875.

The Opéra's interior is decorated with Gobelin tapestries, gilded mosaics, and an eight-ton chandelier that fell on the audience in 1896. The incident, along with rumors of a spooky lake beneath the building, inspired *Le Fantôme de l'Opera (The Phantom of the Opera)*, which began life as a 1910 novel by Gaston Leroux and went through several film incarnations before bursting into song in 1986 with Andrew Lloyd Webber's megamusical. Be sure to pay a visit to the Phantom's box, no. 5. The Opéra's auditorium has 1900 red velvet seats and a ceiling painted by Marc Chagall in 1964. The five-tiered auditorium was designed as a stage not only for operas, but also for social life; balconies were constructed so audience members could watch one another, as well as the show.

Since 1989, most operas have been performed at the **Opéra Bastille,** generally regarded as the Garnier's ugly stepsister (p. 219). The Opéra Garnier is now mainly a venue for ballet. In 1992, Rudolf Nureyev made his last public appearance here.

Guided tours are available in several languages. The Opéra houses a library and museum where temporary exhibits on theatrical personages, such as director Alain Germain and dancer Vaslav Nijinsky, are held throughout the year. The museum also displays a permanent collection that includes sculptures by Degas and scale models of famous opera scenes. Paul Baudry's portrait of Charles Garnier hangs by the entrance to the museum. (Ⓜ *Opéra.* ☎ *08 92 89 90 90; www.operade-paris.fr. Concert hall and museum open Sept. to mid-July daily 10am-4:30pm; mid-July to Aug. 10am-5:30pm. Concert hall closed during rehearsals; call ahead. Admission €7, concessions €4. English tours daily at 10am and 2:30pm: afternoon tours are cancelled during rehearsals; call ahead for more info. See also **Entertainment,** p. 280.)*

CAFE DE LA PAIX. The Café de la Paix, located next to the Opéra Garnier, is the quintessential 19th-century cafe. Like the Opéra, it was designed by Charles Garnier and sports frescoes, mirrored walls, and Neoclassical ceilings with winking "epicurean cherubs." Oscar Wilde frequented the cafe; today it caters to the after-theater crowd and other deep-pocketed patrons (see **Food,** p. 167). *(12, bd. des Capucines.)*

NORTH OF OPÉRA

The upper 9*ème,* with its infamous red-light district, is a destination for those in search of cheap and not-so-cheap thrills, while the less debaucherous visitor will probably choose to stay toward the south. Below Pigalle, the middle 9*ème* is home to a substantial Jewish population. There is a handful of kosher food stores along **rue Notre Dame de Lorette** and **rue du Faubourg-Montmartre.** This lively neighborhood is also filled with discount shops, pizza parlors, and car exhaust.

EGLISE NOTRE DAME DE LORETTE. Built in 1836 to honor "the glory of the Virgin Mary," Eglise Notre Dame de Lorette is an example of Neoclassical architecture, although it's now a bit delapidated. Frescoes inside its elevated chapel depict the four evangelists contemplating Mary, and the four prophets hailing her. Noisy **rue Notre Dame de Lorette** is far less virtuous than the church after which it's named. The street was the debauched hangout of Emile Zola's *Nana* (whose name is now slang equivalent to "chick" or "babe"), while *Lorette* became a nickname for the quarter's young prostitutes in the 1960s. (Ⓜ *Notre Dame de Lorette. Exit the metro and the church will be in front of you on pl. Kossuth. Mass M-F 8am, 12:15, 6:45pm; Sa 6:30pm; Su 9:30, 11am, and 6:30pm.)*

PIGALLE. The home of famous cabarets-turned-nightclubs (Folies Bergère, Moulin Rouge, Folies Pigalle) and well-endowed newcomers with names like "Le Coq Hardy" and "Dirty Dick," this neighborhood is raunchy enough to make even Jacques Chirac blush. Stretching along bd. de Clichy from pl. Pigalle to pl. Blanche, Pigalle earned its reputation as the un-chastity belt of Paris during WWII, when American servicemen stationed in Paris nicknamed it "Pig Alley." Every corner is crammed with sex shops, brothels, porn stores, and lace, leather, and latex boutiques. At "night," which starts well before dark in Pigalle, prostitutes and drug dealers prowl the streets and subway stations in the area; as a result, the district is heavily policed. Though it is supposedly undergoing a slow gentrification, Pigalle shows no signs of shedding its sleazy reputation any time soon. Even the RATP makes regular announcements in neighborhood metro stops warning visitors against pickpockets. The streets north of bd. Clichy and south of pl. Blanche are comparatively calm, but visitors—especially young women—should use caution throughout the area. (Ⓜ *Pigalle.)*

TENTH ARRONDISSEMENT

While probably not the first stop on any tourist's jaunt through Paris, the 10ème offers a surprising wealth of things to see and do for folks who do venture out there. Visitors can marvel at the cultural col-

see map p. 370 lision of pl. de la République or simply take a relaxing stroll along the Canal St-Martin.

PORTES ST-DENIS AND ST-MARTIN. The grand **Porte St-Denis** looms triumphantly at the end of r. du Faubourg St-Denis. Built in 1672 to celebrate the victories of Louis XIV in Flanders and the Rhineland, the gate imitates the Arch of Titus in Rome. The site of the arch was once a medieval entrance to the city; today it serves as a traffic rotary and a gathering place for pigeons and loiterers alike. In the words of André Breton, "c'est très belle et très inutile" (it's very beautiful and very useless). On July 28, 1830, revolutionaries scrambled to the top and rained cobblestones on the monarchist troops below (see **Life and Times,** p. 64). The **Porte St-Martin** at the end of r. du Faubourg St-Martin, constructed in 1674, is a variation on a similar theme, with more subdued architecture and a smaller scale. On the bd. St-Martin side, a herculean Louis XIV dominates the facade, wearing nothing but a wig and a smile. (Ⓜ Strasbourg-St-Denis.)

THÉÂTRES DE LA RENAISSANCE AND DE ST-MARTIN. The stretch from Porte St-Martin to pl. de la République along r. René Boulanger and bd. St-Martin was a lively theater district in the 19th century but is now quite shabby, filled with loiterers and sex shops. Vestiges of the glory days are visible at the intersection of bd. St-Martin and r. René Boulanger in the ornate, sculpted facades of the two theaters, both of which are still active. (Ⓜ Strasbourg-St-Denis or République.)

PLACE DE LA RÉPUBLIQUE. Though Haussmann created it to separate some *beaux quartiers* from the revolutionary *arrondissements*, the pl. de la République is now a bustling meeting point for the vastly different 3ème, 10ème, and 11ème. It also serves as the disorienting junction of av. de la République and bd. Magenta, Voltaire, Temple, Turbigo, and St-Martin. At the center of the *place*, Morice's sculpture of *La République* glorifies France's many revolutionary struggles, and the host of chain restaurants lining it feed the diverse crowds. The area buzzes with people during the day but can be a bit uncomfortable at night. (Ⓜ République.)

CANAL ST-MARTIN. The most pleasant area of the 10ème is unquestionably the tree-lined Canal St-

TOUR DE FORCE

The Tour de France is an event of legendary proportions. Hundreds of cyclists have competed for the *Grand Boucle* every year since 1903, interrupted only by the world wars. The first edition was eight stages, approximately 400km each. It left from Paris, and returned a week later. Much has changed since 1903. The bicycles are no longer made out of steel, but of lightweight carbon fiber. The racers fortify themselves with Gatorade instead of wine, and their wool sweaters and long pants have been replaced by aerodynamic synthetics. One constant has endured throughout: the tour still ends in Paris.

July brings the final stage of the race down the Champs-Elysées, and the entire city halts. The sprinters who have survived the Alps and the Pyrenées have one last shot at glory. The man in the yellow jersey—the overall leader—knocks back a celebratory champagne from the seat of his bike before joining the sprint to the line.

The spectacle is inspiring—stake out a spot along the Champs many hours in advance, but the wait is worth it. The cyclists whiz by as fast as motorcycles, with the entire *peloton* (pack) passing in the blink of an eye.

Martin. Measuring 4.5km, the canal runs from r. du Faubourg du Temple to the Bassin de la Villette. It was built in 1825 as a shortcut for river traffic on the Seine, and it also served to remind the plebeians of their place in the city—that is to say, not in it. In recent years, the city has made efforts to improve water quality in the canal and clean up its banks, and the result has been a sort of local rennaissance. The residential area around the canal is being rediscovered by Parisians and tourists alike, and the tree-lined *quais* boast new, upscale boutiques and restaurants. Children line up along the banks to watch the several working locks lift barges and boats, and Canauxrama runs boat tours on the canal (see **Practical Information,** p. 116). On Sundays, an antique market takes place along the quai de Valmy and the streets along the canal close to traffic, making room for bikes and rollerblades. *(Ⓜ République or Goncourt will take you to the most beautiful end of the canal.)*

ELEVENTH ARRONDISSEMENT

see map p. 373

There are few monumental sights in the 11*ème* aside from the pl. de la Bastille, but you might see some funny drunken antics during a bar crawl at r. Oberkampf.

BASTILLE PRISON. The Bastille Prison is the most visited sight in Paris that doesn't actually exist. A Parisian mob stormed this symbol of royal tyranny on July 14, 1789, sparking the French Revolution. Two days later, the National Assembly ordered the prison demolished. Today, the pl. de la Bastille is a busy intersection, but the ground plan of the fortress is still visible as a line of paving-stones in the *place*, beneath which some of the cellars are said to still be in place.

The prison was originally commissioned by Charles V to safeguard the eastern entrance to Paris. Strapped for cash, Charles "recruited" a press-gang of passing civilians to lay the stones for the fortress. The Bastille towers rose 100 ft. above Paris by the end of the 14th century. Under Henri IV, they became the royal treasury; Louis XIII made them a state prison. Internment there, generally reserved for heretics and political dissidents, was the king's business and, as a result, often arbitrary. But it was hardly the hell-hole that the Revolutionaries who tore it down imagined it to be—the Bastille's titled inmates were allowed to furnish their suites, use fresh linens, bring their own servants, and receive guests: the Cardinal de Rohan held a dinner party for 20 in his cell. Notable prisoners included the mysterious Man in the Iron Mask (made famous by writer Alexandre Dumas), the Comte de Mirabeau, Voltaire (twice), and the Marquis de Sade, who wrote his notorious novel *Justine* here.

Having ransacked the Invalides for weapons, Revolutionary militants stormed the Bastille for munitions. Supposedly an impenetrable fortress, the prison had actually been attacked during other periods of civil unrest. Surrounded by an armed rabble, too short on food to entertain the luxury of a siege, and unsure of the loyalty of the Swiss mercenaries who defended the prison, the Bastille's governor surrendered. His head was severed with a pocket knife and paraded through the streets on a pike. Despite the gruesome details, the storming of the Bastille has come to symbolize the triumph of liberty over tyranny. Its first anniversary was the cause for great celebration in Revolutionary Paris. Since the late 19th century, July 14 has been the official state holiday of the French Republic. It is usually a time of glorious firework displays and consumption of copious amounts of alcohol, with festivities concentrated in the pl. de la Bastille (see **Life and Times,** p. 97). *(Ⓜ Bastille.)*

JULY COLUMN. The column topped by the conspicuous gold cupid at the center of pl. de la Bastille is not connected to the storming of the Bastille. It was erected by King Louis-Philippe in 1831 to commemorate Republicans who died in the *Trois Glorieuses*, three-days of street fighting in July 1830. Victims of the Revolution of February 1848 were subsequently buried here, along with two mummified Egyptian pharaohs. The column is not open to the public. *(⑩ Bastille. In the center of pl. de la Bastille.)*

RUE DE LA ROQUETTE. Quieter than its neighbor, the buzzing r. de Lappe, the winding r. de la Roquette does have some hidden gems. This 17th-century byway was home to poet Paul Verlaine, who lived at no. 17, and is now lined with off-beat cafes, bars, creative boutiques, an avant-garde church, and countless restaurants serving everything from Italian to Thai food. The charming **square de la Roquette** is an ideal endpoint to a stroll along this multi-faceted street. *(⑩ Bastille-Voltaire.)*

TWELFTH ARRONDISSEMENT

The 12*ème* boasts giant monoliths of modern architecture, like the **Opéra Bastille** and the **Palais Omnisports.** Most of the construction is practical and commercial, as befits the working-class background of the arrondissement, but a bit of old-fashioned charm can be seen in the Viaduc des Arts near the Bastille.

see map p. 371

AROUND PLACE DE LA BASTILLE

OPÉRA BASTILLE. President Mitterand made a bold move when he plunked the Opéra Bastille down in the working-class neighborhood around **Place de la Bastille.** The building was engineered by Carlos Ott, a Uruguayan architect, and it opened on July 14, 1989 (the bicentennial of the Revolution) to protests over its unattractive and dubious design (nets still surround parts of the building to catch falling tiles). The "People's Opera" has been described as a huge toilet because of its resemblance to the coin-operated *pissoirs* on the streets of Paris. However, the opera has not struck a completely sour note, as it has helped renew local interest in the arts. The guided tour (expensive but extremely interesting) offers a behind-the-scenes view of the largest theater in the world. The immense granite and glass auditorium, which seats 2703, comprises only 5% of the building's surface area. The rest of the opera houses exact replicas of the stage (for rehearsal purposes) and workshops for both the Bastille and Garnier operas. The building employs almost 1000 people, from technies to actors to administrators to wig- and shoe-makers. *(130, r. de Lyon. ⑩ Bastille. Look for the words "Billeterie" on the building. ☎01 40 01 19 70; www.operadeparis.fr. 1hr. tour almost every day, usually at 1 or 5pm; call ahead for schedule. Tours are in French, but groups of 15 or more can arrange for English. €11, over 60 and students €9, under 18 €6. For concert info, see Entertainment, p. 279.)*

VIADUC DES ARTS AND PROMENADE PLANTÉE. The *ateliers* in the **Viaduc des Arts** house artisans who make everything from *haute couture* fabric to hand-painted porcelain to space-age furniture. Restorators of all types fill the arches of the old railway viaduct, and they can make your oil painting, 12th-century book, grandmother's linen, or childhood dollhouse as good as new. Interspersed among the stores are gallery spaces that are rented by new artists each month (see **Museums,** p. 264). High above the avenue, on the "roof" of the viaduct, runs the lovely, rose-filled **Promenade Plantée,** Paris's skinniest park. It is ideal for a Sunday afternoon stroll among the rooftops. *(9-129, av. Daumesnil. ⑩ Bastille. The viaduct extends from r. de Lyon to r. de Charenton. Entrances to the Promenade are at Ledru Rollin,*

Hector Malot, and bd. Diderot. www.viaduc-des-arts.com. Park opens M-F 8am, Sa-Su 9am; closing hours vary, around 5:30pm in winter and 9:30pm in summer. Stores open M-Sa; hours vary, with many taking a 2-hr. lunch break at noon.)

ELSEWHERE IN THE TWELFTH

BERCY QUARTER. East of the **Gare de Lyon,** the Bercy quarter has seen rapid construction, beginning with Mitterrand's **Ministère des Finances** building, a modern monolith to match the Bibliothèque across the river. Sit in one of the many new cafes and *brasseries* along the **rue de Bercy** and ogle the mammoth grass-and-glass **Palais Omnisports** concert and sports complex. Each of its sloping sides, which local youth and the occasional tourist try (unsuccessfully) to scale, is covered in green grass. The **Parc de Bercy** is not quite the calming getaway some visitors may seek, thanks to uneasy manmade details like its perfectly calibrated hills. A lovelier (and less weird) site is the **Yitzhak Rabin Garden** at the eastern edges of the park, with rose arbors, grape vines, an herb garden, and a playground dedicated to the Nobel Prize-winning Prime Minister of Israel.

To top off this bizarre 21st-century construct, **Frank Gehry** added one of his psychedelic, turreted buildings at **no. 51, rue de Bercy,** to be dedicated to the history of cinema. To one side of the park is what used to be Paris's wine depot; the rows of former wine storage buildings have now been converted into a Club Med (Ⓜ Cour St-Emilion). The club cafes lining Cour St-Emilion are cute in a rather contrived way; one even has hammocks outside instead of chairs. The Cour is jammed with tourists and locals in the summer. *(Ⓜ Bercy.)*

THIRTEENTH ARRONDISSEMENT

The 13*ème*, while not richly endowed with *hôtels particuliers,* has plenty of diverse neighborhoods ranging from historic to ethnic. A self-proclaimed colorful Chinatown lies paces away from the working-class **Butte-aux-Cailles.** This *arrondissement* is a delightful, often overlooked mixed bag of sights that offers an ungilded glimpse of Parisian life.

see map p. 374

MANUFACTURE DES GOBELINS. The Manufacture des Gobelins, a tapestry workshop over 300 years old, is all that is left of the 13*ème*'s manufacturing past. Established in 1662 by Henri IV for his imported Flemish tapestry artists, the Gobelins produced the priceless 17th-century tapestries now displayed in the Musée de Cluny (see **Museums,** p. 254). Still an adjunct of the state, the factory receives commissions from French ministries and foreign embassies. The tours are great if you have an interest in the intricacies of weaving: you can actually see the artists at work during each step of the process. Tours are the only way inside the Gobelins, but it's under construction until early 2007. Tour information subject to change; call for more information. *(42, av. des Gobelins. ☎01 44 08 52 00 or 01 44 54 19 33. Ⓜ Gobelins. 1½hr. tours in French Tu-Th 2 and 2:45pm; arrive 30min. in advance. Call in advance for group tours in English. €8, ages 7-25 €6, under 7 free.)*

QUARTIER DE LA BUTTE-AUX-CAILLES. The Butte-aux-Cailles (Quail Knoll) district is like a mini-village in the heart of the big city, with old-fashioned lampposts and cobblestone streets. Historically a working-class neighborhood, the Butte-aux-Cailles has a long-standing tradition of defiance. The area was one of the first to fight during the Revolution of 1848, and 120 years later it was the unofficial headquarters of the *soixante-huitards,* the student and intellectual activists behind the 1968 riots in Paris. **Rue de la Butte-aux-Cailles** and **rue des Cinq Diamants** share duties as the *quartier*'s main drags. Funky new restaurants and drinking holes have cropped up amongst the old standards, the Butte's cooperative bar **La Folie en Tête** (see **Nightlife,** p. 316), and the intellectual hang-out **Le Temps des Cerises** (see **Food,** p. 172). The nascent gentrification of the entire *arrondissement* has attracted trendsetters, artists, and intellectuals to this area, but, luckily for long-time residents, this process is still slow-moving. *(Ⓜ Corvisart. Exit onto bd. Blanqui, and turn onto r. Barrault, which will meet r. de la Butte-aux-Cailles.)*

EGLISE STE-ANNE DE LA BUTTE-AUX-CAILLES. This Byzantine church owes its completion to the Lombard family who, in 1898, donated funds from their chocolate store on av. de Choisy to finish it. The front of the church is nicknamed *la façade chocolat* in their honor. *(188, r. de Tolbiac. ☎ 01 45 89 34 73. Ⓜ Tolbiac. Open daily 9am-7:30pm. Mass M 7pm, Tu and Th 9am and 7pm, W and F 9am and noon, Sa 9am and 6pm, Su 9, 10:30am, and 6:30pm.)*

CHINATOWN (QUARTIER CHINOIS). Paris's Chinatown lies in the area bounded by r. de Tolbiac, bd. Massena, av. de Choisy, and av. d'Ivry. It is home to large Chinese, Vietnamese, and Cambodian communities, and to a host of Asian restaurants, shops, and markets like Tang Frères (**Food,** p. 172). Chinatown offers fascinating window-shopping along av. de Choisy and av. d'Ivry: beautiful embroidered shoes and dresses, elegant chopstick sets, ceramic Buddha statuettes, and exotic fruits and vegetables. *(Ⓜ Porte d'Ivry, Porte de Choisy, Tolbiac, or Maison Blanche are all near Chinatown.)*

BIBLIOTHÈQUE NATIONALE DE FRANCE: SITE FRANÇOIS MITTERRAND. Opened in 1996, the Bibliothèque de France is the last and most expensive of Mitterrand's *grands projets*. Because construction was hurried in order to complete the building before Mitterrand's death (so he could have the building named after him), it never fully realized its original design. The Site Mitterrand was built to accommodate the ever-increasing number of books housed in the old Bibliothèque Nationale in the *2ème*—since 1642, every book published in France has been required to enter the library's national archives. Most of the Bibliothèque Nationale's 12 million volume collection, including Gutenberg Bibles and first editions dating back to the 15th century, has been transferred to the Site Mitterrand. The L-shaped towers of Dominique Perrault's controversial design are meant to look like open books from above. Inside, the modern building features grand reading rooms, which look out on a dense courtyard of man-made woodland. Multiple galleries show temporary multimedia exhibits on various themes in French history. On sunny days, visitors gaze on views of the Seine from the multitude of stairs that surrounds the building. The MK2 cultural center is an offshoot from the library complex that features a cinema, music library, and numerous airy and modern eateries for a range of budgets. *(Quai F. Mauriac. ☎ 01 53 79 59 79; www.bnf.fr. Ⓜ Quai de la Gare or Bibliothèque François Mitterrand. Reception open M 2-7pm, Tu-Sa 9am-7pm, Su 1-7pm; closed 1st-3rd Su of Sept. Open to those over the age of 16. €3.50. Annual membership €35, €18 for students. MC/V.)*

FOURTEENTH ARRONDISSEMENT

see map p. 376

CIMETIÈRE MONTPARNASSE. The beautiful Montparnasse Cemetery, which sits in the shadow of the less aesthetically pleasing Tour Montparnasse (see p. 223), opened in 1824. It serves as the burial grounds for some of the city's most famous and fashionable former residents. Inhabitants include characters as diverse as Jean-Paul Sartre, Alfred Dreyfus, and Andre Citroën (of angst, Affair, and automobile fame, respectively). The main entrance is off bd. Edgar Quinet. Free maps of the grounds show the locations of celebrities and indicate what brought them to fame. Devotees of hard-living singer-songwriter Serge Gainsbourg have left cigarettes, beer bottle caps, metro tickets, and flowers on his modest concrete tomb. Also buried here are Samuel Beckett, Simone de Beauvoir, Emile Durkheim, Charles Baudelaire, Eugène Ionesco, Marguerite Duras, Robert Desnos, Guy de Maupassant, and sculptors Constantin Brancusi and Frédéric Bartholdi (who designed the Statue of Liberty as well as the imposing lion at nearby pl. Denfert-Rochereau). Cimetière Montparnasse is still an active cemetery, so please be respectful of other visitors. *3, bd. Edgar Quinet.* Ⓜ *Edgar Quinet. With your back to Café Odessa, walk to your left down bd. Quinet, and the cemetery will be on your right, opposite sq. Delambre.* ☎*01 44 10 86 50. Open Apr.-Oct. M-F 8am-6pm, Sa 8:30am-6pm, Su and holidays 9am-6pm; Nov-Mar open daily until 5:30 pm.*

CATACOMBS. A lion sculpted by Bartholdi in commemoration of *La Défense Nationale* of 1870-1871 presides over the intersection of six avenues at pl. Denfert-Rochereau. Visitors might observe Bartholdi's Leo while they wait in line to visit the catacombs, a series of tunnels 20m below ground and 1.7km in length. They were originally excavated to provide stone for the construction of the city, but by the 1770s, much of the Left Bank was in danger of caving in, and digging had to be stopped. The former quarry was turned into a mass grave a decade later in order to relieve the stench of Paris's extremely insalubrious *Cimetière des Innocents*. The entrance warns "Stop! Beyond Here Is the Empire of Death." In 1793, a hapless Parisian got lost and became a permanent resident, so stick to the tour. During WWII, the Resistance set up headquarters among the departed, and rumor has it that a group of young Parisians, called cataphiles, prowls around here these days in a radical kind of urban exploration. The catacombs are like an underground city, with street names on walls lined with the femurs and craniums of almost six million ex-Parisians. Taller visitors should expect to spend much of the visit crouching beneath very low ceilings. Be warned that the catacombs are dark, chilly, and damp, and the morbid proverbs carved into the walls will hardly warm you up. Arriving before 2pm is recommended because the lines are sometimes long. The catacombs are not recommended for the faint of heart or leg: there are 83 steep steps to climb on the way out. Visitors brave enough to venture beneath the city will be rewarded with a one-of-a-kind experience. *1, av. du Colonel Henri Rol-Tanguy* Ⓜ *Denfert-Rochereau. Take exit pl. Denfert-Rochereau, and cross av. du Colonel Henri Rol-Tanguy with the lion on your left. The entrance is the dark green structure straight ahead.* ☎*01 43 22 47 63; www.catacombes.paris.fr. Open Tu-Su 10am-4pm. Tour lasts 45-60min. Exits at 36 r. Rémy-Dumoncel, 2 blocks to the right at av. du Général Leclerc is* Ⓜ *Mouton Duvernet. €5, seniors €3.30, ages 14-26 €2.50, under 14 free.*

CITÉ UNIVERSITAIRE. Cité Universitaire is home to upwards of 5600 students from 122 countries. It was built and still serves as a purely residential campus for students and university affiliates from all nations who want to study in Paris. The **Maison Internationale,** near the main entrance, is the center of Cité, and its topiary mazes and high *mansarde* roofs are modeled on the Chateau de Fontainebleau. The building's old marble halls house the information center and cafeteria for the Cité, where visitors and residents alike can grab a quick bite. The houses (*résidences*) all have distinct personalities, mostly reflecting something cultural of the country they represent. Though the houses are closed to the public, the grounds are free for exploration during the day. The **Fondation Deutsch de la Meurthe** is the oldest *résidence*. More modern and architecturally innovative houses like Le Corbusier's **Pavillon Suisse** (1932) and **Maison du Brésil** (1959) can be found at the eastern end of the Cité. The former reflects the architect's dream of a vertical city, and its roof garden housed anti-aircraft guns during WWII. At the other end of the park lies the delightful **Maison de l'Asie du Sud-Est,** with its quintessentially Asian design. Behind the Maison Internationale, you'll find people picnicking, playing soccer and practicing Tai Chi on the *Grande Pelouse* (Big Lawn). Add a frisbee and some Birkenstocks, and you're back in the US. (*Main entrance 17, bd. Jourdain.* Ⓜ *Porte d'Orléans. Take one of the pl.*

du 25 Août 1944 exits and walk down bd. Jourdain past intersection with r. E. Faguet. RER: Cité Universitaire. Bus #88: Porte d'Arcueil. With your back to r. E.D. de la Meurthe, walk down bd. Jourdain. Guided tours start at the Maison Internationale. For information about staying at the Cité Universitaire, call the Administrative Office ☎01 44 16 64 48; www.ciup.fr. Free. Open daily 7am-10pm. Lunch or dinner €4-10.)

BOULEVARD DU MONTPARNASSE. In the early 20th century, Montparnasse became a center for avant-garde artists like Picasso, Chagall, Modigliani, and Utrillo, many of whom moved from Montmartre to escape rising rents. Political exiles Lenin and Trotsky talked strategy over cognac in the cafes along bd. Montparnasse, including **Le Dôme**, **Le Sélect**, and **La Coupole**. After WWI, the *quartier* attracted American expatriates and artistic rebels like Calder, Hemingway, and Henry Miller. WWII, however, ended the area's bohemian golden age. Montparnasse has since seen heavy commercialization. Chain stores and tourists now crowd the boulevard, but the handful of classic restaurants that have weathered the years still offer a place to sip a *café express*, read Apollinaire, and sigh longingly. (ⓜ *Montparnasse-Bienvenüe or Vavin.*)

FIFTEENTH ARRONDISSEMENT

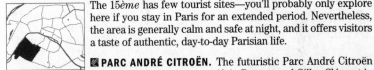

The 15*ème* has few tourist sites—you'll probably only explore here if you stay in Paris for an extended period. Nevertheless, the area is generally calm and safe at night, and it offers visitors a taste of authentic, day-to-day Parisian life.

■ PARC ANDRÉ CITROËN. The futuristic Parc André Citroën **see map p. 375** was created by landscapers Alain Provost and Gilles Clément in the 1970s. These two men were not afraid to use concrete in their designs, but the park is still a lovely place to spend a summer afternoon. Rides in the hot-air balloon that launches from the central garden offer spectacular aerial views of the park and all of Paris (see **Up, Up, and Away,** p. 224). The six gardens alongside the Seine contain a variety of fountains, huge glass greenhouses, and a wild plant exhibit whose inhabitants changes from one year to the next. On sunny days, the grassy expanses of the park are crowded with sunbathers and picnickers of all ages. (*2, r. de la Montagne de la Fage.* ⓜ *Javel or Balard.* ☎*01 44 26 20 00; www.aeroparis.com. Open daily 9am-9:30pm throughout the summer. 10min balloon rides €12, ages 12-17 €10, ages 3-11 €6, under 3 free on weekends and holidays; €10/9/5/free on other days.*)

INSTITUT PASTEUR. Founded by the French scientist Louis Pasteur in 1887, the Institut Pasteur is now a center for biochemical research, development, and treatment. It was here that Pasteur, a champion of 19th-century germ theory, developed pasteurization, a technique for purifying milk products and beer. The institute has turned Pasteur's somber but magnificent home into a museum. Inside, the very instruments with which the scientist discovered a vaccine for anthrax and the cure for rabies will impress even the least scientifically minded visitors. The grand portraits of Pasteur and his family, including several painted by a teenage Louis, offer a closer look at his life, as do the meticulously preserved rooms. It was also here in 1983 that Dr. Luc Montaigner and Robert Gallo first isolated HIV. Pasteur's tomb, an awesome marble and mosaic construction, is also open to visitors as part of the short (45min.) museum tour. (*25, r. du Docteur Roux.* ⓜ *Pasteur. Walk uphill on bd. Pasteur; r. du Docteur Roux is the 1st right.* ☎*01 45 68 82 83; www.pasteur.fr. Before entering the museum, you must obtain a name tag from the small office across from the institute. Open Sept.-July M-F 2-5:30pm. Admission €3, students €1.50. Guided tours in English easily arranged; just ask at reception.*)

TOUR MONTPARNASSE. The modern Montparnasse Tower dominates the 15ème's northeast corner. Standing 59 stories tall and completed in 1973, the building looks jarringly out of place amid Montparnasse's otherwise sedate

THE HIDDEN DEAL

UP, UP, AND AWAY!

Looking out over the expanse of Paris from the top of the Eiffel Tower is a tourist rite of passage. For those more in the know, the view from the Tour Montparnasse offers a similar, less tourist-crammed experience. But the best and most thrilling view comes floating 150m above the French capital in a *mongolfière*, or hot-air balloon.

The Montgolfier brothers launched the first manned hot-air balloon in 1783 in Paris. Earlier in the year, the brothers had run a trial demonstration out at Versailles, loading the craft with a sheep, a duck, and a cockerel to prove to Louis XVI that flight could be safe. A few months later, with the king's permission, Pilâtre de Rozier and the Marquis d'Arlande became the first humans to drift over Paris, at a height of about 100m. It's a fitting nod to tradition to take the trip skyward in the birthplace of human flight.

From the Parc André Citroën, a *mongolfière* takes off every 10min., carrying 8-25 people (capacity depends on wind conditions). For a unique and unforgettable view of Paris, thrill seekers should not miss this. *(Parc André Citroën, 2, r. de la Montagne de la Fage, 15ème (☎01 44 26 20 00; www.aeroparis.com).* Ⓜ *Javel-André Citroën or Balard. Balloon rides €12, ages 12-17 €10, ages 3-11 €6, under 3 free.)*

19th-century architecture. The structure, frequently maligned as an eyesore, spoils countless of Baron Haussmann's carefully considered vistas. Shortly after it was erected, the city forbade the construction of similar monstrosities, designating the outer reaches of the La Défense district (p. 240) as the sole home for future gratte-ciels. For an open-air view of Paris that rivals that from the Eiffel Tower—and lacks the walls of tourists—ride Europe's fastest elevator past 52 floors of office space to the 56th floor, then climb three flights to the rooftop, 207m above the city. After all, this is the only vantage point in Paris from which you don't have to look at the the tower itself. Historical photographs and maps (inside on the 56th floor) help you locate landmarks. On your way down, stop for a meal at Ciel on the 56th floor if you're in the mood for a splurge with a view. Great views but ridiculous prices. *(33, av. du Maine.* Ⓜ *Montparnasse-Bienvenüe. Entrance on r. de l'Arrivée. ☎01 45 38 52 56, Ciel 01 40 64 77 64. Tower open May-Sept. daily 9:30am-11:30pm; Oct.-Apr. M-F 9:30am-10:30pm. Ciel open daily 8:30am-11pm, bar open until 1am. Admission €8.70, student €6.50, ages 7-15 €4.)*

LA RUCHE. Although La Ruche is **not open to visitors,** modern art buffs may still find it interesting. The building was originally constructed as a wine pavilion by Gustave Eiffel for the 1900 World's Fair. Sculptor Albert Boucher then bought the pavilion and converted it into a studio and quasi-artists' colony. The building is called "The Beehive" for its round shape, and its triangular cells prompted resident Ossip Zadkine to call it "a sinister wheel of brie." Over the years, La Ruche provided workspace for Chagall, Soutine, Léger, and countless others, whom Boucher called *ses abeilles* (his bees). Today, the Fondation La Ruche offers grants, studios, and housing to young artists. *(52, r. de Dantzig; on the passage de Dantzig.* Ⓜ *Convention. Follow r. de la Convention toward pl. Charles Vallin; r. de Dantzig will be on the right.)*

SIXTEENTH ARRONDISSEMENT

The stately avenues of the 16ème harbor peaceful parks and lovely architectural gems away from the rush of the central arrondissements. Although bustling around Trocadéro, this otherwise calm

see map p. 378 and leisurely neighborhood offers a delicious glimpse into the daily life of Parisians.

TROCADÉRO AND SURROUNDINGS

PLACE D'IÉNA. The pl. d'Iéna positions you next to the rotunda of the **Conseil Economique** and in front of a sweep of popular museums, including the round Palladian facade of the **Musée Guimet,** which houses an outstanding collection of Asian art. It is a 5min. walk west to the Trocadéro and 5min. east to the museums of the **Palais de Tokyo** (see **Museums,** p. 267). (Ⓜ *Iéna.*)

PALAIS DE TOKYO. Built for the 1937 World Expo, the austere, neoclassical Palais is home to the world-class **Musée d'Art Moderne de la Ville de Paris** (see **Museums,** p. 267), which re-opened in 2006 after two years of renovation. The west wing of the Palais houses the excellent **site de création contemporaine,** which exhibits today's hottest (and most controversial) art. *(11, av. du Président Wilson.* Ⓜ *Iéna.)*

PALAIS GALLIERA. This elegant Italianate structure houses the **Musée de la Mode et du Costume** (see **Museums,** p. 267). Completed in 1892, the Palais was originally conceived as a repository for the Duchess of Galliera's sizable collection of Italian Baroque art, although the works were eventually sent to Genoa instead. *(Across from the Palais de Tokyo.* Ⓜ *Iéna.)*

PLACE DU TROCADÉRO. This square was christened in the 1820s by the Duc d'Angoulême as a memorial to his military victory at the Spanish fortress of Trocadéro. It is flanked by the two colonnaded wings of the **Palais de Chaillot** and centers around a group of spectacular, cannon-shaped fountains. Enigmatic gold inscriptions by Paul Valéry claim, among other things, that "the hand of the artist is equal and rival to thoughts of the artist, and each is nothing without the other." Surveyed by Henri Bouchard's 7.5m bronze *Apollo* and eight other figures, the terrace attracts hordes of tourists who come to survey the panoramic views of the Eiffel Tower and Champs de Mars. Be aware of pickpockets and traffic as you gaze upward. (Ⓜ *Trocadéro.*)

PALAIS DE CHAILLOT. The Palais de Chaillot houses the **Musée de l'Homme,** the **Musée de la Marine** (see **Museums,** p. 268), and the **Théâtre National de Chaillot** (see **Entertainment,** p. 276). It is the last of a series of buildings on the site: Catherine de Médicis had a château here, which was transformed into a convent by Queen Henrietta of England. Napoleon razed the convent and planned a palace for his son, but rotten luck at Waterloo brought construction to a halt. The building's current incarnation was conceived by architect Jacques Carlu for the 1937 World's Fair. His design, which beat out Le Corbusier's in a contest for the commission, is unusual for its lack of a central rotunda. *(17, pl. de Trocadéro.)*

JARDINS DU TROCADÉRO. Below the palace, the green swaths of the Jardins du Trocadéro stretch to the banks of the Seine. The gardens offer a stunning picnic spot, a ride on a two-storied **carousel** (€2) in the pl. de Varsovie, and at night, an incredible view of the Eiffel Tower. In the summer, children frolic in the wide, cool fountains. The unlit parts of the garden are best avoided after dark.

CIMETIÈRE DE PASSY. You can catch a tourist-free (if somewhat obscured) glimpse of the Eiffel Tower from the Passy Cemetery, located diagonally opposite the Palais de Chaillot. The hilly grotto that overhangs pl. du Trocadéro is a pleasant place to wander, listen to the sounds of street performers below, and gaze out over the 16*ème*'s array of stately buildings. Art aficionados can pay homage to painters Edouard Manet and Berthe Morisot and composers Claude Débussy and Gabriel Fauré. The enormous wall that holds up the cemetery on the Trocadéro side was designed in the same Neoclassical style as the Palais de Chaillot. *(2, r. du Commandant-Schloesing.* Ⓜ *Trocadéro.* ☎ *01 47 27 07 56. Walk toward the far wing of the Palais de Chaillot,* *turn right on av. Paul Doumer, and veer right onto r. du Commandant-Schloesing. Open Mar. 16-Nov. 5 M-F 8am-6pm, Sa 8:30am-6pm, Su 9am-6pm; Nov. 6-Mar. 15 M-F 8am-5:30pm, Sa 8:30am-5:30pm, Su 9am-5:30pm. Last entry 15min. before closing. Conservation office open M-F 8:30am-12:30pm, 2-5pm.)*

PASSY AND AUTEUIL

Located southwest of Trocadéro, **Passy** and **Auteuil** were once famous for their restorative waters (which attracted such visitors as Molière, Racine, and Proust) and later for their avant-garde architecture. Now, this famous pair of ex-hamlets is best known as the site where *Last Tango in Paris* was filmed, and as a pricey shopping district. The glitziest in glamour-wear is around the intersection of **rue Passy, rue Mozart,** and **avenue Paul Doumer,** near Ⓜ La Muette. The narrow, winding streets named after famous composers, writers, and artists (Guy de Maupassant, Nicolas Poussin, Donizetti) recall 18th-century *salon* culture and are ripe for free-style exploration on foot. **No. 59, rue d'Auteuil** was the site of Mme. Helvetius's house, where the so-called "Notre Dame d'Auteuil" hosted the Right Bank's well-read and best-dressed at her notorious *salons*.

RUE LA FONTAINE. Its name comes from the sulphurous thermal spring that brought the residents of Auteuil their water, but since the late 19th century, r. la Fontaine has been most famous for its Belle Epoque architecture. Many of the neighborhood's buildings flaunt the designs of Art Nouveau master Hector Guimard. **Castel Béranger** (1898), at no. 14, launched Guimard's career—look for the turquoise iron flourishes, carbuncular seahorses, and columns bulging with floral sea-growth. The red-paneled **Bar Antoine** at no. 17 (1911) has a painted-glass ceiling and is decorated with Art Nouveau tiles. Guimard designed the vine-entangled street signs of **rue Agar,** off r. la Fontaine, as well as the the gnarled iron "branches" of the fence at no. 60 (1911), which now houses the **Ministère de l'Education Nationale.** Proust fans will want to pause at no. 96, where the writer was born on July 10, 1871; look above the first-floor window for the information plaque. *(Ⓜ Michel-Ange Auteuil, Jasmin, or Eglise d'Auteuil, or RER Kennedy. R. la Fontaine extends from the intersection at Ⓜ Michel-Ange Auteuil to the Maison de Radio France, where it turns into r. Raynouard.)*

PLACE D'AUTEUIL. The eclectic **Eglise Notre Dame d'Auteuil,** a Romanesque-Byzantine amalgam of a church, stands at the center of this jumbled intersection. The *place* is surrounded by tempting *traiteurs*, prime for impromptu lunch spreads in the village-style square. *(Ⓜ Eglise d'Auteuil.)*

RUE BENJAMIN FRANKLIN. Rue Benjamin Franklin commemorates the statesman's one-time residence in Passy. Franklin lived at 66, r. Raynouard from 1777 to 1785 while negotiating a treaty between the newly formed US and Louis XVI. The present building was erected long after his stay, but it was on this site that Franklin experimented with his electrifying lightning rod. A statue of Franklin presides opposite the entrance to Cimetière de Passy. *(Ⓜ Passy. After exiting, take r. de l'Albinoni straight up and turn right onto r. Benjamin Franklin, past bd. Pelessert.)*

STATUE OF LIBERTY. On a manmade islet in the middle of the Seine, the **Allée des Cygnes,** stands a very miniature version of the very grand Lady Liberty of New York fame. This version of the monument, by French sculptor Frédéric Bartholdi, was donated by a group of American expats in 1885 and was moved to this spot for the 1889 World's Fair. A wide, paved pedestrian path runs through the shady, sandy island; it is ideal for jogging or wandering, but *Let's Go* advises caution after dark. *(Ⓜ Passy or Mirabeau. From Passy, walk down r. de l'Albinoni toward the Seine and cross av. du Président Kennedy onto the Pont Bir-Hakeim. From Mirabeau, Walk on av.*

de Versailles toward the Eiffel Tower and turn right on the Pont de Grenelle. Fr.
access to the Allée des Cygnes is available.)

JARDIN DE RANELAGH. The lovely Jardin de Ranelagh has playgrounds,
puppets, and donkey rides. The people-watching is excellent: this is v
wealthy residents of the 16ème come out to play. The well-maintained green sp.
perfect for a romantic picnic after a day of sightseeing. (Ⓜ *La Muette. Head away from*
the Eiffel Tower down Chaussée de la Muette, which becomes the pedestrian av. Ranelagh.)

SEVENTEENTH ARRONDISSEMENT

Because the western half of the 17ème is primarily residential,
visitors will find more to do if they stick to the eastern Village
Batignolles area. It's a great place for a leisurely stroll, bargain
shopping, or a stop at the stately cemetery.

see map p. 379

VILLAGE BATIGNOLLES

The Village Batignolles, in the eastern half of the 17ème, is an old-fashioned,
working-class neighborhood of shops and residences. It centers around **rue des
Batignolles,** stretching from bd. des Batignolles at the southern end to **place du Dr.
Félix Lobligeois.** The *place* affords excellent people-watching, with a cluster of hip
cafes overlooking the greenery-filled town square. Just north of the *place,* the
craggy waterfalls and duck ponds of the English-style park, **square des Batignolles,**
recall its more famous neighbor to the south, the Parc Monceau (p. 214). The
meticulously landscaped oasis is among the loveliest parks in Paris; its compact
size is perfect for a *petite promenade.* It was from the park's western end that
Monet painted his train tracks running from the Gare St-Lazare. To the west, **rue
des Dames** is lined with restaurants and cafes, and **rue de Lévis** with shops (Ⓜ Villiers). On the other side of r. des Batignolles, at **rue Lemercier** between r. Clairaut
and r. des Moines (Ⓜ Brochant), is a daily covered market filled with meats,
cheeses, flowers, produce, and old women who have shopped here since WWII. **La
Cité des Fleurs,** 59-61, r. de la Jonquière (at the intersection with r. des Epinettes),
is a row of exquisite private homes and gardens that look like they were lifted out
of a Balzac novel. Designed in 1847, this prototypical condominium required each
owner to plant at least three trees in the gardens.

CIMETIÈRE DES BATIGNOLLES. The Cimetière des Batignolles, sandwiched
between a noisy *lycée* and the car horns of the Périphérique, is surprisingly serene,
given its surroundings. André Breton, Paul Verlaine, and Benjamin Peret are buried here. (*8, r. St-Just.* Ⓜ *Port-de-Clichy. Walk north along av. Port-de-Clichy and turn right onto
av. du Cimetière des Batignolles.* ☎*01 46 27 03 18. Open Mar. 6 to Nov. 5 M-F 8am-6pm, Sa
8:30am-6pm and Su and holidays 9am-6pm; Nov. 6 to Mar. 15 M-F 8am-5:30pm, Sa 8:30am-
5:30pm, Su and holidays 9am-5:30pm. Last entry 15min. before closing. Free.)*

EIGHTEENTH ARRONDISSEMENT

Montmartre is one of the most lively, captivating, and bohemian
areas in Paris. Because the secret of its allure has gotten out,
however, it's also one of the most touristed. Plan to spend at
least a day and an evening here; the 18ème has enough nooks
and crannies to keep you entertained for some time.

see map p. 368-369

MOUNTING MONTMARTRE

One does not merely visit Montmartre; one climbs it. The standard approach is
from the south, via Ⓜ Anvers or Ⓜ Abbesses, although other directions provide

...teresting, less crowded climbs. From Ⓜ Anvers, the walk up r. Steinkerque to the ornate, switchbacked stairway is short but often overcrowded. The longer but more peaceful climb from Ⓜ Abbesses (fans may recognize this as Amélie's metro stop) passes by more worthwhile cafes and shops. Particularly feisty travelers up for a physical challenge should note that Ⓜ Abbesses is also the metro stop with the most steps to its exit, lying 30m. below ground. The walls around the spiral stairway are covered in graffiti, which can provide interesting reading if you need to take a break from the climb. For children, the infirm, and the lazy, the glass-covered **funiculaire** from the base of r. Tardieu offers a painless ascent (from Ⓜ Anvers, walk up r. Steinkerque and take a left on r. Tardieu). Something like a ski lift, it is operated by the RATP and you can ride it with a normal metro ticket.

The **Syndicat d'Initiative de Montmartre** offers 2hr. walking tours of the historic district of Montmartre (€10). Call ahead to join a group for a tour, or organize one of your own if you have a group of 20 or more. The tours offer a unique perspective into some of the less touristed parts of the *butte*, and run in a number of languages. The Syndicat is located in pl. du Tertre (☎01 42 62 21 21). *(Funicular runs cars up and down the hill every 2min. Open 6am-12:40am. €1.50 or metro ticket.)*

BASILIQUE DU SACRÉ-COEUR. Sacré-Coeur is one of Paris's most divisive monuments, politically and architecturally: natives either love it or hate it. Politician Eugène Spuller rightly described the basilica as "a monument to civil war." In 1873, in yet another episode of strife between the supporters and detractors of the 1789 Revolution, the reactionary Assemblée Nationale selected the birthplace of the Paris Commune (see **Life and Times,** p. 65) as the location for Sacré-Coeur, "in witness of repentance and as a symbol of hope." Needless to say, the government of Adolphe Thiers was not repenting for the massacre of 25,000 citizens in the suppression of the Commune, but for the fact that the Commune—and indeed the French Revolution—had occurred in the first place. After a massive fundraising effort, the basilica was completed in 1914 and consecrated in 1919.

Parisians are also divided over the architecture of Sacré-Coeur. Its unusual onion domes, arches, and white color set it apart from the drab grey of most of Paris's buildings. The mosaics inside the basilica are striking, especially the depiction of Christ on the ceiling and the mural of the Passion at the back of the altar. Beneath the basilica, the crypt contains what many believe to be a piece of the sacred heart of Christ. The narrow climb up to the top of the dome offers the highest vantage point in all of Paris and a view that stretches as far as 50km on clear days (although, beware: crowds come with the clear sky). While it's worth climbing the grassy slopes beneath the cathedral for the view, the streets leading up to them are horribly over-touristed. Committed lefties who feel queasy looking at the Basilica can walk over to the west and visit the statue of the Chevalier de la Barre, who had his tongue ripped out and his hands cut off, and was burned alive in 1766 for singing sacreligious songs and refusing to doff his hat to a religious procession. *(35, r. du Chevalier-de-la-Barre. Ⓜ Anvers, Abbesses, or Château-Rouge. ☎01 53 41 89 00. Open daily 6am-11pm. Wheelchair accessible through the back. Free. Dome open daily 9am-6pm. €5. Crypt open periodically; call ahead for details.)*

AU LAPIN AGILE. The Lapin Agile cabaret is still going strong amidst the now-shuttered houses of Montmartre. A favorite of Verlaine, Renoir, Modigliani, and Max Jacob, the establishment was known as the "Cabaret des Assassins" until André Gill decorated its facade with a painting of a *lapin* (rabbit) balancing a hat on its head and a bottle on its paw. The cabaret immediately gained renown as the "Lapin à Gill" (Gill's rabbit). By the time Picasso began to frequent the establishment, walking over from his studio at no. 49, r. Gabrielle, the name had contracted to the "Lapin Agile." Today, the cabaret is a very touristy spot, but you can still sip a *cerises maison* (€7) while taking in a mix of French *chanson* and comedy (see

Entertainment, p. 277). *(22, r. des Saules. ⓜ Lamarck-Caulaincourt. Walk right on r. Lamarck and turn right onto r. des Saules. ☎01 46 06 85 87; www.au-lapin-agile.com. Call for reservations. M-F and Su entrance and 1 drink €24, students under 26 €17. Shows start daily at 9pm and go until 2am. Knock on the door if you arrive after 9pm.)*

BATEAU-LAVOIR. Given its name by sardonic residents Max Jacob and André Salmon, who thought the building's winding corridors resembled the interior of a ship *(bateau)*, the Bateau-Lavoir has been home to several artists' *ateliers* since the turn of the century. Though it still serves as studio space for 25 contemporary painters and sculptors, the building's undisputed heyday was in the first quarter of the 20th century, when great artists like Picasso, Modigliani, Juan Gris, and Max Jacob (among others) stayed there. In his studio here in 1907, Picasso finished his Cubist manifesto, the remarkable *Demoiselles d'Avignon*. Sadly, the original building burned down in 1970, but a display to the left of the gate chronicles the site's history and residents. *(11bis, pl. Emile Godeau. ⓜ Abbesses. Facing the church, head right up r. des Abbesses, and turn right, uphill, on r. Ravignan; follow the steps to pl. Emile Godeau. Closed to the public.)*

LES VIGNES. In the 16th century, the Montmartre vineyards were known for the diuretic wines they produced: a 17th-century saying even promises, "C'est du vin de Montmartre, qui en boit pinte en pisse quarte" (With Montmartre wine, he who drinks a pint pisses a quart). Now this lone surviving winery, perched on the hilly slope across from the Lapin Agile, is one of the few remaining vineyards in all of Paris. The *vignes* of Montmartre have remained intact more for tradition than function (they produce only a few dozen bottles of wine per year), and every October, the vineyard hosts the **Fête des Vendages.** This boisterous festival of wine-drinking, dancing, and folklore is the only time that the wine produced on the grounds is sold to the public (see **Life and Times,** p. 98). The area around the vineyard, on the northern slope of the *butte*, is one of the loveliest in Montmartre. Still largely unspoiled by tourism, the streets around r. St-Vincent have maintained their rural village charm with old stone walkways and farm houses. Sit down for a meal at La Maison Rose (see **Food,** p. 179), and enjoy the serenity away from the tour buses. *(r. des Saules. ⓜ Lamarck-Caulaincourt. Follow directions to the Lapin Agile. On the corner of r. des Saules and r. St-Vincent. Closed to the general public, except during the Fête des Vendages.)*

PLACE DU TERTRE. Place du Tertre teems with tourists, amateur artists, portrait painters, and has-been cafes. Once the haunt of artists and intellectuals, it is still historically interesting and physically beautiful, despite its theme-park atmosphere. It is also chock-full of *crêperies*, which are great for picking up a cheap meal on the go. *(ⓜ Abbesses. With your back to the church in pl. des Abbesses, walk up r. de la Vieuville, turn left on r. Drevet, left again on r. Gabrielle, and go right uphill on r. du Calvaire.)*

DOWNHILL

RUES ABBESSES, LEPIC, AND D'ORSEL. These days, tasty restaurants, trendy cafes, and *boulangeries* crowd the corner of Montmartre around r. des Abbesses and r. Lepic. The international hit film *Amélie* (2002) was filmed in the area, and fans have since been making pilgrimages to the home of the adorable title character. Predictably, longtime residents are complaining about the *"Amélie Poulainization"* of their neighborhood, but truth be told, the damage isn't too conspicuous. Tall iron gates hide the beautiful gardens of several 18th-century townhouses. Walking down r. Lepic will take you past the **Moulin Radet,** one of the last remaining windmills on Montmartre. Farther down is the site of the now-demolished **Moulin de la Galette,** depicted in a painting by Auguste Renoir during one of the frequent dances held there (*Bal au Moulin de la Galette*, 1876; now in the Musée d'Orsay). Even farther down lies one of Vincent van Gogh's former homes at 54, r. Lepic. Attractive boutiques cluster along r. d'Orsel near ⓜ Abbesses.

SIGHTS

CIMETIÈRE MONTMARTRE. Though less star-studded than the legendary Père Lachaise (p. 232), Cimetière Montmartre is beautifully landscaped and more secluded than its famous neighbor. Writers Alexandre Dumas and Stendhal, painter Edgar Degas, physicians André Ampère and Léon Foucault, composer Hector Berlioz, filmmaker François Truffaut, and dancer Vaslav Nijinksy are buried here, among others. The cemetery was also the site of mass graves after the suppression of the Commune in 1871. Emile Zola was interred here until a grateful fatherland transferred his remains to the Panthéon in 1908, with all the other *grands hommes*. Maps of the cemetery are available at the office to the left after the entrance. *(20, av. Rachel. ⓜ Place de Clichy or Blanche. ☎ 01 53 42 36 30. From either metro, walk down bd. de Clichy and turn down av. Rachel. At the end of the avenue is the entrance. Open M-F 8am-6pm, Sa 8:30am-6pm, Su and holidays 9am-6pm; winter closes 5:30pm.)*

BAL DU MOULIN ROUGE. Along the bd. de Clichy and bd. de Rochechouart, you'll find many of the cabarets and nightclubs that were the definitive hangouts of the Belle Epoque, including the infamous cabaret Bal du Moulin Rouge, immortalized by the paintings of Toulouse-Lautrec, the music of Offenbach, and, most recently, Baz Luhrmann's Hollywood blockbuster. At the turn of the century, Paris's bourgeoisie came to the Moulin Rouge to play at being bohemian. After WWI, Paris's artsiest relocated to the Left Bank, and the area around pl. Pigalle became a world-renowned seedy red-light district (p. 216). Today, the crowd at the Moulin Rouge consists of tourists out for an evening of sequins, tassels, and skin. The *revues* are still risqué, but the price of admission is prohibitively expensive—a show and dinner cost €140-170. You can be risky yourself and buy a ticket for a spot at the bar for €72, which includes two drinks but no guarantee that you'll have somewhere to sit. Or come for the 9 and 11pm performances, which include champagne instead of dinner and cost €97 or €87, respectively. *(82, bd. de Clichy. ⓜ Blanche. Directly across from the metro. ☎ 01 53 09 82 82; www.moulin-rouge.com. Shows daily 7 (with dinner), 9, 11pm.)*

LA GOUTTE D'OR. Farther east, toward the railroad tracks, the 18*ème* becomes an immigrant ghetto in the midst of urban renewal. Still filled with crumbling buildings, the *quartier* takes its name, "drop of gold," from the medieval vineyard that once stood here. Today, the area is one of the few refuges for cheap housing in the city. The large Virgin Megastore on bd. Barbès, however, is just one of many indications that the area is changing, and ambitious development plans may soon raise the rents here, too. Discount clothing shops line bd. Barbès, and there are numerous African cloth, food, and gift shops around r. Doudeauville and r. des Poissonniers. **Tati,** a low-end department store good for rummaging, is at 13, pl. de la République (**Shopping,** p. 287). Be watchful of pickpockets in the neighborhood. Those unfamiliar with the area might be uncomfortable at night. *(ⓜ Barbès-Rochechouart, Château Rouge, Marcadet-Poissonniers.)*

NINETEENTH ARRONDISSEMENT

Modern, inventive, and extremely child-friendly, the sights of the 19*ème* are varied enough to keep any family on its toes for a day or more. La Villette showcases some of the Paris's significant architectural and social accomplishments of the past few decades, while the Parc des Buttes-Chaumont provides a wonderful location to have a picnic.

see map p. 380

LA VILLETTE

La Villette is the product of a successful urban renewal project. Once a meat-packing district that provided Paris with much of its pork and beef, the area became outmoded after the advent of refrigerated trucks. A decision was made to replace the neighborhood slaughterhouses with a neighborhood park, and *voilà:* what President Mitterrand inaugurated in 1985 as "the place of intelligent leisure" was born.

■ **PARC DE LA VILLETTE.** Cut in the middle by the **Canal de l'Ourcq** and the **Canal St-Denis,** the Parc de la Villette separates the Cité des Sciences from the Cité de la Musique and is dominated by the steel-and-glass **Grande Halle,** which features frequent plays, concerts, and films. The park's lines of sight are sliced by the angles of funny-shaped red buildings called *folies,* each made from regular 10.8 sq.m cubes. Impressive metal canopies join them in architect Bernard Tschumi's rebuttal of right angles. At least one of the *folies* offers hamburgers (from an outpost of Le Quick, France's answer to McDonald's).

Every July and August from Tuesday to Sunday at sundown (around 10pm), La Villette hosts a free open-air **film festival** that shows foreign, art, and generally funky movies next to the Folie de Charolais. The **Zénith** concert hall hosts major rock bands. Directly behind Zénith is the **Trabendo** jazz and modern music club; the park's yearly jazz festival is extraordinarily popular (see **Life and Times,** p. 98).

Finally, the **Promenade des Jardins** links several thematic gardens, such as the **Garden of Dunes and Wind,** which looks like a very tricky mini-golf course; the **Garden of Childhood Fears,** which winds through a wooded grove resonant with spooky sounds; and the roller coaster **Dragon Garden.** If you can bypass the height requirement and pass yourself off as under 12, then you too can join a gaggle of moppets leaping on trampolines, running on rolling hills, and zooming down slides. (Ⓜ *Porte de Pantin. General info including Grande Halle* ☎ *01 40 03 75 03, Park info office 01 40 03 75 75, Trabendo info* ☎ *01 42 01 12 12, Zénith 01 42 08 60 00; but call FNAC to buy tickets. Info office open daily 10am-7pm. Promenade des Jardins open 24hr. Free.)*

■ **CITÉ DES SCIENCES ET DE L'INDUSTRIE.** The Cité des Sciences et de l'Industrie houses the fabulous **Explora Science Museum** (see **Museums,** p. 270), arguably the best destination for kids in Paris. The enormous **Géode** outside the Cité is a mirrored sphere mounted on a flower bed like a gigantic disco ball. The exterior is coated with 6433 polished stainless steel triangles that reflect every detail of the surroundings. Inside, **Omnimax movies** on volcanoes, glaciers, and other natural phenomena are shown on a 1000 sq. m hemispheric screen. To the right of the Géode, the **Argonaute** submarine details the history of submersibles from Jules Verne to present-day nuclear-powered subs. This 400-ton, 50m long fighter submarine was designed in 1950 as part of the French national fleet. Between the Canal St-Denis and the Cité, **Cinaxe** features innovative movies filmed from the first-person perspective from vehicles like Formula One cars, low-flying planes, and Mars land rovers, while hydraulic pumps simulate every curve and bump. Lunch beforehand is not recommended. (Ⓜ *Porte de la Villette.* ☎ *01 40 05 80 00; www.cite-sciences.fr. Géode:* ☎ *01 40 05 79 99. Open M variable hours, Tu-Su 10:30am-9:30pm. Shows every hr. Tickets €9, under 25 €7. Argonaute: Open Tu-F 10:30am-5:30pm, Sa-Su 11am-6pm. Admission €3. Audioguide tour of the submarine, in English or French, is included. Cinaxe:* ☎ *01 40 05 12 12. Open Tu-Su 11am-1pm and 2-5pm; shows every 15min. Admission €5.40, with a ticket from another exposition €4.80.)*

CITÉ DE LA MUSIQUE. At the opposite end of La Villette from the Cité des Sciences is the Cité de la Musique. Designed by Franck Hammoutène and completed in 1990, the complex of buildings is stunning, full of curves and glass ceilings. The highlight for classical music lovers is the **Musée de la Musique,** a collection of 900 antique instruments and a handful of paintings and sculptures. Visitors don headphones that tune in to musical excerpts and descriptions of each instrument. The Cité de la Musique's two performance spaces—the 1200-seat **Salle des Concerts** and the 230-seat **Amphithéâtre**—host an eclectic range of shows and concerts year-round (see **Entertainment,** p. 279). The Cité de la Musique also has a **music information center** and the **Médiathèque Pédagogique,** with 70,000 books, documents, music journals, and photographs. (Ⓜ *Porte de Pantin.* ☎ *01 44 84 44 84, info 01 44 84 45 45, médiathèque 01*

THE LOCAL STORY

ROMANCE! TRAGEDY! CASTRATION!

Pierre Abélard, born of a noble family near Nantes, was a reputable professor of rhetoric and philosophy in Paris during the Middle Ages. After years of chastity, he fixed his gaze upon the beautiful and intelligent Héloïse, more than 20 years his junior. He convinced her uncle, Canon Fulbert, to hire him as a live-in tutor to the precocious girl. A strong attraction developed, and soon they were spending more time studying one another than any academic material. Unfortunately, Héloïse soon found herself pregnant. To avoid Fulbert's wrath, Abélard spirited Héloïse away to Bretagne, where she gave birth to their son, Astrolabe.

One night, the furious Canon Fulbert dispatched servants to Abélard's home, who broke in and cruelly castrated him. A stricken Abélard wrote to Héloïse of his dismay that "one wretched stroke of fortune" had robbed him of his love. Retreating to a monastery, he encouraged Héloïse to take the veil. For the rest of their lives, the two lovers fervently exchanged spiritually intense letters. Abélard's writings on philosophy and theology during this period earned him a throne among the greatest intellectuals of the 12th century. Upon their deaths, the lovers were re-united in Père-Lachaise Cemetery. Today, their tomb is among the most popular in the cemetery.

44 84 89 45; www.cite-musique.fr. Info center open Tu-Su noon-6pm. Musée de la Musique open Tu-Sa noon-6pm, Su 10am-6pm. Admission €7, under 18 €3.40; €3.40 more for temporary exhibits. €10 guided tours in French; call the info office for times. Médiathèque open Tu-Sa noon-6pm, Su 1-6pm. Free.)

ELSEWHERE IN THE NINETEENTH

■ **PARC DES BUTTES-CHAUMONT.** Parc des Buttes-Chaumont, in the south of the 19ème, is a mix of man-made topography and transplanted vegetation, all of it created on a whim of nostalgia. Napoleon III commissioned it in 1860 out of a longing for London's Hyde Park, where he spent much of his time in exile. Since the 13th century, the *quartier* had been host to a *gibbet* (an iron cage filled with the rotting corpses of criminals), a dumping ground for dead horses, a haven for worms, and a gypsum quarry (the source of "plaster of Paris"). Making a park out of the existing mess took four years and 1000 workers. Designer Adolphe Alphand had all of the soil replaced and the quarried remains built up with new rock to create enormous cliffs around a lake. Today's visitors walk the winding paths surrounded by lush greenery and dynamic hills, and enjoy a great view of the *quartier* from the Roman temple atop cave-filled cliffs. Watch out for the ominously named *Pont des Suicides* (Suicide Bridge). (Ⓜ Buttes-Chaumont and Botzaris are both situated right along the park. Open daily 7am-10:30pm; some gates close early.)

TWENTIETH ARRONDISSEMENT

The 20ème is a largely residential district, but it contains one massive attraction that dominates the area: the **Père Lachaise Cemetery.** This beautiful and historic location renders the long metro ride from see map p. 381 the center of Paris to peruse the graves of legends well worth it. For a more tranquil (and less morbid) place to sunbathe and relax, try the beautiful, layered **Parc de Belleville.**

■ PÈRE LACHAISE CEMETERY

16, r. du Repos. Ⓜ Père Lachaise. ☎ 01 55 25 82 10. Open mid- Mar. to early Nov. M-F 8am-6pm, Sa 8:30am-6pm, Su and holidays 9am-6pm; Nov.-Feb. M-F 8am-5:30pm, Sa 8:30am-5:30pm, Su and holidays 9am-5:30pm. Last entrance 15min. before closing. Free. Free maps at the Bureau de Conservation near Porte Gambetta; ask for directions at guard booths by main entrances if you cannot find it. 2 1/2 hr. guided tour offered, as well as numerous "theme" tours. €9. For info check www.afif.asso.fr.

With its winding paths and elaborate sarcophagi, Cimetière du Père Lachaise has become the final resting place of many French and foreign legends. Balzac, Colette, Jacques Louis David, Delacroix, La Fontaine, Haussmann, Molière, and Proust are buried here, as are Modigliani, Jim Morrison, Gertrude Stein, and Oscar Wilde. With so many tourists, however, they're hardly resting in peace.

The cemetery is a bustling 19th-century neighborhood-of-the-dead, laid out in streets with some sarcophagi that resemble little houses. Many of the tombs in this landscaped grove strive to remind visitors of the dead's worldly accomplishments: the tomb of French Romantic painter **Géricault** wears a reproduction of his *Raft of the Medusa* (the original is in the Louvre); on **Chopin's** tomb sits his muse Calliope. **Oscar Wilde's** grave is marked by a striking, larger-than-life Egyptian fig-

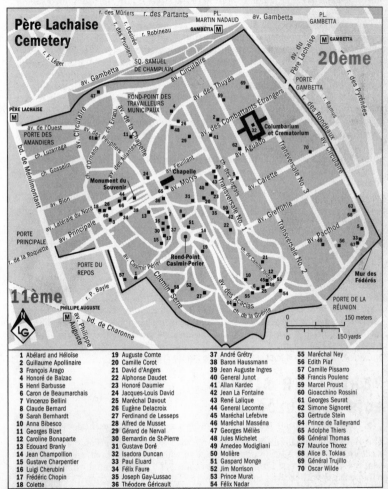

1 Abélard and Héloïse	**19** Auguste Comte	**37** André Grétry
2 Guillaume Apollinaire	**20** Camille Corot	**38** Baron Haussmann
3 François Arago	**21** David d'Angers	**39** Jean Auguste Ingres
4 Honoré de Balzac	**22** Alphonse Daudet	**40** General Junot
5 Henri Barbusse	**23** Honoré Daumier	**41** Allan Kardec
6 Caron de Beaumarchais	**24** Jacques-Louis David	**42** Jean La Fontaine
7 Vincenzo Bellini	**25** Maréchal Davout	**43** René Lalique
8 Claude Bernard	**26** Eugène Delacroix	**44** General Lecomte
9 Sarah Bernhardt	**27** Ferdinand de Lesseps	**45** Maréchal Lefebvre
10 Anna Bibesco	**28** Alfred de Musset	**46** Maréchal Masséna
11 Georges Bizet	**29** Gérard de Nerval	**47** Georges Méliès
12 Caroline Bonaparte	**30** Bernardin de St-Pierre	**48** Jules Michelet
13 Edouard Branly	**31** Gustave Doré	**49** Amedeo Modigliani
14 Jean Champollion	**32** Isadora Duncan	**50** Molière
15 Gustave Charpentier	**33** Paul Eluard	**51** Gaspard Monge
16 Luigi Cherubini	**34** Félix Faure	**52** Jim Morrison
17 Frédéric Chopin	**35** Joseph Gay-Lussac	**53** Prince Murat
18 Colette	**36** Théodore Géricault	**54** Félix Nadar

55 Maréchal Ney	
56 Edith Piaf	
57 Camille Pissarro	
58 Francis Poulenc	
59 Marcel Proust	
60 Gioacchino Rossini	
61 Georges Seurat	
62 Simone Signoret	
63 Gertrude Stein	
64 Prince de Talleyrand	
65 Adolphe Thiers	
66 Général Thomas	
67 Maurice Thorez	
68 Alice B. Toklas	
69 Général Trujillo	
70 Oscar Wilde	

ure. He died destitute, but in 1912, an American admirer of his work provided his grave with the Egyptian adornment. The sculpture was defaced in 1961, prompting false rumors that the cemetery director, finding a part of the sculpture's anatomy to be out of proportion, removed the offending jewels of the Nile and kept them as a paperweight. Though the jewels are gone, dozens of lipstick marks from adoring fans cover the tomb today. Kissing the tomb, however, is strictly forbidden, as lipstick apparently eats away at the stone.

Haussmann, the man of the boulevards, wanted to destroy Père Lachaise as part of his urban-renewal project, but obviously relented; he now occupies a mausoleum in the cemetery. Remembered by plaques here are dancer **Isadora Duncan,** author **Richard Wright,** opera diva **Maria Callas,** and artist **Max Ernst.** The most visited grave is that of **Jim Morrison,** the former lead singer of The Doors. In summer, dozens of people bring flowers, joints, beer, poetry, and Doors paraphernalia to his tomb each day. The sandbox in front of the stone is now the sanctioned site for mourners' creative expression. A guard polices the spot at all times.

Over one million people are buried in the cemetery. Curiously, there are only 100,000 tombs. This discrepancy is due to the old practice of burying the poor in mass graves. Corpses are removed from these unmarked plots at regular intervals to make room for new generations of the dead. Even with such purges, however, the 44 hectares of Père Lachaise are filled to bursting, so the government digs up any grave that has not been visited in a certain number of years. To avoid being disinterred, some rich, solitary souls who sense they are about to kick the bucket resort to hiring a professional "mourner."

Perhaps the most moving sites in Père Lachaise are those that mark collective deaths. The **Mur des Fédérés** (Wall of the Federals) has become a site of pilgrimage for left-wing sympathizers worldwide. In May 1871, a group of Communards, sensing that the end was near, murdered the Archbishop of Paris, who had been taken hostage at the beginning of the Commune. They dragged his mutilated corpse to their stronghold in Père Lachaise and tossed it in a ditch. Four days later, the victorious Versaillais found the body. In retaliation, they lined up 147 Fédérés against the eastern wall of the cemetery, shot them, and buried them on the spot. Since 1871, the Mur des Fédérés has been a rallying point for the French Left, which recalls the massacre's anniversary every Pentecost. Near the wall, a number of moving monuments commemorate the Resistance fighters of WWII and Nazi concentration camp victims.

OTHER SIGHTS IN THE TWENTIETH

■PARC DE BELLEVILLE. Built in the side of a hill, this well-landscaped park is a series of terraces connected by stairs and footpaths. At its highest points, the park offers spectacular views of Parisian landmarks, including the Panthéon, the Centre Pompidou, and the Eiffel Tower. Fountains, flowers, and families dot the park's serene landscape; the only noise comes from the playground located at the entrance. (27, r. Piat, in front of La Maison de l'Air. Ⓜ Pyrénées.)

PERIMETER SIGHTS

BOIS DE BOULOGNE

(Ⓜ Porte Maillot, Sablons, Les Sablons, Porte Dauphine, or Porte d'Auteuil. Open 24hr.)

The Bois de Boulogne is an 846-hectare (over 2000 acres) green canopy at the western edge of Paris. It's a popular place to walk, jog, bike, boat, and picnic. In a past life, it was the vast Forêt de Rouvray, a royal hunting ground where deer and wild boar ran with wolves and bears. By 1852 the *bois* had become "a desert used for dueling and suicides," and was given to the city of Paris by Napoleon III. Acting on imperial instructions, Baron Haussmann dug lakes, created waterfalls, and cut

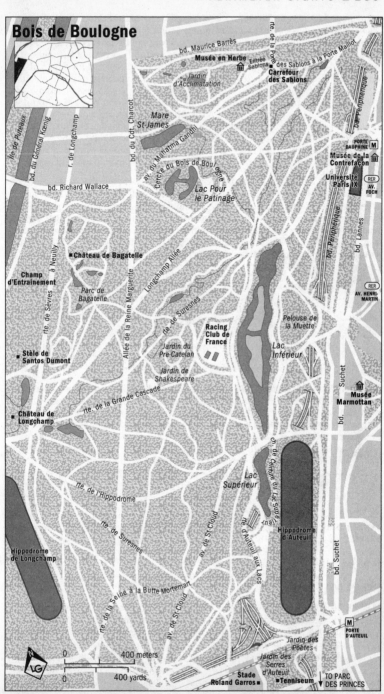

Bois de Boulogne

bd. Maurice Barrès

Musée en Herbe

Entrée Sablons

rte. de la Porte des Sablons à la Porte Maillot

rte. de la Porte des Sablons

Carrefour des Sablons

Jardin d'Acclimatation

Mare St-James

av. du Mahatma Gandhi

Cercle du Bois de Boulogne

Lac Pour le Patinage

rte. du Cdt. Charcot

r. de Longchamp

bd. du Général Koenig

Île de Puteaux

bd. Richard Wallace

à Neuilly

PORTE DAUPHINE Ⓜ

Musée de la Contrefaçon 🏛

Université Paris IX

RER AV. FOCH

bd. Périphérique

bd. Lannes

■ Château de Bagatelle

Longchamp Allée

Champ d'Entrainement

rte. de Sèvres

Parc de Bagatelle

Allée de la Reine Marguerite

rte. de Suresnes

Racing Club de France

Pelouse de la Muette

RER AV. HENRI-MARTIN

Lac Inférieur

■ Stèle de Santos Dumont

Jardin du Pré-Catelan

Jardin de Shakespeare

Suchet

Musée Marmottan 🏛

■ Château de Longchamp

rte. de la Grande Cascade

bd.

rte. de l'Hippodrome

Lac Supérieur

ch. de Ceinture du Lac Supér ieur

rte. de Suresnes

av. de St-Cloud

rte. d'Auteuil aux Lacs

Hippodrome d'Auteuil

Hippodrome de Longchamp

rte. de la Seine à la Butte Mortemart

av. de St-Cloud

bd. Suchet

Ⓜ PORTE D'AUTEUIL

0   400 meters

0   400 yards

Jardin des Poètes

Jardin des Serres d'Auteuil

Stade Roland Garros ■   ● Tenniseum

→ TO PARC DES PRINCES

winding paths through thickly wooded areas. By the turn of the century, the park was tamed enough that aristocratic families rode there to spend a Sunday afternoon "in the country." In harder times, this pleasure park also served a decidedly utilitarian purpose—its trees were felled for firewood during the Revolution; it was occupied by a "ragged army" of starving citizens scrounging for edible plants during the Prussian siege in 1870; it was a site for the execution of political undesirables by the Communards in 1871; and during WWII, people grew vegetable gardens in it to supplement meager rations. In 1991, a flood of newly liberated Eastern Europeans camped in the park. More recently, the *bois* by night has become a bazaar of sex and drugs, complete with transsexual prostitutes and violent crime. Police are stepping up patrols, but the boulevards around the periphery of the *bois* continue to be lined with fleshly wares and are best avoided after dark. Take care if wandering the park alone and try to stay on main paths and roads.

STADIUMS. The Bois de Boulogne contains several stadiums, the most famous of which are the **Hippodromes de Longchamp** and **d'Auteuil,** a flat race course and a steeplechase, respectively. The June Grand Prix at Longchamp was one of the premier annual events of the Belle Epoque. Today, these stadiums host events ranging from music festivals to sports matches. The **Stade Roland Garros,** also within the *bois*, is the home of the **French Open** tennis tournament. A 10min. walk away, the **Parc des Princes** hosts soccer, rugby, and concerts.

LAKES. There are two artificial lakes stretching down the eastern edge of the *bois*. The manicured islands of the **Lac Inférieur** can be reached only by rowboat. There is a path around the waterfalls that cascade from the **Lac Supérieur** into the Lac Inférieur; a stroll along it through the shade makes for a refreshing break from sweltering summer temperatures. At the north end of the islands, facing the boat rental, is a statue of a naked man and woman embracing. Along the length of the lake (and indeed throughout the park) couples can be seen re-enacting this scene, except clothed. Usually. (Ⓜ *Porte Dauphine. Boathouses open daily mid Mar. to early Nov. M-F 12-5:30pm, weather permitting. Rentals €10 per hr., €50 deposit.*)

■**TENNISEUM ROLAND GARROS.** The Tenniseum Roland Garros is a fantastic museum of the history of tennis and the French Open, and a salute to the achievements of French tennis players throughout the ages. A multimedia paradise for serious tennis fans, the museum displays important artifacts like the Coupe des Mousquetaires (the champion's trophy) and the first jacket, worn by the great René Lacoste, adorned with the now-famous crocodile logo. Visitors can also watch the archived matches of all the tennis greats of the Open era or test their tennis knowledge with quizzes on the many computer terminals in the museum. (Ⓜ *Porte d'Auteuil or Michel-Ange Molitor. Enter at 2, av. Gordon-Bennett, off bd. d'Auteuil.* ☎01 47 43 48 48. *Open Tu-Su 10am-6pm mid Feb. to Oct., W, F, Sa-Su Nov. to mid Feb. €7.50, under 18 €4. Tours Tu-Sa, 11am in English, 2:30pm and 4:30pm in French.*)

JARDIN D'ACCLIMATATION. The Jardin d'Acclimatation offers a small zoo, some sports (mini-golf, riding, bowling), carnival rides, educational museums, picnic areas, and outdoor jazz concerts. Perfect for a day with the kids. Pick up a map from the ticket counter as you enter. (Ⓜ *Sablons. Cross the street, pass Monoprix, and walk 3 blocks.* ☎01 40 67 90 82. *Open daily 10am-7pm in summer, 10am-6pm in winter. €3, seniors €1.50, under 3 free.*)

MUSÉE EN HERBE. The Musée en Herbe is a European art-history museum designed for children ages 4-11. Temporary exhibits range from farm animals to artists like Manet, Chagall, and Picasso. The museum also offers studio workshops on sculpture, pottery, *papier mâché*, painting, and collage for children ages two and up. A participatory theater company for children stages plays and puppet shows. *(In the Jardin d'Acclimatation. Directly on your left at the Entrée Sablons. ☎01 40 67 97 66. Open daily 10am-6pm. €4. Call to make reservations for special studio sessions.)*

PRÉ CATELAN. The Pré Catelan is probably named after Théophile Catelan, master of the hunt under Louis XIV, but legend has it that this neatly manicured meadow was actually named after a murdered delivery boy, Arnault Catelan. Catelan was ordered to ride from Provence to Paris to deliver gifts to Philippe le Bel from Beatrice de Savoie, so he hired a group of men to protect him on his journey. The men killed him in the night, believing that Arnault carried gold. In fact, the gifts were only perfumes from the South of France. Authorities later captured the marauders, who, doused in a rare Provençale scent, were easy to identify. Inside the Pré Catelan, the **Jardin de Shakespeare** is a popular open-air theater. *(From Ⓜ Porte Maillot, take exit av. de Neuilly. Take bus #244 to Bagatuel-Pré-Catelan. Jardin de Shakespeare ☎01 40 19 95 33, tours of Pré Catelan 01 40 71 75 60. Jardin open daily 2-4pm. Pré Catelan open daily 9am-8pm. Guided tours €6, reduced €3).*

PARC DE BAGATELLE. The Parc de Bagatelle was once a private estate and became a public park in 1905. In 1777, in an impetuous act that could not have helped his image in pre-revolutionary Paris, the future Charles X bet his sister-in-law, Marie-Antoinette, that he could build the **Château de Bagatelle** in three months. She was game, and Charles employed 1000 workers of all descriptions (including a Scottish landscape artist) to complete the job (see **Garden Party,** p. 326). The **Bagatelle Garden** is now famous for its **rose exhibition** (3rd Th of June). The tulips are magnificent in April, irises bloom in May, and August is the month for the water lilies the gardener added in tribute to Monet. *(Same bus stop as Pré Catelan, above. ☎01 53 64 53 80. Open daily June-Sept. 9am-8pm, closes earlier as winter approaches; Dec.-Jan. 9am-5pm. Ticket office closes 30min. earlier. Reduced price for under age 26 €1.50.)*

JARDIN DES SERRES D'AUTEUIL. The Jardin des Serres d'Auteuil (Greenhouse Garden) represents the merging of two 19th-century passions: iron-and-glass construction and gardens. Here resides one of Paris's first hothouses, built (between 1895 and 1898) to allow the green of summer gardens to bloom all winter long and today it is still in full bloom. The tropical greenhouses also house birds and massive fish. Back when the hothouse was first built, tickets were rationed out according to a person's moral standards; an exception was made for drunkards, whose "condition" the garden was supposed to cure. *(Ⓜ Porte d'Auteuil or Michel-Ange Molitor. Enter at 1, av. Gordon-Bennett, off bd. d'Auteuil. Open daily May-Aug. 10am-6pm, Sept.-Apr. 10am-5pm. Guided tours €6; reduced fare €3.)*

JARDIN DES POÈTES. Smaller and simpler than the Jardin des Serres d'Auteuil (and something of a make-out spot) is the neighboring **Jardin des Poètes.** Here natural beauty reigns instead of human creations. Poems are marked on stones on each flower bed: scan Ronsard, Corneille, Racine, Baudelaire, and Apollinaire. Rodin's sculpture of Victor Hugo can also be found in the garden. *(Open Apr. 16-Oct. 15 daily 9am-8pm; Oct. 16-Apr. 15 W and Sa-Su 10am-7pm.)*

BOIS DE VINCENNES

Ⓜ Château de Vincennes or Porte Dorée. To best enjoy the park, rent a bike from the Lac des Minimes (☎01 30 59 68 38): open W and Sa 1:30-7:30 or 8pm, Su and holidays 9:30 or 10am-7pm (closed 6pm in winter), daily during school holidays; €5 for 1hr. ID deposit required. Lac Daumesnil (☎06 81 34 47 19): open W and Sa-Su 10am-7pm; daily during school holidays 9am-8pm (6pm in winter); €5 for 1hr. ID or €150 required.

Once a royal hunting forest, the Bois de Vincennes is now the largest expanse of greenery in Paris, encompassing nearly 1000 hectares. Until the 19th century, it lay beyond the reach of Parisian authorities, making it a favorite dueling venue. Alexandre Dumas challenged a literary collaborator to a duel in the *bois* for claiming to have written *Le Tour de Nesle*. Although the duel was a debacle—Dumas's pistol misfired—the experience gave the author the inspiration for a scene in *Les Frères Corses*. Like the Bois de Boulogne, the Vincennes forest was given to Paris by Napoleon III, to be transformed into an English-style garden. Not surprisingly, Haussmann (see **Life and Times,** p. 82) oversaw the planning of the lakes and pathways. Annexed to a much poorer section of Paris than the Bois de Boulogne, Vincennes was never as fashionable or as formal. Today, the Bois de Vincennes's bike paths, horse trails, zoo, and Buddhist temple offer an escape from the city. The flat terrain is given definition by two irregularly shaped lakes and numerous thematic gardens. The park also houses the **Vélodrome Jacques Anquetil,** the **Hippodrome de Vincennes,** and other sports facilities.

PARC ZOOLOGIQUE DE PARIS. In a country not known for its zoos, the Parc Zoologique de Paris is considered the best of the bunch. It is the Bois de Vincennes's most popular attraction, and a recent effort has been made to improve the environment in which its 135 species live. The entrance is dominated by a man-made mountain especially designed for the zoo's population of alpine goats. A troupe of Japanese macaques pass the day sliding down rocks, swinging from trees, and chewing on hats that people throw into their habitat (don't feed the animals!). The phoques (the French word for seal, pronounced just like you think it is) are fed daily at 4pm (pelicans at 2:15pm, penguins at 2:30pm, and otters at 3pm). The park is also home to the **Grand Rocher** observatory, which offers a breathtaking view of the surrounding *bois*. The zoo is undergoing comprehensive renovation until 2010, and the elephants, rhinos, and bears have decamped, but it is still open and fun to explore. *(53, av. de St-Maurice. ⓜ Porte Dorée. ☎ 01 44 75 20 10. Open daily Jan. 9am-5pm; Feb.-Mar. 9am-5:30pm; Apr.-Sept. M-Sa 9am-6pm and Su and holidays 9am-6:30pm; Oct. 9am-6pm; Nov.-Dec. 9am-5pm. Ticket office closes 30min. before zoo. Admission €5, under 4 free. Train tour leaves from giraffe enclosure. €1.50, children €1.)*

CHÂTEAU DE VINCENNES. Called "the Versailles of the Middle Ages," the Château de Vincennes was the favored court residence of French kings as early as the 13th century. Although the Louvre was the principal royale abode, every French monarch from Charles V to Henri IV spent at least part of his time at Vincennes. Henri III took refuge here during the Wars of Religion, and Mazarin and the court found the château's defenses useful in the wake of the Fronde. In the 18th century, Vincennes became a country-club prison for well-known enemies of the state like the Comte de Mirabeau and the infamous Marquis de Sade. When Diderot was imprisoned in the château, Rousseau walked through the forest to visit him. In the 19th century, the complex served as fortress, arsenal, and artillery park. In 1917, the infamous spy Mata Hari, convicted of espionage on behalf of the Germans, faced a firing squad within its walls. In 1940, the château was the headquarters of General Maurice Gamelin, Commander of the French Land Forces. Today, the 17th-century apartments house the archives of the French armed forces, and much of the château complex is only accessible by guided tour. *(ⓜ Château de Vincennes. On the northern edge of the park. Château doors open daily Apr.-Sept. 7:30am-7pm and Oct.-Mar. 9am-6:50pm. Information office (Accueil Charles V) located in second building to the right. ☎ 01 48 08 31 20. Open Sept.-Apr. 10am-noon and 1-5pm, May-Aug. 10am-noon and 1-6pm. Tour of Ste-Chapelle and château history (45min.) 11:45am, 1:30, and 5:15pm. €5, ages 18-25 €3.50, under 18 free. Tour of Ste-Chapelle, Etude du Roi, and Donjon (1½hr.) 11am, 2:15, 3, 3:45, 4:30pm. €6.50/ 4.50. Tour information liable to change after the re-opening of the Donjon in spring of 2007.)*

STE-CHAPELLE AND DONJON. Not to be confused with the better-known Ste-Chapelle on Île de la Cité, Ste-Chapelle is looking better than ever these days after restoration of its exterior. Built between 1336 and 1370, the 52m high *donjon* (big square tower) is a striking example of medieval architecture. It has been closed for restoration since 1995, and is expected to have a lavish re-opening in spring of

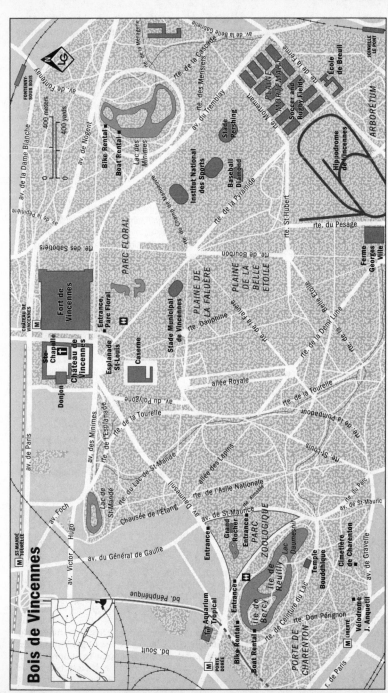

Bois de Vincennes

SIGHTS

2007. Guided tours are the only way to get inside the church for a close-up look at the 16th-century stained-glass windows but most of the tour is devoted to historical background. Much of the structure's beauty can be appreciated from the outside as much as from inside the ramparts.

PARC FLORAL DE PARIS. The Parc Floral de Paris's ultra-modern block-lettered entrance can be seen from the château entrance not facing the metro. The park has a butterfly garden, bonsai display, miniature golf, and assorted games for kids, and hosts festivals and concerts in summer. Check the park's website for details. *(Esplanade du Château. Ⓜ Château de Vincennes. ☎01 49 57 15 15, tours 01 40 71 75 60; www.parcfloraldeparis.com. Open daily Mar.-Apr. 9:30am-6pm; Apr.-Sept. 9:30am-8pm; Oct.-Feb. 9:30am-5pm. Admission €1, ages 7-25 €0.50, under 7 free; during events and concerts €3/ 1.50. €3-6 guided tours meet at the entrance of the park, and are themed by particular flowers .)*

LAC DAUMESNIL AND LAC DES MINIMES. Joggers, cyclists, horseback-riders, and people-watchers share the banks of the lovely Lac Daumesnil, while rowboats paddle around in it. The mysterious caves near the lake—topped off by a small temple—are not to be missed. The more remotely located Lac des Minimes is quiet and great for boating and picnicking. *(Lac Daumesnil boat rental (☎01 60 94 45 75) on av. Daumesnil. Open daily Mar.-Nov. 20 9:30am-6pm in winter and until 8pm in summer. 1-2 people €9.50 per hr., 3-4 people €10.50 per hr.; additional €10 deposit. Lac des Minimes boat rental (☎06 86 08 01 12) on av. de Nogent. Open Mar.-Nov. W and Sa-Su and holidays 1:30-7pm in winter. Open 1:30-8pm in summer daily 1:30-7pm; 1-2 people €9, 3-5 people €10; additional €15 deposit.*

FERME GEORGES VILLE (FERME DE PARIS). Visitors to the farm enjoy the company of chickens, cows, goats, and more. This is a great place to bring the kids. *(☎01 43 28 47 63. Open Nov.-Feb. Sa-Su 1:30-5pm; Oct.-Mar. Sa-Su 1:30-5:30pm; Apr.-June Sa-Su 1:30-6:30 pm; July-Aug. Tu-F 1:30-6pm and Sa-Su 1:30-6:30pm. Free.)*

LA DÉFENSE

Ⓜ/RER La Défense, or the #73 bus. The RER is slightly faster, but the metro is pretty quick and cheaper. If you take the RER, buy your ticket before going through the turnstile. A normal metro ticket may get you into the RER station in Paris, but won't get you out without a fine at La Défense. Consider either coming or going by the Esplanade de la Défense metro stop so you can savor the architecture, gardens, and outdoor sculpture around the arch. Grande Arche open daily 10am-7pm; last ascent 6:30pm. €7.50; under 18, students, and seniors €6. Beyond the small lawn, the Info Défense booth offers free maps, guides, and a free permanent exhibit on the architectural history and future of La Défense. ☎01 47 74 84 24. Open Oct.-Mar. M-F 9:30am-5:30pm, Apr.-Sept. 10am-6pm. Daily French Petit Train tours Apr.-Oct. every hr. 10am-5pm (6pm in Aug.), lasting 35min., from under the Grande Arche. €5, under 16 €3.

Just outside Paris's most exclusive suburbs lies a gleaming, teeming space crammed with eye-popping contemporary architecture, enormous office buildings, and one very geometric arch. Great efforts have been made since La Défense's initial development in 1958—especially by Mitterrand and his *Grands Projets* program—to inject social spaces, monuments, and art into La Défense's commercial landscape. Shops, galleries, gardens, and sculptures by **Miró, Calder,** and **César** cluster around the **Grande Arche de la Défense,** a 35-story building in the shape of a white hollow cube.

After the construction of the Tour Montparnasse was somehow permitted in 1973 (p. 223), Parisian authorities restricted further building of *gratte-ciels* (skyscrapers) within the 20 *arrondissements*, rightly fearing that new high-rises would mar the Paris skyline. As a result, new construction projects moved to La Défense. To maintain the symmetry of the **Historic Axis** (the line that stretches from the arch in front of the Louvre to La Défense, passing up the Champs-Elysées and through the Arc de Triomphe), I.M. Pei suggested a plan for a monument to anchor the La

Défense end of the axis. Danish architect Otto von Spreckelsen's Grande Arche was chosen for the La Défense monument, and Pei was asked to design the eastern terminus in the courtyard of the Louvre. Spreckelsen backed out of the project midway, disheartened by red tape and by his own design, which he deemed a "monument without a soul." British engineer Peter Rice finished the work and designed the canvas tent "clouds" suspended to soften the arch's austere angles.

The arch was inaugurated on the French Republic's bicentennial, July 14, 1989. It took 300,000 tons of steel, 2800 marble and glass facade pieces, 2.6 billion francs and the efforts of 2000 workmen (2 of whom died in construction accidents) to complete the 87,000 sq. m building. The roof of this unconventional office space covers one hectare—Notre Dame could nestle in its hollow core. The arch's walls are covered with white marble and mirrors, so that it gleams in sunlight (bring your shades or you'll be squinting all morning).

THE REAL DEAL. The outdoor glass elevators on the Grande Arche de la Défense make for a unique ride, as you will get fantastic views all the way up. The view from the top of the arch, however, is less than spectacular, given the number of tall buildings between it and the far-off center of Paris. It doesn't quite match the views from the Eiffel Tower, the Basilica of Sacré-Coeur, the Parc de Belleville, or the top of the Centre Pompidou. — Laura Martin

OTHER SIGHTS AT LA DEFENSE. Other La Défense buildings include the **Bull Tower**; the tent-like **Palais Défense**; a space-age **IMAX dome;** and the **CNIT building**, a center for congresses, exhibitions, and conferences that, at age 39, is La Défense's oldest building. Underneath the Arche is the **Sources d'Europe** European information center, which houses a quiet cafe and holds exhibits on topics like the European Union. (Open M-F 10am-6pm. Free.) The arch is surrounded by eight gardens (maps available at Info Défense). The huge **Quatre Temps** shopping center, one of the largest shopping malls in Europe, contains cafes, supermarkets, a cinema, and 30 restaurants. But visitors expecting to find a fashion mecca will probably be disappointed by the stores themselves—serious shoppers will have better luck in Paris proper. *(Enter from the Grande Arche metro or from behind the Miró sculpture. Shops open M-Sa 10am-8pm. Supermarkets open M-F 9am-10pm, Sa 8:30am-10pm. Cinema and restaurants open daily until 11pm.)*

SAINT-DENIS

North of the 18ème and easily accessible by metro, the town of St-Denis is most noted for its stunning 12th-century basilica that has served for centuries as the spiritual home and final resting place of French royalty. The basilica is an architectural marvel—especially in comparison to the rather grubby modern buildings beside it. The town itself has little else to offer in the way of tourist sights, and if you're looking for a bite to eat, you'll find plenty of fast-food outlets and cheap eats but not much in the way of fine dining. Its most recent claim to fame was as the venue for the 1998 World Cup, which necessitated the construction of a new 75,000-seat stadium that today hosts rock concerts and sporting events. An open-air market is held three times a week (Tu, F, Su) in the square by the Hôtel-de-Ville (on the way from the metro stop to the basilica).

PRACTICAL INFORMATION. The most direct route to St-Denis is by metro (Ⓜ Basilique St-Denis, line 13); visitors headed to the stadium should take the RER (RER Stade de France, line B5 or RER St-Denis, line D1). The **tourist office,** 1, r. de la République, has English-speaking guides, info on the basilica and the town of St-Denis, maps, suggested walks, restaurant guides, and a ticket outlet for events in the Stade de France. From the metro, take exit 1; turn left down r. Jean Jaurès, following the signs to the tourist office; and turn right on r. de la République. (☎01 55 87 08 70; www.ville-saint-denis.fr. Open daily Apr.-Sept. 1am-1pm and 2-4pm; Oct.-Mar. 10am-2pm.)

BASILIQUE DE ST-DENIS. Surrounded by modern buildings, markets, and non-Christian communities, the Basilique de St-Denis stands as an anachronistic and archaic symbol of the French monarchy. Buried in the transept, crevet, and crypt are the remains of three royal families (the Capets, the Valois, and the Bourbons), 41 kings, 32 queens, 63 princes and princesses, 10 dignitaries, and the relics of three saints. During the height of the French monarchy, the basilica acted as the national church, housing political artifacts like the *Oriflamme* (the royal banner) and coronation paraphernalia.

The first church on this site was built on top of an existing Gallo-Roman cemetery in honor of Paris's first bishop, St. Denis. St. Denis was martyred by the Romans in AD 260 for trying to Christianize the city. After being beheaded on Mt. Mercury, which was renamed Montmartre (see Mount of the Martyr; p. 227) in his honor, he allegedly picked up his head and walked north with it to the sight of this church, where he collapsed. His tragic tale is told in stained glass on the northern side of the nave. In 475, a small church was built to mark St. Denis's grave. King Pepin the Short built a larger basilica to accommodate the many pilgrimages to this site and was buried here in 768. Over the years, he was joined by the royal remains of Clovis, François I, Catherine de Medicis, Anne d'Autriche, Louis XIV, Louis XVI, and Marie-Antoinette.

The basilica's 12th-century ambulatory was the first appearance of Gothic architecture in Europe (the scornful term "Gothic" was coined by Italian critics to describe St-Denis's extravagant style). Nicknamed "Lucerna" (Latin for "lantern") for its luminosity, the basilica features enormous stained-glass windows, high vaults, and exceptionally wide, airy transepts. These and other innovations were ordered by St-Denis's great patron, **Abbot Suger** (1122-1151), an influential clergyman and politician. Dissatisfied with the dark interiors of Romanesque churches, Abbot Suger famously began rebuilding the basilica in 1136 to open it to the "uninterrupted light of the divine." The vaulted arches and flying buttresses outside freed the walls from the burden of supporting the roof and enabled the architects to replace them with huge stained-glass windows that became the trademark of Gothic style.

Suger's shocked contemporaries worked to outdo him in technical brilliance, building ever more intricate interiors, larger stained-glass windows, and loftier vaults. But few were able to rival the luminous eastern end of the church: Suger's celebrated, color-flooded **crevet.** Dubbed the "manifesto" of the new Gothic style, the crevet was originally built to displace the crowds of pilgrims who flooded into the crypt to view the reliquaries. The crowds became so immense at times that, as rumor has it, some would faint and even suffocate in the tiny, air-deprived vault. The monks were terrified that the reliquaries would be stolen, and had taken to jumping out the windows with the saintly remains in their arms. The crevet is still home to some of the finest stained glass in France, with wall-to-wall ripple effects and intricate patterns. But the price of innovation is high: according to Suger himself, the windows cost more money than the entire building. Almost all of the windows were replaced in the 19th century after the originals were shattered during the Revolution. Some of the 12th-century windows can still be seen, however, in the center of the ambulatory. Abbot Suger ensured his immortality by having his likeness—a small monk prostrate before the Virgin Mother—added to the design.

Suger died in 1151, well before the basilica was finished, but he had already established it as France's seat of theological power. Several queens were crowned here, and in 1593, underneath the nave, Henri IV converted to Catholicism (see **Life and Times,** p. 61). With such a royalist pedigree, St-Denis made a prime target for the wrath of the Revolution. Tombs were destroyed, windows were shattered, and the remains of the Bourbon royal family were thrown into a ditch. With the restoration of the monarchy in 1815, Louis XVIII ordered the re-establishment of the necropolis, and Louis XVI and Marie-Antoinette were buried here with great pomp in 1819. Louis XVIII also retrieved the Bourbons' remains, placing them in a small **ossuary** in the crypt, and replaced the original tombs and funerary monuments. *(1, r. de la Légion d'Honneur and 2, r. de Strasbourg. From the metro, head toward the town square on r. Jean Jaurès and turn left at the tourist office on r. de la République.* ☎ *01 48 09 83 54. Open Apr.-Sept. M-Sa 10am-6:30pm, Su and holidays noon-6:30pm; Oct.-Mar. M-Sa 10am-4:30pm, Su noon-4:30pm. Last entry 30min. before closing. Admission to nave, side aisles and chapels free. Transept, ambulatory, and crypt €6.50, ages 18-25 €4.50, under 18 and first Su of month from Nov.-Mar. free. Open daily Apr.-Sept. 10am-5:45pm; Oct.-Mar. 10am-4:45pm. Enter through the right fence gate of the basilica and go to the ticket kiosk. Audioguide in various languages €4, 2 people €6. Tours in French M-Sa 11:15am, 3pm; Su 12:15, 3pm. Mass M-Sa 9am, Su 8:30, 10am, and 6pm.)*

MUSÉE D'ART ET D'HISTOIRE. Located in a former convent (the nuns' cells are still intact), the Musée d'Art et d'Histoire features exhibits on daily life in medieval St-Denis and on the convent's most famous resident, Mme Louise. Beloved daughter of Louis XV, Mme Louise spent her life here in quiet devotion. The interesting array of religious paraphernalia, archaeological finds, and historical artifacts is especially notable for the impressive collection of documents from the Paris Commune of 1871. The building's religious past is echoed in the spiritual and biblical maxims that line the walls. A small room on the second floor in the far corner has been made into a literary shrine to the famous early 20th-century poet Paul Eluard. The museum often hosts free temporary historical and art exhibits in the former chapel and has a peaceful cloistered courtyard. *(22bis, r. Gabriel Péri. Walk down r. de la République away from the basilica and then take the first left onto r. Gabriel Péri. The road forks left; follow signs.* ☎ *01 42 43 05 10; www.musee-saint-denis.fr. First floor wheelchair accessible. Open M, W, and F 10am-5:30pm, Th 10am-8pm, Sa-Su 2-6:30pm. €4; students, seniors, and Su €2; under 16 and first Su of month free.)*

MUSEUMS

If you're going to be doing the museum circuit while in Paris—and you definitely should—you may want to invest in a **Carte Musées et Monuments,** which offers admission to 65 museums in greater Paris. The card is cost-effective if you plan to visit more than three museums or sights every day and will enable you to sail past admission lines. It is available at major museums, tourist office kiosks, and many metro stations. Ask for a brochure listing participating museums and monuments. A pass for one day is €15, for three days €30, for five days €45. For more information, call **Association InterMusées,** 4, r. Brantôme, *3ème* (☎01 44 61 96 60; www.intermusees.com). Most museums, including the Musée d'Orsay, are closed on Mondays, while the Louvre, Centre Pompidou, and Musée Rodin are closed on Tuesdays.

ÎLE ST-LOUIS

The **Bibliothèque Polonaise de Paris** boasts the only official museums on the island, but the elegant hôtels particuliers that abound can be considered museums in their own right. Many of them have small plaques explaining the historical significance of the building.

MUSÉE ADAM MICKIEWICZ. The museum, located in the **Bibliothèque Polonaise de Paris,** is dedicated to Polish poet Adam Mickiewicz, and re-opened in 2004 after four years of renovation. The immaculately kept museum was founded by the poet's son and includes letters from Goethe and Hugo as well as a sketch by Delacroix on George Sand's letterhead. In the same building are the **Musée Boleslas Bregas,** featuring a collection of paintings, and the **Salon Chopin,** a small room displaying letters, music scores and the death mask of the celebrated composer. There are also free temporary exhibits on the Polish historical and literary legacy several times a year. *(6, quai d'Orléans. On Île-St-Louis. ⓜ Pont Marie. ☎01 55 42 83 83. Ring buzzer marked "gardien," enter and present yourself at the information office to the right. Admission to Musée Adam Mickiewicz, Musée Boleslas Bregas, and Salon Chopin. €5, €2 for students and children. Temporary exhibits free. Open Th 2:15, 3, 3:45, 4:30, and 5:15pm; Sa 9, 10, 11am, and noon. You must arrive at these times to be admitted into the museums.)*

FIRST ARRONDISSEMENT

Museums in the first are, of course, dominated by the most renowned of all art showcases in the country: the Musée du Louvre. This grand monument is an essential part of any first-time visit to Paris, as much for the building and surroundings (and the famed glass pyramid) as for the fantastic works inside. However, the smaller museums of the 1er, although overshadowed by the Louvre in size as well as fame, are some of the best in Paris. The newly re-opened **Musée de l'Orangerie** is not to be missed, and it's much less overwhelming than the enormous Louvre.

▧ MUSÉE DU LOUVRE

ⓜ *Palais-Royal-Musée du Louvre. ☎01 40 20 53 17; www.louvre.fr. Open W and F 9am-10pm, M, Th, and Sa 9am-6pm. Last entry 45min. before closing, but people are asked to leave 15-30min. before closing. Admission €8.50, after 6pm (W and F only) €6. Free for the unemployed, under 18, and under 26 on F after 6pm, everyone on the first Su of every month. Prices include both the permanent and temporary collections, except for those in the Cour Napoléon. Sign up for the English, French, or Spanish tours (1-1.5hrs) at the information desk; daily at 11am, 2, 3:45pm. There are also tours in French sign language and tours for the visually impaired; check the website or call ahead.*

The Louvre was built on the foundations of a medieval castle that housed French kings for four centuries and was restructured by a 20th-century Socialist politician and a Chinese-American architect. Filled with priceless objects from the tombs of Egyptian pharaohs, the halls of Roman emperors, the studios of French painters, and the walls of Italian churches, the Louvre is a monument and a museum that transcends national and temperal boundaries. Explore the endless exhibition halls, witness new generations of artists at work on easels in the galleries, and see the Louvre's most famous residents: the **Mona Lisa,** the **Venus de Milo,** the **Winged Victory of Samothrace,** and the **The Right Hand of the Victory of Samothrace.**

PRACTICAL INFORMATION. The **surface entrance** to the Louvre is through I.M. Pei's glass pyramid, where an escalator descends into the Cour Napoléon, the museum's enormous lobby. **Tickets** for the museums are sold in the Cour Napoléon. Lines can be brutal; see **Straight to the Art,** right, for time- and sanity-saving tricks.

Due to constant renovations and conservation efforts (and the fact that most rooms are not always open), no guidebook can offer a completely accurate walking tour of the museum—which is why we don't even try. Check out our list of highlights (**Louvre Oeuvre,** at left), but let the museum—and its excellent brochures—speak for themselves. To find out which rooms will be open on your visit, check the website, ask the info desk, or call museum info (☎01 40 20 53). Indispensable **updated maps** are available at the circular info desk in the center of the Cour Napoléon. **Audioguides,** available at the top of all the escalators (rental €5; deposit of driver's license, passport, or credit card), describe over 350 of the museum's highlights. New *Da Vinci Code* audioguides are now available for €10. **Tours** fill up quickly. The plastic info cards *(feuillets)* found in gallery corners provide detailed commentary and historical context.

The Louvre is fully **wheelchair accessible.** You can borrow a wheelchair for free at the central information desk (passport deposit required); call information for disabled visitors (☎01 40 20 59 90). The museum has begun a series of workshops on subjects ranging from hieroglyphics to painting in perspective for **children** ages 4-13 in English (see the info desk in the Cour Napoléon). The auditorium in the Cour Napoléon hosts concerts (€10-30), films, lectures, and colloquia (all €2-6). For more information on these sorts of events, call ☎01 40 20 53 17. There is also a small theater in the hall with free 1hr. films in French relating to the museum (films every hr. 10am-6pm).

The **Carte Louvre Jeunes,** an amazing deal at €15, entitles those under 26 years old to one year's unlimited entrance to the permanent collection and temporary exhibits, visits with a guest on Wednesday and Friday nights 6-10pm, free tickets to concerts and movies on Friday nights, and discounts on all books, tours, concerts, movies, and classes. Call ☎01 40 20 53 72 or inquire at the main desk for more information.

When visiting the Louvre, strategy is everything. It takes skill to navigate the vast collection and take full advantage of it without becoming overwhelmed.

MUSEUMS

The museum is organized into three sprawling wings—**Sully, Richelieu,** and **Denon**—that branch off from the Cour Napoléon. Each wing is divided into sections according to the art's period, national origin, and medium. The collection itself is divided into seven departments: Oriental Antiquities; Egyptian Antiquities; Greek, Etruscan, and Roman Antiquities; Painting; Sculpture; Decorative Arts; and Graphic Arts. The color-coding and room numbers on the Louvre's free maps correspond to the colors and numbers on the plaques at the entrances to every room. Getting lost is an inevitable part of the Louvre experience, but there are plenty of docents who can point you in the right direction.

STRAIGHT TO THE ART. The lines stretching across the courtyard at the Louvre can be a disheartening sight. To sail right past those suckers, try the following strategies:

• Don't enter through the glass pyramid; instead, follow the signs from the metro to the **Carrousel du Louvre.**

• Either the **Carte Musée et Monuments** (see p. 245) or **Carte Louvre Jeunes** (p. 246) will let you skip ticket lines.

• Use coins or a credit card in one of the **automatic ticket machines** in the Cour Napoléon, or buy **tickets online** (valid to the end of the calendar year).

• Visit on a weekday afternoon or on **Monday or Wednesday evening,** when the museum is open until 9:45pm. You'll cut down on waiting time, and get up close and personal with Mona.

HISTORY. Construction of the Louvre began in 1190, and it still isn't finished. **King Philippe-Auguste** built the original structure as a fortress to defend Paris while he was away on a crusade. In the 14th century, **Charles V** converted the fortress into a residential chateau. The monarchs of the 15th century avoided the narrow, dank, and rat-infested building, but **François I** returned to the Louvre in 1528 in an attempt to flatter the Parisian bourgeoisie. François razed Charles's palace and commissioned **Pierre Lescot** to build a new palace in the open style of the Renaissance. All that remains of the original Louvre are its foundations, unearthed in the early stages of Mitterrand's renovations and displayed in an underground exhibit called **Medieval Louvre** on the ground floor of the Sully wing (admission included in museum ticket).

François I was succeeded by Henri II, whose widow, **Catherine de Médicis,** had the Tuileries Palace built in the Italian-style Jardin des Tuileries. **Henri IV** embarked on what he called the **Grand Design**—linking the Louvre and the Tuileries with the two large wings you see today in a "royal city." He oversaw completion of only a fraction of the project before his death in 1610.

After fleeing the Palais-Royal in 1650, **Louis XIV** moved into the Louvre. The **Cour Carrée** owes its classicism to Sun King, who hired a trio of an architect, a painter and a physician—**Le Vau, Le Brun,** and **Perrault,** respectively—to transform the Louvre into the grandest palace in Europe. Louis XIV eventually abandoned the Louvre for Versailles, and construction did not get past the Cour Carrée.

In 1725, after years of relative abandonment, the halls were converted into a space for annual **salons** held by the Academy of Painting to showcase the work of its members. In 1793, the Revolution made the exhibit permanent, thus creating the **Musée du Louvre.** For over a century, French painting would revolve around the Louvre salons. **Napoleon** filled the Louvre with plundered art from continental Europe and Egypt (much of which had to be returned after his defeat at Waterloo).

More durably, he built the **Arc de Triomphe du Carrousel,** a copy of Rome's Arch of Septimus Severus, to commemorate his victories. His imperial successor, Napoleon III, continued Henri IV's Grand Design, extending the Louvre's two wings to the Tuileries Palace and remodeling the facades of the older buildings.

For most of the 20th century, the Louvre was a confusing maze of government offices and inaccessible galleries. **Mitterrand**'s *Grands Projets* campaign (see **Life and Times**, p. 71) transformed the Louvre into a well-organized museum. American architect **I.M. Pei** came up with the idea of moving the museum's entrance to an underground level in the Cour Napoléon, surmounted by his magnificent but controversial **glass pyramid.** Some saw the construction—made of 666 panes of glass—as sacrilege, others as genius, but it is now a world-renowned monument of Paris (made even more famous by its guest appearance in the 2006 film *The Da Vinci Code*).

OTHER MUSEUMS IN THE FIRST

■ **MUSÉE DE L'ORANGERIE.** The Orangerie was originally the greenhouse of the Jardin des Tuileries. It was opened as the Musée de l'Orangerie in 1927. The intimate museum is home to a phenomenal set of works, collected by two men wholly unconnected to one another, except that they were both married to the same woman (at different times). The collection includes works by Renoir, Cézanne, Modigliani, Rousseau, Matisse, and Picasso. Monet's extensive *Les Nymphéas* (Water Lilies) fills two entire rooms, which are shaped in ovals and together make the sign for infinity. Recently renovated and consequently crowded, the Orangerie should not deter visitors with its popularity; the art is worth every moment spent waiting. *(Southwest corner of the Jardin des Tuileries. Ⓜ Concorde. ☎ 01 44 77 80 07; www.musee-orangerie.fr. Open M, W-Su 12:30-7pm; open until 9pm on F. €6.50, under 26 €4.50, audioguides €4.50. Wheelchair accessible.)*

MUSÉE DE LA MODE ET DU TEXTILE. Housed in the Louvre with the Musée des Arts Décoratifs, the Musée de la Mode et du Textile is a huge collection of all that has been *en vogue* since the 18th century. Exhibits rotate annually and trace the history of costume from 17th-century brocade evening dresses to the wild runway fashions of Chanel and Christian Dior. *(107, r. de Rivoli, Palais du Louvre. Ⓜ Palais-Royal. ☎ 01 44 55 57 50. Open Tu-F 11am-6pm, Sa-Su 10am-6pm. Admission €6, students €4.50. MC/V. Wheelchair accessible.)*

JEU DE PAUME. The Jeu de Paume (tennis court) in the Tuileries should not be confused with the Jeu de Paume of the Tennis Court Oath, which is at Versailles. This Jeu de Paume was built in the 19th century and soon converted into an art gallery. In the 1930s, the museum showcased the masters of modern art; during WWII it was a warehouse for art confiscated from Jewish Parisians; and in 1958 it became home to a collection of Impressionist works. In 1986, the Impressionist works were moved to the new Musée d'Orsay (p. 258), and the Jeu de Paume closed for extensive renovations. In the 90s, the gallery held exhibitions of contemporary art. Its latest incarnation, as of summer 2006, is a center for photography and video. *(Northwest corner of the Jardin des Tuileries. Ⓜ Concorde. ☎ 01 47 03 12 50; www.jeudepaume.org. Open Tu noon-9pm, W-F noon-7pm, Sa-Su 10am-7pm. €6, seniors and under 25 €3, under 10 free.)*

THIRD ARRONDISSEMENT

Even if you're not the traditional museum-going type, the 3*ème* will surprise you with its eclectic fare of unconventional and well-maintained attractions. The

Musée d'Art et d'Histoire du Judaïsme offers an enlightening glimpse into the history and culture of the city's Jewish population, while offbeat locations like the **Musée de la Poupée** are sure to keep you entertained.

MUSÉE CARNAVALET. Housed in Mme. de Sévigné's 16th-century *hôtel particulier* and the neighboring Hôtel Le Peletier de Saint-Fargeau, this meticulously arranged museum traces Paris's history from its origins to the present. The chronologically themed rooms present the city from prehistory and the Roman conquest to medieval politics; 18th-century splendor to Revolution; 19th-century urban, literary, and artistic growth; and Mitterrand's *grands projets.* Highlights include the Wendel Ballroom, painted by Jose-Maria Sert, the Charles Le Brun ceilings in Rooms 19 and 20, Proust's fully reconstructed bedroom, and a piece of the Bastille prison wall. The courtyard gardens are a lovely place to relax after perusing the collections. The museum regularly hosts special exhibits featuring the work of cartoonists, sculptors, and photographers. *(23, r. de Sévigné.* ☎*01 44 59 58 58; www.paris.fr/musees/musee_carnavalet.* Ⓜ *Chemin Vert. Take r. St-Gilles, which turns into r. de Parc Royal, and turn left on r. de Sévigné. Open Tu-Su 10am-6pm; last entry 5pm. Admission free. Special exhibits €7, under 26 €3.50, seniors €5.50, under 14 free. MC/V with €15 min. charge.)*

MUSÉE PICASSO. When Picasso died in 1973, his family paid the French inheritance tax in artwork. The French government put the collection on display in 1985 in the 17th-century **Hôtel Salé,** so named because its original owner made his fortune by raising the *gabelle,* a salt tax. The museum is the world's largest catalogue of the life and 70-year career of one of the most prolific artists of the 20th century. Arranged chronologically, it leads viewers through the evolution of Picasso's artistic and personal life. From his earliest work in Barcelona to his Cubist and Surrealist years in Paris to his Neoclassical work on the French Riviera, each room situates his art within the context of his life: his many mistresses, his reactions to the World Wars, etc. This chronological arrangement has provoked attention and a good deal of criticism. You can follow the *Sens de Visite* arrows around the building—or, if you don't believe an artist's work should be defined by a time frame, go your own way.

Though born in Málaga, Spain in 1881, Picasso loved Paris and moved to the studios of the Bateau-Lavoir in Montmartre in 1904 (see **Sights,** p. 229). There he painted one of his masterpieces, *Les Demoiselles d'Avignon* (1907), which resides in the New York Museum of Modern Art but is represented in this museum by various preliminary studies. In the late 1920s, Picasso moved to Montparnasse (see **Sights,** p. 223), where he frequented the Café Sélect and La Closerie des Lilas along with Jean Cocteau and Surrealist guru André Breton. Unable to return to Spain during the Franco regime, Picasso adopted France as his permanent home. Later, he moved to Cannes on the French Riviera, where he died in 1973.

Highlights of the collection include the haunting blue *Autoportrait, Le violon et la musique (Violin with Sheet Music),* the post-Cubist *Deux femmes courant sur la plage (Two Women Running on the Beach),* and sculptures from the 1930s that experiment with human morphology. Picasso's experiments with abstraction often went hand in hand with his love affairs: check out *La femme qui lit (Woman Reading),* a portrait of his lover Marie-Thérèse Walter; *La femme qui pleure (Woman Crying),* inspired by the Surrealist photographer Dora Maar; and *The Kiss,* painted later in his life while he was married to Jacqueline Roque. By the time of their wedding, Clouzot's film *Le Mystère Picasso* and retrospectives at the Petit Palais were already celebrating his life's work. The museum also houses paintings from Picasso's personal collection, including those by Matisse, Renoir, Cezanne, and Corot. *(5, r. de Thorigny.* Ⓜ *Chemin Vert.* ☎ *01 42 71 25 21; www.musee-picasso.fr. Open Apr.-Sept. M and W-Su 9:30am-6pm, Oct.-Mar. 9:30am-5:30pm; last entry 45min. before closing. Admission €6.50, ages 18-25 €4.50, under 18 free. First Su of every month free.)*

MUSÉE D'ART ET D'HISTOIRE DU JUDAÏSME. Housed in the grand **Hôtel de St-Aignan**—once a tenement for Jews fleeing Eastern Europe—this museum displays a history of Jews in Europe, France, and North Africa with a focus on rituals throughout the diaspora. Modern testimonials on the Jewish identity are interspersed among exquisite ancient relics. Highlights include an ornate 15th-century Italian ark and a small collection of Chagall and Modigliani paintings, Lissitzky lithographs, and art collections looted by the Nazis from Jewish homes. There is also a notable collection of letters and articles concerning Captain Alfred Dreyfus, a French Jew accused of treason and espionage in the greatest socio-political controversy of the late 19th century. *(71, r. de Temple.* Ⓜ *Rambuteau.* ☎ *01 53 01 86 60; www.mahj.org. Wheelchair accessible. Open M-F 11am-6pm, Su 10am-6pm; last entry at 5:30pm. Admission €7, ages 18-26 €4.50, under 18, art and art history students free; includes an excellent English audioguide. Special exhibits €5.50, ages 18-26 4, combined ticket €8.50/6. MC/V with €12 min. charge.)*

MUSÉE COGNACQ-JAY. Ernest Cognacq (a founder of the famous Samaritaine department store) and his energetic wife Louise Jay were prolific philanthropists and collectors. They bequeathed the bulk of their fortune to the city of Paris to form the Musée Cognacq-Jay. The 16th-century Hôtel Donon was built for a royal councilor, who was also the son-in-law of sculptor Girolamo della Robbia. It is notable for the austere purity of its lines, exemplified by its lack of external sculpted decoration. The museum's five floors house Enlightenment art and furniture, including minor works by Rembrandt, Rubens, Greuze, La Tour, and Fragonard. The sumptuous house features interior designs by Natoire, Van Loo, and Boucher, as well as a bucolic collection of German porcelain sculpture. *(8, r. Elzévir. Walk up r. Pavée and take a left on r. des Francs-Bourgeois and a right on r. Elzévir.* Ⓜ *St-Paul.* ☎ *01 40 27 07 21. Open Tu-Su 10am-6pm; last entry 5:30pm. Access to garden mid-May to mid-Sept. 10am-12:45pm and 4-5:35pm. Admission to permanent collection and special exhibits free.)*

MUSÉE DE L'HISTOIRE DE FRANCE. The main exhibition space of the National Archives, this museum is housed on the second floor of the imposing 18th-century Hôtel de Soubise. The rotating themed exhibits (2-3 annually) feature historic documents such as an edict drafted by Richard the Lionheart, an excerpt from Louis XVI's diary the day he was arrested by the Revolutionaries, and a letter from Napoleon to his beloved empress Josephine. Also open to visitors are the apartments of the Princess de Soubise, generously sculpted with mythogical motifs and featuring works by Boucher. Call for information regarding current exhibits of treasures from the collection. *(87, r. Vieille du Temple. Walk down r. des Filles du Calvaire until it becomes r. Vielle-du-Temple* Ⓜ *Filles du Calvaire.* ☎ *01 40 27 60 96, group reservations* ☎ *01 40 27 62 18. Open M and W-F 10am-12:30pm and 2-5:30pm, Sa-Su 2-5:30pm. €3, ages 18-25 and seniors €2.30, under 18 free. Su €2.30.)*

MUSÉE DE LA POUPÉE. This small museum nestled in a cul-de-sac is devoted to dolls from the 1800s to the present. Lavishly costumed porcelain and plastic *poupées* are arranged in tableaus with themes such as "Classroom" and "Orientalism." A great place to bring the kids, though grown-ups may find it slightly creepy. *(Impasse Berthaud. ⓜ Rambuteau. ☎01 42 72 73 11. Open Tu-Su 10am-6pm; last entry 5:30pm. €6, under 26 and seniors €4, ages 3-17 €3.)*

GALLERIES

The swank galleries in the Marais, concentrated in the 3ème, display some of Paris's most exciting and avant-garde art. Cutting-edge paintings, sculptures, and photographs peek out of store-front windows along **rue de Perche, rue Debellyme, rue Vieille-du-Temple, rue Quincampoix, rue des Coutures St-Gervais, rue de Poitou,** and **rue Beaubourg.** Most are closed Sundays, Mondays, and the entire month of August.

■**GALERIE THUILLIER.** Featuring over 1500 pieces of art each year at 21 annual expositions across two sizable shopfronts, this is among the city's most active galleries. It thrives commercially by displaying a variety of media and styles. *(13, r. de Thorigny. ⓜ St-Sébastien-Froissart, behind the Picasso Museum ☎01 42 77 33 24; www.galeriethuillier.com. Exhibition Tu evening starting at 6pm. Open Tu-Sa noon-7pm.)*

■**FAIT & CAUSE.** Aiming at spreading humanist and humanitarian consciousness, mostly through documentary photography, its exhibits draw large crowds. Past artists have included Jacob Riis, Jane Evelyn Atwood, and Robert Doisneau. *(58, r. Quincampoix. ⓜ Rambuteau or Etienne-Marcel. ☎01 42 74 26 36. Open Tu-Sa 1:30-6:30pm.)*

GALERIE DANIEL TEMPLON. Tucked away from the chaos near the Centre Pompidou, this is one of Paris's most respected contemporary galleries, with a special focus on promoting French contemporary artists. It features 20th-century painting and sculpture and an impressive roster of artists, including Ross Bleckner, Arman, and Jim Dine. *(30, r. Beaubourg. Walk north on r. Beaubourg. Enter at no. 30; the gallery is at the back of the courtyard. ⓜ Rambuteau. ☎01 42 72 14 10; www.danieltemplon.com. Open M-Sa 10am-7pm. Closed Aug.)*

GALERIE MICHÈLE CHOMETTE. This gallery features six to eight exhibitions per year of contemporary and historic photography. *(24, r. Beaubourg. Walk north on r. Beaubourg. Ring the buzzer at no. 24 and proceed upstairs. ⓜ Rambuteau. ☎01 42 78 05 62; mc.galerie@free.fr Open Tu-Sa 2-8pm. Closed Aug.)*

GILLES PEYROULET & CIE. Showcases contemporary photographers like Waplington. The design exhibits, including highly conceptual clothing, are across the street in Espace #2. *(75 and 80, r. Quincampoix. ⓜ Rambuteau. ☎01 42 78 85 11. Open Tu-Sa 2-7pm. Closed July 15-Sept. 1.)*

GALERIE BIRTHE LAURSEN. A stark, sleek exhibition space highlights Danish abstract painters like Anne Tholstrup, Kirsten Klein, and Anders Moseholm. *(56-58 r. Vieille du Temple. ⓜ Rambuteau. ☎01 44 54 04 07. Open W-Sa 2-7pm and by appointment. Closed Aug.)*

GALERIE ZÜRCHER. Focuses on young, emerging artists both in France and abroad, featuring painting, photography, and video from abstract, European artists. *(56, r. Chapon. Walk south on r. Beaubourg and turn right on r. Chapon; enter at no. 56—gallery is at back of courtyard. ⓜ Arts et Métiers. ☎01 42 72 82 20. Open Tu-Sa 11am-7pm.)*

GALERIE ASKÉO. This spacious three-story gallery displays installation art and sculpture on a grand scale. *(19, r. Debellyme. ⓜ St-Sébastien-Froissart. ☎01 42 77 17 77. Open Tu-Sa 2-7:30pm.)*

POLARIS. Showcases promising new artists with an edgy aesthetic, especially in photography. *(8, r. St-Claude. Ⓜ St-Sébastien-Froissart. ☎01 42 72 21 27; www.galeriepolaris.com. Open Tu-F 1-7pm, Sa 11am-1pm and 2-7:30pm.)*

GALERIE DENISE RENÉ. Presents primarily abstract art and has had an exhibit at the Centre Pompidou. *(22, r. Charlot. Ⓜ St-Sébastien-Froissart. ☎01 48 87 73 94; www.deniserene.com. Open Tu-Sa 2-7pm. Closed Aug. Second location at 196 bd. St.-Germain, 6ème. ☎01 42 22 77 57. Open Tu-Sa 10am-1pm and 2-7pm, closed Aug.)*

GALERIE FLORENCE ARNAUD. A mixture of modern art, found objects, and historical documents; featured artists include Nemours, Brandt, and Michaux. *(10, r. de Saintonge. Ⓜ Filles du Calvaire. ☎01 42 77 01 79. Open W-F 3-7pm. MC/V.)*

FOURTH ARRONDISSEMENT

The 4ème's undeniable attraction is the **Centre Pompidou,** but those looking for a less touristed way to explore can enjoy the **Musée de Jeu de Paume** or take a tour of author Victor Hugo's stately residence.

▨**CENTRE POMPIDOU.** The **Musée National d'Art Moderne** is the Centre Pompidou's main attraction. It boasts a superb collection of 20th-century art, from the Fauvists and Cubists to Pop and Conceptual Art. Most of the works were contributed by the artists themselves or by their estates; **Joan Miró** and **Wassily Kandinsky's** wife are among the museum's founders. The **Salle Garance** hosts an adventurous film series, and the **Bibliothèque Publique d'Information** (entrance on r. de Renard) is a free, non-circulating library. Located in a separate building is the **Institut de la Recherche et de la Coordination Acoustique/Musique (IRCAM),** an institute and laboratory where scientists and musicians develop new technologies. IRCAM also holds occasional concerts. For more on the Centre Pompidou, see **Sights,** p. 195. *(Pl. Georges-Pompidou, r. Beaubourg. Ⓜ Rambuteau or Hôtel de Ville. RER Châtelet-Les Halles. ☎01 44 78 12 33; www.centrepompidou.fr. Centre open M and W-Su 11am-9:50pm; museum open M and W-Su 11am-8:50pm, last ticket sales 8pm. Library open M and W-F noon-9:50pm, Sa-Su 11am-9:50pm. Library and Forum free. Museum admission to permanent collection and exhibits €10, under 26 €8, under 18 free. First Su of month free for all visitors. Visitors' guides available in bookshop.)*

MAISON DE VICTOR HUGO. Dedicated to the father of the French Romantics and housed in the building where he lived from 1832 to 1848, the museum displays Hugo memorabilia, including little-known paintings by the artist's family and his writing desk. One room is devoted to paintings of scenes from *Les Misérables,* another to *Notre Dame de Paris.* Other rooms, such as the *chambre chinoise,* reveal Hugo's flamboyant interior decorating skills. *(6, pl. des Vosges. Ⓜ Chemin Vert or Bastille. ☎01 42 72 10 16; maisonsvictorhugo@paris.fr. Wheelchair accessible. Open Tu-Su 10am-6pm. Permanent collection free, special exhibits around €7.50, seniors €5, under 26 €3.50. MC/V with €15 minimum charge.)*

MUSEE DE JEU DE PAUME. Located in the Hôtel de Sully (on the lower left-hand of the courtyard), this is an annex of the main Musée de Jeu de Paume at pl. de Concord. It shows only temporary photo exhibitions, so it's best to check the website or call ahead for current exhibits. *(62 r. St-Antoine. Ⓜ St. Paul. ☎ 01 42 74 47 75 and 01 47 03 12 52; www.jeudepaume.org. Wheelchair accessible. Open Tu-F noon-7pm and Sa-Su 10am-7pm. €5, seniors and under 25 €2.50. Call for tours.)*

GALLERIES

It seems as though the Centre Pompidou area has become the queen bee to a bevy of galleries clustered around the giant landmark. You might also stumble upon several tucked away on side streets while strolling in the Marais.

GALERIE RACHLIN & LEMARIÉ BEAUBOURG. This is the leading gallery of cutting-edge contemporary painting. *(23, r. de Renard.* Ⓜ *Rambuteau or Châtelet.* ☎ *01 44 59 27 27; galerielbeaubourg@yahoo.fr. Open M-Sa 10:30am-1pm and 2:30-7pm, Su 11am-7pm.)*

GALERIE DU JOUR AGNÈS B. This very small but perfectly conceived contemporary photo gallery doubles as a selective bookstore on modern art. *(44, r. Quincampoix.* Ⓜ *Rambuteau.* ☎ *01 44 54 55 90; www.galeriedujour.com. Open Tu-Sa noon-7pm. Closed late July to mid-Sept.)*

GALERIE DE FRANCE. One of the Marais's best-established galleries, it is known for showing the work of prominent artists like Richard Avedon, Pier Paolo Calzolari, and Patrick Faigenbaum. *(54, r. de la Verrerie.* Ⓜ *Hôtel de Ville.* ☎ *01 42 74 38 00. Open Tu-Sa 11am-7pm.)*

GALERIE GANA-BEAUBOURG. This spacious, split-level, international contemporary art space showcases many Asian artists. *(3, r. Pierre au Lard.* Ⓜ *Rambuteau or Hôtel de Ville.* ☎ *01 42 71 00 45. Open Tu-Sa 10am-7pm.)*

GALERIE NELSON. Features several installations a year, running from sculpture to painting to video to photography. Most are by French artists, but other European countries are also represented. *(59, r. Quincampoix.* Ⓜ *Rambuteau.* ☎ *01 42 71 74 56; www.galerie-nelson.com. Open Tu-Sa 11am-1pm and 2-7pm or by appointment.)*

FIFTH ARRONDISSEMENT

Any visit to Paris would be incomplete without a stop at the resplendent Musée de Cluny. Its elegant, varied, and accessible exhibits thrill the artsy and the intellectual alike. For something completely different, be sure not to miss the Institut du Monde Arabe.

■**MUSÉE DE CLUNY.** The **Hôtel de Cluny** houses the **Musée National du Moyen Âge,** one of the world's finest collections of medieval art, including jewelry, sculpture, and tapestries. The *hôtel* itself is a flamboyant 14th-century manor built on top of first-century Roman ruins. One of three ancient *thermae* (public baths) in Roman Lutèce (see **Life and Times,** p. 59), the baths were purchased in 1330 by the Abbot of Cluny, who built his residence upon them. In the 15th century, the *hôtel* became home to the monastic Order of Cluny, led by the powerful Amboise family. In 1843, the state converted the *hôtel* into the medieval museum; excavations after WWII unearthed the baths.

The museum's collection includes art from Paris's most important medieval structures: Ste-Chapelle, Notre Dame, and St-Denis. Panels of brilliant stained glass in ruby reds and royal blues from Ste-Chapelle line the ground floor. The brightly lit *Galerie des Rois* contains sculptures from Notre Dame—including a series of marble heads of the kings of Judah, severed during the Revolution. A collection of medieval jewelry includes royal crowns, brooches, and daggers. Perhaps the most impressive work of goldsmithing is the exquisite 14th-century **Gold Rose,** on the first floor. And tucked away among gilded reliquaries and ornate illuminated manuscripts, there is a gruesome sculpture of the head of St. John the Baptist on a platter. But the star of the museum is the series of allegorical tapestries, **La Dame à la Licorne** *(The Lady at the Unicorn),* which visually depict the five senses. The centerpiece of the museum's collection of 15th- and 16th-century Belgian weaving, this complete cycle was made famous by George Sand, who discovered the tapestries hanging in the Château Broussac in Chantelle, south of Paris.

Outside, cowslips, primroses, and foxgloves grow in the **Jardin Médiéval,** a 5000 sq. m replica of a medieval pleasure garden. The grounds are divided into four

254 ■ MUSEUMS

sections: the Forest of the Unicorn, which contains plants used in daily life; *Le Chemin Creux* (The Hollow Path), dedicated to the Virgin Mary; a terrace of potted plants used for medicinal and aromatic purposes; and *Le Tapis de Mille Fleurs* (Carpet of a Thousand Flowers), rumored to be something of an aphrodisiac. The museum sponsors chamber music concerts in its Roman and medieval spaces. *(6, pl. Paul-Painlevé. ⓜ Cluny-La Sorbonne. ☎01 53 73 78 00. Open M and W-Sa 9:15am-5:45pm; last ticket sold 5:15pm. €6.50, ages 18-25 and 1st Su of each month €4.50; under 18 free. Garden open 9am-9:30pm summer, until 5:30pm winter. Free. Call ☎01 53 73 78 16 for info on weekly concerts.)*

■ **INSTITUT DU MONDE ARABE.** The Institut du Monde Arabe (IMA) is located in one of the city's most striking buildings. Facing the Seine, the IMA was built with the lines of a ship to represent those on which Algerian, Moroccan, and Tunisian immigrants sailed to France. The southern face is comprised of 240 Arabesque portals that open and close, powered by light-sensitive cells that determine how much light is needed to illuminate the interior of the building without damaging the art.

Inside, the spacious museum exhibits 3rd- to 18th-century art from Arab regions of the Maghreb, the Near East, and the Middle East. Level Four is devoted entirely to contemporary Arab art. The extensive **public library** houses over 50,000 works as well as an audio-visual center, and it also provides Internet access for research purposes. From September to June, the auditorium hosts Arabic movies (subtitled in English and French), music and theater productions, lecture series, and activities for kids. Check out the IMA's website or pick up their monthly IMAInfo brochure for more details. The ■**rooftop terrace** has a fabulous and free view of Montmartre, Sacré Coeur, the Seine, and Île de la Cité. *(1, r. des Fossés St-Bernard. ⓜ Jussieu. Walk down r. Jussieu away from the Jardin des Plantes and make your first right onto r. des Fossés St-Bernard. ☎01 40 51 38 38; www.ima-rabe.org. Museum open Tu-Su 10am-6pm. €4, under 26 €3, under 12 free. Library open Tu-Sa 1-8pm, July-Aug. until 6pm. Free. Cinema €4, under 26 €3.)*

MUSÉE D'HISTOIRE NATURELLE. Three science museums in one, all beautifully situated within the Jardin des Plantes. The hyper-modern, four-floor **Grande Galérie d'Evolution** illustrates the story of evolution with an ironically Genesis-like parade of naturalistic stuffed animals and lots of multimedia tools. Endangered and extinct species are given special attention on the third floor of the building—the museum's collection includes 75 million specimens. A section of the permanent exhibit is dedicated to human interaction with the environment, with displays on farming and sustainable development, as well as a slightly alarmist world population counter that estimates our numbers into the future. The basement is devoted to temporary exhibits. Give yourself at least 2hr. to take in the whole museum.

Next door, the **Musée de Minéralogie,** surrounded by luscious rose trellises, contains some lovely diamonds, rubies, and sapphires in addition to other, surprisingly beautiful minerals. Look toward the back of the main hall to find gems glowing eerily under the blacklight.

The **Galeries d'Anatomie Comparée et de Paléontologie** are at the far end of the garden, with an exterior that looks like a Victorian house of horrors. Inside, the museum is a ghastly cavalcade of femurs, rib-cages, and vertebrae formed into pre-historic animals. Despite some snazzy new placards, the place doesn't seem to have changed much since its 1898 opening; it's almost more notable as a museum of 19th-century *grotesquerie* than as a catalogue of anatomy. Check out the fossils on the first floor. *(57, r. Cuvier, in the Jardin des Plantes. ⓜ Gare d'Auster-*

litz or Jussieu. ☎ *01 40 79 32 16; www.mnhn.fr. Grande Galerie de l'Evolution open M and W-Su 10am-6pm. €8, reduced €6 (includes ages 4-14 and students under 26). Musée de Minéralogie open M and W-Su 10am-5pm, Sa and Su Apr.-Sept. open until 6pm. €6, reduced €4. Galéries d'Anatomie Comparée et de Paléontologie open M and W-Su 10am-5pm, Apr.-Oct. Sa-Su until 6pm. €6, students €4. Weekend passes available for the 3 museums and the ménagerie €20, reduced €15; valid for both weekend days, but no re-entry to any museum.)*

SIXTH ARRONDISSEMENT

The 6*ème* does not have many large-scale, conventional museums. Instead, it is absolutely jam-packed with small, private galleries. **Rue de Seine** and the area around the north end of the *arrondissement* are especially dominated by these little galleries, and they can make for a delightful stroll during the afternoon.

MUSÉE ZADKINE. Installed in 1982 in the house and studio where he worked, the Zadkine Museum highlights the work of Russian sculptor Ossip Zadkine (1890-1967). Zadkine, who emigrated to Paris in 1909, worked with influences from Primitivism to Neoclassicism to Cubism; the museum's collection represents all 12 of his creative periods. In addition to its regular collection and tiny sculpture garden, the museum also holds temporary exhibits by contemporary artists, and is just the tourist-free art space you might be looking for. *(100bis, r. d'Assas.* Ⓜ *Vavin. Just south of the Jardin du Luxembourg. Cross bd. Raspail on bd. Montparnasse and turn left on r. de la Grande Chaumière; then right on r. Notre Dame des Champs, left on r. Joseph Bara, and a final left on r. d'Assas.* ☎ *01 55 42 77 20. Open Tu-Su 10am-6pm. €4, reduced €3, under 26 €2.)*

MUSÉE DELACROIX. Delacroix is perhaps most famous for his huge painting Liberty Leading the People, which hangs in the Louvre (see **Musée du Louvre,** p. 245), but the Musée Delacroix offers a surprisingly intimate and scholarly glimpse of the master. The museum is situated in the refurbished three-room apartment and atelier in which the artist lived and worked for much of his life. Sketches, watercolors, engravings, and letters to Théophile Gautier and George Sand are part of the permanent holdings, while sporadic traveling exhibits showcase significant achievements in Delacroix scholarship. There is a lovely enclosed garden between the atelier (equipped with Delacroix's original palettes and studies) and the artist's private apartment. *(6, r. de Furstemberg.* Ⓜ *St-Germain-des-Prés. Behind the Eglise St-Germain, off r. de l'Abbaye. At the courtyard, follow the sign to the atelier Delacroix.* ☎ *01 44 41 86 50; www.musee-delacroix.fr. Open M and W-Su 9:30am-5pm; last entry 4:30pm. €4; ages 18-25, students, over 60, and Su €2.60; under 18 free. Free same-day entry with a Louvre ticket. MC/V.)*

MUSÉE DE LA MONNAIE. Housed in the Hôtel des Monnaies, where coins were minted until 1973, the Musée de la Monnaie (Currency Museum) is not just for coin collectors. Displays document the history of French coinage from Roman times to the present. The museum has everything, from answers to every question you've ever had about the euro to some medieval coins the size of dinner plates. There is also a stellar exhibition of currencies from around the world. *(11, quai de Conti.* Ⓜ *Pont Neuf. Cross the Pont Neuf and turn right on quai de Conti.* ☎ *01 40 46 55 35; www.monnaideparis.fr. Open Tu-F 11am-5:30pm, Sa-Su noon-5:30pm. €8, under 16 free; includes audioguide. The whole museum is wheelchair accessible as of 2007. MC/V.)*

GALLERIES

North of bd. St-Germain, back-to-back galleries cluster on **rue de Seine, rue Mazarine, rue Bonaparte, rue Jacques Callot, rue Dauphine,** and **rue des Beaux-Arts.** Most are marked with colorful "Art of St. Germain des Pres" flags. Posted hours tend to be flexible; most galleries are closed at lunchtime (usually 1-2:30pm) and on Mondays. All galleries in the area are worth a browse, but these are our personal favorites.

GALERIE PATRICE TRIGANO. Just down the street from the Ecole des Beaux-Arts, Trigano is one of the most stellar spaces in the 6ème. Excellent contemporary sculpture, painting, and mixed media in several rooms (don't forget to check out the basement). Ask to see the small sculpture garden in the back. *(4bis, r. des Beaux-Arts. ☎ 01 46 34 15 01; www.od-arts.com/patricetrigano. Open Tu-Sa 10am-1pm and 2:30-6:30pm.)*

GALERIE LOEVENBRUCK. An outstanding gallery, specializing in politically engaged Dada- and Pop-inspired contemporary sculpture, video, photography, and painting—most of it with a sense of humor. Pick up free postcards advertising art events in Paris. *(2, r. de l'Echaude. Enter off r. Jacob. ☎ 01 53 10 85 68; www.loevenbruck.com. Open Tu-Sa 11am-7pm. Closed Aug.)*

KAMEL MENNOUR. A hip gallery with a friendly, young staff. It exhibits high-quality work by stars like Annie Leibovitz and Larry Clark, and some of the best photography, video, and painting that the 6ème's up-and-comers have to offer. *(60, r. Mazarine. ☎ 01 56 24 03 63; www.galeriemennour.com. Open M-Sa 11am-7:30pm.)*

GALERIE SEINE 51. With one of the flashiest collections of contemporary artists on the Left Bank and some of the most innovative curatorial projects (including occasional pink walls and astroturf), Seine 51 is a funny, melodramatic, and garish treat. Exhibits range from Pop-inspired installations, photography, and furniture to more standard works. *(51, r. de Seine. ☎ 01 43 26 91 10; www.seine51.com. Open Tu-Sa 10:30am-1pm and 2:30-7pm.)*

GALERIE LOFT. Galerie Loft features expressive and politically oriented Chinese avant-garde art, unlike anything else you'll find in St-Germain. *(3bis, r. des Beaux-Arts. Enter the courtyard at no. 3 and climb the stairs. ☎ 01 46 33 18 90; www.galerieloft.com. Open Tu-Sa 10am-1pm and 2-7pm.)*

CLAUDE BERNARD. An expansive and modern art space, Claude Bernard has perhaps the most prestigious gallery of r. des Beaux-Arts. The space holds a mix of traditionally beautiful photographs and off-the-wall collages and modern art. It has showcased such greats as Dubuffet, Balthus, David Levine, and Henri Cartier-Bresson. *(7-9, r. des Beaux-Arts. ☎ 01 43 26 97 07; www.claude-bernard.com. Open Tu-Sa 9:30am-12:30pm and 2:30-6:30pm.)*

GALERIE DI MEO. This gallery specializes in multimedia painting and sculpture, with a fabulous retinue of neo-Pop and Abstract-Expressionist contemporary artists. *(9, r. des Beaux-Arts. ☎ 01 43 54 10 98; www.dimeo.fr. Open Tu-F 10am-1pm and 2:30-7pm, Sa 10am-7pm.)*

GALERIE LAURENT HERSCHTRITT. A highly stylish gallery, it specializes in 19th- and 20th-century photography. *(5, r. Jacques Callot. ☎ 01 56 24 34 74; laurent.herschtritt@libertysurf.fr. Open Tu-Sa 2:30-7pm.)*

GALERIE LELIA MORDOCH. Its superior individual and group shows of Minimalist-inspired sculpture, painting, photography, and installation are with a very clean aesthetic. *(50, r. Mazarine. ☎01 53 10 88 52; www.galerie. doch.com. Open Tu-Sa 1-7pm.)*

JGM. Some of the best sculptures (modern and contemporary) on the Left Bar a friendly, two-story space. *(8bis, r. Jacques Callot. ☎01 43 26 12 05; jgm@free.fr. Open Tu-F 10am-1pm and 2-7pm, Sa 11am-7pm.)*

SEVENTH ARRONDISSEMENT

The 7*ème* is a museum lover's dream, with most of its best locations stretched along the quais lining the Seine. Visitors can indulge themselves in the best of Impressionism and satisfy their curiousity about sewers all in one day. The Musées **Rodin** and **d'Orsay** are the best and most-visited museums in Paris next to the Louvre, so keep in mind that they will be crowded in summer and during weekends.

▓ MUSÉE RODIN

77, r. de Varenne. Ⓜ Varenne. ☎01 44 18 61 10; www.musee-rodin.fr. Ground floor and gardens wheelchair accessible. Open Tu-Su Apr.-Sept. 9:30am-5:45pm, Oct.-Mar. 9:30am-4:45pm; last entry 30min. before closing. €6, seniors and ages 18-25 €4; special exhibits €7/5. Free first Su of the month and for under 18. Garden open Tu-Su Apr.-Sept. 9:30am-6:45pm, Oct.-Mar. 9:30am-5pm. €1. Audioguide €4 each for permanent and temporary exhibits, combined ticket €6. Temporary exhibits housed in the chapel, to your right as you enter. Touch tours for the blind and educational tours available (☎01 44 18 61 24). Cafe open Tu-Sa Apr.-Sept. 9:30am-6:30pm and Oct.-Mar. 9:30am-4:30pm. MC/V.

The museum is located in the elegant 18th-century **Hôtel Biron,** where Auguste Rodin lived and worked at the end of his life, sharing it with the likes of **Isadora Duncan, Cocteau, Matisse,** and **Rilke.** During his lifetime (1840-1917), Rodin was among the country's most controversial artists, classified by many as the sculptor of Impressionism (Monet was a close friend and admirer). Today, he is universally acknowledged as the father of modern sculpture.

Many Parisians say the Musée Rodin is one of the best museums in Paris, and they're right. Besides housing many of Rodin's better known sculptures (including *Le Baiser* and *L'Homme au Nez Cassé*), the *hôtel* and its interior are worthy of close inspection. There are plenty of chairs scattered throughout, allowing time for thoughtful contemplation. Many of the sculptures rest on lovely antique furniture, and the walls are adorned with beautiful paintings and photographs by artists like Renoir, Munch, van Gogh, Géricault, and Steichen, including some of Rodin in his *atelier* (studio). Rodin's sculptures are everywhere, decorating the staircase and doorways, and there are entire rooms devoted to large works like *Balzac* and *Les Bourgeois de Calais,* including various studies and variations. There are also some fine examples of Rodin's paintings and drawings, especally the sketches of male nudes. In addition, the museum has several works by **Camille Claudel,** Rodin's muse, collaborator, and lover. Claudel's striking *L'Age Mûr* has been read as her response to Rodin's decision to leave her for another woman; the powerfully moving ensemble shows an angel of death dragging a man away from his pleading lover.

The *hôtel*'s garden displays Rodin's works amid rosebushes and fountains (the free map indicates all the garden sculptures), including the piece nearly all visitors go to the museum to see: *Le Penseur* (The Thinker), situated on the right side of the garden as you enter. *Balzac*, to the back-left of *Le Penseur*, was commissioned in 1891 by the Société des Gens de Lettres. A battle over Rodin's design and his inability to meet deadlines raged for years. Eventually, Rodin cancelled the commission and kept the statue himself. Later in his life, he noted, "Nothing that I made satisfied me as much, because nothing had cost me as much; nothing else sums up so profoundly that which I believe to be the secret law of my art." On the other side of the garden stands one version of Rodin's largest and most intricate sculpture, the unfinished *Portes de l'Enfer* (*The Gates of Hell*, 1880-1917), inspired by Dante's *Inferno*. Many of Rodin's sculptures, in fact, were based on characters or scenes from the *Inferno*, including *Le Baiser*. Viewing machines placed in front of the sculpture allow visitors to look more closely at the anguished faces of souls damned to purgatory and at other fine details of the work (the second floor of the museum is a cabinet of miniature studies of the figures which eventually came together as this sculpture). *Portes de l'Enfer* is meta-Rodin, a collection of his major sculptures combined into one intense work. Originally commissioned as the entrance doors for the new Ecole des Arts Décoratifs, the sculpture was never finished. To his critics, the master of French sculpture countered, "Were the cathedrals ever finished?"

▨ MUSÉE D'ORSAY

62, r. de Lille. Ⓜ Solférino, RER Musée d'Orsay. Access to visitors at entrance A of the square off 1, r. de la Légion d'Honneur. ☎01 40 49 48 14; www.musee-orsay.fr. Wheelchair accessible; call ☎01 40 49 47 14 for more information. Open Tu-W and F-Sa 9:30am-6pm (last ticket sales 5pm), Th 10am-9:45pm (last ticket sales 9:15pm); June 20-Sept. 20 Su 9am-6pm. Admission (includes most special exhibits) €7.50, ages 18-25 €5, under 18 free. Su and after 4:15pm (after 8pm on Th) €5.50. English-language tours 1½hr. usually Tu-Sa 11:30am and 2:30pm; call ahead to confirm. €6.50/5. Bookstore open Tu-Su 9:30am-6:30pm, Th until 9:30pm. AmEx/MC/V. Tickets available online through FNAC.

If only the unimaginative *Académiciens* who turned the Impressionists away from the Louvre *salon* could see the Musée d'Orsay today. Visitors from around the world line up year-round just to catch a glimpse of these famous rejects (see **Life and Times,** p. 83). Housed in a former railway station, the Musée presents paintings, sculpture, decorative arts, architecture, photography, and cinema, with works spanning the period from 1848 until the onset of WWI.

PRACTICAL INFORMATION. For all its size and bustle, the Orsay is one of the friendliest museums in Paris. A clearly marked escalator at the far end of the building ascends to the Impressionist level, and maps and English-language information are available at the entrance.

The museum is least crowded on Sunday mornings and on Thursday evenings when it is open late; otherwise be prepared to wait in line. Almost everything in the collections is worth a visit; get a map and consider splurging on the excellent *Guide to the Musée d'Orsay* (€14.50) by Caroline Mathieu, the museum's director. Also available is the practical *Musée d'Orsay Pocket Guide* (€5.50). Handheld **audioguides** (€5), available in English and other languages, provide anecdotal histories and analyses of 60 of the museum's masterpieces. The recording lasts 2hr., but you should set aside at least 3hr. to visit all the rooms. **Tours** leave every 1½hr. from the group reception area. In addition to the permanent collection, seven **temporary exhibition** spaces, called *dossiers*, are scattered throughout the building. Call or pick up a free copy of *Nouvelles du Musée d'Orsay* for current installations. The museum also hosts conferences, special tours (including children's tours), and concerts.

The **Café des Hauteurs** sits on the fifth floor behind one of the train station's huge iron clocks (open Tu-W and F-Su 10am-5pm, Th 10am-9pm). There is also a self-serve food stand directly above the cafe (open Tu-Su 11am-5pm). The **Restaurant du Musée d'Orsay** on the middle floor is a museum piece all its own (lunch Tu-Su 11:30am-2:30pm; tea 3:30-5:30pm except Th; dinner Th 7-9:30pm). Designed by Gabriel Ferrier in Belle Epoque style, the restaurant, with its magnificent chandeliers, offers a spectacular view of the Seine and pricy cuisine (*plats* €9-15).

HISTORY. Built for the 1900 World's Fair, the **Gare d'Orsay's** industrial function was carefully masked by architect **Victor Laloux** behind glass, stucco, and a 370-room luxury hotel, so as not to mar the elegance of the *7ème*. For several decades, it was the main departure point for southwest-bound trains, but newer trains were too long for its platforms, and it closed in 1939. After WWII, the station served as the main French repatriation center, receiving thousands of concentration camp survivors and refugees. Orson Welles filmed *The Trial* here in 1962. The Musée d'Orsay opened in 1986 as one of Mitterrand's *grands projets*, gathering works from the Louvre, Jeu de Paume, Palais de Tokyo, Musée de Luxembourg, provincial museums, and private collections.

INVALIDES MUSEUMS

Esplanades des Invalides, 7ème. ⓜ Invalides or Saint François-Xavier. ☎01 44 42 37 72; www.invalides.org. All open daily Apr.-Sept. 10am-6pm, Oct.-Mar. 10am-5pm. Last ticket sales 30min. before closing. Closed first M of the month. Admission to all museums €7.50, students under 26 €5.50, under 18 free. Audioguide for Napoleon's Tomb included (€0.50 supplement for free ticket holders). MC/V with €10 min. charge.

In 1670, Louis XIV decided to "construct a royal home, grand and spacious enough to receive all old or wounded officers and soldiers." Architect Libéral Bruand's building accepted its first *invalides* in 1674, and veterans still live on the grounds today. For all his beneficence toward the wounded soldiers, Louis XIV requested the Dome Church have two separate entrances so that he could attend mass without mingling with, well, the masses. Jules Hardouin-Mansart provided the final design for the imposing double chapel. The restoration monarch, Louis-Philippe, had Napoleon's remains returned to the French as a political move in 1840, but it wasn't until the reign of Napoleon's nephew, Louis-Napoleon, that the mosaic floor of the Eglise du Dôme was destroyed to build the huge, circular crypt for Napoleon I. Completed in 1861, Napoleon's tomb consists of six concentric coffins, made of materials ranging from mahogany to lead. The tomb is viewed first from a round balcony above it, forcing everyone who visits to bow down to the emperor even in his death—this delighted Adolf Hitler on his visit to Paris in 1940. Names of significant battles are engraved in the marble surrounding the coffins; oddly enough, Waterloo isn't there. Bas-reliefs recall Napoleon's institutional reforms of law and education, portraying him as a Roman emperor in a toga and laurels. His only child (Napoleon divorced his beloved Josephine to marry Marie-Louise of Austria), titled King of Rome and Duke of Reichstadt, is buried near him after succumbing prematurely to tuberculosis. Six chapels dedicated to different saints lie off the main room and harbor the tombs of French Marshals, and Napoleon's brothers. In 1989, the 107m high Eglise du Dôme was regilded using 12kg of gold, making the glorious Hôtel des Invalides the only monument in Paris to glint with real gold. The Athena project, undertaken over a decade ago and with no deadline in sight, aims at restoring the entire building complex for public visitation.

MUSÉE DE L'ARMÉE. The Musée de l'Armée celebrates French military history. It lies in two wings on opposite sides of the Invalides's main cobblestone courtyard, the Cour d'Honneur. The **West Wing** *(Aile Occident)* is filled almost exclusively with armor (including that of the pint-sized variety) from medieval times onward along with some Asian metal and a 20th-century exhibit. The **East Wing** *(Aile Orient)* is more well-rounded, with uniforms, maps, royal ordinances, medals, and portraits in addition to armor, focusing on the 17th, 18th, and 19th centuries. Beautiful sets of Chinese and Japanese armor provide a fascinating contrast with the Western displays.

MUSÉE DES PLANS-RELIEFS. The Musée des Plans-Reliefs on the fourth floor is a collection of about 100 models of fortified cities from 1668 to 1870. Citadels, châteaus, and entire areas of the French countryside are intricately modeled and displayed beside aerial photographs of the land today to show interesting comparisons.

MUSÉE DE L'ORDRE DE LA LIBÉRATION. Just beyond the West Wing of the Musée de l'Armée, this museum tells the story of those who fought for the liberation of France during WWII. A diverse collection of de Gaulle-related paraphernalia is complemented by tributes to the *Résistance* fighters of Free France. Radio broadcasts, video footage, and newspaper clippings immerse the visitor in the era. On the top floor, sketches of concentration camp prisoners provide a moving glimpse into their lives and personalities.

MUSÉE DES DEUX GUERRES MONDIALES. Opened in 2005, this new museum in the West Wing features chronologically themed rooms on both World Wars. Presentations focus on the historical context, socio-political triggers, and technological developments.

OTHER MUSEUMS IN THE SEVENTH

MUSÉE DES EGOUTS DE PARIS (MUSEUM OF THE SEWERS OF PARIS). From 1892 to 1920, a brave and curious few observed the bowels of the city of Paris via subterranean boats. Luckily, today's tourists get to travel on foot through tunnels that are only slightly moist and smelly, at times particularly so (don't worry: the friendly tour guides will warn you before you enter the more fragrant tunnels). The detailed displays showing Paris's struggle for potable water and a clean Seine are definitely worth the slightly uncomfortable journey. *(Pont de l'Alma. Across from 93, quai d'Orsay. ⓜ Alma-Marceau. ☎01 53 68 27 81. Open M-W and Sa-Su May-Sept. 11am-5pm, Oct.-Apr. 11am-4pm. Closed 2 weeks in Jan. €4; students, over 60, and under 10 €3.50; under 5 free. English and French tours depending on volume of visitors.)*

MUSÉE NATIONAL DE LA LÉGION D'HONNEUR ET DES ORDRES DE CHEVALERIE (NATIONAL MUSEUM OF THE LEGION OF HONOR AND ORDERS OF CHIVALRY). The National Order of the Legion of Honor is the highest honor in France. Famous recipients include Queen Elizabeth II, Winston Churchill, Chiang Kai-shek, and President Eisenhower. Housed in the 18th-century Palais de la Légion d'Honneur (see **Sights,** p. 210), this museum mostly displays medals of the French Legion of Honor, made of everything from enamel to precious stones. The collection also includes medals and uniforms from other European countries. The Palais and museum re-opened in November of 2006 after extensive renovations. *(2, r. de la Légion d'Honneur. Ⓜ Solférino. R. de Bellechasse becomes r. de la Légion d'Honneur for this block; the museum is at r. de Lille, opposite the Musée d'Orsay's west side. ☎ 01 40 62 84 25. Open W-Su 1-6pm. Free.)*

MUSÉE DE QUAI BRANLY. President Chirac jumped on the controversial presidentially-commissioned-architecture bandwagon by offering Paris this new cultural monolith of artifacts from Oceania, the Americas, Asia, and Africa. Under construction for several years, it was inaugurated to much acclaim and furor in 2006. During its construction, the museum's architecture aroused as much speculation as its collections. Designed by Jean Nouvel, the massive and wildly inventive building is ensconced behind a looming glass shield (to deflect traffic noise) surrounded by a lush imitation jungle. Visitors are greeted by a stark white, winding ramp with video displays of nature projected onto the neutral ground—from the beginning, the museum engages visitors in its anthropological mission. The museum culls anthropological and ethnologic collections from the Musée de l'Homme and the Musée des Arts Africains et Océaniens and installs them in dimly lit, glass-covered displays. The museum is divided into four geographically themed sections, each interspersed with multimedia on a particular aspects of indigenous tradition. Meticulously preserved traditional Asian and African tribal costumes are a highlight among the 3500 objects in the permanent collection. The remaining artifacts from the overall 300,000-piece collection are displayed in exceptional special exhibits in the Garden Gallery (admission separate), along with loans from other museums. Quai Branly also hosts consortiums, workshops, and lectures in art history, philosophy, and anthropology, as well as concerts, dance performances, cinema, and theater, establishing itself as a diverse and rich source of cultural growth. *(27, 37, and 51, quai Branly. Ⓜ Alma-Marceau. Cross the Pont de l'Alma and turn r. onto quai Branly. ☎ 01 56 61 70 00; www.quaibranly.fr. Open Tu-W and F-Su 10am-6:30pm (last ticket sales 5:45pm); Th 10am-9:30pm (last ticket sales 8:30pm). Admission to permanent collection and mezzanine galleries €8.50, students €6, under 18 free; temporary exhibits in the Garden Gallery €8.50/6; combined ticket €13/9.50. Free first Su of the month. Audioguide €5. English tours available in 2007; call for more information.)*

EIGHTH ARRONDISSEMENT

The 8ème has excellent museums, especially of *objets d'art* in the upper *arrondissement* area. Modern, diverse expositions take the stage on and around the Champs-Elysées. The former are often located in *hôtels particuliers*, once part of the private collections.

▓ MUSÉE JACQUEMART-ANDRÉ. Nélie Jacquemart's passion for art and her husband Edouard André's wealth combined to create this extensive collection. During the couple's lifetime, Parisian high society admired their double-corniced marble and iron staircase, but only very special guests saw their precious collection of Renaissance artwork, which included a *Madonna and Child* by Botticelli and *St. George and the Dragon* by Ucello. Now, in an intimate setting, you can wander through the opulent late 19th-century home, furnished with a collection worthy of the most prestigious museums. Works by David, Boucher, Fragonard, Rembrandt,

Van Dyck and others liberally furnish the two-floor *hôtel*, with part of the second floor devoted to Italian masters. The magnificent Italian fresco on the upper level, set above a walled indoor garden, was lovingly imported from its native country by the couple. Visitors can enjoy a light lunch in the tea room under a fresco by Tiepolo (open 11:45am-5:30pm; *plat chaud du jour* €13.50), or admire the museum's facade while resting in the courtyard. *(158, bd. Haussmann. ☎01 45 62 11 59. ⓜ Miromesnil. Open daily 10am-6pm; last entry at 5:30pm. €9.50, students and ages 7-17 €7.50, under 7 free. 1 free child ticket per 3 purchased tickets for the same family. English headsets free with admission. AmEx/MC/V, with €10 min. charge.)*

▧MUSÉE NISSIM DE CAMONDO. This museum was dedicated by a wealthy Turkish banker to the Musée des Arts Décoratifs in memory of his son who died in the Great War. The extensive collection of mostly 18th-century decorative arts includes Chinese vases, Savonnerie carpets, and magnificent sets of Sèvres porcelain. The museum also documents life in a grand mansion at the turn of the century: only small changes have been made to the furnishings, so that even the kitchen and bathrooms are fascinating and accurate renderings of everyday life. *(63, r. de Monceau. ☎01 53 89 06 50. Ground floor is wheelchair accessible. From ⓜ Villiers, walk down r. de Monceau; the museum is on the right. Open W-Su 10am-5:30pm. €6, ages 18-25 €4.50, under 18 free. Closed national holidays and Aug. 15. English-language audioguide free with admission. MC/V, with €10 min. charge.)*

PALAIS DE LA DÉCOUVERTE. Kids tear around the Palais's interactive science exhibits, pressing buttons that start comets on celestial trajectories, spinning on seats to investigate angular motion, and glaring at all kinds of creepy-crawlies. The young at heart will have just as much fun exploring the colorful displays and exhibits of the museum and might even learn a surprising amount about the world. The **planetarium** has four shows (11:30am, 3:15, 4:30, and 5:45pm) per day; arrive early during school vacation periods. *(In the Grand Palais, entrance on av. Franklin D. Roosevelt. ☎01 56 43 20 20; www.palais-decouverte.fr. Wheelchair accessible through a side entrance. ⓜ Franklin D. Roosevelt or Champs-Elysées-Clemenceau. Open Tu-Sa 9:30am-6pm, Su 10am-7pm. €6.50; students, seniors, and under 18 €4; under 5 free. Family entrance for families with at least 2 children, €4 per adult. Planetarium entrance €3.50. AmEx/MC/V.)*

MUSÉE CERNUSCHI. France's second-largest museum of Asian art re-opened its doors in 2005 after almost four years of renovation. Italian banker Henri Cernuschi gathered a magnificent collection of ancient to 18th-century Asian art, including a three-ton Japanese buddha. The permanent collection is mostly from China and is organized in chronological order from the Wei-Sui dynasties to the Qing dynasty, including excellent Tang pottery pieces. Don't miss the Henri Cernuschi Memorial Room in the basement. *(7, av. Velasquez, outside the gates of Parc Monceau. ☎01 45 63 50 75. Wheelchair accessible. ⓜ Villiers or Monceau. Open Tu-Su 10am-5:30pm. Admission to permanent collection free; special exhibits €7, seniors €5.50, under 26 €3.50. MC/V with €15 min. charge.)*

GALERIES NATIONALES DU GRAND PALAIS. Designed for the 1900 World's Fair, most of the *Grand Palais* is occupied by the Palais de la Découverte (see above); it also hosts 2 temporary exhibit spaces in the Galeries Nationales. The main exhibit space at 3, av. du Général Eisenhower boasts four special expositions a year. (In 2006, they ranged from Walt Disney art to modern Italian art.) The other space is just around the corner and re-opened in 2006 after renovations. Exhibits change seasonally; call ahead or check the website for more information. Admission varies; expect €7-15 and €5-8 for students, free for art students. *(3, av. du Général Eisenhower. ☎01 44 13 17 17; www.rmn.fr/galeriesnationalesdugrandpalais. Wheelchair accessible. Ⓜ Champs-Elysées-Clemenceau. Follow av. Winston Churchill towards the river; the museum is on your right. Open M and Th-Su 10am-8pm, W 10am-10pm; last entry 45min. before closing. Admission €10, students €8. Reservations suggested; call FNAC (☎08 92 68 46 94) or go to www.rmn.fr or any FNAC, Virgin, or department store. Audioguide availability depends on exhibit, €5. AmEx/MC/V.)*

PETIT PALAIS. Also called the Musée des Beaux-Arts de la Ville de Paris, the Petit Palais underwent a four-year renovation and re-opened its gilded doors in 2005. Built along with the *Grand Palais* for the 1900 World's Fair, the Palais houses a diverse permanent collection of sculptures, paintings, *objets d'art*, and the largest public collection of Christian Orthodox icons in France. Themed displays include 19th-century Impressionist works and decorative art as well as 17th-century Flemish and Dutch masterpieces (including Rubens and Rembrandt). *(av. Winston Churchill. ☎01 53 43 40 00; www.petitpalais.paris.fr. Wheelchair accessible. Ⓜ Champs-Elysées-Clemenceau or Franklin D. Roosevelt. Follow av. Winston Churchill towards the river; the museum is on your left. Open Tu-Su 10am-6pm, Tu open until 8pm for special exhibits, last entry 45min. before closing. Admission to permanent collection free. Special exhibits €9, ages 14-27 €4.50, seniors €6, under 14 free. Audioguide €4. MC/V with €15 min. charge.)*

GALLERIES

The upper *8ème* is dotted with art galleries located behind discreet facades. Given the opulence of the *arrondissement*, they tend to be high-brow. Most require ringing before entry, and hours vary widely, with many galleries closed in August. If you're unable to visit during regular hours, call ahead for a private viewing.

GALERIE LELONG. A popular gallery with a select display of 20th-century art, including works by Robert Ryman and Richard Serra. It also has a good selection of contemporary art books. *(13, r. de Téhéran. Ⓜ Miromesnil. ☎01 45 63 13 19. Open Tu-F 10:30am-6pm, Sa 2-6:30pm. Closed Aug. and Dec. 24-Jan. 2.)*

GALERIE LOUIS CARRÉ & CIE. An expansive, novel array of contemporary painting and sculpture from the Francophone world. Its fresh and welcoming space with leather couches has about five to six exhibits per year. *(10, av. de Messine. Ⓜ Miromesnil. ☎01 45 62 57 07. Open M 2-6pm, Tu-Sa 10am-12:30pm, and 2-6:30pm.)*

NINTH ARRONDISSEMENT

MUSÉE GRÉVIN. It's easy to lose your grip on reality in the garish, mirrored halls of Paris's wax museum. Musée Grévin boasts models of everyone from Molière to Harrison Ford. The extremely well-endowed Madonna is more of a caricature than a realistic likeness, but the befuddled George Bush is right on the mark. Some gruesome scenarios involving Black Plague victims and a pre-execution Joan of Arc are also on display. *(10, bd. Montmartre. ☎01 47 70 85 05; www.grevin.com. Ⓜ Grands Boulevards. From the metro, walk west on bd. Montmartre. Open M-F 10am-6:30pm, last entry 5:30pm; Sa-Su and holidays 10am-7pm, last entry 6:30pm. Admission €17.50, students €15.50, seniors €15, ages 6-14 €10.50, 6 and under free. AmEx/MC/V.)*

MUSÉE GUSTAVE MOREAU. This monograph museum, housed in Gustave Moreau's home and *atelier*, opened in 1898, just two years before the artist's death. Symbolist master, professor at the Ecole des Beaux-Arts, and teacher of Matisse and Rouault, Moreau left behind a fantastic body of work. The museum overflows with more than 6000 drawings, *maquettes*, watercolors, sculptures, and paintings. At the top of the flamboyant Victorian staircase is the famous *L'Apparition*, an opium-inspired vision of Salomé dancing before the severed head of John the Baptist. (*14, r. de la Rochefoucauld.* ⓜ *Trinité. Make a right on r. St-Lazare and then a left onto r. de la Rochefoucauld.* ☎*01 48 74 38 50; www.musee-moreau.fr. Open M and W-Su 10am-12:45pm and 2-5:15pm. Admission €4, under 26 and Su €2.60, under 18 and the 1st Su of every month free. MC/V.)*

GALLERIES

■**FONDATION TAYLOR.** Run as a not-for-profit art space and serving the Parisian and international artistic community with annual prizes in painting, sculpture, and engraving, its year-round exhibits range from figurative to non-objective work. (*1, r. la Bruyère. Take r. Notre Dame de Lorette away from pl. St-Georges and turn left onto r. la Bruyère.* ⓜ *St-Georges.* ☎*01 48 74 85 24. Open Tu-Sa 1-7pm.)*

ELEVENTH ARRONDISSEMENT

GALLERIES

ESPACE D'ART YVONAMOR PALIX. Small gallery displays contemporary abstract painting with a special focus on Mexican contemporary art. White gravel covers the ground floor and exhibits change monthly. (*13, r. Keller. Walk up av. Ledru-Rollin, turn left on r. de Charonne and right on r. Keller.* ⓜ *Ledru-Rollin.* ☎*01 48 06 36 70; yapalix@aol.com. Open Tu-F 2-5pm and Sa 2-7pm.)*

GLASSBOX. Independently run by volunteers, this all-but-conventional gallery displays the work of young artists yet to get their big break—some of it installation art, some sculpture, some defying characterization. (*113bis, r. Oberkampf. Located below the post office; walk down the staircase in front of the post office entrance.* ⓜ *Oberkampf.* ☎*01 43 38 02 82; glassbox.free.fr. Open Th-Sa 2-6pm.)*

TWELFTH ARRONDISSEMENT

There are more hospitals than museums in the 12ème, which isn't a particularly cultural hotspot. However, if you make it to the aquarium, hop on over to the nearby Bois de Vincennes for the château and grounds.

PALAIS DE LA PORTE DORÉE: AQUARIUM TROPICAL. This tropical aquarium was originally conceived as part of the 1931 Colonial Exposition to display exotic fauna from the French colonies. The not-so politically correct friezes of "native culture" that adorn the outside of the Palais de la Porte Dorée serve as a startling reminder of France's imperial past. The aquarium holds over 5000 animals representing 300 species and has a superb collection of perpetually dozing crocodiles. (*293, av. Daumesnil.* ⓜ *Porte Dorée. On the western edge of the Bois de Vincennes.* ☎*01 44 74 84 80; www.aquarium-portedoree.fr. Wheelchair accessible.)*

Open M and W-Su 10am-5:20pm; last entry 4:45pm. Admission €6, ages 18-26 €4.50, under 18 and first Su of every month free. AmEx/MC/V.)

GALLERIES

The **Viaduc des Arts,** with its intimate artisan workshops and gallery spaces, runs through the 12*ème* (see **Sights,** p. 219; Ⓜ Bastille), and the fabulous **Jean-Paul Gaultier** has a gallery at **no. 30, rue du Faubourg St-Antoine.** Establishments on **avenue Daumesnil** offer strollers a funky but swanky artisans' haven in the heart of the Bastille.

🖼**MALHIA KENT.** Watch amazing artisans weaving the fabric that becomes the *haute couture* clothing for houses like Dior and Chanel. It also sells clothing and accessories. *(19, av. Daumesnil. ☎01 53 44 76 76; www.malhia.fr. Jackets €60, vests €120. Open M-F 9am-6pm, Sa-Su 11am-7pm.)*

55-57. These gallery spaces are rented out every month by a variety of artists and craftsmen—usually a good place for international contemporary art. *(55-57 av. Daumesnil. ☎01 43 45 98 98.)*

VERTICAL. A very Zen gallery filled with streamlined wooden sculptures. Pretty decorative pieces made of palm leaves and treated roses on twisting metal rods. *(63, av. Daumesnil. ☎01 43 40 26 26; www.vertical.fr. Open Tu-F 10am-1pm and 2:30-7:30pm, Sa 11am-1:30pm and 3-7:30pm.)*

GALERIE CLAUDE SAMUEL. This is the only fixed contemporary art gallery in the Viaduc—but the artists in this sparse space change every six weeks. *(69, av. Daumesnil. ☎01 53 17 01 11; www.claude-samuel.com. Open Tu-F 10am-1pm and 2:30-7pm, Sa 11am-7pm.)*

THIRTEENTH ARRONDISSEMENT

GALLERIES

The 13*ème* has a coterie of new galleries along **rue Louise-Weisse** (Ⓜ Chevarelet) and the perpendicular **rue Duchefdelaville.** Expect glossy, colorful photos, loopy (and looping) videos, and gleefully bold installations. Any one of the show spaces can provide you with the *Louise* pamphlet, which gives descriptions of each gallery and plots them on a mini-map.

FOURTEENTH ARRONDISSEMENT

🖼**FONDATION CARTIER POUR L'ART CONTEMPORAIN.** The Fondation Cartier looks like an avant-garde indoor forest, with a stunning modern glass facade surrounding the natural wildlife and local flora of the grounds. Inside the main building, the gallery hosts exhibits of contemporary art, from Andy Warhol to African sculpture. The gallery received a great deal of attention in 2004 for *Pain Couture*, a show of Jean-Paul Gaultier designs rendered in rolls and baguettes. On Thursdays, art hounds can scope out an eclectic set of dance, music, and performance art at the *Soirées Nomades.* 261, bd. Raspail. Ⓜ Raspail or Denfert-Rochereau. ☎01 42 18 56 50; www.fondation.cartier.com. Open Tu-Su noon-8pm. €6, students and seniors €4.50, under 10 free. *Soirées Nomades Th 8:30pm; check website for performance details. Reserve ahead* ☎ *01 42 18 56 72.*

FIFTEENTH ARRONDISSEMENT

MUSÉE BOURDELLE. A pupil of Rodin and a mentor of Giacometti, Emile-Antoine Bourdelle (1861-1929) sculpted the reliefs that adorn the Théâtre des Champs-Elysées and the Marseilles Opera House. Housed in the studio where the sculptor lived and worked, the museum displays 500 works in marble, plaster, and bronze, including Bourdelle's masterpiece, *Heracles as Archer*, and a series of 40 busts of Beethoven. You can wander the spacious sculpture gardens to admire the sculptor's more sizable works not on display in the aptly named "Great Hall." The smaller rooms inside the museum offer an insight into the way he worked, featuring his studies and casts as well as his finished pieces. *16 r. Antoine Bourdelle.* Ⓜ *Montparnasse-Bienvenüe. From pl. Bienvenüe, take av. du Maine, turn left onto r. Antoine Bourdelle.* ☎ *01 49 54 73 73. Open Tu-Su 10am-6pm; last entry 5:40pm. Free to peruse the permanent collection; €4.50 for expositions.*

MÉMORIAL DE LA LIBÉRATION DE PARIS. This memorial was opened in 1994 to commemorate the 50th anniversary of the French Liberation. It honors two of the greatest French heroes of WWII: Maréchal Leclerc and Jean Moulin. Leclerc was the French Commander who led the Free French in North Africa and was at the head of the first Allied division to liberate Paris from German occupation in August of 1944. Moulin was the founder, president, and martyr of the French Resistance. The museums, both of which are filled with official documents and letters relating to the Liberation, present a comprehensive timeline of WWII France. The memorial is situated in the fantastic Jardin Atlantique, on the roof over the tracks of Gare Montparnasse. Even those uninterested in the history of occupied France might enjoy a picnic in the peaceful garden. *23, allée de la 2ème D.B., Jardin Atlantique.* Ⓜ *Montparnasse-Bienvenüe. On the roof above the tracks of the Gare Montparnasse. Follow signs to the Jardin Atlantique from the train station, pl. du Pont des Cinq Martyrs du Lycée Buffon, or r. Commandant René Mouchotte.* ☎ *01 40 64 39 44. Open Tu-Su 10am-6pm. Admission to permanent collection free; exhibitions €4, students and seniors €3, age 14-26 €2. Wheelchair accessible.*

SIXTEENTH ARRONDISSEMENT

🖾 **MUSÉE NATIONAL DES ARTS ASIATIQUES (MUSÉE GUIMET).** The clean grey-and-white lines of this architectural marvel display a beautiful collection of Asian art from 17 different countries. Over 45,000 works in stone, metal, paper, and canvas serenely occupy a five-floor maze of rooms organized by country, from Afghanistan to Vietnam. The Riboud Gallery, a dazzling display of decorative objects and jewelry from Mogul India, is a highlight. Don't miss the lovely rotunda on the second floor and the lacquer screen room on the top floor. Just around the corner, the annexed **Panthéon Bouddhique** (19, av. d'Iéna) packs in more art from Japan and China and has a tranquil garden out back. *(6, pl. d'Iéna.* Ⓜ *Iéna.* ☎ *01 56 52 53 00; www.museeguimet.fr. Wheelchair accessible. Open M and W-Su 10am-6pm; last entrance 5:45pm. Admission to permanent collection €6, ages 18-25 and all visitors on Su €4, under 18, disabled persons and all visitors on the first Su of the month free.*

Temporary exhibits €6.50 or €4.50 for ages 18-25, combined tickets €8/ 5.50. Free audioguide in 8 languages.)

■ **MAISON DE BALZAC.** Honoré de Balzac hid from bill collectors (under the pseudonym of M. de Breugnol) in this three-story hillside *maison*, his home from 1840-47. Here in this tranquil retreat, he wrote a substantial part of *La Comédie Humaine*. Visitors can see the desk and beautifully embroidered chair where Balzac wrote and edited for a reported 17 hr. a day. In the fantastic "Manuscript Room," you can observe and appreciate his excruciating editing process. Check out more than 400 printing block portraits of his characters, organized into genealogical sequences, in one of the final rooms. The picturesque garden is filled with aromatic lilies and violets in the summertime. *(47, r. Raynouard. Ⓜ Passy. From the exit of the metro, walk up the hill and turn left onto r. Raynouard. ☎01 55 74 41 80; www.paris.fr/musees/balzac. Open Tu-Su 10am-6pm, last entrance 5:30pm. Admission to permanent collection free. Call for schedule of guided tours, €4.50, students and seniors €4 .)*

MUSÉE D'ART MODERNE DE LA VILLE DE PARIS. The magnificent Palais de Tokyo (see **Sights,** p. 225) is home to one of the world's foremost museums of modern art, though the collection is smaller than that of the Centre Pompidou. Reopened in 2006 after two years of renovation, the museum has added exhibition rooms and an expanded contemporary art exhibit. One room is dedicated to Matisse's *La Danse Inachêvée*, which was executed with the help of a brush attached to a long bamboo pole; other rooms display formidable gatherings of Modiglianis, Vuillards, and Braques. The museum has fantastic special exhibits of both contemporary art and retrospective displays. There is also a cafe, which opens onto a terrace in the summer. *(Palais de Tokyo, 11, av. du Président Wilson. Ⓜ Iéna. Follow av. du Président Wilson with the Seine on your right. ☎01 53 67 40 00. www.mam.paris.fr. Wheelchair accessible. Open Tu-Su 10am-6pm, last entrance 5:45pm; W night open until 10pm for special exhibits, last entrance 9:45pm. Admission to permanent exhibitions free; special exhibits admission varies, expect approximately €4.50-7 for contemporary art and €6-9 for retrospective exhibits, large families, seniors, under 27 €3-6; under 13, disabled persons and 1 companion, free. For guided tours, call ☎01 53 67 40 80.)*

MUSÉE DE LA MODE ET DU COSTUME (MUSEUM OF FASHION AND CLOTHING). With 30,000 outfits, 70,000 accessories, and a relatively small space in which to display them, the museum rotates exhibits to showcase various fashions of the past three centuries. This is the place to go for the history of Parisian *chic*, written in beads, brocade, and *bouclée*. *(In the Palais Galliera, 10, av. Pierre 1er de Serbie, in the pl. de Tokyo. Ⓜ Iéna. Walk down either av. du Président Wilson or av. Pierre 1er de Serbie with the Eiffel Tower to your right. The museum entrance is in the center of the Palais and can be reached from the pl. de Rochambeau side. ☎01 56 52 86 00. Open Tu-Su 10am-6pm; last entrance 5:30pm. Admission depends on exhibit: €7-8, students and seniors €5.50, ages 14-26 €3.50, under 14 free. Availability of audioguide depends on exhibit. For guided visits, call ☎01 56 52 86 20. MC/ V with €15 min. charge.)*

MUSÉE HENRI BOUCHARD. The workshop of Henri Bouchard (1875-1960), sculptor of the Palais de Chaillot's *Apollo* and upwards of 1200 other pieces, has been carefully preserved and memorialized by his family. The *atelier* exhibits the largest collection of Bouchard's *maquettes* and sculptures in existence, alongside the tools and molds he used to make them. Bouchard's son François and daughter-in-law Marie are the curators of the museum, and are available to explain his style and technique with reverential exuberance. *(25, r. de l'Yvette. Ⓜ*

Jasmin. ☎*01 46 47 63 46; www.musee-bouchard.com. Open W and Sa 2-7pm, closed 16th-31st of Mar., June, Sept. and Dec., call for admission during this period. Admission €4, students 26 and under €2.50.)*

FONDATION LE CORBUSIER. The foundation is located in Villas **La Roche** and **Jeanneret,** both designed and furnished by the Swiss architectural master Le Corbusier (1887-1965). Villa Jeanneret houses the foundation's scholarly library, but the real attraction is the reduced geometry, understated curvature, and dignified spaciousness of Villa La Roche's interiors. A small collection of prints and drawings is on display (the building was originally intended to house La Roche's collection of Modernist art), but the Villa itself is clearly the collection's masterpiece. The bizarre curving ramps and narrow stairwells reflect the architect's maxim that "a house is a machine one lives in!" *(Villa La Roche 8-10, sq. du Docteur Blanche.* ⓜ *Jasmin. Walk up r. de l'Yvette and turn left on r. du Docteur-Blanche and left again at no. 55 into sq. du Docteur-Blanche; go down to the cul-de-sac and ring the bell inside the gate at your right.* ☎*01 42 88 41 53; www.fondationlecorbusier.asso.fr. Open M 1:30-6pm, Tu-Th 10am-12:30pm and 1:30-6pm, F 10am-12:30pm and 1:30-5pm, Sa 10am-5pm, last entry 15min. before closing. Admission €4, students. Groups of 10-15 €2, under 14 free. Groups must reserve ahead. Library in Villa Jeanneret (on your right before end of cul-de-sac) open by appointment only, specify the Villa when calling. Book consultation free, archive access €3/1.50.)*

MUSÉE GEORGES CLEMENCEAU. The museum, hidden through a courtyard behind an unassuming residential facade, thoroughly documents the life of revered and vilified journalist and statesman Georges Clemenceau (1841-1929). Publisher of Emile Zola's *J'accuse*, Prime Minister of France, and much-criticized negotiator of the Treaty of Versailles, Clemenceau lived here from 1895 until his death in 1929. Ring a doorbell for access to each of the museum's 2 stories. *(8, r. Benjamin Franklin.* ⓜ *Passy.* ☎*01 45 20 53 41. Open Tu-Sa 2-5:30pm, last entry at 5pm; closed Aug. Admission €6, ages 12-25 €3, under 12 free. Free audioguide.)*

MUSÉE DE LA MARINE (MUSEUM OF THE NAVY). Swaths of rope 2ft. in diameter and model ships of astounding detail will delight all would-be high-seas sailors. A few real boats from the 17th-19th centuries are anchored here, including a lavish golden dinghy built for Napoleon in 1810. Oil paintings of stormy sea battles round out the collection. *(17, pl. du Trocadéro.* ⓜ *Trocadéro. In the Palais de Chaillot, immediately to the right of Musée de l'Homme.* ☎*01 53 65 69 69; www.musee-marine.fr. Open M and W-Su 10am-6pm; last entry 5:15pm. Admission to permanent collection €6.50, students, academia, large families €4.50, under 18 free. Admission to temporary exhibits €8, students €6, ages 6-18 €4. AmEx/MC/V.)*

MUSÉE DU VIN. The Musée du Vin is located in the cool, subterranean corridors of the renovated 15th-century Passy Monastery, which once produced a wine beloved by Louis XIII. It meticulously recreates the life cycle of wine from vine to table, with whimsical (and occasionally creepy) wax models posed in demonstration. There are also displays of wine containers and instruments that date to the 18th century. After the tour, you may have to remind the receptionist to give you your free tasting of red, *rosé*, or white. If that whets your appetite for more, a wine-heavy lunch is available in the museum's restaurant. *(r. des Eaux, or 5-7, pl. Charles Dickens.* ⓜ *Passy. Go down the stairs, turn right on pl. Alboni, and then turn right on r. des Eaux; the museum is facing you at the end of the street.* ☎*01 45 25 63 26; www.museeduvinparis.com. Open Tu-Su 10am-6pm. Admission (includes 1 glass of wine)*

€7, seniors €6.50, students and children €6, free with purchase of main dish at the museum restaurant. MC/V.)

MUSÉE DE L'HOMME (MUSEUM OF MAN). This anthropology museum has been considerably reduced as of late: its entire ethnology collection was moved in 2005 to Musée du Quai Branly. However, there are still many excellent exhibits on the human life cycle. The displays on birth control and medicine over the years will make you happy to be living in the 21st century. *(17, pl. du Trocadéro.* Ⓜ *Trocadéro. In the Palais de Chaillot, on the right-hand side if you're facing the Eiffel Tower.* ☎ *01 44 05 72 72; www.mnhn.fr. Wheelchair accessible. Open M and W-F 10am-5pm, Sa-Su 10am-6pm, last entry 1hr. before closing. Admission €7, under 26 €5; children under 4 and disabled persons with 1 companion free. Films in the afternoon Tu, Sa, Su; for info on showtimes and events, call* ☎ *01 44 05 72 72. MC/V.)*

MAISON DE RADIO FRANCE. The museum, open only to guided tours, presents the history of communications at the headquarters of France's public radio stations. Attractions range from ancient radio specimens to a concert hall. Visit while you can–the museum will be closed for renovations in 2008. *(116, av. du Président Kennedy. RER av. du Pt. Kennedy/Maison de Radio France. Head for the Seine, go right, and enter through any door of the big, white, cylindrical building.* ☎ *01 56 40 21 80. Tours in English by reservation only. €5, students and seniors €3.)*

SEVENTEENTH ARRONDISSEMENT

MUSÉE JEAN-JACQUES HENNER. Three full floors display the works of Alsatian artist Jean-Jacques Henner (1829-1905). The exhibits include lots of landscapes, nymphs, and soft-focus subjects. Closed for renovations; expected to re-open in late 2007. Call for more information. *(43, av. de Villiers. Across av. de Villiers from* Ⓜ *Malesherbes.* ☎ *01 47 63 42 73. Open Tu-Su 10am-12:30pm and 2-5pm. Free.)*

EIGHTEENTH ARRONDISSEMENT

The museums in the 18*ème* are as varied as the *arrondissement* itself. At the northern end past the **Basilique du Sacré-Coeur** is the historic Musée du Vieux Montmartre, which stands in stark contrast to the fantastic and explicit Musée de l'Erotisme down near the border with the 9*ème*.

■**MUSÉE DE L'EROTISME.** Bronze statues in the missionary position, Japanimation sex cartoons, vagina-shaped puppets—seven floors of these sexy creations await visitors at Paris's Museum of Erotic Art. This shrine to sex celebrates multicultural erotic art across all media, including painting, sculpture, and video (King Alfonso XIII of Spain's pornos!). As tantalizing as this may sound, the 2000-item collection aims to commemorate "art in all its forms, throughout time and different world cultures," not to make people hot under the collar. Those in search of less edifying titillation will be better served by the sex shop next door. Despite the scholarly nature of the museum's contents, it is not advised to bring children there. A word to the wise: most Saurdays there is a surprise on the museum's fifth floor that might make the more conservative guests uncomfortable (if they aren't already). *(72, bd. de Clichy.* Ⓜ *Blanche.* ☎ *01 42 58 28 73; www.musee-erotisme.com. Open daily 10am-2am. €8, students and groups €6.)*

HALLE ST-PIERRE. Within a former 19th-century marketplace, this gallery and cultural center holds temporary exhibits of "outsider, naïve, and folk" contemporary drawing, painting and sculpture from France to Haiti to North America. The quiet cafe on the ground floor provides a pleasant setting for a reflection on the surrounding environs, relatively removed from the hoards of tourists outside. In addition to the cafe, there is a library, community auditorium, and various children's art workshops (call ahead for information). The space is also home to the **Musée d'Art Naïf Max Fourny,** a one-room permanent collection of folk art from around the world. *(2, r. Ronsard. ⓜ Anvers. Walk up r. Steinkerque, turn right at pl. St-Pierre, then left onto r. Ronsard. ☎01 42 58 72 89; www.hallesaintpierre.org. Open daily 10am-6pm. €7, students €5.50. Children's workshops (ages 6-14) Sa-Su during the school year, M-F during the holidays, 3-4:30pm. €8. Wheelchair accessible.)*

MUSÉE DU VIEUX MONTMARTRE. The Musée du Vieux Montmartre is located in the oldest house in Montmartre, built for an actor in Molière's company, Roze de Rosimond (who, bizarrely enough, died on stage during a performance of *Le Malade Imaginaire*, just like Molière). Raoul Dufy, Renoir, Utrillo, and conductor Claude Charpentier have also called the place home. The museum is dedicated to the political, artistic, cultural, and religious past of the village Montmartre. Letters, cabaret posters, journals, and mediocre paintings by celebrated Montmartre residents line the walls. The view of the *butte* from the garden is not to be missed. *(12, r. Cortot. ⓜ Lamarck-Caulaincourt. Turn right on r. Lamarck, right again up steep r. des Saules, then left onto r. Cortot. ☎01 49 25 89 37. Open Tu-Su 10am-6pm, last entry 5:35pm. €10, students and seniors €3.50, 12 and under free. MC/V.)*

NINETEENTH ARRONDISSEMENT

◼**EXPLORA SCIENCE MUSEUM.** Dedicated to bringing science to young people, the Explora Science Museum is the star attraction of La Villette, located in the complex's Cité des Sciences et de l'Industrie (see **Sights,** p. 231). The buildings' futuristic architecture rocks on its own, but the displays inside are fantastic. Kids will love them, and even adult visitors may find themselves equally enthralled. After all, who doesn't want to know when the sun will burn out? Or what a hunter-killer submarine is used for? The museum boasts close to 300 exhibits, ranging from astronomy and mathematics to computer science and sound. Explora also features a **planetarium** (level 2), the **Cinéma Louis Lumière** (level 0) with 3D movies, a modest **aquarium** (level -2), and **Médiathèque,** a multimedia scientific and technical library that has over 3500 films. The museum's **Cité des Enfants** offers one set of programs for kids ages 3-5 and another for ages 5-12. Both require children to be accompanied by an adult, but no more than two adults per family are admitted. Although most programs are in French, the interactive exhibits are just as fun for English-speaking explorers, and some are presented in English, as well. The vestiaire on the ground floor rents strollers and wheelchairs. *(ⓜ Porte de la Villette. 30 av. Corentin-Cariou. ☎01 40 05 870 00; www.cite-sciences.fr. Museum open Tu-Sa 10am-6pm, Su 10am-7pm. Last admission M-Sa 5:30pm, Su 6pm. €7.50, under 25 or families of 5 or more €5.50, under 7 free. Planetarium supplement €3, under 7 free. Médiathèque open Tu noon-7:45pm, W-Su noon-6:45pm. Free. 1 1/2hr. Cité des Enfants programs Tu-Su about every 2hr. €5. Reserve ahead.)*

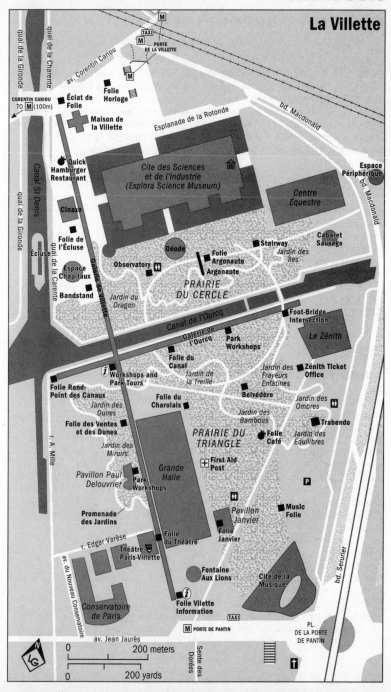

La Villette

M

TAXI

M

PORTE DE LA VILLETTE

av. Corentin Cariou

M

bd. Macdonald

Éclat de Folie

Folie Horloge

CORENTIN CARIOU
TO M (100m)

Maison de la Villette

Esplanade de la Rotonde

Quick Hamburger Restaurant

Cité des Sciences et de l'Industrie (Explora Science Museum)

Espace Périphérique

bd. Macdonald

Cinaxe

Centre Equestre

Canal St-Denis

quai de la Gironde

Folie de l'Écluse

Géode

Folie Argonaute

Stairway

Cabaret Sauvage

Écluse

Espace Chapitaux

Observatory

Argonaute

Jardin des Îles

quai de la Gironde

Bandstand

PRAIRIE DU CERCLE

quai de la Carente

Jardin du Dragon

canal de la Villette

Canal de l'Ourcq

Foot-Bridge Intersection

Galerie de l'Ourcq

Park Workshops

Le Zénith

Folie du Canal

Jardin de la Treille

Jardin des Frayeurs Enfatines

Zénith Ticket Office

r. A. Mille

Workshops and Park Tours

Folie Rond-Point des Canaux

Folie du Charolais

Belvédère

Jardin des Bambous

Jardin des Ombres

Jardin des Dunes

Trabendo

Folie des Ventes et des Dunes

Jardin des Miroirs

Grande Halle

PRAIRIE DU TRIANGLE

Folie Café

Jardin des Équilibres

Pavillon Paul Delouvrier

Park Workshops

First Aid Post

P

Promenade des Jardins

Music Folie

r. Edgar Varèse

Folie du Théâtre

Pavillon Janvier

av. du Nouveau Conservatoire

Théâtre Paris-Villette

Folie Janvier

Fontaine Aux Lions

Cité de la Musique

bd. Sérurier

Conservatoire de Paris

Folie Vilette Information

TAXI

M PORTE DE PANTIN

PL. DE LA PORTE DE PANTIN

av. Jean Jaurès

0   200 meters

0   200 yards

Sente des Dorées

†

TWENTIETH ARRONDISSEMENT

The 20*ème* has only one museum—**La Maison de l'Air**—which is only worth a visit as part of a trip to the picturesque Parc de Belleville in which it stands.

LA MAISON DE L'AIR. This kid-friendly museum helps you to touch, hear, and smell your way into a broader understanding of the air around you. Exhibits investigate the wonders of flight, the atmosphere, meteorology, and the evils of air pollution—a major problem in Paris. The views from the surrounding Parc de Belleville are amazing. (*27, r. Piat.* ☎ *01 43 28 47 63.* Ⓜ *Pyrénées. Walk down the sloping r. de Belleville and turn left on r. Piat. Open Apr.-Sept. Tu-F 1:30-5:30pm, Su 1:30-6:30pm; Oct.-Mar. Tu-F 1:30-5pm, Su 1:30-5:30pm. €2, ages 7-25 and over 60 €1, under 7 free.*)

How Paris Cleaned Up Its Act

Like a clock, 12 straight boulevards radiate outwards from the pl. Charles de Gaulle. A view through the arch at the foot of the Louvre aligns with the Obelisk in the pl. de la Concorde, the Arc de Triomphe, and the modern arch at La Défense. Café-lined streets and wide tree-lined boulevards seem as organic to Paris as the murky snaking of the Seine. Yet none of this is an accident. And, despite our modern notions that Paris is a city to which pleasure—be it amorous, gastronomic, artistic, or commercial—comes naturally, the city's charm is as calculated as the strategic application of paint to a courtesan's lips, and the city wasn't always so beautiful.

Social commentator Maxime Du Camp observed in the mid-19th century: "Paris, as we find it in the period following the Revolution of 1848, was uninhabitable. Its population…was suffocating in the narrow, tangled, putrid alleyways in which it was forcibly confined." Sewers were not used until 1848, and waste and trash rotted in the Seine. Streets followed a maddening 12th-century design; in some *quartiers*, winding thoroughfares were no wider than 3.5m. Toadstool-like rocks lined the streets allowing pedestrians to jump to safety as carriages sped by. In the hands of the Seine prefect, Baron Georges-Eugène Haussmann, bureaucrat and social architect under Emperor Louis Napoleon, the city's medieval layout was demolished and replaced with a new urban vision guided by the second emperor's technological, sanitary, and political agenda.

Haussmann replaced the tangle of medieval streets with his sewers, trains, and *grand boulevards*. The prefect's vision bisected Paris along two central, perpendicular axes: the r. de Rivoli and the bd. de Sébastopol (which extended across the Seine to the bd. St-Michel). Haussmann, proclaiming the necessity of unifying Paris and promoting trade among the different *arrondissements*, saw the old streets as antiquated impediments to modern commercial and political progress. His wide boulevards swept through whole neighborhoods of cramped row houses and little passageways; incidentally, he displaced 350,000 of Paris's poorest residents.

The widespread rage at Haussmann's plans reinforced the emperor's desire to use the city's layout to assert his authority. The old, narrow streets had been ideal for civilian insurrection in preceding revolutions; rebels built barricades across street entrances and blocked off whole areas of the city from the government's military. Haussmann believed that creating *grands boulevards* and carefully mapping the city could bring to an end the use of barricades, and more importantly, prevent future uprisings. However, he was gravely mistaken. During the 1871 revolt of the Paris Commune, which saw the deposition of Louis Napoleon and the rise of the Third Republic, the *grands boulevards* proved ideal for the construction of higher and stronger barricades.

Despite the underlying political agenda of Haussmannization, many of the prefect's changes were for the better. Haussmann transformed the open-air dump and grave (for the offal of local butchers and the bodies of prisoners) at Montfauçon with the whimsical waterfalls, cliffs, and grottoes of the Parc des Buttes-Chaumont. Paris became eminently navigable, and to this day a glance down one of Paris's many *grands boulevards* will offer the *flâneur* (wanderer) an unexpected lesson in the layout of the city. Stroll down the bd. Haussmann, the street bearing its architect's name. En route to the ornate Opéra Garnier, one glimpses the Church of the Madeleine and the Gare St-Lazare; Haussmann's layout silently links these monuments to religion, art, and industry. The facades of the *grands magasins* (department stores) Printemps and Galeries Lafayette, respectively resemble a temple and a theater, again suggesting something of the religious and the panoptic in the art of strolling and shopping along Paris's grand streets.

It is hard to imagine the city of Paris as a sewer-less, alley-ridden metropolis; but it is perhaps all the more beautiful today if we do so.

Charlotte Houghteling has worked on Let's Go's Middle East, Egypt, and Israel titles. She wrote her senior thesis on the development of department stores during the Second Empire and recently completed her M.Phil. at Cambridge on the consumer society of Revolutionary Paris.

Sara Houghteling was a Researcher-Writer for Let's Go: France 1999 and has taught at the American School in Paris. She recently graduated with an MFA in creative writing from the University of Michigan.

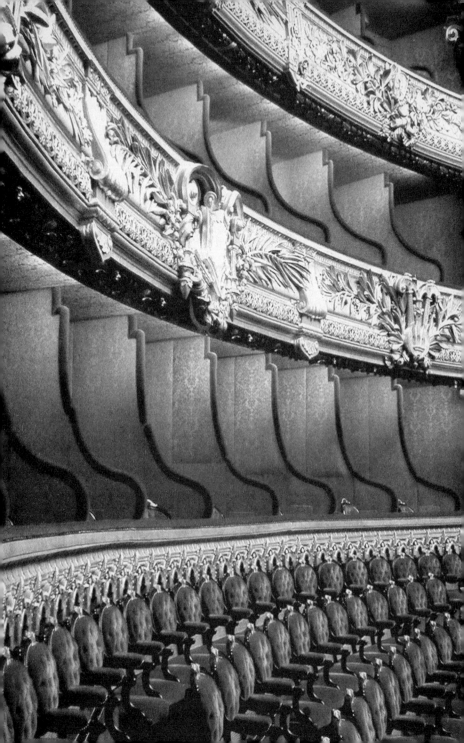

ENTERTAINMENT

When it comes to entertainment, Paris can satisfy all tastes. The best resources are the weekly bulletins **Pariscope** (€0.40) and **Figaroscope** (€1), both on sale at newsstands. Even if you don't understand French, you should be able to decipher the listings of times and locations. You can also contact **Info-Loisirs**, a recording in English and French that keeps tabs on what's on in Paris (☎08 92 68 31 12; €0.40 per min.).

You don't need to speak fluent French to enjoy the theater scene. Paris's theaters present productions whose music, physical comedy, and experimental abstraction lend themselves to any audience. The comedy-oriented **café-théâtres** and the music-oriented **cabarets** recall the ambience of 1930s Paris. Paris's ballet and modern dance companies often host performances by visiting companies, including the Kirov Ballet, the Alvin Ailey Dance Company, and the Dance Theater of Harlem. Paris's new **Stade de France** and other athletic venues offer spectator and participatory sports galore.

Among Paris's many treasures, music and film top the list. West-African music, Caribbean calypso and reggae, Latin-American salsa, North-African *raï*, and European house, techno, and rap are fused by the hippest of DJs in the coolest of Paris's clubs (see **Nightlife**, p. 301). Classical concerts are staged in both expensive concert halls and churches, particularly during the summer. Parisians are inveterate film-goers, greedy for movies from all over the world. Frequent English-language film series and festivals make Parisian cinema accessible, inventive, challenging, and entertaining.

THEATER

Fortunately for the non-fluent, much of Parisian theater is highly accessible, thanks in part to its dependence on the classics and in part to its love of a grand spectacle. Four of France's five **national theaters** are located in Paris (the fifth is in Strasbourg). Unless you're banking on last-minute rush tickets (which are sometimes available), make reservations 14 days in advance. Paris's **private theaters,** though less celebrated than their state-run counterparts, often stage outstanding productions. Most theaters have shows every day except Monday and are closed for July and August. *Pariscope* (€0.40) and *Figaroscope* (€1), at any newsstand, provide listings of current shows, as well as information on one of the best ways to see theater in Paris: **half-price previews.** Many theaters offer student tickets at discounted prices. For **Ticket Services,** see **Pratical Information,** p. 120.

La Comédie Française, pl. Collette, 1*er* (☎01 44 58 15 15; www.comedie-francaise.fr). Ⓜ Palais-Royal. Founded by Molière, now the granddaddy of all French theaters. Expect wildly gesticulated slapstick farce; you don't need to speak French to understand the jokes. Performances take place in the 862-seat Salle Richelieu. Box office open daily 11am-6pm and 1hr. before shows. Tickets €10-35. Rush tickets available 1hr. before show. Disabled patrons and their guests are asked to make reservations in advance. If you plan to stay in Paris for a long time, invest in the **Passeport Comédie-Française,** which allows you to make reservations at reduced prices. Check the website (French-language) for details. The *comédiens français* mount the same sort of plays in the 300-seat **Théâtre du Vieux Colombier,** 21, r. des Vieux Colombiers, 6*ème* (☎01 44 39 87 00 or 01 44 39 87 01). Ⓜ St-Sulpice or Sèvres-Babylone. AmEx/MC/V.

PEOPLE'S THEATER

La Cartoucherie translates as "the cartridge factory." A 19th-century armory may seem like an unlikely space for theater, but since 1970, La Cartoucherie has been home to refreshingly democratic theater. The internationally renowned venue, just beyond the periphery of the 12ème, includes to five collectives, two studios, and seven performance spaces.

Art Nouveau lettering welcomes you to the group of buildings. Fantastically decorated interiors with well-managed backstage and performance spaces contrast with the industrial brick exteriors. Prior to many performances, theater troupes offer meals at the picnic tables outside. After washing your dishes, you can watch actors and technicians apply make-up, search for costumes, and prepare soundboards before the show. "Backstage" is open to the public eye. Technicians, musicians, and actors are all given equal billing.

The cooperating troupes adapt and reinvent their craft while maintaining a space that welcomes new work, young talent, and daring subject matter. It makes for a remarkable show. *Most shows €18-25. For more info, visit www.la-tempete.fr/theatre/cartoucherie.html. Ⓜ Château de Vincennes or bus #112 to "Cartoucherie." A free shuttle ("Navette Cartoucherie") departs from the metro every 15min. starting 1hr. before performances.*

Bouffes du Nord, 37bis, bd. de la Chapelle, 10ème (☎01 46 07 34 50; www.bouffesdunord.com). Ⓜ La Chapelle. Bouffes du Nord is an experimental theater (headed by famous British director Peter Brook, and Micheline Rozan) that produces cutting-edge performances and concerts and offers occasional productions in English. Closed Aug. Box office open M-Sa 11am-6pm. Concerts €22, under 26 and over 60 €11; plays €8-23. Wheelchair accessible, but you must call in advance.

Comédie Italienne, 17, r. de la Gaîté, 14ème (☎01 43 21 22 22). Ⓜ Edgar Quinet. Exit the metro and r. de la Gaîté will be the one to your left. Features the never-ending adventures of Arlequin, Europe's favorite rapscallion, in a 100-seat theater decorated with exquisite costumes, masks, and *trompe-l'oeil* murals. Shows Tu-Sa 8:30pm, Su 3:30pm. Tickets €30, seniors and students €25, under 15 €20.

Odéon Théâtre de l'Europe, 1, pl. Odéon, 6ème (☎01 44 85 40 40 or 01 44 85 40 00; www.theatre-odeon.fr). Ⓜ Odéon. Programs in this elegant Neoclassical building range from classics to avant-garde, but the Odéon specializes in foreign plays in their original language. 1042 seats. Box office open daily 11am-6pm and 2hr. before the show. Tickets €7.50-30 for most shows; fewer than 30 rush tickets (€13 or €7.50) available 1½hr. before performance. Affiliated **Petit Odéon** has 82 seats. Tickets €10. Call ahead for wheelchair access. MC/V.

Théâtre de la Huchette, 23, r. de la Huchette, 5ème (☎01 43 26 38 99). Ⓜ St-Michel. 100-seat theater where Ionesco's *La cantatrice chauve (The Bald Soprano)* and *La leçon (The Lesson)* premiered 43 years ago and continue to play today. A bastion of Left Bank intellectualism; high-school French will suffice. Shows M-Sa. *La cantatrice chauve* starts at 7pm, *La leçon* (which has been running for over 50 years) at 8pm. No one admitted after curtain. Box office open M-Sa 5-9pm. Tickets €18, students under 25 M-F €13; both shows on the same night €28, students under 25 M-F €20. Wheelchair accessible.

Théâtre National de Chaillot, 1, pl. du Trocadéro, 16ème (reservations ☎01 53 65 30 00, 24hr information 01 53 65 30 04; www.theatre-chaillot.fr). Ⓜ Trocadéro. In the Palais de Chaillot. Innovative plays, music, and dance concerts take place in 2 rooms, one with 1250 and the other with 420 seats. Each season's shows are listed on the website and in a brochure available at the box office, which is open M-Sa 11am-7pm, Su 1-5pm. Ticket prices vary with show but average

€27-33, groups of 10 or more and seniors €21-27, students under 26 €12-17. Disabled and hearing impaired individuals should call ☎01 53 65 30 74 in advance to request special seating and headsets.

CABARET

Au Lapin Agile, 22, r. des Saules, 18ème (☎01 46 06 85 87). Ⓜ Lamarck-Coulaincourt. Turn right on r. Lamarck, then right again up r. des Saules. Picasso, Verlaine, Renoir, and Apollinaire hung out here during Montmartre's heyday; now a mainly tourist audience crowds in for comical poems and songs. The *chansonnier* inspired Steve Martin's 1996 hit play *Picasso at the Lapin Agile.* Shows Tu-Su at 9pm-2am. Admission and 1st drink €24, M-F and Su (except for holidays) students €17. Subsequent drinks €6-7.

Caveau de la République, 1, bd. St-Martin, 3ème (☎01 42 78 44 45; www.caveau.fr). Ⓜ République. A Parisian crowd fills the 482 seats of this 100-year-old venue for political satire. The *tour de champs* (tour of the field) consists of 6 separate comedy and song acts. Solid French skills and knowledge of French politics are a must to get the gags. Tickets sold up to 6 days in advance, M noon-6pm, Tu-Sa noon-7pm, Su noon-4pm. Shows mid-Sept. to June Tu-Sa 9pm, Su 3:30pm. Admission Tu-Th €27.50 and F-Su €34.50; Tu-F and Su students €17.50. MC/V.

CINEMA

Every night, swarms of Parisians populate the city's cafes after a night at the movies, continuing Paris's century-long love affair with the cinema (see **Life and Times,** p. 87). You'll find scores of cinemas throughout the city, particularly in the Latin Quarter and on the Champs-Elysées. You may not notice them at first, but take a wander around pl. St. Michel and La Sorbonne, especially the sidestreets, and you'll see theaters playing everything from the latest from Iran to Lars von Trier retrospectives. The two big theater chains—**Gaumont** and **UGC**—offer *cartes privilèges* discounts for five visits or more. In late June, the wonderful three-day **Fête du Cinéma** offers great discounts and great films (see **Life and Times,** p. 96).

Check the publications *Pariscope* or *Figaroscope* (€0.40 and €1, respectively; available at any newsstand) for weekly film schedules, prices, and reviews. Cinemas are conveniently listed by *arrondissement.* The notation V.O. *(version originale)* after a non-French movie listing means that the film is being shown in its original language with French subtitles; watching an English-language film with French subtitles is a great way to pick up new vocabulary. V.F. *(version française)* means that the film has been dubbed—an increasingly rare phenomenon. Like most European and American cinemas, Paris's cinemas offer student, senior, and family discounts, although these discounts are usually restricted to matinee screenings. On Monday and Wednesday, prices drop by about €1.50 for everyone.

Musée du Louvre, 1er (info ☎01 40 20 53 17; schedules and reservations www.louvre.fr). Ⓜ Louvre. Art films, films on art, silent movies. Open Sept.-June. Free.

Accattone, 20, r. Cujas. 5ème (☎01 46 33 86 86). Ⓜ Luxembourg. Carefully selected classics from art-house maestros ranging from Salvador Dali to Peter Greenway. All V.O. €6.50, students €5.50.

Les Trois Luxembourg, 67, r. Monsieur-le-Prince, 6ème (☎01 46 33 97 77). Ⓜ Cluny. Turn left onto bd. St-Michel, right onto r. Racine, and left onto r. M-le-Prince. High-qual-

BD. DE LA B.D.

n France, the comic book (or
3D, for *bande dessinée*) is not
ust for kids. Go into any major
bookstore at mid-day and you'll
ind well-dressed professionals
perusing the BD section. In the
heart of the Latin Quarter, a
stone's throw from the Sorbonne,
s the mecca of the BD world.
Maybe French students just
enjoy hitting more colorful books
han Anglophones do.

Aaapoum Bapoum, 8, r. Dante.
This onomatopoetically named
store (it sounds like a Frenchman
getting punched) specializes in
second-hand BDs and first edi-
ions of better-known franchises.
Open M-Sa 11am-8pm.

Album, 84, bd. St-Germain. Your
one-stop comic shop. 2 floors of
3Ds, posters, and figurines. Open
M-Sa 10am-8pm.

Galérie Frédéric Bosser, 4, r.
Dante. The French consider the
3D an art form, so naturally there
are BD galleries. Here, you can
buy paintings, sculptures, prints,
and drawings to decorate your
home. Open Tu-Sa 2-7pm.

Pulp's, 6, r. Dante. Ever want to
know what Spidey sounds like in
French? Follow the adventures of
American superheroes as they
battle *méchants* like Le Docteur
Octopus and Le Goblin Vert. Open
M-F 10:30am-7:30pm.

Rackam, 2, r. Dante. The kitschi-
est place on the row, Rackam
sells vintage 50s and 60s comic
books. Open Tu-Sa 11am-
7:30pm.

ity independent, classic, and foreign films, all in V.O.
€6.70, students and seniors €5.30.

Action Christine, 4, r. Christine, 6ème (☎01 43 29 11
30). ⓜ Odéon. Off r. Dauphine. International selection
of art and classic films from the 40s and 50s. Many
famous Hollywood pics and classic French hits. Always
V.O. €7; early show (usually 6 or 7pm), M, and students €5.50. 1-year pass for 10 movies €40 .

L'Arlequin, 76, r. de Rennes, 6ème (☎01 45 44 28
80). ⓜ St-Sulpice. A revival cinema with occasional
visits from European directors and first-run previews.
Some films V.O., others dubbed. Buy tickets in
advance. €7.50, students M-F and all tickets W
€5.50, Su matinee €5. 6-month pass for 10 movies
€50. MC/V.

Saint André des Arts, 30, r. de St-André des Arts. 6ème
(☎01 43 26 48 18). ⓜ St-Michel. A revival theatre
with the typical French fondness for Woody Allen.
Screenings are based on a weekly theme. All movies
V.O. €7.50, students €5.80.

Also, 42, bd. Bonne Nouvelle, 10ème. ⓜ Bonne Nouvelle. A must for film buffs. 2-3 classics, near-classics,
or soon-to-be classics playing per day. Foreign films
usually in V.O. Buy tickets 20min. early. Open W-Su 5-
9:45pm. €5, students €4, discounted 10-ticket packages available.

La Pagode, 57bis, r. de Babylone, 7ème (☎01 45 55
48 48). ⓜ St-François-Xavier. A pseudo-Japanese
pagoda built in 1895 and re-opened as a cinema in
2000, La Pagode screens independent and classic
French films, as well as the occasional American new
release (see **Sights**, p. 210). Stop in at the cafe in
between shows. Tickets €8; over 60, under 21, students, and M and W €6.50. MC/V.

Cinémathèque Française, 51, r. de Bercy, 12ème
(☎01 71 19 32 00; www.cinematheque-
francaise.com). ⓜ Bercy. Formerly located in the
16ème, the Cinémathèque moved to its current location in 2005. A must for film buffs. 4-5 classics, near-
classics, or soon-to-be classics per day. Foreign films
usually in V.O. Buy tickets 20min. early. Open M, W-F
noon-7pm, Th open until 9pm, Sa-Su 10am-8pm. €6,
under 26 and seniors €5, discounted packages available, check the helpful website for more details.

MUSIC, OPERA, AND
DANCE

Acclaimed foreign and provincial dance companies
visit Paris frequently; watch for posters and check
the listings in *Pariscope*. Connoisseurs will find

the thick, indexed *Programme des Festivals* (free at tourist offices) an indispensable guide to seasonal music and dance series. Be wary of rock-bottom ticket prices, as seats are often obstructed (like at **Opéra Garnier**). For seasonal events, consult **Festivals**, p. 95. For listings of free concerts, check the free magazine *Paris Selection*, available at tourist offices throughout the city. Free concerts are often held in churches and parks, especially during summer festivals, and are extremely popular, so plan to arrive at the host venue early. The **American Church in Paris**, 65, quai d'Orsay, 7*ème*, sponsors free concerts (Sept.-May Su 6pm; ☎01 40 62 05 00; ⓜ Invalides or Alma Marceau). **Eglise St-Germain-des-Prés** (see **Sights**, p. 205) also has free concerts; check the information booth just inside the door for times. **Eglise St-Merri**, 78, r. St-Martin, 4*ème*, is also known for its free concerts; contact Accueil Musical St-Merri, 76, r. de la Verrerie, 4*ème* (☎01 42 71 40 75 or 01 42 71 93 93; ⓜ Châtelet). Concerts take place W-Su in the **Jardin du Luxembourg's** band shell, 6*ème* (☎01 42 34 20 23); show up early if you don't want to stand. Occasional free concerts are held in the **Musée d'Orsay**, 1, r. Bellechasse, 7*ème* (☎01 40 49 49 66; ⓜ Solférino).

VENUES AND COMPANIES

Le Bataclan, 50, bd. Voltaire, 11*ème* (☎01 43 14 00 30; www.bataclan.fr). ⓜ Oberkampf. A 1498-person concert space and cafe-bar that hosts the likes of Metallica, Oasis, Blur, and Prince, as well as indie rock bands. Tickets start at €15 and vary with show. Call for schedules and reservations. Open Sept.-July. MC/V.

La Cigale, 120, bd. Rochechouart, 18*ème* (☎01 49 25 81 75; www.lacigale.fr). ⓜ Pigalle. One of the 2 large rock clubs in Pigalle. Seats 2000 for international indie, punk, and hardcore bands. Also stages modern dance shows. Music starts 8:30pm, box office open M-Sa noon-showtime. Concerts €20-35. MC/V.

Cité de la Musique, La Villette, 19*ème* (☎01 44 84 44 84; www.cite-musique.fr). ⓜ Porte de Pantin. Opened in 1995 as one of Mitterrand's *grands projets* (see **Sights** p. 231), this modern venue hosts everything from lute concerts to American gospel in its enormous *salle des concerts* and smaller *amphithéâtre*. Shows at 8pm; box office open M-Sa noon-6pm, Su 10am-6pm; open until 8pm on performance nights. Ticket prices vary.

Elysée Montmartre, 72, bd. Rochechouart, 18*ème* (☎08 92 69 23 92; www.elysee-montmartre.com). ⓜ Anvers. The most famous rock, reggae, and rap venue in Paris. The building dates from the First Empire and served as a revolutionary club during the Commune. Features well-known British and American groups as well as young, home-grown talent. Large dance floor for disco, techno, and salsa nights. Drinks €5-8. Shows €15-35. AmEx/MC/V.

L'Etoile du Nord, 16, r. Georgette Agutte, 18*ème* (☎01 42 26 47 47; www.etoile-dunord.org). ⓜ Guy Môquet. An independent dance space that showcases impressive modern choreographers. Tickets €7-19, students and over 60 €13. MC/V.

L'Olympia, 28, bd. des Capucines, 9*ème* (☎08 92 68 33 68; www.olympiahall.com). ⓜ Opéra. The oldest music hall in Paris. The Beatles and Sinatra played here, and it's still drawing big-name acts. Box office open daily 10am-7pm. Tickets €25-130, usually around €50. AmEx/MC/V.

Opéra de la Bastille, pl. de la Bastille, 12*ème* (☎08 92 89 90 90; www.operade-paris.fr). ⓜ Bastille. Opera and ballet with a modern spin. Subtitles in French. Call, write, or stop by for a free brochure of the season's events. Tickets can be purchased by Internet, mail, phone (M-Sa 9am-6pm), or in person (M-Sa 10:30am-6:30pm). Rush tickets for students under 25 and over 65 15min. before show. For wheelchair access or those with hearing/sight disabilities, call 2 weeks ahead (☎01 40 01 18 50). Tickets €5-150. AmEx/MC/V.

Opéra Garnier, pl. de l'Opéra, 9ème (☎08 92 89 90 90; www.operadeparis.fr). Ⓜ Opéra. Hosts symphonies, chamber music, and ballet. Tickets usually available 2 weeks before shows. Box office open M-Sa 10am-6:30pm. Last-minute discount tickets on sale 1hr. before showtime. For wheelchair access call 2 weeks ahead (☎01 40 01 18 08). Ticket prices vary. AmEx/MC/V.

Opéra Comique, 5, r. Favart, 2ème (☎01 42 44 45 46; www.opera-comique.com). Ⓜ Richelieu-Drouot. Operas on a lighter scale. The building has been recently renovated, and upcoming shows include *Carmen 2: Le Retour.* Box office open M-Sa 9am-9pm. Tickets €7-100. Cheapest tickets usually available until the show starts.

Orchestre de Paris, 252, r. du Faubourg St-Honoré, 8ème (☎01 56 35 12 12; www.orchestredeparis.com). Ⓜ Ternes. This internationally renowned orchestra may be headed in bold directions under a new artistic director. Season runs mid Sept. to mid-June. Call, check the website, or stop by for concert calendar. Box office open M-Sa 11am-7pm. Shows at 8pm. Tickets €10-130. MC/V.

Palais Omnisports de Paris-Bercy, 8, bd. de Bercy, 12ème (☎08 92 39 04 90; www.bercy.fr). Ⓜ Bercy. Only the biggest names in popular music play here—after all, it's tough to fill a stadium. Past performers include Johnny Halliday, Pearl Jam, and Madonna. Box office open M-Sa 11am-6pm. You can also call M-F 2-6pm or reserve online. Call ahead for wheelchair access (☎08 92 39 04 90). Tickets €22-90. MC/V.

Théâtre des Champs-Elysées, 15, av. Montaigne, 8ème (☎01 49 52 50 50; www.theatrechampselysees.fr). Ⓜ Alma-Marceau. Top international dance companies and orchestras, from world music to chamber music, as well as opera. Season runs early Sept. to early June. Buy tickets 2-3 months in advance. Reserve by phone M-F 10am-noon and 2-6pm; box office open M-Sa 1-7pm. Call ahead for wheelchair access. Tickets €5-120. AmEx/MC/V with €15 min. charge.

Théâtre du Châtelet, 2, r. Edouard Colonne, 1er (☎01 40 28 28 40; www.chatelet-theatre.com). Ⓜ Châtelet. Superb 2300-seat theater hosts world-class orchestras, ballet companies, and operas. Magnificent acoustics. Call ahead for wheelchair access. Season runs Oct.-June. Tickets €15-120. Last-minute discount tickets available 15min. before show. AmEx/MC/V.

Théâtre de la Ville, 2, pl. du Châtelet, 4ème (☎01 42 74 22 77; www.theatredelaville-paris.com). Ⓜ Châtelet. Primarily known for its innovative dance productions, this venue also offers a selection of classical and world music concerts. Season runs Sept.-June. Call for program and discounts. Tickets sold by phone M-Sa 11am-7pm; box office open M 11am-7pm, Tu-Sa 11am-8pm. Call ahead for wheelchair access. Tickets €16-22. AmEx/MC/V.

Zénith, 211, av. Jean-Jaurès, Parc de la Villette, 19ème (☎01 42 08 60 00; www.le-zenith.com). Ⓜ Porte de Pantin. This loud, large venue on the edge of the city hosts major rap and rock artists. Tickets start at €16 (often around €45) and are available only from ticket agencies; try FNAC (www.fnacspectacles.com). MC/V.

GUIGNOLS

Grand-Guignol Theater features the *guignol,* the classic stock character of the traditional Parisian marionette show. It's like Punch and Judy, but without the domestic violence. Although the puppets speak French, they're very urbane, and you'll have no trouble understanding the slapstick, child-geared humor. Nearly all parks have *guignols;* check *Pariscope* for more info. During the months of July and August, all *guignols* switch to a daily schedule to accommodate the French school vacations.

Marionnettes du Luxembourg, in the Jardin du Luxembourg (see **Sights,** p. 204), 6ème (☎ 01 43 26 46 47 or 01 43 29 50 97 for groups). Ⓜ Vavin. The best *guignol* in Paris. This theater has played the same classics since its opening in 1933, including *Little Red Riding Hood, The Three Little Pigs,* and others. Running time 45min. Arrive 30min. early for good seats. Performances during the summer months at 4pm daily with a second performance at 11am on Sa and Su. €4.

SHOPPING

Fashion is born by small facts, trends, or even politics, never by trying to make little pleats and furbelows, by trinkets, by clothes easy to copy, or by the shortening or lengthening of a skirt.
  —Elsa Schiaparelli

In a city where Hermès scarves function as slings for broken arms and department store history stretches back to the mid-19th century, shopping is nothing less than an art form. Be prepared to expend every ounce of your energy while out in the boutique battlefield, but take comfort in the knowledge that your efforts will pay off. Almost everything in this city, from the world's most expensive dresses to kitchen appliances, is astoundingly stylish. The brave and experimental, willing to splurge on the independent designs of off-the-beaten path boutiques in the 18ème or the Marais, will be especially rewarded with one-of-a-kind pieces—wearable evidence of your exploits in the fashion capital of the world.

A BRIEF HISTORY OF PARISIAN FASHION

Paris has been at the vanguard of fashion since the Romans got tunic-making tips from the Gauls. Things really took off during the 17th century, when the extravagant costumes of royals and aristocrats inspired the envy of both the wealthy and the lowly, who eventually got so fed up with those 5ft. high powdered wigs and 10ft. wide bejeweled skirts that they started a Revolution. Post-Revolutionary **Empire** style, perhaps aware of the decadent fastidiousness of the previous century, was all about a "simple" Neoclassical ideal. Fashion as we know it today came into being in the 1800s, when the first department stores were built (p. 294). The bourgeoisie became consummate consumers; artists like **Edouard Manet** and writers like **Charles Baudelaire** began to represent fashion as a harbinger of modernity—a unique expression of the "the moral and aesthetic feeling" of the era. Soon thereafter, the *couturier* (designer; see **Couture Culture**) was born.

  The first modern *couturier* was **Charles Frederick Worth,** whose House of Worth opened in Paris in 1858. Worth invented the fashion show, the designer-as-celebrity (clothing-makers had previously been considered lowly artisans), and the fashion label as a status symbol. In the early 20th century, designers like **Madeliene Vionnet** and **Paul Poiret,** influenced by Art Nouveau and Orientalist trends, "liberated" women from corsets and heavy petticoats, designing whimsical shapes and flowing bias-cut dresses. In the 1920s, the iconic **Coco Chanel** revolutionized women's dress with her boyish elegance, insistence on comfort, legendary suits, and invention of the "little black dress." Meanwhile, the designs of innovators like **Elsa Schiaparelli** echoed radical art movements like Surrealism and Cubism (Salvador Dalí designed the fabric for some of her dresses). During WWII, strict regulations were enforced on fabric and design, and patriotic self-denial came into fashion. But in 1947, **Christian Dior** aroused shock, anger, and delight with the cinched waists and outlandishly full skirts of his New Look, re-establishing Paris as the center of the fashion world and, once again, reinventing the way the female form was idealized. In the 1960s, **André Courrèges** and **Paco Rabanne** moved fashion in fantastically futuristic directions, employing bold shapes and radical new materials. **Yves Saint Laurent** dominated

Parisian fashion throughout the second half of the 20th century with his embrace of androgynous style and Left Bank beatnik chic.

Today, designers like **Jean-Paul Gaultier** and **Christian Lacroix** display their creations in extravagant bi-annual spectacles, the Paris fashion shows. Fashion continues to exist at the crossroads of art and consumerism; to reinvent the past and imagine the future; and to shape—and be shaped by—the way we perceive our desires, bodies, and eras. And Paris is where it happens.

ÎLE DE LA CITÉ

▨ **Le Marché aux Fleurs,** pl. Louis-Lépine. ⓜ Cité. The market is to your left as you exit the metro station. An open secret to Parisians for many years, this covered flower marketplace is open year-round, rain or shine. Dangling wicker baskets, quaint garden knicknacks and straw-hat wearing cacti are just some of the attractions. This leafy oasis turns into the Marché aux Oiseaux (bird market) on Su, attracting delighted children who poke at cuddly furballs and chirpy birds nestled in cages. Open year-round daily 8am-7pm.

ÎLE ST-LOUIS

Shopping on Île St-Louis is not for the faint of heart—one could easily spend a fortune on antiques or rare books. Small, unusual boutiques can be found all over the island, however, and you just might find that one-of-a-kind hat (or toaster) you've been looking for. Most stores cluster on **rue St-Louis-en-l'Île.**

CLOTHING AND ACCESSORIES

Pylônes, 57, r. St-Louis-en-l'Île (☎01 46 34 05 02). ⓜ Pont Marie. Sells all the crazy items that you'll never really need (but will certainly want). Exuberantly youthful, whimsical, artful, and adorable concept. Bright and spunky housewares such as plastic Nutella stirrers (€3.50), dog-shaped pie spatulas (€18), and the slightly sinister "voodoo knife holder" (€90). Open daily 10:30am-7:30pm. Also at 13, r. Ste-Croix-de-la-Brettonerie, 4ème. AmEx/MC/V.

Sobral, 79, r. St-Louis-en-l'Île (☎01 43 25 80 10; www.rsobral.com.br). ⓜ Pont Marie. This boutique features funky, chic accessories influenced by pop art with a dash of retro Italian flavor. Fabulous and creative belts in unusual combinations of leather, ceramic, and raffia (€50-55). Bright and chunky earrings (€10-15) and key chains (€12-21). For those with deep pockets, the stools covered with sea flora and fauna are unique artsy pieces (€240). Open daily 11am-8pm. AmEx/MC/V.

Le Grain de Sable, 79, r. St-Louis-en-l'Île (☎01 46 33 67 27). ⓜ Pont Marie. Hats of every color, shape, and size imaginable (beginning at €45) are displayed throughout the shop. *Parisiennes* bring in dresses to match colors when ordering their latest piece, and staff are more than willing to spend hours with each customer. Also stocks brightly colored espadrilles, dressy knits, and costume jewelry. Open daily 11am-7pm. MC/V.

FIRST AND SECOND ARRONDISSEMENTS

Sugar and spice, and all things naughty. In these two tourist-packed *arrondissements,* the fabrics are a little cheaper and the style is younger, especially around **rue Tiquetonne.** A stroll down **rue Etienne-Marcel** will delight shoe fetishists. The popular **Forum Les Halles** (p. 285) and the streets that surround it offer everything you'll need for a full urban-warrior aesthetic.

MEN'S AND WOMEN'S CLOTHING

🟦 **Le Shop,** 3, r. d'Argout, 2ème (☎01 40 28 95 94). Ⓜ Etienne-Marcel. Whatever you buy here, you'll be the only one with it back home. 2 levels, 1200 sq. m and 24 "corners" of sleek club wear plus a live DJ. Shirts and pants start at around €50. Open M 1-7pm, Tu-Sa 11am-7pm. AmEx/MC/V.

🟦 **Espace Kiliwatch,** 64, r. Tiquetonne, 2ème (☎01 42 21 17 37). Ⓜ Etienne-Marcel. Walk east down r. Etienne-Marcel and turn right onto r. Tiquetonne. One of the coolest, most popular shops in Paris. Secondhand *(fripe)* shirts from around €20, pants from €30. New and pricier clothes, books, furnishings, and other funky stuff also for sale. Open Tu-Sa 11am-7pm, Su 2pm-7pm. MC/V.

🟦 **Zara,** 75 r. de Rivoli, 1er (☎01 40 13 70 17). Zara is an immense Spanish chain, but it still manages to produce unique pieces in tune with the latest looks from the runways. Lots of bright and fabulous shoes, accessories, and lingerie. Some men's and children's apparel. Open M-Sa 10am-8pm. Also at 45, r. de Rennes, 6ème (☎01 44 39 03 50); 38 and 44, av. des Champs-Elysées, 8ème (☎01 45 61 52 80) *and throughout Paris.* AmEx/MC/V.

H&M, 118-120 r. de Rivoli, 1er (☎01 55 34 96 86). Ⓜ Châtelet. Other locations throughout the city. This funky and fabulous Swedish chain has disposable fashion down to an art. Bargain basement prices for fabulous items, though you may have to search through some less delightful articles. Open M-Sa 10am-8pm. AmEx/MC/V.

Zadig & Voltaire, 15, r. du Jour, 1er (☎01 42 21 88 70). Ⓜ Etienne-Marcel. 6 other locations in the city. Funky, sleek, and expensive women's designs by Paul & Jack, Holly, etc. Their own label does soft, feminine designs. A big selection of handbags. Opening hours vary by branch. Main branch open M 1-7:30pm, Tu-Sa 10:30am-7:30pm. AmEx/MC/V.

Celio, 65, r. de Rivoli, 1er (☎01 42 21 18 04). Ⓜ Palais-Royal. Other locations throughout the city. Exhaustive collection of shirts, jeans, pants, and sweaters. The Celio Sport section of the store carries basic athletic wear. Everything is more than reasonably priced. Most stores open M-Sa 11am-7pm. AmEx/MC/V.

Forum des Halles, Ⓜ Les Halles or RER: Châtelet-Les Halles, 2ème (☎01 44 76 96 56). Why anyone thought Paris needed an American-style shopping mall is a puzzling question. The 4 main entrances lead down to over 200 boutiques, including FNAC, the cosmetics wonderland Sephora, boutiques featuring independent

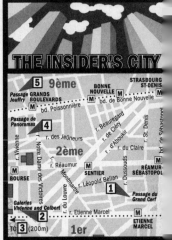

THE INSIDER'S CITY

SHOPPING A L'ANCIENNE

Easy to miss, these mid-block 19th-century passages are the world's first indoor malls. The best time to go is the afternoon.

1 Passage du Grand Cerf, 10, r. Dussoubs to 145, r. St-Denis. The most beautiful of the passages.

2 Galerie Vivienne and Galerie Colbert, 4 r. des Petits Champs to 6 r. Vivienne. The *grande dame* of the passages, with mosaic-covered floors and bad-boy designer Jean-Paul Gaultier's boutique.

3 Passage Choiseul, r. St-Augustin to r. des Petits Champs. You can find everything here, from clothing boutiques to Vietnamese restaurants to artists' painting and sculpture shops.

4 Passage de Panoramas, 10 r. St-Marc to 11 bd. Montmartre. The stores at no. 8 and 47 have been open since the 1830s.

5 Passage Jouffry, across bd. Montmartre. Bookstores, toy shops, a jewelry store, and a phenomenal *pâtisserie:* Le Valentin at no. 32.

designers, and a 4-story H&M. It can get confusing, so pick up a map from the welcome desks. Open M-Sa 10am-7:30pm (later during the *soldes*).

Samaritaine, 67, r. de Rivoli, on the quai du Louvre, 1er (☎01 40 41 20 20). Ⓜ Pont Neuf, Châtelet-Les Halles, or Louvre-Rivoli. 4 large, historic Art Deco buildings between r. de Rivoli and the Seine, connected by tunnels and bridges (see **Sights**, p. 192). Not as chic as Galeries Lafayette or Bon Marché, as it dares to sell souvenirs (gasp!) and merchandise at down-to-earth prices (the horror!), but a calmer, pleasant shopping experience. The rooftop observation deck provides one of the best views of the city; take the elevator to the 9th floor and climb the short, spiral staircase. Some hotels offer 10% discount coupons for use in the store. Open M-W and F-Sa 9:30am-7pm, Th 9:30am-10pm. AmEx/MC/V.

Kookaï, pl. Carrée, Forum des Halles, 1er (☎01 40 26 40 30). Quintessential French fashion chain for fun-loving *jeune filles*. Beware the notoriously small sizing. Open M-Sa 10:30am-7pm. Also at 155, r. de Rennes, 6ème (☎01 45 48 26 36); 66, bd. de Montparnasse, 14ème (☎01 45 38 98 46); and other locations throughout the city. MC/V.

Esprit, 99, r. de Rivoli, 1er (☎01 42 60 41 51). Ⓜ Châtelet. Other locations throughout the city. Modern, sporty basics for the whole family done with a trendy twist. AmEx/MC/V.

SHOES AND ACCESSORIES

Jacques Le Corre, 193, r. St-Honoré, 1er (☎01 42 96 97 40). Ⓜ Tuileries. Stunning high-end women's handbags and hats. Seasonal shoe displays. Le Corre's designs are sold only at 3 stores worldwide: here, New York, and Tokyo. Staff is friendly—even if you don't look like you could buy the whole store. Hats €130-500. Handbags €350-550 (but, as in the rest of Paris, everything is discounted June-July). All handmade in France. Open M-Sa 10am-7pm. AmEx/MC/V.

Longchamp, 404, r. St-Honoré, 1er (☎01 43 16 00 16). Ⓜ Concorde. Sells classic leather-strapped canvas totes that fold up into miniature, flat bags when not in use. Basic bags start at €45. Also sells wallets and other, more conventional totes. Open M-Sa 10am-7pm. AmEx/MC/V. Also at 21, r. du Vieux-Colombier, 6ème (☎01 42 22 74 75).

Colette, 213, r. St-Honoré, 1er (☎01 55 35 33 90; www.colette.fr). Ⓜ Tuileries. Unthinkably cool lifestyle store whose bare display tables feature an eclectic selection of art books, make-up, jewelry, music, magazines, and food. A lifeline for those with a lot of money and little taste. 2nd fl. has high-priced fashion items. Downstairs cafe has free Internet. Open M-Sa 11am-7pm. AmEx/MC/V.

La Droguerie, 9-11 r. du Jour, 1er (☎01 45 08 93 27). Ⓜ Etienne Marcel. Every sewing supply you could possibly need, whether you're patching a hole in your backpack or creating a ballgown. Open M 2-6:45pm, Tu-Sa 10:30am-6:45pm.

BOOKS AND MUSIC

W.H. Smith, 248, r. de Rivoli, 1er (☎01 44 77 88 99; www.whsmith.fr). Ⓜ Concorde. Large general selection includes many scholarly works in English. A solid array of magazines and tourist guidebooks. The *New York Times* is available daily. Open M-Sa 9am-7:30pm, Su 1-7:30pm. AmEx/MC/V.

Brentano's, 37, av. de l'Opéra, 2ème (☎01 42 61 52 50; www.brentanos.fr). Ⓜ Opéra. An American and French bookstore with an extensive selection of English-language literature, guidebooks, and greeting cards. Open M-Sa 10am-7:30pm. AmEx/MC/V.

Monster Melodies, 9, r. des Déchargeurs, 1er (☎01 40 28 09 39). Ⓜ Les Halles. Downstairs supplies used CDs, while upstairs overflows with records. Mostly American pop and rock, but some techno and indie rock. Open M-Sa noon-7pm.

THIRD AND FOURTH ARRONDISSEMENTS

Shopping in the Marais is a complete aesthetic experience: boutiques of all colors and flavors pop out along medieval streets and among chic, tree-shaded cafes. (Ⓜ **St-Paul** or **Hôtel-de-Ville.**) What the Marais does best are independent designer shops selling truly unique creations, as well as vintage stores that line **rue Vieille-du-Temple, rue de Sévigné, rue du Roi de Sicile** and **rue des Rosiers.** The best selection of affordable-chic menswear in Paris can be found here, especially along **rue Ste-Croix-de-la-Bretonnerie,** in stores that outfit a largely GLBT clientele—but anyone, queer or otherwise, who wants to absorb a bit of metrosexual Euro-style should check them out. Womenswear runs the gamut from downtown deconstructed to all-out glamor, often in the same edgy boutique. Most stores are open Sundays.

SHOPPING

MEN'S AND WOMEN'S CLOTHING

Free 'P' Star, 8, r. Ste-Croix-de-la-Bretonnerie, 4ème (☎01 42 76 03 72). Ⓜ Hôtel de Ville. Enter as Plain Jane and leave as a star. Wide selection of vintage dresses (€20), velvet blazers (€40), and a €10 jean pile. Worn military-style blazers €20. Open M-Sa noon-11pm, Su 2-11pm. MC/V with €20 min. charge.

Loft Design by, 12, r. de Sévigné, 4ème (☎01 48 87 13 07). Ⓜ St-Paul. Men's and women's clothing, including well-tailored shirts and fine-gauge casual sweaters (from €50 for men, from €55 for women) and pants in a palette of neutrals. Loft's selling points are refinement and style rather than innovation, but it has a popular local following. Open daily 10:30am-7pm. Additional locations at 12, r. du Faubourg-St-Honoré, 8ème (☎01 42 65 59 65) and 56 r. de Rennes, 6ème (☎01 45 44 88 99). AmEx/MC/V.

Tati, 13, pl. de la République, 3ème (☎01 48 87 72 81). Ⓜ République. A kitschy, chaotic, crowded, and cheap department store. Low-end, but worth rummaging through for basic casual wear and disposable knick-knacks. Get your sales slip made out by one of the clerks (who stand around for just that purpose) before heading to the cashier. All branches open M-Sa 10am-7pm. Additional locations at 76, av. de Clichy, 17ème (☎01 58 22 28 90), Ⓜ La Fourche; and 4, bd. de Rochechouart, 18ème (☎01 55 29 50 00). Ⓜ Barbès-Rochechouart.

BHV, 52-64, r. de Rivoli across from the Hôtel de Ville, 4ème (☎01 42 74 90 00). Ⓜ Hôtel-de-Ville. Wheelchair accessible. Dior, Lacoste, and John Deere? An immense, all-encompassing, and completely unpretentious department store scattered over several streets. Clothes, accessories, books, home furnishings, and the best hardware store in central Paris. Sporadic access to roof, but if it's available, ascend for a stellar view of Paris. A classy and inexpensive cafe is located in the flower shop on 11, r. des Archives (menu €9-11). Open M-Tu and Th-Sa 9:30am-7:30pm, W 9:30am-9pm. AmEx/MC/V.

WOMEN'S CLOTHING

▨**Culotte,** 7, r. Malher, 4ème (☎01 42 71 58 89). Ⓜ St-Paul. The deconstructed is de rigeur at this eclectic vintage boutique. Designs range from ripped, printed tees to 40s-

COUTURE CULTURE

Every year, in January and July, the stars collide: models, designers, actresses, and heiresses descend on Paris for the fashion shows. Journalists and groupies follow in their wake—and the world, or at least the part of it that cares about fashion, watches.

Haute couture (high fashion) is a strictly defined business, subject to regulations of French Department of Industry. Only 18 houses qualify as *haute couturiers* today, employing 4500 designers and craftspeople. Every *haute couture* garment is made entirely by hand and fitted precisely to the body of the model or client. Due to the astronomical price tags—a dress can cost up to $100,000—there are only 1500 *couture* clients in the world today (there were 15,000 in 1947). Many of the designs are totally unwearable, made only for the spectacle of the runway. *Couture* houses gain most of their profit from less expensive *prêt-a-porter* (ready-to-wear) lines and from cosmetics that commoners can afford, purchasing a little glamor with their lipsticks.

With dwindling profits and supposedly lessening creativity, many are convinced that *haute couture* is fated to die out. But it continues to be defended by designers and scholars, who see it as art, and by the government, which sees it as a part of French cultural heritage. And it continues to influence, however indirectly, what the world wears.

style dresses, all handmade and reasonably priced. Bold and funky vintage jewelry, especially of the mod and 80s variety, will ensure that any outfit makes a statement. Most items under €100. Open Tu-Sa 12:30-7pm, Su 2-7pm. AmEx/MC/V.

Bel'Air, 2, r. des Rosiers, 4*ème* (☎01 48 04 82 16). Ⓜ St-Paul. At the intersection with r. Malher. Beads, sequins, and *appliqué* flowers abound. Casual, flowing cotton-based frocks and smocks with a flirty, whimsical edge (€50-100). Open M-Sa 10:30am-7:30pm, Su 2-7:30pm. MC/V.

Abou d'abi Bazar, 10, r. des Francs-Bourgeois, 3*ème* (☎01 42 77 96 98). Ⓜ St-Paul. Flirty, feminine French fashion in simple and chic styles and natural fabrics. Most items €50-150. Features lots of Paul & Joe as well as some Chloé, Tara Jarmon, Etoile by Isabel Marant, and smaller French labels. The accessories are not to be missed, especially the adorable shoes. Open M 2-7:15pm, Tu-Sa 10:30am-7:15pm, and Su 2-7pm. Second location at 125, r. Vieille-du-Temple (☎01 42 87 36 64). Closed Su. AmEx/MC/V.

MEN'S CLOTHING

Boy'z Bazaar, 5, r. Ste-Croix-de-la-Bretonnerie, 4*ème* (☎01 42 71 94 00 or 01 42 71 67 00). Ⓜ Hôtel de Ville. A large selection of all that's elegant and trendy in casual menswear, including Energie, Paul Smith, and Sonia Rykiel. Caters to a largely GLBT clientele, though anyone who wants to soak up the Euro-metro vibe is welcome. Piles of Replay denim from €100. D&G tees from €100. Athletic wear down the street at no. 38. Open M-Th noon-9pm, F-Sa noon-midnight, Su 2-8pm. AmEx/MC/V.

IEM, 16, r. Ste-Croix-de-la-Bretonnerie, 4*ème* (☎01 42 74 01 61; www.iem.fr). Ⓜ Hôtel de Ville. This sexy boutique flies the rainbow flag—as well as rainbow keyrings, belts, and other paraphernalia—but is popular with a mixed crowd looking for a kinky kind of chic. Leather bracelets (€11-13) and iron dog collars (€79-100). A museum-like display of leather masks and sex paraphernalia in the basement is worth a visit. Extensive collection of queer porn in the back room. "Sexy Boy" t-shirt €30. Open M-Th 1-8pm, F-Sa 1-10pm, Su 2-9pm. AmEx/MC/V.

Fabien Nobile, 7, r. Ferdinand Duval (☎01 42 78 51 12). Ⓜ St-Paul. In a recent attempt to streamline his own line, the designer no longer carries other brands, and caters only to men. Emphasis on simple, artfully cut shapes in solid colors. Roomy linen trousers and chemises €100-200. Open Tu-Sa noon-8pm. AmEx/MC/V.

VINTAGE AND CONSIGNMENT CLOTHING

Alternatives, 18, r. du Roi de Sicile, 4ème (☎01 42 78 31 50). Ⓜ St-Paul. This upscale secondhand shop sells an eclectic collection of quality clothes, including many designers at reasonable prices. Most bottoms under €100. Christian Louboutin heels as low as €50. Limited entry; only a few customers allowed at a time to ensure quality of service. Open M-Sa 1-7pm. MC/V.

Vertiges, 85, r. St-Martin, 3ème (☎01 48 87 36 64). Ⓜ Rambuteau. A bit musty, but a consignment shopper's heaven—well-organized racks of shirts, skirts (€5), dresses, pants (€10), fabulous leather jackets, and velvet blazers (€40). Small selection of Burberry trenches at €120. Open M-Sa 10:30am-7:30pm and Su noon-7:30pm. Cash only.

SHOES AND ACCESSORIES

Monic, 5, r. des Francs-Bourgeois, 4ème (☎01 42 72 39 15). Ⓜ Chemin Vert or St-Paul. A fantastic, transgenerational boutique selling all types of jewelry. Silver, gold, precious, and semi-precious stones; from handmade Bohemian antique pieces to up-to-date Nina Ricci (€1-300; most under €50). Large selection of charms from €9. Open M-Sa 10am-7pm and Su 2:30-7pm. Second location at 14, r. de l'Ancienne-Comedie, 6ème (☎01 43 25 36 61). Ⓜ Odéon. AmEx/MC/V.

Brontibay, 4, r. de Sevigné, 4ème (☎01 42 76 90 80). Ⓜ St-Paul. Vibrant and artistic bags come in all shapes and sizes; materials range from canvas to leather to delicate silk. Most bags €100-200, printed silk clutches €35, leather and silk wallets in delicious shades €78. Open M-Sa 11am-8pm and Su 1:30-7:30pm. AmEx/MC/V.

Tokyoite, 12, r. du Roi de Sicile, 4ème (☎01 42 77 87 01). Ⓜ St-Paul. Spend €100 for the ultimate sporty chic. A large selection of new and vintage Nike. Also stocks hard-to-find Converse (albeit at wince-worthy prices), the Parisian casual footwear of choice. Sleek, Japanimation-style motorcycle helmets €200-600 (pricy, but so practical!). Open Tu-Su 1-7pm. MC/V.

BOOKS

⊠ **Les Mots à la Bouche,** 6, r. Ste-Croix de la Bretonnerie, 4ème (☎01 42 78 88 30; www.motsbouche.com). Ⓜ Hôtel de Ville. Walk with traffic along r. du Temple, turn right onto r. Ste-Croix-de-la-Bretonnerie. A 2-level bookstore offering queer literature, photography, magazines, and art. Don't miss the international DVD collection (with titles somewhere between art and porn) in the corner of the bottom level (€10-28). Open M-Sa 11am-11pm, Su 1-9pm. AmEx/MC/V.

 SHOPPING FOR POCKET CHANGE. Twice a year, Parisians and tourists alike hit the pavement for what is the shopper's version of the Tour de France. As during the famed bicycle race, Paris's semi-annual sales will take you down winding roads and through superstores to find that last pair of beaded mules at a quarter of their original price in your size. The two great *soldes* (sales) of the year start right after New Year's and at the very end of June. If you don't mind slimmer pickings, the best prices are at the beginning of February and the end of July. And if at any time of the word *braderie* (clearance sale) appears in a store window, that is your signal to enter said store without hesitation.

FIFTH AND SIXTH ARRONDISSEMENTS

While you'll find plenty of chain clothing and shoe stores around **boulevard St-Michel** and numerous little boutiques selling scarves and jewelry, the bookstores are the truly exceptional shopping attraction of the 5ème.

Wealthy St-Germain-des-Prés, meanwhile, is saturated with high-budget names, particularly in the triangle bordered by **boulevard St-Germain, rue St-Sulpice** and **rue des St-Pères**. **Rue du Four** (Ⓜ St-Germain-des-Prés) has fun and more affordable designers like **Paul and Joe** (men's, no. 40; ☎01 45 44 97 70; open daily 11am-7:30pm) and **Sinéquanone** (women's, no. 16; ☎01 56 24 27 74; open M-Sa 10am-7:30pm).

CHILDREN'S CLOTHING

Bill Tornade, 32 r. du Four, 6ème (☎01 45 48 73 88). Ⓜ St-Germain-des-Prés. This clothing boutique for fashion-plates-in-training sells the latest runway styles sized down for toddlers and small children. Open M-Sa 10:30am-7pm. AmEx/MC/V.

MEN'S AND WOMEN'S CLOTHING

🖩 **Petit Bateau,** 26, r. Vavin, 6ème (☎01 55 42 02 53). Ⓜ Vavin or Notre-Dame-des-Champs. Locations throughout the city. A children's store, but fashionistas flock here for the soft cotton t-shirts and tanks. A kid's size 16 is about an American 6; sizes go up to 18. Tees €6.50. Open M-Sa 10am-7pm. AmEx/MC/V.

Moloko, 53, r. du Cherche-Midi, 6ème (☎01 45 48 46 79). Ⓜ Sèvres-Babylone, St-Sulpice, or Rennes. Simple, Asian-inspired women's clothing with surprising colors, shapes, and closures. Buy a piece here and wear it for life—the compliments will keep coming. Dresses from €120. Branches in the 4ème and Forum des Halles. Open Tu-Sa 11am-1pm and 2-7pm. Closed Aug. MC/V.

Tara Jarmon, 18, r. du Four, 6ème (☎01 46 33 26 60). Classic, feminine styles in lovely fabrics. Open M-Sa 10:30am-7:30pm. Also at 73, av. des Champs-Elysées, 8ème (☎01 45 63 45 41) and 51, r. de Passy, 16ème (☎01 45 24 65 20).

Vanessa Bruno, 25, r. St-Sulpice, 6ème (☎01 43 54 41 04). Ⓜ St-Sulpice. Chic, trendy, simple, exotic, conservative, wild—all describe Vanessa Bruno's beautiful, well-cut clothing creations. Color schemes and fabrics that will fit any wardrobe—even if the prices won't fit any budget. Blazers and skirts around €150. Open M-Sa 10:30am-7:30pm. AmEx/MC/V.

agnès b., 6 and 12, r. du Vieux-Colombier, 6ème (☎01 44 39 02 60). Ⓜ St-Suplice. Men's apparel at 12, women's at 6, plus several other locations throughout the city. Legendary knitwear and other separates in classic cuts and colors. Stylish rather than fashionable, this Parisian staple represents understated elegance at its best. Open daily 10am-7pm. AmEx/MC/V.

Naf Naf, 25, bd. St- Michel, 5ème (☎01 43 29 36 45). One of the two big French chains (along with Kookaï), Naf Naf sells consistently affordable, generally fashionable clothes to a teenage crowd. Open M-Sa noon-7pm. MC/V. Also at 52, av. des Champs-Elysées, 8ème (☎01 45 62 03 08), 34, r. du Faubourg St-Antoine, 12ème (☎01 53 33 80 12), and other locations throughout the city.

Mango, 3, pl. du 18 Juin, 6ème (☎01 45 48 04 96). Festive, fashionable European styles at reasonable prices. Sizable range of basics. Open M-Sa 10am-8pm. AmEx/MC/V. Also at 82, r. de Rivoli, 8ème (☎01 44 59 80 37) and 6, bd. des Capucines, 9ème (☎01 53 30 82 70).

Cacharel, 64, r. Bonaparte, 6*ème* (☎01 40 46 00 45). Ⓜ St-Germain-des-Prés. The house of Cacharel has gone upscale and more mature of late. Emphasis is on retro-inspired patterns and bright colors. Dresses €180-400. Open M-F 10am-7pm, Sa 10am-7:30pm. AmEx/MC/V.

SHOES AND ACCESSORIES

Om Kashi, 7, r. de la Montagne Ste-Geneviève, 5*ème* (☎01 46 33 46 07; www.omkashi.com). Ⓜ Maubert-Mutualité. Imported boxes of henna, more than 300 kinds of incense, and shelves of clothing and jewelry mix with 18th-century furniture in this welcoming shop. Carries the unusual scarves and fabrics with which Parisians love to accessorize. Open M 2-7pm, Tu-Sa 10:30am-1:30pm and 2:30-7pm.

Muji, 27 and 30, r. St-Sulpice, 6*ème* (☎01 46 34 01 10 and 01 44 07 37 30). Ⓜ Odéon. Affordable, modern, and minimalist bric-a-brac made in Japan. Everything from bathroom candles to magazine racks and bathrobes. Great picture frames and colored pens. Lots under €15. Open M-Sa 10am-8pm. AmEx/MC/V.

No Name, 8, r. des Canettes, 6*ème* (☎01 44 41 66 46). Ⓜ St-Sulpice. Stylish sneakers in every color, fabric, and shade of glitter possible. Sandals €53-61, sneakers €60-90. Open M-Tu 10am-1pm and 2-7:30pm, W-Sa 10am-7:30pm. AmEx/MC/V.

Free Lance, 30, r. du Four, 6*ème* (☎01 45 48 14 78). Ⓜ St-Germain-des-Prés or Mabillon. Some great and stylish shoes alongside a few less posh picks. *Très cher* rainbow stilettos and patterned knee-high leather boots call to the stylistically outrageous, or at least to the strong of heart. Some more basic merchandise falls just below the €200 mark. Come for the sales, when prices become infinitely more reasonable. Open M-Sa 10am-7pm. AmEx/MC/V.

BOOKS AND MUSIC

🕮 **Abbey Bookshop,** 29, r. de la Parcheminerie, 5*ème* (☎01 46 33 16 24; www.abbeybookshop.net). Ⓜ St-Michel or Cluny. Located on a road steeped in literary history, this laid-back shop overflows with new and used English-language titles and Canadian pride, furnished by its friendly expat owner Brian. A good selection of travel books (including *How to Survive at the North Pole*). Impressive basement collection of anthropology, sociology, history, and literary criticism titles. Also carries English-language fiction and French-Canadian work. Happy to take special orders. Ask about the Canadian club's author events and Su hikes, or get

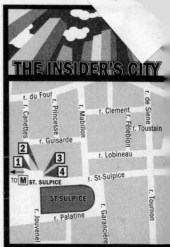

THE INSIDER'S CITY

LÈCHE-VITRINES

Translation: window-shopping, or, literally, "window-licking." The long streets of the 6*ème* hold an amazing array of clothing shops, but the smaller streets around St-Sulpice showcase truly gorgeous window displays and minimalist clothing collections. Go to discover what money really can buy.

1 **Yves Saint Laurent.** The *haute couture* house famous for its haughty clientele as well as its clothes. Mens's store at no. 12. (☎01 43 29 43 00).

2 **Lola.** Browse among feminine dresses and soft sweaters (☎01 46 33 60 21).

3 **Christian Lacroix.** Fabulous (and completely unaffordable) fashion. (☎01 42 68 79 00).

4 **Tabula Rasa.** Try on that pink, tutu-skirted cocktail number—the next Little Black Dress? (☎01 53 10 80 74).

FROM THE ROAD

WHO DOESN'T WEAR SHORT SHORTS

f living in Paris has taught me one thing, it's what clothing to avoid if I don't want to be labeled as a tourist before opening my mouth. Through endless hours of clubbing purely in the name of research, I have realized the secrets of Parisian style. Here are my simple rules to avoid being the "obvious tourist":

Rule number one: No sneakers. Parisian women, especially, never wear sneakers outside the gym, a location with which most remain thoroughly unfamiliar. If you want to blend in, flats are probably the way to go.

Rule number two: No shorts. Shorts absolutely scream "tourist!" in Paris. Granted, not all shorts scream at the same volume. A nice pair of knee-length shorts matched with an appropriately colored belt is fine. But whether they're short, tattered, denim, or sporty, most shorts are a dead giveaway.

Rule number three: No sweats. Ever. Perhaps this falls in line with the no-shorts deal, given the lack of French exercise culture. The one day I wore a sweatshirt in Paris this summer, I was never addressed in French.

–Olivia Brown

your name on their email list. Open M-Sa 10am-7pm, sometimes open later.

▨ Shakespeare & Co., 37, r. de la Bûcherie, 5ème. Ⓜ St-Michel. Across the Seine from Notre-Dame. Run by *bon vivant* George Whitman (alleged great-grandson of Walt), this shop seeks to reproduce the atmosphere of Sylvia Beach's 1920s expat hangout at no. 8, r. Dupuytren. The current location has accumulated a wide and quirky selection of new and used books (and a wide and quirky selection of kids who crash in the back room). Bargain bins outside include French classics in English (all prices written in pencil on the inside cover). Open daily noon-midnight. €10 credit card min. See **Sights**, p. 203.

▨ Gibert Jeune, 5, pl. St-Michel, 5ème (☎01 56 81 22 22). Ⓜ St-Michel. Main location plus 7 specialized branches clustered around the Fontaine St-Michel (you can't miss the yellow canopies). The main place for books in any language, including lots of reduced-price choices. Extensive stationary department downstairs. **University text branch,** 27, quai St-Michel, 5ème (☎01 56 81 22 22). Open M-Sa 10am-7pm. **General books branch,** 15bis, bd. St-Denis, 2ème (☎01 55 34 75 75). Open M-Sa 9:30am-7:30pm. AmEx/MC/V.

▨ L'Harmattan, 16 and 21bis, r. des Ecoles, 5ème (☎01 46 34 13 71; www.editions-harmattan.fr). Ⓜ Cluny-La Sorbonne. Walk with traffic down bd. St-Germain, make a right on r. St-Jacques, and a left onto r. des Ecoles. Over 90,000 titles of Francophone literature from Africa, the Indian Ocean, Antilles, the Middle East, Asia, and Latin America. A good place to go for classic novels. So packed with books that it's hard to navigate. General catalogue available on the website; ask any sales staff for help. Open M-Sa 10am-12:30pm and 1:30-7pm. MC/V.

Présence Africaine, 25bis, r. des Ecoles, 5ème (☎01 43 54 15 88). Ⓜ Cluny-La Sorbonne. Both a publisher and a shop, this was the first bookstore in Paris to specialize in African literature, history, and social science. The well-organized shelves have everything from contemporary political analysis to children's stories from Francophone Africa. Open M-Sa 10:30am-6:30pm. MC/V.

The Village Voice, 6, r. Princesse, 6ème (☎01 46 33 36 47; www.villagevoicebookshop.com). Ⓜ Mabillon. Takes its name less from the Manhattan paper than from the Parisian neighborhood. An excellent Anglophone bookstore and the center of the city's English literary life, featuring 3-4 readings, lectures, and discussions every month (Sept.-June). A good selection of English-language travel books. Open M 2-7:30pm, Tu-Sa 10am-7:30pm, Su 1-6pm. Closed Su in Aug. AmEx/MC/V.

San Francisco Book Co., 17, r. Monsieur le Prince, 6ème (☎01 43 29 15 70). ⓜ Odéon. The towering shelves of this old bookshop hold scads of secondhand English-language books, both literary and pulp—including some rare and out-of-print titles. This is a great place to trade in used paperbacks. Open M-Sa 11am-9pm, Su 2-7:30pm.

Tea and Tattered Pages, 24, r. Mayet, 6ème (☎01 40 65 94 35; tandtp@hotmail.com). ⓜ Duroc. This place's funky collection of secondhand English-language books is a lot of fun to browse through. Sell books at €0.30-0.80 per paperback, and get a 10% discount on your next purchase. Books €3-11. If they don't have what you want, sign the wish list and you'll be called if it comes in. Tea room serves root beer floats, brownies, and American coffee with free refills. Occasional poetry readings, and lots of info for English speakers in Paris. Particularly useful is the free *Insider's Guide*, available in a box just inside the store's door. Open M-Sa 11am-7pm, Su noon-6pm. MC/V with a €15.25 min.

Gibert Joseph, 26-34, bd. St-Michel, 6ème (☎01 44 41 88 88). ⓜ Odéon or Cluny-La Sorbonne. A gigantic *librairie* and music store with new and used selections. Frequent sidewalk sales with crates of books and notebooks from €2. Good selection of used dictionaries and guidebooks. There are several branches along bd. St-Michel. Open M-Sa 10am-7:30pm. MC/V.

La Chaumière à Musique, 5, r. de Vaugirard, 6ème (☎01 43 54 07 25; www.chaumiereonline.com). ⓜ Odéon. As if attending a concert, the sophisticated patrons at this classical music store move quietly and speak softly. Knowledgeable and friendly staff. Bargain bin CDs start at €4. Will buy back and trade used CDs. Open M-F 11am-8pm, Sa 10am-8pm, Su and holidays 2-8pm.

Crocodisc, 40-42, r. des Ecoles, 5ème (☎01 43 54 47 95 or 01 43 54 33 22). ⓜ Maubert-Mutualité. Music from the enormous speakers entertains patrons browsing through 2 rooms of used CDs, tapes, and records. Mainly stocks rock, pop, techno, reggae, funk, and classical. Buys CDs for €8-15. Nearby **Crocojazz,** 64, r. de la Montagne-Ste-Geneviève (☎01 46 34 78 38) stocks jazz and blues. Both stores open Tu-Sa 11am-7pm. MC/V. €10 credit card min.

SEVENTH ARRONDISSEMENT

Affordable luxury goods are not to be found in the 7ème, but that shouldn't stop you from looking. Specialty shops abound, and it's easy to spend an entire day window-shopping. Begin your trek along **rue du Bac** (entire guidebooks have been written about the shops on this street), taking in everything from fountain pens to baby clothes, until you arrive at **Au Bon Marché** (p. 294) at r. de Sèvres. Stroll down **rue de Sevres,** and if you're tired and hungry, pop into one of the many cafes to recharge.

CLOTHING AND ACCESSORIES

■ **La Femme Ecarlaté,** 42, av. Bosquet (☎01 45 51 08 44). ⓜ Ecole Militaire. Forgot to pack your €3000 evening gown? Friendly and attentive salesladies will help you select a Lacroix, Azzaro, Balmain, or other designer evening gown to rent. Biannual sales (Jan.-Feb. and July-Aug.) offer dresses for around 10% of the original price. Also rents bridal gowns, €300-600 per day. 1-night rentals €150-300. Open Tu-Sa 11am-7pm. Cash only.

Misia Rêve, 87, r. du Bac (☎01 42 34 20 52). ⓜ Rue du Bac. Accessories for grown-up girls, all designed by the very quirky but tasteful Misia. Whimsical coin purses featuring cherries, polka dots, and geisha girls (€15); leather bags with colorful *appliqués* and whimsical patterns (from €50); and patchwork t-shirts in primary colors (from €25). Open Tu-Sa 11am-7:15pm. AmEx/MC/V.

Au Bon Marché, 24, r. de Sèvres, 7*ème* (☎01 44 39 80 00). ⓜ Sèvres-Babylone. Paris's oldest department store, Au Bon Marché has it all, from scarves to smoking accessories, designer clothes to home furnishings. Don't be beguiled by the name (*bon marché* means cheap)—this is the most exclusive and expensive department store in Paris. Look out for the shoes on the top floor, which get their own display cases, lights, and guards. Across the street is ▨ **La Grande Epicerie de Paris** (38, r. de Sèvres), Bon Marché's celebrated gourmet food annex, featuring all things dried, canned, smoked, and freshly baked. Store open M-W and F 9:30am-7pm, Th 10am-9pm, Sa 9:30am-8pm. La Grande Epicerie open M-Sa 8:30am-9pm. AmEx/MC/V.

BOOKS, ETC.

▨ **Ciné-Images,** 68, r. de Babylone (☎01 47 05 60 25; www.cine-images.com). ⓜ St-François Xavier. A cinephile's paradise, this boutique has endless catalogues of stock: original movie posters from the beginning of film history to the late 1970s. Prices range from €30 to as high as €20,000, but it's worth a browse through the shelves even if you can't afford a thing. The kind, English-speaking owner also does amazing restorations and mounting work *(entoilage)* for around €120. Open Tu-F 10am-1pm and 2-7pm, Sa 2-7pm. MC/V.

Florent Monestier, 47bis, av. Bosquet (☎01 45 55 03 01). ⓜ Ecole Militaire. All manner of nostalgic bric-a-brac to perfect that cluttered, shabby-chic look. Nautical baubles nestle against Chinese vintage-inspired porcelain. A mix of classic toiletry items and retro household goods, this is a treasure trove of quintessentially Parisian gifts for anyone fed up with tacky souvenirs. Open M-Sa 10:30am-7pm.

Librairie Gallimard, 15, bd. Raspail (☎01 45 48 24 84; www.librairie-gallimard.com). ⓜ Rue du Bac. The main store of this famed publisher of French classics features a huge selection of pricey Gallimard books. Basement filled with folio paperbacks. Open M-Sa 10am-7pm. AmEx/MC/V.

 Pickpockets and con artists often work in groups, and children are among the most effective extortionists in Paris. Pickpocketing is common at department stores, particularly on the escalators.

EIGHTH ARRONDISSEMENT

The 8*ème* is not wallet-friendly, but it is perfect for a day of window shopping. Take a break from the exhausting Champs-Elysées and walk along **avenue Montaigne** to admire the great couture houses. Their collections change every season, and they're always innovative, gorgeous, and jaw-droppingly expensive. Check out **Chanel** at no. 42, **Christian Dior** at no. 30, **Emanuel Ungaro** at no. 2, and **Nina Ricci** at no. 39. **Rue du Faubourg Saint-Honoré** is home to **Lanvin** at no. 22 and **Jean-Paul Gaultier** at no. 30. Around the **Madeleine,** you'll find **Burberry** and some big American names. Keep in mind that many of these shops have an unspoken dress code. You'll find it difficult to browse their collections if you don't look like you can afford them. A more accessible way to peruse *couture* collections is in department stores (p. 294).

Back on the **Champs-Elysées,** you can purchase everything from CDs (check out the **Virgin Megastore,** open until midnight) to perfumes to chocolates, usually until a much later hour than in the rest of Paris.

Sephora, 70-72, av. des Champs-Elysées (☎01 53 93 22 50). Ⓜ Charles de Gaulle-Etoile. The fairest cosmetics store of them all: an enormous array of beauty products to color your world pretty. The welcoming carpeted corridor is lined with almost every *eau-de-toilette* on the market, both for men and women. The perfect place to go wild and transform yourself before a night at the clubs. Frequent makeover promotions by prestigious cosmetics companies on the premises. Prices run the gamut from reasonable to absurd. French cosmetics aren't necessarily less expensive in France, so check before you buy. Open daily 10am-midnight. AmEx/MC/V.

Monoprix, 52, av. de Champs Elysees, 8è*me* (☎01 53 77 65 65). Ⓜ George V. Many locations throughout Paris. Monoprix means "one price"—a cheap one. From *pâté* to bathing suits to wine glasses. Most locations open daily 9:30am-7:30pm, some open until 10pm. MC/V.

FNAC (Fédération Nationale des Achats et Cadres), is the big Kahuna of music chains in Paris and has 10 locations throughout the city. The Champs-Elysées (74, av. des Champs-Elysées; ☎01 53 53 64 64), Bastille (4, pl. de la Bastille; ☎01 43 42 04 04), Italiens (24, bd. des Italiens; ☎01 48 01 02 03), and Etoile (26-30, av. des Ternes; ☎01 44 09 18 00) branches are the largest, with a comprehensive selection of music, stereo equipment, and, in some cases, books. Use scanners to listen to any CD in the store. Tickets to nearly any concert and many theater shows can be purchased at the FNAC ticket desk located on the ground level of the store. For detailed and helpful information (in French), visit the website at www.fnac.com. All branches open at 10am and most close at 7:30 or 8pm. The Champs-Elysées and Italiens branches close at midnight. MC/V.

 SHOPPING FOR POCKET CHANGE. A *stock* is the French version of an outlet store, selling big name clothing for less—often because it has small imperfections or dates from last season. Many are on r. d'Alésia in the 14è*me* (Ⓜ Alésia), including **Cacharel Stock,** no. 114 (☎01 45 42 53 04; open M-Sa 10am-7pm; AmEx/MC/V); **S.R. Store** (Sonia Rykiel) at no. 112 and no. 64 (☎01 43 95 06 13; open Tu 11am-7pm, W-Sa 10am-7pm; MC/V); **Stock Patrick Gerard,** no. 113 (☎01 40 44 07 40). A large **Stock Kookaï** bustles at 82, r. Réamur, 2è*me* (☎01 45 08 17 91; open M 11:30am-7:30pm, Tu-Sa 10:30am-7pm); **Apara Stock** sits at 16, r. Etienne Marcel (☎01 40 26 70 04); and **Haut-de-Gomme Stock,** with names like Armani, Christian Dior, and Dolce & Gabbana, has two locations, at 9, r. Scribe, 9è*me* (☎01 40 07 10 20; open M-Sa 10am-7pm; Ⓜ Opéra) and 190, r. de Rivoli, 1*er* (☎01 42 96 97 47; open daily 11am-7pm; Ⓜ Louvre-Rivoli).

NINTH ARRONDISSEMENT

Au Printemps, 64, bd. Haussmann, 9è*me* (☎01 42 82 50 00). Ⓜ Chaussée d'Antin-Lafayette or Havre-Caumartin. One of the two biggies on the Parisian department store scene. Visitors to this mega-complex can escape into air-conditioned bliss with hundreds of other Parisians and tourists, but should be prepared to be pushy or be pushed. Bringing your credit card is advisable if you want to hit the 2nd floor. Open M-Sa 9:30am-7pm. AmEx/MC/V.

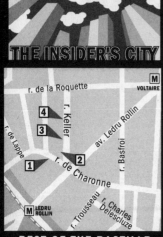

THE INSIDER'S CITY

BEST OF THE BASTILLE

Tucked away behind the Bastille are the newest names in Paris fashion. Up-and-coming labels are conceptual but relatively inexpensive, making this boutique block a magnet for the young and trendy.

1 Roucou Paris, 30 bis, r. de Charonne. Sleek, sporty bags for 60s-style mods.

2 Des Petits Hauts, 5, r. Keller. Delicate knits in sorbet colors, from €40.

3 Anne Willi, 13, r. Keller. A zen haven of minimalist linen looks.

4 Gaele Barré, 17, r. Keller. Madcap juxtapositions of prints and polka dots on sweatshirt materials, cut to wispy shapes. Vintage-style sundress €150.

Galeries Lafayette, 40, bd. Haussmann, 9ème (☎01 42 82 34 56). ⓜ Chaussée d'Antin. Chaotic (the equivalent of Paris's entire population visits here each month), but carries it all, including mini-boutiques of Kookaï, agnès b., French Connection, and Cacharel. The astounding food annex on the first floor, Lafayette Gourmet, has everything from a sushi counter to a mini-*boulangerie*. Haussmann open M-W and F-Sa 9:30am-7:30pm, Th 9:30am-9pm; Montparnasse open M-Sa 9:45am-7:30pm. AmEx/V.

ELEVENTH AND TWELFTH ARRONDISSEMENTS

The 11ème and 12ème collectively form one of the best shopping areas in Paris. Emerging designer labels and alternative music stores cling to the edgy **rue Keller,** while nearby **rue de Charonne** hosts a variety of eclectic, feminine boutiques. **Rue de la Roquette** is a one-stop shop for young, funky fashion that occasionally veers toward Eurotrash territory but always makes for cute clubbing gear.

WOMEN'S CLOTHING

Doria Salambo, 38, r. de la Roquette, 11ème (☎01 47 00 06 30). ⓜ Bastille. Lots of cotton and linen sundresses in bohemian, tie-dye, and African patterns (€80-100) with a smattering of jackets. Open M 3-8pm, Tu-Sa 11am-8pm. MC/V.

Incognito, 41, r. de la Roquette, 11ème (☎01 40 21 86 55). ⓜ Bastille. Tiny boutique stocked with trendy dresses (€140), tops (€60-80) and fur-trimmed leather jackets (€300). Menswear also available. Open Tu-Sa 11am-8pm. MC/V.

Planisphere, 19, r. de la Roquette, 11ème (☎01 43 57 69 90). ⓜ Bastille. Miss Sixty rules the roost in this store, with a smattering of Diesel, D&G, and We Are Replay. Jeans €120-280 and tops €50-120. Open M-Sa 11am-8pm and Su 2-8pm. AmEx/MC/V. Additional location at 19, r. des Rosiers (☎01 48 04 01 05). Men's location at 78, r. de la Roquette (☎01 48 05 10 55) and 32, r. des Rosiers (☎01 40 27 07 31).

Atelier 33, 33, r. du Faubourg Ste-Antoine, 11ème (☎01 43 40 61 63). ⓜ Bastille. If you can flash the cash: choose from over 200 designs, wait one month, and take home a glamorous gown (€300-3000) in any fabric imaginable. Evening gown showroom accessible by appointment only. All clothes can be tailored, including the ready-made jackets (€35-200), pants (€80-100), and flirty frocks. The floral prints, liberal sequinning, and wild colors resemble the most outlandish Versace styles. Prices negotiable. Open M-Sa 10:30am-7:30pm. AmEx/MC/V.

MEN'S CLOTHING

Stone Company, 6, r. Bréguet, 12ème (☎01 47 00 56 81). Ⓜ Bastille. Swiss owned and operated but specializing in all things Italian. Shoes (€180), shirts (€60), and leather jackets (up to €2500) by Alkis, Portland, and others. No wardrobe is complete without a cheetah-print belt (€78). Open M 1-8pm, Tu-Su 10am-noon and 1-8pm. MC/V.

ACCESSORIES

Total Eclipse, 40, r. de la Roquette, 11ème (☎01 48 07 88 04). Ⓜ Bastille. It's time to accessorize. Purchase you-can't-find-me-anywhere-else jewelry with chunky stones in bright colors. One-of-a-kind necklaces (from €30), where-did-you-get-that bracelets (€30-50). Also a wide range of men's and women's watches from the likes of Diesel, Fossil, and Opex (from €30). Open M-F 11am-7:30pm and Sa 10:30am-8pm. AmEx/MC/V.

La Baleine, 11, r. Boulle, 11ème (☎01 43 14 94 94). Ⓜ Bastille. Classic toys and accessories by Hello Kitty and Groovy Girls, animal- and food- shaped lamps (penguin, rabbit, *champignon*...) €39-70, and porcelain figurines €4. Check out the remote-controlled mobiles €30-69. Open M-Sa noon-8pm. MC/V.

Automates & Poupées, 97, av. Daumesnil (☎01 43 42 22 33). Dolls, dolls, and more dolls—Automates & Poupées offers restorations as well as a moderate selection for purchase. The prices aren't child's play, though: some dolls exceed €1000 (prices begin around €40). Open Tu-Sa 10:30am-6:30pm.

BOOKS AND MUSIC

Les Soeurs Lumière, 18, r. St-Nicolas, 12ème (☎01 43 43 13 15; www.soeurslumiere.fr). Ⓜ Ledru Rollin. With the motto "Un livre, un film," this cinema-centered bookstore sells DVDs and the books that they are based on. The selection includes classics like *The Importance of Being Earnest* and more recent works like *Harry Potter,* with an emphasis on English-language titles. Open M-Sa 11am-7pm. MC/V.

L'Arbre à Lettres, 62, r. du Faubourg St-Antoine, 12ème (☎01 53 33 83 23). Ⓜ Bastille. A vast, well-presented selection of French and other European literature. Regular readings and lectures. Consult store for details, and pick up their gazette at the desk. Open daily 10am-8pm (closed Su July-Aug.). MC/V.

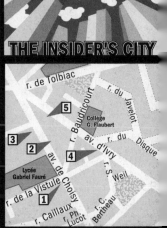

THE INSIDER'S CITY

LE QUARTIER CHINOIS

While the edges of the 13ème pursue a trendy rebirth, Chinatown manages to preserve its traditions. These are some of its gems:

1 **Dong Nam A,** 64, av. de Choisy (☎01 45 84 68 44). An amazing selection of exotic produce.

2 **Hoa Ly,** 84, av. de Choisy (☎01 45 83 96 63). Beautiful Mandarin dresses (*cheongsams*), blouses, and jackets.

3 **Ka Sun Sas,** 89-97 av. de Choisy (☎01 56 61 98 89). No Ming vases here, but plenty of shiny porcelain and basic housewares at basic prices.

4 **Kim Thanh,** 69, av. d'Ivry. Shimmering *cheongsams,* reversible kimonos, and golden teapots.

5 **L'Empire des Thés,** 101, av. d'Ivry (☎01 45 85 66 33). A ritzy tea shop. Sesame eclairs and 220 Chinese teas, to try there or take home.

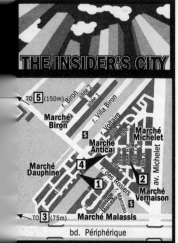

THE INSIDER'S CITY

Marché Biron

r. Biron

allée 1

allée 2

r. Villa Biron

L. Voltaire

Marché Michelet

Marché Antica

allée 3

Les Rosiers

av. Michelet

Marché Dauphine

4

1

2

Marché Vernaison

passage Marceau

impasse Marceau

r. Marceau

TO **5** (150m)

TO **3** (75m) Marché Malassis

bd. Périphérique

PUCES DE ST-OUEN
The fairest of the flea markets, the famous Puces de St-Ouen will sell you anything from antiques to the latest hip-hop attire:

1 **Fidalgo, Stall #147, Marché Dauphine.** Start high-class with this collection of antique jewelry, silver dinner sets, and antique statues and mirrors.

2 **La Toile D'Araignée, Stall #100, Marché Vernaison.** An eclectic mix of modern furniture, lights, and other household objects.

3 **Stall #79, Marché Malik.** The genius combination of dance music and jeans for sale in a market already vibrant and noisy.

4 **Lili et Daniel, Stall #6, Marché Vernaison.** More beads than you can imagine, alongside threads, and curtain ropes.

5 **Stall #42, Marché Paul Bert.** This stall brandishes intimidating deer heads and other unfortunate victims of taxidermists lining the wall. Some skulls have been made into lamps.

Born Bad Record Shop, 17, r. Keller, 11ème (☎01 43 38 41 78). Ⓜ Bastille. Vintage records from all genres, including soul, funk, ska, gothic, and more. Also sells music miscellany (stickers, badges, zines) and comic books. Open M-Sa noon-8pm. **Born Bad Exotica** (11, r. St-Sabin; ☎01 49 23 98 05) sells rebellious t-shirts and gothic accessories and clothing. Open M-F 1-7:30pm and Sa noon-7:30pm. MC/V.

Downtown Records, 57, r. du Faubourg St-Antoine, 11ème (☎01 44 74 64 18). Ⓜ Bastille. House, garage, techno, disco, hip-hop (the entire upper floor is devoted to it), jazz, and R&B on tape, CD, and vinyl. Learn to spin records with instructional videos or DVDs (€20-30) or just go ahead and buy your turntables (€800). Open M noon-8pm, Tu-Sa 11:30am-8pm. AmEx/MC/V.

Wave, 36, r. Keller, 11ème (☎01 40 21 86 98). Ⓜ Bastille. This tiny store packs a great selection of techno, house, electronic, jungle, and ambient music. Record and CD players for those who want to listen before buying. Also has a board with posters and flyers listing upcoming shows and other events. Open M-F 1-7:30pm and Sa noon-7:30pm. MC/V.

EIGHTEENTH ARRONDISSEMENT

The 18ème is just south of the granddaddy of all flea markets, the Puces de St-Ouen—an overwhelming and eclectic mix of stuff. It opens early and shuts down late, and serious hunters should allow themselves the better part of a day to cover significant ground. In general, merchandise is either dirt-cheap and shoddy or expensive and antique, but those with patience might find incredible deals in the mix. The market began during the Middle Ages, when merchants resold the cast-off clothing of aristocrats (crawling with fleas—*puces*—hence the name) to peasant-folk. At today's market, aristocratic clothing is hard to come by, but you can still find style at prices that can't be matched anywhere else in Paris.

PUCES DE ST-OUEN

Renegade Market, the 10min. walk along av. de la Porte de Clignancourt, under the highway, and left on r. Jean Henri Fabre to the official market. Jammed with tiny unofficial stalls. From the moment you exit the metro, you will be surrounded—and hassled—by sellers. These stalls sell flimsy new clothes, African masks, fake designer get-up, and cheap, colorful jewelry. If the renegade bazaar turns you off, continue on to the official market, where you'll be able to browse more leisurely in a slightly less crowded setting. Although many of the official stalls close early, renegade vendors may open at 5am and stay open until 9pm.

Official Market (www.parispuces.com) Ⓜ Porte-de-Clignancourt. On r. des Rosiers and r. Jules Vallès, the regular market is officially divided into 15 sub-markets, each theoretically specializing in a certain type of item. Don't try to follow a set path or worry about hitting every *marché,* as they all generally have the same eclectic collection of everything antique you could ever imagine. Your best bet is to get lost and then keep browsing. Most of the official markets have posted maps of their layout and stalls which are very helpful once inside. Open M and Sa-Su 7am-7:30pm (although most stalls open around 9am and close at 6pm); on M, most vendors are open even fewer hours.

COMMENT DIT-ON "RIP-OFF"? First-time flea market visitors should note some important tips. There are no €1 diamond rings here. If you find the Hope Diamond in a pile of schlock jewelry, the vendor planted it. Be prepared to bargain; sellers at flea markets don't expect to get their starting prices. Pickpockets love crowded areas, especially the one around the unofficial stalls. Three Card Monte con artists proliferate. Don't be pulled into the game by seeing someone win lots of money: he's part of the con, planted to attract suckers. If you are a savvy rock 'n' roll connoisseur with a sense of patience, this is the place to find rare records. Record peddlers seem not to know what they have, and if you look long enough, you might just find a priceless LP for next to nothing.

NIGHTLIFE

It comes as no surprise that the City of Love offers ample opportunities to while the night away over drinks at a mellow **bar** or a rowdy **pub.** Bars in Paris are either chic nighttime cafes bursting with people-watching potential or more laid-back neighborhood spots that often double as Anglo havens. In the 5*ème* and 6*ème*, bars draw French and foreign students, while the Bastille and Marais teem with Paris's young and hip, queer and straight. Les Halles and surroundings draw a slightly older set, while the outer *arrondissements* cater to the full range of locals in tobacco-stained bungalows and yuppie drinking holes. Paris also harbors a host of quality **jazz bars,** the best of which are listed in this chapter. For more information on jazz bar culture and etiquette, see **Life and Times,** p. 85.

Clubbing in Paris is less about hip DJs and cutting-edge beats than it is about dressing up, getting in, and being seen. Drinks are expensive, and Parisians drink little beyond the first round, included·in most cover charges. Many clubs accept reservations, which means that on busy nights, there is no available seating. It is advisable to dress well and be confident but not aggressive about getting in. Come early and in a couple if you can. Bouncers like tourists because they generally spend more money inside, so it helps to speak English. Clubs are usually busiest between 2 and 4am. Tune in to *Radio FG* (98.2 FM) or *Radio Nova* (101.5 FM) to find out about upcoming events.

One of Europe's most queer-friendly cities, Paris boasts a plethora of **GLBT nightlife** hotspots, both calm and cruisy. The Marais is the center of GLBT life in Paris. Most queer bars and clubs cluster around r. du Temple, r. Ste-Croix de la Bretonnerie, r. des Archives, and r. Vieille du Temple in the 4*ème* (p. 305). A number of lesbian bars can be found in the 3*ème* (p. 304). For the most comprehensive listing of GLBT restaurants, clubs, hotels, organizations, and services, consult *Illico* (free at queer bars and restaurants), *Gai Pied*'s annually updated book *Guide Gai* (€15 at kiosks and bookstores), or Zurban magazine's annual *Paris Gay and Lesbian Guide* (€5 at any kiosk). **Les Mots à la Bouche,** Paris's largest queer bookstore, serves as an unofficial information center for GLBT life; they can tell you what's hot now (see **Shopping,** p. 289).

FIRST ARRONDISSEMENT

Nightlife in the 1*er* is dominated by the many jazz bars in the area. R. des Lombards is home to three of the best, as well as other bars and cafes, and crêpe stands for that essential after-drinking snack. The 1*er* is a great area to go out at night, as it's mostly safe and the bars are fun and full. Getting home can be a chore, however, as on busy nights cabs are difficult to find. If France wins a football game by day, tired clubbers might find themselves walking home by night.

🏴 **Banana Café,** 13, r. de la Ferronerie (☎01 42 33 35 31; www.bananacafeparis.com). ⓂＣhâtelet. Take r. Pierre Lescot to r. de la Ferronerie. This *très branché* (way cool) evening arena is the most popular GLBT bar in the 1*er*, and it draws an extremely mixed group. Patrons can enjoy the loud dance music and tropical decor while watching a scantily-clad male pole dance. Head downstairs for a lively piano bar and more dancing space. Legendary theme nights. "Go-Go Boys" Th-Sa midnight-dawn. 2 for 1 drinks during happy hour 6-9pm; mixed drinks excluded. Beer €5.50. Mixed drinks €8.50. F-Sa €10 cover with a drink. Open daily 5:30pm-6am. AmEx/MC/V.

Le Fumoir, 6, r. de l'Amiral Coligny (☎01 42 92 00 24; www.lefumoir.com). Ⓜ Louvre. As cool and ritzy by night as it is by day. 30-something crowd. Extra dry martini €11-12.

THE HIDDEN DEAL

BEST LATE NIGHT...

Can't sleep? Neither can we. Check out the following for all of your 4am needs.

Anglo fun: Party with the late-night Anglo crowd at **Mustang Café** in the 14*ème* until 5am.

Cheap food and coffee: Hang out with the cab drivers at **Taxi Club** in the 1*er*, open until 6am. (8, r. Etienne Marcel; ☎01 42 36 28 30.)

Cigarettes: Most *tabacs* close around 6pm, but the one at **10, r. Washington** in the 8*ème* is open till 2:30am. Look for the long line of desperate smokers.

Dinner: Babylone Bis in the 2*ème* is open till 8am and serves food and fun all night. (p. 153.)

Flowers: Romantic emergency at dawn? **Elyfleur** in the 17*ème* is open 24hr. (82, av. de Wagram; ☎01 46 66 87 19).

Museum: For that midnight museum fix, the **Musée de l'Érotisme** in the 18*ème* is open until 2am. (p. 269.)

Music: At **Aux Trois Mailletz** in the 5*ème* you can enjoy smoky jazz till dawn with the Latin Quarter's coolest. (p. 310.)

Packing tape and stamps: Need to mail a letter at 5am? No worries. **Poste du Louvre** in the 1*er* is open 24hr. (p. 121.)

Posh, Pricey Cocktails: Drink with the it-boys and girls of St-Germain until 6am at **Café Mabillon** in the 6*ème*. (p. 311.)

Champagne-infused mixed drinks €12. Happy hour 6-8pm; €6 mixed drinks. See full listing in **Food**, p. 151.

Café Oz, 18, r. St-Denis (☎01 40 39 00 18; www.cafe-oz.com). ⓜ Châtelet. Take the r. de Rivoli exit, walk down r. de Rivoli, and make a left onto r. St-Denis. Huge, friendly Australian bar with pine benches, big tables, and obliging bartenders. Pint €6.50. Mixed drinks €8. Happy hour daily 6-8pm; pint €5.50, mixed drinks €5. Open M-Th and Su 5pm-3am, F 5pm-5am, Sa 1pm-5am. Sa €10 cover includes drink and coat check. MC/V. Also at 1, r. de Bruxelles 9*ème* (☎01 40 16 11 16). ⓜ Blanche.

Le Slow Club, 130, r. de Rivoli (☎01 42 21 18 51). ⓜ Châtelet. This cellar used to be a banana-ripening warehouse, and it now looks like a cave with plush seating and a DJ. Once a jazz venue, Le Slow Club is now a private club with a great mix of music, from 60s to the present. Lots of dancing and a 25+ crowd, so you won't find any 17-year-olds trying to bend lax liquor laws. There isn't any cover, so be sure to look good and be nice to the bouncer. Some nights host private functions, so it can be worth calling in advance; weekends are usually open but selective. Open W-Sa midnight-6am.

JAZZ CLUBS

🎵 **Au Duc des Lombards,** 42, r. des Lombards (☎01 42 33 22 88; www.ducdeslombards.com). ⓜ Châtelet. From r. de Rivoli exit, walk down r. des Lavandières St-Opportune. Cross the street to follow r. St-Opportune, and turn right onto r. des Lombards. Murals of Ellington and Coltrane cover the exterior of this premier jazz joint. Still the best in French jazz, with occasional American soloists and hot items in world music. 3 sets each night—lower cover and *concessions* if you reserve in advance by phone. Cover €19-23, student €12 if you call in advance. Couples €30 also in advance. Beer €7-10. Mixed drinks €10. Music 10pm-1:30am. Open M-Sa 5pm-2am. MC/V.

🎵 **Le Baiser Salé,** 58, r. des Lombards (☎01 42 33 37 71; www.lebaisersale.com). ⓜ Châtelet. A few doors down from Au Duc des Lombards; see directions above. Cuban, African, and Antillean music featured together with modern jazz and funk in a welcoming, mellow space. Month-long African music festival in July. Jazz concerts start at 10pm, *chanson* before, music until 2:30am (typically 3 sets); mainly new talent. Cover usually around €20. Free M jam sessions at 10pm with 1-drink min. Beer €6.50-11.50. Mixed drinks €9.50. Happy hour 5-8:30pm. Open daily 5pm-6am. AmEx/MC/V.

Le Sunside, Le Sunset, 60, r. des Lombards (☎01 40 26 21 25; www.sunset-sunside.com). ⓜ Châtelet. Next door to the Baiser Salé, down the street from Au Duc des Lombards. An easy-going double club with an old and widespread reputation, Le Sunside and Le Sunset are in fact 2 separate jazz venues; Le Sunside is above Le Sunset and opens 1hr. earlier. Sometimes both have concerts, sometimes only one; check online to be sure. Beer €5-6. Mixed drinks €8.50-9.50. Cover €12-25, occasional student discount. Concerts M-Sa 9:30pm-1am. MC/V.

WINE BARS

Willi's Wine Bar, 13, r. des Petits Champs (☎01 42 61 05 09; www.williswinebar.com). ⓜ Palais-Royal. Behind the Palais. Popular since its opening in 1980, this place is fancier than its name suggests. Exposed wood beams, chic decor, and huge windows looking out onto the Palais and apartment of author Colette. Friendly staff and international clientele. Huge selection of French wines €13.50-17 per glass. Open M-Sa noon-midnight. MC/V.

SECOND ARRONDISSEMENT

When it comes to throwing a great party, few *arrondissements* can top the 2*ème*. A welcoming destination for English-speaking expats from around the globe, the neighborhood is home to several Anglophone pubs and some of the best dancing in Paris. It's also the most GLBT-friendly nightspot outside of the Marais.

🏠 **Le Champmeslé,** 4, r. Chabanais (☎01 42 96 85 20). ⓜ Pyramides. Walk down ave. de l'Opéra and make a right on r. des Petits Champs and a left onto r. Chabanais. This welcoming lesbian bar is Paris's oldest and most famous. Both men and women come to enjoy the popular cabaret shows Th 10pm, the Tu *soirée voyance*, and the monthly art exhibits. Beer €4 before 10pm, €5 after. Mixed drinks €8. Enjoy a free drink on your birthday. No cover. Open M-Sa 3pm-dawn.

Le Café Noir, 65, r. Montmartre (☎01 40 39 07 36). ⓜ Sentier. Turn down r. d'Aboukir and make a left onto r. Montmartre. Crazy plastic alien creatures hanging from the ceiling, a leopard-skin-covered bike, and bartenders leaping onto the bar to perform comedy. A true mix of locals and Anglophones: patrons gladly overcome language barriers to meet one another. Beer €2.50-3.50. Open M-F 8am-2am, Sa 4pm-2am. MC/V.

Harry's New York Bar, 5, r. Daunou (☎01 42 61 71 14). ⓜ Opéra. Walk down r. de la Paix and turn left onto r. Daunou. Claiming to be the "oldest cocktail bar in Europe," Harry's tries to make international students feel at home with college flags and foreign currencies on the walls, but it generally draws a slightly older crowd. Beer €5.50. Open daily 10:30am-4am. Downstairs is a 1920s-style piano bar (open Tu-Sa 10pm-3am), with live jazz piano nightly, accompanied by other instruments Th and F. No cover for the live music, so drink prices are slightly higher. AmEx/MC/V.

Frog and Rosbif, 116, r. St-Denis (☎01 42 36 34 73). ⓜ Etienne-Marcel. At the corner of r. St-Denis and r. Tiquetonne. One of several "Frog and..." Anglo-French pubs in Paris and around France, but each has its own flavor. The Frog and Rosbif shows live rugby and football broadcasts, which can get pretty intense when England plays. Frog pubs also brew their own lagers and bitters in a brewery downstairs. A great mix of French and English drinkers congregate here. Happy hour 6-8pm. Th students €4.50 beer and mixed drinks. Beer €6. Mixed drinks €7. Free but cranky wireless Internet. Open daily 10am-1:30am. MC/V.

DANCE CLUBS

Le Pulp, 25, bd. Poissonnière (☎01 40 26 01 93; www.pulp-paris.com). ⓜ Grands Boulevards. This legendary lesbian club feels like an old-school movie theater, with red couches, drapes, and an intimately low ceiling. Men welcome, but it is a predominantly female crowd, especially F and Sa (lesbian night). F is mixed night, Th electronic, and W rock. Weekends mostly house and techno fill the dancefloor. During Paris (GLBT) Pride, movies of the parade are projected on the walls. Beer €7. Mixed drinks €13. Cover varies but is usually around €10-15. Open W-Sa midnight-6am.

Rex Club, 5, bd. Poissonnière (☎01 42 36 10 96; www.rexclub.com). ⓜ Bonne-Nouvelle. A non-selective club that presents the most selective of DJ line-ups. Young clubbers crowd this casual venue to hear cutting-edge techno, jungle, and house fusion from international DJs on one of the best sound systems in Paris. Large dance floor and lots of seats. Beer €7.50-8. Mixed drinks €9-10. Cover €8-13 (some nights free). Open W-Th 11:30pm-6am, F-Sa midnight-6am.

Le Vinyl, 25, bd. Poissonnière (☎01 40 26 28 30; www.vinyl-paris.com). ⓜ Grands Boulevards. A GLBT-friendly dance club located underneath the famed Le Pulp. Big dance floor with raised seating areas on either side; glowsticks all around, and the inevitable discoball takes center stage. Th *Oh là là* (French songs) GLBT night; weekends vary. Cover (includes 1st drink) Th €10; weekends €15-20. Open Tu-Su 11pm-7am.

THIRD ARRONDISSEMENT

Nightlife in the *3ème* is more subdued than the scene found in the neighboring *4ème*—for the most part, women (and men, too) can leave their stiletto heels at home. There are a number of GLBT bars in the area on and around **rue aux Ours, rue St-Martin,** and **rue Michel Le Comte,** but the area's focus is on casual bar-cafes with live music.

■ **Andy Wahloo,** 69, r. des Gravilliers (☎01 42 71 20 38). ⓜ Arts et Métiers. Walk down r. Beaubourg and turn left onto r. des Gravilliers. The happening and hip lounge bar of the moment, this place is an offshoot of the popular 404 restaurant next door. The environment is funky and eclectic, featuring ingenious paint-bucket seats and a cushioned corner poised on plastic crates. The tiny bar stirs after 11pm, but come early to claim a seat on the casual terrace and smoke hookah to the beat of DJs spinning tunes. Beer €5-6. Mixed drinks €9-10. Happy hour 5-8pm; beer and mixed drinks €5. Open M-Sa 5pm-2am, Su 11am-5pm. AmEx/MC/V.

■ **L'Apparement Café,** 18, r. des Coutures St-Gervais (☎01 48 87 12 22). ⓜ Chemin Vert. Beautiful wood and red lounge with games and a chill, young crowd. Display of local artists' paintings that you can buy if the fancy strikes. Late-night meals €12-15, served until 11:30pm. Mixed drinks €9 (see **Food,** p. 154).

■ **Le Duplex,** 25, r. Michel Le Comte (☎01 42 72 80 86) ⓜ Rambuteau. A great place to make friends instead of trouble. Small and intimate atmosphere features a computer where the 30-something patrons can snap photos to remember their evening. Local artists display photographs and paintings in rotating exhibits on the walls. Not an exclusively male bar—anyone is welcome—but few women hang out here. The bar becomes lively after 11pm and plays lots of jazz and electronic music. Beer €2.50 until 10pm, €3.50 after. Mixed drinks €7.50. Open M-Th and Su 8am-2am and Fri-Sa 8am-4am. MC with €15 min. charge.

Le Connétable, 55, r. des Archives (☎01 42 77 41 40). ⓜ Arts et Métiers. Walk down r. Beaubourg and turn left onto r. Michel Le Comte; restaurant is at corner of r. des Archives and r. des Haudriettes. Housed in a former *hôtel particulier*, this 3-level bar-restaurant boasts exposed ceiling beams presiding over the dimly lit classic decor. The unpretentious but cultured ambience lends itself to popular nightly concerts in the basement, starting at 8:30 and 10pm. Come early to secure a good seat in the tiny concert room. Beer €4-7. Mixed drinks €8. Dinner menu €21. Main dishes €15-20. Open M-F noon-3pm and 7pm-3am, Sa-Su 7pm-3am. Food served noon-3pm and 7-11pm. AmEx/MC/V.

Villa Keops, 58, bd. de Sébastopol (☎01 40 27 99 92). ⓜ Etienne-Marcel. Walk east on r. Etienne-Marcel; Villa Keops is on the corner with bd. de Sébastopol. Stylish, candlelit bar populated with sexy brass-studded purple leather seats and beautiful waiters serving designer drinks. A posh spot to stop for a drink before heading to one of the many GLBT clubs in the Marais. Wine €3.50-5.50, divine *Rose du Nil* €8.50. Happy hour 6-9pm; buy 1 drink, get 1 free. Also serves food. Open daily noon-2am. AmEx/MC/V.

L'Enchanteur, 15, r. Michel Le Comte (☎06 17 11 90 13). ⓜ Rambuteau. This laid-back bar works its magic with plenty of purple fittings and psychedelic lighting. Club downstairs Sa; festivities begin at 9pm. Older men are the predominant species, but women are welcome. Beer €2.50. Mixed drinks €7. Open M-Th and Su 4pm-2am, F-Sa 4pm-4am. V.

DANCE CLUBS

Le Dépôt, 10, r. aux Ours (☎01 44 54 96 96; www.ledepot.com). ⓜ Etienne-Marcel. Take r. Etienne-Marcel east; it becomes r. aux Ours. A pleasure complex for queer men. Dance for inspiration to everything from disco to house to techno but don't waste time on small talk; just take your boy toy of the night to one of the rooms in the downstairs labyrinth. Find said boy toy in the designated "cruising" area while watching porno on mounted TVs. Women not welcome (exceptions include Pride Week, when a few lesbians can enter). The 5pm post-Su brunch Gay Tea Dance is especially popular. Cover (includes 1st drink) M-Th €8.50, F €10, Sa €12, Su €10. Open daily 2pm-8am. V.

WINE BARS

◙ **L'Estaminet,** 39 r. de Bretagne, Marché des Enfants Rouges (☎01 42 72 34 85). ⓜ Temple. Walk down r. du Temple and turn left on r. de Bretagne. Enter the Marché des Enfants Rouges; the bar is on the upper right corner, marked by an arching grapevine and cheerful geraniums growing in wooden barrels. This tiny, clean-scrubbed and airy wine bar features a delightful selection of inexpensive wines by the glass (€3-3.50) or bottle (€5-25). Accompaniments available, or better yet, traipse through the market and pick up some nibbles. In summer, the yellow-checkered picnic tables are a great way to meet friendly locals. MC/V. ❶

FOURTH ARRONDISSEMENT

No matter where you are in the 4*ème*, a bar is close by. Spots with outdoor seating are piled on top of one another on **rue Vieille du Temple,** from r. des Francs-Bourgeois to r. de Rivoli. GLBT bars crowd **rue Ste Croix de la Bretonnerie.** The bars on **rue des Lombards** have a more rough and convivial atmosphere.

◙ **Raidd Bar,** 23, r. du Temple. ⓜ Hôtel de Ville. Take the ⓜ Hôtel de Ville exit and walk up r. du Temple. The most hip and happening GLBT club in the Marais and perhaps Paris. Spinning disco globes cast undulating shadow and light in the intimate space, illuminating the muscular, topless torsos of the sexy bartenders. Watch performers strip and shower for the clients in a glass shower cubicle built into the wall (yes, they take it *all* off in shows at 11:30pm, midnight, 12:30, and 1am). Tu disco night, W 80s and house and Su house mix. Beer €4. Notoriously strict door policy–women are allowed in with men on weekdays, but might not be so lucky on weekends.

◙ **Chez Richard,** 37, r. Vieille-du-Temple (☎01 42 74 31 65). ⓜ St-Paul or Hôtel de Ville. Inside a courtyard off r. Vieille-du-Temple, this bar reminds patrons of *Casablanca* with its stone interior, hidden balcony, slowly spinning ceiling fan, and shadow-casting palm leaves. A hot place to people-watch on weekends, but ideal for chilling on weekdays, with suave bartenders and mellow beats. Happy hour 6-8pm; mixed drinks €5. Open daily 6pm-2am. AmEx/MC/V.

◙ **Amnésia Café,** 42, r. Vieille-du-Temple (☎01 42 72 16 94). ⓜ St-Paul or Hôtel de Ville. A largely queer crowd comes to lounge on plush sofas in Amnésia's classy wood-paneled interior. 1st fl. cafe, 2nd fl. lounge and basement club with music beginning 9pm. This is one of the top see-and-be-seen spots in the Marais, especially on Sa nights. Espresso €2. Kir €4. Mixed drinks €7.50-8.50. Open Tu-Th and Su 11am-2am, M and F-Sa 11am-3am. MC/V.

Open Café, 17, r. des Archives (☎01 42 72 26 18). ⓜ Hôtel de Ville. The most popular of the Marais GLBT bars draws a large crowd of loyal customers to its corner. Always crowded, this is one of the most hip and classy GLBT bars in Paris. Most patrons are

NIGHTLIFE

TAXI TALE

It was a dark and stormy night somewhere west of Bastille. Broke, bedraggled, and done for the night, a girlfriend and I decided to head home. As it was well after 1am, the metro was closed, leaving us little choice but to take a cab. This was to be my rude introduction to the perilous world of Parisian taxis.

You can tell that a taxi is available when the main light atop the car is illuminated. If a taxi is full, the main light will be off. One of the three smaller lights below the main one, however, should be illuminated. These correspond to the rate being charged. Rates in Paris are determined by time of day and distance from the city center; police can stop a taxi if its lights show it applying an inappropriate rate.

But just because a taxi is empty doesn't mean the driver will stop for you. For a start, you can't hail a taxi mid-block. It's against the law, and cabs risk a big fine if they try it. After a half-hour of frantic hand-waving in the pouring rain, we were still *sans transport*, so we headed for a stand.

There are hundreds of taxi stands throughout Paris, indicated by bright blue street signs. But don't be deceived by any genteel connotations of orderly lines, or even the expectation that taxis will search out the taxi stand. After the bars close at 2am, the taxi stand transforms

men, but women are welcome. Happy hour 6-9pm; helf-price beer only. Beer €3.50-6.50, mixed drinks €7.50. Open daily 11am-2am. AmEx/MC/V.

Les Etages, 35, r. Vieille du Temple (☎01 42 78 72 00). ⓜ St-Paul or Hôtel de Ville. Set in an 18th-century hotel-turned-bar. 4 *étages* populated by dressed-down, nonthreatening 20-somethings. Limited selection of €4 mixed drinks during happy hour (3:30-9pm)—they'll bring it to you with a side of nuts and olives. Open daily 3:30pm-2am. MC/V with €15 min. charge.

Lizard Lounge, 18, r. du Bourg-Tibourg (☎01 42 72 81 34). ⓜ Hôtel de Ville. A happening split-level space for rowdy American college kids. Underground cellar has DJs every night from 10pm. Happy hour on ground floor 5-8pm, underground 8-10pm; select pints and mixed drinks €5. Lizard Juice €7.50. Open daily noon-2am. Good, if somewhat pricey American grub served M-F noon-3pm and 7:30-10:30pm, Sa-Su noon-4pm, 7:30-10:30pm. Sa-Su brunch €12-14. MC/V with €15 min. charge.

Le Café du Trésor, 5, r. du Trésor (☎01 42 74 35 17). ⓜ St-Paul. Walk along r. de Rivoli in the direction of traffic, turn right onto r. Vieille-du-Temple and right onto the pedestrian r. du Trésor. This plush and luxurious restaurant/bar/club complex takes up most of the block. Its ultra-sophisticated plush velvet interior and tranquil terrace are havens for the bourgeois bohemian set. Happy hour 5-8pm; half-price mixed drinks and beer. Beer €4-5. Mixed drinks €7. Open daily 9am-2am. Food served M-F 12:30-3pm and 8-11:30pm, Sa-Su 12:30-11:30pm. MC/V.

Le Carré, 18, r. du Temple (☎01 44 59 38 57). ⓜ Hôtel de Ville. Take the Hôtel de Ville exit and walk up r. du Temple. Stained glass, a red back-lit bar, and smoky taupe velvet chairs mark this happening bar of the moment. It is a favorite drinking hole for chic and well-dressed 20somethings, both queer and straight. Beer €3.40-4. Mixed drinks €8-10. Happy hour 6-9pm. Lunch menu €13.50. Brunch €18 every Su 11am-5pm. Open M-Su 11am-4am. AmEx/MC/V.

Okawa, 40, r. Vieille-du-Temple (☎01 48 04 30 69). ⓜ St-Paul. Walk up r. de Pavée, turn left onto r. des Rosiers and turn left onto r. Vieille-du-Temple. This friendly and casual Franco-Québécois bar-cafe is run by a Canadian expat. Plop down on one of the leather tufted stools and ogle passersby, or check out a cabaret-concert in the basement (W-Th only, no concerts during summer; €5 cover charge in addition to meal), which features chunky stone wells from the reign of Philippe-Auguste. The €7 speed-dating nights on Tu (includes 1 drink) are popular with singletons; sign up beforehand. Happy hour 7-9pm; beer €3.50-3.70. Coffee €2.50. Mixed drinks €8.50. Open daily 11:30am-2am. MC/V.

3W Kafé, 8, r. des Ecouffes (☎01 48 87 39 26). ⓜ St-Paul. Walk with traffic along r. de Rivoli and turn right onto r. des Ecouffes. Formerly "Les Scandaleuses," the Marais's hippest lesbian bar got a face-lift and a new name—3W stands for "women with women." Sleek interior, smooth beats. Men welcome accompanied by women. Downstairs club with DJ F-Sa from 10pm. Beer €3.30-5. Mixed drinks €8-9. Open daily 5:30pm-2am. MC/V.

Au Petit Fer à Cheval, 30, r. Vieille-du-Temple (☎01 42 72 47 47; www.cafeine.com). ⓂHôtel de Ville. A Marais institution with a horseshoe bar, sidewalk terrace, and small restaurant in back. Serves up the best mojito in Paris (€7.50-8.50). Beer €2.50-10. Mixed drinks €7.50-8.50. Drinks cheaper if served at bar. See also **Food**, p. 155. Open daily 10am-2am. MC/V.

Mixer Bar, 23, r. Ste-Croix de la Brettonerie (☎01 48 87 55 44). ⓂSt-Paul. Boys, boys, and more boys, but this is a "mixed" bar, and the friendly bartender-owner Miloud welcomes all. Packed even early in the night, with Marais crawlers soaking in the beer and 3 nightly DJs (from 6pm). Bartenders speak English and distribute GLBT-friendly maps of Paris. Happy hour 5-9pm and all night Tu. Beer €3. Mixed drinks €7. Open daily 5pm-2am. MC/V with €16 min charge.

Le Quetzal, 10, r. de la Verrerie (☎01 48 87 99 07). ⓂHôtel de Ville. Nicknamed *l'Incontournable* (it's been around for 20 years), this spacious, black-lit men's bar plays everything from rap to techno and runs the gamut from stylish to shady. Opposite the r. des Mauvais Garçons (Bad Boys). Women welcome. Happy hour 5pm-midnight. Beer €3.50. Mixed drinks €7.50-9. Open daily 5pm-5am. MC/V.

Bliss Kfé, 30, r. du Roi de Sicile (☎01 42 78 49 36). ⓂSt-Paul. This "sensitive lounge bar's" mellow atmosphere contrasts with its fashionably gritty and sharp decor. Soft red candlelight flickers over metal seating, and mellow lounge music washes over a funky, alternative, and all-female clientele. A DJ spins techno and house tunes in the basement after 10pm. Men discouraged. Beer €3.50-4. Mixed drinks €9. Open daily 5:30pm-2am. MC/V.

Cox, 15, r. des Archives (☎01 42 72 08 00). ⓂHôtel-de-Ville. As the name suggests, this is a buns-to-the-wall men's bar with an older clientele. So crowded that the guys who gather here block traffic on the street. Cruisy and hypersexualized, with a slightly seedy tang; not the place for a quiet weekend cocktail. Happy hour 6-9pm; draft beer half-price. Beer €3.50-4.50. Open daily 12:30pm-2am.

Stolly's, 16, r. Cloche-Perce (☎01 42 76 06 76). ⓂSt-Paul. On a dead-end street off r. du Roi de Sicile. This small Anglophone hangout, run by the same folks who own Lizard Lounge, does dive-bar cool. The €13.50 pitchers of cheap blonde ensure that the bar lives up to its motto, "Hangovers installed and serviced here." Life-size papier-mâché animals and a decidedly non-trendy

into a field of urban combat. Only the strongest, pushiest, and most willing to jump the queue manage to procure a ride from the trickle of passing cabs. Taxis refused passengers for no apparent reason, and passengers refused taxis if the meter on the back window showed that the driver had been on the road for more than the legal limit of ten hours.

When we finally landed a cab, sure enough, the driver proclaimed that our destination was too close by and kicked us out. I didn't know this then, but it is actually illegal for taxis to refuse passengers based on their destination. The minimum fare is €4.50, but the trip can be as short as you like beyond that, so stand your ground and stay seated, regardless of where you want to go.

Finally, we tried to call a cab, only to discover that the meter begins when you call, not when the taxi arrives. We ended up paying an absurd amount for a brief journey.

The moral of the story? Take the Noctambus if you're out late (see Essentials, p. 43). There may be 20,000 taxis in Paris, but finding one on a rainy Saturday night is like finding the proverbial needle in a haystack.

— *Amelia Lester*

crowd. Happy hour 4-8pm; mixed drinks and beer €5. Open daily 4:30pm-2am (but last call comes early). MC/V.

Café Klein Holland, 36, r. du Roi de Sicile (☎01 42 71 43 13). ⓜ St-Paul. From St-Paul, take r. de Pavée and turn left onto r. du Roi de Sicile. A Dutch bar with a friendly, lively atmosphere. Happy hour all night; pints €3. Beer €3-3.50, special mixed drinks such as the "multiple orgasm" €8. Open daily 5pm-2am. MC/V.

L'Unity, 176-178, r. St-Martin (☎01 42 72 70 59). ⓜ Rambuteau. Walk down r. Rambuteau and turn right on r. St-Martin. This women's club features a pool table, cards and boardgames, and a soundtrack of reggae, folk, rock, and techno. Straight men not encouraged. Happy hour M-F 4-8pm; €1 off draft beer. Beer €3.50-7. Mixed drinks €3.50-8. Open daily 4pm-2am. MC/V.

Le Tango, 11, r. au Maire (☎01 42 72 17 78; www.tangoparis.com). ⓜ Arts et Métiers. This 70 year-old establishment is the last vestige of the traditional *musette* (accordion) club. The columns and bar and the casual, down-to-earth ambience have changed little since the club's inception. Managed by the GLBT organization "La Boite à Frissons" (The Thrill Box), this is not your typical sweaty, over-sexed queer club. Partners' dancing to tango and chacha before 12:30am, and world music (with lots of Madonna) thereafter on Fridays and Saturdays. Sunday parties are organized by various GLBT organizations; check website for details. Every two months, a popular singles ball takes over. Cover €7, drinks €4-7.50. Open F-Sa 10:30pm-5am, Su 6-11pm. No credit cards.

WINE BARS

La Belle Hortense, 31, r. Vieille du Temple (☎01 48 04 71 60). ⓜ St-Paul. Walk with traffic along r. de Rivoli and turn right onto r. Vieille du Temple. A breath of fresh air for those worn out by the hyper-chic scene along the rest of the *rue*, but this is not an all-inclusive crowd: its intellectualism strikes some as snobby. Coffee €1.30-2. Varied wine selection from €4 a glass, €8 a bottle. Walls and walls of books (literature, art, philosophy) and mellow music to go with your merlot. Frequent exhibits, readings, lectures, signatures, and discussions in the small leather-couch-filled back room advertised on the front window. Open daily 5pm-2am. MC/V.

Wine and Bubbles, 15, r. des Lombards (☎01 42 72 01 52; www.wineandbubbles.com). ⓜ Châtelet. Walk north on bd. de Sébastopol and turn right on r. des Lombards. Taste-test bubbly without breaking the bank. The communal seating area has a cozy, kitchen-table feel. If you like what you try, you can buy the bottle—this classy wine bar doubles as a *marchand de vin*. From €3.50 a glass and €16 a bottle, cheese accompaniments €5-16. Bar open Tu 6pm-midnight, W-Sa 6pm-2am; shop open 11am-9pm. AmEx/MC/V. Second location at 3, r. Française, 1er (☎01 44 76 99 84). ⓜ Etienne Marcel.

FIFTH ARRONDISSEMENT

A decidedly student-dominated scene, the 5ème offers an astoundingly diverse array of nightlife, much of it with a retro pastiche. Come here to down a rowdy pint with the intellectuals at **Finnegan's Wake** or to swing the night away at **Le Caveau de la Huchette.**

🏴 **Le Caveau des Oubliettes,** 52, r. Galande (☎01 46 34 23 09). ⓜ St-Michel. Head away from pl. St-Michel on quai de Montebello and turn right on r. Petit Pont, then left onto r. Galande. 2 scenes in 1, both with a mellow, funky vibe: the upstairs bar (La Guillotine) has sod carpeting, ferns, and a real guillotine. The downstairs cellar is an outstanding jazz club. This cellar's previous incarnation was an actual *caveau des oubliettes* (cave of the forgotten ones), where criminals were locked up and forgotten. Free *soirée boeuf* (jam session) M-Th and Su 10pm-1:30am; F-Sa concerts free. Drinks from €5. Happy hour daily 5-9pm. Open daily 5pm-2am.

■ **Le Reflet,** 6, r. Champollion (☎01 43 29 97 27). Ⓜ Cluny-La Sorbonne. Walk away from the river on bd. St-Michel, turn left on r. des Ecoles, then right on r. Champollion. Crowded with students and workers stopping by for a post-cinema drink (it's opposite 3 theaters). ½ pint beer €2.50-4. Mixed drinks €5. Salads €7-9. Open M-Sa 10am-2am, Su noon-2am. Closed mid-July to mid-Aug. MC/V.

Le Who's Bar, 13, r. Petit Pont (☎01 43 54 80 71). Ⓜ St-Michel. Walk away from pl. St-Michel on quai Montebello and make a right onto r. Petit Pont. This hopping bar is right in the swing of things, by r. de la Huchette and the Seine. Live music, some of it not too terrible (think Placebo covers), starts nightly at 10:30pm; dance club in the basement on weekends. Beer €5.50-6. Mixed drinks €11-12. Happy hour daily 6:30-10pm, all drinks half-price. Open M-Th and Su 6pm-5am, F-Sa 6pm-6am.

Finnegan's Wake, 9, r. des Boulangers (☎01 46 34 23 65). Ⓜ Jussieu. An Irish pub set in a renovated ancient wine cellar with low, black-beamed ceilings. Have a pint (€6) with the boisterous crowd of students. F night traditional Irish music, jazz, R&B, and rock in the *cave* from 5pm. Happy hour daily 6-8pm, all pints €4.50. Open M-F 11am-1am, Sa-Su 6pm-1am.

Le Piano Vache, 8, r. Laplace (☎01 46 33 75 03). Ⓜ Cardinal Lemoine or Maubert-Mutualité. From Maubert, walk up r. de la Montagne Ste-Geneviève and make a right on r. Laplace. Once a butcher shop, now a dim, poster-plastered bar hidden behind the Panthéon and decorated with cow paraphernalia. Not a good choice if you're scared of the dark, but a great one if you're scared of your date. Happy hour 6-9pm. Beer €3.50. Mixed drinks €7. W Manic Depression night. Th 80s night. *Soirée Chewing-Gum des Oreilles* (don't ask us) rock night Sa-Su. Theme nights 9pm-2am. Japanese rock night every second Tu of the month. Open July-Aug. M-F 6pm-2am, Sa-Su 9pm-2am; Sept.-June M-F noon-2am, Sa-Su 9pm-2am.

Le Rive Gauche, 1 r. du Sabot (☎01 42 22 51 70, night 01 40 20 43 23 day; www.rivegauche-maryse.com). Ⓜ St-Germain-des-Prés. Walk down r. de Rennes, turn right onto r. du Sabot, and continue to the end of the road; look for a door on the corner on the right. A club exclusively for women and gay men (and quite a few come), Le Rive Gauche is spacious and well-decorated. Recently opened and not extremely well-known, the club is not always full, but the music and atmosphere are great. Red lighting sets off disco-

ON THE MENU

GREEN PARTY

Degas's painting *L'absinthe* (1875) features the green concoction absinthe being downed at a Pigalle cafe. Some think Van Gogh owed much of his inspiration—and madness—to it. Ernest Hemingway wrote: "that opaque, bitter, tongue-numbing, brain-warming, stomach-warming, idea-changing liquid alchemy." Picasso, Toulouse-Lautrec, and hordes of Parisians once drank it fanatically.

First distilled in 1792 from the wormwood plant (Artemisia absinthium) and chlorophyll, which makes it green, the 120-proof, licorice-flavored drink was first used by French soldiers in Algeria to foil dysentery. They returned to France in the 1830s with a taste for the stuff, and soon all of Paris was riding the green wave. Bars had *l'heure verte* (green hour), where water was poured onto a sugar cube and into the green liquor. Some spoke of the *fée verte* (green fairy) that stole the drinker's soul, while others warned of *le péril vert*. In 1915, it was outlawed in France. Pernod tastes similar, but for the real thing, most of us will probably have to settle for anecdotes—maybe for the best. "After the first glass," wrote Oscar Wilde, "you see things as you wish they were. After the second, you see things as they are not. Finally you see things as they really are, and that is the most horrible thing in the world."

ball-type mirrors on the walls, and there are seats both around the dance floor and in more private rooms past the bar. Beer €10. Champagne €12. Cover €10 on F, €15 on Sa. Open F-Sa 11pm-6am.

JAZZ CLUBS

Le Petit Journal St-Michel, 71, bd. St-Michel (☎01 43 26 28 59; www.petitjournal-saintmichel.com). ⓜ Cluny-La Sorbonne, RER Luxembourg. Follow bd. St-Michel away from the Seine. Le Petit is another of the early jazz strongholds, now popular with a middle-aged crowd. First-class New Orleans and Big Band acts frequently perform here. Concerts start at 9:15pm. Obligatory 1st drink €17-20 (students €11-15), subsequent drinks €6.50. Open M-Sa 9pm-1:15am. Closed Aug.

Le Caveau de la Huchette, 5, r. de la Huchette (☎01 43 26 65 05; www.caveaudelahuchette.fr). ⓜ St-Michel. From bd. St-Michel, turn down r. de la Huchette. Come prepared to listen, watch, jitterbug, swing, jive, and sweat in this extremely popular (if touristy) club. Bebop dance lessons Sept.-June; call for times. Crowd covers a wide range of ages. Live music 10pm-2am. Drinks €5-10.50. Cover M-Th and Su, F-Sa €13; students €9; no cover after 2am. Open daily 9:30pm-2:30am, Th-Sa until dawn. AmEx/MC/V.

Aux Trois Mailletz, 56, r. Galande (☎01 43 54 00 79; before 5pm 01 43 25 96 86). ⓜ St-Michel. Walk along the Seine on the Quai St-Michel, make a right on r. du Petit Pont and a left on r. Galande. What you'd expect a cool jazz club to look like. The crowded basement cafe features world music and jazz vocals. The upper floor is packed with a well-dressed mix of students and 40-somethings. Weekend cover for club €13-19; bar cover free. Grog €9. Mixed drinks €12.50. Bar open daily 5pm-dawn; *cave* 10pm-dawn.

SIXTH ARRONDISSEMENT

The *6ème* has great nightlife, although it is definitely oriented toward bars and pubs, not clubs. Around **Carrefour Buci** and **Carrefour de l'Odéon** are lots of great little bar-cafes, and also some *crêpe* stalls for the journey home at the end of the night.

🎵 **Le 10 Bar,** 10, r. de l'Odéon (☎01 43 26 66 83). ⓜ Odéon. Walk against traffic on bd. St-Germain and make a left on r. de l'Odéon. Le 10 Bar is a classic student hangout, where Parisian youth indulge in philosophical and political discussion. After several glasses of their famous spiced sangria (€3.50), you might feel inspired to join in. Jukebox plays everything from Edith Piaf to Aretha Franklin. Open daily 6pm-2am.

🎵 **Bob Cool,** 15, r. des Grands Augustins (☎01 46 33 33 77). ⓜ Odéon. Walk up r. de l'Ancienne Comédie, turn right on r. St-André-des-Arts and left on to the small r. des Grands Augustins. Bob Cool has laid-back clientele, a friendly vibe, and a reputation as one of the best bars in the city. The music is at the discretion of the bartender and veers all over the spectrum, from salsa to The Corrs. Happy hour 5-9pm; pint €4.50, mixed drinks €5-6. Open daily 5pm-2am.

Fu Bar, 5, r. St-Sulpice (☎01 40 51 82 00). ⓜ Odéon. Take Carrefour d'Odéon to r. de Condé, then turn right on r. St-Sulpice. A multilevel haven for a boisterous Anglophone crowd, this hip bar serves an astounding array of tantalizing martinis (€7.50) along with the regular bar fare. Tu is student night, when martinis are €2 off, and those under 25 pack the place almost to bursting. Happy Hour daily 5-9pm. Open daily 5pm-2am.

The Moose, 16, r. des Quatre Vents (☎01 46 33 77 00; www.mooseheadparis.com). ⓜ Odéon. Head toward r. d'Odeon and go right on r. des Quatre Vents. Decorated in typical Canadian fashion—that is to say, with hockey sweaters and bilingual beer posters—The Moose is the place to rub elbows with friendly Canadian expats. Restaurant serves North American bar fare—nachos, burgers, and wings—until midnight. Those yearning for Canadian beer can treat themselves to an ice-cold bottle of Moosehead (€5.50).

Happy hour 4-8:30pm. Tu happy hour all night; mixed drinks €5.50, Moosehead €3.50. Bar open M-Sa 4pm-2am, Su 11:30pm-2am.

Chez Georges, 11, r. des Cannettes (☎01 43 26 79 15). ⓜ Mabillon. Walk down r. du Four and turn left on r. des Cannettes. Upstairs, Chez Georges is a small wine bar with a mixed crowd; downstairs, it's a smoky, candlelit cellar rampant with students drinking and dancing. Beer €3.50-4.50. Wine €1.50-3.20. Upstairs open Tu-Sa noon-2am, cellar 10pm-2am. Closed Aug.

Café Mabillon, 164, bd. St-Germain (☎01 43 26 62 93). ⓜ Mabillon. This fast-track cafe-bar with lavender lights and hard techno draws the area's Gucci-wearing girls and black-clad boys. Fancy mixed drinks €12-13. Happy hour 7-9pm. Open daily 8am-5:30am. MC/V.

SEVENTH ARRONDISSEMENT

The 7ème may be the poshest address in town, but its respectable citizens retreat early, and quality nightlife spots are thus sparse. A few wannabe-cool corner cafe-bars at Ecole Militaire are expensive and touristy, but the r. St-Dominique has a couple of cafes and bars staked out by locals.

▨ Le Club des Poètes, 30, r. de Bourgogne (☎01 47 05 06 03; www.poesie.net). ⓜ Varenne. Walk up bd. des Invalides with the Invalides behind you and to your left; go right on r. de Grenelle and left onto r. de Bourgogne. Since 1961, Jean-Pierre Rosnay has been making "poetry contagious and inevitable—vive la poésie!" A restaurant by day, Le Club des Poètes is transformed at 10pm each night when a troupe of readers and comedians, including Rosnay's family, bewitch the audience with poetry from Villon, Baudelaire, Rimbaud, and others. If you arrive after 10pm, wait to enter until you hear clapping or a break in the performance. Le Club is not cheap (dinner without wine €20), but come for a post-dinner drink to be part of the fun. Lunch menu €15. Drinks €7.50. Open Tu-Sa noon-3pm and 8pm-1am. Food served until 10pm. Closed Aug. MC/V.

Malone's, 64, av. Bosquet (☎01 45 51 08 99). ⓜ Ecole Militaire. Chic mahogany decor and candlelight create a surprisingly easy-going atmosphere, enhanced by the warm waitstaff, Jazz and rhythm downstairs several nights per week. Beer €5. Mixed drinks (try the grasshopper) €8. Snacks like bacon chevre croques and rillette tartines served until closing, €5-6. Happy hour 5-8pm; mixed drinks €5.50. Open M-Sa 5pm-2am, Su 5pm-1am. MC/V.

O'Brien's, 77, r. St-Dominique (☎01 45 51 75 87). ⓜ La Tour-Maubourg. Follow traffic along bd. de La Tour Maubourg. A bustling Irish pub with a horseshoe-shaped bar and a largely English-speaking clientele. TV plays sports matches in the evenings (everything from darts to football). Happy hour M-F 5-8pm; pints €5.50. 25cl beer €3.50-4.50, 50cl beer €6.50-7. Mixed drinks €8. Open daily 5pm-2am (3am weekends). MC/V with €15 min. charge.

EIGHTH ARRONDISSEMENT

Glam is the word at the trendy, expensive bars and clubs of the 8ème. Whether you're going for a mystical evening at buddha-bar or a surprisingly more accessible evening at Le Queen, your wallet and dashing good looks are a must.

▨ buddha-bar, 8, r. Boissy d'Anglas (☎01 53 05 90 00; www.buddha-bar.com). ⓜ Madeleine or Concorde. The legendary buddha-bar has to be the most glamorous drinking-hole in the world (Madonna drops by when she's in town). Hypnotic and vibration global rhythms diffuse over 2 dim, candlelit levels populated by the beautiful and the well-heeled. A giant buddha watches over the expensive ground-floor restaurant while an elegant bar serves creative mixed drinks and martinis (€16-17) to the exclusive clientele lounging on intimate couches. Drowning yourself in the surreal atmosphere for a night might just be worth breaking the bank, but be sure to look your best for optimum service. Beer €8-10. Wine €10-12. Open M-F noon-3pm and 6pm-2am, Sa-Su 6pm-2am.

THE BIG SPLURGE

DINE LIKE THE GODS

Tucked between historic hotels and the American embassy is the **buddha-bar**, two floors of pure delight where you can spend a few hours living like the rich and famous (which just might be worth a few days' budget). Swanky, candlelit, and expensive, yet surprisingly welcoming, buddha will seduce you with its stunning atmosphere, food, and clientele. The afternoon *menu degustation* (€32) includes three courses, wine, and coffee. The menu treats you to appetizers like avocado sushi or crispy spring-rolls, and a main dish that frames rice with a light curry or *steak tartare* and a spring salad. For dessert, expect something fresh and fruity that looks like artwork and awakens new tastebuds.

Gawk at the drink menu, which lists a particular bottle of cognac at over €1000 (you could just take a 2cl shot for €122!). For ordinary humans, the fantastic "experimental" mixed drinks, which include such unconventional ingredients as aniseed and cucumber, are around €12. So that you can relive the experience at home, a line of buddha-bar CDs and dining accessories are for sale at reception.
buddha-bar, 8, r. Boissy d'Anglais, 8ème (☎01 53 05 90 00). Ⓜ *Concorde or Madeleine. Lunch M-F noon-3pm. Open nightly 6pm-2am.* ❺

Charlie Birdy, 124, r. la Boétie (☎01 42 25 18 06; www.charliebirdy.com). Ⓜ Franklin D. Roosevelt. Walk toward the arch on the Champs; r. la Boétie will be the second street on your right. The third incarnation of this bar-restaurant formerly known as the Chesterfield Café and the House of Live. A friendly, spacious bar with an Anglo-Indian design concept that serves up affordable drinks (mixed drinks €8, special drinks €11) and fusion food in a chill and casual atmosphere. Come on Sa nights to shimmy to Latin music, hip-hop, rap and R&B on the dance platform in the back. Happy hour M-F 4-8pm with half-price drinks. Wine €3-5. Beer €4-6.50. Open daily 10am-5am. AmEx/MC/V.

Mandala Ray, 34 r. Marboeuf (☎01 56 88 36 36; www.manray.fr). Hyper-trendy bar-restaurant named after the famous photographer Man Ray and owned by Johnny Depp, John Malkovich, and Sean Penn, among others. The upper level houses a busy bar (beer €7, mixed drinks €12), with a daily happy hour from 6-8pm (€6 drinks). Live jazz, salsa, soul, and Latin music featured Tu at 10pm. On weekends, DJs spin tunes to jammed crowds after 11pm, with a cover charge of €15-20. There is also a restaurant in the lower level presided over by Asian-inspired goddess statues. This place is exclusive; come with your hottest outfit and a surplus of confidence. Open M-F 6pm-3am, Sa-Su 6pm-5am.

DANCE CLUBS

Le Queen, 102, av. des Champs-Elysées (☎01 53 89 08 90). Ⓜ George V. Where drag queens, superstars, models, moguls, and go-go boys get down to the mainstream rhythms of a 10,000-gigawatt sound system. Her Majesty is one of the cheapest and most accessible GLBT clubs in town, but it caters to a mix of tastes. Women have the better luck with the bouncer if in the company of at least one man. In summer, some nights are rumored to end in a wild foam bath. M disco, Th-Sa house, Su 80s. Cover M-Th and Su €15, F-Sa €20, includes 1 drink. W night Ladies' Night. Bring an ID with birthdate, and avoid coming in large groups. All drinks €10. Open daily 11pm-dawn. AmEx/MC/V.

NINTH ARRONDISSEMENT

In this notoriously scandalous *arrondissement*, expect to find nightlife as spicy as its surroundings. Dance clubs range from the classy to the crude.

Folies Pigalle, 11, pl. Pigalle (☎01 48 78 55 25; www.folies-pigalle.com). Ⓜ Pigalle. The largest, wildest club in the sleazy Pigalle *quartier*—not for the faint of heart. A former strip joint, the Folies is popular with both GLBT and straight clubbers and is probably the most trans-friendly club in the city. Mostly house and techno. *Soirées Transsexuelles* Th and Su, although all nights welcome all types. Usually crowded. Open M-Th and Su midnight-8am, F-Sa midnight-noon. Drinks €10. €20 cover includes 1st drink. AmEx/MC/V.

Bus Palladium, 6, r. Fontaine (☎01 42 23 18 62; www.lebuspalladium.com). From Ⓜ Pigalle, walk down r. Jean-Baptiste Pigalle (on the left of Folies Pigalle), turn right on r. Fontaine, and look for the bright blue facade. Getting past the bouncers can be tough, as this trendy club is rented out to private organizations that often have a guest list (sometimes more for show than anything). Call ahead or check online to be sure of what is going on during a particular evening; but most F and Sa are open to the public. Cover depends on the night, but is usually €12-15. AmEx/V.

TENTH ARRONDISSEMENT

While it's relatively safe during the day, the 10*ème* becomes a haven of pickpocketing and prostitution after sundown, so *Let's Go* recommends avoiding the area if at all possible. For intrepid travelers who feel particularly inclined to hear some jazz, **New Morning** is the best option for nightlife in the area.

JAZZ CLUBS

New Morning, 7-9, r. des Petites-Ecuries (☎01 45 23 51 41; www.newmorning.com). Ⓜ Château d'Eau. This 400-seat former printing plant now plays host to some of the biggest American headliners in the city. Dark, smoky, and crowded, New Morning is everything a jazz club should be. The venue's best acoustics are in the lower front section or near the wings of the stage. All the greatest names in jazz have played here—from Chet Baker to Stan Getz and Miles Davis. These days it continues to attracts big names like Wynton Marsalis, Betty Carter, and John Scofield. Tickets can be purchased from the box office, any branch of FNAC, or the Virgin Megastore; they average €16-20. Drinks €6-10. Open Sept.-July from 8pm, though exact times vary. Concerts begin at 9:30pm. MC/V.

ELEVENTH ARRONDISSEMENT

Nightlife in the 11*ème* is a tale of two scenes. With a few exceptions, **rue de Lappe** and its neighbors offer a big, raucous night on the town dominated by Anglophiles, while **rue Oberkampf** is more eclectic, low-key, and local. Both streets are definitely worth your time, even if you have only one night in the area.

▧ **Favela Chic,** 18, r. du Faubourg du Temple (☎01 40 21 38 14; www.favelachic.com). Ⓜ Republique. Walk down r. du Faubourg du Temple, turn right into an arch at no. 18, and the club is to your left. This self-proclaimed Franco-Brazilian joint has little Franco and lots of brassy Brazilian: it's a mini Brazilian nightlife paradise plopped in the middle of working class Republique. Wildly popular with locals, this restaurant-bar-club is decorated with eclectic decor and equally colorful clients. Dinner time in the restaurant segues fluidly into unbridled and energetic table-dancing to thumping salsa-latino-brazilian rhythms. Exceedingly crowded with gyrating bodies during the weekend, and a long line snaking out the door. Mixed drinks that pack a strong dollop, €9; cover Fri-Sa €10, includes a drink. Open Tu-Th 7:30pm-2am and Fri-Sa 7:30pm-4am. MC/V.

▧ **Berimbar,** 131, r. Oberkampf (☎01 43 57 80 61). Ⓜ Parmentier. A popular Brazilian bar-restaurant (Berimbor is Portuguese for "bar-restaurant") with trendy and attractive waitstaff, jungle decor, and avant-garde art. Flip-up benches transform the small space into a spontaneous late-night dance floor. Munch on free homemade potato chips while you sip a delicious Boteco (€4), made with the traditional Brazilian rum *cachaça*, pineapple juice, and vanilla extract. 3-course lunch *menu* with coffee €11. Beer €3-4.50. Happy hour 6-9pm (house special mixed drink €3). Open daily 9am-2am. MC/V with €18 min. charge.

▧ **Le Bar Sans Nom,** 49, r. de Lappe (☎01 48 05 59 36). Ⓜ Bastille. Take r. de la Roquette and make a right onto r. de Lappe. The No-Name Bar is a laid-back oasis amid the clamor of r. de Lappe. Dim, seductive lounge famous for its creative mixed drinks (some *flambé*), posted on oversized wooden menus. Older and calmer crowd than at most r. de Lappe establishments. Don't leave Paris without trying their mojito (€8.50). Free tarot-card reading Tu 5:30pm (but come early to grab a seat), when the bar is mobbed by young Parisian women in search of their future. Beer €5-6.50. Shots €6.50. Mixed drinks €8.50-9.50. Open Tu-Th 6pm-2am and F-Sa 6pm-4am. MC/V with €12 min. charge.

Le Lèche-Vin, 13, r. Daval (☎01 43 55 98 91). ⓜ Bastille. This irreverent bar greets visitors with a large statue of a praying nun and various religious-tinged paraphernalia. The holy kitsch doesn't prevent anyone from enjoying their beers (€5.50), downed with the approval of several Virgin Marys surveying from the wall. Draws an alternative and artsy crowd. Happy hour 6-10pm; beer and mixed drinks €4. Open M-Sa 6pm-2am.

Sanz Sans, 49, r. du Faubourg St-Antoine (☎01 44 75 78 78). ⓜ Bastille. Popular, upbeat bar/club/restaurant with moderate bouncer control (during peak hours, there must be a female in your group) but thankfully no cover. It's not particularly classy, but a lot of fun on weekend nights when the dance floor gets crowded. For the voyeur in each of us: a large, baroque-framed screen projects scenes from the bar like a black-and-white movie. DJs spin funk/groove on M, R&B Tu, house W and F-Sa, hip-hop Th, and reggae Su. Outdoor seating; indoor A/C. Happy hour before 9pm; beer €2.50. Drink prices go up after 9pm. Open M-Sa 9am-5am and Su 6pm-2am. MC/V.

Café Charbon, 109, r. Oberkampf (☎01 43 57 55 13). ⓜ Parmentier or Ménilmontant. The beautiful, soaring ceiling and burnished mirrors are proud traces of this place's *fin-de-siècle* dance-hall days, but these days, the cafe maintains a casual, modern atmosphere. The crowd varies with the act playing at the attached Nouveau Casino (p. 314). Happy hour daily 5-7pm. Open M-W and Su 9am-2am and Tu-Sa 9am-4am. Mixed drinks €6-7. Salads €8. Food served noon-3pm and 8pm-midnight. MC/V.

Les Abats Jour à Coudre, 115, r. Oberkampf (☎ 06 16 24 08 54). ⓜ Parmentier or Ménilmontant. A lively bar that grabs attention with its equally enthusiastic fetishes for sewing machines and Frank Zappa. Vintage Singers serve as tables, while Zappa's artwork presides benevolently over the crazy and colorful decor. Tu-W cafe-theater play night, W Frank Zappa night, and F-Sa live blues and jazz. Happy hour 4-8pm; mixed drink €3.50. Open Tu-Su 5pm-2am.

Bar à Nénette, 26, r. de Lappe (☎01 48 07 08 18). ⓜ Bastille. Walk down r. de la Roquette and make a right onto r. de Lappe; look for the sparkling lights. Saloon-style bar with wooden facade and a cool, casual vibe. Friendly owner and pretty bartenders complement the welcoming atmosphere. The never-ending happy hour is popular with locals (5-10pm; mixed drinks €5, *apéritifs* €3). Open daily 5pm-2am. AmEx/MC/V.

Le Kitch, 10, r. Oberkampf. ⓜ Oberkampf or Filles-du-Calvaire. A crazy patchwork dream of a cafe with painted clouds scudding across the ceiling and rainbow brooms flying across the wall. Eclectic, slightly eccentric crowd. Happy hour 5:30-9pm; mixed drinks and beer €5. Open daily Tu-Su 5:30pm-2am.

Barbat, 23, r. de Lappe (☎01 43 14 26 06). ⓜ Bastille. A hip bar and restaurant that attracts a mix of 20-somethings. Chill-out area with sofas near the entrance seems more characteristic of a cafe than a bar. The restaurant specializes in Corsican cuisine that visitors can eat while gazing upon cheerful paintings of the sunny isle. *Plats* €11-16. Happy hour daily 5-8pm in the back; beer €3 and mixed drinks €4.50. Open M-Th 5pm-2am and F-Su 5pm-4am. Food served M-Th 5-11:30pm and F-Su 5pm-midnight. MC/V with €20 min. charge.

DANCE CLUBS

▨ **Wax,** 15, r. Daval (☎01 48 05 88 33). ⓜ Bastille. Head north on bd. Richard Lenoir and make a right on r. Daval. One of those rare Parisian miracles: a place that is always free and fun. Set up in a concrete bunker with retro orange, red and white couches, this mod bar/club gets very crowded at night with a mix of locals and tourists. W and Su disco/funk, Th R&B, weekend house. Open daily 9pm-dawn. Beer €5.50-6.50. Mixed drinks €9.50. MC/V with €15 min. charge.

Nouveau Casino, 109, r. Oberkampf (☎01 43 57 57 40; www.nouveaucasino.net). ⓜ Parmentier or Ménilmontant. This hot-spot draws in the crowds of the 11ème with

concerts and clubbing. Music ranges from electropop to hip-hop to rock. Some evenings feature art exhibits and video shows, as well; check the website or call for a
weekly schedule. Cover €5-10. Tickets available through FNAC. Open midnight-dawn
when there are events.

WINE BARS

■ **Jacques Mélac,** 42, r. Léon Frot (☎01 43 70 59 27). Ⓜ Charonne. Walk down r.
Charonne, and turn left onto r. Léon Frot. A cozy, family-owned wine bar and bistro open
since 1938. In mid-Sept., Mélac lets children harvest, tread upon, and extract wine
from grapes grown in vines hanging from the bar's storefront. Wine €3 per glass, bottles
€15-38. Open Sept.-July Tu-Sa 9am-3pm and 7:30pm-midnight. MC/V.

Le Clown Bar, 114, r. Amelot (☎01 43 55 87 35). Ⓜ Filles du Calvaire. Cross bd. du
Filles du Calvaire to r. Amelot; across from the Cirque d'Hiver. A neighborhood hangout
that has attracted considerable buzz for its reasonable prices, friendly service, and delicious sampler menu. Those afraid of clowns should stay far, far away—clown paintings,
posters, and sculptures adorn every surface. Wine by the glass from €3.50. Dinner
menu €18. Open M-Sa noon-3:30pm and 7pm-midnight, Su 7pm-midnight.

La Muse Vin, 101, r. de Charonne (☎01 40 09 93 05). Ⓜ Charonne. Younger and
trendier than your standard wine bar. A ready-to-party crowd can taste or takeout from
the huge selection lining the fuschia walls. Wine by the glass from €4; bottles from
€15. Lunch *menu* of main dish with a glass of wine for only €10. Open M-Sa
10:30am-11pm. MC/V.

TWELFTH ARRONDISSEMENT

R. du Faubourg St-Antoine is the dividing line between the lively 11*ème* and its
tamer 12*ème* sister. Buzzing nightlife spills out from both sides of the road,
and you can hop from one club-lounge to another all night, but it won't be
cheap in the 12*ème*.

■ **Barrio Latino,** 46-48, r. du Faubourg St-Antoine (☎01 55 78 84 75; www.buddha-
bar.com). Ⓜ Bastille. Shares the same swanky owners as buddha-bar. No wallflowers
on this hot Latin dance floor, and not an empty barstool on weekends. Shove the flip-
flops in the closet; the bouncers are picky with footwear. Potent mixed drinks like the
strawberry margarita, €11.50. Shake it on the packed ground floor, or take your drink
for a stroll up to the 4th fl. to relax in the leather couches. Su brunch is an institution
among stylish locals (noon-4pm, €28) and includes a free salsa lesson. Open daily
noon-2am; DJ arrives at 10pm. AmEx/MC/V.

■ **China Club,** 50, r. de Charenton (☎01 43 43 82 02; chinaclub.cc). Ⓜ Ledru-Rollin or
Bastille. Swank, red-lit club with a *fumoir chinois* look. High-class prices, but the classic
mixed drinks and creative concoctions like the "Roasted Almond" (€9) are worth it.
Weekend jazz after 10pm. Concerts 9:30pm (ask for a program). Games and a bar
upstairs. Happy hour daily 7-9pm (Su 7pm-2am); drinks €6. Downstairs club closes for
3 weeks at the end of July and in early Aug. Call ahead. 3-course dinner *menu* €28. Dinner reservations recommended. Open daily 7pm-2am; last call 1:30am. AmEx/MC/V.

WINE BARS

Le Baron Rouge, 1, r. Théophile-Roussel (☎01 43 43 14 32). Ⓜ Ledru-Rollin. Follow the
r. du Faubourg St-Antoine away from the opera and take a right on r. Charles Baudelaire. Théophile-Roussel is your first left. The boisterous bartender will suggest one of
the dozens of wines on the menu (a steal at €1-3 a glass). Light snacks €5. Open Tu-F
10am-2pm and 5-10pm, Sa 10am-2pm, Su 10am-3pm. MC/V.

NIGHTLIFE

SKETCH IN THE CITY

Sometime past 2am, as smoke pumped onto the dance floor (and alcohol pumped through my veins), I watched the over-60-bar-prowler giving the you-can't-touch-me-twink. A fresh-out-of-the-closet wallflower was hiding in his corner, gawking at shirtless muscle queens. Here, at one of Paris's most popular gay clubs, the usual cast of characters was present. But though the players were wearing the same clothes and dancing to the same music as anywhere else, the game was completely different.

When a friend and I entered the club (in the name of research, I assure you), sultry neon signs presented us with two options: "clubbing" or "cruising." Feeling a bit uptight, I decided to claim my complimentary drink at the bar. As I sat sipping my vodka tonic, I felt a hand on my left thigh, and then on my right. Two buff boys were groping me. "Are you innocent?" they asked. Of course I am. "Do you want to come with us to our château tomorrow?" Dream on.

Less inhibited after a second drink, I ventured into the designated "cruising" area. Stepping through fake vines, I entered a labyrinth of dark rooms and darker corridors, the only light coming from pornographic films playing on mounted TVs. All around me, shadowy figures entered cell-like rooms together. I didn't hear any talking—just the

THIRTEENTH ARRONDISSEMENT

Rue de la Butte-aux-Cailles has a few local bars that are perfect for kicking back. If you'd rather kick up your heels, head for the new boat bars along the **Quai de la Gare.**

🏳️ **La Folie en Tête,** 33, r. de la Butte-aux-Cailles (☎01 45 80 65 99). ⓜ Corvisart. The artsy axis mundi of the 13ème. World music and exotic instruments line the walls of this beaten-up wood-fronted hole in the wall. Crowded concerts on Sa nights, usually Afro-Caribbean music (€8); no concerts July-Aug. Beer €3. Ti punch €5. Happy hour 6-8pm; kir €1.50. Open M-Sa 6pm-2am, service ends at 1:30am. MC/V.

Bateau El Alamein, Port de la Gare (☎01 45 86 41 60; elalamein.free.fr). ⓜ Quai-de-la-Gare. This docked boat is like a floating Eden, with everything from orange trees to morning glories blooming on its wide deck. The stage downstairs features local performers nightly at 9pm, with an emphasis on vocals, but call ahead to be sure. Entrance €8. Popular drinks include a mean mojito and the TGV (tequila, gin, vodka), both €8. Open daily 7pm-2am.

Le Merle Moqueur, 11, r. de la Butte-aux-Cailles. ⓜ Corvisart. Take r. Bobillot south until r. de la Butte-aux-Cailles branches right. Bamboo walls, African music, and shabby-cool ambience in the back room. A primarily locals scebe with cheap drinks (beer €2.50-3, kir €3). Happy hour 5-8pm. Open daily 5pm-2am.

La Guinguette Pirate, Porte de la Gare (☎01 43 49 68 68; www.guinguettepiratecom). This outdoor bar is a favorite of locals who sip cheap booze at picnic tables. The pirate ship behind the bar features live music from 9pm. Drink specials nightly, mixed drinks €7.50. Cover Tu-Th €8, students €6; F-Sa €10/8. Open Tu-F 7:30pm-2am, Sa 7:30pm-5am.

DANCE CLUBS

🏳️ **Batofar,** facing 11, quai François-Mauriac (☎01 53 60 17 42). ⓜ Quai de la Gare. Facing the river, walk right along the quai—Batofar has the red lights. This 45m long, 520-ton barge/bar/club has made it big with the electronic music crowd but maintains a friendly vibe. Live artists daily; check out website for more information. Open M-Th 11pm-6am, F-Su 11pm until the next day; hours change for special film and DJ events. Buy tickets through FNAC, ☎01 3 60 17 30. Cover €8-15, which usually includes first drink. "Electronic brunch" on Su afternoon. MC/V.

FOURTEENTH ARRONDISSEMENT

■ **L'Entrepôt,** 7-9, r. Francis de Pressensé (☎01 45 40 07 50, film schedule 08 36 68 05 87, restaurant reservations 01 45 40 07 50; www.lentrepot.fr). Ⓜ Pernety. From the metro, turn right, walk down r. Raymond Losserand and turn right onto r. Francis de Pressensé. Proving that intellectualism and good times can indeed go together, this savvy establishment offers a quadruple combo: a 3-screen cinema; a restaurant with a garden patio; an art gallery; and a trendy bar that features live jazz, Latin, and world music. You may need to (and should!) come a few times to see it all. Jazz (Th at 9:30pm) and poetry readings (most Th, before the jazz). Ciné-Philo—a screening, lecture, and discussion cafe—is held every other Su at 2:20pm; check the monthly schedule in the main foyer. Improvisational theatre takes up the alternate Sundays at 6:30pm. World music concerts F-Sa; cover €5-7. Beer €3.50. Su brunch noon-3pm (€22). Open M-Sa 11am-1am (though usually stays open later F and Sa), Su 11am-midnight. Kitchen open daily noon-3pm and 8-11pm.

Smoke Bar, 29, r. Delambre (☎01 43 20 61 73). Ⓜ Vavin. Walk down r. Delambre past sq. Delambre; the bar is to the left. A place where you might be able to strike up a conversation with a stranger without feeling like an outsider. Or come with a couple friends and calmly drink the night away. Jazz and blues posters line the walls of this intimate bar. Occasional Su bring performers from jazz musicians to Albanian poets. Beer €3.50-5.50. Mixed drinks €6. Open M-Sa noon-3pm and 6pm-2am. MC/V.

Café Tournesol, 9, r. de la Gaîté (☎01 43 27 65 72). Ⓜ Edgar Quinet. From the metro, turn left on r. de la Gaîté; the bar is on the left, at the corner of impasse de la Gaîté and r. de la Gaîté. At this ultra-mod cafe-bar, some of the 14ème's most stylish come out to drink, read, and mingle. The chic evening clientele praise the easy-going, open atmosphere. Maybe it's the piped-in techno and industrial-chic decor. The alcohol can't hurt either. Beer €2.50-6. Wine €2.50-3. Open M-F 8:30am-2am, Su 9:30am-2am. MC/V.

FIFTEENTH ARRONDISSEMENT

The 15ème is largely residential and does not have much to offer in terms of nightlife. There are a few good cafe-bars, popular with businessmen during the week, but the weekends are generally very quiet.

opening and closing of doors. In each room, a lubricant dispenser was visible on the wall. Condoms could be purchased from vending machines in the hall.

Walking through the corridor, I saw men lined up against the wall. By watching the men in front of me, I learned the rules of engagement. A walker expresses his desire for a rendezvous by staring at a man against the wall. After a five to ten second confirmation stare, the two go on their merry way.

Knowledge of this simple courting technique is critical to preventing misunderstandings. Searching for a clock, I found one on the cruising wall. Little did I know that a man's eyes were in my line of vision. I wanted the time (3:45am), not a cheap thrill. He stared back, assuming that the mating ritual was underway; a prompt *"Non, merci!"* ended his advance.

After unsuccessfully searching for my friend, I decided that he had succumbed to temptation, and I left the club. Watching strangers stumble home together, I realized that the French *joie de vivre* can take scintillating forms. At Le Dépôt, the desire for pleasure streamlines social foreplay. Bluntness replaces pretense and talk is unnecessary. The players here know the rules of this game—and before you decide to play in their arena, you should, too.

– *William Lee Adams*

Au Roi du Café, 59, r. Lecourbe (☎01 47 34 48 50). Ⓜ Sèvres-Lecourbe. This is a great little cafe/bar frequented by both Parisians and expats. Super friendly staff gives it a great atmosphere, and the drinks are generous. Simple but delicious café food served until 11pm; try the classic *sandwich mixte* (€4). You can enjoy a quiet drink at the bar or come with friends and sit at an outside table on summer evenings. Happy hour 6-9pm. Open M-F 7am-1am, Sa-Su 7am-midnight.

33 Latino, 33, r. Blomet. Ⓜ Sèvres-Lecourbe or Volontaires. Break out your salsa moves on the weekends at 33 Latino. No need to be embarrassed about shaking your hips among the throng of dancers; there are as many rhythm-challenged dancers as there are virtuosos. When you get tired of the dance floor, you can watch from the tables around the sides while sipping a slightly overpriced mixed drink (€8). Tu rock; W 70s; Th-F salsa; Sa *Soirée Dominicaine.* Cover €10 includes a drink and coat check. Open Tu-Sa 8pm-2am.

Mix Club, 24, r. de l'Arrivée (www.mixclub.fr). Ⓜ Montparnasse-Bienvenüe. The club is underground and the entrance is right next to the Tour Montparnasse. This club is horribly cheesy but can be amusing for the open-minded. €15 for entrance, a drink, and a healthy lungful of the ambient, machine-generated smoke. The DJ pumps out an eclectic mix of house, rock, German ska, Greek tunes, oldies and hip-hop to please the tourists (who get in free before midnight on Th). Huge neon signs flash "party," just in case you forget. The drinks are expensive and the alcohol is undetectable, but the atmosphere is fun and the party goes on until 6am. Mixed drinks from €8.

SIXTEENTH ARRONDISSEMENT

The 16ème is a mostly residential district, and most of its paltry nightlife lies on the edge of the upper half bordering the more lively 8ème. What sparse nightlife there is tends to be hard on the pocket.

Duplex, 2bis, av. Foch (☎01 45 00 45 00; www.leduplex.com). Ⓜ Charles de Gaulle-Etoile. Take the av. Foch exit; the entrance is marked by a red awning leading to the underground nightclub. Although the once-glamorous clientele has been diluted with tourists, weekends still bring businessmen displaying their arm-candy here. 2 separate rooms play music ranging from techno to R&B to hip-hop to house. Also houses an expensive restaurant (open Tu-Su 9pm-1am), which stands in contrast to the strip-club-esque vibe of the rest of the club. Tu students; W airline night or Charmed (free champagne for ladies before 1am); F "mucho-much"; Su Asian night. Cover and first drink Su and Tu-Th €15, F-Sa €20. Women in free before midnight Tu-Th and Su. All drinks €10. Open Tu-Su 11:00pm-dawn. Closed July 30-Aug. 25.

Sir Winston, 5, r. de Presbourg (☎01 40 67 17 37). Ⓜ Kléber. Walk toward the Arc de Triomphe, take a right, and take the first right again. This hip bar/restaurant/lounge/club is the watering hole for young Parisian *bobos* (the French version of American yuppies) to lounge and be seen. The Anglo-Indian inspired decor boasts Indian shrines, romantically dim lighting, wrought-iron lanterns and superb ceiling frescos. Downstairs is a dance space with a DJ spinning lounge and jazzy tunes. The food menu is pricey, but come here at night to escape the touristy Odéon area and mix with the locals. Wine €4-9 per glass. Beer €4.50-7. Mixed drinks €9-11.50. The virgin mixed drinks (€8) are especially good. Open daily 9am-4am. MC/V.

SEVENTEENTH ARRONDISSEMENT

The 17ème, like its sedate neighbor, the 16ème, has not much to offer in nighttime revelry. The cafes near the pl. du Dr. Félix Lobligeois are filled night and day with crowds of young things sipping cocktails and chatting away, which is about as wild as the neighborhood gets.

▨ **L'Endroit,** 67, pl. du Dr. Félix Lobligeois (☎01 42 29 50 00). Ⓜ Rome. Follow r. Boursault to r. Legendre, and make a right. Hip, young 17ème-ers come for the snazzy bar and idyllic location in the tree-lined *place.* Wine €3.50-4. Beer €4. Mixed drinks €8-8.50. Classics include the mojito and the apple martini. Open daily 10am-2am (often open later on weekends). MC/V. See also **Food,** p. 177.

EIGHTEENTH ARRONDISSEMENT

Much of the 18*ème*'s nightlife lies in the sleazy southern end of the *butte*, in the red light district around **Place Pigalle** and **boulevard Rochechouart.** The streets are lined with peep-show hawkers and the odd drug dealer; stay in well-lit, busy areas if you want to avoid hassles. Tourists traveling alone, especially women, should avoid Ⓜ Pigalle, Ⓜ Anvers and Ⓜ Barbès-Rochechouart at night. For live music in Montmartre, see **Entertainment,** p. 277.

La Fourmi, 74, r. des Martyrs (☎01 42 64 70 35). Ⓜ Pigalle. Head east on bd. Rochechouart; La Fourmi is on the corner of r. des Martyrs. An artsy atmosphere with a large zinc bar and industrial-chic decor, complete with a chandelier made of green chianti bottles and sprawling black-and-white drawings. A hyper-hip, energetic, and scrappy young crowd takes refuge here from the sleazy surroundings of bd. Rochechouart. Beer €2.50-3.50. Wine €2.50-3. Mixed drinks €5.50-9. Open M-Th 8am-2am, F-Sa 8am-3:30am, Su 10am-1:30am. MC/V.

Chez Camille, 8, r. Ravignan (☎01 42 59 21 02). Ⓜ Abbesses. Facing the church in pl/ des Abbesses, head right down r. des Abbesses and go right (uphill) on r. Ravignan. Small, bright yellow bar on the upper slopes of Montmartre with a small terrace looking down the *butte* to the Invalides dome (especially dramatic at night). Come for the view, not for the aging and lethargic crowd. Cheap coffee (€1.50) and tea (€2.50). Beer €2.50-4. Wine €3. Mixed drinks €5.50. Open Tu-Su 5pm-2am.

TWENTIETH ARRONDISSEMENT

A laid-back place to enjoy a drink and possibly a little bit of live music, the 20*ème* provides visitors with nightlife that is mellow yet still hip. Come here on a Friday night to wind down like the locals do.

Café Flèche d'Or, 102bis, r. de Bagnolet (☎01 44 64 01 02; www.flechedor.fr). Cool, intense, and a little rough around the edges. Live music nightly, from reggae to hip-hop to Celtic rock. Art videos, dance classes, and crazy theater on the tracks below the terrace. Live music nightly, from rock and alternative to trip-hop and electro-pop (cover €5-20, but often free). DJ set Th-Sa midnight-6am. Concerts: beer €3, mixed drinks €7. Club: beer €4-5, mixed drinks €8. Happy hour 7-9pm. Open W-Sa 10am-3am, Th-Sa open until 6am. MC/V. See also **Food,** p. 180.

Lou Pascalou, 14, r. des Panoyaux (☎01 46 36 78 10; www.loupascalou.com). Ⓜ Ménilmontant. Follow bd. de Belleville and make a left on r. des Panayaux. Lou Pascalou is a little bit out of the way, but aside from the brusque management, it can be a pleasant place to drink. Features open-air terrace seating, occasional concerts, and art displays. Attracts a local crowd. Beer €2.50. Wine €2-3. Open daily 9am-2am. MC.

NIGHTLIFE

DAYTRIPS

TRIP	TRAVEL TIME
Versailles	40-60min.
Chartres	65-75min.
Fontainebleau	55-65min.
Chantilly	45-75min.
Giverny	1-1¼hr.
Vaux-le-Vicomte	1¼-2hr.
Auvers-sur-Oise	1-1½hr.
Disneyland Resort Paris	45-50min.

VERSAILLES

By sheer force of ego, the Sun King converted a simple hunting lodge into the world's most famous palace. The sprawling château and gardens testify to the absolute power of Louis XIV, who lived, entertained, and governed here on the grandest of scales. A century later, the extravagant court of Louis XVI and Marie-Antoinette gave the unhappy citizenry a lightning rod for their resentment (see **Life and Times,** p. 62).

⚡ PRACTICAL INFORMATION

Transportation: RER trains beginning with "V" run from Ⓜ Invalides or any stop on **RER Line C5** to the Versailles Rive Gauche station (30-40min., departs approx. every 15min., €5.30 round-trip). Buy your RER ticket before going through the turnstile to the platform (quickest from the machines; look for the Île-de-France ticket option); although a metro ticket will get you through these turnstiles, it will not get you through RER turnstiles at Versailles and could get you fined by the *contrôleurs*. From the RER Versailles station, turn right down av. de Général de Gaulle, walk 200m, and turn left at the first big intersection on av. de Paris; the entrance to the château is straight ahead.

Tourist Office: Office de Tourisme de Versailles, 2bis, av. de Paris (☎01 39 24 88 88; www.versailles-tourisme.fr). From the RER Versailles train station, follow directions to the château; the office will be on your left on av. de Paris before you reach the château courtyard. The tourist office is a great place to get a patient explanation of your options in Versailles before reaching the tourist mayhem in the palace. The office sells tickets for tourist options such as the hop-on, hop-off bus and provides brochures on accommodations, restaurants, and events in town. There is also a currency exchange. Open in summer M 10am-6pm, Tu-Sa 9am-7pm; in winter M and Su 11am-5pm, Tu-Sa 9am-6pm.

Food: While there are a number of tourist dining options (including a *McDo*) along the walk from the train station to the palace, your best warm-weather bet is to bring a picnic (and a blanket) to enjoy by the canal in the gardens after you tour the palace. On the weekends many French do the same, minus the palace visit. Should you forget your *pique-nique*, there are moderately priced snack bars tucked in various corners of the gardens, as well as over-priced restaurants with generally mediocre food.

👁 SIGHTS

PALACE HISTORY. Louis XIV's bedroom was invaded by a Parisian mob during the Fronde when he was just 10 years old. Traumatized by the malodorous commoners, he determined to move his government away from the politically unreliable capital to the safety of Versailles. In 1661, the Sun King renovated the small hunting lodge in Versailles and enlisted the help of architect Louis Le Vau, painter Charles Le Brun, and landscape architect André Le Nôtre (all of Vaux-le-Vicomte fame) just months after their previous patron, Nicolas Fouquet, had been sentenced to lifetime imprisonment (see Vaux-le-Vicomte, p. 339). Indeed, Versailles's Vaux-esque fountains and grandiloquent scale were a not-so-subtle reminder to Paris of who was in charge. The court at Versailles became the nucleus of noble life, where France's aristocrats vied for the king's favor.

No one knows just how much it cost to build Versailles; Louis XIV burned the accounts to keep the price a mystery. Though every aspect of life was a minutely choreographed public spectacle, things there were less luxurious than one might imagine: courtiers wore rented swords and urinated behind statues in the parlors, wine froze in the drafty dining rooms, and dressmakers invented the color *puce* (literally, "flea") to camouflage the bugs crawling on the noblewomen. Louis XIV died on September 1, 1715 and was succeeded by his great-grandson Louis XV. He commissioned the opera in the North Wing for the marriage of Marie-Antoinette to his grandson, the Dauphin (crowned prince). The newlyweds inherited the throne and Versailles when Louis XV died in 1774. The new king Louis XVI (formerly the Dauphin) and Marie-Antoinette changed little of the château's exterior, but they did create Marie-Antoinette's personal pretend playland, the *Hameau*. On October 5, 1789, 15,000 angry Parisian women and National Guardsmen marched out to the palace and brought the royal family back to Paris, where they would eventually be victims of the Revolution.

During the 19th century, King Louis-Philippe established a museum to preserve the château, against the wishes of many Frenchmen, who wanted Versailles demolished just as the Bastille had been (see **Sights**, p. 218). In 1871, the château took the limelight once again, when King Wilhelm of Prussia became Kaiser Wilhelm I of Germany in the Hall of Mirrors. That same year, as headquarters of the conservative Thiers regime, Versailles sent an army against the Paris Commune. The *Versaillais* pierced the city walls and crushed the Communards. On June 28, 1919, the Hall of Mirrors was again the setting for a historic occasion, this time the signing of the Treaty of Versailles, which ended WWI with a flawed peace.

GUIDED TOURS. It's best to arrive early in the morning to avoid the crowds, which are worst on Sundays from May to September, especially in late June. Pick up a map at one of the entrances. Figuring out how to get into the château is the hardest part, as there are half a dozen entrances. Most visitors enter at **Entrance A**, located on the right-hand side in the north wing, or **Entrance C**, located in the archway to the left. Both locations have audioguide options for an extra €4.50 or free with the day pass. **Entrance B** is for groups, **Entrance D** is where guided tours begin, and **Entrance H** is for visitors in wheelchairs. **General admission** allows entrance to the following rooms: the *Grands Appartements*, the War and Peace Drawing Rooms, the *Galerie des Glaces* (Hall of Mirrors), and Marie-Antoinette's public apartment. From Entrance D, at the left-hand corner as you approach the palace, you can choose between four excellent and scholarly **guided tours** (in English or French) of different parts of the château. The best is the 1½hr. tour of the Louis XV apartments and opera. After the tour, you'll be able to explore the rest of Versailles on your own, without waiting in the general admission line. To avoid a long wait for guided tours, arrive before 11am. *(☎01 30 83 78 00; www.chateauversailles.fr. Château open Tu-Su Apr.-Oct. 9am-6:30pm, Nov.-Mar. 9am-5:30pm. Last admission 30min. before closing. Admission to palace and self-guided tour through entrance A €8, after 3:30pm €6, under 18 free. Supplement for 1hr. audio tour €4.50, under 7 free. Alternatively, you can opt for the 1-day pass which is still self-guided but includes entrance to the private apartments, temporary exhibitions, and the Grand and Petit Trianons, as well as the usual Grand Apartments, Hall of Mirrors, and, on weekends only, Mesdames Apartments. This pass also includes audioguides for both the Grand and private apartments, for €20 total. Guided tours through entrance D: 1hr. tour of Chambres du Roi €4, under 18 €2.70; 1½hr. tour of the apartments of Louis XV and the opera €6, ages 7-17 €4.20. Full-day tour "A Day at Versailles" (2*

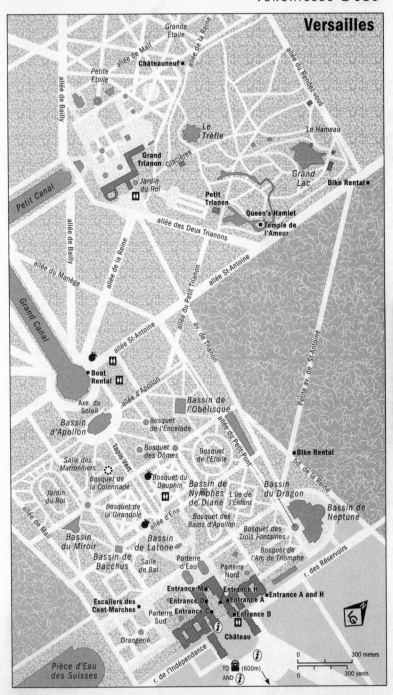

Versailles

Grande
Étoile

allée de Mall

Châteauneuf ■

Petite
Étoile

allée de la Reine

allée du Rendez-vous

allée de Bailly

Le
Trèfle

Le Hameau

Grand
Trianon

Glacières

Grand
Lac

Bike Rental ■

Jardin
du Roi

Petit
Trianon

Queen's Hamlet

allée des Deux Trianons

■ Temple de
l'Amour

Petit Canal

allée de Bailly

allée de la Reine

allée St-Antoine

allée du Petit Trianon

av. de Trianon

allée du Manège

Grand Canal

allée St-Antoine

Petite av. de St-Antoine

● Boat
Rental

allée d'Apollon

Axe. du
Soleil

Bassin de
l'Obélisque

Bassin
d'Apollon

Bosquet
de l'Encelade

allée du Petit-Pont

Bosquet
des Dômes

Bosquet
de l'Etoile

Salle des
Marronniers

● Bike Rental

Bosquet de
la Colonnade

● Bosquet du
Dauphin

Bassin de
Nymphes
de Diane

L'île de
l'Enfant

Bassin
du Dragon

Jardin
du Roi

Bosquet de
la Girandole

allée d'Enu

Bassin de
Neptune

Bassin
du Miroir

Bassin
de Latone

Bosquet des
Bains d'Apollon

Bosquet des
Trois Fontaines

allée de Mall

Bassin de
Bacchus

Salle
de Bal

Parterre
d'Eau

Bosquet de
l'Arc de Triomphe

r. des Réservoirs

Escaliers des
Cent-Marches

Parterre
Sud

Parterre
Nord

Entrance M ■

Entrance H

Entrance D

Entrance A

Entrance A and H

Entrance C

Entrance B

bd. de la Reine

Orangerie

Château

Pièce d'Eau
des Suisses

r. de l'Indépendance

TO 🔒 (600m)
AND ℹ

0   300 meters
0   300 yards

1½hr. segments, 1 in the morning, 1 in the afternoon) is the most comprehensive; €20. Make advance reservations with the Bureau d'Action Culturelle ☎01 30 83 77 88.)

THE LOCAL STORY

LET THEM STEAL FURNITURE

October 5, 1789 was a good day for the French Revolution and a very bad one for Versailles. Taking their cue from the crowd that stormed the Bastille prison, another, even larger one made its way to Versailles, hijacked the King and Queen, and brought them back to Paris.

After those shenanigans, the Revolutionaries auctioned off many of the chests, chairs, and tables that filled the Versailles palace. All of the artwork was transported to the Louvre for safe-keeping. Many of the rooms and buildings at Versailles were later restored to their pre-Revolutionary glory, with reproductions put in place of the original furnishings, but of the roughly 17,000 items sold off at public auction, the majority are lost forever.

Gerald van Kemp, a French curator who died in January 2002, made it his life's work to track down missing pieces and return them to their rightful place. Nicknamed "The Man Who Gave Us Back Versailles," he retrieved some Riesener commodes made for Marie-Antoinette and a Savonniere carpet, for which the Versailles estate paid millions of dollars. Versailles's most prized former possession is Leonardo da Vinci's *Mona Lisa*, but let's hope she doesn't leave the Louvre anytime soon—the lines at Versailles are long enough already.

SELF-GUIDED TOURS. With a general admission ticket or day pass, begin at **Entrance A** and start your visit in the **Musée de l'Histoire de France,** created in 1837 by Louis-Philippe to celebrate his country's glory. Along its textured walls hang portraits of men and women who shaped French history. The 21 rooms, arranged in chronological order, lay out a historical context for the château, helpful for those not taking a guided tour. However, this museum is only open on some days, with no fixed schedule, so call ahead to be sure not to miss it.

Up the staircase to the right is the dual-level **royal chapel** where the king heard mass. The chapel was constructed by architect Hardouin-Mansart from 1699-1710. Back toward the staircase and to the left is a series of gilded **drawing rooms** in the **State Apartments** that are dedicated to Roman gods such as Hercules, Mars, and the ever-present Apollo (the Sun King identified with the sun god). The ornate **Salon d'Apollo** was Louis XIV's throne room, and the king's prestige was so great that people had to bow or curtsey when passing the throne, even when it was empty. Framed by the **War and Peace Drawing Rooms** is the **Hall of Mirrors** (under renovation until 2007; until then, only portions are open to visitors), originally a terrace until Mansart added a series of mirrored panels and windows to double the light in the room and reflect the gardens outside. These mirrors were the largest that 17th-century technology could produce and therefore an unthinkable extravagance. Le Brun's ceiling paintings (1679-1686) tell the history of Louis XIV's heroism, culminating with *The King Governs Alone*.

The **Queen's Bedchamber,** where royal births were public events in order to prove the legitimacy of the heirs, is now furnished as it was on October 6, 1789, when Marie-Antoinette left the palace for the last time. A version of the David painting depicting Napoleon's self-coronation dominates the **Salle du Sacré** (also known as the Coronation Room). The **Hall of Battles,** installed by Louis-Philippe, is a monument to 14 centuries of France's military.

GARDENS. Numerous artists, including Le Brun, Mansart, and Coysevox, created statues and fountains for Versailles's gardens, but master gardener André Le Nôtre provided the overall plan. Louis XIV wrote the first guide to the gardens, entitled the *Manner of Presenting the Gardens at Versailles*, and today the grounds remain a spectacular example of obsessive landscaping: neatly trimmed rectangular hedges line the geometric *bosquets* (groves), as if proving Louis XIV's mastery over nature. The Sun King even proved his control over his visitors' vision: the cross-shaped canal is wider on the western-most end, creating a perspective-defying illusion when viewed from the terrace.

Though the château offers a decent 2hr. **Discovering Groves Tour** of the gardens (covering Le Nôtre's work with an emphasis on Greco-Roman mythology), the best way to visit the park is during the spectacular summer festival, **Les Grandes Eaux Musicales,** when the fountains are turned on and chamber music groups per-form among the groves (see **Festivals,** p. 95). Any self-guided tour of the gardens must begin, as the Sun King commanded, on the terrace. To the left of the terrace, the **Parterre Sud** graces the area in front of Mansart's **Orangerie,** once home to 2000 orange trees; the temperature inside still never drops below 6°C (43°F). In the cen-ter of the terrace lie the fountains of the **Parterre d'Eau,** while down the steps, the **Bassin de Latone** features Latona, the mother of Diana and Apollo, shielding her children as Jupiter turns villains into frogs.

Past the Bassin de Latone and to the left is one of the Versailles Gardens' undisputed gems: the fragrant, flower-lined sanctuary of the **Jardin du Roi,** accessi-ble only from the easternmost side facing the Bassin du Miroir. Still near the south gate of the grove is the magnificent Bassin de Bacchus, one of four sea-sonal fountains depicting the Greek god of wine crowned in vine branches reclining on a bunch of grapes. Working your way north toward the center of the garden brings you to the exquisite Bosquet de la Colonnade, where the king used to take light meals amid 32 violet and blue marble columns, sculptures, and white marble basins. The north gate to the Colonnade exits onto the 330m long **Tapis Vert** (Green Carpet), the central mall linking the château to the garden's conspicuously central fountain, the Bassin d'Apollon, whose charioted Apollo rises out of the water to enlighten the world.

On the north side of the garden is the incredible Bosquet de l'Encelade. When the fountains are turned on, a 25m high jet bursts from Titan's enormous mouth, which is plated with shimmering gold and half buried under rocks. Flora reclines on a bed of flowers in the Bassin de Flore, while a gilded Ceres luxuriates in sheaves of wheat in the Bassin de Cérès. The **Parterre Nord,** full of flowers, lawns, and trees, overlooks some of the garden's most spectacular fountains. The **Allée d'Eau,** a fountain-lined walkway, provides the best view of the Bassin des Nymphes de Diane. The path slopes toward the sculpted Bassin du Dragon, where a beast slain by Apollo spurts water 27m into the air. Next to the Bassin du Dragon, 99 jets of water issue from seahorses encircling Neptune in the **B**assin de Neptune, the gardens' largest fountain.

Beyond Le Nôtre's classical gardens stretch wilder woods, meadows, and farmland perfect for a *pique-nique* away from the manicured perfection of Ver-sailles. Stroll along the **Grand Canal,** a rectangular pond beyond the Bassin d'Apollon that measures an impressive 1535m long. To explore destinations far-ther afield around Versailles, rent a **bike** or a **boat,** or go for a **horse-drawn car-riage** ride. *(Open daily sunrise-sunset. Apr.-Oct. M-F €3, under 18 and after 6pm free. Fountains turned on for special displays, such as the Grandes Eaux Musicales, Apr.-Sept. Sa-Su, and some holidays 11am-noon and 3:30-5pm. €6. The most convenient place to rent bikes is across from the base of the canal. ☎01 39 66 97 66. Open Feb.-Nov. daily 10am-7pm. 30min. €4, 1hr. €6. There are 2 other bike rental locations: one to the north of the Parterre Nord by the Grille de la Reine, another by the Trianons at Porte St-Antoine. Rent a 4-person electric car next to entrance C2 on the terrace. ☎01 39 66 97 66. 1hr. €28; driver must be over 18. Rent boats for 4 at the boathouse to the right of the canal. ☎01 39 66 97 66. Open daily 10am-6:30pm. 30min. €10, 1hr. €14; refundable deposit €10. Horse-drawn carriages depart Tu-Su from right of the main ter-race. ☎01 30 97 04 40.)*

Nature as Social Theater in 18th-Century Paris

You don't have to be a Francophile to know that when it came to Versailles, Louis XIV was something of a control freak. After assuming sole leadership of the French state upon the death of Cardinal Mazarin in 1661, the 22-year-old king quickly set about re-fashioning all of France into an integrated symbol of his new regime. At the top of the list was the establishment of a centralized court, and to that end Louis hired scores of artists to refurbish his father's old hunting pavilion and transform it into what would become Versailles, epicenter of courtly culture for the next hundred years and emblem of the Sun King's reign for hundreds more.

Although Louis left his mark throughout the palace, from the grand Hall of Mirrors to the small solar motifs that adorn the walls, perhaps the best evidence for Versailles as a manifestation of the king's power is the garden designs by Le Nôtre. Appearing to extend infinitely from the main building, the Versailles garden represents a triumph of engineering, a marshaling of immense resources, and, in its rigid geometry and strict bilateral symmetry, an image of nature brought under man's control. Not only is nature tamed, but it's served up for the gaze of the king: recalling the one-point perspective system of Renaissance painting, the "vanishing point" of the garden is perfectly on axis with the king's bedroom. Like Louis's famous statement, "I am the state," the Versailles garden testifies to the fact that careful management of one's image is not just a product of our own media-saturated age.

To ensure that this carefully calibrated message was clear, Louis penned a guidebook, the *Manière de montrer les jardins de Versailles* (1689), which required that all visitors follow in the king's footsteps while touring his gardens. Although Versailles would remain for many the paragon of French garden design in the one hundred years between the publication of the *Manière* and the outbreak of the Revolution, there appeared in the 18th century a number of alternatives to the formal garden system, just as there were an increasing number of alternative proposals to the ideology of absolutism. Whereas courtiers had formerly spent a great deal of time ambulating through the gardens at Versailles and performing their loyalty to the king, during the Regency period (1715-23), certain members of the court avoided Versailles in favor of more intimate rendezvous at their country houses outside of Paris. We can observe them today in the delightfully ambiguous paintings of Antoine Watteau (many of which reside in the Louvre), where aristocrats mix with wealthy financiers, and it's never quite clear whether the courtiers are watching a play, mingling with actors, or donning theatrical costumes and playing the roles themselves. What is clear in these improvisational

gatherings is that the idea of the garden as a space of self-representation not only survives Louis XIV's reign but emerges as a crucial means of expression—personal and political—in the waning days of the Old Regime.

Far from the politically neutral spaces that we think of today, gardens in France in this period comprised quite a contested terrain. One major controversy was the debate between France and England over who had invented the more "naturalistic" style of gardening that became popular around the middle of the 18th century. Across the Channel, the Prime Minister's son Horace Walpole published a treatise on garden design, insisting that the new preference for untamed nature, serpentine walkways, and meandering streams was an indisputably English phenomenon, and reflected his government's ties to liberty and free expression. French writers similarly praised this new trend but argued not only that *they* had developed the style independently of the English, but that whatever devices the English were exhibiting in their gardens had been cribbed from the Chinese. No one went so far as to point out that this "natural" style was built upon a paradox—the idea that one would spend an enormous amount of money transforming a piece of nature into a garden that, in its painstaking attempt at informality, recalled a piece of nature.

Whether they admitted it or not, wealthy Frenchmen and Frenchwomen of the second half of the 18th century closely monitored developments in England before commissioning artists to transform their Louis XIV-style gardens into landscapes that embraced the new taste for the "natural." In Paris, three projects from the 1770s indicate the immense popularity of the new style as well as its relative diversity in contrast to Versailles. Two gardens were constructed in the Bois de Boulogne, which at that time served as a quasi-public space to promenade, duel, see and be seen, and engage in illicit sexual activity (that this last association persists today is evidenced by the recent publication of Catherine Millet's scandalous memoir *The Sexual Life of Catherine M*). One sight belonged to the king's rakish younger brother, the Comte d'Artois, and was the result of a bet he made with Marie-Antoinette that he could entertain her in a sparkling new Parisian pavilion constructed in three months' time. Luckily for Artois, his land was located near a major thoroughfare entering Paris from the west, allowing him to commandeer all building supplies headed toward the city and redirect them toward his own building site. Artois took a keen interest in every aspect of the design, devising a decorating scheme for his bedroom along the lines of an extended military metaphor, which spoke both to his prowess in the armed forces and his famed erotic conquests. Ultimately the pavilion, named "Bagatelle," was completed in just 64 days. It still stands in the Bois de Boulogne, and is best visited in June, when the site's famous roses are in full bloom.

Bagatelle's gardens were attacked by architect François Bélanger and his Scottish collaborator Thomas Blaikie with the same militaristic zeal. Following the latest "Anglo-Chinese" fashion, the gardens contained the requisite winding walkways studded with small buildings knows as "follies," which reference previous eras and other cultures, like an encyclopedia in three dimensions (recalling the ambitious Encyclopedic publishing project of Diderot and d'Alembert). Among the structures were an Egyptian obelisk, rustic hermitage, and Gothic-style philosopher's pavilion, the windows of which allowed visitors to view the garden through different-colored panes of glass, depending on one's mood. Overall, the gardens represented a shift from the idea of nature reconstituted in one man's image—the king's—to nature as an infinitely diverse yet private experience of individual contemplation. Of course, one still had to write to Artois's secretary to obtain permission to visit Bagatelle, a fact later redressed by the Revolutionary government, which in 1793 declared the gardens open to *all* members of the French citizenry.

Bagatelle's designers created an even more elaborate Anglo-Chinese garden adjacent to it for Charles Baudard de Saint-James, the wealthy financier and newly appointed treasurer of the American colonies. In addition to the more conventional follies, the gardens of the "Folie Saint-James" contained a mock dairy for the banker's daughter to entertain in—suggesting that Marie-Antoinette's obsession with playing milkmaid was not an isolated phenomenon—as well as a structure known as the *Grand Rocher*, referred to by contemporaries as the "Eighth Wonder of the World." This great rock (all that remains of the garden today) consisted of an enormous grotto surrounding a Doric portico that stood as the facade for the luxuriously appointed rooms behind it. The structure recalled an ancient archaeological ruin, signifying an interest in origins as well as a desire on the part of the *arriviste*

Saint-James to "naturalize" his connection to the land and to the social position that ownership of such an estate implied. The public responded favorably to his garden by visiting it in droves, but Artois was less than pleased and, rumor has it, instructed Bélanger to ruin Saint-James financially by proposing ever-more elaborate building schemes. The plan apparently worked: Saint-James declared bankruptcy in 1787.

The final example, the Parc Monceau, was also constructed in the western part of the city, near the Champs-Elysées. Although many of Monceau's follies were destroyed in the Revolution, several remain, and the site is now a public park and jogging track (but don't be surprised if you draw stares from incredulous Parisians while attempting to run there). In the early 1770s King Louis XVI's cousin, the Duc de Chartres (later the Duc d'Orléans), commissioned the designer Carmontelle to lay out a garden which loosely followed the Anglo-Chinese program, complete with hermitage, obelisk, and decorative farm, where cows were tended by servants dressed in "Turkish" costume. Some commentators have declared Monceau to be the anti-Versailles, an emblem of the duke's self-professed Anglomania as well as his public criticism of the monarchy: during the Revolution the duke voted to have Louis XVI beheaded and, in 1793, ended up losing his own head as well. But one should not be too quick to ascribe a political message to Monceau, for, as its designer insisted, it followed no particular formula but was rather a "landscape of illusion," where visitors could "change the scenes in a garden like the stage sets at the Opéra." Carmontelle's statement adequately captures the status of Old Regime gardens as pieces of social theater, where aristocrats and their hangers-on eagerly performed for an audience of the King, as much as for themselves. In addition, it also speaks to the climate of unreality that surrounded these 18th-century spaces and their hangers-on eagerly performed for an audience of the King, as much as for themselves. In addition, it also speaks to the climate of unreality that surrounded these 18th-century spaces and their inhabitants, who despite such fertile imagination could scarcely have dreamed up what would befall their nation in 1789.

Meredith Martin is a Ph.D. candidate in the Department of the History of Art and Architecture at Harvard University.

LOCAL LEGEND

GOD SAVE THE KING'S ASS

n 1686, King Louis XIV developed an anal fistula (Google it) hat became so painful and nfected that he could not even sit down. The Sun King, who had been living in excruciating pain, was forced to undergo an operation to deal with the fistula. Unfortunately for Louis, anal fistulae are very uncommon ailments, so his surgeons were not experienced in the procedure at hand. His fate was seen as largely in the hands of God. When the unfortunate monarch miraculously recovered and was again fit to reign (sitting down), the Superior of the Ladies of Saint-Cyr, Mme de Brinon, wrote some verses to thank God for the King's recovery, which were then set to music by Lully. They were, as it turns out, shockingly similar to the words of "God Save the King."

Handel, in his capacity as court musician to King George I of England, came to Versailles and was so inspired by Lully and Brinon's hymn that he took a note of the tune and lyrics and translated them into their current form. The hymn was apparently so popular that it was played at all official ceremonies and was eventually declared the national anthem.

This tale, of course, is simply a favorite legend among Parisians, but tell it to a gullible British expat, and the results are well worth the effort.

TRIANONS AND MARIE-ANTOINETTE'S HAMEAU.

The Trianons and particularly Marie-Antoinette's *hameau* provide an interesting perspective on what monarchs did when they wanted to get away from the hassle of all that ruling: build palaces, tryst with lovers, and pretend to be peasants.

On the right down the wooded path from the château is the **Petit Trianon,** built between 1762 and 1768 for Louis XV and his mistress Mme de Pompadour. Marie-Antoinette took control of the Petit Trianon in 1774, and it soon earned the nickname "Little Vienna." The Petit Trianon was later inhabited by Napoleon's sister and the Empress Marie-Louise. In 1867, the Empress Eugénie, who for some reason admired Marie-Antoinette, turned it into a museum devoted to the hapless queen.

If you exit the Petit Trianon, turn left, and follow the marked path, you will find yourself at the libidinous **Temple of Love,** a domed rotunda with 12 white marble columns and swans. Marie-Antoinette held many intimate nighttime parties in the small space, during which thousands of torches would be illuminated in the surrounding ditch. The queen was perhaps at her happiest and most ludicrous when spending time at the *hameau*, her own pseudo-peasant "hamlet" down the path from the Temple of Love. Inspired by Jean-Jacques Rousseau's theories on the goodness of nature and the *hameau* at **Chantilly** (*p. 336*), the queen aspired fashionably to a so-called "simple" life. She commissioned Richard Mique to build a compound of 12 buildings (including a mill, dairy, and gardener's house, all surrounding a quaint artificial lake) in which she could play at country life. The result is something of a cross between English Romanticism and Disneyland Paris. At the center of the complex is the **Queen's Cottage.** Any naïve illusions of rough living disappear after crossing through her cottage doors. The rooms are filled to the brim with ornate furniture, polished marble fireplaces, and walk-in closets where Marie-Antoinette kept her monogrammed linens and frolicsome footmen.

The single-story, stone-and-pink-marble **Grand Trianon** was intended as a château-away-from-château for Louis XIV. Here the King could be reached only by boat from the **Grand Canal.** The palace, which consists of two wings joined by a large central porch, was designed by Mansart and erected in 1687. Lovely and simple **formal gardens** located behind the colonnaded porch are a relief from the rest of Versailles's showy *bosquets*. The mini-château was stripped of its furniture during the Revolution, but was later restored and inhabited by Napoleon and his second wife. President Charles de Gaulle installed presidential apartments and rooms for visiting heads of state, and the constitutional amendment for the Maastricht Treaty was also written here.

(Shuttle trams from the palace to the Trianons and the hameau leave from behind the palace next to entrance C2 on the left of the château facing the gardens. Round-trip €5.80, ages 11-18 €4, audioguides for the ride through the gardens €1.20 with a deposit of an ID. The walk takes 25min. Both Trianons open Tu-Sa Nov.-Mar. noon-5:30pm; Apr.-Oct. noon-6:30pm; last entrance 30min. before closing. Admission to the Trianons €5, Sa-Su after 3:30pm €3, under 18 free.)

CHARTRES

Nothing compares to Chartres. It is the thinking of the Middle Ages itself made visible.
   —Emile Male

Were it not for a scrap of fabric, the cathedral and town of Chartres might still be a sleepy hamlet. But the cloth the Virgin Mary supposedly wore when she gave birth to Jesus made Chartres a major medieval pilgrimage center. The spectacular cathedral that towers over the city isn't the only reason to visit: the *vieille ville* (old city) is also a masterpiece of medieval architecture, which almost lets you forget the zooming highways that have encroached upon it.

Founded as the Roman city Autricum, Chartres is an ancient hilltop village at heart. Its oldest streets, still named for the trades once practiced there, cluster around the cathedral and gaze over the tranquil Eure River. These winding paths offer some of the best views of the cathedral and are navigable using the well-marked tourist office circuit (map available at tourist office). Chartres's medieval tangle of streets can be confusing, but getting lost here can only be enjoyable.

Timing is important if you want to fully enjoy your visit to Chartres, as everything closes during lunch time, casual visits to the cathedral are not permitted during mass, and English tours are only given twice a day. For an ideal daytrip, arrive around 10 or 10:30am, pick up the invaluable walking-tour map of the *vieille ville* from the tourist office, and head straight for the **Musée des Beaux-Arts** to catch it before it closes at noon (those particularly interested in stained glass can walk through the smaller **Centre International du Vitrail** afterward; it closes at 12:30pm). You can start your walking tour in the northward direction after visiting the museum and stop en route for lunch at the beautiful **Moulin de Ponceau**, on the banks of the river (be sure to make reservations the day before). A stop at the **Maison Picassiette** makes for an enjoyable detour. Finish with a trip to some of the still-spectacular smaller churches, and make it back to the cathedral in time for **Malcolm Miller's English tour** (p. 330) or for your own afternoon visit. Visitors can rest at one of the cafes surrounding the cathedral, and finish the day with brief visits to any of the small museums.

■ PRACTICAL INFORMATION

Transportation: Chartres is accessible by frequent trains from **Gare Montparnasse, Grandes Lignes,** on the Nogent-le-Rotrou line. About 1 train per hr. during the summer; best to pick up a schedule ahead of time in both summer and winter, as times are irregular. (50-75min.; round-trip €25, under 25 and seniors €18.50, under 12 €12.50. Discount of 20-40% available if bought up to 2 weeks ahead of time.) To reach the cathedral from the train station, walk straight along av. Jehan de Beauce to pl. de Châtelet and turn left into the *place*, right onto r. Ste-Même, and left onto r. Jean Moulin (head toward the massive spires).

Tourist Office: The tourist office, (☎02 37 18 26 26; www.chartres-tourisme.com), located in front of the cathedral's main entrance at pl. de la Cathédrale, helps find accommodations (€2 surcharge) and supplies visitors with a free and helpful **map** that includes a walking tour and a list of restaurants, hotels, and sights. Visitors can also purchase the **Chartres Pass** (€14.50), which includes free or reduced admission to sights—a worthwhile investment if you are staying overnight or longer. For those with difficulty walking or who want a relaxed tour of the town, **le petit train Chart'train** runs late Mar. to early Nov. with 35min. narrated tours (in French and English) of the old city.

(☎02 37 25 88 50). Tours begin in front of the tourist office every hr. starting at 10:30am and running until 6pm. €5.50, under 12 €3. English-language **walking tours** (1½hr.) depart from the tourist office every Sa from July-Aug. at 4:15pm (€5, young children free). **Audioguide** of the *vieille ville* (1½hr.) available for €5.50, and €3 for the second. Tourist office open Apr.-Sept. M-Sa 9am-7pm, Su and holidays 9:30am-5:30pm; Oct.-Mar. M-Sa 10am-6pm, Su and holidays 10am-1pm and 2:30-4:30pm. Closed Jan. 1 and Dec. 25.

▐ FOOD

Le Moulin de Ponceau, 21/23, r. de la Tannerie (☎02 37 35 30 05; www.lemoulindeponceau.fr). Located on one of the lower medieval stone landings along the town's beautiful stream, this classic French restaurant is worth every penny. 3-course *menus* at €25, €35, and €45, as well as a €12 children's *menu*. Make reservations before visiting Chartres—you'll regret it if you don't. Open daily 12:15-2pm and 7:30-10pm. Closed Su evenings in the summer. Oct. 1-Mar. 31, closed W and Sa lunch and Su dinner. AmEx/MC/V. ❸

Epicerie de la Place Billard, 19, r. des Changes (☎02 37 21 00 25). A friendly grocery store with bottles of perfumed *limonade* (a fizzy drink) and flavored *sirops* (€6) stacked in the window. Choose from over 40 flavors of *limonade* (€3.50), ranging from cotton candy to violet to praline. Open M-Sa from 6am-7:30pm and Su 6am-noon. ❶

Les Trois Lys, 3, r. Porte Guillame (☎02 37 28 42 02). This casual *crêperie,* right by the river and just off the walking tour, serves a formidable assortment of crêpes (€2.00-6.50) and *galettes* for a delicious price (€5.50-8.50). Try the *salade Sud-Ouest* (smoked duck, *foie gras,* apples, and greens; €10). Open Tu-Su noon-2pm and 7-10pm (weekend open until 11pm). Reservations suggested F-Sa evenings. MC/V. ❶

◉ SIGHTS

THE CATHEDRAL

☎02 37 21 75 02; www.cathedrale-chartres.com. Open daily 8:30am-7:30pm. No casual visits during mass. Mass M-F 11:45am and 6:15pm (9am on T and F); Sa 11:45am and 6pm; Su 9:15 (Latin), 11am, 6pm (in the crypt). Call the tourist office for info on concerts in the cathedral, the annual student pilgrimage in late May, Chartres in Lights in high summer, and other events throughout the year. English-language audioguides available at the gift shop (€3.50, €4.50, €6.50, depending on version) require a piece of identification as a deposit. English tours of the cathedral by Malcolm Miller (see below) begin outside the gift shop in the cathedral. 1¼hr. Easter to early Nov. M-Sa noon and 2:45pm; call ☎02 37 28 15 58 for tour availability during winter months. €10.

The Cathédrale de Chartres is the best-preserved medieval church in Europe, having miraculously escaped major damage during the French Revolution and WWII. A patchwork masterpiece of Romanesque and Gothic design, the cathedral was constructed by generations of masons, architects, and artisans. Its grand scale dominates the town—with spires visible from most locations—and its history is strongly bound to that of France. It was here, for example, that Henri IV was crowned in 1594 (see **Life and Times,** p. 61). Approaching from the pl. de la Cathédrale, you can see the discrepancy between the two towers: the one on the left, finished in 1513, is Late Gothic (or Flamboyant); the one on the right, built just before an 1194 fire, is Romanesque and octagonal (the tallest of its kind still standing). The 12th-century statues of the Portale Royale present an assembly of Old Testament figures. The 13th-century *Porche du Nord* depicts the life of Mary, while the *Porche du Sud* depicts the life of Christ.

The only English-language **tours** of the cathedral are given by **Malcolm Miller,** an authority on Gothic architecture who has been leading visitors through the church for over 40 years. His presentations on the cathedral's history and symbolism are intelligent, witty, and enjoyable for all ages. If you can, take both his morning and afternoon tour—no two are alike.

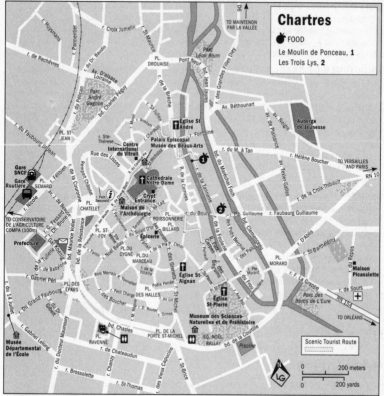

Chartres

🍴 FOOD

Le Moulin de Ponceau, **1**
Les Trois Lys, **2**

SANCTA CAMISIA. The year after he became emperor in AD 875, Charlemagne's grandson, the unfortunately named Charles the Bald, donated to Chartres the Sancta Camisia, the cloth believed to have been worn by the Virgin Mary when she gave birth to Christ. Although a church dedicated to Mary had existed on the site as early as the mid-700s, the emperor's bequest required a new cathedral to accommodate the growing number of pilgrims. Thousands journeyed to the church to kneel before the sacred relic in hope that it would heal them and answer their prayers. The sick were nursed in the crypt below the sanctuary. The powers of the relic were confirmed in AD 911 when the cloth supposedly saved the city from invading Goths and Vikings; the Viking leader Rollon converted to Christianity and became the first Duke of Normandy. Today, the relic is preserved behind glass and is on display in the back of the church on the left-hand side.

STAINED GLASS. At a time when books were rare and the vast majority of people illiterate, the cathedral served as a multimedia teaching tool. Most of the 172 stained-glass windows date from the 13th century and were preserved through both World Wars by heroic town authorities, who dismantled over 2000 sq. m of glass and stored the windows pane by pane in Dordogne. The famous **Blue Virgin, Tree of Jesse,** and **Passion and Resurrection of Christ** windows are among the surviving originals. The medieval merchants who paid for the windows are represented in the lower panels, which provide a record of daily life in the 13th century. The windows are characterized by a stunning color known as "Chartres blue," which has not been reproduced in modern times. The center window depicts the story of Christ from the Annunciation to the ride into Jerusalem. Stories read from bottom to top, left to right.

LABYRINTH. The windows of Chartres often distract visitors from the treasure below their feet: a winding labyrinth pattern that is carved into the floor in the rear of the nave. Designed in the 13th century, the labyrinth was laid out for pilgrims as a substitute for a journey to the Holy Land. By following this symbolic journey on their hands and knees, the devout would enact a symbolic voyage to Jerusalem.

TOUR JEHAN-DE-BEAUCE. The adventurous, the athletic, and the non-claustrophobic can climb the narrow staircase to the cathedral's north tower, Tour Jehan-de-Beauce (named after its architect), for a stellar view of the cathedral roof, the flying buttresses, and the city below. If you don't make it all the way to the top, the first viewing platform offers a slightly obstructed but nonetheless impressive sight. *(Open May-Aug. M-Sa 9:30am-12:30pm and 2-5:30pm, Su 2-6pm, last entry 30min. before closing; Sept.-Apr. M-Sa 9:30am-12:30pm and 2-5pm, Su 2-5pm, last entrance 30min. before closing. Access to roof structure May-Aug. starting at 4pm, Sept.-Apr., Sa-Su and school holidays starting at 3pm. Tours of the upper stained-glass windows available upon request. ☎02 37 21 75 02. Closed Jan. 1 and 5 and Dec. 25. €6, ages 18-25 €4, under 18 free.)*

CRYPT. Visitors may enter the 110m long subterranean crypt only as part of a guided tour. Parts of the crypt, including a well down which Vikings tossed the bodies of their victims during raids, date back to the 9th century. Information sheets in English are available at the La Crypte store. ☎02 37 21 56 33. Tours (in French) leave from La Crypte, the store opposite the cathedral's south entrance at 18, Cloître Notre Dame. *(☎02 37 21 56 33. French-language tours 30min. Apr.-Oct. M-Sa 11am (except Su and bank holidays), 2:15, 3:30, 4:30pm; Nov.-Mar. 11am (except Su and bank holidays) and 4:15pm; additional 5:15pm tour June 22-Sept. 21. €3, students €2, under 7 free. Groups should call ahead ☎02 37 21 75 02.)*

ELSEWHERE IN THE CATHEDRAL. Inside the church, the intricate Renaissance choir screen, begun by Jehan de Beauce in 1514, depicts the life of the Virgin Mary. The lovely, candlelit shrine to *"Notre Dame de Pilier"* is near the Sancta Camista. Both are worth a visit.

OTHER SIGHTS

MUSÉE DES BEAUX-ARTS. The Musée des Beaux-Arts is housed in the former Bishop's Palace, which is itself an impressive sight. Built principally in the 17th and 18th centuries (on a site occupied by bishops since the 11th century), the palace houses a wildly eclectic collection of painting, sculpture, and furniture, including works by Vlaminck, Navarre, and Soutine. A harpsichord collection dating back to the 17th century and a collection of Oceanic art are also on display. The multi-terraced park is perfect for wandering or picnicking. It includes a miniature labyrinth and plenty of shady spots overlooking the town. *(29, Cloître Notre-Dame. Behind the cathedral. ☎02 37 90 45 80. Open May-Oct. M and W-Sa 10am-noon and 2-6pm, Su 2-6pm; Nov.-Apr. M and W-Sa 10am-noon and 2-5pm, Su 2-5pm, last entry 30min. before closing. Closed Jan. 1, May 1 and 8, Nov. 1 and 11, and Dec. 25. €2.50, students and seniors €1.50, under 12 free.)*

OTHER MUSEUMS. Chartres has a number of small museums that cater to specific interests. The small **Centre International du Vitrail,** 5, r. du Cardinal Pie , housed in a small 13th-century barn once used by the clergy, hosts two temporary exhibitions on stained glass each year. *(☎02 37 21 65 72; www.centre-vitrail.org. Open M-F 9:30am-12:30pm and 1:30-6pm, Sa-Su 10am-12:30pm and 2:30-6pm. €4, students €3, under 14 free).* English-language tours available upon reservation (€6.50-17.50). The **Maison Picassiette,** 22, r. du Repos, is an extraordinary house covered entirely in mosaic tiles, inside and out. *(☎02 37 34 10 78. Open Apr.-Oct. M and W-Sa 10am-noon and 2-6pm, Su 2-6pm. €4.50, students €2.50; combination ticket with the Musée des Beaux-Arts €6, students €3.)* There is also a substantial natural history museum, the **Muséum des Sciences Naturelles et de Préhistoire,** 5bis, bd. de la Courtille. *(☎02 37 28*

36 09. Open July to mid-Sept. and school holidays M-Sa 2-6pm; mid-Sept. to June W and Su 2-5pm. Free.) The **Maison de l'Archéologie**, 1 r. de l'Étroit Degré, has a fascinating collection of archaeological finds relating to the history of the town. (☎02 37 30 99 38. Open Oct.-June W and Su 2-5pm and by appointment; July-Sept. M and W-Su 2-6pm. Closed Dec. 19-Jan. 8 and May 1, July 14 and Aug. 15. €1.50; under 18, students, disabled persons free.) The **Musée Départemental de l'Ecole**, 1, r. du 14 Juillet, is a replica of a turn-of-the-century village classroom. Under renovation until 2007. (☎02 37 30 07 69. Open M-F 10am-noon and 2-6pm except holidays. €3, under 16 €2, under 6 free.) The **Conservatoire de l'Agriculture COMPA**, Pont de Mainvilliers, the largest agricultural museum in France, displays a huge array of tractors and other farm machinery, as well as one temporary exhibit at a time, on subjects like horses and farm life. (☎02 37 84 15 00; www.lecompa.com. Open T-F 10am-12:30pm and 1:30-6pm, Sa-Su and holidays 10am-12:30pm and 1:30-7pm. €4, students €3, ages 6-18 €1.50, under 6 free. French-language guided tours holidays, Sa and Su 11am, 3, 5pm.).

CHURCHES. Rebuilt in the 16th century, the feudal ▓ **Eglise St-Aignan**, on r. des Greniers, has magnificent ceiling frescoes, a true rarity. Also offers summer concerts and exhibits. (Open daily 8am-noon and 2-6pm. Mass daily at 9am.) The 12th-century Romanesque **Eglise St-André** sits on r. St-André on the banks of the Eure River. (Open daily 10am-noon and 2-6pm.) Once part of a Benedictine monastery, the **Eglise St-Pierre**, on pl. St-Pierre, is a 12th-century Gothic masterpiece. (Open daily 10am-noon and 2-6pm, mass at 10:30am.) All three churches are on the tourist office's walking tour.

MONUMENT TO JEAN MOULIN. A monument to WWII Resistance hero Jean Moulin, on r. Jean Moulin off bd. de la Résistance, consists of a giant stone hand gripping the hilt of a broken sword. Moulin, who was Prefect of Chartres before the war, attempted suicide to avoid signing a Nazi document accusing French troops of atrocities. Tortured and killed by the Gestapo in 1943, he was eventually buried in the Panthéon. The monument is plotted on the tourist office's walking tour.

FONTAINEBLEAU

More digestible and less crowded than Versailles, the Château de Fontainebleau achieves nearly the same grandeur while preserving a distinctive charm among the great royal châteaux. With lush gardens and luxuriously decorated apartments, the estate ranks among the best daytrips from Paris. Kings of France have hunted on these grounds since the 12th century, when the exiled Thomas à Becket consecrated Louis VII's manor chapel. In 1528, François I rebuilt the castle to be closer to the game he loved to hunt. Fontainebleau's masterfully rendered galleries and frescoes are considered the first manifestation of Renaissance art in France. François I, a great patron of the arts, sought out Italian artists to design and decorate his pet project; among them was Leonardo Da Vinci, whose *Mona Lisa* hung here. Subsequent kings commissioned magnificent new rooms and wings. At Fontainebleau, Louis XIII was born in 1601, Louis XIV revoked the Edict of Nantes in 1685, and Louis XV was married in 1725. Napoleon, who visited frequently, called it *"la Maison des Siècles"* (the House of Centuries). In 1814, Napoleon bid goodbye to the Empire from the central courtyard, now called the **Cour des Adieux** in his honor.

🛈 PRACTICAL INFORMATION

Transportation: Hourly trains from **Gare de Lyon** on the *banlieue sud-est* line (45min., €15.50 round-trip; keep your ticket to be punched on the train). At Gare de Lyon, follow signs to the *Grandes Lignes*, and buy your ticket from the *"Billets Île de France"* counter. From the station, **Connex** (☎01 64 23 71 11) runs buses (€1.50) after each train arrival from Paris; take the bus in direction "Château-Lilas" and get off at the château stop. Otherwise, the château is a 30min. walk away (follow the signs from the station), through the small towns of Avon and Fontainebleau.

Tourist Office: 4, r. Royal (☎01 60 74 99 99; www.fontainebleau-tourisme.com). Turn right from château entrance and left up r. Royal. Finds accommodations, organizes tours of the village, sells audio tours of the château's exterior, and distributes maps of Fontainebleau and Barbizon. Open M-Sa 10am-6pm; Su and holidays 10am-1pm and 2-5:30pm.

◘ FOOD

The bistros immediately surrounding the château are not the only dining options when visiting Fontainebleau. Walk a couple of minutes into town, following r. de Ferrare, and you'll find several quality establishments serving up traditional French cuisine. There are also many pizza, sandwich, and *crêpe* places along r. Grande and r. de France.

Le Caveau des Ducs, 24, r. de Ferrare (☎01 64 22 05 05; www.lecaveaudesducs.com). At this medieval-style bistro, the €21 *menu* includes either appetizer and *plat* or *plat* and dessert. Taller patrons at the Duke's Cave should keep their eyes open for the arches and hanging candles. Many classic dessert choices (€6). Giant salads €13-17. Open daily noon-2pm and 7-10:30pm. AmEx/MC/V. ❸

La Petite Alsace, 26, r. de Ferrare (☎01 64 23 45 45). Warm yellow walls, lace curtains, and flowery tablecloths welcome you to this traditional restaurant with an €11 lunch *formule* (M-F) and *menus* €15-31. The terrace is lovely when it's nice out. Open daily noon-2pm and 7-10:30pm. AmEx/MC/V. ❸

◉ SIGHTS

CHÂTEAU DE FONTAINEBLEAU

☎01 60 71 50 60; www.musee-chateau-fontainebleau.fr. Wheelchair accessible. Château open May-Sept. M and W-Su 9:30am-6pm; Oct.-Apr. 9:30am-5:30pm. Gardens open Nov.-Feb. 9am-5pm; May-Sept. 9am-7pm; Oct. 9am-6pm. Last entry 45min. before closing. €6.50, ages 18-25 €4.50, under 18 free, and 1st Su of the month free. Useful printed guide available in gift shop to the right of the central courtyard staircase. 60min. audioguides €3. 1hr. tours of the Petits Appartements in French €3. Call ahead for tour schedule. Admission to Musée Chinois de l'Impératrice Eugénie is included, but it is sometimes closed due to low staffing, so call ahead. The information office (right wing of the château) features a superb model of the château with English descriptions.

GRANDS AND PETITS APPARTEMENTS. The Grands Appartements provide a lesson on the history of French architecture and decoration. Napoleon III commissioned the **Celebration Gallery,** which brings together works depicting historical events witnessed by the château. Dubreuil's **Gallery of Plates** represents the history of Fontainebleau on a series of 128 porcelain plates fitted into the woodwork, and it includes an exquisitely rendered cabinet of Sèvres porcelain. The **Galerie de François I** both glorifies the king's royal egotism and serves as a testament to his patronage of the arts: it is flanked with his initials and personal salamander emblem, and it boasts vivid mythological frescoes by Il Rosso and Le Primatice. The *galerie* is brilliantly illuminated by windows that look out onto the **Fountain Courtyard.** The bay windows of the **ball room,** which features an octagonal ceiling and heavy wood paneling, face out onto the **Oval Courtyard.** The elaborate gilded rostrum above the entrance was intended for musicians. The **King's Cabinet** (also known as the Louis XIII Salon because Louis XIII was born there) was the site of *le débotter*, the king's post-hunt boot removal. Napoleon pored over the volumes in the sunlit **Diana Gallery.** Since Marie de Médicis, every queen and empress of France has slept in the gold-and-green **Queen's Bed Chamber;** the gilded wood bed was built for Marie-Antoinette. The "N" on the red and gold velvet throne of the

Throne Room is a testament to Napoleon's humility in what is today the only existing throne room in France. The **Council Chambers** feature a representation of the *Christ of Apollo* by Boucher, to inspire the king in his rule. Sandwiched between two mirrors, **Napoleon's bed chamber** is a monument to both narcissism and eroticism, while his austere **small bed chamber** contains a narrow military bed. In the Emperor's Private Room, known today as the **Abdication Chamber**, Napoleon signed off his empire in 1814 before bidding farewell to his troops in the château's entry courtyard. The tour ends with the 16th-century, Italian-frescoed **Trinity Chapel**, where visitors can sit on red velvet benches and listen to classical hymns piped into the beautiful room. Paintings of the vault illustrate the theme of the Redemption of Man. The Petits Appartements feature the private rooms of Napoleon and the Empress Josephine, as well as the impressive **Map Room** and **Galerie des Cerfs**; they can be seen only by guided tour.

MUSÉE NAPOLÉON. The Musée Napoléon features an extensive collection of the Emperor's personal effects: his toothbrush, tiny shoes, field tent, and gifts from European monarchs. (☎*01 60 71 50 60. Only open to guided 1hr. tours; average of 8 per day, but call ahead for exact tour schedule; in French. €3, under 18 free.*)

▧ GARDENS. Fontainebleau's serene **Jardin Anglais** and **Jardin de Diane** shelter quiet grottoes guarded by statues of the huntress Diana. The **Etang des Carpes,** a carp-filled pond, can be explored by rowboat. (Boat rental available on an irregular basis. Coach driving in the park, €4, children €3. ☎01 64 22 92 61 or 01 81 50 09 20.) The lake was formerly a swamp, which François I altered into an ornamental body of water. On the outskirts of the garden is a 1200m canal perfect for picnicking. The **Forêt de Fontainebleau** is a thickly wooded 20,000-hectare preserve with hiking trails, bike paths, and sandstone rock-climbing. The tourist office provides maps.

CHANTILLY

The 14th- to 19th-century **Château de Chantilly** is a whimsical amalgam of Gothic extravagance, Renaissance geometry, and flashy Victorian ornamentalism. The triangular-shaped château is surrounded by a moat, lakes, canals, and the simple, elegant Le Nôtre gardens. Between the architecturally masterful **Grandes Ecuries** (stables) and the world-class **Musée Condé**, it's a wonder that this lovely château and its surroundings have stayed a hidden treasure for so long. The whole package makes for a delightful foray into the French countryside, where just 30min. from the city, visitors can stroll through the dense woodland surrounding the château and hear nothing but the melodious singing of the *tilleul*, the bird from which the town derives its name.

A Roman citizen named Cantilius originally built his villa here, and a succession of medieval lords constructed elaborate fortifications. In the 17th century, Louis XIV's cousin, the Grand Condé, commissioned a château and asked André Le Nôtre to create the gardens. It was while the Prince played at peasantry in these magnificent grounds that the now-famed *crème chantilly* (whipped cream) was invented. The Grand Château was razed during the Revolution. In the 1870s, the château was rebuilt under the orders of the Duc d'Aumale, fifth son of King Louis-Philippe, complete with the eclectic facade, modern wrought-iron grillwork, copies of Michelangelo marbles, lush greenery, and extravagant entrance hall you see today.

▨ PRACTICAL INFORMATION

Transportation: Take the **train** from the Gare du Nord RATP (Grand Lignes) to Chantilly Gouvieux (up to 35min., approximately every hr. 6am-10pm, round-trip €13.50, under 25 €10.50). Schedule varies with season. The château is a scenic 30min. walk from the train station—go straight up r. des Otages about 50m, and the well-marked path (1.5km) runs directly through the woodland opposite. Alternatively, by road (2km), turn left on av. du Maréchal Joffre, and then right on r. de Connetable, the town's main street. There is also a free but irregular **navette** (shuttle) service; catch one just to the left as you exit the train station. M-Sa until 6pm.

Tourist Office: 60, av. du Maréchal Joffre (☎03 44 67 37 37; www.chantilly-tourisme.com). From the train station, go straight up r. des Otages about 50m. Offers brochures and maps. The tourist office can also call a taxi (€6) (☎03 44 57 10 03). Open May-Sept. daily M-Sa 9:30am-12:30pm and 1:30-5:30pm, Su 10am-1:30pm. Oct.-Apr. M-Sa 9:30am-12:30pm and 1:30-5:30pm.

FOOD

R. de Connetable runs through the middle of the town of Chantilly to the Grandes Ecuries, offering a number of reasonable dining options—cafes, *crêperies*, and *boulangeries*. Near the entrance to the château grounds, you'll find ice cream and sandwich stands. The château itself has a pricy restaurant. In the gardens, have a dessert or meal at **Les Gouters Champetres ❸** (☎03 44 57 46 21). From the château, bear left toward the fountains, turn right, and walk along le Canal des Morfondus. Cross the canal by one of the two woodplanked bridges, and you'll see the restaurant on your right once you clear the woods. It offers a full *menu* starting at €17.50; or for a filling farm-style lunch, try the *assiette gourmande* (€20), piled high with *foie gras*, *terrine*, and *pâté*. Various *crème chantilly* and fruit concoctions start at €4 (see **A Good Whipping**, p. 337). (Beer €4.50. Plenty of outdoor seating. Reservations suggested in the summer. Open mid-Mar. to mid-Nov. daily noon-6pm; lunch service stops after 3pm. MC/V.)

Whatever you do, don't miss the small strawberry patch behind the snack shop in Le Hameau. The berries are yours for the picking while they're in season.

SIGHTS

CHÂTEAU, GARDENS, AND MUSÉE CONDÉ. Maps of the **gardens** suggest a walking tour of the grounds, but wandering is just as effective. A bike can help you explore the château's 115 hectares of parks and grounds. Directly in front of the château, the gardens' central expanse is designed in the French formal style, with neat rows of carefully pruned trees, calm statues, and geometric pools. To the left, hidden within a forest, the Romantic English garden attempts to re-create untamed nature. Here, paths meander around pools where lone swans glide elegantly. Windows carved into the foliage allow you to see fountains in the formal garden as you stroll. To the right, the gardens hide an idyllic play- village **hameau** (hamlet), the inspiration for Marie-Antoinette's hamlet at Versailles. Farther in, a statue of Cupid reigns over the "Island of Love." A 2003 addition is the kangaroo enclosure—the 15 or so wallabies gathered in the far right corner of the formal gardens represent the park's first hop towards recreating the *ménagerie* that existed during the château's heyday.

Chantilly's biggest attraction lies inside the château: the spectacular **Musée Condé** houses the Duc d'Aumale's private collection of pre-modern paintings and is one of only two museums in France to boast three Raphaels (the other is the Louvre). The skylit picture galleries contain 800 paintings; 3000 drawings; and hundreds of engravings, sculptures, and tapestries, among them works by Titian, Corot, Botticelli, Delacroix, Reynolds, Watteau, and Ingres. Marble busts and drawings of royals and nobles attest to the château's illustrious litany of owners: the powerful noble Montmorency family, and the royal Bourbon and Condé princes. Following the Duke's will, the paintings and furniture are arranged as they were over a century ago, in the distinctively 19th-century frame-to-frame (academic) style. The absolute gem is the tiny velvet-walled **sanctuario.** This hidden gallery contains what the Duke himself considered the finest works in his collection: illuminated manuscripts by Jean Fouquet, a painting by Fra Filippo Lippi, and two Raphaels. Alas, the museum's two most valuable pieces, a Gutenberg Bible and the illuminated manuscripts of the *Très Riches Heures* (1410), are too fragile to be kept in public view—but a near-perfect digitized facsimile of the latter can be seen in the illustrious **library,** second only to the Bibliothèque Nationale in prestige. The rest of the château's **appartements** can be visited only by taking a guided tour in French. (☎ *03 44 62 62 62; www.chauteaudechantilly.com. Château open Nov.-Mar. M and W-F 10:30am-12:45pm and 2-5pm, Sa-Su and holidays 10:30am-5pm, last entry 45min. before closing. Gardens open Nov.-Mar. M and W-Su 10:30am-6pm, last entry 5pm; Apr.-Nov. M-Su 10am-10pm, last entry 8pm. Gardens €4, large families, seniors, disabled persons, students €3.50, ages 4-12 €2.50; to gardens and château (the Musée Condé) €8/7/3.50. Various ticket packages available: gardens, château, and boat or train ride €12/10.50/6.50; gardens and train or boat ride €9/7.50/5.50; carriage and garden (weekend and holidays only) €10/8/5.50; garden, château and carriage €13/11/6.50. Miniature trains offer 30min. tours of the gardens and grounds in French and English. Frequent, free 45min. tours of the château's appartements in French leaving from inside the château. Audioguide €2 in English and French. Program of daily children's activities available at ticket office. AmEx/MC/V.)*

GRANDES ECURIES. Another great (if slightly less sweet-smelling) draw to the château is the Grandes Ecuries (stables), whose immense marble corridors, courtyards, and facades are masterpieces of 18th-century French architecture. Commissioned by Louis-Henri Bourbon, who hoped to live here when he was reborn as a horse, the Ecuries boast extravagant fountains, domed rotundas, and sculptured patios that are enough to make even the most cynical believe in reincarnation. From 1719 to the Revolution, the stables housed 240 horses and hundreds of hunting dogs, and now are home to the **Musée Vivant du Cheval,** an extensive collection (supposedly the largest in the world) of all things equine. In addition to the stables' 30 live horses, donkeys, and ponies, the museum displays saddles, merry-go-rounds, and a horse statue featured in a James Bond film. Equestrian shows such as "Horses, Dreams, and Poetry" are a fanciful highlight (on the first Su of every month and at Christmas; call for schedule). The **Hippodrome** on the premises is a major racetrack: two of France's premier horse races are held here in June. (☎ *03 44 57 13 13; www.museevivantducheval.fr. Open Apr. and Sept.-Oct. M and W-F 10:30am-5:30pm, Sa-Su 10:30am-6pm; Nov. and Jan.-Mar. M and W-F 2-5pm, Sa-Su 10:30am-5:30pm; Dec. M, W-F Sa-Su 10:30am-*

ON THE MENU

A GOOD WHIPPING

As frothy as a cloud on a summer's day, the vanilla-infused *crème de Chantilly* is a sublime accompaniment to any dessert. The cream, which has the consistency of melted ice cream, originated on the grounds of the Chateau de Chantilly in the *hameau* (hamlet) constructed by the Prince of Condé in 1774. The Prince invited *la crème de la crème* of European royalty to join him in playing at peasants and to sample the fruits of the forest. Berries were topped with a cream developed at the on-site dairy.

The *hameau* of Chantilly quickly became known for its delicious whipped cream, the popularity of which has outlived the age of indulgence when aristocrats dressed up as shepherds and milkmaids. The secret of the cream, which mixes cold, non pasteurized cream, vanilla sugar, and icing sugar, is all in the whipping. The mixture must be beaten until it has reached twice its original volume. When the mixture is thick enough, waves created by the vigorous stirring will stay rigid when the whip is taken out of the cream. It's a fine art, though whip too long, and it will turn to butter. Today, you can enjoy the cream at the very spot where it was invented, at the restaurant **Les Gouters Champetres** (p. 336), nestled amid the buildings of the *hameau.*

5pm; May-June M-F 10:30am-5:30pm, Sa-Su 10:30am-6pm; July-Aug. M and W-F 10:30am-5:30pm, Sa-Su 10:30am-6pm. Museum €8.50, students €7.50, children €6.50. Educational demonstration equestrian shows Sept.-Oct. and Apr.-June M and W-Su 11:30am, 3:30, and 5:15pm; Nov. and Jan.-Mar. M and W-F 3:30pm, Sa-Su 11:30am, 3:30, and 5:15pm; Dec. M and W-F 3:45pm, Sa-Su 11:30am except holidays; July-Aug. M and W-Su 11:30am, 3:30, and 5:30pm. Hippodrome matches €3, schedule upon request at the tourist office.)

LE POTAGER DES PRINCES (THE PRINCES' KITCHEN GARDEN). The Prince's Kitchen Garden is a cultivated 2½-hectare expanse of greenery modeled on the château's original 17th-century working garden. It was first designed by Le Nôtre as a pheasantry for the Grand Duke Condé in 1682 and was later converted into a "Roman pavilion" of terraced gardens. Abandoned during the Revolution's pruning of excess, the gardens were restored in 2002 to their former verdant glory, this time as a public attraction. The garden is arranged in themed areas, including a fantasy region replete with bridges and grottoes, a romantic and aromatic rose garden, and a *ménagerie* that features goats, squabbling chickens, and over 100 varieties of pheasant. (☎ 03 44 57 40 40; www.potagerdesprinces.com. Wheelchair accessible. 300m from the stables down r. Connetable toward the town, turn onto r. des Potagers; garden is at end of road. Open mid-Mar. to mid-Oct. M and W-F 2-6:30pm, Sa-Su and holidays 11am-12:30pm and 2-7pm; last entry 1hr. before closing. Gardener talks in French for children M and W-F 2:30pm; free with entry. €7.50, ages 13-17 €7, ages 4-12 €6.)*

GIVERNY

Drawn to the verdant hills, woodsy haystacks, and lily-strewn Epte River, painter Claude Monet and his eight children settled in Giverny in 1883. By 1887, John Singer Sargent, Paul Cézanne, and Mary Cassatt had placed their easels beside Monet's and turned the village into an artists' colony. Today, the vistas depicted by these artists remain undisturbed. The cobblestone street that was the setting for Monet's *Wedding March* is instantly recognizable. In spite of the tourists, who come in droves to retrace the steps of the now-famous Impressionists (see **Life and Times,** p. 83) who found inspiration here, Giverny retains its rustic tranquility.

⑦ PRACTICAL INFORMATION

Transportation: From Paris to Vernon: The **SNCF** runs trains regularly from Paris's **Gare St-Lazare** to **Vernon,** the station nearest Giverny. To get to the Gare St-Lazare, take the metro to St-Lazare and follow the signs to the Grandes Lignes. From there, proceed to any ticket line marked "France," or use an SNCF machine to avoid the lines (MC/V). To schedule a trip ahead of time, call the SNCF (☎ 08 36 35 35 35) or look up the schedule on the web at www.sncf.fr. Round trip around €24, ages 18-25 €17.50. **From Vernon to Giverny:** The fastest way to Giverny is by **bus** (☎ 08 25 07 60 27; 10min.; Tu-Su.) Buses leave every day for Giverny just a few minutes after the train arrives in Vernon, so hurry over. 3 buses per day go from Giverny to Vernon; look for the schedule inside the information office in the train station; €3 return (as many times as you want in a day). You can rent a **bike** (☎ 02 32 21 16 01) from many of the restaurants opposite the Vernon station for €10 per day, plus deposit. The 6km **pedestrian and cyclist path** from the Vernon station to Giverny is unmarked: it begins as the dirt road that intersects r. de la Ravine above the highway (free **map** at most bike rental locations). **Taxis** run from the train station for a flat rate: M-F €11 for up to 3 people; €12 for 4 people; sometimes more on Sa-Su and holidays.

🍴 FOOD

🦪 **Ancien Hôtel Baudy,** 81, r. Claude Monet (☎ 02 32 21 10 03). From the Fondation, walk 500m up r. Claude Monet (when facing the Fondation, walk right). In addition to its delicious Normandy-style cuisine, this renovated hotel (once frequented by Monet, Cézanne, and Cassatt) has an exquisite terraced garden. Also on the premises is a reconstructed ivy-covered artist's *atelier*. *Menus* €20.50. Salads €7.50-13.50. Open Tu-Su 10am-9pm. MC/V.

Les Nymphéas, r. Claude Monet (☎02 32 21 20 31). Adjacent to the parking lot opposite the Fondation. After a day of roses and honeybees, visitors can decompress at Les Nymphéas, named, of course, after Monet's famous waterlilies. The building was originally part of the artist's farm. *Cuisine nouvelle-Normandie* is served in an indoor terrace decorated with Toulouse-Lautrec posters. *Menu* €20.50, wine €3-4.50. The *salade Monet* (€10.90) is a masterpiece: mixed greens with mushrooms, smoked salmon, crab, tomatoes, green beans, asparagus, and avocado. Open Apr.-Oct. Tu-Su 9:30am-6pm. MC/V.

👁 SIGHTS

FONDATION CLAUDE MONET. From 1883 until 1926, Claude Monet, the leader of the Impressionist movement, resided in Giverny. His home, with its thatched roof and pink, crushed brick facade, was surrounded by ponds and immense gardens, two features central to his art. Today, Monet's house and gardens are maintained by the Fondation Claude Monet. From April to July, the gardens overflow with wild roses, hollyhocks, poppies, and fragrant honeysuckle. The Orientalist Water Gardens contain the water lilies, weeping willows, and Japanese bridge recognizeable from Monet's paintings. To avoid the rush, go early in the morning and, if possible, early in the season. Inside the house, with its big windows and pastel hues, the original decorations have been restored or recreated. Highlights include the artist's cheerful, brimming kitchen and his collection of 18th- and 19th-century Japanese prints. The house also boasts a great view of the gardens from Monet's bedroom window. *(84, r. Claude Monet. ☎02 32 51 28 21; www.fondation-monet.com. Open Apr.-Oct. Tu-Su 9:30am-6pm, last entry 5:30pm. €5.50, students and ages 12-18 €4, ages 7-12 €3. Gardens €4.)*

MUSÉE D'ART AMÉRICAIN. The modern Musée d'Art Américain, near the Fondation Monet, is the sister institution of the Museum of American Art in Chicago. It houses a small number of works by American expats like Theodore Butler and John Leslie Breck, who came to Giverny to study Impressionist style. Outside the museum, a garden designed by landscape architect Mark Rudkin features an array of flowers separated by large, rectangular hedges. While not as impressive as Monet's garden, this smaller labyrinth is worth a visit (and free). It affords a scenic view of Giverny Hill, the inspiration for many Impressionist œuvres. *(99, r. Claude Monet. ☎02 32 51 94 65; www.maag.org. Open Apr.-Oct. Tu-Su and holiday M, 10am-6pm. €5.50; students, seniors, and teachers €4; ages 12-18 years €3; under 12 free. Free the first Su of each month. Audioguides available for €1.50.)*

VAUX-LE-VICOMTE

Nicolas Fouquet, Louis XIV's Minister of Finance, assembled the triumvirate of Le Vau, Le Brun, and Le Nôtre (architect, artist, and landscaper) to build Vaux-le-Vicomte in 1641. On August 17, 1661, upon the completion of what was then France's most ornate chateau, Fouquet threw an extravagant party in honor of Louis XIV. King Louis and his mother Anne of Austria were among the 6000 guests at the event, which premiered poetry by Jean de la Fontaine and a comedy-ballet, *Les Fâcheux*, by Molière. After novelties like elephants wearing crystal jewelry and whales in the canal, the evening concluded with an exhibition of fireworks that featured the King and Queen's coat of arms and pyrotechnic squirrels (squirrels were Fouquet's family symbol). But the housewarming bash was the beginning of the end for Fouquet. Since his appointment to the office in 1653, the ambitious young Minister of Finance had fully replenished the failing Royal treasury. His own lavish lifestyle, however, sparked rumors of embezzlement that were nourished by jealous underlings like Private Secretary Jean-Baptiste Colbert, Fouquet's eventual successor as master of Vaux-le-Vicomte. The 1661 revels gave 22-year-old Louis XIV an opportunity to publicly question the Minister's source of income, and shortly after the fête he ordered Fouquet's arrest. In the words of Voltaire, "At six o'clock in the evening, Fouquet was king of France; at two the next morning, he was nothing." In a trial that lasted three years, Fouquet was found guilty of embezzlement, and the judges voted narrowly for banishment over death. Louis XIV overturned the sentence in favor of life imprisonment—the only time in French history that the head of state overruled the court's decision in favor of a more severe punishment. Fouquet was to remain imprisoned at Pignerol, in the French Alps, until his death in 1680. The Fouquet intrigue has been repeatedly dramatized by the popular and literary imagination. Alexandre Dumas retells the story in *Le Vicomte de Bragelonne*. Some have postulated that Fouquet was the legendary "man in the iron mask," and while evidence refutes the claim, Hollywood's 1999 film *The Man in The Iron Mask* starring Leonardo diCaprio was filmed in part at Vaux-le-Vicomte.

🛈 PRACTICAL INFORMATION

Vaux is one of the most exquisite French châteaux, and it's less crowded than Versailles, whose construction it reputedly inspired. Getting there during the week can be an ordeal, as there is no shuttle service from the train station in Melun to the chateâu 7km away, but the trek is worth it.

Transportation: Take the **RER** (D line) to Melun from Châtelet-Les Halles, Gare de Lyon, or Gare du Nord (50min.; round-trip €13.80). Then catch a shuttle to the château (€6-8 roundtrip, weekends only) or take a taxi (around €15). The château staff will phone you a cab for the return trip. By **car,** take Autoroute A4 and exit at Troyes-Nancy by N104. Head toward Meaux on N36 and follow the signs. The château is about 50km from Paris.

Tourist Office: Service Jeunesse et Citoyenneté, 2, av. Gallieni (☎01 60 56 55 10). By the train station in Melun. Information on accommodations and sight-seeing, plus free maps. Open Tu-Sa 10am-noon and 2-6pm.

Tour Groups: Several tour companies run trips to the château with varying frequencies and prices; call ahead to book a trip. **ParisVision** (☎01 42 60 30 01; www.parisvision.com; trips for *visites aux chandelles* run every Sa May-Oct.) offers regularly scheduled trips.

📷 SIGHTS

CHÂTEAU. The château does not appear ostentatious when viewed from the front, but it is quite Baroque in the back. The garden facade is covered with ornate, scripted "F"s, squirrels (Fouquet's symbol), and the family motto, *"Quo non ascendit"* (What heights might he not reach). The inside is even more opulent. **Madame Fouquet's Closet,** once lined with tiny mirrors, was the decorative precedent for Versailles's Hall of Mirrors. The **Room of the Muses** is one of Le Brun's most famous decorative and detailed displays. The artist had planned to crown the cavernous, Neoclassical **Oval Room** (or **Grand Salon**) with a fresco entitled *The Palace of the Sun,* but Fouquet's arrest halted all decorating activity, and only a single eagle and a patch of sky were painted in to fill the space. The tapestries once bore Fouquet's menacing squirrels, but his great enemy and eventual successor as King's minister, Colbert, seized them and replaced the rodents with his own adders. The ornate **King's Bedchamber** boasts an orgy of cherubs and lions circling the centerpiece, Le Brun's *Time Bearing Truth Heavenward.* (☎01 64 14 41 90;

www.vaux-le-vicomte.com. Open Mar. 25-Nov. 12, and Dec. 23-Jan. 7 daily 10am-5:30pm; visits by appointment for groups of 20 or more the rest of the year. Admission to château, gardens, and carriage museum €12.50; students, seniors, and ages 6-16 €9.90; under 6 free. On Sa evenings from May to mid-Oct., and F in July and Aug., the château is open for visites aux chandelles (candlelight visits) 8pm-midnight. €15.50, concession €13.40. Fountains Apr.-Oct., 2nd and last Sa of each month 3-6pm. Château audio tour includes good historical presentation in English; €1.50. Golf carts stationed to the right of the garden from the entrance; €15 for 45min. ride. The château is not wheelchair accessible. AmEx/MC/V.)

GARDENS. At Vaux-le-Vicomte, Le Nôtre invented the classical French garden, forcing nature to conform to strict geometric patterns (see **Garden Party,** p. 326). Vaux's multilevel terraces, fountained walkways, and fantastical *parterres* (literally "on the ground;" these are low-cut hedges and crushed stone arranged in arabesque patterns) are still the most exquisite example of 17th-century French gardens. The collaboration of Le Nôtre with Le Vau and Le Brun ensured that the same patterns and motifs were repeated with astonishing harmony in the gardens, the château, and the tapestries inside. Vaux owes its most impressive *trompe l'oeil* effect to Le Nôtre's adroit use of the laws of perspective. From the back steps of the château, it looks as if you can see the entire landscape at a glance. The grottoes at the far end of the garden appear directly behind the large pool of water. But as you walk toward the far end of the garden, the grottoes seem to recede, revealing a sunken canal known as **La Poêle** (the Frying Pan), which is invisible from the château. The **Round Pool** and its surrounding 17th-century statues mark an important intersection: to the left, down the east walkway, are the **Water Gates,** the backdrop for Molière's performance of *Les Fâcheux.* The **Water Mirror,** closer to the château along the central walkway, was designed to reflect the building perfectly, but the reflection can be marred on a windy day. A climb to the **Farnese Hercules** earns the best vista of the grounds. The tremendous Hercules sculpture at the top was at the center of Fouquet's trial; in an age when kings enjoyed divine rights to their royalty, the beleaguered Fouquet had to defend likening himself to Hercules, the only mortal to become a god. The old stables, **Les Equipages,** also house a fantastic **carriage museum.** But by far the best way to see Vaux's gardens is during the ■**visites aux chandelles,** when the château and grounds are lit up by thousands of candles, and classical music plays through the gardens in imitation of Fouquet's legendary party; arrive around dusk to see the grounds in all their glory. The gardens, like the château, are not wheelchair accessible.

AUVERS-SUR-OISE

I am entirely absorbed by these plains of wheat on a vast expanse of hills—like an ocean of tender yellow, pale green, and soft mauve.
    —Vincent van Gogh, 1890

This once-sleepy little hamlet has transformed into a self-proclaimed "Cradle of Impressionism," proud of having hosted famed artists such as Daubigny, Corot, Daumier, Cézanne, and a certain van Gogh. The 70 canvases van Gogh produced during his 10-week stay in Auvers bear testimony to what he called the "medicinal effect" of this bit of countryside, only 30km northwest of Paris. Fleeing Provence, where he had been diagnosed with depression and possible epilepsy, van Gogh arrived in May 1890 at Auvers-sur-Oise, where he would be treated by a Dr. Gachet. But neither the doctor nor the countryside were enough to lift his depression. On the afternoon of July 27, he set off with his paints to the fields above the village, crawling back into his room that evening with a bullet lodged deep in his chest. Gachet, van Gogh's brother Théo, and even the police had a chance to demand an explanation from the painter as he lay smoking his pipe and bleeding for two days. "Sadness goes on forever," he told his brother, and died. Visitors to this tranquil town will find a number of vistas remarkably unchanged from those portrayed in van Gogh's work. Auvers-sur-Oise also features a handful of interesting museums that pay tribute to the town's artistic heritage, as well as a small but charming château. Various festivals and fairs are held here throughout the year; check www.auverscama.com for more information.

◪ PRACTICAL INFORMATION

Transportation: Take the **RER C** from Gare d'Austerlitz (☎01 30 36 70 61) toward Pontoise. Disembark at St-Ouens L'Aumone (approx. 1hr.). Then switch to the Persan Beaumont Creil line (walk downstairs and change to opposite platform; consult screen for departures) and get off at Gare d'Auvers-sur-Oise (approx. 15min.). €9.50 round-trip.

Tourist Office: Manoir des Colombières, r. de la Sansonne (☎01 30 36 10 06; www.tourisme.fr/office-de-tourisme/auvers-sur-oise.htm). Helpful free walking maps and event brochures. Open Tu-Su Apr.-Oct. 9:30am-12:30pm and 2-6pm, Nov.-Mar. 9:30am-12:30pm and 2-5pm. 1½hr. guided tours in French Apr.-Oct. Su 3pm; €5.50. Free audiovisual guide (15min.) in the office.

◉ SIGHTS

The following walk should take around 2hr. Turn left directly from the train station.

The small **Parc van Gogh** on your right offers a shady rest and a great picnicking spot, as well as a Zadkine statue of the artist. Farther down on the right is the **Auberge Ravoux** where van Gogh stayed while in Auvers-sur-Oise and where he ultimately killed himself. While the **Maison de van Gogh,** 8, r. de la Sansonne, is just around the corner and a good place to start your tour, it has little to offer beyond a glimpse of van Gogh's bare room and a pretty (and pretty uninformative) slide show. However, the cost of admission includes an elegant souvenir "passport" to Auvers-sur-Oise that details the history of the *auberge* and van Gogh's sojourn here. There is also a booklet available that gives information on the other museums and self-guided walking tours in the region, as well as offers discounts to four of the museums. (☎01 30 36 60 60. Open Mar.-Oct. W-Su 10am-6pm; last entry 5:30pm. Van Gogh's room/Auberge Ravoux €5, ages 12-18 years €3, under 12 free. House/Dr. Gachet's Garden €4 (open Apr.-Oct.).

A visit to the **Cimetière d'Auvers,** where van Gogh and his brother Théo are buried, is worth the 15min. walk from the Maison de van Gogh. To get to the cemetery, take the uphill path past the tourist office, following the signs labeled *"Les tombes de Théo et Vincent."* After the path becomes r. Daubigny, you will reach a narrow staircase on your left. Follow the steps to the elegant **Notre Dame d'Auvers** (open daily 9:30am-6pm), which served as the 12th-century subject of van Gogh's 1890 *Eglise d'Auvers*, which currently hangs in the Musée d'Orsay (see **Museums,** p. 258). The entrance to the church is on the left side.

From the right side of the church, take the steep road curving uphill, which levels with a wheat field. The cemetery is on your right, and the tombs are located against the far left wall, covered by an uimpressive ivy bush. Outside the cemetery, facing the field, take the dirt path to your right labeled "Château par la Sente du Montier." The wheat field, where van Gogh painted his *Champs de Blé aux Corbeaux (Wheatfields with Crows),* dips into a shady slope. Turn left at the end of the road and you will see on your right the **Atelier de Daubigny,** 61, r. Daubigny, once the home and studio of pre-Impressionist painter Charles-François Daubigny. (☎01 34 48 03 03. Open Apr. 10.-Nov. 1 W-Su 2-6:30pm, closed mid-July to mid-Aug. €5.) Turn right onto r. de Léry and on a side street to the left is the **Musée de l'Absinthe,** 44, r. Callé, a tribute to the potent green liqueur (see

Green Party, p. 309) immortalized in various paintings by Degas and Manet. Samples of a legal but much less toxic (read: less fun) version of the supposedly psychedelic drink that van Gogh liked so much are on sale at the museum's small gift shop. (☎01 30 36 83 26. Open Mar. to mid-Sept. W-F 1:30-6pm and Sa-Su 11am-6pm; mid-Sept. to mid-Dec. Sa-Su 11am-6pm. €4.50, students €3.80, under 14 free.) Follow r. de Léry up to the Château d'Auvers, which houses a modest collection of engaging Impressionist paintings and also features a tranquil *orangerie*. (☎01 34 48 48 45; www.chateau-auvers.fr. Open Oct.-Mar. M-F 10:30am-4:30pm and Sa-Su 10:30am-5:30pm; Apr.-Sept. M-F 10:30am-6pm and Sa-Su 10:30am-6:30pm. Closed mid-Dec. to mid-Jan. €10.50, students and ages 6-18 €6.50, families €25.50.)

FOOD

Inexpensive cafes and *crêperies* can be found throughout the town, but visitors willing to splurge should experience the Auberge Ravoux ❹, 52, r. de Général-de-Gaulle (☎01 30 36 60 60), in all its historical glory. For the ultimate van Gogh experience, dine in style at the same *auberge* where the painter lived and died over 100 years ago. Elaborate glasswork, lace curtains, and old-fashioned wooden benches complement €28 two-course or €35 three-course *menus* of classic French dishes such as 7hr. leg of lamb, beef Bourguignon, and homemade *foie gras*. (Open W-F noon-3pm for lunch and 3-6pm (*salon de thé*); Sa-Su first lunch service noon and second lunch service 2:15pm. Serves dinner only to groups of 30-45; reservations required. Closed Nov.-Feb. AmEx/MC/V.)

DISNEYLAND RESORT PARIS

It's a small, small world, and Disney is hell-bent on making it even smaller. When EuroDisney opened on April 12, 1992, Mickey Mouse, Cinderella, and Snow White were met by the jeers of French intellectuals and the popular press, who called the Disney theme park a "cultural Chernobyl." Resistance seems to have subsided since Walt & Co. renamed it Disneyland Paris and started serving wine. Pre-construction press touted the complex as a vast entertainment and resort center covering an area one-fifth the size of Paris. In truth, the current theme park doesn't even measure the size of an *arrondissement*, though Disney owns (and may eventually develop) 600 hectares. But this Disney park is the most technologically advanced yet, and the special effects on some rides will blow you away. If you have bottomless pockets, indulging in one of the park's seven world-class

THE LOCAL STORY

OF BATHS AND BIDETS

Befuddled American tourists have found an array of uses for the mysterious porcelain fixture lurking near the sink in their Paris hotel room: an ice-bucket for chilling champagne, a home for their globe-trotting goldfish. Good thing Goldie has no short-term memory because he'd be pretty shocked to learn that his fishbowl was in fact a *bidet*, used for centuries to bathe Europeans' nether-regions.

The French are notorious for their lackadaisical attitude toward personal hygiene. While the stereotype is outdated, it's true that they don't hold showers (*douches*, in French) as sacred as super-sanitized Americans do. France uses the smallest amount of soap per capita in Europe, and in older Paris apartments the stand-up, curtained-off shower is a rare amenity. In a culture that considers it normal to go a few days without bathing, the *bidet* is an economical way to clean where it counts.

The word *bidet* comes from the French word for "pony." To saddle up, squat on the *bidet* with your front toward the fixture. Newer apparatuses have jets that squirt water upward, like a drinking fountain, but most use a simple faucet. *Bidets* should never be used as a toilet or—in Europe anyway—in place of toilet paper. Today, however, as modern plumbing gains prominence, many Parisians use their *bidets* for washing feet, babies, and delicate laundry.

hotels (like the palatial Disneyland Hotel—a "lavish Victorian fantasy") may be worth the extra euros. For the more frugal (and those with a low tolerance for toddlers), a daytrip will more than suffice.

⑦ PRACTICAL INFORMATION

Everything in Disneyland Paris is in English and French. The detailed park map is free from the entrance and around the park and contains not only a map, but also information on everything from restaurants and attractions to bathrooms and park safety. The *Guests' Special Services Guide* has info on wheelchair accessibility. For more info on Disneyland Paris, call ☎01 60 30 60 81 (from the US) or 01 60 30 63 53 from all other countries, or visit their website at www.disneylandparis.com.

Transportation: Take **RER A4** from either Ⓜ Gare de Lyon, Opéra (RER: Auber) or Châtelet-Les Halles (dir. Marne-la-Vallée) to the last stop, Ⓜ Marne-la-Vallée-Chessy. Before boarding the train, check the boards hanging above the platform to make sure there's a light next to the Marne-la-Vallée stop and not the Boissy-Saint-Leger stop (40min., departs every 30min., round-trip from Opéra-Auber €12.50). The last train to Paris leaves Disney at 12:20am, but the metro closes just before 1am, so you'll have to catch an earlier train to make it to the metro in time. **TGV** service from de Gaulle reaches the park in a mere 15min., making Disneyland Paris easily accessible for travelers with Eurail passes and international visitors. Certain **Eurostar** trains now run directly between Waterloo Station in London and Disneyland. (☎00 44 1233 617 575 from outside the UK, from within the UK 08705 186 186; www.eurostar.co.uk). Prices from around €70 return per person. Reserve far in advance. By **car,** take the A4 highway from Paris and get off at Exit 14, marked "Parcs Disney/Bailly-Romainvilliers" about 30min. from the city. Parking €8 per day; 11,000 spaces.

Tickets: Instead of selling tickets, Disneyland Paris issues **passeports,** valid for 1 day and available online and at the entrance. *Passeports* are also sold at Paris tourist office kiosks (see **Practical Information,** p. 116), FNAC, Virgin Megastores, any Disney Store, many hotels in Paris, or at any of the major stations on RER line A, such as Châtelet-Les Halles, Gare de Lyon, or Charles de Gaulle-Etoile. Any of these options beats buying tickets at the park, as ticket lines can be very long. Buy online in advance for the best deals at www.disneylandparis.com.

Admission: A 1-day ticket allows entry to either Disneyland Park or Walt Disney Studios. For around an extra €10, you can visit both theme parks. Apr.-Nov. €43, child €35. 2- and 3-day *passeports* also available (€95-114, child €78-94); days do not need to be consecutive. ▨**Fastpasses** allow guests to make reservations to ride attractions, shaving up to 45min. off of the wait for selected rides. Pick up your Fastpass from the Fastpass counters outside of each attraction.

Hours: Open July-Aug daily 9am-11pm; Sept.-May daily 10am-8pm; June M-F 10am-11pm, Sa-Su until 9pm.

⑥ SIGHTS

DISNEYLAND PARK. Divided into five areas, each filled to bursting with families, Disneyland Park showcases American cultural imperialism in action. Main Street, Frontierland, Adventureland, Fantasyland, and Discoveryland circle around the park's central plaza—a flowery garden in front of Sleeping Beauty Castle. "Main St., U.S.A." attempts to recreate "the charm of a small American town at the turn of the 20th century." Old-fashioned streetcars and the Main Street Railroad Station are employed in this venture. Each day at 4pm the **Disney Parade**—a parade of Disney characters marching to a loud fanfare of Disney tunes—takes place on Main St. Finally, at 11pm, Disney caps off the night with **fireworks.**

The park's main draws, of course, are its 45 **rides** and attractions. For children, slow-moving and colorful attractions like **Pinocchio's Fantastic Journey** (through a toyshop) and **Peter Pan's Flight** (through the Isle of Never Land) are perennial favorites. For guests seeking more action, or those simply hoping to feel nauseous, **Indiana Jones and the Temple of Peril** and **Space Mountain** are sure to thrill. The latter is the more modern and technologically savvy counterpart to Space Mountain at DisneyWorld (US). Passengers ride on a turbulent "rocket-powered" spaceship that loops, twists, drops, and climbs through complete darkness. If that doesn't scare you, check out **Phantom Manor**—a mansion haunted by 999 ghosts and witches. Visitors in wheelchairs should have someone to help transfer them to rides, as Disneyland employees are not permitted to do so.

WALT DISNEY STUDIOS. More technical than Disneyland Park, Walt Disney Studios features motor stunt shows (3 shows daily, times change; check the free map for details), an Armageddon special effects exhibit, and an entire building dedicated to the art of Disney animation. Coaster-enthusiasts fret not: the **Rock 'N' Roll Roller Coaster with Aerosmith** is a thrilling indoor coaster with loud music, strobe lights, and loops. Lines in Walt Disney studios are usually much smaller than those in its big-sister park, but with good reason: the thrills in this park are few and far between. It is mostly worth visiting as a later stop in a longer Disneyland trip. Each day at 10:30, 11:30am, 12:30, 2:30, 3:15, 4:15pm, children can enjoy an Animagique show with Mickey, Donald, and the rest of the gang. Daily cinema parades at 3:30pm.

APPENDIX

CLIMATE

While spring and autumn in Paris have been known to deliver unpredictable precipitation, temperatures throughout the year remain palatably moderate. Summer highs rarely rise above 80°F; winters, while often wet, hardly ever see temperatures colder than 30°F. From October through April, it may be a good idea to pack outerwear. In all seasons, remember comfortable rain gear.

Avg Temp (lo/hi), Precipitation	January			April			July			October		
	°C	°F	mm	°C	°F	mm	°C	°F	mm	°C	°F	mm
Paris	1/6	34/43	56	6/16	43/61	42	15/25	59/77	59	8/16	46/61	50
Versailles	1/6	34/43	56	6/14	43/57	42	14/24	58/75	59	8/15	46/59	50
Reims	-1/4	30/40	46	4/16	40/60	48	13/24	56/76	66	6/14	43/58	66

MEASUREMENTS

Paris (and the rest of France) uses the metric system. The basic metric unit of length is the **meter (m)**, which is divided into 100 **centimeters (cm)**, or 1000 **millimeters (mm)**. One thousand meters comprise one **kilometer (km)**. Fluids are measured in **liters (L)**, each divided into 1000 **millileters (ml)**. A liter of pure water weighs one **kilogram (kg)**, one-thousandth of which is a **gram (g)**. 1000 kilograms make a singe **metric ton.**

1 in. = 25.4mm	1mm = 0.039 in.
1 ft. = 0.30m	1m = 3.28 ft.
1 yd. = 0.914m	1m = 1.09 yd.
1 mi. = 1.61km	1km = 0.62 mi.
1 oz. = 28.35g	1g = 0.035 oz.
1 lb. = 0.454kg	1kg = 2.202 lb.
1 fl. oz. = 29.57ml	1ml = 0.034 fl. oz.
1 gal. = 3.785L	1L = 0.264 gal.

FRENCH PRONUNCIATION AND GRAMMAR

French pronunciation has been duping Anglophones since well before the Hundred Years' War. A few tricks, though, can decode some of the intricacies of this absurdly non-phonetic Romance language. Final **consonants** are often silent, but are always pronounced when followed by an E (e.g., *muet* is mew-AY but *muette* is mew-ET). The S at the end of a plural noun is silent. The letter H is rarely aspirated, the French CH sounds like *SH*, and J is pronounced like the S in "pleasure." Rs are perhaps the trickiest phoneme of anyone's French-learning experience, as they originate in the throat, with the tongue arched and blocking the nasal passage. C sounds like *K* if it precedes A, O, or U; it sounds like *S* if it precedes E or I. A ç always sounds like *S*. **Vowels** are pronounced precisely: A as the *O* in "mom"; E as in "help" (é becomes the a in "hay", è the ai in "air"); I as the *ee* in "creep"; *O* as in "oh." UI sounds like the word "whee." U is a short, clipped *oo* sound; hold your lips as if you were about to say "ooh," but say *ee* instead. OU sounds like *oo*. With few exceptions, all syllables in French words receive equal emphasis.

Le (pronounced like "look" without the K) is the masculine singular definite article (the); *la* is the feminine. Both are abbreviated to *l'* before a vowel, and *les* (pronounced "lay") is the plural definite article for both genders. Where a noun or adjective can take masculine and feminine forms, the masculine is listed first and the feminine in parentheses; often the feminine form consists of an additional "e" on the end of a word (e.g., étudiant(e)). In general, the plural is formed by adding an "s" to the singular form. *Tu* is the familiar form of second-person address, and *vous* serves as both the plural and the formal singular forms. *Vous* should always be used to address strangers, authority figures, and older people; *tu* is traditionally used only for close friends and family, although it is now frequently used among young people.

FRENCH PHRASEBOOK

ENGLISH	FRENCH	PRONUNCIATION
THE BASICS		
Hello/Good day	Bonjour	bohn-ZHOOR
Good evening	Bon soir	bohn-SWAH
Hi!	Salut!	SAH-LU
Goodbye	Au revoir	oh ruh-VWAH
Good night	Bonne nuit	buhn NWEE
Yes/No/Maybe	Oui/Non/Peut-être	wee/nohn/p'TET-ruh
Please	S'il vous plaît	see voo PLAY
Thank you	Merci	mehr-SEE
You're welcome	De rien/je vous en prie	duh rhee-AHN/zh'VOOS on PREE
There you go!	Voilà!	vwah-LAH
Pardon me!	Excusez-moi!	ex-KU-zay-MWAH
Go away!	Allez-vous en!	ah-lay vooz AHN
What time do you open/close?	Vous ouvrez/fermez à quelle heure?	vooz ooVRAY/ferhMAY ah kel-UHR
Help!	Au secours!	oh-skOOR
I'm lost (m/f).	Je suis perdu(e).	zh'SWEE pehr-DU
I'm sorry (m/f).	Je suis désolé(e).	zh'SWEE day-zoh-LAY
Do you speak English?	Parlez-vous anglais?	PAR-lay-voo ahn-GLAY

JUST BEYOND THE BASICS			
Who?	Qui?	No, thank you.	Non, merci.
What?	Quoi?	What is it?	Qu'est-ce que c'est?
When?	Quand?	this one/that one	ceci/cela
How?	Comment?	Stop/Stop that!	Arrête! (familiar) Arrêtez! (polite)
Why?	Pourquoi?	Please repeat.	Répétez, s'il vous plaît.
I don't understand.	Je ne comprends pas.	How do you say ( ) in French?	Comment dit-on ( ) en Français?

Leave me alone.	Laissez-moi tranquille.	**I am a student (m/f).**	Je suis étudiant/étudi-ante.
How much does this cost?	Ça coûte combien?	**Please, where is ...?**	S'il vous plaît, où se trouve...?
Please speak slowly.	S'il vous plaît, parlez moins vite.	**...an ATM?**	...un distributeur d'argent?
Please help me.	Aidez-moi, s'il vous plaît.	**...the bathroom?**	...les toilettes?
I am (20) years old.	J'ai (vingt) ans.	**...the train station?**	...la gare?
What is your name?	Comment vous appelez-vous?	**...the beef?**	...le boeuf?

EMERGENCY			
Where is the nearest hospital?	Où est l'hôpital le plus proche?	**Someone pick-pock-eted me!**	J'ai été victime d'un pickpocket!
It's an emergency!	C'est urgent!	**Someone raped me (m/f).**	J'étais violé(e).
Where is the nearest emergency pharmacy?	Où est la pharmacie de garde la plus proche?	**Someone stole...**	Quelqu'un ma volé...
Where is the police station?	Où est la station de police?	**...my camera.**	...mon appareil photo.
I am ill/I am hurt (m/f).	Je suis malade/Je suis blessé(e).	**...my purse.**	...mon sac.
I think I broke my leg.	Je pense que j'ai cassé une jambe.	**...my wallet.**	...ma portefeuille.
My friend has gone mad.	Mon ami(e) est dev-enu(e) fou/folle.	**...my weasel.**	...ma belette.

DIRECTIONS			
(to the) right	(à) droite	**south**	sud
(to the) left	(à) gauche	**east**	est
straight	tout droit	**west**	ouest
near to/far from	près de/loin de	**north**	nord

NUMBERS			
one	un	**ten**	dix
two	deux	**fifteen**	quinze
three	trois	**twenty**	vingt
four	quatre	**twenty-five**	vingt-cinq
five	cinq	**thirty**	trente
six	six	**forty**	quarante
seven	sept	**fifty**	cinquante
eight	huit	**hundred**	cent
nine	neuf	**thousand**	mille

TIMES AND HOURS			
What time is it?	Quelle heure est-il?	**today**	aujourd'hui
It's (11) o'clock.	Il est (onze) heures.	**tomorrow**	demain
open (m/f)	ouvert(e)	**yesterday**	hier
closed (m/f)	fermé(e)	**until**	jusqu'à
January	janvier	**public holidays**	jours fériés (j.f.)
February	fevrier	**morning**	le matin
March	mars	**afternoon**	l'après-midi
April	avril	**evening**	le soir
May	mai	**night**	la nuit
June	juin	**Monday**	lundi

July	juillet	**Tuesday**	mardi
August	août	**Wednesday**	mercredi
September	septembre	**Thursday**	jeudi
October	octobre	**Friday**	vendredi
November	novembre	**Saturday**	samedi
December	décembre	**Sunday**	dimanche

COMMON SIGNS			
sortie de secours	emergency exit	**complet**	no vacancy
voie sans issue	dead end	**en panne**	out of order
pelouse interdite	stay off the grass	**entrée interdite**	stay out
à emporter	to go/takeout	**stationnement interdit**	no parking

SIGHTSEEING			
vieille ville	old town	**Quel dommage que tu n'aies qu'un guide Lonely Planet.**	What a shame you only have a Lonely Planet guide.
visite guidée	guided tour	**appareil photo**	camera
Y a-t-il une visite guidée en anglais?	Is there a guided tour in English?	**Pourriez-vous nous prendre une photo?**	Could you take our picture?

PLANES, TRAINS, AND AUTOMOBILES			
gare SNCF	train station	**faire la correspon-dence**	transfer (between subway lines, trains, or flights)
gare routière	bus station	**billet aller simple**	one-way ticket
arrêt de taxi	taxi stand	**billet aller-retour**	round-trip ticket

PLANES			
vol	flight	**enregistrer les bagages**	check baggage
place côté fenêtre/côté couloir	window/aisle seat	**Dois-je enregistrer ceci?**	Do I have to check this?

TRAINS			
TGV	high speed train	**guichet**	ticket window
composter la billet	validate a ticket	**quai**	platform
consigne	luggage locker	**voie**	track
faire la correspon-dence	transfer between lines	**À quelle heure part le train?**	What time does the train leave?

AUTOMOBILES			
voiture	car	**car**	coach bus
bus	city bus	**autoroute**	highway
essence (sans plomb/diesel)	gasoline (unleaded/diesel)	**limite de vitesse**	speed limit
boîte de vitesse automatique/man-uelle	automatic/manual transmission	**citation**	speeding ticket
station de service	gas station	**Je n'amène que des stoppeurs mignons/mignonnes.**	I only pick up cute hitchhikers.
thermes	hot springs	**forêt**	forest

ARCHITECTURAL TERMS			
abbaye	abbey	**haute-ville**	upper town
basse-ville	lower town	**hôtel particulier**	town house, mansion
cave	cellar, often for wine	**hôtel de ville**	city hall

centre-ville	center of town	monastère	monastery
chapelle	chapel	mur	wall
château	castle, mansion, or headquarters of a vineyard	palais	palace
cimitière	cemetery	parc	park
cité	walled city	place	town square
clocher	church tower	pont	bridge
cloître	cloister	quartier	neighborhood, section of town
couvent	convent	tour	tower
église	church	vielle-ville	old town
fontaine	fountain	vitraux	stained-glass windows

À L'HÔTEL (AT THE HOTEL)			
a bedroom with...	une chambre avec...	single/double room	une chambre simple/ double
...a double bed	...un grand lit	room on the street/on the courtyard	une chambre sur la rue/ sur la cour
...two single beds	...deux lits	Breakfast is included.	Le petit déjeuner est compris.
...a shower	...une douche	Where is the youth hostel?	Où est l'auberge de jeunesse?
...a bath tub	...bains	May I see the room?	Puis-je voir la chambre?
bed and breakfast	chambre d'hôte	country home	gîte

AU CAFÉ, AU RESTAURANT (AT A CAFE, AT A RESTAURANT)			
I would like...	Je voudrais...	The check, please.	L'addition, s'il vous plaît.
What is this?	Qu'est que c'est que ceci?	I'm a vegetarian (m/f).	Je suis végétarien(ne).
Do you have kosher food?	Avez-vous des plats kashers?	I'm a vegan (m/f).	Je suis végétalien(ne).
Is service included?	Est-ce que le service est compris?	I really need a whisky right now.	Il me faut un whiskey tout de suite.

BOISSONS (DRINKS)			
café (crème/au lait)	coffee (with cream/ milk)	vin rouge/blanc	red/white wine
chocolat chaud	hot chocolate	bière	beer
thé	tea	carafe d'eau	pitcher of water
eau platte/gazeuse	flat/sparkling water	une bouteille de champagne exquisite	a bottle of exquisite champagne

VIANDE (MEAT)			
agneau	lamb	faux-filet	sirloin steak
andouillette	tripe sausage	foie gras d'oie/de canard	liver pâté of goose/duck
bavette	flank (cut of meat)	jambon	ham
boeuf	beef	lapin	rabbit
brochette	kebab	poulet	chicken
canard	duck	rillettes	meat hash (usually pork or rabbit)
cervelles	brains	steak...	a steak
côte	rib or chop (cut of meat)	...saignant	...rare
coq au vin	rooster stewed in wine	...à point	...medium
dinde	turkey	...bien cuit	...well done

entrecôte	chop (cut of meat)	**steak tartare**	raw steak mixed with raw egg
escalope	thin slice of meat	**veau**	veal
saucisson	sausage	**cuisses de grenouilles**	frog legs
FRUITS DE MER (SEAFOOD)			
poisson	fish	**homard**	lobster
coquilles st-jacques	scallops	**huîtres**	oysters
crevettes	shrimp	**moules**	mussels
escargots	snail	**thon**	tuna
FRUITS ET LÉGUMES (FRUITS AND VEGETABLES)			
ananas	pineapple	**figue**	fig
asperges	asparagus	**fraise**	strawberry
aubergine	eggplant	**framboise**	raspberry
champignons	mushrooms	**haricots verts**	green beans
citron	lemon	**petits pois**	peas
citron vert	lime	**poire**	pear
choufleur	cauliflower	**poireaux**	leeks
compote	stewed fruit	**pomme**	apple
cornichon	pickle	**pomme de terre**	potato
épinards	spinach	**raisins**	grapes
PAIN (BREAD)			
baguette	baguette	**pain au chocolat**	chocolate-filled pastry
brioche	light, buttery roll	**feuilleté**	puff pastry
gaufre	waffle	**galette**	savory dinner crêpe
OTHER			
oeuf	egg	**crème Chantilly**	whipped cream
l'ail	garlic	**crème fraiche**	thick cream
le beurre	butter	**froid**	cold
chaud	hot	**la moutarde**	mustard
le sel	salt	**le poivre**	pepper
AU BAR (AT THE BAR)			
Puis-je t'acheter un demi?	Can I buy you a beer?	**Dis donc, quel est ton numéro?**	So, what's your number?
Mon copain/ma copine m'attend dehors.	My boyfriend/girlfriend is waiting for me outside.	**Qu'est-ce que tu feras avec tous ces déchets?**	What are you going to do with all that junk?

MAP LEGEND

- ✚ Hospital
- ✪ Police
- ✉ Post Office
- ⓘ Tourist Office
- $ Bank
- ⚑ Embassy/Consulate
- ■ Sight or Point of Interest
- ☎ Telephone Office
- ♨ Theater

- ✈ Airport
- 🚌 Bus Station
- 🚂 Train Station
- Ⓜ METRO Station
- ▬ METRO Line
- RER RER Station
- 🚻 Public Restroom
- ✝ Church
- ✡ Synagogue

- 🕌 Mosque
- ♜ Castle
- 🏛 Museum
- ⛫ Arch
- ⌂ Hotel/Hostel
- 🍴 Food & Drink
- 🛍 Shopping
- ★ Nightlife
- 💻 Internet Café

- ▦▦▦ Pedestrian Zone / Steps
- Park
- Water
- Forest
- The Let's Go compass always points NORTH.

Paris: Overview and Arrondissements

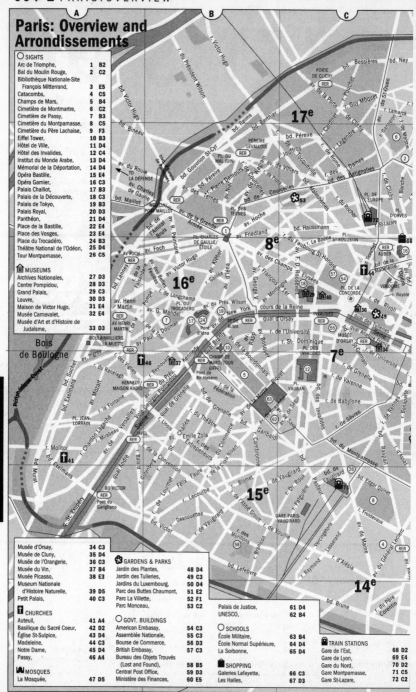

APPENDIX

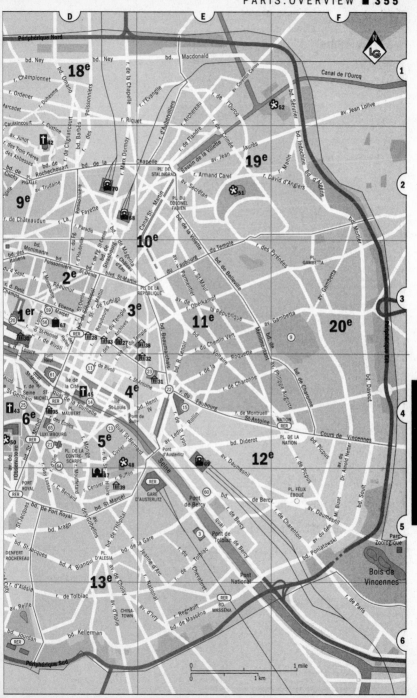

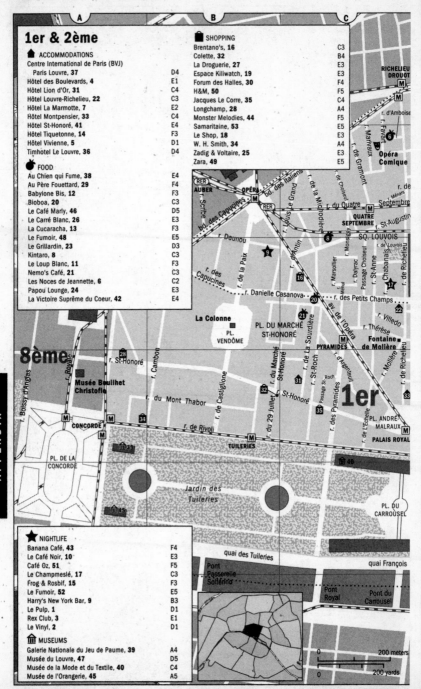

1er & 2ème

🏠 ACCOMMODATIONS

Centre International de Paris (BVJ) Paris Louvre, 37	D4
Hôtel des Boulevards, 4	E1
Hôtel Lion d'Or, 31	C4
Hôtel Louvre-Richelieu, 22	C3
Hôtel La Marmotte, 7	E2
Hôtel Montpensier, 33	C4
Hôtel St-Honoré, 41	E4
Hôtel Tiquetonne, 14	F3
Hôtel Vivienne, 5	D1
Timhotel Le Louvre, 36	D4

🍎 FOOD

Au Chien qui Fume, 38	E4
Au Père Fouettard, 29	F4
Babylone Bis, 12	F3
Bioboa, 20	C3
Le Café Marly, 46	D5
Le Carré Blanc, 26	E3
La Cucaracha, 13	F3
Le Fumoir, 48	E5
Le Grillardin, 23	D3
Kintaro, 8	C3
Le Loup Blanc, 11	F3
Nemo's Café, 21	C3
Les Noces de Jeannette, 6	C2
Papou Lounge, 24	E3
La Victoire Suprême du Coeur, 42	E4

🛍 SHOPPING

Brentano's, 16	C3
Colette, 32	B4
La Droguerie, 27	E3
Espace Kiliwatch, 19	E3
Forum des Halles, 30	F4
H&M, 50	F5
Jacques Le Corre, 35	C4
Longchamp, 28	A4
Monster Melodies, 44	F5
Samaritaine, 53	E5
Le Shop, 18	E3
W. H. Smith, 34	A4
Zadig & Voltaire, 25	E3
Zara, 49	E5

★ NIGHTLIFE

Banana Café, 43	F4
Le Café Noir, 10	E3
Café Oz, 51	F5
Le Champmeslé, 17	C3
Frog & Rosbif, 15	F3
Le Fumoir, 52	E5
Harry's New York Bar, 9	B3
Le Pulp, 1	D1
Rex Club, 3	E1
Le Vinyl, 2	D1

🏛 MUSEUMS

Galerie Nationale du Jeu de Paume, 39	A4
Musée du Louvre, 47	D5
Musée de la Mode et du Textile, 40	C4
Musée de l'Orangerie, 45	A5

8ème

1er

RICHELIEU DROUOT

Opéra Comique

r. d'Amboise

r. Favart

Marivaux

r. de Gramont

AUBER

RER

OPÉRA

bd. des Italiens

Louis Le Grand

de la Michodière

de Choiseul

r. du Quatre Septembre

Ménars

r. de Septembre

QUATRE SEPTEMBRE

RER

r. St-Augustin

SQ. LOUVOIS

r. de Louvois

Chabanais

r. de Richelieu

r. Scribe

bd. des Capucines

r. Daunou

d'Antin

Marsollier

Monsigny

Méhul

r. Dalayrac

Passage Choiseul

r. St-Anne

r. de la Paix

r. des Capucines

r. Danielle Casanova

r. des Petits Champs

r. Villedo

r. Thérèse

Fontaine de Molière

r. Molière

r. de Richelieu

La Colonne

PL. VENDÔME

PL. DU MARCHÉ ST-HONORÉ

r. de la Sourdière

av. de l'Opéra

PYRAMIDES

r. Royale

r. St-Honoré

r. Cambon

r. du Marché St-Honoré

r. St-Roch

r. d'Argenteuil

r. de Richelieu

Musée Bouilhet Christofle

r. du Mont Thabor

r. de Castiglione

St-Honoré

Passage St. Roch

r. des Pyramides

PL. ANDRÉ MALRAUX

r. de l'Echelle

PALAIS ROYAL

CONCORDE

r. Boissy d'Anglas

r. du 29 Juillet

r. de Rivoli

TUILERIES

PL. DE LA CONCORDE

Jardin des Tuileries

PL. DU CARROUSEL

quai des Tuileries

quai François

Pont Passerelle Solférino

Pont Royal

Pont du Carrousel

	0	200 meters
	0	200 yards

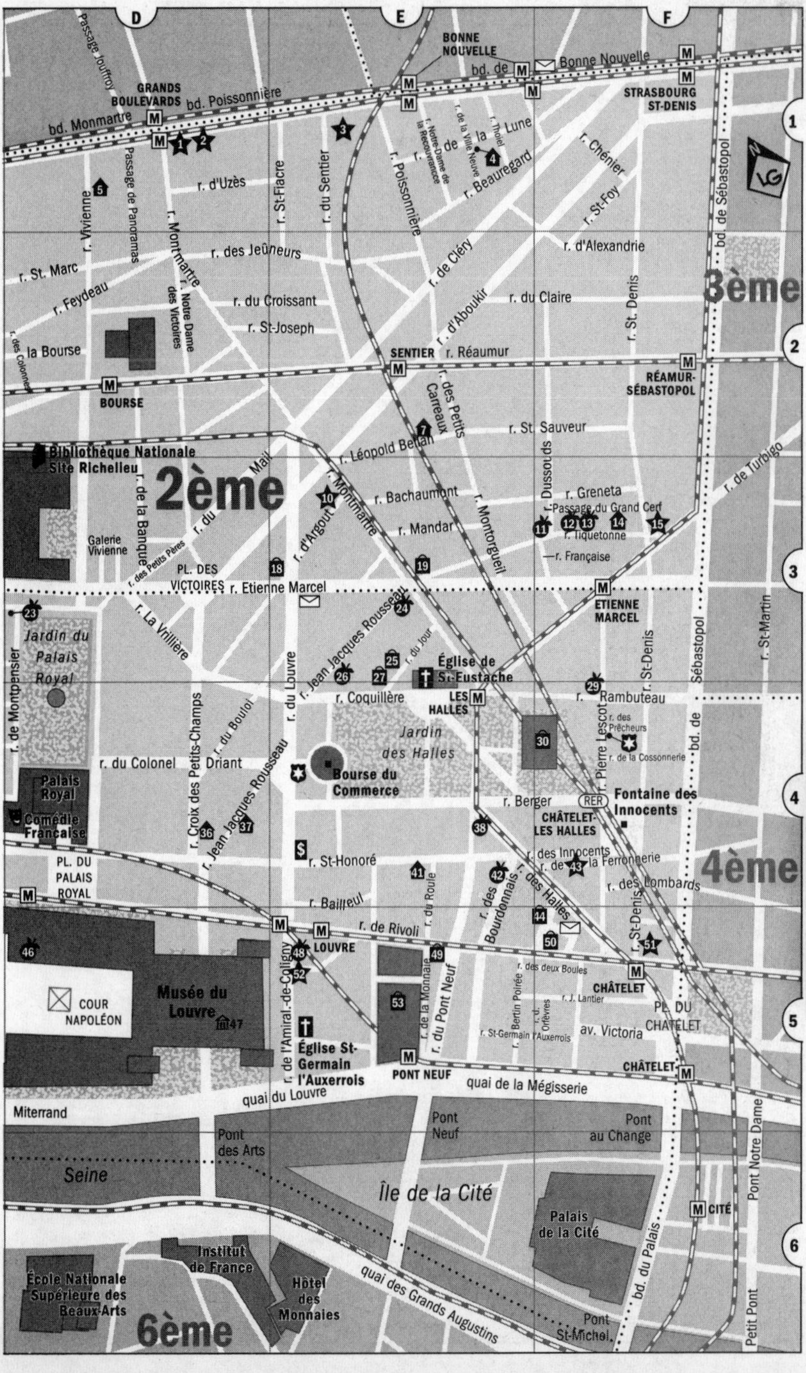
D
E
F
1
2
3
4
5
6
Passage Jouffroy
GRANDS BOULEVARDS
bd. Monmartre
bd. Poissonnière
BONNE NOUVELLE
bd. de
Bonne Nouvelle
STRASBOURG ST-DENIS
r. Notre-Dame de la Recouvrance
r. de la Ville Neuve
r. Thorel
r. de la Lune
r. Beauregard
r. Chénier
r. St-Foy
r. d'Alexandrie
r. d'Uzès
Passage de Panoramas
r. Vivienne
r. Montmartre
r. St-Fiacre
r. du Sentier
r. Poissonnière
r. de Cléry
r. des Jeûneurs
r. St. Marc
r. Feydeau
r. Notre Dame des Victoires
r. du Croissant
r. St-Joseph
r. d'Aboukir
r. du Claire
r. St. Denis
bd. de Sébastopol
3ème
r. des Colonnes
la Bourse
BOURSE
SENTIER
r. Réaumur
RÉAMUR-SÉBASTOPOL
r. des Petits Carreaux
r. St. Sauveur
Bibliothèque Nationale Site Richelieu
2ème
r. de la Banque
r. du Mail
r. Léopold Bellan
r. Montmartre
r. Bachaumont
r. Dussouds
r. Greneta
Passage du Grand Cerf
r. Tiquetonne
r. Française
r. de Turbigo
r. Mandar
r. d'Argout
r. Montorgueil
Galerie Vivienne
r. des Petits Pères
PL. DES VICTOIRES
r. Etienne Marcel
ETIENNE MARCEL
Jardin du Palais Royal
r. La Vrillière
r. Jean Jacques Rousseau
r. du Jour
Église de St-Eustache
r. St-Denis
Sébastopol
r. St-Martin
r. de Montpensier
r. du Louvre
r. Coquillère
LES HALLES
r. Rambuteau
r. Croix des Petits-Champs
r. du Bouloi
Jardin des Halles
r. Pierre Lescot
r. des Prêcheurs
r. de la Cossonnerie
bd. de
r. du Colonel Driant
Bourse du Commerce
Palais Royal
Comédie Française
r. Berger
RER
Fontaine des Innocents
CHÂTELET-LES HALLES
APPENDIX
r. des Innocents
r. de la Ferronnerie
r. St-Honoré
4ème
PL. DU PALAIS ROYAL
r. des Lombards
r. Bailleul
r. du Roule
r. des Bourdonnais
r. des Halles
r. de Rivoli
LOUVRE
r. de l'Amiral-de-Coligny
r. de la Monnaie
r. du Pont Neuf
r. des deux Boules
CHÂTELET
COUR NAPOLÉON
Musée du Louvre
r. J. Lantier
r. Bertin Poirée
r. d. Orfèvres
PL. DU CHÂTELET
r. St-Germain l'Auxerrois
av. Victoria
Église St-Germain l'Auxerrois
PONT NEUF
CHÂTELET
quai du Louvre
quai de la Mégisserie
Miterrand
Pont Neuf
Pont au Change
Pont Notre Dame
Pont des Arts
Seine
Île de la Cité
CITÉ
Palais de la Cité
Institut de France
École Nationale Supérieure des Beaux-Arts
Hôtel des Monnaies
quai des Grands Augustins
bd. du Palais
Pont St-Michel
Petit Pont
6ème

APPENDIX

APPENDIX

3ème & 4ème
see key p. 360

10ème

11ème

3ème

200 meters
200 yards

PARMENTIER
OBERKAMPF
RÉPUBLIQUE
TEMPLE
RÉAUMUR-SÉBASTOPOL
ARTS ET MÉTIERS
FILLES DU CALVAIRE
ST-SÉBASTIEN FROISSART
RICHARD LENOIR
ST-AMBROISE
CHEMIN VERT
RAMBUTEAU

bd. Richard Lenoir
BRÉGUET SABIN
r. du Chemin Vert
r. de la Folie Méricourt
r. Oberkampf
ST-AMBROISE
r. Amelot
r. St-Sébastien
bd. Beaumarchais
bd. des Filles du Calvaire
des Arquebusiers
r. St-Claude
r. St-Gilles
Villehardouin
r. St-Gilles
Église St-Denis du St-Sacrement
r. de Turenne
r. du Parc Royale
vigne
r. Elzévir
enne
Hôtel Salé
r. Ste-Anastase
r. du Roi Doré
r. Debelleyme
r. de Thorigny
Hôtel Libéral Bruant
des Coutures St-Gervais
r. de la Perle
r. Vieille du Temple
r. Barbette
Hôtel de Rohan
Hôtel de la Tour du Pin
Archives Nationales
r. des Archives
r. des-4-Fils
r. des Haudriettes
r. de Braque
Pecquay
Passage Ste-Avoie
r. Rambuteau
Imp. Berthaud
r. Michel Le Comte
r. Beaubourg
r. de Montmorency
r. du Grenier St-Lazare
r. Brantôme
r. aux Ours
r. St-Martin
r. Quincampoix
r. Molière
bd. de Sébastopol
r. du Bourg l'Abbé
r. de Turbigo
Grételle
r. Réaumur
SQ. ÉMILE CHAUTEMPS
Conservatoire Nationale des Arts et Métiers
r. St-Martin
r. Vaucanson
r. Conté
r. Montgolfier
r. du Vertbois
r. Volta
r. Notre Dame de Nazareth
r. Meslay
bd. St-Martin
r. Bona
r. des Gravilliers
r. au Maire
r. des Vertus
ap. Rome
r. Chapon
r. des Fontaines
du Temple
r. Portefoin
r. Pastourelle
r. Charlot
r. Perrée
r. de Bretagne
r. Dupetit Thouars
r. Dubois
Vicaire
r. Dupetit Thouars
SQ. DU TEMPLE
r. Spurlier
r. de la Corderie
Gourdes
r. Béranger
r. du Temple
bd. du Temple
bd. Voltaire
av. de la République
pl. de la République
l. Turenne
r. de Picardie
r. de Beauce
r. de Caffarelli
r. de Saintonge
r. de Normandie
Froissart
Commines
du Pont aux Choux
r. de Poitou
Elzache Comte
PL. DE LA RÉPUBLIQUE
RÉPUBLIQUE

Port de l'Arsenal

bd. Bourdon

PL. DE LA BASTILLE

Colonne de Juillet

BASTILLE

r. Jean Beausire

r. St-Antoine

r. Castex

r. de la Cerisaie

r. de Schomberg

r. de Sully

bd. Morland

r. Crillon

r. Mornay

quai Henri IV

Seine

Pavillon de l'Arsenal

Tournelles

r. Roger Verlomme

PL. DES VOSGES

r. de Turenne

r. du Pas-de-la-Mule

r. de Béarn

r. des Minimes

r. du Foin

Hôtel de Sully

r. Necker

bd. Henri IV

r. du Petit Musc

r. Beautreillis

17 r. Beautreillis

r. St-Paul

r. des Lions St-Paul

r. Charles v

4ème

Pont de Sully

SULLY MORLAND

Institut du Monde Arabe

Hôtel Carnavalet

Hôtel de Lamoignon

r. de Sévigné

r. d'Ormesson

PL. DU MARCHÉ STE-CATHERINE

Église St Paul-St-Louis

r. de Jarente

r. St-Paul

r. Charlemagne

r. de l'Ave Maria

quai des Célestins

Voie G. Pompidou

Église St-Louis en l'Île

Pont Marie

quai d'Anjou

Pont de Sully

r. Malher

ST-PAUL

r. Pavée

r. du Prévôt

r. du Fauconnier

r. du Figuier

Hôtel de Sens

quai de Béthune

Pont de la Tournelle

Île St-Louis

r. des Rosiers

r. des Hospitaliers St-Gervais

r. des Écouffes

r. du Roi de Sicile

Duval

r. du Bourg Tibourg

PONT MARIE

r. de l'Hôtel de Ville

Hôtel de Ville

La Maison Européenne de la Photographie

r. Geoffroy l'Asnier

quai de l'Hôtel de Ville

quai de Bourbon

quai d'Orléans

Île St-Louis

quai de la Tournelle

Hôtel Hérovet

r. des Francs-Bourgeois

r. Vieille du Temple

r. des Guillemites

r. du Trésor

Hôtel de Beauvais

r. François Miron

r. des Barres

Mémorial du Martyr Juif Inconnu

Voie G. Pompidou

r. des Deux Ponts

Pont St-Louis

Pont de la Tournelle

Pont Louis Philippe

Musée de l'Assistance Publique

r. des Blancs Manteaux

r. du Platre

r. Ste-Croix de la Bretonnerie

r. des Archives

r. de Moussy

r. des Mauvais Garçons

PL. BAUDOYER

Église St-Gervais-St-Protais

PL. ST. GERVAIS

r. de Rivoli

Pont Louis Philippe

Île de la Cité

Notre Dame

r. des Guillemites

r. de la Verrerie

r. du Renard

Hôtel de Ville

HÔTEL DE VILLE

PL. DE L'HÔTEL DE VILLE

quai de l'Hôtel de Ville

Pont d'Arcole

Pont Notre Dame

Île de la Cité

quai de Montebello

quai de la Tournelle

r. Simon LeFranc

r. St-Merri

r. du Temple

r. de la Coutellerie

av. Victoria

Théâtre de la Ville

r. de la Ville

Pont d'Arcole

Cloître Notre Dame

r. St-Jacques

Beaubourg

Centre Pompidou

PL. IGOR STRAVINSKY

Église St-Merri

St-Bon

St-Martin

av. Victoria

quai de Gesvres

Pont au Change

r. de la Cité

r. St-Jacques

bd. de Sébastopol

PL. E. MICHELET

r. du Cloître-de-St-Merri

r. des Lombards

PL. DU CHÂTELET

Pont au Change

bd. du Palais

r. de Lutèce

Tour St-Jacques

Châtelet Central Nightbus Hub

CHÂTELET

CITÉ

ST-MICHEL RER

ST-MICHEL

APPENDIX

3ème & 4ème
see map p. 358-359

🏠 ACCOMMODATIONS

Castex Hôtel, **95**	F5
Le Fauconnier, **94**	D5
Le Fourcy, **92**	D5
Grand Hôtel Jeanne d'Arc, **84**	E4
Hôtel Andréa Rivoli, **45**	A4
Hôtel Bellevue et du Chariot d'Or, **5**	A2
Hôtel de la Herse d'Or, **88**	F4
Hôtel du Marais, **11**	C2
Hôtel de Nice, **69**	C4
Hôtel Paris France, **2**	B2
Hôtel Picard, **10**	D2
Hôtel Pratic, **83**	D4
Hôtel Rivoli, **67**	C4
Hôtel de Roubaix, **4**	A2
Hôtel du Séjour, **17**	B3
Maubuisson, **93**	C5
Sully Hôtel, **86**	E4

🍎 FOOD

404, **7**	A2
L'Apparement Café, **21**	D3
Les Arts et Métiers, **3**	B2
L'Às du Falafel, **60**	D4
Au Petit Fer à Cheval, **63**	C4
Bistrot du Dome, **89**	F4
Café Beaubourg, **40**	A4
Caves St-Gilles, **29**	E3
Chez Janou, **38**	E4
Chez Omar, **9**	C2
La Cure Gourmande, **42**	A4
Curieux Spaghetti Bar, **46**	B4
Le Divin, **49**	B4
L'Estaminet, **12**	C2
Georges, **39**	A4
Le Grizzli, **44**	A4
Izrael, **91**	C5
Jadis et Gourmande, **32**	B3
Little Italy Trattoria, **31**	B3
Mariage Frères, **61**	C4
Pain, Vin, Fromage, **30**	B3
Petit Bofinger, **90**	F4
Le Petit Pamphlet, **28**	E3
Piccolo Teatro, **75**	C4
Le Réconfort, **14**	D3
Taxi Jaune, **13**	B3

⭐ NIGHTLIFE

3W Kafé, **73**	C4
Amnésia Café, **58**	C4
Andy Wahloo, **6**	A2
L'Apparement Café, **22**	D3
Au Petit Fer à Cheval, **64**	C4
La Belle Hortense, **70**	C4
Bliss Kfé, **76**	D4
Le Café du Trésor, **71**	C4
Le Carré, **48**	B4

Chez Richard, **56**	C4
Le Connétable, **20**	C3
Cox, **50**	B4
Le Dépôt, **16**	A3
Le Duplex, **18**	B3
L'Enchanteur, **19**	B3
Les Etages, **57**	C4
Lizard Lounge, **68**	C4
Mixer Bar, **52**	B4
Okawa, **59**	C4
Open Café, **51**	B4
Le Quetzal, **66**	B4
Raidd Bar, **47**	B4
Stolly's, **72**	C4
Le Tango, **8**	B2
L'Unity, **23**	A3
Villa Keops, **15**	A3
Wine and Bubbles, **43**	A4

🛍 SHOPPING

Abou d'abi Bazar, **36**	E4
Alternatives, **77**	D4
Bel ' Air, **79**	D4
BHV, **65**	B4
Boy'z Bazaar, **62**	C4
Brontibay, **82**	D4
Culotte, **80**	D4
Fabien Nobile, **74**	D4
Free 'P' Star, **54**	C4
IEM, **53**	C4
Loft Design By, **81**	D4
Monic, **37**	E4
Les Mots à la Bouche, **55**	C4
Tati, **1**	C1
Tokyoite, **78**	D4
Vertiges, **41**	A4

🏛 MUSEUMS

Centre Pompidou, **33**	A4
Maison de Victor Hugo, **87**	E4
Musée d'Art et d'Histoire du Judaïsme, **26**	B3
Musée Carnavalet, **35**	D4
Musée Cognacq-Jay, **34**	D4
Musée de l'Histoire de France, **27**	C3
Musée de Jeu de Paume, **85**	E4
Musée Picasso, **25**	D3
Musée de la Poupée, **24**	B3

APPENDIX

5ème, 6ème, & Islands (see map p. 362-363)

♠ ACCOMMODATIONS

Centre International de Paris (BVJ) Paris Quartier Latin, **73**	D3
Delhy's Hôtel, **23**	C2
Foyer International des Etudiantes, **92**	C5
Hôtel des Argonauts, **25**	C2
Hôtel le Central, **76**	D3
Hôtel de Chevreuse, **98**	B6
Hôtel Esmerelda, **27**	C2
Hôtel Gay-Lussac, **90**	C5
Hôtel du Lys, **38**	C3
Hôtel Marignan, **67**	C3
Hôtel des Médicis, **88**	C4
Hôtel de Nesle, **20**	B2
Hôtel St-André des Arts, **36**	B2
Hôtel St-Jacques, **69**	D3
Hôtel Stella, **63**	B3
Young and Happy Hostel, **91**	D5

🍎 FOOD

Au Port Salut, **86**	C4
Le Bistro Ernest, **19**	A2
Le Bistro d'Henri, **51**	A3
Café Delmas, **84**	D4
Café de Flore, **40**	A3
Café de la Mosquée, **89**	E4
Café Vavin, **95**	A6
Chez Henri, **72**	D3
Comptoir Méditerranée, **77**	D3
Così, **35**	A2
La Crêpe Rit du Clown, **50**	A3
Crêperie Saint Germain, **22**	B2
Les Deux Magots, **41**	A3
Les Editeurs, **55**	B3
Le Grenier de Notre-Dame, **30**	D2
Guen-Maï, **34**	A2
Le Jardin des Pâtes, **85**	E4
Le Machon d'Henri, **54**	A3
Octave, **93**	E5
Le Perraudin, **82**	C4
Le Petit Vatel, **59**	B3
Le Procope, **37**	B2
Le "Relais de L'Entrecôte," **32**	A2
Savannah Café, **83**	D4
Le Sélect, **97**	A6

⭐ NIGHTLIFE

Le 10 Bar, **62**	B3
Bob Cool, **21**	B2
Café Mabillon, **42**	A3
Le Caveau des Oubliettes, **29**	C2
Chez Georges, **48**	A3
Finnegan's Wake, **78**	E3
Fu Bar, **61**	B3
The Moose, **60**	B3
Le Piano Vache, **75**	D3
Le Reflet, **65**	C3
Le Rive Gauche, **44**	A3
Le Who's Bar, **28**	C2

🛍 SHOPPING

Abbey Bookshop, **39**	C2
agnès b., **52**	A3
Bill Tornade, **45**	A3
Cacharel, **53**	A3
Crocodisc, **68**	C3
Free Lance, **46**	A3
Gibert Jeune, **24**	C2
Gibert Joseph, **64**	C3
L'Harmattan, **74**	D3
Moloko, **79**	A4
Muji, **57**	B3
No Name, **47**	A3
Om Kashi, **71**	D3
Petit Bateau, **94**	A6
Présence Africaine, **70**	D3
San Francisco Book Co., **56**	B3
Shakespeare and Co., **26**	C2
Tara Jarmon, **43**	A3
Tea and Tattered Pages, **80**	A4
Vanessa Bruno, **58**	B3
The Village Voice, **49**	A3

🏛 MUSEUMS

Institut du Monde Arabe, **31**	E2
Musée de Cluny, **66**	C3
Musée Delacroix, **33**	A2
Musée d'Histoire Naturelle, **87**	F4
Musée du Luxembourg, **81**	B4
Musée de la Monnaie, **18**	B2
Musée Zadkine, **96**	B6

Islands

♠ ACCOMMODATIONS

Hôtel Henri IV, **2**	B1

🍎 FOOD

Amorino, **13**	D3
Au Rendez-Vous des Camionneurs, **1**	B1
Auberge de la Reine Blanche, **16**	E2
Berthillon, **15**	E2
Brasserie de l'Île St-Louis, **4**	B1
Café Med, **9**	D2
Le Caveau du Palais, **6**	D1
L'Épicerie, **11**	D2
Les Fous de l'Île, **14**	E1
La Petite Scierie, **12**	D1
Place Numéro Thé, **3**	B1

🛍 SHOPPING

Le Grain de Sable, **8**	D2
Le Marche aux Fleurs, **5**	C1
Pylônes, **10**	D2
Sobral, **7**	D2

🏛 MUSEUMS

Musée Adam Mickiewicz, **17**	E2

A   B   C

1er

Palais du Louvre

PONT NEUF

CHÂTELET Ⓜ

Quai du Louvre

Pont du Carrousel

Pont des Arts

Pont au Change

Pont Notre Dame

SQ. DU VERT GALANT

qual de l'Horloge

Conciergerie Palais de Justice Ste-Chapelle

CITÉ Ⓜ

Hôtel Dieu

quai Malaquais

Institut de France

1 2 3 4 PL. DAUPHINE

quai d'Orfèvres

Île de la Cité

RER

Pont d'Arcole

École Nationale Superieure des Beaux Arts

quai de Conti

🏛18

Hôtel de Monnaies

r. des Beaux Arts   19

20

r. Dauphine   r. du Pt. de Lodi

quai des Grands Augustins

Pont St-Michel

ST-MICHEL Ⓜ RER

RER

r. Visconti

r. Jacob

r. J. Callot

r. de Nesle

r. de Savoie

r. Seguier

23

PL. ST-MICHEL

24

de la Huchette

25 26

r. de l'Hirondelle

r. du Petit Pont

28

Église St-Julien-le-Pauvre

r. de Furstemberg

PL. de l'Abbaye

33 34

35

r. de Buci

36

r. St-André des Arts   22

21

27 29

r. St Séverin

Église St-Séverin   39

r. des Sts-Pères

r. Bonaparte

32

ST-GERMAIN-DES-PRÉS

St-Germain Des Prés

r. de Seine

r. Grégoire de Tours

r. de l'École de Médecine

Hôtel Cluny

🏛66 pl. Paul Painlevé

r. du Sommerard

40 41

bd. St-Germain

37

42

M ODÉON

bd. St-Germain   38

CLUNY-LA SORBONNE Ⓜ

65

67 68

ST-GERMAIN DES PRÉS Ⓢ

MABILLON

55

56

63

64

La Sorbonne

Collège de France

r. du Dragon

43

r. du Four

44 45 46 47 48 49 50 51 52 53 54

r. Mabillon   r. Princesse   r. des Canettes   r. Guisarde

r. Lobineau

59

60

61 62

r. de l'Odéon

r. de Condé

r. Monsieur-le-Prince

r. Racine

r. Champollion

PL. DE LA SORBONNE

r. Cujas

Lycée Louis le Grand

r. de Sèvres

r. du Vieux Colombier

57 58

St-Sulpice

r. St-Sulpice   r. Garancière

r. de Tournon

PL. DE L'ODÉON

Odéon Théâtre de l'Europe

Ⓢ

r. de Médicis

r. Soufflot

82

Ⓢ

ST-SULPICE Ⓜ

PL. ST-SULPICE

r. du Cherche Midi

TO 79 (350m) 80 (700m)

r. Cassette

r. d'Assas

bd. Raspail

r. de Rennes

r. Guynemer

r. de Vaugirard

🏛81

r. Férou

r. Madame

r. Jean Bart

Palais du Luxembourg

PL. EDMOND ROSTAND

LUXEMBOURG RER

r. Royer Collard

86

88

r. P. et M. Curie

90

r. St-Jacques

r. Gay Lussac

RENNES Ⓜ

✚

Fontaine des Médicis

6ème

Marionettes de Luxembourg

Jardin du Luxembourg

LUXEMBOURG RER

92

ST-PLACIDE Ⓜ

NOTRE-DAME DES CHAMPS Ⓜ

r. Auguste Compte

✚

r. d'Assas

r. des Ursulines

r. des Feuillan

r. du Montparnasse

94 95

r. Bréa

r. Notre-Dame des Champs

r. Jean Chaplain   r. de la Grande Chaumière   r. de Chevreuse

🏛96

r. J. Bara

✚

r. Henri Baptiste

r. Pierre Nicole

✚

97 VAVIN Ⓜ

MONTPARNASSE BIENVENÜE Ⓜ

bd. Raspail

14ème

bd. du Montparnasse

av. de l'Observatoire

PORT ROYAL

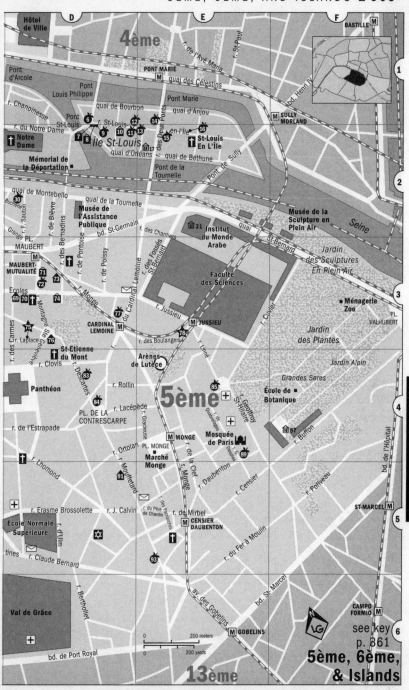

5ème, 6ème, & Islands

APPENDIX

see key p. 361

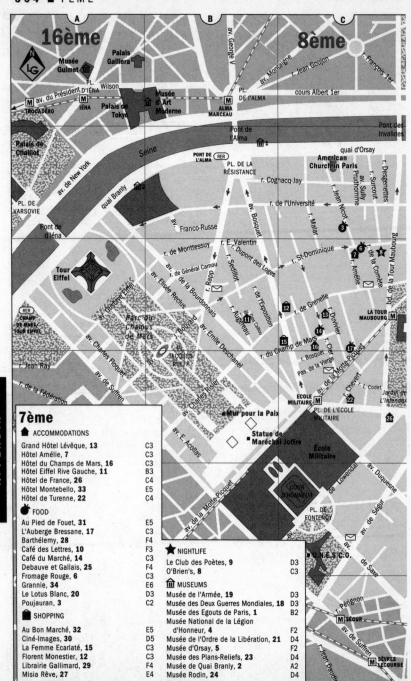

7ème

ACCOMMODATIONS

Grand Hôtel Lévêque, 13	C3
Hôtel Amélie, 7	C3
Hôtel du Champs de Mars, 16	C3
Hôtel Eiffel Rive Gauche, 11	B3
Hôtel de France, 26	C4
Hôtel Montebello, 33	E5
Hôtel de Turenne, 22	C4

FOOD

Au Pied de Fouet, 31	E5
L'Auberge Bressane, 17	C3
Barthélemy, 28	F4
Café des Lettres, 10	F3
Café du Marché, 14	C3
Debauve et Gallais, 25	F4
Fromage Rouge, 6	C3
Grannie, 34	E6
Le Lotus Blanc, 20	D3
Poujauran, 3	C2

SHOPPING

Au Bon Marché, 32	E5
Ciné-Images, 30	D5
La Femme Ecarlaté, 15	C3
Florent Monestier, 12	C3
Librairie Gallimard, 29	F4
Misia Rêve, 27	E4

★ NIGHTLIFE

Le Club des Poètes, 9	D3
O'Brien's, 8	C3

🏛 MUSEUMS

Musée de l'Armée, 19	D3
Musée des Deux Guerres Mondiales, 18	D3
Musée des Egouts de Paris, 1	B2
Musée National de la Légion d'Honneur, 4	F2
Musée de l'Ordre de la Libération, 21	D4
Musée d'Orsay, 5	F2
Musée des Plans-Reliefs, 23	D4
Musée de Quai Branly, 2	A2
Musée Rodin, 24	D4

1er

D E F

CONCORDE

Grand Palais/
Palais de
la Découverte

Petit
Palais

Obélisque

PL. DE
LA CONCORDE

Galerie
Nationale du
Jeu de
Paume

r. St-Honoré

r. de Rivoli

TUILERIES

cours la Reine

Musée de
l'Orangerie

Jardin des
Tuileries

Pont Alexandre III

Pont de
la Concorde

Seine

quai des Tuileries

quai Anatole France

Assemblée
Nationale

Palais de la
Légion d'Honneur

MUSÉE
D'ORSAY

Passerelle
Solférino

INVALIDES

ASSEMBLÉE
NATIONALE

PL. DU
PALAIS BOURBON

Pont
Royal

quai Voltaire

7ème

Esplanade
des
Invalides

SOLFÉRINO

r. St-Dominique

SQ. S.
ROSSEAU

Basilique
Ste-Clotilde

St-Thomas
d'Aquin

PL. DES
INVALIDES

r. de Grenelle

VARENNE

COUR
D'HONNEUR

St-Louis

Hôtel
des
Invalides

Hôtel Biron

RUE DU BAC

Église
du Dome

Fontaine des
Quatre Saisons

bd. St-Germain

av. de Tourville

Hôtel
Matignon

r. de Varenne

PL.
VAUBAN

SQ. CHAISE
RÉCAMIER

Esplanade
du Souvenir
Français

La Pagode

r. de Babylone

Jardin Catherine
Labouré

SÈVRES
BABYLONE

r. de Sèvres

ST-SULPICE

ST-FRANÇOIS
XAVIER

Église St-
François-Xavier

VANEAU

6ème

PL. A.
TARDIEU

RENNES

PL.
DE BRETEUIL

DUROC

bd. du Montparnasse

200 meters
200 yards

PL. HENRI
QUEUILLE

APPENDIX

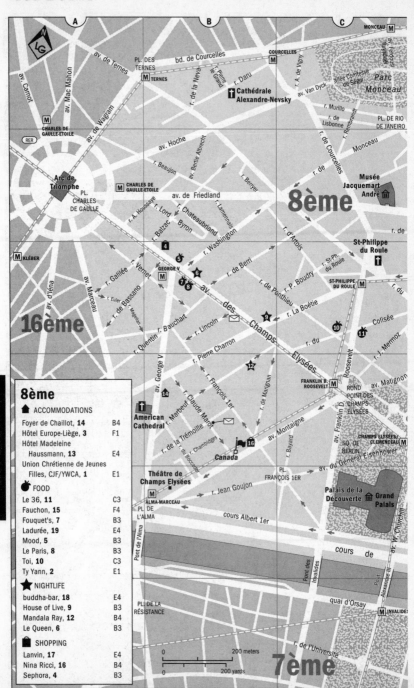

APPENDIX

8ème

🏠 ACCOMMODATIONS

Foyer de Chaillot, 14	B4
Hôtel Europe-Liège, 3	F1
Hôtel Madeleine	
Haussmann, 13	E4
Union Chrétienne de Jeunes	
Filles, CJF/YWCA, 1	E1

🍎 FOOD

Le 36, 11	C3
Fauchon, 15	F4
Fouquet's, 7	B3
Ladurée, 19	E4
Mood, 5	B3
Le Paris, 8	B3
Toi, 10	C3
Ty Yann, 2	E1

⭐ NIGHTLIFE

buddha-bar, 18	E4
House of Live, 9	B3
Mandala Ray, 12	B4
Le Queen, 6	B3

🛍 SHOPPING

Lanvin, 17	E4
Nina Ricci, 16	B4
Sephora, 4	B3

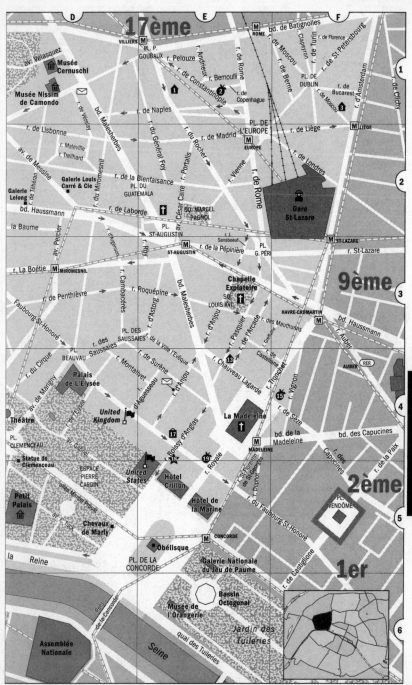

17ème

VILLIERS M

PL. P.
GOUBAUX

av. Velasquez

Musée
Cernuschi

Musée Nissim
de Camondo

r. de Lisbonne

r. de Naples

av. de Messine

r. Maleville
r. Treilhard

bd. Malesherbes

r. du Général Foy

Galerie
Lelong

av. de Téhéran

Galerie Louis
Carré & Cie

r. de la Bienfaisance
PL. DU
GUATEMALA

r. du Miromesnil

r. de Laborde

bd. Haussmann

la Baume

av. Percier

r. de Verzeny

r. Pelouze

r. Andreu
r. Bernoulli

r. de Constantinople

r. de Naples

r. du Rocher

r. de Rome

r. de Copenhague

r. de Madrid

av. César Caire

r. Portalis

PL. DE
L'EUROPE

r. de Moscou
bd. de Batignolles
Clapeyron

r. de Berne

PL. DE
DUBLIN

r. de Liège

ROME M

r. de Turin
r. de Florence
r. de St-Pétersbourg

r. de Moscou

r. d'Amsterdam

r. de Clichy

r. de Bucarest

EUROPE M

r. de Liège

LIÈGE M

r. de Londres

17ème

PL.
ST-AUGUSTIN

SQ. MARCEL
PAGNOL

av. César Caire

r. de Madrid

r. Vienne

r. de Rome

Gare
St-Lazare

ST-AUGUSTIN M

r. de la Pépinière

PL.
G. PÉRI

r. J.
Sansboeuf

ST-LAZARE M

r. St-Lazare

r. La Boétie

MIROMESNIL M

av. Percier

r. de Penthièvre

r. d'Argenson

Faubourg-St-Honoré

r. de Cambacérès

r. Roquépine

r. d'Astorg

r. d'Anjou

bd. Malesherbes

Chapelle
Expiatoire

SQ.
LOUIS XVI

r. Pasquier

r. des Mathurins

r. de l'Arcade

HAVRE-CAUMARTIN

r. Greffulhe

bd. Haussmann

r. Auber

9ème

PL. DES
SAUSSAIES

r. des Saussaies

r. de la Ville l'Evêque

r. de Surène

r. Cambon

r. de Castellane

AUBER RER

r. du Cirque

PL.
BEAUVAU

r. de Miromesnil

r. Montalivet

r. d'Aguesseau

r. d'Anjou

Chauveau Lagarde

r. Tronchet

r. Vignon

r. de Sère

Palais
de L'Elysée

av. de Marigny

av. Gabriel

United
Kingdom

Boissy d'Anglas

r. d'Anjou

La Madeleine

bd. de la
Madeleine

bd. des Capucines

Théâtre

PL.
CLEMENCEAU

Statue de
Clemenceau

ESPACE
PIERRE
CARDIN

allée Marcel Proust

r. Boissy d'Anglas

r. Royale

MADELEINE M

r. de la Paix

2ème

United
States

Hôtel
Crillon

r. St-Florentin
de Ste-Croix

r. Duphot

r. du Faubourg-St-Honoré

PL.
VENDÔME

Petit
Palais

av. F. Luel

Chevaux
de Marly

Hôtel de
la Marine

CONCORDE M

r. de Castiglione

la Reine

Obélisque

PL. DE LA
CONCORDE

Galerie Nationale
du Jeu de Paume

1er

Pont de la Concorde

Musée de
l'Orangerie

Bassin
Octogonal

Jardin des
Tuileries

Assemblée
Nationale

Seine

quai des Tuileries

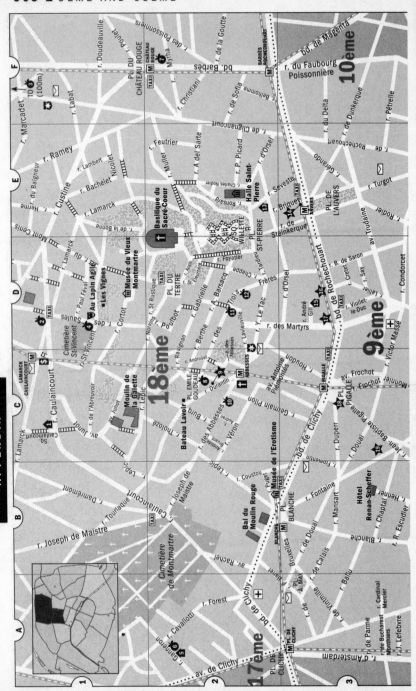

APPENDIX

9ème & 18ème

▲ ACCOMMODATIONS

Hôtel André Gill, 15	D3
Hôtel Caulaincourt, 1	C1
Hôtel Chopin, 30	D6
Modial Hôtel Européen, 26	C4
Perfect Hôtel, 23	D4
Style Hôtel, 5	A2
Le Village Hostel, 13	E2
Woodstock Hostel, 24	E4

◆ FOOD

Anarkali Sarangui, 21	C4
Au Général La Fayette, 27	D5
Au Grain de Folie, 11	D2
La Bodega, 3	F1
Café de la Paix, 32	B6
Chartier, 31	D6
Chez Ginette, 2	D1
Chez Haynes, 25	D4
Comme Par Hasard, 20	C4
Djerba Cacher Chez Guichi, 7	F2
La Maison Rose, 4	D1
No Stress Café, 22	C4
Refuge des Fondues, 12	D2
Le Sancerre, 10	C2
Le Soleil Gourmand, 8	C2
Wassana, 6	A2

★ NIGHTLIFE AND ENTERTAINMENT

Bus Palladium, 19	C3
Chez Camille, 9	C2
La Cigale, 16	D3
Elysée Montmartre, 14	E3
Folies Pigalle, 18	C3
La Fourmi, 17	D3

♦ SHOPPING

Au Printemps, 28	A5
Galeries Lafayette, 29	B5

APPENDIX

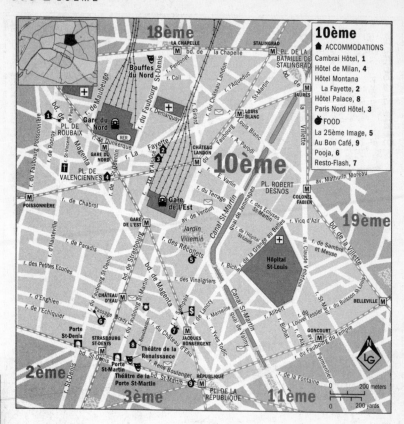

12ème

▲ ACCOMMODATIONS

Centre International du Séjour de Paris, **18**	G3
Hôtel de l'Aveyron, **12**	B2
Hôtel Printania, **17**	F2
Hôtel de Reims, **14**	C2
Mistral Hôtel, **16**	C2
Nièvre-Hôtel, **13**	C2
Nouvel Hotel, **11**	B2

◆ FOOD

Les Broches à l'Ancienne, **4**	B1
Le Cheval de Troie, **6**	C2
La Connivence, **10**	C2
L'Ebauchoir, **7**	C1
Les Grands Marchés, **1**	B1

● SHOPPING

L'Arbre à Lettres, **3**	B1
Marché Beauvau, **9**	C1
Automates + Poupées, **15**	C2
Les Soeurs Lumière, **5**	B1

★ NIGHTLIFE

Barrio Latino, **2**	B1
China Club, **8**	B1

300 meters

300 yards

11ème

▲ ACCOMMODATIONS	
Auberge de Jeunesse "Jules Ferry", **2**	C1
Hôtel Beaumarchais, **8**	C2
Hôtel de Belfort, **17**	E3
Hôtel Notre-Dame, **3**	C1
Hôtel Rhetia, **15**	D3
Modern Hôtel, **16**	E3
Plessis Hôtel, **4**	C1
● FOOD	
La Banane Ivoirienne, **40**	C5
Le Bistrot du Peintre, **36**	C4
Café de l'Industrie, **19**	B4
Chez Paul, **33**	C4
Juan et Juanita, **6**	E2
Pause Café, **35**	C4
Polichinelle, **37**	C4
Restaurant Assoce, **14**	E3
Le Troisième Bureau, **5**	D2
★ NIGHTLIFE	
Les Abats Jour à Coudre, **12**	E2
Bar à Nénette, **29**	B4
Le Bar Sans Nom, **34**	C4
Barbat, **27**	C4
Berimbar, **13**	E2
Café Charbon, **10**	C2
Le Clown Bar, **7**	C2
Favela Chic, **1**	C1
Jacques Mélac, **39**	E4
Le Kitch, **9**	C2
Le Lèche-Vin, **18**	B4
La Muse Vin, **38**	D4
Nouveau Casino, **11**	E2
Sanz Sans, **31**	B4
Wax, **20**	B4
▲ SHOPPING	
Atelier 33, **32**	B4

12ème

Cimetière Père Lachaise

SQ. DE LA ROQUETTE

PL. LÉON BLUM

Opéra Bastille

Gare de Lyon

PL. DE LA NATION

Metro stations:
Charonne
Alexandre Dumas
Avron
Philippe Auguste
Nation
Boulets Montreuil
Voltaire
Charonne
Reuilly Diderot
Ledru Rollin
Faidherbe Chaligny
Bastille
Gare de Lyon
Quai de la Rapée

Streets:
r. de la Folie
bd. de Charonne
av. Philippe Auguste
r. de Tunis
imp. Monet
Montreuil
r. des Immeubles industriels
r. Cheu... de
r. de Nice
r. Nueve des Boulets
r. Alexandre Dumas
r. des Boulets
bd. Diderot
r. de Reuilly
r. C. Desmoulins
r. Léon Frot
r. Mercoeur
r. A. Laurent
r. de Belfort
bd. Voltaire
Titon
r. J. Macé
Godefroy Cavaignac
r. Richard Lenoir
r. Chanzy
r. Faidherbe
r. du Faubourg St-Antoine
av. Ledru Rollin
r. Basfroi
r. de Charonne
St. Bernard
r. de Chaligny
r. Ch. Delescluze
Trousseau
Forge Royale
r. de Reuilly
r. Keller
r. des Taillandiers
pas. Thiéré
r. de la Roquette
r. de Lappe
r. Daval
r. de Crozatier
r. Crozatier
r. de Charenton
av. Daumesnil
r. Villiot
r. de Cîteaux
r. de Charenton
r. de Lyon
r. Traversière
bd. Diderot
r. de Bercy
av. Ledru Rollin
bd. de la Bastille
quai de la Rapée
bd. Bourdon

Seine

RER

4

5

6

APPENDIX

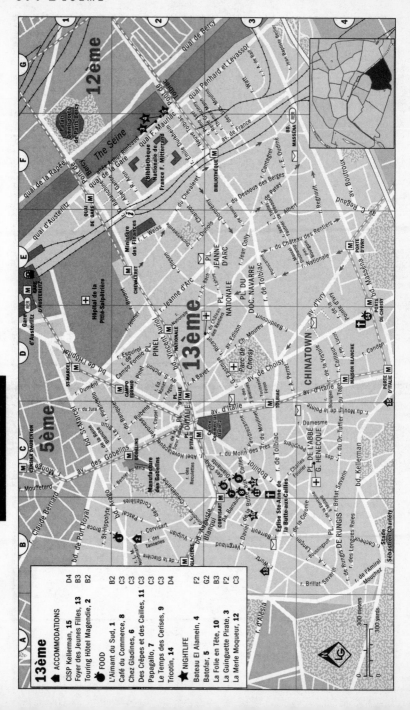

13ème

🔺 ACCOMMODATIONS

CISP Kellerman, 15	D4
Foyer des Jeunes Filles, 13	B3
Touring Hôtel Magendie, 2	B2

● FOOD

L'Aimant du Sud, 1	B2
Café du Commerce, 8	C3
Chez Gladines, 6	C3
Des Crêpes et des Cailles, 11	C3
Papagallo, 7	C3
Le Temps des Cerises, 9	C3
Tricotin, 14	D4

★ NIGHTLIFE

Bateau El Alamein, 4	F2
Batofar, 5	G2
La Folie en Tête, 10	B3
La Guinguette Pirate, 3	F2
La Merle Moqueur, 12	C3

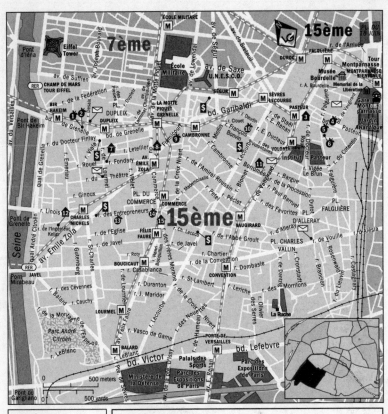

15ème

🏠 **ACCOMMODATIONS**

Aloha Hostel, **11**
Hôtel Camélia, **3**
Hôtel Printemps, **8**
Pacific Hôtel, **7**
Pratic Hôtel, **12**
Three Ducks Hostel, **15**

🍅 **FOOD**

Au Coin du Pétrin, **14**	Thai Phetburi, **2**
Aux Artistes, **6**	Le Tire Bouchon, **13**
Chez Fung, **9**	Le Troquet, **10**
Le Dix Vins, **5**	Ty Breiz, **4**
Samaya, **1**	

14ème
see map p. 376-377

🏠 **ACCOMMODATIONS**

FIAP Jean-Monnet, **7**	F3
Hôtel de Blois, **9**	C3
Hôtel du Midi, **6**	E2
Hôtel du Parc, **5**	B1
Ouest Hôtel, **11**	A4

🍅 **FOOD**

L'Amuse Bouche, **8**	C3
Aquarius Café, **12**	B4
Au Rendez-Vous	
Des Camionneurs, **13**	C4
Chez Papa, **5**	C2
La Coupole, **1**	C1

⭐ **NIGHTLIFE**

Café Tournesol, **4**	B1
L'Entrepôt, **10**	B3
Smoke Bar, **2**	B1

14ème
see key p. 375

13ème

14ème

15ème

r. Ferrus

Hôpital St-Anne

r. de la Santé

Villa de Lourcine

r. Cabanis

7

r. Broussais

r. du St-Gothard

Hôpital Cochin

r. Méchain

bd. Arago

r. Jean Dolent

bd. St-Jacques

Émile Dubois

Darau

av. René Coty

r. du Faubourg St-Jacques

bd. de Port Royal

PL. ST-JACQUES

ST-JACQUES

r. de la Tombe Issoire

Bezout

Maternité Port Royal Clinique Baudelocque

r. Cassini

Observatoire de Paris

The Catacombs

SQ. DE L'ABBÉ MIGNE

6

Hôpital La Rochefoucauld

r. Hallé

r. du Coëdic

r. Rémy-Dumoncel

av. de l'Observatoire

av. Denfert Rochereau

PL. DENFERT ROCHEREAU

TAXI

SQ. CLAUDE NICOLAS LEDOUX

DENFERT ROCHEREAU

r. Sophie Germain

MOUTON DUVERNET

av. du Général Leclerc

$

Hôpital St-Vincent de-Paul

Fondation Cartier pour l'Art Contemporain

bd. Raspall

r. Victor Considérant

r. Schœlcher

SQ. GEORGES LAMARQUE

r. E. Cresson

SQUARE H. DELORMEL

Duvernet

r. Brézin

14ème

bd. du Montparnasse

r. Campagne Première

Passage d'Enfer

r. Boissonade

r. Lalande

Danville

r. Charles Divry

Mairie

SQ. F. BRUNOT

r. Mouton

r. Saillard

Duro-

r. Boulard

PL. F. PERROY

9

G. SÉVERO

PL. PABLO PICASSO

1

VAVIN

r. Huyghens

RASPAIL

J.L. Robert

r. Émile Richard

Cimetière du Montparnasse

5

r. Froidevaux

r. Daguerre

r. Liancourt

r. Gassendi

r. Maurice Ripoche

r. de la Sablière

r. Delambre

SQ. Delambre

bd. Edgar Quinet

EDGAR QUINET

r. Fermat

r. Depercieux

r. Cels

av. du Maine

r. du Château

Maindron

r. de l'Eure

r. d'Odessa

Impasse de la Gaîté

4

Comédie Italienne

r. de la Gaîté

r. Jolivet

3

r. Poinsot

GAÎTÉ

TAXI

±

r. Vercingétorix

r. Lebouis

r. Raymond Losserand

r. Maison Dieu

Asseline

r. Bénard

PL. DE LA GARENNE

r. Pernety

r. de Plaisance

PERNETY

r. du Montparnasse

PL. DU 18 JUIN 1940

MONTPARNASSE BIENVENÜE

Tour Montparnasse

Gare Montparnasse

r. du Départ

r. de l'Arrivée

av. du Maine

Antoine Bourdelle

Musée Bourdelle

Musée de la Poste

bd. de Vaugirard

bd. Pasteur

TAXI

TAXI

r. du Cdt. René Mouchotte

PL. DE CATALOGNE

r. Jean Zay

r. Guesde

r. de Texel

r. du Château

CAL-WYSZYNSKI

Église Nôtre Dame du Travail

†

r. Alain

r. Croce Spinelli

r. Niepce

r. Des Prez

r. du Cagne

r. de l'Ouest

r. du Moulin les Lapins

r. Francis de Pressensé

PORT ROYAL

RER

RER

2

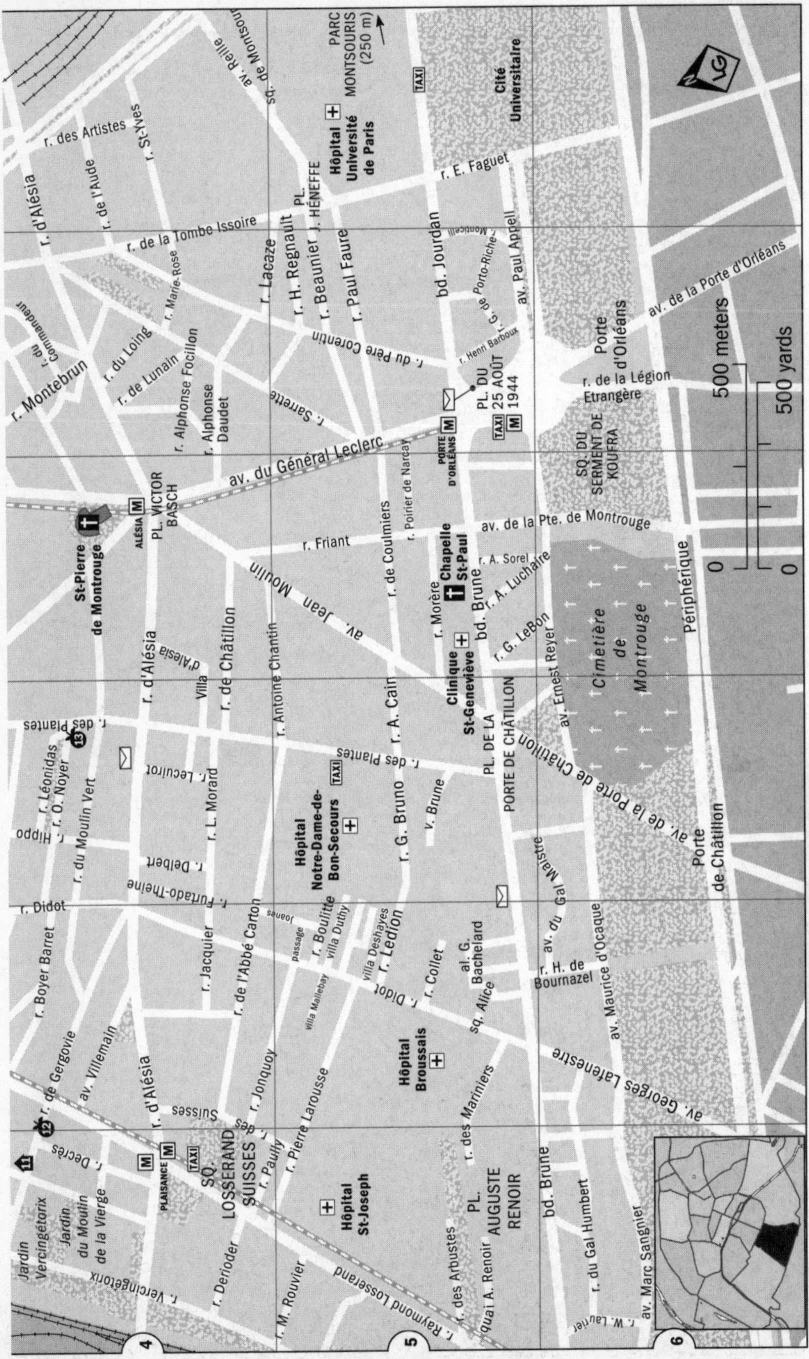

PARC MONTSOURIS (250 m)
Cité Universitaire
Hôpital Université de Paris
r. des Artistes
r. St-Yves
r. d'Alésia
r. de l'Aude
r. de la Tombe Issoire
r. E. Faguet
PL. J. HÉNEFFE
r. H. Regnault
r. Beaunier
r. Paul Faure
bd. Jourdan
r. Lacaze
r. Marie-Rose
r. du Commandeur
r. Montebrun
r. du Loing
r. de Lunain
r. Alphonse Focillon
r. Alphonse Daudet
r. du Père Corentin
r. Sarrette
r. Henri Barboux
r. G. de Porto-Riche
av. Paul Appell
PL. DU 25 AOÛT 1944
PORTE D'ORLÉANS
av. du Général Leclerc
Porte d'Orléans
av. de la Porte d'Orléans
r. de la Légion Etrangère
SQ. DU SERMENT DE KOUFRA
St-Pierre de Montrouge
ALÉSIA
PL. VICTOR BASCH
r. Poirier de Narçay
av. de la Pte. de Montrouge
r. Friant
r. de Coulmiers
Chapelle St-Paul
r. A. Sorel
r. A. Luchaire
av. Jean Moulin
r. Morère
Clinique St-Geneviève
bd. Brune
r. G. LeBon
Cimetière de Montrouge
Périphérique
500 meters
500 yards
r. de Châtillon
Villa d'Alésia
r. Antoine Chantin
r. A. Cain
PL. DE LA PORTE DE CHÂTILLON
av. Ernest Reyer
av. de la Porte de Châtillon
r. des Plantes
r. Léonidas
r. O. Noyer
r. du Moulin Vert
r. Hippo
r. Lecuirot
r. L. Morard
Hôpital Notre-Dame-de-Bon-Secours
r. G. Bruno
v. Brune
r. Delbet
r. Furtado-Heine
r. Didot
av. du Gal Maistre
Porte de Châtillon
r. Boyer Barret
r. Jacquier
r. de l'Abbé Carton
passage Joanes
r. Boulitte
villa Duthy
villa Deshayes
r. Ledion
r. Collet
al. G. Bachelard
r. H. de Bournazel
av. Maurice d'Ocaque
villa Mallebay
sq. Alice
r. de Gergovie
av. Villemain
r. d'Alésia
r. Jonquoy
r. des Suisses
r. Pierre Larousse
Hôpital Broussais
r. des Mariniers
av. Georges Lafenestre
r. Decrès
PLAISANCE
SQ. LOSSERAND SUISSES
r. Pauly
Hôpital St-Joseph
PL. AUGUSTE RENOIR
bd. Brune
r. du Gal Humbert
av. Marc Sangnier
Jardin Vercingétorix
Jardin du Moulin de la Vierge
r. Vercingétorix
r. Deriodier
r. M. Rouvier
r. Raymond Losserand
r. des Arbustes
quai A. Renoir
r. W. Lautier
4
5
6

APPENDIX

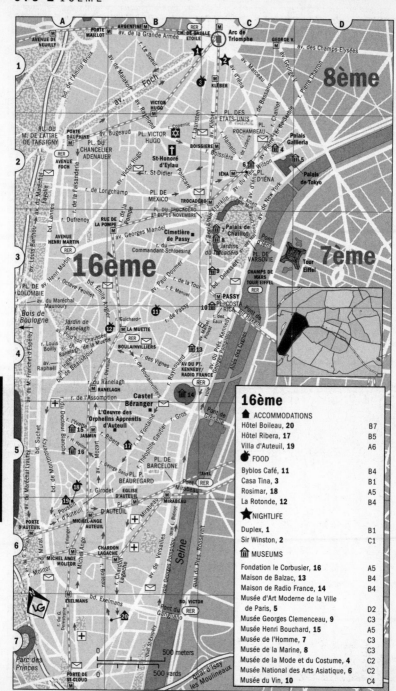

16ème

🏠 ACCOMMODATIONS

Hôtel Boileau, **20**	B7
Hôtel Ribera, **17**	B5
Villa d'Auteuil, **19**	A6

🍎 FOOD

Byblos Café, **11**	B4
Casa Tina, **3**	B1
Rosimar, **18**	A5
La Rotonde, **12**	B4

⭐ NIGHTLIFE

Duplex, **1**	B1
Sir Winston, **2**	C1

🏛 MUSEUMS

Fondation le Corbusier, **16**	A5
Maison de Balzac, **13**	B4
Maison de Radio France, **14**	B4
Musée d'Art Moderne de la Ville de Paris, **5**	D2
Musée Georges Clemenceau, **9**	C3
Musée Henri Bouchard, **15**	A5
Musée de l'Homme, **7**	C3
Musée de la Marine, **8**	C3
Musée de la Mode et du Costume, **4**	C2
Musée National des Arts Asiatique, **6**	C2
Musée du Vin, **10**	C4

17ème

ACCOMMODATIONS

Hôtel Belidor, 12	B3
Hôtel Champerret Héliopolis, 1	C2
Hôtel Prince Albert Wagram, 3	E2
Hôtel Riviera, 13	C4

FOOD

Au Vieux Logis, 8	F3
Le Bistrot de Théo, 7	F3
L'Endroit, 4	F2
Les Hortensias, 2	D2
The James Joyce Pub, 11	B3
Le Patio Provençal, 6	F3
Restaurant Natacha, 10	B3
Le Niv's, 9	G3

NIGHTLIFE

L'Endroit, 5	F2

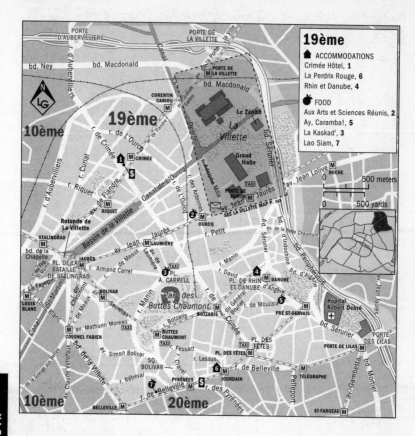

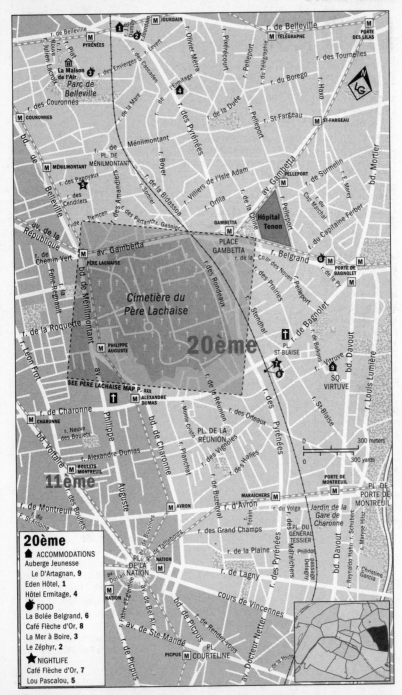

INDEX

Numerics

10 Bar, Le 310
1968 student uprising 79
25ème Image, La 168
3 334
33 Latino 318
36, Le 164
3W Kafé 306
404 153
968 69

A

Abbey Bookshop 291
Abou d'abi Bazar 288
absinthe 309
absurdist theater 77
Académie Française 75, 204
Académie Royale 81
accommodation agencies 115
Accommodations 123–143
accommodations
    long-term 51
accommodations agencies 51
ACT-UP Paris 118
adapters 26
aerogrammes 48
aéroports. See airports.
affairs
    Sarko and Chirac 73
agnès b 290, 296
AIDS (SIDA) 121
AIDS awareness 105
Aimant du Sud, L' 172
Air France Buses 38, 39, 116
Airhop 54
airplane travel
    airlines 33
    courier 34
    fares 32
    standby 35
    ticket consolidators 35
airports
    Beauvais 40
    Orly 39, 116
    Roissy-Charles de Gaulle 38, 116
    shuttles 39, 116
alcohol 27

drinking age 27
Alcoholics Anonymous 121
Algeria 69, 78
    Algerian War 79
Algerian Cultural Center 119
Algerian War 69
Allée des Cygnes 226
Allô Logement Temporaire 51, 115
Alternatives 289
Althusser, Louis 79
Amélie 10, 88, 229
American Cathedral 120
American Church in Paris 51, 120, 209, 279
American Express 23, 49, 115
American House 51
American Red Cross 30
Americanization 79
Amnésia Café 305
Amorino 149
Ampère, André 230
Amuse Bouche, L' 173
An American in Paris 79
Anarkali Sarangui 166
Ancien Hôtel Baudy 338
Andy Wahloo 304
Angelina's 151
anglophone community
    bars 303, 307, 309, 310, 311
    bookstores 286, 291
    churches 120, 209
    hospital 121
    libraries 119
    publications 51, 95
Anne d'Autriche 189, 197, 242, 339
anti-Semitism 66, 67, 73
aparelli 283
apartments 51
apéritifs 91
Apparemment Café, L' 154, 304
Appendix 347–352
aquariums 264, 270
Aquarius Café 174
Arab art 254
Aragon, Louis 77
Arbre à Lettres, L' 297

Arc de Triomphe 64, 81, 211
Arc de Triomphe du Carrousel 64, 188, 248
architecture 350
    history 80–84
Archives Nationales 194
Arènes de Lutèce 59, 80, 203
Armstrong, Lance 89
arrondissement rouge 10
Art Deco 192
art history 80–84
Art Nouveau 83, 195, 206, 213, 226, 283
artificial nature 326
Arts et Métiers, Les 154
Asian art 266
Asian cultural center 119
Assemblée Nationale 62, 210
Association des Foyers de Jeunes 138
Association InterMusées 245
Atelier 33 296
Atelier de Daubigny, Auvers-sur-Oise 342
Attila and the Huns 59
Au Bon Café 168
Au Bon Marché 162, 293, 294
Au Chien qui Fume 150
Au Coin du Pétrin 175
Au Duc des Lombards 302
Au Franc-Pinot 187
Au Général La Fayette 167
Au Grain de Folie 179
Au Lapin Agile 228, 277
Au Père Fouettard 150
Au Petit Fer à Cheval 155, 307
Au Pied de Fouet 163
Au Port Salut 158
Au Printemps 295
Au Rendez-Vous des Camionneurs 148, 173
Au Roi du Café 318
Au Vieux Comptoir 150
Au Vieux Logis 177
Auberge 143
Auberge Bressane, L' 163
Auberge de la Reine Blanche 149

INDEX

INDEX

MAP INDEX

MAP LEGEND

✛ Hospital	✈ Airport	🕌 Mosque
✪ Police	🚌 Bus Station	♜ Castle
✉ Post Office	🚉 Train Station	🏛 Museum
ⓘ Tourist Office	Ⓜ METRO Station	⌒ Arch
$ Bank	METRO Line	⌂ Hotel/Hostel
⚑ Embassy/Consulate	RER RER Station	🍎 Food & Drink
▪ Sight or Point of Interest	🚻 Public Restroom	🛍 Shopping
☎ Telephone Office	✝ Church	★ Nightlife
♖ Theater	✡ Synagogue	💻 Internet Café

Pedestrian Zone
Steps

Park

Water

Forest

The Let's Go compass always points NORTH.